How to Read Chinese Prose

HOW TO READ CHINESE LITERATURE

HOW TO READ CHINESE LITERATURE

ZONG-QI CAI, GENERAL EDITOR

YUAN XINGPEI, EDITORIAL BOARD DIRECTOR

How to Read Chinese Poetry: A Guided Anthology
(2008)

How to Read Chinese Poetry Workbook
(2012)

How to Read Chinese Poetry in Context:
Poetic Culture from Antiquity Through the Tang
(2017)

How to Read Chinese Prose: A Guided Anthology
(2022)

How to Read Chinese Prose in Chinese: A Course in Classical Chinese
(2022)

How to Read Chinese Drama: A Guided Anthology
(2022)

How to Read Chinese Prose

A GUIDED ANTHOLOGY

EDITED BY ZONG-QI CAI

Columbia University Press   New York

**CENTER FOR LANGUAGE
EDUCATION AND COOPERATION
中外语言交流合作中心**

Columbia University Press wishes to express its appreciation for assistance given by the Center for Language Education and Cooperation in the publication of this series.

Columbia University Press
Publishers Since 1893
New York   Chichester, West Sussex
cup.columbia.edu

Library of Congress Cataloging-in-Publication Data
Names: Cai, Zong-qi, 1955– editor.
Title: How to read Chinese prose : a guided anthology / edited by Zong-qi Cai.
Description: New York : Columbia University Press, [2022] | Series: How to read Chinese literature | Includes index
Identifiers: LCCN 2021007654 (print) | LCCN 2021007655 (ebook) | ISBN 9780231203647 (hardback; acid-free paper) | ISBN 9780231203654 (trade paperback; acid-free paper) | ISBN 9780231555166 (ebook)
Subjects: LCSH: Chinese prose literature. | Chinese prose literature—Translations into English. | Chinese prose literature—History and criticism. | LCGFT: Literary criticism. | Creative nonfiction.
Classification: LCC PL2452.H67 2022 (print) | LCC PL2452 (ebook) | DDC 495.186/421—dc23
LC record available at https://lccn.loc.gov/2021007654
LC ebook record available at https://lccn.loc.gov/2021007655

Columbia University Press books are printed on permanent and durable acid-free paper.

Printed in the United States of America

Cover design: Milenda Nan Ok Lee
Cover image: Susii © Shutterstock

CONTENTS

PART II: THE HAN DYNASTY AND THE SIX DYNASTIES

6. Han Historical Prose: Sima Qian and the *Grand Scribe's Records* (*Shiji*)   **129**

WILLIAM H. NIENHAUSER, JR.

7. Han and Six Dynasties Epistolary Prose: Memorials and Letters   **148**

LIU YUCAI, TRANSLATED BY BENJAMIN RIDGWAY

8. Six Dynasties Informal Prose: *A New Account of the Tales of the World* (*Shishuo xinyu*)   **181**

XINDA LIAN

PART IV: THE MING AND QING DYNASTIES

---

* This text is also featured, accompanied by modern Chinese translation and extensive annotation, in
How to Read Chinese Prose in Chinese: A Course in Classical Chinese (New York: Columbia University
Press, 2022).

THEMATIC CONTENTS

1. NARRATIVE GENRES

Commentaries

- Diplomatic rhetoric (C1.1; ☞ *HTRCProse-CCC*, L02)
- Family conflicts and their political consequences (C2.1)
- Arguments for and against centralizing power (C2.1)
- Woman and conflict of loyalties (C2.2)
- Woman as victim or historical agent in *Zuo Tradition* (C2.2–2.5)
- Strategic calculations on the battlefield (C2.6; ☞ *HTRCProse-CCC*, L01)
- What is good governance? (C2.8)

Commentaries

- Categorical biographies (chap. 6)
- Loyal retainer (or loyalty to a ruler) (chap. 6)
- Strategy and force as part of treaty negotiations (C6.1)
- Self-mutilation as a means to attempt assassination (C6.2)
- Ritual death as an expression of loyalty (C6.2)
- Violation of trust leading to death (C6.3)
- Waiting for the right moment as an assassin (C6.3)
- Selection of an accomplice leading to failure (C6.3)
- Attempt to stop the encroachment of Qin on neighboring states (C6.3)
- Leitmotif of the dedication of retainers to lords who recognize their skills (C6.1–6.3)
- Recognition of a worthy man (C6.2–6.3)
- Vertical and horizontal alliances (*Springs and Autumns of Mr. Lü*) (C5.2)
- Foolish lords and kings depicted in *Grand Scribe's Records* (C5.8)

Commentaries

- Historical origins of Tang and Song biographical writings (chap. 13)
- Impact of "Tang and Song Poetry and Prose Modernization Movement" on biographical writings (chap. 13)
- Biographical writings as literature (chap. 13)
- Tang biographical writings as metaphor, political allegory, and moral persuasion (C13.1–13.3)
- The playfulness and humor in Tang biographical writings (C13.1)
- The strange and the fantastical in Tang biographical writings (C13.4)
- The cultural shift in Tang and Song biographical writings (C13.5–13.6)
- Song biographical writings as personal narrative and cultural commentary (C13.5–13.6)
- Logical clarity and authorial control in Song biographical writings (C13.5–13.6)
- The art of storytelling in Tang and Song biographical writings (chap. 13)
- Teacher–student relationship (C15.2)

2. DISCURSIVE GENRES

2.1. Recorded Conversations (*yüluti* 語錄體)

Commentaries

- The *Odes* and the education of the noble man (C3.1, C3.6)
- Self-cultivation and the achievement of perfected spontaneity (C3.5)
- Confucius as the model of sagacity (C3.9)
- Moral courage and the primacy of the mind (*xin*) (C3.9)
- Learning as remolding and self-improvement (C3.9, C3.11)
- The nature of human nature (C3.10–3.13)
- Understanding discourse (C3.12)
- The ideal of musical harmony (C3.13)

Commentaries

- Ritual, music, and the channeling of human affections (C3.13)
- Rulership through charismatic suasion (C3.13)
- Faithless rhetoric in *Han Feizi* (C5.3)
- Vertical and Horizontal alliances (*Han Feizi*) (C5.3)
- The need for competent advisors (*Han Feizi*) (C5.3–4)
- Pursuit of self-interest (*Han Feizi, Sunzi*) (C5.3, C5.5)
- Suppressing evidence of one's plans and purposes (*Han Feizi, Sunzi*) (C5.3, C5.6)
- Foolish lords and kings depicted in *Han Feizi* and *Mozi* (C5.3, C5.7)
- Efficient use of troops (*Sunzi*) (C5.5–5.6)
- Appeal to the Sage Kings (*Mozi*) (C5.7)
- Punishing minor offenses but glorifying great ones (*Mozi*) (C5.7)

Commentaries

- Confucian perspectives on social order (C10.1)
- Confucian critique of Buddhism/Daoism (C10.1)
- Confucian ideas of self-cultivation (C10.1)
- "Chinese" and "foreign/barbarian" identity (C10.1)
- Historical analysis as political critique (C10.3)
- Heaven as mechanistic/moral (C10.2)
- Social functions of expository prose writing (chap. 10)
- The features of the ancient-style expository prose (chap. 10)
- Prose rhythm of Han Yu's "Origin" (C10.1)
- War and peace (C10.3)
- Interstate relations (C10.3)
- The use of dialogs and analogies in Liu Zongyuan's "Heaven" (C10.2)

2.4 Eight-Legged Essay (*baguwen* 八股文)

Commentaries

- The development of civil service examinations (C14.1–14.2)
- The establishment of the eight-legged essay as an examination genre (C14.1–14.2)
- Eight-legged essays devoted to the exegesis of the Confucian canon (C14.1–14.2)
- Eight-legged essay and neo-Confucianism orthodoxy (C14.1–14.2)
- The standard structure of the eight-legged essay (C14.1–14.2)
- Playful eight-legged essays as popular literary pastime and parody (C14.1–14.2)
- The criticism and abolishment of the eight-legged essay (C14.1–14.2)

3. DESCRIPTIVE GENRES

3.1 Metaphorical Description (*yuyan* 寓言)

Commentaries

- Zhuangzi's achievement as a writer (C4.1)
- Three modes of discourse (C4.1–4.2)
- Metaphorical words (*yuyan*): fable about roaming (C4.3)
- Goblet words (*zhiyan*): ad hoc comments and random or unpremeditated discourse (C4.3, C4.5, C4.6a–4.6c, C4.8, C4.10)
- Spiritual cultivation (C4.4)
- The concept of the heart (*xin*) (C4.5)
- Weighty words (*zhongyan*): parables and masks (C4.4, C4.6b, C4.11)
- Loss of self (C4, C6b)
- The piping of heaven (C4.6b)
- Nurturing life (C4.7)
- Zhuangzi on fame and punishment (C4.9)
- Zhuangzi on life and death (C4.7, C4.11–4.13)

3.2 Character Sketches (*Shishuo ti* 世說體)

FROM *A NEW ACCOUNT OF THE TALES OF THE WORLD* (*SHISHUO XINYU*):

Commentaries

- *Carpe diem* sensibility in prefaces (C11.1)
- Officialdom and reclusion (C11.2)
- The imperative to serve the state (C11.2)
- Finding contentment in the simple life (C11.5)
- Memory and remembrance in prefaces (C12.2)
- Song dynasty capital life (C12.2)
- Gender and literary identity (C12.3)
- Games (C12.3)
- Women's writing (C12.3)
- Achievements of occasional essay (*xiaopin wen*) (chap. 16)
- Travelogue as marginalized history (chap. 16)
- Gui Youguang as the transitional figure in Ming and Qing prose (C16.1)
- The three Yuan brothers as forerunners of modern Chinese prose (C16.2)
- Hypnotic allure of Zhang Dai's dreamy nostalgia (C16.3)
- Yao Nai and canonization of ancient-style prose (C16.5)
- Xu Fucheng and the demise of classical Chinese prose (C16.6)

4 COMMUNICATIVE GENRES

4.1 Memorials (*biao* 表)

Commentaries

- The origins of the epistolary genre (chap. 7)
- The popularization of paper use and the increase in epistolary writings (chap. 7)
- Differences between official and private correspondence (chap. 7)
- Crafting and diction in memorials written in parallel prose (chap. 7)
- The flaws of excessive formalism in memorials and letters (chap. 7)

- Equal importance of descriptive and affective language in memorials (chap. 7)
- Literary works and governance (chap. 7)
- The model of a loyal minister's advice on governing (Zhuge Liang's memorial) (C7.1)
- Mourning in familial relationships in Li Mi's memorial (C7.2)

4.2 Letters (*shu* 書): Expository Contents

SUPPLEMENTAL READINGS FROM HRTCPROSE–CCC

Commentaries

- Categorizing and appreciating private letters as literary works (chap. 7)
- The impassioned confession of the humiliated (Sima Qian's letter) (C7.4)
- The sincerity of an iconoclast (Ji Kang's letter) (C7.5)
- Affective and persuasive language in Qiu Chi's call for surrender (C7.7)
- Eulogies for departed friends by royal brothers, Cao Pi and Cao Zhi (C7.8–7.9)

4.3 Letters: Descriptive and Narrative Contents

5 FORMS: EXTRATEXTUAL PATTERNING

5.1 Extratextual Patterning: Narrative Texts

5.2 Extratextual Patterning: Descriptive Texts

6 FORMS: TEXTUAL PATTERNING

6.1 Repetitive Patterning

ADDITIONAL EXAMPLES FROM HRTCPROSE–CCC

6.2 Aggregative Patterning

PREFACE TO THE HOW TO READ CHINESE LITERATURE SERIES

Welcome to the How to Read Chinese Literature series, a comprehensive collection of literary anthologies and language texts covering all the major genres of Chinese literature. When completed, the series will consist of ten volumes: five guided literary anthologies, one book on poetic culture, and four language companions. Together, they will promote the teaching and learning of premodern Chinese poetry, fiction, drama, prose, and literary criticism.

In particular, the five guided anthologies offer innovative ways of overcoming some barriers that have long hindered the teaching and learning of Chinese literature. While fine scholarly monographs on Chinese literature abound, they are usually too specialized for classroom use. To make that scholarship more accessible, guided anthologies present the highlights of scholarship on major genres, subgenres, and writers through commentary on individual texts as well as broad surveys.

Every reader of Chinese literature is aware of the gap between English translations and Chinese originals. Because most existing anthologies offer only an English translation, however, students often find it hard to see how diverse linguistic elements work together in the original. To remedy this, each guided anthology presents the Chinese text alongside an English translation, with detailed remarks on the intricate interplay of word, image, and sound in Chinese.

So far, scant attention has been given to the relation between sound and sense in English-language studies of Chinese literature. As a corrective, the poetry anthology explains in detail the prosodic conventions of all major poetic genres and marks the tonal patterning in regulated verse and *ci* poetry. Samples of reconstructed ancient and medieval pronunciation are also given to show how the poems were probably pronounced when first composed. For the poetry and prose anthologies, we offer a sound recording of selected texts, read in Mandarin. For the drama and prose anthologies, video clips of traditional storytelling and dramatic performance will be provided free of charge online.

For decades, the study of Chinese literature in the West was a purely intellectual and aesthetic exercise, completely divorced from language learning. To accommodate demand from an ever-increasing number of Chinese-language learners, we provide tone-marked romanizations for all poetry texts, usually accompanied by sound recording. For any text also featured in the accompanying language text, cross-references allow the reader to quickly proceed to in-depth language study of the original.

Designed to work with the guided anthologies, the four language texts introduce classical Chinese to advanced beginners and above, teaching them how to appreciate Chinese literature in its original form. As stand-alone resources, these texts illustrate China's major literary genres and themes through a variety of examples.

Each language companion presents a select number of works in three different forms—Chinese, English, and tone-marked romanization—while also providing comprehensive vocabulary notes and prose translations in modern Chinese. Subsequent comprehension questions and comments focus on the artistic aspect of the works, while exercises test readers' grasp of both classical and modern Chinese words, phrases, and syntax. An extensive glossary cross-references classical and modern Chinese usage, characters and compounds, and multiple character meanings. Sound recording is provided for each selected text in the poetry and prose companions. Along with other learning aids, a list of literary or grammar issues addressed throughout completes each volume.

To achieve a seamless integration of literary anthologies and language texts, we draw from the same corpus of canonical texts and provide an extensive network of cross-references. Moreover, by presenting the ten books as a coherent set, we aim to help readers cross the divide between literary genres and between literary and language learning, thereby achieving a kind of experience impossible with traditional approaches. Thanks to these innovative features, we hope the series will reinvigorate—if not revolutionize—the learning and teaching of Chinese literature, language, and culture throughout the English-speaking world for decades to come.

Zong-qi Cai

A NOTE ON HOW TO USE THIS ANTHOLOGY

The goal of this anthology is to introduce students and general readers to the rich heritage of Chinese nonfiction prose, a major literary genre long neglected in Western-language studies of Chinese literature.

This anthology features 115 famous texts, representing major prose genres and dynastic periods from antiquity through the Qing, the last of the Chinese dynasties. Presentation of each text is composed of an English translation, its Chinese original, and a critical commentary. Reading this book cover to cover, students will acquire a comprehensive picture of both the historical development of Chinese prose and the prominent artistic features of its major genres. This combination of breadth and depth makes the anthology a fine core text for developing an undergraduate or graduate course in Chinese prose, which is conspicuously absent from current Chinese literature curricula in the Western world.

The 115 texts are organized first by dynastic period, then by genre. To make the myriad genres and texts manageable, I have introduced four broad genre clusters—narrative, expository, descriptive, and communicative—and listed selected texts accordingly in the thematic table of contents. The four clusters' interrelatedness, as well as their symbiotic relationship with certain prose forms, are noted in my introduction.

This anthology (like others in the series) helps readers go beyond translation to understand what is it that has made selected texts canonical in the Chinese literary traditions. To this end, the Introduction presents the notions of extratextual and textual patterning as a broad paradigm for probing the inner secrets of Chinese prose art. This is followed in chapter 1 by a demonstration of how these two types of patterning work in eight texts drawn from different periods and genres. Additionally, the deployment of extratextual and textual patterning in other texts is identified in the thematic table of contents. Within the chapters, four major forms of textual patterning are clearly marked by typographical symbols.

While mainly serving readers who do not know Chinese, this anthology also seeks to assist learners of Chinese. For them, two important pedagogical aids have been introduced. The first is an extensive network of cross-references, in both the thematic table and individual chapters, to the companion book *How to Read Prose in Chinese: A Course in Classical Chinese*. Twenty of the 115 texts are also featured in that language companion, each with exhaustive glossary and grammar notes and language exercises. These 20 texts are marked by an asterisk in the main table of contents. The remaining 95 texts can be fruitfully studied along with related lessons in the companion book. Second, we provide sound recordings (accompanied by tone-marked romanizations for all 115 texts), accessible and downloadable free of charge at **https://cup.columbia.edu/supplemental-materials-for-how-to-read-chinese-prose.**

This anthology also offers a good source of supplemental readings for courses in Chinese history, philosophy, or general culture. Prose is the direct, primary medium for narrating historical events, depicting social conditions, and advancing political and philosophical ideas. It is only natural, then, that these 115 texts yield vivid glimpses of major developments in politics, philosophy, and religions as well as literati life throughout Chinese history. Guided by the primary and thematic tables of contents, readers can easily find material closely related to their subjects of study in and beyond literature.

Having benefited so much from readers' feedback on the three poetry volumes through social media, we wish to engage the readers of this book in the same way. We encourage everyone to send in comments and suggestions on our Facebook page (**facebook.com/HowtoReadChinesePoetryZongqiCai**). We will do our best to foster and maintain an informative dialogue on all matters about this and other books in the series and about the teaching and learning of Chinese literature in general.

Zong-qi Cai

MAJOR CHINESE DYNASTIES

Xia	ca. 2100–ca. 1600 BCE
Shang	ca. 1600–ca. 1028 BCE
Zhou	ca. 1046–ca. 256 BCE
Western Zhou	ca. 1046–771 BCE
Eastern Zhou	ca. 771–256 BCE
Spring and Autumn Period	770–ca. 475 BCE
Warring States Period	ca. 475–221 BCE
Qin	221–206 BCE
Han	206 BCE–CE 220
Former Han	206 BCE–CE 8
Later Han	CE 25–220
Three Kingdoms	220–265
Shu	221–263
Wu	222–280
Wei	220–265
Jin	265–420
Western Jin	265–317
Eastern Jin	317–420
Southern and Northern Dynasties	
Southern	420–589
(Liu) Song	420–479
Southern Qi	479–502
Southern Liang	502–557
Southern Chen	557–589
Northern	386–581
Sui	581–618
Tang	618–907
Five Dynasties	907–960
Song	960–1279
Northern Song	960–1127
Southern Song	1127–1279
Yuan	1206–1368
Ming	1368–1644
Qing	1616–1911

Six Dynasties

SYMBOLS, ABBREVIATIONS, AND TYPOGRAPHIC USAGES

❀ ❀ ❀

chap. 8	Chapter eight
C8.4	Chapter eight, the fourth selected text
L01	Lesson 1 in *HTRCProse—CCC*
✂	A cross-reference marker
	Example: (✂ *HTRCProse-CCC*, L1; *HTRCP* ch. 8)
HTRCProse-CCC	Cui, Jie, Liu Yucai and Zong-qi Cai. *How to Read Chinese Prose in Chinese: A Course in Classical Chinese.* New York: Columbia University Press, 2022.
HTRCP	Cai, Zong-qi, ed. *How to Read Chinese Poetry: A Guided Anthology.* New York: Columbia University Press, 2008.
HTRCPIC	Cai, Zong-qi, ed. *How to Read Chinese Poetry in Context: Poetic Culture from Antiquity Through the Tang.* New York: Columbia University Press, 2012.
Straight underline in a Chinese text	Marking the use of repetitive patterning in a Chinese text, unless indicated otherwise. Example: "知之者不如好之者，好之者不如樂之者。"
Wavy underline in a Chinese text	Marking the use of parallel phrasing in coupled sentences, unless otherwise indicated. Example: 寂然 凝慮，思接 千載；悄焉 動容，視通 萬里。
Superscript numbers at the beginning of a line	Marking the use of aggregative patterning in a Chinese text, unless indicated otherwise. Example: ⁴歲月不居，⁴時節如流。⁴五十之年，⁴忽焉已至。⁴公爲始滿，⁴融又過二。⁴海內知識，⁴零落殆盡，惟會稽盛孝章尚存。⁶其人困於孫氏，⁴妻孥湮沒，⁴單子獨立，⁴孤危愁苦。⁶若使憂能傷人，此子不得復永年矣！

How to Read Chinese Prose

Introduction

The Literary and Cultural Significance of Chinese Prose

In Western-language (Sinological) studies of Chinese literature, an extraordinary lacuna has eluded the attention of most scholars: the absence of any comprehensive anthology of artistic, nonfiction prose (hereafter just prose). In China, prose is an independent literary genre privileged (with poetry) over fiction and drama. Compounding this neglect, all general anthologies of Chinese literature in translation, to date, have relegated prose to the margins. Monograph studies of Chinese prose are practically nonexistent. The rich heritage of Chinese prose art has been reduced to mere samples of famous prose works in unguided translations. Thus, as a first step toward restoring prose to its rightful place in Sinological literary studies, we created this comprehensive guided anthology.

CAUSES FOR THE NEGLECT OF PROSE IN SINOLOGICAL LITERARY STUDIES

To embark on a serious study of Chinese prose art, it seems appropriate first to reflect on both the extrinsic and intrinsic causes of the genre's long marginalization in the West. We need a clear idea of the obstacles that must be overcome.

Of various possible external causes, one seems to stand out: the near-universal neglect of prose as a genre in Western literary scholarship, regardless of origin. Essentially a branch of Western academia, Sinological literary studies is naturally informed and guided by Western critical concerns, paradigms, approaches, and methodologies. So the Sinological marginalization of the prose genre inevitably has much to do with general trends of Western literary scholarship. Since its establishment as a discipline in the early twentieth century, English studies has largely lost sight of the art of prose. For instance, most major nineteenth-century British and American nonfiction prose writers have focused on content over form. Whether it is American transcendentalist authors like Ralph Waldo Emerson and Henry David Thoreau or English authors like Samuel Taylor Coleridge and his Victorian successors Thomas Carlyle, Matthew Arnold, and John Ruskin, emphasis has almost always fallen on what they say, rather than how they say it. The powerful originality in content has given these nineteenth-century prose writers a decided edge over authors from an earlier period (from the Renaissance to the eighteenth century) who worried about form as much as content, eventually leading to a loss of interest of prose as a form of art.

In fact, the genre Western literary scholars call artistic prose goes all the way back to classical antiquity, and it is not surprising perhaps that the fullest awareness of it as a genre should still be found in classical scholarship. But it was also a thriving genre in the Renaissance and continued thus virtually to the end of the eighteenth century. Everyone knows the great French essayist Michel Montaigne, but artistic prose was equally an English genre. So we think of the Age of Samuel Johnson, who in his time was famous for his Rambler essays. Earlier, in the English Renaissance, we have such sermon writers as John Donne or, later, Jeremy Taylor. English prose writers also made forays into many other fields as well—witness Robert Burton's *Anatomy of Melancholy*, or Thomas Browne's *Religio Medici*. All these writers were well aware of the *topoi* or topics derived from Greek and Latin literature in antiquity and of all the rhetorical ways and means by which these topics were expressed. Nor did they worry overmuch about originality. On the contrary, being in agreement with respected orators like Cicero (i.e., borrowing from him) was thought to be a very smart move. Even the great German critics of the Romantic period, such as Friedrich Schlegel and August Wilhelm Schlegel, who discussed classical literature were already aware of it. That awareness of artistic prose as a genre continued to grow in nineteenth-century German classical scholarship, culminating in the magisterial study by Eduard Norden, *Die antike Kunstprosa* (*Antique Artistic Prose*), from which Western literary scholars now derive the name for this genre. So to understand these writers, it is necessary to contemplate the rhetorical ways and means they themselves were often concerned about. And if we do that, we might then find ourselves on the road to recovering the cultural values that lay behind artistic prose as a genre.

The same if not more promise holds for Sinological literary studies. In China, prose studies fell into neglect around the same time (first decades of the twentieth century) and for a rather similar reason: disdain for the concerns of the prose form. If traditional Western appreciation of literary artistry was trumped by a quest for originality, traditional Chinese prose forms were denounced and jettisoned as conveyers of feudal thought during the New Culture and May Fourth movements.

The neglect of Chinese prose cannot be attributed to external causes alone. Among intrinsic obstacles to Sinological studies of prose, the most noteworthy is perhaps the dearth of distinctive form markers. This difficulty may be best illustrated through a comparison with the readily recognized forms of Chinese poetry. All Chinese poetic forms display distinct configurations with an array of ostensible markers: line and composition length, stanza division, end-rhymes, and parallel phrasing. Most of these form markers come through nicely in English translation, enabling translators and readers alike to break and parse lines in ways faithful to the originals.[1] In my view, this essentially faithful presentation of original poetic forms provides a solid foundation for general appreciation as well as in-depth inquiry into Chinese poetic art. By contrast, lacking such form markers, Chinese prose writings tend to translate all the same so that only their contents separate an ancient Chinese text from a modern one. Such translational homogenization of Chinese prose is no doubt a major factor in the apathy this literature has long received in Sinological scholarship.

UNDERSTANDING CHINESE PROSE GENRES

To mitigate the homogenization of Chinese prose, we have undertaken two major endeavors in preparing this anthology. The first is to introduce readers to a rich diversity of prose genres developed from antiquity through the Qing dynasty. In traditional Chinese literary criticism, prose genres are named and defined according to their specific content, function, or context of composition, thus leading to the proliferation of several hundreds of genres. These genres have not been codified with a vertical genus-species scheme and are therefore overwhelming and confusing even to seasoned scholars of Chinese literature. To help readers view the contours of Chinese prose, I have devised a new fourfold scheme for codifying Chinese prose genres. In the thematic table of contents, I have classified the 115 selected texts under four broad genre categories—narrative, discursive, descriptive, and communicative—each of which features three or four of its most important genres.

Four major narrative genres are introduced in the order of their appearance. We begin with *Zuo Tradition* and other pre-Qin histories (*shi*), presenting excerpts known for their vivid portrayal of famous historical figures through dialogs and actions. Next, in Sima Qian's *Grand Scribe's Records*, we observe a morphing of such character sketches into full-fledged official biographies (*zhuan*). Coming to Tang and Song times, we witness the rise of less formal biographical accounts (*zhuanji*), some real, some allegorical, and some fictive. In writing these biographical accounts, Tang and Song prose masters seem to have been more interested in conveying their Confucian views and beliefs than revealing the inner lives of biographical subjects. Once we have grasped this point, we can understand why most of their biographical subjects are not figures worthy of historical memory like those depicted by Sima Qian. Steele inscription (*bei*), a genre that became rather popular starting in Tang and Song times, represents a return to formal biographical writing, although in a highly condensed form.

Discursive genres are primarily media of advancing and expounding abstract ideas. In this anthology, readers will observe the emergence of four distinctive discursive genres, revealing a trajectory from oral speeches to highly formalized essay writing. The earliest discursive genre is that of recorded conversations (*yulu*), as exemplified by *Analects* in which Confucius articulates his moral ideas through conversations with his disciples (C3.1–9). Then, in *Mencius*, this conversational genre evolves into a prototype of argumentative essay (*yilunwen*), as Mencius habitually expands his replies and speeches into short essays (C1.4; *HTRCProse-CCC*, L07; C3.10). When its conversational framework was dispensed with, this Mencian prototype would become a full-fledged argumentative essay (*yilunwen*). Such a metamorphosis is clearly evident in *Xunzi* (C3.11–12). Many argumentative essays written during the Warring States period and the Han dynasty still retain vestiges of conversation: writers often engage an intellectual opponent as an interlocutor in a debate. With the exit of debating interlocutors, other essays become less argumentative than expository. In these essays, writers dispassionately and objectively expound a concept or theory from multiple perspectives. Such expository prose flourished during the mid– and late–Six Dynasties period, during which the newly developed parallel prose form was exploited to illuminate dynamic bipolar relationships crucial to the elucidation of a theory. Examples par excellence are Zong Bing's (375–443) analysis of the spirit in landscape painting (C9.2) and Liu Xie's (ca. 465–ca. 522) analysis of the creative process (C9.4). Best known for their accomplishments in narrative and descriptive genres (chap. 11, 12), Tang and Song prose masters were not particularly fascinated with formal expository writing even though some of them left behind influential expository essays in the nonparallel ancient style (C10.1; *HTRCProse-CCC*, L25–27). The last major discursive genre is the examination essay, popularly known as the "eight-legged essay," emerging in the mid-Ming dynasty. This genre is in many ways an amalgam of the other three discursive genres. First, the author is required to speak in the voice of a Confucian sage, thus reminding us of recorded conversations, the earliest discursive genre. This genre's debt to the argumentative and expository genres is even more prominent. Its phrasing is typically that of the ancient nonparallel style prevalently used in pre-Qin and Han argumentative and expository prose. In the meantime, its paragraphing style, noted for its mandatory use of six or eight parallel legs (paragraphs), harks back to the Six Dynasties expository prose in the parallel form (C14.1).

Descriptive genres are devoted to depicting nature scenes and events of the human world. In China, full-fledged descriptive genres emerged considerably later than narrative and discursive genres. Although vivid and sometimes extended descriptive passages appear in early pre-Qin texts, nature is hardly an object of exclusive interest in major pre-Qin historical and philosophical writings. For instance, in *Zhuangzi*, we find detailed and vivid descriptions of fauna and flora, but they are primarily metaphorical words (*yuyan*) as called by Zhuangzi's disciples, intended to convey philosophical ideas (C4.2). For all intents and purposes, they should be treated as a prototype of a descriptive genre. Then, in *A New Account of the Tales of the World*, written about six hundred years after *Zhuangzi*, we see another prototype, this time focused on human characters. This book comprises hundreds of stand-alone character sketches or rather character entries, usually just a few sentences each, focused on the transcendent conduct, behaviors, and manners of famous Wei–Jin figures (C8.1–34). The Six Dynasties witnesses the rise of the full-fledged descriptive prose genre—depiction of landscape, real or fictional, as the site of aesthetic enjoyment (C9.2), utopian imagination (*HTRCProse-CCC*, L23), or religious contemplation. Tang and Song times are perhaps the golden age of Chinese descriptive prose, with a full blossoming of not only landscape-focused travel writings but also *ji* and *xu* genres that depict various aspects of literati's semiprivate or private lives (chap. 11, 12). It is largely in these descriptive genres that the Tang and Song prose masters earned their literary eminence. Descriptive genres continued to flourish in Ming-Qing times, achieving new breakthroughs in broadening thematic scope, amplifying lyrical intensity (C15.1, C15.4), and capturing aesthetic pleasure of sensory impressions (C16.3; *HTRCProse-CCC*, L33).

Communicative genres include two broad types of epistolary writing: formal correspondence between officials and their rulers, and informal correspondence between friends and family members. The former consists of many subtypes defined based on the specificity of occasions, functions, and addresser–addressee relationship. Of these types, memorials (*biao*) are considered to have the greatest literary value thanks to the lyrical intensity with which many writers argue for one cause or another. For this reason, three famous memorials are included in this anthology (C7.1–3), even though our focus is on informal letters (*shu*) between friends and family members.

Examining the selected memorials and letters, it is not hard to see what distinguishes Chinese epistolary prose from other genres: its communicative framework, made up of a letter writer's self-effacing, stylized pleasantries that open and end a letter. This communicative framework ultimately could be traced to the dialogic framework of pre-Qin recorded conversations. With the addressee being physically absent, however, a letter writer no longer faces the exigency of ongoing questions and answers and can put down whatever he or she wants, whether an exposition of ideas, a description of nature scenes, or an account of events. Consequently, letters are the most versatile of all prose genres because they can effectively perform, albeit in a miniature form, narrative, discursive, and descriptive functions, as indicated in the thematic table of contents (4.1–4.3).

UNDERSTANDING CHINESE PROSE FORMS

To further mitigate the translational homogenization of Chinese prose, we have undertaken a second endeavor: to make manifest the hidden form markers of Chinese prose. Chapter 1 is devoted to codifying manifold Chinese prose forms based on the employment of extratextual and textual patterning.

Extratextual patterning refers to an author's *global* organizing act, unaided by any textual device, of selecting, cutting, and integrating diverse material in a way that best conveys his or her thematic conception. It may be in some way compared to a kaleidoscopic integration of fragments into an aesthetically pleasing whole. A brainchild of the author, extratextual patterning does not allow further categorization but always can be vicariously experienced by a perceptive reader. To discern and describe a prose master's invisible, cerebral extratextual patterning behind a seemingly disjointed text is an abiding endeavor in traditional Chinese prose criticism. By contrast, textual patterning refers to a largely *local* act of organizing individual words into larger units of lines, sentences, and paragraphs. It has been employed for a broad array of purposes—to enhance the sensory impact of scene description, to amplify the emotional intensity of self-expression or communication, to enhance the persuasiveness of an oratory, and to facilitate an argumentative or expository process. Textual patterning could be quantitatively verified and classified. In my view, textual patterning consists of four major types: repetitive (pre-Qin times), aggregative (Han and Wei–Jin periods), parallel (Qi–Liang period), and parallel-repetitive (Ming-Qing times). As marked by the parentheses, these four patterns emerged in a clear historical sequence. But after its emergence, each type continues to be employed and refined in subsequent times.

The ubiquity of extratextual and textual patterning in Chinese prose is beyond question. Most of the 115 selected texts in this book employ extratextual patterning, textual patterning, or a mixture of both and are accordingly classified in the thematic table of contents. To help readers better recognize and appreciate prominent prose forms, I have clearly marked the use of textual patterning in individual texts—using straight underline for repetitive patterning, superscript numbers for aggregative patterning, and wavy underline for parallel patterning.

INTERCONNECTEDNESS OF CHINESE PROSE GENRES, FORMS, AND THEMES

As we read through the 115 selected texts, we will see an unusually high degree of interconnectedness among prose genres, forms, and, to a lesser degree, themes.

As we look at "Forms: Extratextual Patterning" in the thematic contents, we cannot fail to see that narrative genres almost exclusively employ extratextual patterning. Contrary to our common association of narration with linear sequence, the most acclaimed of Chinese narrative texts are those that deftly utilize extratextual patterning to organize diverse narrative elements in a kaleidoscopic fashion. By exploiting the gaps between narrative elements, writers aim to subtly reveal their understanding of pivotal human factors behind the unfolding of historical events. This symbiosis between narrative genres and extratextual patterning seems to stem from and in turn enhance the human-focused feature of the Chinese narrative tradition. This defining feature figures prominently in pre-Qin historical texts and eventually leads to a proliferation in subsequent times of biographical writings in varying forms. Going hand in hand with this profuse use of extratextual patterning is a notable avoidance of textual patterning in most narrative texts except in isolated citations of oratory speeches.

In discursive genres, the balance between extratextual and textual patterning is just the reverse. The inherent linear nature of reasoning renders irrelevant any use of kaleidoscopic *global* extratextual patterning. Most full-fledged discursive writings naturally follow a beginning-middle-end process, and therefore there is little need for global organization. In most circumstances, a writer needs to enhance the transition within this tripartite structure with various connectives. By the Ming and Qing times, the beginning-middle-ending structure has become so internalized by writers and readers alike that obtrusive use of connectives largely disappears in eight-legged essays. In proportion to the decreasing need of global patterning, *local* textual patterning within paragraphs becomes ever more pronounced in discursive genres, as a means of advancing political and philosophical theories, illuminating bipolar relationships, and achieving maximum rhetorical impact. In discursive genres, we see a crescendo moving from repetitive patterning in pre-Qin argumentative essays, through aggregative and parallel patterning in Six Dynasties expository prose, toward the merging of parallel and repetitive patterning in the Ming-Qing eight-legged essays. In terms of themes, discursive genres are no doubt a good place for readers to get acquainted with Confucian, Moist, Legalist, and other philosophies. The marking of textual patterning in selected discursive texts should make it easier for readers to follow the thoughts of Chinese thinkers.

As compared with narrative and discursive genres, descriptive genres are more malleable and syncretic regarding the use of patterning. In depicting a nature scene or a social occasion, a writer may opt to exclusively use extratextual patterning (C11.1–2) or textual patterning (C12.1–2) or to blend the two (C11.3), all with an impressive effect. Consequently, descriptive genres do not display the kind of close genre-form symbiosis evident in narrative and discursive genres. Descriptive genres also exhibit the same border-crossing capabilities in thematic alignment. While primarily used to convey sensory perceptions and emotional response to scenes, occasions, and events, descriptive genres also readily take on discursive functions by means of analogy or allegory (C4.3, C4.13).

With the communicative framework removed, memorials and letters are practically discursive, descriptive, and narrative writings writ small. So what has been said about the interconnectedness of genres, forms, and themes in the other three genres applies to letters as well. One point worthy of mention is a personalization and lyricization when discursive, descriptive, and narrative contents are put in the letter form. Readers may see, for instance, how abstract philosophical ideas get transmuted to burning existential issues in Sima Qian's and Ji Kang's letters (C7.4–5). It is to this magic power of personalization and lyricization that epistolary genres owe their enduring value.

THE CULTURAL SIGNIFICANCE OF CHINESE PROSE

In addition to its symbiotic integration of genres, forms, and contents, Chinese prose displays an even more important cultural specificity: its embodiment of culture at large. In promoting a new prose form, critics almost invariably make grandiose cosmological claims, enshrining it as the essence of the Dao. This line of reasoning is strictly adhered to by prominent prose critics of all persuasions and in all eras, from Liu Xie and Xiao Tong in the Six Dynasties to the Eight Masters of Tang–Song prose, the Ming–Qing critic Fang Bao, and many others. Their effusive claims for prose are far too numerous to cite here. Moving down to the less rarified ethico-sociopolitical plane, we never cease to hear arguments for or against certain prose forms couched in the strongest of glorifying or condemning terms. As time passed, forms were by turns lionized as the epitome of cultural accomplishment and condemned as decadence leading to the fall of dynasties. The dramatically changing fortunes of parallel prose are a classic case in point. At different times, polemic arguments for or against certain prose forms ushered in broad new literary and cultural movements, such as the Tang–Song Ancient-Prose movement.

Endowed with so much cultural significance, it is little wonder that traditional prose forms became a prime target of attacks during the New Culture movement and the May Fourth movement in the early twentieth century. Deemed preservers of feudal thought and obstacles to language reform, all three dominant classical prose forms—ancient-style, parallel prose, and the eight-legged essay—were relentlessly castigated and resolutely jettisoned. The eight-legged essay was rendered obsolete by the abolition of the civil service examination in 1905, leaving the other two prose forms to bear the brunt of hostile attacks by revolutionary-minded intellectuals, who deftly galvanized broad support through the famous name-calling of Qian Xuantong (1887–1939). He railed against "the evils of the Xuanxue [studies of parallel prose] and the curse of Tongcheng [school of the ancient-style prose]."[2] Vernacular Chinese, presumably untainted by traditional prose forms, has ever since been adopted as the standard prose form. As if to mark this triumph of natural, untutored vernacular prose, the term *sanwen* literally meaning "loose writing," and although it originally designated nonpatterned writing as opposed to parallel prose, it has since been elevated to name the prose genre in its entirety.

But traditions die hard and some even have a way of coming back. Thanks to the revived appreciation of traditional culture since the 1990s, traditional Chinese prose forms have staged an amazing comeback both as a means of literary composition and as a subject of scholarly research. Today, the ability to write in traditional prose forms is taken to attest to one's erudition and literary talent. In the academy, the study of prose, known as *wenzhang xue* (studies of literary compositions), has become one of the most popular areas of research. Considering these recent developments, in addition to prose's intrinsic literary and cultural significance, it seems opportune now to bring prose into the purview of Sinological literary studies and introduce its splendid art to English readers.

Zong-qi Cai

NOTES

1. Poetry boasts a sophisticated taxonomy of formal differentiations based on line syllabic counts (e.g., pentasyllabic poetry, heptasyllabic poetry), tonal regulations (e.g., regulated quatrains, regulated verse), poem lengths and so on.
2. Chen Yongbao, ed., *Qian Xuantong wusi shiqi pinglunji* (*A Collection of Qian Xuantong's Commentaries Written During the May Fourth Movement*) (Beijing: Dongfang chuban zhongxin, 1998), 1.

PART I

Overview and Pre-Qin Times

I

Anatomy of the Chinese Prose Form

An Overview

To help English readers get beyond the translational homogeneity noted in the introductory essay, we first give an overview of all major Chinese prose forms, demonstrating how they were developed for expressive, communicative, and other purposes as well as how they were consciously perfected as a medium of artistic creation over the millennia. To give such an overview, however, is easier said than done for one simple reason: As of today, Chinese prose forms have not been satisfactorily codified into a systematic whole. All existing classifications of prose forms are too broad, incomplete, and not analytical enough to illuminate the historical development of Chinese prose art.

This absence of a workable codification of prose forms is not for lack of trying by Chinese critics. In fact, codifying literary forms is an endeavor as old as Chinese literary criticism itself. During the Six Dynasties, the formative era of literary and art criticism, such codifying endeavors were all the rage, culminating in a series of amazing achievements not superseded by later critics.[1]

While adapting the term *wen* as a broad designator encompassing all rhymed poetic genres, Liu Xie (ca. 465–ca. 522) and other Six Dynasties critics use the term *bi* (literally meaning "writing brush") to designate all unrhymed prose genres.[2] This exclusive identification of *wen* with poetry effectively closed off the possibility of taking "patterning" as the differentia of prose, as I will attempt to do shortly. So, when Liu proceeds to distinguish prose genres and subgenres, he has no option but to forgo formal differentiation and classify according to the specific content, function, and context of writing, as we see in his naming of eighteen prose genres in chapters 16–25 of *Literary Mind and the Carving of Dragons*.[3]

During the Tang and Song, *wen*, originally reserved for rhymed poetry, evolved to denote, often exclusively, unrhymed prose such as *guwen* (ancient-style prose) as opposed to *shi* or poetry. Yet, even as prose wrested the exalted term *wen* for itself, forms continued to be overlooked as a source for prose classification. It was not until the Qing dynasty that critics began a serious effort to reclassify prose writings according to their formal features. But they came up with an overly broad twofold division: parallel prose (*pianwen*) versus nonparallel prose, which is considered to be "loosely constructed" (*san*). Before long, this *pian–san* division was found to be too limiting, and critics like Wang Kaiyun (1833–1916) replaced this with a new twofold division: *dan* (singular; uncoupled) versus *fu* (reduplicative; coupled). The *dan* category is largely the same as the earlier *san* category, encompassing prose writings whose sentences are not coupled. These *dan* sentences typically vary in length, sometimes quite drastically, and bear little correspondence to one another. In contrast, the *fu* category refers to prose writings whose sentences mostly conform to fixed lengths (usually four- and six-character lines) and are more often than not paired like couplets in poetry. This newly minted *fu* category differs significantly from the *pian* category noted earlier. If *pian* narrowly refers to the heavily regulated parallel prose of the Qi–Liang period, *fu* is broad enough to accommodate both parallel prose and earlier Han and Wei–Jin prose writings whose paired four-character lines do not strive for morphological and semantic correspondence.

This *dan–fu* division, arguably the most serviceable scheme available for classifying prose writings, is far from sufficient to differentiate manifold prose forms developed over millennia. It behooves us to try to construct a new codifying scheme for Chinese prose, whether our goal is in-depth research on the form or a guided anthology for English readers.

To construct such a codifying scheme may actually be easier than we think. All we have to do is go back to where Liu Xie veered off course and adopt patterning (*wen*) as a means of differentiating major prose forms. Constructing a codifying scheme for any subject entails two essential tasks: discern a common denominator and establish differentia for descending levels of organization—from genus to species to subspecies. Although Liu Xie identified patterning as the common denominator of all refined writings, he failed to take the next step and institute it as the differentia to classify prose writings. As we set out on this attempt, it may be helpful first to reflect on Liu Xizai's (1813–1881) remarks on patterning as the cardinal principle of prose writing:

> The *Commentary on the Book of Changes* writes, "Things are mixed with one another and therefore called 'patterning' " (*wen*). *Discourses of the States* writes, "If things are one and the same, there is no patterning." Xu Xie's *Comprehensive Discussion on Wen* writes, "The strong and the weak complete each other; the hard and the soft give form to each other. Therefore, the character *wen* 文 is compounded of the 人 radical [at the top] and the *yi* 乂 radical [at bottom]."

> 《易‧系傳》：“物相雜故曰文。”《國語》：“物一無文。”徐諧《說文通論》：“強弱相成，剛柔相形，故於文人乂為文。”4

> The *Discourses of the States* says that "If things are one and the same, there can be no patterning," but what people of later times should all the more know is this: if there is no "oneness" among things, there is no patterning. So "oneness" is the essence of a composition. First there must be "oneness" in a composition before one can make use of things that are not the same.5

> 《國語》言“物一無文”，後人更當知物無一則無文。蓋一乃文之真宰，必有一在其中，斯能用夫不一者也。

The first passage repeats the traditional views that (1) patterning is contingent upon prior existence of diverse components, and (2) ideal patterning emerges from a yin-yang interplay of opposing yet complementary components. The second passage presents Liu's own view of what is missing in the traditional conception of patterning: a recognition of the cardinal importance of unity, a principle much more important than that of diversity. Patterning is significant only to the extent that it brings about unity in diversity, a principle of oneness he enshrines as the essence of prose compositions.

In light of Liu's insightful expositions on patterning, we could attempt a pattern-based codification of Chinese prose by asking the following questions: Which components of a text are patterned—the entire text, paragraphs, sentences, or lines? Is this patterning achieved through textual or extratextual means? What kind of unity does patterning bring about: global or local?

Guided by these questions, we can conceptualize two broad categories of prose forms developed over millennia of Chinese writing: one based on extratextual patterning, the other on textual patterning. Extratextual patterning constitutes a global organization of content through nontextual means. In an extratextually patterned composition, loosely related or even unrelated segments are brought together as a whole, unaided by ostensible connectives or established structuring conventions. This extratextual patterning is invisible and cerebral, achieved through the author's ingenious selection, cutting, and composing of contents. This patterning is also virtual in the sense that it can, like virtual reality, be vicariously experienced by the reader through his or her mental enactment of the authorial patterning process. The brainchild of an author's conception of a given topic, extratextual patterning has infinite variety and admits no subdivision. As we will see, extratextual patterning is most frequently used in narrative writing, especially historical and biographical texts, in various different periods.

In contrast, textual patterning operates through a regular recurrence of specific textual elements. In textually patterned prose, textual elements being patterned vary greatly in almost all aspects. In length, they may be as short as binomes (i.e., bisyllabic or two-character words) or as long as sections, with lines and paragraphs between. The modes of their recurrence vary greatly as well, ranging from verbatim repetitions to nonverbatim correspondence or contrast. Nonverbatim correspondence or contrast appears in many different forms, including prosodic, semantic, and syntactic forms. Unlike extratextual patterning, however, textual patterning is visually manifested and can be easily subdivided according to what and how textual elements are patterned. Broadly speaking, we can posit four basic types of textual patterning, dominating their respective historical periods: (1) repetitive patterning in pre-Qin argument prose, (2) aggregative patterning in the discursive prose of the Han and early Six Dynasties periods, (3) parallel patterning in late–Six Dynasties descriptive and discursive prose, and (4) the parallel-repetitive patterning found in Ming–Qing examination essays.

EXTRATEXTUALLY PATTERNED NARRATIVE WRITINGS: FROM ANTIQUITY THROUGH THE QING

Applying this proposed patterning-based codification, we will now examine eight famous works of extratextually and textually patterned prose and hope thereby to provide a historical survey of Chinese prose art's evolution. In this section, I trace the trajectory of extratextual patterning as reflected by three examples drawn from antiquity, the Tang–Song, and the Qing.

EXTRATEXTUAL PATTERNING IN PRE-QIN HISTORICAL TEXTS

This type of patterning has served as a primary means of compositional organization since antiquity. A classic, early example of this is found in the *Zuozhuan* (*Zuo Tradition*) where Zhu Zhiwu's diplomatic success in thwarting the imminent invasion of the Zheng state is described:

《左傳》燭之武退秦師
燭之武退秦師

晉侯、秦伯圍鄭，以
其無禮于晉且貳于楚
也。晉軍函陵，秦軍氾
南。

佚之狐言于鄭伯曰：
「國危矣，若使燭之武
見秦君，師必退。」公
從之。辭曰：「臣之壯
也，　猶不如人；今老
矣，無能為也已。」公
曰：「吾不能早用子，
今急而求子，是寡人之
過也。然鄭亡，子亦有
不利焉！」許之。

夜縋而出，見秦伯，
曰：「秦、晉圍鄭，鄭
既知亡矣。若亡鄭而
有益于君，敢以煩執
事。越國以鄙遠，君知
其難也，焉用亡鄭以
陪鄰？鄰之厚，君之
薄也。若舍鄭以為東道
主，行李之往來，共其
乏困，君亦無所害。
且君嘗為晉君賜矣，

C1.1 *Zuo Tradition*, "Zhu Zhiwu Convinced the Qin Army to Retreat"

1. The Prince of Jin and the Liege of Qin laid siege to Zheng: this was because Zheng had acted without appropriate ritual in regard to Jin and had additionally switched allegiance to Chu. Jin was encamped at Hanling, and Qin stationed its army south of the Fan River.

2. Yi Zhihu, a Zheng minister, said to the Liege of Zheng, "The domain is in peril! If you send Zhu Zhiwu to have an audience with the ruler of Qin, their troops will surely withdraw." The Liege of Zheng followed this advice, but Zhu Zhiwu declined the mission, saying, "Even when I was in the prime of life, I was not as good as others. Now I am old, there is simply nothing I am able to do!" The Liege of Zheng said, "That I was not able to employ you, sir, early on, and only now seek you out because of an emergency is indeed my error. Still, if Zheng perishes, you too will suffer from it." So he agreed.

3. During the night, Zhu Zhiwu left the city by letting himself over the wall by rope. He had an audience with the Liege of Qin and said, "Qin and Jin are laying siege to Zheng, and Zheng already knows it will perish. If there were some advantage for you to gain, my lord, by destroying Zheng, would I dare to trouble your functionaries? You know how difficult it is to cross over a domain and join distant lands to one's frontiers. What is the use of destroying Zheng to enhance a neighbor? A neighbor's strength is your weakness, my lord. But if you release Zheng and make them the hosts of your road to the east, then as your envoys come and go, Zheng would supply what they lacked, and you, my lord, would in no way suffer harm. Moreover, you once did a favor for the ruler of Jin, and he promised you Jiao and Xia. In the morning he crossed the Yellow River to return home, and by evening he had begun laying down frames to build walls in those places. This is something

you know. How will Jin ever be satisfied? After it has extended its boundaries to the east and annexed Zheng, it will want to give free rein to expansions of its western boundary. If it does not carve away Qin, where will it get land? Carving away at Qin to benefit Jin: this is something you should consider carefully."

4. The Liege of Qin was pleased. He swore a covenant with Zheng, dispatching Qizi, Fengsun, and Yangsun to garrison Zheng, and he then turned toward home. Hu Yan requested permission to strike at the Qin forces, but the Prince of Jin said, "This cannot be done. Were it not for that man's effort, I would not have reached this position. To rely upon another's strength and then to injure him is not noble. To lose one with whom you have been allied is not wise. To replace good order with disorder is not martial. We should just return home." He also left Zheng.

[ZZ 435–437]

許君焦、瑕，朝濟而夕
設版焉，君之所知也。
夫晉，何厭之有？既東
封鄭，又欲肆其西封，
若不闕秦，將焉取之？
闕秦以利晉，唯君圖
之。"

秦伯說，與鄭人盟。使
杞子、逢孫、楊孫戍
之，乃還。子犯請擊
之。公曰："不可。微
夫人之力不及此。因人
之力而敝之，不仁；失
其所與，不知；以亂
易整，不武。吾其還
也。"亦去之。

This text displays a conspicuous absence of textual patterning. Its sentences vary in length and do not form any pattern of recurrent repetition, with the exception of the three consecutive negations in the last paragraph (indicated by straight underline). Its words are mostly monosyllabic and do not form substantive binomes. The few binomes found in this text are merely proper names of people or places (marked by boldface). With its dearth of textual patterning, why is this text so frequently anthologized and hailed as one of the finest examples of narrative prose?

To answer this question, we need to look at how extratextual patterning integrates four discrete narrative segments into a meaningful whole. This text is composed of two component parts: narrative statements and dialogues. In the Chinese text, narrative statements are highlighted in gray against the unhighlighted dialogues. Comparing the two, we note that the author is short on the former (translation is much wordier than the original) and long on the latter. Narration is reduced to a mere sketch, accentuating a chain of external causes and effects:

Qin and Jin troops' pending invasion → the meeting between Zhu Zhiwu and the Zheng ruler → Zhu Zhiwu breaking through the siege → his meeting with the Qin ruler → the withdrawal of the Qin troops → the withdrawal of the Jin troops.

By contrast, the dialogues interwoven into the narrative sketch are much longer and full of vivid details. They are meant to shed light on the human factors—or internal causes—that ultimately propel the chain of the narrated events.

As indicated in the title given to this text, Zhu Zhiwu is the most obvious human factor influencing the course of historical events. If not for his tactful diplomatic persuasion, history would have been rewritten, with the Zheng state vanquished by the allied troops of Qin and Jin. But there is a much more important human factor behind Zhu Zhiwu's diplomatic success: an intense desire, shared by individuals and states alike at the time, to uphold (or be seen as upholding) the code of honor (*yi*) and simultaneously to advance actual self-interest (*li*). Zhu Zhiwu overcame his initial reluctance and agreed to risk his life to go to the Qin as an envoy. This decision was made partly because he felt honor bound to reciprocate the Liege of Zheng's honorable apology and partly because he saw the Qin invasion threatening his self-preservation. Then, in the Qin court, he tried to talk the Qin out of its alliance with the Jin on the grounds of both self-interest and honor. His no-nonsense analysis of the Qin-Jin geopolitical rivalry undoubtedly guided the Qin ruler to see where his self-interest lay. In the same breath, Zhu Zhiwu reminded the Qin ruler of the Jin's dishonorable breach of a past agreement and thus convinced him of the moral impeccability of an annulment of the current alliance with the Jin. Surprisingly, the Jin ruler explained his decision against chasing the Qin troops also on the ground of honor. The heavy debt he owed to the Qin would make his military action against the troops unjustifiable and hence doomed to failure. It is quite a twist for the author to put these high-sounding words into the mouth of the Jin ruler, whom Zhu Zhiwu accused of violating the code of honor. Whose words should the reader believe? The author has provided no clues. Maybe, in creating this ambiguity, he wants us to take with a grain of salt all claims to moral action made in this time of ruthless self-interest by the warring states.

This story displays extratextual patterning at its best: a deft cutting and combining of narrative statements and dialogues in ways that guide the reader beyond dry historical fact to probe both external and internal causes for the historical events in question and even reflect on the complex issue of honor. From a broader historical perspective, the extratextual patterning exemplified in this *Zuozhuan* story should be seen as a continuation of what we might call the literary approach to history pioneered by *Spring and Autumn Annals* (*Chunqiu*). Both texts dispense with discursive statements and seek to pass moral judgments on historical figures and events through literary maneuvering—semantic exploitation in *Spring and Autumn Annals* and extratextual patterning in the *Zuo Tradition*. Commenting on this lineage between these texts, Liu Xizai writes, "In *Spring and Autumn Annals*, we see have the literal text right before us, but its meaning lies hidden elsewhere. Master Zuo has grasped this secret, and therefore his own writings exhibit an interplay of the literal and implied, with neither being fully fathomable."[6]

EXTRATEXTUAL PATTERNING IN TANG–SONG ANCIENT-STYLE PROSE

The next example of extratextual patterning is Han Yu's (768–824) "A Prose Farewell to Dong Shaonan," a short piece written nearly a millennium and a half after the *Zuo Tradition*. Within this long intervening period, roughly the six hundred years after the start of the common era (from the Eastern Han through the Chen dynasties) often are referred to as the "Eight Dynasties"—a period that witnessed the steady ascendancy of parallel textual patterning and the eventual absolute dominance of parallel prose. After the Sui dynasty, parallel prose began to be censured by many as "a form of decadence" responsible for the rapid fall of the Qi and Liang dynasties. To counter what he considered the pernicious influence of parallel prose, Han Yu consciously reverted to pre-Qin prose forms before the eight dynasties and, galvanizing support from like-minded scholars, succeeded in launching *Guwen yundong* (an ancient-style prose movement) that lasted through the Tang and Song dynasties. Thanks to his decisive role in pivoting away from parallel prose, he earned lavish praise from Su Shi (1037–1101): "His prose reverses the decadence of the eight dynasties" (*wenqi badai zhi shuai*).[7] To accomplish this pivot, Han adapted both extratextual and textual patterning invented in pre-Qin prose. Although his discursive writings usually employ repetitive textual patterning in the pre-Qin vein, his narrative writings are often a tour de force of extratextual patterning, as shown by this short piece:

C1.2 Han Yu, "A Prose Farewell to Dong Shaonan: Departing for North of the Yellow River"

Yan and Zhao have since ancient times been known as regions where men with deep feelings express their frustrations in ardent song. Master Dong was recommended for the Presented Scholar degree here in the capital. But the examining officials repeatedly prevented him from achieving his aims. Now, keeping his "sharpened blade" to himself, he is setting off for that region, filled with melancholy. I know he is sure to find patrons there who appreciate him. Do your best, Master Dong!

Since you have not met favor in your time, gentlemen who esteem what is right and strive to be humane will all cherish you. These traits, moreover, are inborn in the gentlemen of Yan and Zhao. Nevertheless, I have heard that local customs may change with the temper of the age. How can we be sure the region is the same today as it was in ancient times? Now that you are going there, please look into this for me. Do your best, Master Dong!

Your journey there has given me an idea: kindly go perform the mourning ritual on my behalf at the tomb of the Lord of Wangzhu. Go also to observe in the marketplace: Is there still anyone there like the dog butcher of ancient times? If so, please tell him this for me: "Today an enlightened Son of Heaven sits on the throne. You can come out of reclusion and serve!"[8]

韓愈 送董邵南遊河北序

燕趙古稱多感慨悲歌之
士。董生舉進士，連不
得志於有司。懷抱利
器，鬱鬱適茲土。吾知
其必有合也。董生勉乎
哉！
　夫以子之不遇時，苟
慕義彊仁者皆愛惜焉。
矧燕趙之士出乎其性者
哉？然吾嘗聞：風俗與
化移易。吾惡知其今不
異於古所云邪？聊以吾
子之行卜之也。董生勉
乎哉！
　吾因子有所感矣：為
我弔望諸君之墓。而觀
於其市，復有昔時屠狗
者乎？為我謝曰：“明
天子在上，可以出而仕
矣。”

[*HYWJHJJZ* 3.10.1055]

The title of this piece includes the genre title *xu*, designating a short narrative or narrated description piece composed on a specific occasion, like sending off a friend, as here. Han begins by mentioning Dong's failure in the civil service examination and his pending departure from the capital city to find a more appreciative political patron. What follows is a raft of future happenings anticipated or rather imagined by the author: Dong's encountering appreciative patrons in a land historically known for its righteousness; his paying homage (at Han's request) at the tombs of historical figures; his search for high-minded figures like Gao Jianli (the "dog butcher," failed assassin of the first emperor of China) in the marketplace; and, finally, his relaying of Han's words to the buried heroes. This vivid narrative moves by leaps and bounds, punctuated by exclamations and questions calculated to undermine his approval of Dong's journey.

Twice, he exhorts, "Do your best, Master Dong!"—as if to say, "Good luck! (you'll need it)." In the same vein, Han's polite, indirect questions about whether righteous Yan-Zhao customs have endured and such high-minded heroes may still be found are, in essence, suggestions of disapproval tactfully couched in the interrogative form.

By so structuring this short narrative, Han manages to accomplish what seems to be an impossible task: to express sincere good wishes and at the same time advise against making the trip. Han is undoubtedly against his friend's leaving the capital, thereby switching loyalty from imperial court to local vassals. Han's advice becomes clear with his final message: "Today an enlightened Son of Heaven sits on the throne. You can come out of reclusion and serve!" The real addressee is Dong, not the buried heroes.

Comparing this piece with the *Zuozhuan* excerpt (C1.1), we notice some generic and thematic changes. In contrast to pre-Qing grand historical narratives focused on intrigue and war among rival states and the lives of extraordinary political figures, Tang–Song narrative works like Han Yu's usually provide a stand-alone account of individuals—real or fictive, famous or obscure—living their lives in a less sublime setting. But as far as prose forms are concerned, many Tang–Song writers of ancient-style prose unswervingly adhere to the *Zuozhuan* way of extratextual patterning. They, too, freely truncate the temporal continuum and stitch together loosely related episodes or occasions for pretty much the same purpose: to convey their subjective judgment or views on narrated events.

EXTRATEXTUAL PATTERNING IN THE TONGCHENG ANCIENT-STYLE PROSE

For one more example of extra-textual patterning, we fast forward to the Qing dynasty and look at the prose writings of the Tongcheng school (*Tongcheng pai*). In many ways, this school may be seen as a new incarnation of the Tang–Song ancient-style prose movement as it follows in the latter's footsteps in espousing Confucian thought and championing pre-Qin prose forms. Of course, some minor differences are worthy of our attention. In content, the Tongcheng school adheres to the orthodox Song neo-Confucianism, many advocates of which were harshly critical of the Tang–Song ancient-style prose movement. In form, the Tongcheng school shows a strong tendency to exclusively use extratextual patterning in its narrative and descriptive writings. This tendency is not because Tongcheng masters eschewed textual patterning, but rather because they reserved it for the examination essay, in which many of them excelled. Another minor formal difference is that Tongcheng masters were reluctant to turn narrative and descriptive accounts, real or fictional, into moral allegory as Liu Zongyuan (773–819) had done. Instead, they were fond of writing short narratives describing occasions, events, and personages in real life, without explicit moral comment. The finest Tongcheng writers assiduously sought to fuse moral ideas into the narration—letting them shine through actions and words of real people in real-life situations—as well shown in this celebrated composition by Fang Bao (1668–1749), founder of the Tongcheng school:

C1.3 Fang Bao, "Anecdotes Concerning Zuo the Loyal and Steadfast"

方苞　左忠毅公逸事

1. My father told me that Zuo the Loyal and Steadfast, from our county [of Tongcheng, in Anhui], served as supervisor of education for the capital district. One windy, bitter cold winter day, dressed in unofficial garb, he set out on horseback along with several companions to visit an old temple. In a side room, they came upon a student slumped over his desk, having just completed a draft of an essay. No sooner had Zuo read it than he removed the ermine cloak he had been wearing and placed it over the student's shoulders. Shutting the door, he inquired of a monk at the temple who the student might be. It turned out to be Shi Kefa.

先君子嘗言，鄉先輩左忠毅公視學京畿，一日，風雪嚴寒，從數騎出，微行入古寺。廡下一生伏案臥，文方成草。公閱畢，即解貂覆生，爲掩戶。叩之寺僧，則史公可法也。

2. At the next examination, when the official calling the roll spoke Shi Kefa's name, Zuo stared in astonishment. The papers were submitted, and as soon as he read Shi Kefa's exam, he assigned it the highest mark. He then summoned Shi Kefa to his home to pay respects to his wife, saying, "Our sons are all quite mediocre. Someday this student alone will carry on my legacy."

及試，吏呼名至史公，公瞿然注視，呈卷，即面署第一。召入，使拜夫人，曰："吾諸兒碌碌，他日繼吾志事，惟此生耳。"

3. When Zuo Guangdou was imprisoned by the [eunuch's] secret police, Shi Kefa kept watch by the [prison] door day and night. But the tyrannical eunuch's guards were extremely vigilant; not even a servant from Zuo's own household could sneak past them. After a long time, Shi Kefa heard Zuo Guangdou had been tortured with a branding iron and might die any day. In tears, and offering 50 taels of silver, Shi Kefa approached a guard. The guard was moved [and relented]: one day he instructed Shi Kefa to put on a tattered coat and straw sandals. Dressed like a janitor, carrying a large bamboo basket on his back and a spade in his hands, Shi Kefa was led into the prison. The guard indicated where Zuo Guangdou was sitting on the floor, propped up against the wall; his face was singed beyond recognition, and the flesh below his left knee had been completely torn from the bone. Shi Kefa knelt before him and, clasping him by the knees, wept bitterly.

及左公下廠獄，史朝夕獄門外。逆閹防伺甚嚴，雖家僕不得近。久之，聞左公被炮烙，旦夕且死，持五十金涕泣謀於禁卒。卒感焉；一日，使史更敝衣，草屨，背筐，手長鑱，爲除不潔者，引入，微指左公處。則席地倚牆而坐，面額焦爛不可辨，左膝以下筋骨盡脫矣。史前跪，抱公膝而嗚咽。

4. Zuo Guangdou recognized Shi Kefa's voice but was unable to open his eyes. So he raised his arm and, using his fingers, pried his eyelid open. Then, with a fiery glare, he barked: "Imbecile! What are you doing here?! Our country is putrefying before our very eyes. I'm an old man whose life is already over. But look at you—risking your life [by coming here], while neglecting what really matters. Who will support the world?! If you don't get out of here immediately, those bastards won't have time to bring charges

公辨其聲，而目不可開，乃奮臂以指撥眥，目光如炬。怒曰："庸奴！此何地也！而汝來前？國家之事糜爛

至此。老夫已矣，汝復
輕身而昧大義，天下事
誰可支拄者！不速去，
無俟姦人構陷，吾今即
撲殺汝！＂因摸地上刑
械作投擊勢。史噤不敢
發聲，趨而出。後常流
涕述其事以語人，曰：
＂吾師肺肝，皆鐵石所
鑄造也。＂

崇禎末，流賊張獻忠出
沒蘄、黃、潛、桐間，
史公以鳳廬道奉檄守
禦。每有警，輒數月不
就寢，使將士更休，而
自坐幄幕外。擇健卒十
人，令二人蹲踞而背倚
之，漏鼓移則番代。每
寒夜起立，振衣裳，甲
上冰霜迸落，鏗然有
聲。或勸以少休，公
曰：＂吾上恐負朝廷，
下恐愧吾師也。＂

史公治兵，往來桐城，
必躬造左公第，候太
公、太母起居，拜夫人
於堂上。余宗老塗山，
左公甥也，與先君子
善，謂獄中語乃親得之
于史公云。

[*MQSWX* 269–272]

against you; I'll kill you myself—right now!" So saying, he groped his way on the ground until he found an instrument of torture and flung it at Shi Kefa. Shi Kefa fled, not daring to make a sound. Later, he often shed tears as he recounted these events, saying, "My teacher's conviction was rock solid; he had an iron will."

5. In the final years of the Chongzhen reign [1627–1644], the roving bandit Zhang Xianzhong preyed on the regions of Qichun and Huanggang [in modern-day Hubei province], as well as Qianshan and Tongcheng [in modern-day Anhui province]. Shi Kefa, as Military Circuit Intendant of Fengyang and Lujiang [in modern-day Anhui], was ordered to defend these areas. Whenever an incident was reported, he would not go to bed for several months. He instructed his men to rest in shifts, and he himself sat outside the tent. He would choose ten strong men and make two of them kneel on the ground; he would lean against them until the drum sounding the hour was beaten. Then two more men would take their place. On cold nights, he would stand and shake his cloak, and the frost and ice that had accumulated on his armor would fall to the ground with a crash. If anyone urged him to rest, he would reply: "I fear betraying my country and disgracing my teacher."

6. When Shi Kefa led an army through Tongcheng, he insisted on visiting Zuo's home, personally inquiring into the well-being of his parents, and paying respects to Zuo's widow in the formal hall. My senior kinsman [Fang] Tushan, Zuo's son-in-law, maintained cordial relations with my late father and told me that Shi had personally related to him what happened in prison.[9]

These touching encounters between Zuo the Loyal and Steadfast (Zuo Guangdou, 1575–1625) and his protégé Shi Kefa (1602–1645) were not included in official records: hence the *yishi* (anecdotes) in the composition's title. With its five episodes set in different locales over time, the text offers vivid snapshots of action and speeches that, by turns, warm, break, and uplift our hearts.

The first episode depicts Zuo's first speechless encounter with Shi: Zuo the examiner spots Shi, a poor examination candidate slumped over a desk, and puts his ermine cloak over him. In the second episode, Zuo discovers Shi to be the top examinee and announces to his wife that Shi, rather than his own less-talented sons, will be his successor. These two episodes reveal Zuo's gentler side—his selfless love for a young talent who he believes will shoulder the hope of his country.

Against this gentleness, we are then stunned by Zuo's almost superhuman fortitude in the face of unthinkable torture and his rejection of Shi's consolation when he needs it most. This episode presents a dramatic clash of two equally touching sights: Shi bursting out crying at the sight of his teacher singed beyond recognition, and Zuo scolding, even threatening to kill, Shi for coming to see him at the risk of arrest and ultimate forfeit of his sacred mission for the country. With Zuo's gentleness and fierce strength thus juxtaposed, we are led to ponder and discover where these two sides of his character meet: an unswerving loyalty to his country as immortalized by his posthumous title "loyal and steadfast."

Even after his death, Zuo continues to loom large in the narrative, as Shi's endurance of physical hardship (fourth episode) and gentle, respectful attention to Zuo's family (final episode) function as a reincarnation of Zuo's steely and gentle character, grounded in unwavering loyalty. Once we understand this, we realize the fourth and fifth episodes are not anticlimactic at all, but lift the narrative to a higher plane: Zuo's steadfast loyalty is transformed into a moral force that survives him to profoundly shape Shi's character and that of many others.

Fang Bao's account of Zuo's life undoubtedly attains the ideal of *yifa* (moral meaning and formal methods) he established for the Tongcheng school. Explaining what he means by *yi*, he cites the *Commentaries on the Book of Changes*: "What's said has substance" (*Yan zhi you wu*). To elucidate the meaning of *fa*, he cites another remark from the *Commentaries on the Book of Changes*: "What's said is orderly" (*Yan zhi you xu*). Traditionally, *yi* and *fa* have been seen as dichotomous concepts akin to content and form in modern literary criticism. But this analysis of "Anecdotes Concerning Zuo the Loyal and Steadfast" certainly invalidates such a dichotomous understanding of *yifa*. To begin with, the text does not rely on abstract moral concepts or discursive statements to depict Zuo's and Shi's character. So we cannot speak of any self-contained tenor (content) being carried by the vehicle (form). Instead, the import of what is said is completely infused in its orderliness. As shown by this text, the "orderliness" Fang and other Tongcheng writers sought is anything but an orderly linear sequence. Rather, it is a combination of loosely connected episodes unified by a central thematic conception—in this case, the inner character of loyalty and steadfastness, complemented by the gentlest of love.

These three examples (C1.1–C1.3) reveal the hallmark of the finest Chinese narrative prose: a productive, dynamic interplay between diversity and oneness. If "diversity" pertains to the selection of narrative material, "oneness" refers to the act of extratextual patterning to unify diverse narrative elements into an artistic whole. Explaining what propels this exercise of oneness, Liu Xizai writes, "A narrative work must have a central thematic conception, just as a commentary must have a canonical text [prior to its coming into being]."[10] In the long Chinese narrative tradition following the *Zuo Tradition*, this authorial thematic conception (*zhuyi*) is seldom conceptually articulated and usually left embedded in the structuring of a composition. At its best, such a thematic conception can be seen as an act of envisagement that transcends conceptual thinking and breathes a living presence, subjective or otherwise, into a composition. Speaking of this great potential, Liu Xizai writes, "A narrative work must have an indwelling principle, emotion, vital breath, or insight. Without such an indwelling presence, it will be like a lifeless figurine."[11]

TEXTUALLY PATTERNED DISCURSIVE AND DESCRIPTIVE WRITINGS FROM PRE-QIN TIMES THROUGH THE QING

If extratextual patterning reigns supreme in Chinese narrative prose, textual patterning figures prominently in Chinese discursive and descriptive prose. The latter is created through a regular recurrence of textual elements: repeated words, phrases, or sentences; and correspondence (prosodic, morphological, semantic, or syntactic) between two coupled lines or twin lines.

The ascendancy of four basic patterning forms follows a sequential timeline: repetitive patterning in pre-Qin times, aggregative in the Han–Wei and Jin periods, parallel in the [Liu] Song and Qi–Liang, and parallel-repetitive in the Ming–Qing. If the first three patterning forms took turns dominating non-narrative prose before the Tang, they entered a phase of conscious, intense rivalry in the Tang. This sectarian competition was initiated by Tang and Song proponents of ancient-style prose who castigated parallel patterning as decadent and consciously revived the unadorned repetitive patterning developed by pre-Qing prose masters. Yet parallel patterning continued to evolve as new subforms of parallel prose arose during the Tang and Song and, later, the Qing. Out of the prolonged rivalry between repetitive and parallel patterning, a hybrid of the two emerged in the Ming: parallel-repetitive patterning adopted for the examination or so-called eight-legged essay (*baguwen*). This fourth form of textual patterning was all the rage until its sudden demise in the final years of the Qing. Having sketched the four basic patterning forms in the broadest strokes, I next demonstrate the distinct features of each through an analysis of one well-known example.

REPETITIVE PATTERNING IN PRE-QIN ARGUMENT WRITINGS

Repetitive patterning entails the repetition of words, word clusters, or even entire sentences, usually more than twice. Such verbatim repetitions can occur in a one-line sentence or a long sentence spanning multiple lines. Repetitive patterning is a primary mode of expression commonly found in the earliest oral traditions. For instance, English and Scottish ballads extensively employ what is termed "incremental repetition": a device involving the "repetition of lines or stanzas with small but crucial changes made to a few words from one to the next, and has an effect of narrative progression or suspense."[12] A similar kind of repetitive patterning, which we might very well call "incremental repetition," is prodigiously used in the folk songs of the *Book of Poetry*, China's oldest collection of poems. But here, beyond the effect of "narrative progression and suspense," it serves as the primary means of emotional expression and dramatic performance. Moreover, unlike its English counterpart, this repetitive patterning is used as much in prose as poetry, as often by educated elites as illiterate oral performers. When used in prose as opposed to poetry, does repetitive patterning assume a different form and serve new functions? To find an answer, we turn to a well-known excerpt from the *Mencius*:

C1.4 *Mencius*, "Fish Is What I Want" 《孟子》魚我所欲也魚我所欲也

孟子曰：

Mencius says:

1. 魚，我所欲也，熊掌，亦我所欲也；二者不可得兼，舍魚而取熊掌者也。
   生，亦我所欲也，義 亦我所欲也； 二者不可得兼，舍生而取義者也。

   Fish is what I want; bear's palm is also what I want. If I cannot have both, I would rather take the bear's palm than fish. Life is what I want; righteousness is also what I want. If I cannot have both, I would rather take righteousness than life.

2. 生亦我所欲，所欲有甚於生者，故不為苟得也；
   死亦我所惡，所惡有甚於死者，故患有所不辟也。

   On the one hand, though life is what I want, there is something I want more than life. That is why I do not cling to life at all costs. On the other hand, though death is what I loathe, there is something I loathe more than death. That is why there are troubles I do not avoid.

3. 如 使人之所欲莫甚於生，則凡可以得生者，何不用也？
   使人之所惡莫甚於死者，則凡可以辟患者，何不為也？
   由是則生而有不用也，
   由是則可以辟患而有不為也，

   If there is nothing a man wants more than life, then why should he have scruples about any means, so long as it will serve to keep him alive? If there is nothing a man loathes more than death, then why should he have scruples about any means, so long as it helps him to avoid this bane? Yet there are ways of remaining alive and ways of avoiding death to which a man will not resort.

4. 是故 所欲有甚於生者，
   所惡有甚於死者。
   非獨賢者有是心也，人皆有之，賢者能勿喪耳。

   Given this In other words, there are things a man wants more than life, and there are also things he loathes more than death. This is an attitude not confined to the moral man but common to all men. The moral man simply never loses it."[13]

[*MZYZ* 265–266]

N.B. Straight underline indicates the use of repetitive patterning. The boldfaced parts are words, phrases, and sentences that are not repeated.

For clearer analysis, the text is divided into four segments. In each, the underlined parts are verbatim repetitions of words, phrases, and sentences, all of which are "correspondingly aligned" (*paibiju*), that is, cast in corresponding positions in two paired sentences. The boldfaced parts are words, phrases, and sentences that are not repeated. This lopsided ratio between underlined and boldfaced parts shows how heavy the repetitive patterning is in this passage—much more so than in most *Shijing* folk songs. The connectives (italicized) used to link up the four discrete segments betrays yet another fundamental difference in the use of repetitive patterning in prose as opposed to poetry in pre-Qin times.

The Peach Tree Tender 詩經•桃夭

桃之夭夭，灼灼其華, /之子于歸，宜其室家。//
桃之夭夭，有蕡其實, /之子于歸，宜其家室。//
桃之夭夭，其葉蓁蓁, /之子于歸，宜其家人。//

The peach tree budding and tender, vivid and bright its flowers./This girl is
   going to be married, and fit for her chamber and house.//
The peach tree budding and tender, quite large its fruit./This girl is going to
   be married, and fit for her house and chamber.//
The peach tree budding and tender, its leaves luxuriant and lush./This girl is
   going to be married, and fits with all in the family.//[14]

In the *Book of Poetry*, as shown by this folk song, each stanza is repetitively patterned and constitutes what is called *bi*, *xing*, or *bixing* in traditional Chinese
poetics—a structure marked by a juxtaposition of an imagistic and a discursive part, with a conspicuous gap between the two (indicated by single slashes).
In addition to such an intrasegment gap, there are also gaps between different
segments (indicated by double slashes). These intrasegment and intersegment
gaps have long been lauded by Chinese critics for evoking rich poetic association
or even imagination. In contrast, repetitive patterning in the *Mencius* excerpt
allows no gaps within each segment. Moreover, it seeks to close any possible
gaps between segments by inserting connectives to lock up the four discrete
parts. This enhanced cohesiveness reveals repetitive patterning's new and opposite function in prose: to facilitate a linear, step-by-step process of argumentation, instead of breaking up the continuum to evoke poetic imagination in the
Shijing fashion.

   This *Mencius* excerpt is a perfect example of argumentation aided by repetitive patterning. Mencius launches into a sustained argument to validate his view
that goodness, shown as a love of righteousness, is the ultimate nature of human
beings, superseding their physical nature. To validate this view, Mencius spares
no effort to prove that man yearns for righteousness more than preservation of
his physical life. He begins by stating the obvious: man desires fish, but a rare and
expensive delicacy (bear paw), even more. Next, he draws an analogy between this
natural choice and another of a higher kind: the choice of righteousness over one's
physical life. In the second segment, he asserts the lesser desirability of one's physical life versus something more valuable, but then the lesser fear of death versus
something worse. In the third segment, he puts the same assertion in a different
modality—that of questioning. "Why should he have scruples about" is just an
emphatic way to state that people do have scruples about life saving or death avoiding means, namely their worries about whether these means would harm something more important than life—righteousness. To amplify this point, he restates
these two choices as natural, inevitable ones. In the last segment, he restates this
assertion once more, adding that this love of righteousness is innate in us all, but
only the moral retain it. Such an interlocking of repetitive patterning dominates

pre-Qin argumentative prose and exerts considerable influence on the prose of all subsequent periods with the exception of the Six Dynasties.[15]

AGGREGATIVE PATTERNING IN HAN AND WEI–JIN DISCURSIVE WRITINGS

Aggregative patterning refers to a cumulative use of binomes to form successive lines of equal length—primarily four- and six-character lines. It differs from repetitive patterning in that it no longer yokes sentences together through the heavy use of verbatim repetition. This shift was made possible through the explosive growth of binomes during the Han. Thanks to this sudden abundance of binomes, Han and Wei–Jin prose writers begin to pile up binomes to form four- and six-character lines, laying the foundation for subsequent conscious exploitation in parallel prose of morphological and semantic correspondence between coupled lines. In chapter 7, I have marked out, with superscript numbers [4] and [6], the prodigious use of four-character and six-character lines in all selected texts. The variant superscripts [4+1] and [6+1] indicate variant four-character and six-character lines with an addition of one function word that has no meaning in itself.

In Chinese prose criticism, aggregative patterning is identified by many as an early form of parallel patterning. In my opinion, the absence of persistent, conscious exploitation of morphological and semantic correspondence is a qualitative difference that warrants a differentiation of aggregative versus parallel patterning. With this differentiation, we can clearly perceive a three-stage trajectory (repetitive → aggregative → parallel) in the development of textual patterning from pre-Qin times through the Six Dynasties.

To see this transition from repetitive to aggregative patterning, we look at a short family letter written by Zhuge Liang (181–234), the famed strategist for the Shu of the Three Kingdoms.

C1.5 Zhuge Liang, "A Letter Admonishing My Son" 諸葛亮 誡子書

1. 夫 [4]君子/之行, [4]靜以/修身, [4]儉以/養德。
   This is how a superior man conducts himself: cultivating the self through mental tranquility and fostering morality through frugal living.

2. 非/[6]澹泊/無以/明志,
   非/[6]寧靜/無以/致遠。
   If one is not free of mundane desires, one cannot know what his true aspiration should be; if one's mind isn't tranquil and peaceful, one cannot achieve any far-reaching success.

3. 夫 [4]學/須靜/也,
   [4]才/須學/也。
   Learning requires a peaceful mind; talent requires constant learning.

4. [6]非學/無以/廣才,
   [6]非志/無以/成學。
   Without learning, one cannot reach the fullest potential of one's talents; without aspiration, one cannot achieve goals of learning.

5. ⁶⁺¹淫慢/則/不能/勵精，
⁶⁺¹險躁/則/不能/治性。

If one dawdles, one cannot invigorate his spirit; if one acts impetuously, one cannot forge one's character.

6. ⁴年/與時/馳，
⁴意/與日/去，
⁴遂成/枯落，⁴多不/接世，⁴悲守/窮廬，⁴將復/何及！

One's years gallop with time; one's aspiration dwindles with each passing day. As a result, like a leaf withering away, one becomes disengaged from the world and finds oneself pitifully trapped in a humble hut, lamenting the squandered time that will never come back.[16]

[ZGLJ 28]

This family letter, among the best known of its kind in China, presents a to-do list along with how-to-do advice, all couched in pithy and memorable binomes. The to-do list includes exhortations to cultivate oneself, foster one's morality, and reach one's potential. These exhortations are all expressed with verbal binomes that are "bonded" (i.e., having fixed meanings) and display a verb + object combination: cultivate (*xiu*) + oneself (*shen*); foster (*yang*) + one's virtues (*de*); know (*ming*) + one's intent (*zhi*); reach (*zhi*) + a distant place/goal (*yuan*); broaden (*guang*) + one's talent (*cai*); complete (*cheng*) + one's learning (*xue*); invigorate (*li*) + one's spirit (*jing*); forge (*ye*) + one's character (*xing*). The how-to-do advice spells out the essential conditions required for achieving the exhorted goals: freedom from mundane desires (*danpo*), mental tranquility (*ningjing*), intellectual training (*xue*), and temperament flaws to be avoided (*taoman, xianzao*). To achieve the maximum impact, these conditions are twice stated, first in the emphatic double-negative form "If not . . . one cannot . . ." (*fei . . . . . . wuyi. . . .*) and then in plain supposition "[If] . . . then one cannot . . ." (. . . *ze* . . .). Ending this letter, Zhuge Liang warns his son of the pathetic consequences that will befall him should he not heed his father's admonition and squander his precious time.

With the Chinese text parsed with slashes, the preponderance of binomes becomes all the more conspicuous. Of the binomes marked out by slashes, those set in boldface have stable, fixed meanings, whereas those not marked in boldface are not yet bonded but make sense contextually. The bonded binomes outnumber the unbonded. By doubling binomes, the author constructs four-character lines for his declarative statements (segments 1, 3, and 6). Alternately, by tripling binomes, he produces six-character lines to accommodate complex cause-effect suppositions cast in the double negative (segments 2 and 4) or simple affirmative form (segment 5). This doubling and tripling binomes is a pronounced feature of prose from the Han–Wei and Jin periods.

The dominance of four-character (and, to a lesser extent, six-character) lines in Han–Wei and Jin prose is a development of profound significance in the history of Chinese prose. These types of lines are often coupled, inviting prose writers to exploit morphological and semantic correspondence between them, just as they did in poetry. Generally speaking, the writers of the Han–Wei period were less preoccupied with morphological and semantic correspondence than those closer to the Qi–Liang period. But Zhuge Liang seems to offer an exception. In "A Letter Admonishing My Son," we observe his persistent effort to establish morphological and semantic correspondence. Indeed, segments 2–5 are all coupled sentences, with morphological categories and semantic tenor neatly matched. For instance, in segment 5, *taoman* (dawdling and slow) and *xianzao* (reckless and impetuous) match each other perfectly, both are adjectival binomes and synonymous in meaning. The same could be said of his pairing the verbal binomes *lijing* (invigorating one's spirit) and *yexing* (forging one's character). To accentuate such morphological and semantic correspondence, I have marked all coupled lines by setting them in two lines in the Chinese text and separating them with a semicolon in the English translation.

In many ways, aggregative patterning can be seen as a transitional form between pre-Qing repetitive patterning and the Song-Qi-Liang parallel patterning. Zhuge Liang's letter seems on the cusp of morphing into the latter. In fact, if the alternate-line parallelism (*geju dui*) (the hallmark of parallel prose examined in the next example) were employed as well, it very well could be taken as parallel prose composition. Besides its transitional role, aggregative patterning exerts a great influence on renowned Qing prose masters like Wang Zhong (1744–1794), Li Zhaoluo (1769–1841), and Wang Kaiyun, who consciously adapted it for their narrative and descriptive writings and produced masterpieces like Wang Zhong's "Lamenting the Salt Boat."[17]

PARALLEL PATTERNING IN DESCRIPTIVE AND EXPOSITORY WRITINGS OF THE SIX DYNASTIES

Parallel patterning is a natural outgrowth of aggregative patterning because it is built on the latter's staple of four- and six-character lines. Coming to the Qi–Liang period, parallelistic patterning practically became the standard rubric for writing prose as well as poetry, at least as far as literati writings are concerned. Considering the prevalence of such patterning, it is no surprise that the term "parallel prose" (*pianwen*) was minted during the Qing to characterize the well-wrought prose of this period. [18]

Qi–Liang parallel prose can be divided, thematically and formally, into two broad types: the descriptive and the expository. To demonstrate first the unique features of descriptive parallel prose, we turn to a famous landscape depiction by Wu Jun (469–520).

C1.6 Wu Jun, "A Letter to Zhu Yuansi" (excerpt) 吳均 與朱元思書(摘錄)

| 1. 風煙 俱淨
　\| \|　\| \|
天山 共色。

There was not a whiff of smoke or mist, and the color of the sky matched the hills. | 2. 從流 飄蕩，
　\| \|
任意 東西。

We drifted with the current, which bore us now in one direction, now in another. | 3. 自富陽至桐廬，一百許里，
Along the hundred-odd li we traversed from Fuyang to Tunglu, |

4. 奇山異水， 　天下獨絕。 There are spectacular mountains and water, unrivaled in the world.	5. 水皆縹碧，千丈見底； 　游魚細石，直視無礙。 The water was throughout a clear green, and over the deepest pools, we fancied we saw to a depth of hundreds of feet; for we could see the fish swimming and the pebbles on the riverbed.	6. 急湍 甚箭， 　｜｜　｜｜ 　猛浪 若奔。 At times the current was swift as an arrow, and angry waves surged forward.
7. 夾岸高山， 　皆生寒樹， The hills on either bank were planted with coniferous trees	8. 負勢 競上，互相 軒邈， 　｜｜　｜｜ 　爭高 直指，千百 成峯。 and rose to a great height, seeming to vie with one another in steepness or eminence. There were hundreds of jutting peaks.	9. 泉水激石，泠泠 作響； 　｜｜　　　｜｜　｜｜ 　好鳥相鳴，嚶嚶 成韻。 The torrents dashed against the rocks as they came rushing down the hillsides, humming and gurgling. The birds sang melodiously in chorus.
10. 蟬 則 千轉 不窮， 　｜　　　｜｜　｜｜ 　猿 則 百叫 無絕。 The chirping of cicadas was interrupted now and then by the ape's shrill cries.	11. 鳶飛戾天者，望峯 息心； 　　　　　　　｜｜　｜｜ 　經綸世務者，窺谷 忘返。 Even as the eagle desists from its soaring flight when confronted with a massive mountain, so those engaged in governmental affairs would forgo their worldly ambitions if they set eyes on one of the mysterious ravines,	12. 橫柯 上蔽，在晝猶昏； 　｜｜　｜｜ 　疏條 交映，有時見日。 shrouded in perpetual twilight by thick overhanging trees forming a screen through which the sun but seldom penetrates.[19] [WJNBCWXSCKZL 652]

N.B. Wavy underline indicates the use of parallel patterning. Vertical lines indicate character-to-character paralleling.

Of the thirty-four lines in this text, twenty-nine lines (85 percent) are four-character lines, and three lines (9 percent) are six-character lines. An addition of one extra character creates two variants of the two basic line types: five-character lines and seven-character lines. These paralleled parts make up 94 percent of the lines in this text.

Breathtaking scenes stretch over a hundred *li* as we follow the narrator in his boat, drifting aimlessly down the mountain stream. The composition consists of eleven units of coupled lines along with one uncoupled unit (the italicized third). The first four units are informational, telling us when, how, and where the boat journey took place and present the topic of description: spectacular scenery of water and mountains. The next four units alternate between river and mountain scenes, which contain alternating, contrasting subscenes. First, still and transparent pools (unit 5) are set against swift rapids and surging waves (unit 6); and then motionless mountains (unit 7) are followed by imagined soaring of the mountains (unit 8). Then, units 9–10 turn from the world of sights to that of sounds: the bubbling of a spring, chirping of birds and cicadas, and cries of apes blending into perfect harmony. The final two units (11–12) return to the mountain view, now lifted skyward to where the eagle dares not soar, inspiring a wish to forgo worldly affairs and find refuge in these mountains.

This piece of descriptive parallel prose vividly reminds us of the landscape poetry written by Xie Lingyun (385–433) just decades earlier; its salient formal features may be best demonstrated through a comparison of their similarities and differences. First, we note their similar exploitation of the morphological and semantic correspondence between coupled lines. In presenting the delightful sights and sounds of his excursion, Wu does exactly what Xie has done, casting them all in well-wrought parallel lines. In this prose piece, all its coupled lines entail morphological and semantic correspondence, with segments 1, 2, 6, and 8–11 containing the neatest kind. First, as indicated by wavy underlines, all binomes in these segments are *both* morphologically and semantically matched: nouns with nouns (e.g., *jituan* [swift current] with *menglang* [surging waves] and verbal phrase with verbal phrase (e.g., *wangfeng* [seeing peaks] with *kuigu* [peeking into ravines]). Moreover, this matching penetrates to the level of single characters. In segment 11, for instance, the paralleled binomes (*wangfeng* with *kuigu*) entail a matching of verbs (*wang* with *kui*) and a matching of object-nouns (*feng* with *gu*). Such character-to-character matching is indicated by vertical lines linking matched characters.

What, then, distinguishes Wu's prose landscape description from Xie's poetic counterpart? The absence of rhyme, of course, is the most obvious. The second most obvious is perhaps the change from Xie's five-character lines to Wu's four-character lines. The profound significance of this one-character reduction, however, is rarely discussed, although it leads, in my view, to a fundamental change in authorial presentation and reader reception. In a five-character line, the odd fifth character is often a verb flexibly deployed from any position within the line. Most frequently it appears as the third character with two noun binomes (mostly natural images) on either side. In this position, the author uses it to convey the dynamic interplay of two natural phenomena, grand or minuscule.[20] Alternatively, two verbs are employed in a line, one appearing in the first- or second-character position, the other in the third-, fourth-, or fifth-character position.[21] In such a two-verb line, two snapshots of nature's action are sequentially presented, inviting us to perceive them in a cause-effect relationship. In both types of lines, the lone verb character enables Xie to convey to the reader his intense perception or imagination of the interplay between natural images or scenes. [22]

In Wu's prose, the disappearance of this free-floating one-verb character necessitates a fundamental change of presentation and reception. In a four-character line, the one-character verb almost invariably appears with a noun after it or an adverb before it. This leaves space only for a noun binome. If a line can accommodate just one natural image, we cannot speak of any perceived interaction between natural phenomena. Consequently, Wu had to report his sense impressions of nature in an aggregative fashion—one line for one impression, using as many lines as he had impressions.

To mitigate this lack of interplay of images, Wu and other parallel prose writers resurrected what is called "fanlike parallelism" (*shandui*), an ancient module of parallelism tracing back to the *Book of Poetry*, that can be considered an extension of a normal couplet. When each line of a couplet is extended to two lines to accommodate more content, we have a four-line parallel module in which the first line is paralleled with the third and the second with the fourth. This can be accurately called "alternate-line parallelism" (*geju dui*). Although it was used only sporadically in the *Book of Poetry* and dispensed with altogether in pentasyllabic poetry, it caught on in Six Dynasties parallel prose and became one of its defining features. In descriptive parallel prose like Wu's piece, it primarily functions to accommodate more images and to set them in dynamic interplay. In segment 9, for instance, it is only through an alternate-line parallelism that Wu Jun managed to blend four delightfully heard sounds—from the bubbling spring, chirping birds and cicadas, and crying apes—in perfect harmony. This newfound popularity of alternate-line parallelism also has much to do with its special usefulness for discursive writings, as shown by the next example.

In turning our attention to expository parallel prose, we examine the following excerpt from the "Spirit Thought" (Shensi) chapter of the *Literary Mind*, in which Liu Xie analyzes the dynamic interplay of transcendental roaming with physiological and linguistic intervention in the creative mind:

C1.7 Liu Xie, *Literary Mind*, "Spirit Thought" 《文心雕龍》神思

1.
　　　　³古人云：⁶**形** 在 **江海** 之上，
　　　　　　　│ │　　　│ │
　　　　　　⁶**心** 存 **魏闕** 之下。
⁵神思之謂也。⁴文之思也，⁴其神遠矣。

An ancient said, "while one's body is on the rivers and lakes, his mind remains at the foot of the high palace tower." *This is what is called "spirit and thought." In the exercise of the literary mind, the spirit travels afar.*

2.　故
　　　　⁴寂然 **凝慮**，⁴思 接 **千載**；
　　　　　│ │ │ │　 │ │ │ │
　　　　⁴悄焉 **動容**，⁴視 通 **萬里**。
　　　　⁴吟詠 之 間，⁶吐納 珠玉 之 聲；
　　　　　│ │　│ │　 │ │ │ │　│ │
　　　　⁴眉睫 之 前，⁶卷舒 風雲 之 色。

Quietly attaining concentration, his thinking may go through one thousand years; slightly stirring his countenance, his seeing may traverse ten thousand *li*.

In the midst of his chanting and singing, the sounds of pearls and jade issue forth. Right before his brows and lashes, the spectacle of windblown clouds spreads out.

3.
其思理之致乎！⁶故思理為妙，⁴⁺¹神與物遊。⁴

All this is made possible by the workings of the mind. With the workings of the mind at its most miraculous, the spirit wanders along with things.

4.
^{4}神 居 胸臆，$^{6+1}$而 志氣 統 其 關鍵；
^{4}物 沿 耳目，$^{6+1}$而 辭令 管 其 樞機。
^{4}樞機 方通，$^{4+1}$則 物無 隱貌；
^{4}關鍵 將塞，$^{4+1}$則 神有 遯心。

The spirit dwells in the bosom, with intent (*zhi*) and vital breath (*qi*) being the pivot of its outlet. Things come to us through ear and eye, with words and phrases controlling the hinge and trigger [for their influx].

When the hinge and trigger allow passage, no external things can have hidden appearance. When the pivot of its outlet is closed, the spirit is impeded.

5. 是以
For this reason,

^{4}陶鈞 文思，^{4}貴在虛靜；
^{4}疏瀹 五藏，^{4}澡雪精神。
^{5}積學 以 儲寶，^{5}酌理 以 富才，
^{5}研閱 以 窮照，^{5}馴致 以 懌辭。

in shaping and developing literary thought, the greatest importance lies in "emptiness and stillness": so, remove obstructions in the five viscera and cleanse the spirit!

One must accumulate learning to store up treasures; one must contemplate the principles [of things] to enrich his talent; one must sharpen his perceptual power to bring things to the fullest light; one must master literary art to make his phrasing felicitous.

6. 然後使
Only after all these

^{4}玄解 之 宰，^{6}尋 聲律 而 定墨；
^{4}獨照 之 匠，^{6}闚 意象 而 運斤。

does one exercise the power of "the mysterious butcher" within him to search for metric patterns and set down words. Only then does he call up the "master wheelwright" within him to wield the axe [of phrasing] in accord with the image of his mind.

7. 此蓋
This, in short,

^{5}馭文之首術，
^{5}謀篇之大端。

is the cardinal principle of writing and the primary guide for drafting a composition.[23]

[*WXDLSY* 338]

N.B. Wavy underline indicates the use of parallel patterning.

Superscripted number indicates the number of characters in a line. Of the thirty-nine lines in this text, nineteen lines (49 percent) are four-character lines, and 7 (18 percent) are six-character lines. An addition of one extra character creates two variants of the two basic line types: five-character lines and seven-character lines. These paralleled parts make up 82 percent of the lines in this excerpt.

Comparing this excerpt with Wu Jun's piece, we can discern two features that distinguish expository parallel prose from descriptive parallel prose. The first is the more extensive use of nonparallel sentences and connectives (indicated by italics). In segments 1 and 3, nonparallel sentences set forth the two main topics of discussion: the mind's transcendental flight (*shen, shensi*) versus conscious thinking (*sili*).

Placed at the head of other segments (second column), short connectives spell out the temporal or logical relationships between adjacent parallel blocks, thus effectively advancing a sustained linear expository process.

The second distinguishing feature is the use of a much richer variety of parallel patterning. In expository parallel prose, with nonparallel sentences and connectives providing global organization, parallel patterning primarily serves as a means of local organization—that is, to provide an optimal grid, with which an author can present multiple concepts and statements and illuminate their intricate relationship. As expository contents vary greatly in complexity, a corresponding repertoire of parallel forms are developed and deployed in the Six Dynasties parallel prose. Liu is undoubtedly a superb master of these forms. In this excerpt, each choice of parallel form is best suited to a specific need in a given stage of exposition.

Segment 1 begins with a parallel form of the simplest kind: a coupling of two single lines: "while one's body is on the rivers and lakes, his mind remains at the foot of the high palace tower." Nonetheless, this parallelism is more sophisticated than what was seen in Wu Jun's piece, as it operates through not a double correspondence in morphology and semantics, but rather a tension between morphological correspondence and semantic antithesis (shown in boldface). As shown by the vertical lines in the block citation, all corresponding characters have the same parts of speech. In meaning, however, all major characters are antithetically set (again, in boldface): the physical form (*xing*) versus the heart (*xin*); rivers and lakes (*jianghai*) versus the Wei tower (*weique*); above (*shang*) versus below (*xia*). This simple antithetical parallelism serves Liu's purpose perfectly: to capture the transcendental flight of the mind unhindered by geographical separation.

In segment 2, Liu provides a fuller description of this transcendental flight. For this, he employs two units of alternate-line parallelism. In the first, the first and second lines contrast a cessation of thought (*ninglü*) with a stirring of one's countenance (*dongrong*), while the second and fourth lines create a contrast between "one thousand years" (*qianzai*) and "ten thousand *li*" (*wanli*). If the first unit introduces a new dimension of time, the second tells us that this transcendental flight is a two-way journey, eventually returning to appear before the author, in the virtual form of sounds and sights.

Segment 4 turns to discuss the physiological and linguistic mediation needed to launch a transcendental flight of the mind. It consists of two units of alternate-line parallelism, which have a gap between them and therefore do not read as smoothly as other parallel units. On closer examination, we discover that these units are actually constructed by breaking up a longer, four-line parallelism:

¹神居胸臆，²而志氣統其關鍵；³關鍵將塞，⁴則神有遯心。
⁵物沿耳目，⁶而辭令管其樞機。⁷樞機方通，⁸則物無隱貌。

The intended meaning comes through much more clearly in this extended parallelism. The first four lines explain three essential points regarding the spirit's outward flight: (1) the spirit resides in the mind before its outward flight; (2) the vital energy is the conduit of spirit; (3) if the conduit is blocked, transcendental flight will be thwarted. Similarly, the next four lines explain three essential points pertaining to the spirit's inward flight: (1) spirit courses back with things (i.e., images), through ears and eyes, to the author; (2) phrasing competence is the crucial medium through which this inbound flight must pass; and (3) if this medium is wide open, things will reveal their true form. But if Liu were to present his ideas in this way, he would be writing ancient-style prose rather than parallel prose, which allows only four lines in an alternate-line parallelism. A seemingly simple solution would be to break the eight lines in this way:

神居胸臆[1]，而志氣統其關鍵[2]；
關鍵將塞[3]，則神有遯心[4]。
物沿耳目[5]，而辭令管其樞機[6]。
樞機方通[7]，則物無隱貌[8]。

But this would not work either, because all parallel lines must be of equal length. Here, the second and fourth lines and the sixth and eighth lines are of different lengths. So, the only solution left is to reposition the third and fourth lines after the seventh and eighth lines, as Liu has actually done. In this case, we witness an uncommon instance of the required parallel form impeding the expository process.[24]

Segment 5 features yet another example of a long nonparallel sentence pigeonholed into parallel form. What Liu means to say is this: 陶鈞文思，貴在虛靜，[貴在]疏瀹五藏，[貴在]澡雪精神. In other words, the last two lines are actually object clauses of the second line's verbal phrase "the importance lies in" (guizai). But the rules of parallelism force him to break up this sentence and turn it into an imperfect alternate-line parallelism. This is followed by a "to-do" list for any writer who wishes to embark on the two-way flight of spirit and reach the optimal state for compositional execution, the final creative stage adumbrated in segment 6.

Having examined the entire excerpt, we cannot but admire Liu's virtuosity in parallel patterning. Taking advantage of allowable expandability of line length, he masterfully varies his lines to best advance his expository process, and in this excerpt, uses no parallel form twice. When he has run out of choices toward the end, he unexpectedly employs enumerative cataloging, a device associated with the rhapsody (fu) genre, as he lists the writer's four tasks of learning. This constant length variation, slight though it is, effectively mitigates the boredom of recurrent textual patterning and injects cadence and energy into what easily could have been a monotonous exposition.

PARALLEL-REPETITIVE PATTERNING: MING–QING EXAMINATION ESSAYS

The Ming–Qing examination essay, called *shiwen*, *shiyi*, *zhiyi*, and so on, may be seen as a hybrid of parallel and ancient-style prose. In content, it faithfully adheres to Confucian thought as championed by Song neo-Confucians. The examinee must assume the persona of a Confucian sage and expound the significance of a phrase, line, or small section from a canonic Confucian text in ways that illuminate contemporary sociopolitical issues. In form, the examination essay bears imprints of both parallel prose and Tang–Song ancient-style prose. Its most distinctive features are structural standardization and a merging of repetitive and parallel patterning, as illustrated in this famous essay by Chen Zilong (1608–1647).[25]

C1.8 Chen Zilong, "A Superior Man Detests Dying Without Achieving Renown" 陳子龍　君子疾沒世而名不稱焉

1.	破題 Breaking open the topic	無後世之名，聖人之所憂也。 That he will lack renown in posterity, this is what worries the sage.
2.	承題 Developing the topic	夫 一時 之名 不必有也， 　後世 之名 不可無也。 故君子不求名，而又不得不疾乎此。 Indeed, short-lived renown is dispensable; renown in later times is requisite. Therefore, the superior man does not seek renown, yet he cannot but suffer concern about it.
3.	起講 Beginning discussion	夫子若曰：好名者，人之恒情也，故下士求名，人亦不得以為躁，但我恨其急一時之名，而非千秋萬世之名耳，若君子則知所以審處於此矣。 The Master [Confucius] would say: To love renown is people's normal inclination. Thus, when a low-status gentleman seeks renown, people should not regard him as impetuous. I would just regret his hastening after short-lived renown, rather than the renown of ten thousand generations. A superior man would reflect seriously in managing this.

4.	起股 Initial legs	**4a.**以為一時之名，自我 為之，而其權在人，苟我之聰明才力，注乎名則有名，而 皆倚人 以為重，盛 與 衰我不得而知之，此名而 名者也； Speaking more specifically, while short-lived renown is shaped by oneself, the ultimate power lies with others. If I pour my wisdom and talent into pursuing such renown, I will attain it. But that [kind of] renown relies heavily on others, and I cannot know whether it will rise or fall. This is renown in name only.	**4b.**千秋萬世 之名，自人 為之，而其權在我，苟我之聰明才力，注乎名未必有名，而常修己以自立，高與下我將得而定之，此名而 實者也。 Though renown that lasts ten thousand generations is shaped by others, the ultimate power lies in oneself. If I pour my wisdom and talent into pursuing such renown, I will not necessarily attain it. But with regular self-cultivation to establish myself, I get to determine whether it is lofty or lowly. This is renown with substance.
5.	中股 Middle legs	**5a.**名而 名者，無之在於 未沒世之前，君子豈可以徒疾乎？ Renown in name only: lacking it before death, how could a superior man disapprove of this?	**5b.**名而 實者，無之在於 既沒世之後，君子豈得而不疾乎？ Renown with substance: lacking it after death, how could a superior man not be distressed by this?
6.	後股 Penultimate legs	**6a.**人之生也有愛有憎，故有幸而 有名者，有不幸而 無 名者，至於身沒之後，與其人不相接，則不可曰愛憎之所為也，而寂寂者竟如斯，則將何以自異於里巷之子耶？	**6b.**人之生也有失勢有得勢，故有幸而 無 名者，又有不幸而 有名者，至於身沒之後，與其時不相及，則又有非得勢失勢之可論矣，而泯泯者遂如斯，則又何以自別於草木之儔耶？

In life, people have their loves and hates. [Accordingly] the fortunate become famous, and the unfortunate become obscure. After death, they have no contact with people [of later times], so [their reputations] cannot be said to result from [latter-day people's] loves or hates. In a situation like this, if one becomes forgotten [posthumously], how can he distinguish himself from the riffraff of alleys and lanes?

In life people can hit or miss the trend of the times. So some have luck but not renown, while others have no luck but do gain renown. After death, they become irrelevant to contemporary times, so there is no matter of hitting or missing the trend to discuss. In a situation like this, if one becomes obscure [posthumously], how can he distinguish himself from the common run of folk?

7. 束股
Last legs

7a. 人之貴乎榮名者，貴其有益生之樂也；君子之貴榮名者，貴其有不死之業也。死而無聞，則其死可悲矣；死而可悲，則其生更可悲矣。是以君子抗節礪行，惟恐不及耳。

An [ordinary] man, in valuing great renown, is valuing its increase to life's enjoyment. A superior man, in valuing great renown, is valuing its [mark of] immortal accomplishment. A death in obscurity is a lamentable death. If one's death is lamentable, then one's life is even more lamentable. So a superior man upholds principles and refines his conduct, fearing only that [renown] may not be reached.

7b. 人之以為沒世之名者，是我身後之計也；君子以為沒世之名者，是我大生之事也。死而無聞，則其死不及憂矣；死不及憂，則其生大可憂矣。是以君子趨事赴功，惟日不足耳。

To an [ordinary] man, posthumous renown concerns one's plan for what happens after one dies. To a superior man, posthumous renown constitutes the challenge of one's whole life. A death in obscurity is a death not worth concern. If one's death is not worth concern, then one's life is greatly concerning. So a superior man hastens to [handle] affairs and strives for success, [worrying] only that there is not sufficient time.

8. 大結
Grand conclusion

人但見君子之為人也，譽之而不喜，毀之而不懼，以為君子之忘名也如此，而不知有所甚不忘也；不大言以欺人，不奇行以駭俗，以為君子之遠名也如此，而不知有所甚不遠也。蓋有大於此者而已，有久於此者而已。若夫營營於旦夕之間，是求速盡者也，好名者豈如是乎？

People merely observe a superior man's behavior: He is neither happy when praised nor scared when maligned. So people take this to be his indifference to renown, not knowing what it is that he never forgets. He does not exaggerate to deceive others nor act strangely to astound the world. So people take this to be his distancing himself from renown, not knowing that from which he never is distant. There simply is something greater than [what they perceive], and more lasting as well. If one bustles about from dawn to dusk [hoping to gain a short-term reputation], it is simply the pursuit of a quick demise. How could one who loves [true] renown be like that? [26]

[*QDSSW* vol. 14, 5.3a–4b]

N.B. Straight underline indicates the use of repetitive patterning.

Structural standardization is a form of textual patterning unseen in earlier prose forms. Although parallel prose standardized its line length, its structure remained unstandardized. Only the Ming–Qing examination essay adopts a highly rigorous and rigid structural standardization. As shown by this essay, its sections are standardized, each bearing a name designating its specific function in the expositional process (as shown in the second column). The length of the examination essay, too, is largely standardized, to a range of three hundred to five hundred characters. Its sections can be subsumed under three parts: beginning, middle, and end.

The beginning contains three (as in the current essay) or four sections. The first section is meant to "Break Open the Topic," usually one or two sentences performing two functions: to identify the speaker in the examination topic (a quote from the Five Confucian Classics or the Four Great Books) without explicitly naming him and to pinpoint the significance of the topic. Chen uses the word "sage" to subtly identify Confucius as the speaker expressing the fear of dying without leaving behind a name. The second section, "Developing the Topic," sets forth antithetical notions, dimensions, or positions pertaining to the topic. Here, Chen introduces a dichotomy between short-lived and lasting renown and tells us what a superior man dreads lacking on his death. The first two sections ("Break Open the Topic" and "Developing the Topic") appear in all examination essays, but the remainder of the beginning could be a single section (as in the current essay) or two sections, in which the examinee begins to assume the persona of a Confucian sage and elucidate the topic. Here, speaking in the voice of Confucius, Chen spells out the contrast between the two types of renown pursued by low-status scholars and a superior man.

The middle is the core of an examination essay and is composed of six or eight neatly paralleled sections (marked "a" and "b"). Each section in this core middle part is called a "leg"; hence, the examination essay becomes known as the eight-legged essay even though some essays contain only six legs. In each pair of legs, the examinee is expected to contrast antithetical notions or positions from a fresh perspective to reaffirm the superiority of one notion or position over its antithetical other.

In the initial legs (sections 4a and 4b), Chen begins by contrasting the two types of renown in paradoxical terms of attainment and nonattainment. Present-day renown may very well be attained by those who are talented and hard-driving but at the cost of not attaining lasting renown because of the neglect of moral cultivation in their headlong pursuit of present-day renown. Moreover, insofar as present-day renown cannot be attained without other people—specifically, those in power—it is but an empty name. Conversely, one does not have to depend on other people in pursuing posthumous renown. Although one may not attain posthumous renown despite his talent and endeavors, he is at least assured that what he strives for is real and lasting, not an empty name.

If the initial legs focus on differentiating these two types of renown in terms of substance (or lack of it), the penultimate legs (sections 6a and 6b) compare the superior man's worries about not attaining the two types of renown. The "middle legs" (section 5) provide a perfect transition between the initial and middle legs because it introduces not only the new topic of worry or fear but also a new perspective—now comparative rather than contrastive—for exploring it. Instead of contrasting the low-status scholar's and superior man's pursuits of renown, this transitional section compares the superior man's worries about not attaining the two types of renown. In section 5a, Chen uses the adverb "only" (*tu*) in the rhetorical question "how could a superior man *only* worry about this?" to subtly endorse a superior man's interest in or even pursuit of present-day renown. This endorsement is consistent with what he has said about the legitimacy of pursuing present-day renown in the "Beginning Discussion" (section 3) and projects a superior man as a true human being with his natural mundane interest and concerns. In section 4b, he talks about a superior man's greater worry or rather fear of not attaining lasting posthumous renown with a more emphatically phrased rhetorical question "how could a superior man *not* worry about this?"

The penultimate legs (section 6) continue to place the superior man and the ordinary man on the same plane as it dwells on their shared misery in not attaining posthumous renown. The first half of 6a depicts an alignment between fortunate life circumstances and attainment of present-day renown, and between unfortunate life circumstances and nonattainment of present-day renown. By contrast, the first half of section 6b presents a dis-alignment of these two sets of relationship. In the second half of both sections 6a and 6b, Chen dismisses the significance of present-day renown for a simple reason: attained through favors bestowed by contemporaries or opportune circumstances in one's lifetime, it will cease to exist with the disappearance of these favorable temporal factors. So, with or without present-day renown, one is condemned all the same to the obscurity of "riffraff of alleys and lanes" and "the likes of wood and weeds."

Having stated the ultimate meaninglessness of present-day renown, Chen moves to expound the paramount significance of posthumous renown in the last legs (section 7). He reverts to contrasting the ordinary with the superior man's views. In section 7a, he projects the image of the superior man standing high above the ordinary man, taking pity on the latter for leading his life completely oblivious to the possibility of lasting renown or existence. In section 7b, he further lauds the superior man's pursuit of posthumous renown through stark contrast with the ordinary man's indifference to it.

The grand conclusion (section 8) sums up this sustained, multistage argument on renown in a most tactful way. The examinee is allowed to step out of the voice of the sage and offer his personal reflections. Taking advantage of this convention, Chen ingeniously shifts his role from an interlocutor to a silent, omniscient spectator, observing how ordinary men perceive at once correctly and erroneously the superior man's renown-forgetting conduct. They do so correctly because they sense in a superior man's conduct the forgetting of present-day renown ordinary men obsess over. They do so erroneously because they fail to see that unlike a Daoist master forgetting, even denouncing all renown, a Confucian superior man dedicates himself to earning posthumous renown, an immortality that rises above all worldly values. Through this penetrating ridicule of ordinary people's misperception, Chen neatly posits the Confucian ideal of immortal renown while simultaneously effecting a formal tour de force: the two antithetical threads running throughout the essay—ordinary versus superior man, present-day versus posthumous renown—are naturally and almost imperceptibly tied together in a seemingly simple act of third-person observation.

The standardized structure of the examination essay exemplified here strikes us as a prose version of the highly regulated examination poetry (*shitie shi*) developed in the Tang, particularly in their shared tripartite structure. In both, the beginning and the ending are much shorter than the core/middle. The avoidance of parallel patterning is another shared feature, although less strict in the examination essay than in examination poetry. The middle of the two genres bears even greater resemblance: the essay's middle is composed of six or eight legs (subsections) cast in three or four paralleled sections, whereas the poetry's middle consists of six or eight lines that form three or four parallel couplets. All of these structural resemblances leave no doubt that the examination essay was modeled, at least in part, on earlier examination poetry. [27]

The tripartite structure of the examination essay may be traced back to expository parallel prose. If we compare the three parts of Chen's essay with those in the excerpt above by Liu Xie (C1.7), we easily see that Chen is following a three-stage expository process similar to Liu's: to set forth a topic with straightforward, unadorned (slightly parallel at most) statements; expound two different aspects of the topic with correspondingly paralleled sections; and, finally, sum up the sustained exposition in a succinct and forceful manner.

If its structure bears the indelible imprint of parallel patterning from Tang examination poetry and Six Dynasties parallel prose, the eight-legged essay is indebted for its phrasing to the earlier repetitive patterning of pre-Qin prose. If we compare the paralleled subsections (sections 4a and 4b, sections 5a and 5b, sections 6a and 6b, and sections 7a and 7b) in Chen's essay, we notice this intrasection parallelism operates through verbatim repetitions rather than subtle exploitation of intricate morphological-semantic correspondence as in Liu's essay. As shown by the underlined text, the preponderance of verbatim repetitions is dramatic, as in the *Mencius* excerpt (C1.4), while persistent, contrived parallel phrasing is practically absent. What has made such phrasing impossible is the constant varying of line length, which is another distinguishing feature of ancient-style prose. As indicated by wavy underlined text, however, simple parallel phrasing, ranging from one to four characters long, does occur within larger repetitive syntax and often is cast antithetically to emphasize contrasts in meaning.

Given its equal debts to repetitive and parallel patterning, the eight-legged essay may be appropriately regarded as a hybrid of parallel prose and ancient-style prose, with a distinct parallel-repetitive patterning.[28]

PROSE FORMS AND PROSE GENRES: INTERPLAY OF EXTRATEXTUAL AND TEXTUAL PATTERNING

The eight well-known examples examined in this chapter trace the evolution of Chinese prose along its dual paths of patterning. The path of extratextual patterning is that of continual structural innovation aiming to turn, like a kaleidoscope, narrative fragments into a unified, enchanting vision, through which the author can convey historical moral judgment (C1.1), express complex, ineffable sentiment (C1.2), or reveal the innermost world of a biographical subject (C1.3). In other words, extratextual patterning exemplifies an art of spatializing temporal narration as subjective vision. By contrast, the path of textual patterning is a dazzling, ceaseless display of linguistic virtuosity, exploiting textual repetition, correspondence, and contrast—one form after another and at one level after another—to produce the maximum descriptive and discursive impact.

The paths of extratextual and textual patterning are perfectly synced with the development of three main prose genres: narrative, descriptive, and discursive. We might even speak of a symbiosis between extratextual patterning and narrative writings by literati or literary-minded historians. These writings rarely employ textual patterning in the narrative proper and mainly depend on extratextual patterning to unify narrative components as a whole. The symbiosis between textual patterning and descriptive and discursive genres is no less obvious. In the descriptive genre, textual patterning introduces recurring repetitions and correspondence on prosodic, semantic, syntactic, and other levels, thus creating a one-step-forward-and-half-step movement that allows the reader to pause to take in the interplay of words and images.

In a discursive genre, textual patterning is primarily employed to advance thought processes. Pre-Qin philosophical writings employ a rich repertoire of repetitive patterning for purposes ranging from enumerative comparison to analogical thinking to inductive reasoning. These writings are often argumentative in nature, intended to convince the targeted reader to accept certain ethico-sociopolitical ideas and positions. Late–Six Dynasties discursive writings mostly take the form of parallel prose, marked by heavy, multilayered parallel patterning; they tend to be expository in nature, aiming to explain and analyze the interplay of bipolar ideas, positions, and relations. As epitomized by the examination essay, Ming–Qing discursive writings often exhibit a combination of pre-Qin-style repetitive patterning and Six Dynasties–style parallel patterning to create a standardized beginning-middle-end module that sustains a prolonged process of exposition.

The paths of extratextual and textual patterning, while advancing on their own, do cross, as amply evidenced by their mixing in narrative writings of all periods. In this regard, textual patterning is the less accommodating of the two. As a rule, discursive writings are tightly textually patterned and contain few breaks where an extended narration or description might be inserted. Descriptive writings tend to be tightly textually patterned as well even though a discursive ending is often appended to them. Extratextual patterning is far more flexible and accommodating than textual patterning. Extratextual, by default, means an absence of textual patterning and implies, ironically, an open space for adding textually patterned elements. In the pre-Qin conversation-style writings like the *Analects*, for instance, we most frequently see nonpatterned narrative segments juxtaposed with pithy, neatly patterned remarks by Confucius. For more examples, we may look at the patterned phrasing in the ending parts of Sima Qian's (ca. 145–ca. 86 BCE) "Biography of

Boyi" (☛ *HTRCProse-CCC*, L13–14) and Tao Qian's (ca. 352–427) "The Biography of Mr. Five Willows" (☛ *HTRCProse-CCC*, L15). In Han and Six Dynasties historical texts, this bifurcation of the nonpatterned narrative proper and meticulously patterned encomiums is so conspicuous and prevalent that Xiao Tong (501–531) deems fit to treat the encomiums in these texts as a discrete subgenre and include it in his *Anthology of Refined Literature*, while expunging the narrative proper from this exclusive collection of textually patterned writings.

In addition to their ability to accommodate alien patterned passages, narrative texts display extraordinary versatility by taking on roles normally belonging to the discursive genre. For instance, in his "On Fiefdom" (*Fengjian lun*), Liu Zongyuan expounds his view of fiefdom with narrative material framed by a few abstract statements. In "On Liu Hou" (*Liuhou lun*), Su Shi goes one step further and dispenses with discursive statements altogether. By deftly weaving narrative fragments around Zhang Liang's life, Su elucidates the redemptive virtue of forbearance much more forcefully than discursive statements would have allowed. These two texts, we may very well say, are narrative in form but discursive in essence.

We return, in conclusion, to the artistic and cultural uniqueness of Chinese prose. In a nutshell, Chinese prose art is a kind of artistic patterning that could be adapted in endlessly varied ways to all sorts of genres—even the most utilitarian—while still yielding aesthetic pleasure. Because of this, Chinese writers have continued over millennia to invent new variations on that patterning, through textual and extratextual maneuvers. In the realm of criticism, they have continually engaged in collecting, preserving, anthologizing, and critiquing prose as an esteemed form of art.

Zong-Qi Cai

NOTES

1. See Zong-qi Cai, ed., *Chinese Aesthetics: The Ordering of Literature, Arts, and the Universe in the Six Dynasties* (Honolulu: University of Hawai'i Press, 2004), 1–28.

2. Of the fifty chapters in Liu Xie's *Literary Mind and the Carving of Dragons* (*Wenxin diaolong*; hereafter the *Literary Mind*), twenty chapters are devoted to surveying the evolution of thirty-five major genres. Of these twenty chapters, the first ten chapters focus on rhymed (*wen*) genres and the other ten chapters on unrhymed (*bi*) genres.

3. Observe the emphasis on content, mode, and function in genre names such as "Histories and Biographies" (*Shizhuan*), "Treatises and Speeches" (*Lunshuo*), "Edicts and Decrees" (*Zhaoce*), "War Proclamations and Dispatches" (*Xiyi*), "Sacrificial Addresses to Heaven and Earth" (*Fengchan*), and so on.

4. Liu Xizai, *Yigai* (*Essentials of the Arts*) (Shanghai: Shanghai guji chubanshe, 1978), 47.

5. Liu Xizai, *Yigai* (*Essentials of the Arts*), 48.

6. Liu Xizai, *Yigai* (*Essentials of the Arts*), 1.

7. Su Shi, *Su Shi quanji* (*Complete Works of Su Shi*) (Shanghai: Shanghai guji chubanshe, 2000), 988.

8. Translated by Ronald Egan in chap. 11, "Tang and Song Occasional Prose: Accounts of Place, Thing, and Events."

9. Translated by Rivi Handler-Spitz in chap. 15, "Ming and Qing Occasional Prose: Letters and Funerary Inscriptions.,"

10. Liu Xizai, *Yigai* (*Essentials of the Arts*), 42.

11. Liu Xizai, *Yigai* (*Essentials of the Arts*), 42.

12. Chris Baldick, *The Concise Oxford Dictionary of Literary Terms* (Oxford: Oxford University Press, 1996), 167.

13. D. C. Lau, trans., *Mencius* (Hong Kong: Chinese University Press, 2003), 253–255. Slightly modified.

14. *Mao shi Zheng jian* (*Zheng Xuan's Comments on the Mao Edition of* The Book of Poetry), *Sibu beiyao edition*, 1.6b–7a, trans. William H. Nienhauser, in *HTRCP*, 16.

15. For more examples of repetitive patterning, see for instance C5.3, *Hanfeizi*, "The Five Kinds of Vermin"; C5.7, *Mozi*, "The Will of Heaven, Part C"; and C10.1, Han Yu, "On the Origin of the Way."

16. My translation.

17. For more examples of aggregative patterning, see the writings included in chap. 7, "Han and Six Dynasties Epistolary Prose: Memorials and Letters Memorials and Letters," and C11.3, Fan Zhongyan, "Yueyang Tower Inscription."

18. For succinct introductions to parallel prose, see James R. Hightower, "Some Characteristics of Parallel Prose," in *Studies in Chinese Literature*, ed. John Bishop (Cambridge, MA: Harvard University Press, 1965), 108–139; C. Bradford Langley, "Pien wen" ["Parallel Rose"], in *Indiana Companion to Traditional Chinese Literature*, ed. William H. Nienhauser (Bloomington: Indiana University Press, 1986), 656–660.

19. Translated by H. C. Chang in John Minford and S. M. Lau, eds., *Classical Chinese Literature: An Anthology of Translations* (Hong Kong: Chinese University Press and New York: Columbia University Press, 2000), 613–614. Slightly modified.

20. See, for instance, lines 6–7, 13–17 of "What I Observed as I Crossed the Lake on My Way from Southern Mountain to Northern Mountain," in *HTRCP*, 133.

21. See, for instance, lines 2–4, 10–11, 17–20 of "What I Observed as I Crossed the Lake on My Way," in *HTRCP*, 133.

22. See my comments on Xie's famous couplet "pond bank grow spring grass, garden willow change crying birds" (literal translation) in *HTRCP*, 385–386.

23. My translation.

24. On the constraints of the parallel form faced by Liu Xie, see Stephen Owen, "Liu Xie and the Discourse Machine," in *A Chinese Literary Mind: Culture, Creativity, and Rhetoric in Wenxin diaolong*, ed. Zong-qi Cai (Stanford, CA: Stanford University Press, 2001), 175–191.

25. For succinct introductions to the eight-legged essay, see Jin Kemu, *Bagu xinlun* and Andrew Plaks, "Pa-ku wen" ["Eight-Legged Essays"], in *Indiana Companion to Traditional Chinese Literature*, ed. William H. Nienhauser (Bloomington: Indiana University Press, 1986), 641–643.

26. Translated by Manling Luo in chap. 14, "Ming and Qing Eight-Legged Essays.".

27. The relationship between these two examination genres is that of mutual, rather than one-way, influence. In Qing times, some examinees consciously imitated the structure of the eight-legged essay by correlating the sequence of poetic lines with the sequence of sections in an eight-legged essay.

28. For a parody of the eight-legged essay, see C14.2, You Tong, "How Irresistible That Parting Glance of Her [Eyes, Like] Autumn Ripples?"

SUGGESTED READING

ENGLISH

Cai, Zong-qi, ed. *A Chinese Literary Mind: Culture, Creativity, and Rhetoric in Wenxin diaolong*. Stanford, CA: Stanford University Press, 2001.

——. ed. *Chinese Aesthetics: The Ordering of Literature, Arts, and the Universe in the Six Dynasties*. Honolulu: University of Hawai'i Press, 2004.

Hightower, James R. "Some Characteristics of Parallel Prose." In *Studies in Chinese Literature*, edited by John Bishop, 108–139. Cambridge, MA: Harvard University Press, 1965.

Langley, C. Bradford. "Pien wen" ["Parallel Prose"]. In *Indiana Companion to Traditional Chinese Literature*, edited by William H. Nienhauser, 656–660. Bloomington: Indiana University Press, 1986.

Nienhauser, William H. "Prose." In *Indiana Companion to Traditional Chinese Literature*, edited by William H. Nienhauser, 93–120. Bloomington: Indiana University Press, 1986.

Owen, Stephen. "Liu Xie and the Discourse Machine." In *A Chinese Literary Mind: Culture, Creativity, and Rhetoric in Wenxin diaolong*, edited by Zong-qi Cai, 175–191. Stanford, CA: Stanford University Press, 2001.

Plaks, Andrew H. "Pa-ku wen" ["Eight-Legged Essays"]. In *Indiana Companion to Traditional Chinese Literature*, edited by William H. Nienhauser, 641–643. Bloomington: Indiana University Press, 1986.

Richter, Antje. *Letters and Epistolary Culture in Early Medieval China*. Seattle: University of Washington Press, 2013.

CHINESE

Deng Yunxiang 鄧雲鄉. *Qing dai baguwen* 清代八股文 (*The Eight-Legged Essays of the Qing Dynasty*). Beijing: Zhonghua shuju, 2015.

He Shihai 何詩海. "Wenzhang mo nan yu xushi shuo jiqi wenzhangxue yiyi" "文章莫難於敘事" 說及其文章學意義" (The Claim That "No Literary Writing Is More Difficult Than the Narrative" and Its Significance in the Study of Literary Compositions). *Wenxue yichan* 文學遺產 (*Literary Heritage*), no. 1 (2018): 106–118.

Jin Kemu 金克木. *Bagu xinlun* 八股新論 (*A New Treatise on the Eight-Legged Essay*). Beijing: Sanlian shudian, 2017.

Liu Linsheng 劉麟生. *Zhongguo pianwen shi* 中國駢文史 (*History of Chinese Parallel Prose*). Beijing: Dongfang chubanshe, 1996.

2

Pre-Qin Historical Prose

Zuo Tradition (Zuozhuan)

It is hard to overstate the foundational role of *Zuo Tradition* (*Zuozhuan*) in the Chinese tradition. On the most obvious level, countless idioms and allusions in the Chinese language are derived from this ancient text. *Zuozhuan* established the form of annalistic historical narrative; its notions of causality and patterns, use of speeches to frame ideas and explain events, and juxtaposition of narrative and judgment (as framed comment) have become standard practice in Chinese historiography. The importance of *Zuozhuan* for the literary tradition is no less profound. Many of the prose genres discussed by Liu Xie (ca. 465–ca. 522) in *Literary Mind and Carvings of Dragons* (*Wenxin diaolong*; hereafter *Literary Mind*), such as remonstrance, exposition, biography, ordinance, persuasion, disputation, inscription, recitation, eulogy, prayer, and lamentation, look back to examples from *Zuozhuan*. Revered as a model of classical prose for its conciseness and power of symbolic concentration, its excerpts appear repeatedly in imperial prose anthologies to explain principles of literary composition. Movements of renewal in Chinese prose also invariably invoke *Zuozhuan*. The text has even exerted a profound influence on the form and method of fiction, if only because of the long tradition of continuity between history and fiction, evident in the terms "unofficial history" (*baishi*) and "lesser history" (*yeshi*) for what we would categorize as fiction. Indeed, *Zuozhuan*'s interest in ghosts, spirits, dreams, omens, prophecies, and secret communication has led some scholars to hail it as a key source of the Chinese fictional imagination.

Zuozhuan is the largest text to survive from pre–imperial China (i.e., from the period when China was divided into many states, before unification in 221 BCE). It comes to us as a commentary on the annalistic *Spring and Autumn Annals* (*Chunqiu*), traditionally associated with Confucius as its supposed author or editor. Spanning 242 years and the reigns of twelve Lu rulers (722–481 BCE), *Chunqiu* tersely records sacrifices, covenants, battles, intrigues, rebellions, accessions, marriages, formal state visits, and births and deaths among the ruling elite, as well as astronomical movements and disasters, such as fires, floods, droughts, and locust plagues. Entries were probably compiled as the events took place or shortly thereafter; some seem to be transcriptions of interstate notifications. Their information is by and large reliable. Following the year-by-year chronology of *Chunqiu* but covering a longer period (722–468 BCE), *Zuozhuan* elaborates many of its incidents with narrative details and rhetorical flourishes, often conveying a sense of temporal and geographical precision. The exact relationship between *Zuozhuan* and *Chunqiu*, however, remains a matter of debate. Some argue that *Zuozhuan* is an amalgamation of Warring States materials rearranged to present a narrative elaboration of and exegetical commentary on *Chunqiu* entries. The traditional view of *Zuozhuan* as a commentary on *Chunqiu* affirms the role of narrative elaboration in articulating moral ideals. Those who draw attention to its deviations from a Confucian vision appeal to *Zuozhuan*'s complex textual history, arguing that its different sources and layers result in a range of perspectives. The product of a long period of accretion and transmission, *Zuozhuan* resists precise dating. Probably already in existence by fourth century BCE, it has much to tell us about both the years it purports to chronicle as well as the era of its own textual formation.

Zuozhuan has long been read as a reliable history of the period it covers, a repository of Confucian values, and a foundational text in the Chinese literary tradition. If we question *Zuozhuan*'s historical veracity (at least in the literal sense—e.g., we do not believe a speech was uttered exactly as recorded, or prophetic dreams necessarily occurred), or recognize that this complex text cannot be reduced to a simple set of Confucian values, we can hardly question the raw power of its narrative and the rhetorical brilliance of its speeches. Liu Xie praised *Zuozhuan* prose as "the winged glory of the sages' writings, the crowning achievements of records and texts."[1] *Zuozhuan* is famous for its linguistic economy, whereby high drama is concentrated in a few words. To name just one example: In the account of the battle of Bi between Jin and Chu in 597 BCE, the Jin commander, anxious to gather the remnants of his defeated army, issues a panicked order: "Those who cross the river first will be rewarded!" Predictably, Jin soldiers fight to board the boats. Soldiers already in the boat, fearing pursuit by the Chu army and afraid the boats will sink under excessive weight, try to fend off those struggling to climb aboard by chopping off their fingers. "The fingers in the boats were so numerous that they could be scooped up."[2] This single gruesome detail captures the disarray and demoralization of the retreating Jin troops as well as the barbarity of warfare. Such stylistic economy coexists with the pleasure in rhetoric, evident in lengthy and elaborately patterned speeches in *Zuozhuan*.

With an aesthetics of reticence and symbolic concentration, a gesture, an utterance, or a descriptive line can capture a person's character and destiny or sum up a complex historical situation. Han historian Sima Qian (ca. 145–ca. 86 BCE) develops this focus on emblematic moments and uses them to create unity, resonance, and momentum in *Grand Scribe's Records* (*Shiji*, ☞ chap. 6). In many later examples of prose and fiction, significant moments often become the focal points of a narrative, sometimes defying the logic of plot or teleology. At the same time, *Zuozhuan*'s chronological arrangement, sometimes breaking up continuous development and separating cause and consequence, encourages habits of weaving and decoding plots that place special emphasis on the interplay of associations and discontinuities, clues and signs and temporal and spatial shifts.

In the following excerpts from *Zuozhuan*, I have added titles for the sake of clarity. In the original, they are of course unmarked beyond the historical year of the narrative. The arrangement follows Yang Bojun's (1902–1992) annotated *Zuozhuan* (*Chunqiu Zuozhuan zhu*), thus "Yin 1.4" indicates the fourth entry for the first year in the reign of Lord Yin of Lu (722 BCE), and the translation follows *Zuo Tradition*, with some modifications. In the original, a character is often called multiple names; the translators have unified the names to make the narrative easier to follow. Days in traditional China were named by a sequence of characters recurring in a cycle of sixty combinations, the so-called sexagenary cycle. In *Zuo Tradition*, the cyclical date names are used and the sequence day of the month is put in parenthesis.

FAMILY AND POLITY: LORD ZHUANG OF ZHENG (R. 744–701 BCE), HIS BROTHER, AND HIS MOTHER

C2.1 *Zuo Tradition*, "The Zheng Ruler Overcame Duan at Yan," Yin 1.4 (722 BCE)

Earlier, Lord Wu of Zheng had taken a wife in Shen. Known as Wu Jiang, she gave birth to Lord Zhuang and Gongshu Duan.[1] Lord Zhuang was breech born, and Lady Jiang was shaken. For this reason, she named him Wusheng [Breech Born] and consequently hated him. She loved Gongshu Duan and wanted to establish him as ruler. Time and again she asked this favor of Lord Wu, but the lord would not grant it. When Lord Zhuang acceded to his position, she requested Zhi for Duan. The lord said, "Zhi is a strategic settlement. Guo Shu died because of it.[2] For any other place, you need only issue a command!" She requested Jing, and the lord sent Duan to live there. Duan came to be called "The Senior Younger Brother of the Walled City Jing."

Zhai Zhong said, "For the wall of an outlying city to exceed one hundred *zhi* is a danger for the capital.[3] In the system of the former kings, large cities did not exceed one-third of the capital, middle-sized cities did not exceed one-fifth, and small cities, one-ninth. Now Jing, failing to conform to this standard, is not in accordance with the rules. You, my lord, will not be able to bear that." The lord said, "Since Lady Jiang wanted this, how am I to avoid harm?" Zhai Zhong replied, "How will Lady Jiang ever be satisfied? It would be better

---

[1] Wu Jiang's name combines the clan name of her natal domain Shen (Jiang) and the posthumous honorific of her husband (Lord Wu). "Lord Zhuang" is the posthumous honorific; his given name is Wusheng. Gong is the name of the place to which Gongshu Duan will eventually flee. "Shu" means "younger brother" and Duan is his given name. So he is literally "Duan the Younger Brother who fled to Gong." For this excerpt, I have unified his name as "Duan." In *Zuo Tradition*, his name is unified as "Gongshu Duan."

[2] According to the commentators, Guo Shu (the lord of Guo), relying on the strategic advantages of Zhi, acted defiantly, and Zheng destroyed Guo.

[3] *Zhi* is a unit of measure for the height and length of a city wall. Some scholars argue that one *zhi* equals about ten meters.

《左傳》鄭伯克段于鄢

初，鄭武公娶于申，曰武姜，生莊公及共叔段。莊公寤生，驚姜氏，故名曰寤生，遂惡之。愛共叔段，欲立之。亟請於武公，公弗許。及莊公即位，為之請制。公曰："制，巖邑也，虢叔死焉。佗邑唯命。"請京，使居之，謂之京城大叔。

祭仲曰："都，城過百雉，國之害也。先王之制：大都，不過參國之一；中，五之一；小，九之一。今京不度，非制也，君將不堪。"公曰："姜氏欲之，焉辟害？"對曰："姜氏何厭之有？不如早為之所，無使滋蔓！蔓，難圖也。蔓草猶不可除，況君之寵弟乎？"公曰："多行不義必自斃，子姑待之。"

既而大叔命西鄙、北鄙貳於己。公子呂

曰：「國不堪貳，君將
若之何？欲與大叔，臣
請事之；若弗與，則請
除之，無生民心。」
公曰：「無庸，將自
及。」

大叔又收貳以為己
邑，至于廩延。子封
曰：「可矣。厚將得
眾。」公曰：
「不義，不暱。厚將
崩。」

大叔完、聚，繕甲、
兵，具卒、乘，將襲
鄭，夫人將啟之。公聞
其期，曰：「可矣。」
命子封帥車二百乘以伐
京。京叛大叔段。段入
于鄢。公伐諸鄢。五月
辛丑，大叔出奔共。

書曰：「鄭伯克段于
鄢。」段不弟，故不言
弟；如二君，故曰克；
稱鄭伯，譏失教也；謂
之鄭志。不言出奔，難
之也。

遂寘姜氏于城潁，
而誓之曰：「不及黃
泉，無相見也！」既而
悔之。潁考叔為潁谷封
人，聞之，有獻於公。
公賜之食。食舍肉。
公問之。對曰：「小
人有母，皆嘗小人之
食矣；未嘗君之羹，請
以遺之。」公曰：「爾
有母遺，繄我獨無！」
潁考叔曰：「敢問何謂
也？」公語之故，且告
之悔。對曰：「君何患
焉？若闕地及泉，隧而
相見，其誰曰不然？」
公從之。

to settle this matter right away. Do not encourage creeping vines to spread! Once they spread, they are difficult to control. If even creeping vines cannot be rooted out, then how much less the favored younger brother of a ruler?" The lord said, "He who commits many undutiful acts will surely bring himself down. You, sir, should just wait."

Shortly thereafter Duan ordered the western and northern marches to switch their allegiance to him. Gongzi Lü said, "A domain cannot bear divided allegiance. What are you, my lord, going to do about this? If you want to give the domain to Duan, then I beg to serve him. If not, then I beg to root him out so as not to give the people the wrong idea!" The lord said, "No need. He will bring about his own downfall."

Duan went on to turn the disaffected ones into his own settlements, reaching as far as Linyan. Gongzi Lü said, "Now we can act! If he gets any stronger, he will gain the multitudes!" The lord said, "If he is not dutiful, the people will not draw close to him. If he gets stronger, the whole thing will collapse."

Duan reinforced walls, gathered provisions, repaired his armor and weapons, and prepared his infantry and chariots. He was going to make a surprise attack on Zheng, and Lady Jiang was going to open the city gate for him. When the lord heard that a date had been set, he said, "Now we can act!" He ordered Gongzi Lü to lead two hundred chariots to attack Jing. Jing turned against Duan, who entered Yan. The lord attacked him at Yan. In the fifth month, on the *xinchou* day (23), Duan left Yan and fled to Gong.

The text says, "The Liege of Zheng overcame Duan at Yan." Duan did not behave like a younger brother, so it does not speak of a younger brother. They were like two rulers, so it says "overcome." That it labels him "the Liege of Zheng" is to criticize his neglect of instruction: what happened is judged to have been Zheng's intention.[4] That the text does not say he left Yan and fled is to express disapproval of him.

Consequently, the lord placed Lady Jiang in Chengying the walled city Ying and swore an oath: "Until we reach the Yellow Springs, we will not see each other!" Shortly thereafter he regretted this.

Ying Kaoshu was the border officer in charge of Ying Valley. When he heard of these events, he offered gifts to the lord. The lord granted him a meal, but as Kaoshu ate, he put aside the meat. The lord asked about this, and Kaoshu responded: "Your humble servant has a mother. She has always partaken of my meals, but she has never tasted my lord's stew. I beg leave to give some to her." The lord said, "You have a mother to give things to. Alas, I alone have none!" Ying Kaoshu said, "Dare I ask what you meant?" The lord explained what happened and also admitted his regret. Kaoshu replied, "Why should you worry about this? If you dig into the earth as far as the springs and meet each other in the tunnel, who could say this goes against the vow?" The lord took his advice.

---

[4] That is, it is Lord Zhuang's intention all along to incriminate Duan so he could expel him. *Zhi* can mean either hidden or manifest intent in *Zuozhuan*.

On entering the tunnel, the lord recited, "Within the great tunnel, / Our joys flow together." On exiting the tunnel, Lady Jiang recited, "Outside the great tunnel, / Our joy spreads abroad."[5] And consequently they became mother and son as before. The noble man said, "Ying Kaoshu was pure in his filial piety. He loved his mother and tendered his example to Lord Zhuang. As it says in the *Book of Poetry*, 'The filial son is unstinting, / And forever blesses your kind.'[6] Surely this is what is meant!"

[ZZ 1:8–13]

公入而賦："大隧之中，其樂也融融。" 姜出而賦："大隧之外，其樂也洩洩。" 遂為母子如初。君子曰："潁考叔，純孝也，愛其母，施及莊公。《詩》曰："'孝子不匱，永錫爾類'，其是之謂乎！"

[CCZZZ 10–16]

This narrative is supposed to explain one line from *Chunqiu*: "The Liege of Zheng overcame Duan at Yan." How and why did that happen? What were the consequences and implications? To explain this almost fratricidal conflict, we need to go back to the beginning and understand the pivotal role of their mother, Lady Jiang. The narrative begins with the word *chu* (earlier, at the beginning): marker of the first or prior event that explains what follows. This word will continue to introduce retrospective causal sequences in later classical prose. Here *chu* takes us to the marriage of Lord Zhuang's parents and the cause of estrangement between him and his mother. On account of Lord Zhuang's breech birth, Lady Jiang favors his younger brother Duan and repeatedly plots with Duan to usurp Lord Zhuang's position. Against all counsel to forestall or thwart the rebellion before it is too late, Lord Zhuang refuses to act until Duan's rebellion is full-fledged and the evidence damning. Then he crushes it and drives Duan into exile. The consequent estrangement from his mother, whom he vows never to see again until they reach the Yellow Springs (the underworld), is healed only when an ingenious border officer, Ying Kaoshu, suggests Lord Zhuang dig a tunnel and meet his mother there. By substituting the literal for the metaphorical meaning of Yellow Springs, Ying Kaoshu allows reconciliation without undoing Lord Zhuang's vow. He manages to offer this advice by the affective force of his own filial conduct. Such moral persuasion through example and skillful rhetoric becomes a powerful trope in the tradition.

One can easily read this as family drama focusing on fraternal conflict and the mother–son relationship. The arc of the narrative moves from random or fated estrangement to willed reconciliation, marked by the three occurrences of the word *sui* (consequently): they explain, in turn, the cause of Lady Jiang's aversion toward Lord Zhuang, the relocation of Lady Jiang to the walled city Ying at the nadir of their relationship, and their reconciliation after the meeting in the tunnel. The emotional intensity and complexity of the situation notwithstanding (we can easily imagine a toxic brew of jealousy, resentment, ambition, disappointment, and hunger for power and control), the tone is remarkably reticent. In the first half of this narrative, is Lord Zhuang passive or active? We do not know whether Lord

---

[5] Both couplets rhyme in Old Chinese and follow the typical four-character line pattern of the *Book of Poetry* (*Shijing*).

[6] Quoted from the *Book of Poetry* (*Maoshi* 247), "Ji zui" ("Having Become Inebriated"), (*Maoshi zhengyi* 17B.606).

Zhuang is indecisively and helplessly trying to mollify his mother or deliberately abetting Duan's rebellion so he can justify his expulsion. Almost nothing is said about the inner life of Lord Zhuang, Duan, and Lady Jiang. Is the narrator interested in motives and intentions? Is he withholding information from the reader, or has he already conveyed his judgment, albeit obliquely? The consensus view is that judgment is indirectly yet pointedly conveyed. Subtlety is linked with rhetorical control, which comes to be upheld as an ideal in classical prose.

Once Duan is out of the picture, the relationship between Lord Zhuang and Lady Jiang deteriorates further, but Ying Kaoshu's skillful remonstrance sets the stage for ending the estrangement between mother and son. Is Lord Zhuang's filial piety a natural expression or a staged performance? The dominant reading over the centuries has Lord Zhuang indeed plotting his younger brother's downfall, but filial emotions triumph in the end to bring about the reconciliation of son and mother. This interpretation follows the cue of comments embedded in the account: the concluding judgment of the "noble man" and the exegetical passage beginning with "the text says" (shuyue, i.e., Chunqiu says). The term "noble man" (junzi) literally means "the lord's son," but by the time of Zuozhuan's compilation, its valence is less sociopolitical than moral. The "noble man" or "superior man" embodies moral integrity and voices authoritative judgment.[3] Here filial piety is lauded for spreading its affective power and healing division. The disquisition on what "the text says" parses word choice in the line from Chunqiu, which is believed to convey "momentous meanings through subtle language" (weiyan dayi). To call someone by his proper relational name or title is supposed to sharpen awareness of the imperative to conform to normative roles (e.g., a younger brother should behave like one or be denied that designation). Lord Zhuang and Duan act like rival heads of state rather than brothers, hence the word "overcame" (ke). Lord Zhuang is called "Liege of Zheng," presumably to unmask his failure to fulfill his duty as an older brother to Duan. The reasoning behind such judgments may seem arbitrary or mysterious to the modern reader; they stem from the belief that every word (or omission) is significant in Chunqiu because it represents the voice of Confucius. The exegetical passage, which bears some resemblance to the Gongyang and Guliang commentaries (the other two extant exegetical traditions of Chunqiu, dated ca. third century BCE), probably belongs to a later layer in the textual formation of Zuozhuan.

Zuozhuan contains a passage eulogizing Chunqiu: "Subtle yet clear, forceful yet indirect, restrained yet richly patterned, exhaustive yet not excessive, chastising evil and encouraging goodness. Who but the sage could have shaped it?"[4] This actually better describes Zuozhuan. Later writers often aspire to its mixture of subtlety and clarity: a stylistic ideal embodying moral purpose and authoritative judgment. More generally, this intersection of narrative and discursive elements becomes a common feature of historical writings as well as other genres of classical prose.

Both the exegetical comments and the noble man's judgment focus on family relations—kinship ties are tested, distorted, and then partially restored. They do not address another key concern in this account: the balance of power in a domain and the proper boundaries of political authority. The ministers who plead with

Lord Zhuang and urge intervention to curb Duan's power paint a stark either–or picture: either share power and risk being deposed or eliminate potential rivals in the interest of political stability. If Lord Zhuang demurs, he is not disputing the doctrine but rather the mode of implementation. Zheng seems to have expanded its power under Lord Zhuang: he manages, for example, to turn the small domain of Xu into a Zheng protectorate, and deals with external and internal foes with similar dexterity.[5] Many passages in *Zuozhuan* echo the arguments of the remonstrating ministers. (On the importance of remonstrance in the relationship between rulers and their advisors in Warring States writings, ☞ chap. 5.) We see recurrent speeches on the danger of having "branches" (*zhi*) larger than the "trunk" (*ben*) (in effect, the tail that wags the dog or, in the words of *Zuozhuan*: "When a tail is large, it will not wag" [*wei da budiao*]) and the need to forestall or eradicate subversion in the interest of greater unity and centralization. The teller of this story, even while implying Lord Zhuang's complicity in Duan's downfall, simultaneously seems to present it as a positive example of triumphant unification. Some imperial commentators also defend Lord Zhuang's action against Duan as cautious, effective, and ultimately justified.[6] Is it possible that Lord Zhuang is being praised for biding his time and maintaining the appearance of fraternal tolerance even while rooting out opposition? Pushing the cynical reading further, one may be tempted to read the mother–son reconciliation as masterful moral rhetoric and a convincing public display of virtue rather than as a sincere change of heart. That the tone is restrained and modulated enough to support these different interpretations accounts in part for the abiding fascination of *Zuozhuan*.

A WOMAN'S CHOICE: FATHER OR HUSBAND?

C 2.2 *Zuo Tradition*, "Yong Ji's Dilemma," Huan 15.2 (697 BCE)

《左傳》父與夫孰親

Zhai Zhong was monopolizing power, and the Leige of Zheng (Lord Li) worried about this. He sent Zhai Zhong's son-in-law Yong Jiu to kill him. Yong Jiu was to offer Zhai Zhong ceremonial toasts in the outlying district [and execute the assassination]. His wife Yong Ji[1] learned of the plot and said to her mother: "Whom should one hold dearer, a father or a husband?" Her mother said, "Any man can be a husband, but one has only a single father. How can they be compared?" And so Yong Ji reported to Zhai Zhong: "Yong Jiu did not use his house and is instead going to offer you ceremonial toasts in the outlying district. I am mystified by this and so report." Zhai Zhong killed Yong Jiu and exposed his corpse near the pond of the Zhou lineage. Lord Li loaded the corpse into his carriage and took it with him as he left the domain, saying, "He let his wife in on his plans; it is fitting that he died." In the summer, Lord Li departed and fled to Cai.

[ZZ 1:124–125]

祭仲專，鄭伯患之，使其壻雍糾殺之。將享諸郊。雍姬知之，謂其母曰："父與夫孰親？"其母曰："人盡夫也，父一而已，胡可比也？"遂告祭仲曰："雍氏舍其室而將享子於郊，吾惑之，以告。"祭仲殺雍糾，尸諸周氏之汪。公載以出，曰："謀及婦人，宜其死也。"夏，厲公出奔蔡。

[CCZZZ 143]

---

[1] Yong Ji's name combines the name of her husband's lineage (Yong) and the clan name of her natal lineage (Ji).

Zhai Zhong, who shows political acumen as Lord Zhuang's loyal minister in the previous entry, here appears in an adversarial relationship with Li Zhuang's son, Lord Li (r. 701–697, 680–673 BCE).[7] Lord Zhuang's heir apparent, Lord Zhao, became ruler in the summer of 701 BCE, but was driven into exile in the autumn by his younger brother, who became Lord Li (*Zuo Tradition*, Huan 11.3, 1:112–15). Zheng's neighboring state, Song, played a crucial role in installing Lord Li, whose mother belonged to the Yong lineage of Song. Song also forced Zhai Zhong to take part in the plot to depose Lord Zhao and establish Lord Li. As a result of his role in the coup, Zhai Zhong monopolizes power in Zheng, much to the chagrin of Lord Li, who enlists the help of Yong Jiu (likely from his mother's lineage) to assassinate Zhai Zhong. Yong Jiu's wife, Yong Ji, is also Zhai Zhong's daughter. Having learned of the plot, she presents her dilemma to her mother, who declares that a woman owes greater loyalty to her father than to her husband. (Of course Yong Ji's mother is primarily interested in defending her own husband here: the choice between a husband and a son-in-law is an easy one.)

This prose of this passage is typically terse and restrained. Complex power relations must be inferred through familiarity with related episodes. This can heighten the difficulty of the text, but such economy also instills a sense of epigrammatic finality into the judgment of Yong Ji's mother: "Any man can be a husband, but one has only a single father." A biological fact is invoked to override the sexual, emotive, social, and ritual bond of marriage. Yong Ji tells her father to be careful, without directly incriminating her husband. All the same, Yong Jiu is killed, and Lord Li has the last word on the folly of sharing political secrets with one's wife. Structurally, his utterance engages with that of Yong Ji's mother. His judgment of the danger represented by a woman functions as a response to Yong Ji's question.

Zuozhuan offers examples of both women siding with their husbands and with their fathers when forced to choose between them. In some cases, this translates into women's divided loyalty toward different lineages and domains, and explains in part the notion that women can be a potential source of political instability; their supposedly wayward emotions (as in the case with Wu Jiang in the first entry) also account for the negative judgment. In his classification of female characters in *Zuozhuan*, the Qing scholar Gu Donggao (1679–1759) lists twelve in the highest rank of "moral probity" (*jiexing*), eleven in the middle rank of "sound judgment" (*mingzhe*), and thirty-four in the lowest rank of "unscrupulous excess" (*zongzi budu*).[8] Gu relegates Yong Ji to the lowest category, castigating her choice as an example of "the total destruction of normative human relationships and heavenly principle." Yong Ji's mother makes her case with incontrovertible logic, but later defenders of patriarchy cannot accept the idea that husbands are replaceable.

Some moral dilemmas in stories about conflicting ties seem more easily resolved. In another example from *Zuozhuan*, a father brings about the arrest and execution of his own son when the latter participates in a rebellion against the rightful ruler. The noble man praises the father: "For the sake of a great duty, he smote his kin" (*dayi mieqin*).[9] In the father-versus-husband story, the moral contours are much less clear. The husband Yong Jiu is after all, assisting Lord Li, a vindictive and ruthless usurper. Exiled at the end of the story, he manages to return to Zheng seventeen years later and rules for another seven years, but not before killing the minister who maneuvered his reinstatement and another Zheng noble who served interim Zheng rulers during his exile.[10] His posthumous honorific, "Li," means "violent." Zhai Zhong, for his part, is an opportunist and a survivor. He bows to Song pressure to oust Lord Zhao and establish his brother Lord Li as ruler. After driving Lord Li into exile, he brings Lord Zhao back, but does not protest when a Zheng minister murders Lord Zhao two years later.[11] Expediency and self-preservation guide Zhai Zhong's conduct, but we see no disparagement and even tacit approval. In other words, neither Zhai Zhong nor Yong Jiu (and by extension Lord Li) can claim to represent a just cause. Both sides are motivated by raw power calculations, and Yong Ji's choice between biological and marital ties cannot be moralized beyond her mother's logic. Indeed, the choice is uncomfortable enough for this account to be excluded from Han and later anecdotal collections offering exemplars and warnings. The idiom derived from the line "any man can be a husband" (ren jin fu ye) leaves the original story behind and comes to refer to a licentious woman whose indiscriminate bestowal of sexual favors suggests that "she can make any man her husband" (ren jin ke fu).

A WOMAN'S SILENCE: THE CLAIMS OF TWO HUSBANDS

C2.3 *Zuo Tradition*, "Cai and Xi At Odds Because of Xi Gui," Zhuang 10.3 (684 BCE)

Prince Ai of Cai took a wife in Chen. The Prince of Xi also took a wife there. When Xi Gui (the wife of the Xi ruler) was about to be married, she passed through Cai. The Prince of Cai said, "She is my sister-in-law." He detained her and met with her but did not treat her like a guest. When the Prince of Xi heard this, he was furious and sent someone to tell King Wen of Chu: "Attack us, and when we seek help from Cai, you can then attack them." The Chu king acted accordingly. In autumn, in the ninth month, Chu defeated Cai troops at Shen. They took Xianwu, the Prince of Cai, back with them.

[ZZ 1:162–163]

C2.4 *Zuo Tradition*, "Xi Gui Had Not Spoken," Zhuang 14.3 (680 BCE)

Because of what happened at Shen, Prince Ai of Cai praised Xi Gui while speaking to the Master of Chu. The latter went to Xi, and on the pretext of carrying in food supplies for a ceremonial feast, extinguished Xi. He took Xi Gui back home, and she eventually gave birth to Du Ao and the future King Cheng.[1] But she had not yet spoken a word.[2] The Master of Chu asked her

《左傳》息媯啟釁

蔡哀侯娶于陳，息侯亦娶焉。息媯將歸，過蔡。蔡侯曰：「吾姨也。」止而見之，弗賓。息侯聞之，怒，使謂楚文王曰：「伐我，吾求救於蔡而伐之。」楚子從之。秋九月，楚敗蔡師于莘，以蔡侯獻舞歸。

[CCZZZ 184]

《左傳》息媯未言

蔡哀侯為莘故，繩息媯以語楚子。楚子如息，以食入享，遂滅息。以息媯歸，生堵敖及成王焉。未言。楚子問之。對曰：「吾一婦人，而事二夫，縱弗能死，其又奚言？」

楚子以蔡侯滅息，遂伐蔡。秋七月，楚入蔡。

---

[1] According to Sima Qian, Du Ao became king after King Wen's death in 677 BCE (*Shiji* 14.573) and Hun (later King Cheng) assassinated his older brother Du Ao and ascended the throne in 672 BCE (*Shiji* 14.575). This seems implausible, however, because King Wen married Xi Gui only in 680 BCE, making King Cheng not more than seven in 672 BCE.

[2] Some scholars have suggested that the line "she had not yet spoken" refers to how Xi Gui had not said anything about the past. Others read this as a kind of "inner mourning" (xinsang). See Qian Zhongshu, *Guanzhui bian*, 1:178.

君子曰： "《商書》
所謂　'惡之易也，如
火之燎于原，不可鄉
邇，其猶可撲滅'者，
其如蔡哀侯乎！ "

[*CCZZZ* 198–99]

about this, and she replied, "I, as one woman, have served two husbands. Even though I have not been able to kill myself, what more is there to say?"

The Master of Chu, having extinguished Xi on account of the Prince of Cai, then attacked Cai. In autumn, in the seventh month, Chu entered Cai.[3]

The noble man said, "What the *Shang Documents* says—'The spread of iniquity is like the blazing of fire on grassland; since one cannot even get near it, is there any chance one can still extinguish it?'[4]—surely this fits Prince Ai of Cai!"

[*ZZ* 1:174–175]

The rise and dominance of the southern state Chu is one of the major developments in the period covered by *Zuozhuan*. In *Chunqiu*, Chu rulers are consistently referred to by the noble title *zi* (master); in *Zuozhuan*, they are called both *zi* and *wang* (king). Traditional commentaries see great significance in such designations, averring the principle of "praise and blame expressed through one word" (*yi zi baobian*). Classical prose, especially in disquisitions (*lunzan*), continues to emphasize the mode of appellation. In the *Zuozhuan* passages, however, it is difficult to discern evaluations implied by the varying designations of the Chu ruler, King Wen of Chu (r. 689–677 BCE). His subjugation of two small states, Cai and Xi, is presented in a neutral tone. Xi is "extinguished" (*mie*), which means its ruling lineage ceased to control the domain. Chu forces "entered" (*ru*) Cai—that is, they overran the Cai capital. (Small states during this period were not much more than city-states.) Chu eventually annexed Cai 149 years later.[12]

Instead of focusing on Chu aggression, the author or compiler exposes the ill-fated machinations of the rulers of Cai and Xi, who both try to use Chu's might to attack each other. The noble man singles out Lord Ai of Cai for blame, probably because he instigates the conflict and wreaks vengeance by destroying Xi. The prose is typically concise, even cryptic. What does it mean that the Cai ruler "did not treat her (Xi Gui) like a guest" (*fubin*)? Is sexual impropriety involved? According to the recently excavated text *Chronological Accounts* (*Xinian*), the Cai ruler detains Xi Gui and "took her as wife" (*qi zhi*), which angers the Xi ruler and launches Cai and Xi on a path of mutual destruction.[13]

Xi Gui wreaks havoc because powerful men covet her beauty, but she has little control over her own fate. When she submits to a new master, she registers her pain through silence and then eloquently explains her silence. In *Accounts of Notable Women* (*Lienü zhuan*, first century BCE), Xi Gui appears under "Chaste Submissiveness" (*zhenshun*); there she commits suicide out of loyalty to the Xi ruler, who likewise kills himself. Awed by such heroic martyrdom, the Chu king buries them

---

[3] An account in *Lüshi chunqiu* (*LSCQXJS* 14.791) claims that King Wen of Chu planned to annex both Xi and Cai from the beginning. In that account, the Cai ruler came up with the pretext of the feast to enter Xi, only to become the Chu king's victim instead of co-conspirator.

[4] *Shangshu* (*Book of Documents*), "Pan Geng shang," 9.129. The four characters *e zhi yi ye* ("the spread of iniquity") are not included in the transmitted version of *Shangshu*. These lines also appear in *Zuo Tradition*, Yin 6.4 (717 BCE), 1:40–43.

together with proper ritual. In Feng Menglong's (1574–1646) vernacular retelling of the story, Xi Gui refrains from committing suicide in exchange for Chu preserving the Xi ruler's life and the Xi lineage, and the Chu king attacks Cai to mollify the resentful Xi Gui.[14]

These later versions recognize Xi Gui's inner conflict and dramatize her virtuous intention and agency accordingly. *Zuozhuan* rests its case with her shame and regret. Spurring debate over political choices and definitions of political integrity (including its figural ties with female chastity), Xi Gui has continued to fascinate readers for centuries.[15] The following poem by Wang Wei (699–761) is but one of the numerous poems about her:

Lady Xi	息夫人
Do not think, just because of today's favor,	莫以今時寵
She can forget the ties of yesteryear.	能忘舊日恩
Looking at the flowers, her eyes filling with tears,	看花滿眼淚
She would not speak with the king of Chu.	不共楚王言

In Wang Wei's poem, the idea of emotions too intense or contradictory for words, of not speaking or speaking only to explain silence, is enacted by the aesthetics of reticence underlying the quatrain (*jueju*) form. Wang Wei's restraint in "Lady Xi" is sometimes adduced as proof of his lack of political courage. He held office in the rebel government during the An Lushan Rebellion (756–763), and later cleared himself of charges of treason with a poem—supposedly written when rebels occupied the capital—indirectly avowing loyalty to the Tang house. A ninth-century anecdote also claims that Wang Wei used this poem to remonstrate with a prince who had taken a commoner's wife into his harem.

Zuozhuan records how, eleven years after King Wen's death, Xi Gui resists the advances of King Wen's younger brother, the Chu chief minister Ziyuan.

C2.5 *Zuo Tradition*, "Ziyuan Wanted to Seduce King Wen's Wife," Zhuang 28.3 (666 BCE)

《左傳》子元欲蠱文夫人

Ziyuan, the chief minister of Chu, wanted to seduce King Wen's wife. He built a lodge near her palace and shook clappers there to the rhythm of the *wan* dance.[1] When the king's wife heard this, she wept and said: "When our former ruler used this dance, it was as training for military preparation. Now the chief minister uses it not to pursue our enemies but to be by the side of this soon-to-perish person.[2] Is this not an aberration?" An attendant reported this to Ziyuan. Ziyuan said, "A woman has not forgotten the need to strike at our enemies, while I, by contrast, have forgotten it!"

[ZZ 1:212–213]

楚令尹子元欲蠱文夫人，為館於其宮側而振萬焉。夫人聞之，泣曰：「先君以是舞也，習戎備也。今令尹不尋諸仇讎，而於未亡人之側，不亦異乎！」御人以告子元。子元曰：「婦人不忘襲讎，我反忘之！」

[CCZZZ 241]

---

[1] The *wan* dance is mentioned in the *Book of Poetry* (*Maoshi* 38, "Jian xi" ["Grand Indeed"]), where the dancers hold flutes and pheasant feathers. It might have been a large-scale court dance with martial overtones.

[2] The "soon-to-perish person" (*wei wang ren*) became a conventional way for a widow to refer to herself.

Xi Gui's name combines the name of domain she married into (Xi) and the clan name (Gui) of her natal domain, Chen. Here she is called "King Wen's wife" (Wen *furen*), and she speaks accordingly as a wise woman concerned with the welfare of Chu. At this point, her young son has become king (King Cheng of Chu, r. 671–626 BCE). Nomenclature is determinative: this idea will continue to hold sway in classical prose (especially historical prose). The force of the anecdote depends on the polyvalence of music and the reversal of its meanings: a symbol of pleasure and indulgence, it is also linked to ritual order and military preparation. (On the importance of music, ☛ chap. 3.) Ziyuan tries to seduce (the word *gu* can also mean "to bewitch" or "to cast a spell over") King Wen's widow with music, but she manages to remind him of its ritual and military significance. Her rebuttal also functions as effective remonstrance, for Ziyuan resumes Chu's earlier military expedition against Zheng. Ironically, a woman remembered (and implicitly commended) for her silence speaks forcefully on two occasions. In the earlier excerpt, she preserves a kind of inner loyalty to the Xi ruler; here, she is loyal to the memory of King Wen of Chu. Xi Gui's double loyalty poses a problem for imperial commentators. Gu Donggao could not decide where to place Xi Gui in his classificatory scheme for women in the *Spring and Autumn Annals* and thus left her out: "Xi Gui gave herself to the enemy and was even worse [than those who simply lost their chastity]. But after she entered Chu, we do not hear of any misconduct. Even when Ziyuan moved into the Chu palace, there was no record of her licentious conduct."[16]

This kind of situational or practical morality is quite common in *Zuozhuan*, and it stands in contrast to other texts with a starker approach to morality. For example, Gong Ji, the widow of Lord Gong of Song (r. 588–576 BCE), dies in a fire because she would not leave the burning palace without her chaperone. "The noble man said of Gong Ji that she acted like a young girl, not a married woman. A young girl should wait for others, but a married woman should attend to her duties judiciously."[17] Gong Ji married Duke Gong of Song in 582 BCE and was widowed six years later. She must have been sixty around the time of the fire (543 BCE). *Zuozhuan* is critical of such a rigid adherence to ritual decorum. By contrast, the *Gongyang* and *Guliang* commentaries on *Chunqiu*, *Accounts of Notable Women*, and *Master Huainan (Huainan zi)* all praise her exemplary modesty and ritual propriety.

CAO GUI ON MILITARY STRATEGY

C2.6 *Zuozhuan*, "Cao Gui on Military Strategy," Zhuang 10.1 (648 BCE)

《左傳》曹劌論戰

十年春，齊師伐我。公將戰。曹劌請見。其鄉人曰："肉食者謀之，又何間焉？"劌曰："肉食者鄙，未能遠謀。"

In the tenth year, in spring, the Qi army attacked us.[1] The lord (Lord Zhuang of Lu, r. 693–662 BCE) was going to fight. Cao Gui asked for an audience. A person from his locality said, "The meat-eaters have planned this. Why would you interfere?" Cao Gui said, "The meat-eaters are limited and incapable of long-range plans."

[1] The newly installed Lord Huan of Qi was punishing Lu for supporting Gongzi Jiu, a rival claimant to the Qi throne. According to the *Spring and Autumn Annals*, the battle took place at Changshuo.

Cao Gui then entered to have an audience with our lord and asked what he would use to fight. The lord said, "For food and clothing wherein one finds comfort, I do not dare to keep all for myself and am sure to share with others." Cao Gui responded, "Such small acts of kindness do not yet reach all. The people will not follow you for this."

"In regard to sacrificial animals and ceremonial jades and silks, I do not dare to exaggerate and am sure to abide by good faith."

"Such small acts of good faith do not yet cover all. The spirits will not bless you for this."

"In both minor and major legal cases, even when I am unable to investigate thoroughly, I am sure to go by actual circumstances."

"This counts as a kind of integrity—with it you may indeed engage in battle. If you do, I beg leave to follow you."

The lord rode with Cao Gui in his chariot. The battle took place at Changshao. The lord was about to sound the drums to attack, but Gui said, "Certainly not yet." The Qi men beat the drums and advanced three times. Gui said, "Now we can!" The Qi troops were completely defeated. The lord was going to race after them, but Gui said, "Certainly not yet." He got down from the chariot and looked at the ruts. Then he stood on the crossbar of the chariot, looked into the distance, and said, "Now we can!" So they pursued the Qi troops.

Having overcome Qi, the lord asked Cao Gui the reasons for his actions. He replied, "In doing battle, it all comes down to the vital energy of courage. Drumming once arouses the energy;[2] but at the second drumming, it declines; and by the third, it is spent. Their vital energy was spent while ours was full; that is why we overcame them. Now, a big domain is difficult to fathom. I was afraid there would be an ambush, but I saw that their ruts were in disarray and I observed that their banners were cast down. That is why we pursued them."

[ZZ 1:160–161]

乃入見，問何以戰。
公曰："衣食所安，弗
敢專也，必以分人。"
對曰："小惠未徧，
民弗從也。"公曰：
"犧牲、玉帛，弗敢加
也。必以信。"對曰：
"小信未孚，神弗福
也。"公曰："小大之
獄，雖不能察，必以
情。"對曰："忠之屬
也，可以一戰。戰，則
請從。"

公與之乘。戰于
長勺。公將鼓之。劌
曰："未可。"齊人三
鼓。劌曰："可矣！"
齊師敗績。公將馳之。
劌曰："未可。"下，
視其轍，登軾而望之，
曰：   "可矣！"遂逐
齊師。

既克，公問其故。對
曰："夫戰，勇氣也。
一鼓作氣，再而衰，三
而竭。彼竭我盈，故
克之。夫大國，難測
也，懼有伏焉。吾視其
轍亂，望其旗靡，故逐
之。"

[CCZZZ 182–83]

This account combines three themes that will recur in later writings: political advice from an unlikely source, debates on the source of legitimate authority, and post-facto explanation of military strategy. The noble lineages in Lu were all related to the ruling house, and Cao was not one of them. "Not being in the position (of power and responsibility) means not planning the policy" (*Analects* 8.14, 14.26). A noble man "thinks about not exceeding the limits of his position" (*Analects* 14.26, *Book of Changes* [*Yijing*], commentary on "Gen," hexagram 52). Should Cao Gui then presume to intervene in affairs of state? An interlocutor is introduced so that Cao Gui can explain his reasoning: the "meat-eaters" (*rou shi zhe*)[18]—that is, the wellborn, perhaps the only people with the means to eat meat on a regular basis—are "limited" (*bi*), and will require the assistance of the humble to make

---

[2] This becomes a common idiom describing how a person is spurred to act with pent-up vigor or determination.

good decisions. The word *bi* refers to the area beyond the boundaries of cities and settlements. Cao Gui, as one who lives far from the center of power, is literally at the margins (*bi*). By redefining *bi* in moral and metaphorical terms as "limited" or parochial, or perhaps even base, vulgar, far-fetched, or ignorant, he reverses the balance of authority between himself and those "meat-eaters." This wordplay is typical. Recall that our first excerpt also shifts between the literal and metaphorical meanings of Yellow Springs. Such manipulation of meanings signals a delight in language and forms the basis of rhetorical prowess.

Zuozhuan includes several examples of commoners or minor officers offering sound advice. (Note that in the first excerpt, Ying Kaoshu, who helps the Zheng ruler reclaim filial ties, is also a border officer.) If power can corrupt or blind its wielders, disempowerment may grant clarity and moral authority. This idea has multiple iterations. The rise of humble persons from obscurity, recluses who see through the game of politics, unlikely advisers whose worth is recognized, and political disappointment and exile that result in new insights are but a few of the plot lines that develop from the potential opposition between power and moral or intellectual authority. (On the theme of having one's worth recognized (or not), ☞ chap. 5, 7, 11, 13).

Cao Gui challenges the Lu ruler to consider his wherewithal for engaging in battle. "Benefiting the people" (*limin*) is consistently upheld as a paramount concern in *Zuozhuan*, but the Lu ruler's claim to share the comfort of "food and clothing" obviously does not rise to that standard, especially as such beneficence likely extends only to Lu nobles or to the ruler's associates and servants. Honesty in not overstating his offerings while sacrificing to the spirits also fails as a guarantee of victory. Cao Gui calls these "small acts of good faith" (*xiaoxin*), perhaps implicitly comparing them with the more momentous issue of keeping faith with the people. *Zuozhuan* repeatedly avers the importance of ritual propriety in serving the spirits, but also asserts that lavish rituals bring no benefits and shows fickle spirits fooling their supplicants. What Cao Gui considers to be an adequate basis for engaging in battle is the Lu ruler's commitment to be judicious, attentive, and impartial in legal cases. This counts as "a kind of integrity": *zhong* is translated as "integrity," which often is rendered as "loyalty" and understood as a hierarchical virtue (e.g., a subject's fealty to his lord). In *Zuozhuan* (and other early texts), however, *zhong* is best understood as the fulfillment of proper duty. A ruler who "thinks of benefiting the people" is *zhong*.[19] Of the three things the Lu ruler enumerates, the last has a most tangible benefit for the people. *Discourses of the States* (*Guoyu*) articulates this point more explicitly in its version of the story: "For so long as the ruler sincerely applies himself to planning for the people, he will certainly arrive at the right course even if his wisdom is not equal to the task."[20] (On principles of governance, ☞ chap. 3, 5, 13).

Cao Gui turns out to be a master strategist. His excursus on timing, knowing the enemy, divining traces, and manipulating the ebb and flow of "vital energy" (*qi*) on both sides finds parallels in military writings like *Master Sun's Art of War* (*Sunzi bingfa*). Postponing explanation to heighten suspense as well as the strategist's mystique becomes a standard literary ploy in later narratives. The reputation of *Zuozhuan* as a book about military strategy is augmented by numerous accounts of battle. Many are protracted, with vignettes and anecdotes resolutely focused on strategies for winning, but they also can be moralized, treating victory as the reward of virtue or a potential hazard. This account is concise and conjoins the outsider's insight, good governance, and military success. Cao Gui's military acumen is inseparable from his judgment of the Lu ruler's "political capital" arising from his impartiality in judicial matters, and both are rooted in his disdain for "meat-eaters."

Cao Gui is featured in another *Zuozhuan* passage, in which he attempts to dissuade the Lu ruler from attending the ceremonies at the altar of earth in Qi. Cao Gui juxtaposes two kinds of "viewing" (*guan*): instead of being fascinated by an unworthy spectacle (Qi ceremonies tainted by a hint of sexual impropriety), the Lu ruler should be mindful of his role as exemplar observed by posterity: "When the ruler travels, it must be recorded. If that which is recorded does not accord with the rules, what will posterity have to observe?"[21] In some late Warring States and Han texts, Cao Gui accompanies Lord Zhuang of Lu to the swearing of a covenant with Qi at Ke three years after the battle at Changshao (Zhuang 13; 681 BCE). By threatening Lord Huan of Qi (r. 685–643 BCE) with a weapon, Cao Gui forces Qi to return Lu territories (☞ chap. 6).[22] The Qi minister Guan Zhong persuades his ruler to adhere to the promise despite its coercive origins, and such good faith is said to pave the way for Lord Huan's rise to the position of hegemon (*ba*) among the lords. (Indeed, some of these stories are told to glorify Guan Zhong and Lord Huan.) Perhaps Cao Gui has just the right mixture of propriety and defiance, caution and daring that allows his image to be associated with both the ritual specialist and the potential assassin.

THE ASSASSINATION OF LORD LING OF JIN (R. 620–607)

C2.7 *Zuo Tradition*, "The Assassination of Lord Ling of Jin," Xuan 2.3 (607 BCE)

《左傳》晉靈公之弒

Lord Ling of Jin was no ruler. He levied heavy taxes in order to lavishly decorate his palace walls.[1] From atop his terrace he shot pellets at people, so that he could watch them dodging the pellets.[2] When the cook did not stew bear paws until they were well done,[3] Lord Ling had him killed and put in a reed basket, and he had women pass through court carrying the basket.[4] When Zhao Dun

晉靈公不君：厚斂以彫牆，從臺上彈人，而觀其辟丸也；宰夫胹熊蹯不熟，殺之，寘諸畚，使婦人載以過朝。趙盾、士季見其手，問其故，而患之。將諫，士季曰："諫而不入，則莫之繼也。會請先，不入，則子繼之。"　三進及溜，而後視之，曰："吾知所過矣，將改之。"稽首而對曰："人誰無過，過而能改，善莫大焉。

---

[1] Literally, "so that he could have the palace walls lavishly carved (or painted)."

[2] This seems more like a prank than a heinous crime. The pellets are probably made of mud or clay. The *Gongyang* and *Guliang* traditions specify that Lord Ling is taking aim at officials, perhaps to make the misdemeanor more serious. If, however, the terrace is inside the palace, it is not likely that officials would be present.

[3] Bear paws, considered a great delicacy, take a long time to cook. In another episode in *Zuozhuan*, King Cheng of Chu, when surrounded by his enemies, asks to have a meal of bear paws before he dies to buy time, but his request is denied (ZZ, Wen 1.7 [626 BCE], 1:464–65).

[4] According to *Springs and Autumns of Mr. Lü* (*LSCQXJS* [23].1599, Lord Ling intends in this way to intimidate his officials. The women should not be passing through court, and Lord Ling is either oblivious or deliberately defiant.

《詩》曰：「靡不有
初，鮮克有終。」夫如
是，則能補過者鮮矣。
君能有終，則社稷之固
也，豈惟群臣賴之。又
曰：「袞職有闕，惟仲
山甫補之」，能補過
也。君能補過，袞不廢
矣。」

猶不改。宣子驟諫，
公患之，使鉏麑賊之。
晨往，寢門闢矣，盛
服將朝。尚早，坐而
假寐。麑退，歎而言
曰：「不忘恭敬，民
之主也。賊民之主，
不忠；棄君之命，不
信。有一於此，不如死
也。」觸槐而死。

秋九月，晉侯飲
趙盾酒，伏甲，將攻
之。其右提彌明
知之，趨登，曰：
「臣侍君宴，過三爵，
非禮也。」遂扶以下。
公嗾夫獒焉，明搏而殺
之。盾曰：「棄人用
犬，雖猛何為！」鬥且
出。提彌明死之。

初，宣子田於首山，
舍于翳桑，見靈輒餓，
問其病。曰：「不食三
日矣。」食之，舍其
半。問之。曰：「宦三
年矣，未知母之存否，
今近焉，請以遺之。」
使盡之，而為之簞食與
肉，寘諸橐以與之。既
而與為公介，倒戟以禦
公徒而免之。問何故。
對曰：「翳桑之餓人
也。」問其名居，不告
而退，遂自亡也。

and Fan Hui saw the dead man's hand [sticking out of the basket] and asked what had happened, they were deeply dismayed. They were about to remonstrate, when Fan Hui said, "If our remonstrance is not heeded, there is no one who can follow us. I beg leave to go first. If I am not heeded, then you can follow." Over three stages he advanced,[5] but only when he reached the eaves did the lord look at him. The lord said, "I know my errors, and I will correct them." Fan Hui bowed, touching the ground with his forehead, and replied, "Who among men is without errors? Having erred and being capable of correction— there is no good greater than that. As it says in the *Book of Poetry*, 'There is none who does not have beginnings, / Few are those who fulfill them as endings.'[6] For if it is so, then those who can make good their errors are few. If my lord can persist to the end, the altars of the domain will have a solid foundation. Surely it is not only your subjects who rely on that! As it also says in the *Book of Poetry*, 'The ritual vestments had holes—/ It was Zhong Shanfu who mended it.'[7] This is about being able to make good one's errors. If my lord can do so, the ritual vestments will not fall into disuse."

Still the lord did not correct his errors. Zhao Dun remonstrated with him several times. The lord loathed this and sent Chu Mi to murder him. When Chu Mi went just before sunrise, the doors of the bedchamber were open. Zhao Dun was fully dressed in official robes and was about to go to court. It was still early, and he was sitting with closed eyes. Chu Mi withdrew and sighed, saying, "He who does not forget reverence is the master of the people. To murder the master of the people is not loyal; to discard the ruler's command is faithless. To be guilty of either of these is worse then death." He smashed his head against a locust tree and died.

In autumn, in the ninth month, the Jin ruler entertained Zhao Dun with wine. The lord had hidden armored soldiers who were going to attack him. Zhao's aide on the right, Shi Miming, learned of this, rushed forward, and ascended the steps, saying, "For a subject waiting on a ruler at a feast to drink more than three rounds is not in accordance with ritual propriety." He then helped Zhao Dun step down. The lord whistled for his fierce hounds.[8] Shi

---

[5] Shen Qinhan (1775–1832) identifies the "three stages" (*sanjin*) as the gate, the inner courtyard, and the steps to the audience chamber. Fan Hui and Zhao Dun were both Jin ministers.

[6] *Maoshi* 255, "Dang" ("Vast"), (*Maoshi zhengyi* 18A.641).

[7] *Maoshi* 260, "Zhengmin" ("Multitudes of People"), (*Maoshi zhengyi* 18A.676). Zhong Shanfu was a minister who helped King Xuan of Zhou (r. 828–782 BCE) revive the fortunes of Zhou. The vestment refers to embroidered robes of office for the king and the highest ministers. Here it is a synecdoche for the king: holes refer to royal errors that Zhong Shanfu repairs by remonstrating with the king. Fan Hui is using the vestment to refer to both the dignity of Lord Ling's office and the stability of the Jin domain.

[8] *Erya* (*Approaching Correct Meanings*) identifies the *ao* as a large hound of about three feet in height; see *Erya zhushu*, with commentaries by Guo Pu and Xing Bing, in *Chongkan Song ben Shisan jing zhushu fu jiaokan ji*, edited by Ruan Yuan et al. (Taipei: Yiwen yinshu guan, 1973), 10.195. *Shuowen jiezi* (*Explanation of Simple Graphs and Analysis of Composite Characters*) describes the *ao* as a hound trained to do its master's bidding; see Xu Shen, *Shuowen jiezi zhu*, annotated by Duan Yucai (Shanghai: Shanghai guji chubanshe, 1981), 10A.5b.

Miming wrestled with them and killed them. Zhao Dun said, "He deserts men and uses hounds—fierce, to be sure, but to what avail?" All the while fighting and struggling, they came out. Shi Miming died defending Zhao Dun.

Earlier, Zhao Dun had hunted at Mount Shou. While lodging at Yisang then, he saw Ling Zhe, who was starving, and asked what ailed him. Ling Zhe said, "I have not eaten for three days." Zhao Dun gave him food, but Ling Zhe set half of it aside. When asked about it, he said, "For three full years I have been in service. I do not yet know whether my mother is still alive. Now that I am close to home, I beg leave to send her this food."[9] Zhao Dun had him finish eating, then prepared for him a bamboo basket filled with food and meat, put it in a sack, and gave it to him. Later, Ling Zhe joined the ranks of the lord's armored attendants. He turned his dagger-axe against the lord's men to defend Zhao and thereby saved him. Zhao asked why he did that, and he replied, "I was the starving man at Yisang." Zhao asked his name and where he lived, but he withdrew without telling him. Then Zhao himself fled.

On the *yichou* day (26), Zhao Chuan killed[10] Lord Ling at Taoyuan. Zhao Dun returned before leaving the mountains of Jin. The scribe wrote, "Zhao Dun assassinated his ruler," and showed the record at court. Zhao Dun said, "This was not so." He replied, "You are the chief minister. Yet fleeing you did not cross the domain border; upon returning you did not chastise the culprit. If you are not responsible, who would be?" Zhao Dun said, "Alas! As it says in the *Book of Poetry*, 'I so cherish this / That I bring sorrow upon myself.' That describes me indeed!"[11] Confucius said, "Dong Hu was a worthy scribe of ancient times: he did not conceal anything in his rules of writing. Zhao Dun was a worthy high officer of ancient times: he bore a guilty verdict for the sake of those rules. What a pity! Had he crossed the domain border, he would have been absolved."

Zhao Dun sent Zhao Chuan to welcome Gongzi Heitun at Zhou and established him as ruler.[12] On the *renshen* day (third day of the tenth month), they offered sacrifices at the Martial Temple.[13]

[ZZ 1:592–597]

乙丑，趙穿（攻）
殺　靈公於桃園。宣子
未出山而復。大史書
曰　"趙盾弒其君"，
以示於朝。宣子曰：
"不然。"對曰："子
為正卿，亡不越竟，反
不討賊，非子而誰？"
宣子曰："嗚呼！
《詩》曰：'我之懷
矣，自詒伊慼。'其我
之謂矣。"孔子曰：
"董狐、古之良史也，
書法不隱。趙宣子、
古之良大夫也，為法
受惡。惜也，越竟乃
免。"

宣子使趙穿逆公子黑
臀于周而立之。壬申，
朝于武宮。

[CCZZZ 655–663]

---

[9] Note the use of this trope also in the first excerpt.

[10] The Kanazawa bunko edition has *sha* (to kill). All other extant editions have *gong* (to attack). Yang Bojun follows the Kanazawa bunko edition.

[11] The *Zuozhuan* scholar Du Yu (222–285) classifies this an "uncollected ode" (*yishi*), that is, a poem not included in the received text of the *Book of Poetry*. Similar lines, however, appear in *Maoshi 33*, "Xiongzhi" ("Male Pheasant"), (*Maoshi zhengyi* 2B.86) and *Maoshi 207*, "Xiaoming" ("Lesser Brightness"), (*Idem* 13A.447).

[12] Gongzi Heitun ("Black Buttocks") got his name because his mother dreamed that the gods drew with ink on his buttocks, see *Guoyu*, "Zhou yu 3" (3.99). He was Lord Ling's uncle and became Lord Cheng of Jin (r. 607–600 BCE).

[13] The Martial Temple was the Ancestral Temple of Lord Wu, ancestor of the Jin House. All Jin rulers offered sacrifices there upon accession to the throne.

This intriguing account of regicide and its historical judgment begins with a categorical denunciation of Lord Ling of Jin. He is "no ruler" or "does not act like a ruler" (*bujun*). In a role-based moral system, does this mean he has forfeited the right to be treated like a ruler? Good government obtains when "the ruler acts as a ruler; the subject, as a subject; the father, as a father; the son, as a son" (*Analects* 12.11). The killing of a tyrant is no longer "regicide" but rather the slaying of "one lone man (rejected by his subjects)" (*dufu, yifu*).[23] That the justification of rule lies in the people's welfare is a recurrent theme in *Zuozhuan* and is echoed in various early texts.[24]

In another passage in *Zuozhuan*, Lord Dao of Jin asks the music master Kuang about the expulsion of Lord Xian of Wei by Wei leaders: "Is that not going too far?"

C2.8 *Zuo Tradition*, "The Music Master Kuang on the Expulsion of a Ruler," Xiang 14.6 (559 BCE)

Kuang replied, "Perhaps it was their ruler who had gone too far . . . Now the ruler is the master of the spirits and the hope of the people. If he ruins the livelihood of the people and deprives the spirits of sacrifices, so that all the clans lose hope and the altars of the domain have no master, of what use is he? What is to be done but have him expelled? Heaven gives birth to the people and establishes rulers to oversee them and take care of them, not letting them lose their livelihood. There being rulers, Heaven establishes helpers for them to act as their teachers and guardians, not letting them exceed limits . . . Scribes make their writings, blind music masters make their odes, musicians recite admonitions and remonstrance, high officers rectify and instruct, officers transmit opinions, commoners complain, merchants and travelers argue in the marketplace, and all kinds of artisans present their views through their skills . . . Great indeed is heaven's love for the people! Why would it let one person exert his will over the people and indulge his excesses while abandoning the nature of heaven and earth? This would certainly not be allowed."[25]

[ZZ 2:1022–1025]

《左傳》師曠論出君

對曰：〝或者其君實甚。……夫君，神之主而民之望也。若困民之主，匱神乏祀，百姓絕望，社稷無主，將安用之？弗去何為？天生民而立之君，使司牧之，勿使失性。 有君而為之貳，使師保之，勿使過度。……史為書，瞽為詩，工誦箴諫，大夫規誨，士傳言，庶人謗，商旅于市，百工獻藝。……天之愛民甚矣，豈其使一人肆於民上，以從其淫，而棄天地之性？必不然矣。〞

[CCZZZ 1016–1018]

The music master Kuang, known elsewhere in *Zuozhuan* for his good judgment, divinatory skills, and musical and military knowledge, justifies the expulsion of Lord Xian of Wei. In Kuang's long speech (partially excerpted here), the balanced cadence complements a political vision wherein a ruler's power has inherent limits. Authority is based on just rule and reciprocity. Remonstrance is the necessary corrective, and opinions from various levels of society are supposed to constrain the ruler's decisions. Compared with the ruination of the people described in music master Kuang's speech, the failings of Lord Ling seem less momentous and more wayward or perverse. All the same, his extravagance, gratuitous cruelty, indifference to remonstrance, and murderous intention toward Zhao Dun mark him as an unworthy ruler. The explicit justification of the Wei ruler's expulsion also finds no parallel in the account of Lord Ling's murder. Instead, insinuations of how the assassination may be justified color the judgment of that violent act.

If loyalty should be based on reciprocity, Zhao Dun owes Lord Ling none. By contrast, the loyalty Zhao Dun inspires foils the Jin ruler's vindictive plots. Chu Mi, sent to assassinate Zhao, is so impressed by his reverence and commitment to duty that he chooses suicide over violence against "the master of the people" (*min zhi zhu*), a term that implicitly elevates him above Lord Ling. Shi Miming dies fending off fierce hounds, which dramatizes the baseness of the Jin ruler's attack. A past act of generosity toward the filial son Ling Zhe earns the latter's requital at a critical moment. Zhao Dun is presented as a victim and a virtuous official who earns the devotion of his loyal defenders. Unlike other characters in this account, Zhao Dun is granted a measure of interiority: being espied in solitude confirms his dutiful reverence as "inner truth," and gaining reprieve through past generosity adds temporal depth to his character.

Zhao Dun, head of the powerful Zhao lineage and chief minister in Jin, is a multifaceted character in *Zuozhuan*.[26] He is praised for his competence and good governance but also is criticized for his harshness. A Jin official describes him as "the sun in summer," unlike his kinder father Zhao Cui, who is compared to "the sun in winter."[27] He had facilitated the accession of Lord Ling of Jin (then a mere infant or very young child) in 620 BCE after initially upholding the claim of another candidate for the throne (an older son who enjoyed the support of the powerful Qin). The subtext of our excerpt is the precarious balance of power between a powerful minister and a young lord in his teens.

This account is supposed to explain one line from *Chunqiu*: "In autumn, in the ninth month, on the *yichou* day (26), Zhao Dun of Jin assassinated his ruler, Yigao (the given name of Lord Ling of Jin)." As told in our excerpt, the actual murderer is Zhao Dun's kinsman Zhao Chuan. The word employed in *Zuozhuan* to describe Zhao Chuan's act is *sha* (kill), or, in some versions of the text, *gong* (attack), whereas the lines from *Chunqiu* and in Dong Hu's record use the word *shi*, translated in *Zuo Tradition* as "assassinate" but whose precise meaning refers to an act of killing that violates the hierarchical order of ruler and subject or father and son. The Jin scribe Dong Hu's recording of the event, which assigns responsibility in the same way as *Chunqiu* and is presumably the source for the latter (or vice versa), offers an opportunity to debate the issue of guilt. Dong's reasoning is compelling. Zhao Dun's half-hearted flight and pardon of Zhao Chuan indicate complicity. By making Zhao Chuan instrumental in establishing the new Jin ruler, Zhao Dun also protects him from future prosecution. Dong Hu is remembered as an example of the unflinchingly impartial historian, and his record is upheld in the tradition as historical writing that "targets the intention" (*zhuxin*). Intention, however, implies deliberation, but this account is elusive on the question of whether Zhao Dun is directly or indirectly, purposefully or inadvertently responsible for Lord Ling's death.

Zhao Dun responds by quoting lines that seem to both acknowledge his responsibility and exonerate himself: "I so cherish this / That I bring sorrow upon myself." What does he "cherish" (*huai*)? Is it his good name, the power and preservation of his lineage, the Jin ruling house, the people of Jin, or something else? The second line asserts that he brings about his own woes, but it is a gesture of both self-pity and self-accusation. Confucius's comments add another level of self-conscious deliberation. He praises Dong Hu for "not concealing anything" (*buyin*), although he may more appropriately be described as "plucking out what is concealed" (*jueyin*). Confucius also commends Zhao Dun for being a good minister, apparently taking into account Zhao's attempts to remonstrate with Lord Ling and his subsequent persecution.

The line that invites the most controversy is this assertion: "Had he [Zhao Dun] crossed the domain border, he would have been absolved." Does Confucius mean that a technical detail of location would have absolved Zhao Dun even if he were guilty? One Qing commentator, Gao Tan, believes that "by leaving the state and not coming back, the duty binding ruler and subject would have been cut off."[28] More probably, Confucius means that he wishes for exonerating evidence: he wishes he could believe that Zhao Dun was not complicit, and his flight across the border would have supported that idea. The idea of possible justification for Zhao Dun was anathema for many imperial commentators. The neo-Confucian thinker Zhu Xi (1130–1200), for example, uses this passage to criticize the *Zuozhuan* author for his "base views": he does not believe that Confucius, known for "instilling fear in rebellious subjects and miscreant sons by creating *Chunqiu*,"[29] could have uttered such evasive judgments.[30] Gu Yanwu (1613–1682), writing as a Ming loyalist in the aftermath of the Ming-Qing dynastic transition in the mid-seventeenth century, emphasizes loyalty as absolute: "Zhao Dun was the mastermind behind Zhao Chuan's assassination of Lord Ling. Even had Zhao Dun punished Zhao Chuan, he could not have absolved himself. There is no escape from the principle of duty tying ruler and subject together anywhere between heaven and earth. How can one escape it by going beyond the border?"[31]

In the aftermath of Lord Ling's death, the Zhao lineage expanded its influence in Zhao. Thirty-seven years later, intralineage tensions and calumny from other lineages almost destroyed the Zhao lineage completely.[32] Could the political reality of the fifth or fourth century BCE—such as voices for or against the Zhao house—have shaped this narrative? Seventeenth-century thinker and scholar Wang Fuzhi (1619–1692), for example, considered the defense of Zhao Dun "partisan words" (*dangci*), evidence that Zhao sources played a role in the sympathetic portrayal of Zhao Dun.[33] It is also possible that our account is responding to debates on the parameters of the ruler-minister relationship flourishing during the period of *Zuozhuan*'s formation. Whether the assassination of an errant ruler is justified remains an unanswered question in this account, but the question undeniably shapes our perspectives. Most importantly, Dong Hu's record and Confucius' comments establish the importance of probing motives, going beyond appearances, adjudicating responsibility, and determining the truth in retrospection on the past (☛ chap. 6). The moral authority based on these concerns becomes an ideal enshrined in the tradition.

It is customary to regard the historical and literary values of *Zuozhuan* as distinct categories, if not indeed incommensurate attributes. But if we think of "the sense of history" as the conscious formulation of patterns and principles to understand the past, then narrative devices, rhetorical constructions, even the use of what we now consider supernatural or suprarational elements represent such patterns and principles. Form is inseparable from content. For us to appreciate the literary complexities of *Zuozhuan* is to explore the different intellectual currents that shape the text. We see competing solutions to problems of instability, conflict, and disintegration dominating the world of *Zuozhuan*. The excerpts in this chapter show that silence, ellipsis, ambiguity, and rhetorical manipulation in *Zuozhuan*'s lapidary prose can illuminate moral and political debates. Stylistic analysis engages with key questions of power and authority, truth and falsehood and judgment and its evasion. Many of the texts discussed in subsequent chapters, particularly *Grand Scribe's Records*, will take up these issues raised in *Zuozhuan*.

Wai-yee Li

NOTES

1. Liu Xie, *Wenxin diaolong yizheng* (*Annotated* Literary Mind and Carvings of Dragon), compiled by Zhan Ying (Shanghai: Shanghai guji chubanshe, 1989), 569.

2. *ZZ*, Xuan 12.2 (597 BCE), 1:656–657. This detail also appears in the *Gongyang* tradition, which, however, does not provide the circumstantial context of Jin retreat that allows it to serve as the climax to the episode. The battle of Bi is mentioned only in passing in the *Guliang* tradition. (The *Gongyang* and *Guliang* are the other two extant commentaries on *Chunqiu*.)

3. There are seventy-eight occurrences of the "noble man" offering judgment in *Zuozhuan*. The term *junzi* is often translated as "gentleman" in modern Chinese.

4. *ZZ*, Cheng 14.4 (577 BCE), 2:814–815.

5. See *ZZ*, Yin 11.3 (712 BCE), 1:60–63. Historians refer to Lord Zhuang of Zheng as a "proto-hegemon" (*xiaoba*).

6. See Gu Donggao, "Zheng Zhuanggong lun" (On Lord Zhuang of Zheng), in *Chunqiu dashi biao* (Tables of Major Events in the *Spring and Autumn Annals*), edited by Wu Shuping and Li Jiemin (Beijing: Zhonghua shuju, 1995), *juan* 49, 3:2618–2619.

7. Such inconsistencies are not uncommon and might have been a result of disparate sources. Thus, Ying Kaoshu, presented as a filial son and good adviser in the previous entry, appears as a vain and combative character in the account of the Zheng siege of Xu, see *ZZ*, Yin 11.2–3 (712 BCE), 1:60–61.

8. See Gu Donggao, "Chunqiu lienü biao" (*Table of Women in the* Spring and Autumn Annals), in *Chunqiu dashi biao, juan* 50, 3:2628–2630.

9. *ZZ*, Yin 4.5 (719 BCE), 1:32–33. This becomes a common idiom in Chinese.

10. *ZZ*, Zhuang 14.2 (680 BCE), 1:172–175.

11. *ZZ*, Huan 17.8 (695 BCE), 1:132–133.

12. *ZZ*, Zhao 11.8 (531 BCE), 3:1468–1469. Cai fortunes briefly revived thereafter, but Chu finally annexed it in 447 BCE.

13. *Xinian* is part of the cache of bamboo manuscripts acquired by Tsinghua University in 2008. On *Xinian*, see *Qinghua er Xinian jijie* (Annotations on *Chronological Accounts*), compiled by Su Jianzhou, Wu Wenwen, Lai Yixuan (Taipei: Wanjuanlou, 2013); Yuri Pines, "Zhou History and Historiography: Introducing the Bamboo *Xinian*," *T'oung Pao* 100, no. 4–5 (2014): 287–324; *Zhou HIstory Unearthed*, NY: Columbia University Press, 2020; Hou Wenxue and Li Mingli, *Qinghua jian "Xinian" yu "Zuozhuan" xushi bijiao yanjiu* (A Comparative Study of the Qinghua Bamboo Strips Chronological Accounts *and* Zuo Commentary) (Shanghai: Zhongxi shuju, 2015).

14. See Feng Menglong, *Xin lieguo zhi* (*A New Account of the Various States*), later published as *Dong Zhou lieguo zhi* (*Account of the Various States During Eastern Zhou*) with revisions by Cai Yuanfang, edited by Liu Bendong (Taipei: Sanmin shuju, 1999), ch. 17, 19, 142–145, 159.

15. On Xi Gui's treatment in the literary tradition, see Wai-yee Li, *Women and National Trauma in Late Imperial China* (Cambridge, MA: Harvard University Asia Center, 2014), 28–32.

16. Gu Donggao, *Chunqiu dashi biao*, 3:2630.

17. ZZ, Xiang 30.7 (543 BCE), 2:1258–1259.

18. In a Han text (first century BCE), an anecdote about political counsel from the humble also uses "meat-eaters" and "betony (a common plant)-eaters" (*huo shi zhe*) to refer to the ruler and ruled. See Liu Xiang, *Shuoyuan jinzhu jinyi* (Annotated and Translated *Garden of Anecdotes*), annotated by Lu Yuanjun (Taipei: Shangwu yinshu guan, 1995), 11.356–357.

19. ZZ, Huan 6.2b (706 BCE), 1:96–97.

20. *Guoyu*, with commentaries by Wei Zhao, annotated by Shanghai Shifan daxue guji zhengli yanjiu suo (Shanghai: Shanghai guji chubanshe, 1988), "Lu yu 1," 4.151.

21. ZZ, Zhuang 23.1 (671 BCE), 1:198–199. Lord Zhuang may be going to Qi to arrange his marriage with Ai Jiang, the daughter of a Qi ruler (their betrothal was arranged the previous year, and the marriage takes place the following year). Lord Zhuang's mother, Wen Jiang, committed adultery with her brother, Lord Xiang of Qi, and brought about the murder of her husband, Lord Huan of Lu (Huan 18.1 [694 BCE], 1:132–135). Ai Jiang would later commit adultery with Lord Zhuang's brother Qingfu and wreak havoc in Lu succession (Min 2.3 [660 BCE], 1:236–237). Attention to how one's action is recorded by scribes can influence choices, as several examples in *Zuozhuan* demonstrate.

22. This story is told in many late Warring States and Han texts, including *Shiji* (*Grand Scribe's Records*), annotated by Pei Yin, Sima Zhen, and Zhang Shoujie (Beijing: Zhonghua shuju, 1959), 32.1487, 86.2515–16.

23. *Mengzi yizhu* (*Translated and Annotated* Mengzi), annotated by Yang Bojun (Hong Kong: Zhonghua shuju, 2000), 2.7–8, 41–43; *Xunzi jishi* (Xunzi, *with Collected Annotations*), annotated by Li Disheng (Taipei: Xuesheng shuju, 1979), 15.317, 18.388.

24. For example, *Mengzi yizhu* 14.14, 328–329, *Xunzi jishi* 18.389, *Shuoyuan* 1.39.

25. ZZ, Xiang 14.6 (559 BCE), 2:1022–1025.

26. As noted earlier, this is a function of the varying sources and the "layering" of the text.

27. ZZ, Wen 7.5 (620 BCE), 1:502–503.

28. Gao Tan, *Chunqiu jigu zhuan zhu* (*Siku quanshu cunmu congshu*, vol. 143), cited in *Siku quanshu zongmu tiyao* (*Annotated Catalog of the Complete Imperial Library*), compiled by Yongrong, Ji Yun et al., edited by Zhou Ren et al. (Haikou: Hainan chubanshe, 1999), 31.641.

29. *Mengzi* 3B.9.

30. Zhu Xi, *Zhuzi yulei* (*Classified Conversations of Zhu Xi*), compiled by Li Jingde, edited by Wang Xingxian (Beijing: Zhonghua shuju, 1994), 83.2150–2151.

31. Gu Yanwu, *Rizhi lu jishi* (*Records of Knowledge Daily Acquired, with Collected Annotations*), compiled by Huang Rucheng (Zhengzhou: Zhongzhou guji chubanshe, 1990 [1936]), 4.94.

32. ZZ, Cheng 8.6 (583 BCE), 2:772–773. A different account of the Zhao lineage's near extinction and miraculous continuation, told in *Shiji* 43.1783–1785, is the basis of the Yuan play *The Orphan of Zhao* (*Zhao shi gu'er*) by Ji Junxiang (thirteenth century).

33. Wang Fuzhi, *Chunqiu jia shuo* (*The Wang Tradition on the* Spring and Autumn Annals), in *Chuanshan quanshu* (*The Complete Works of Wang Fuzhi*), edited by Chuanshan quanshu bianji weiyuan hui (Changsha: Yuelu shushe, 1988), 5:218.

SUGGESTED READING

ENGLISH

Durrant, Stephen, Wai-yee Li, and David Schaberg, trans. and annot. *Zuo Tradition / Zuozhuan, Commentary on the* Spring and Autumn Annals. 3 vols. Seattle: University of Washington Press, 2016.

Li, Wai-yee. *The Readability of the Past in Early Chinese Historiography*. Cambridge, MA: Harvard University Asia Center, 2007.

——. *Women and National Trauma in Late Imperial Chinese Literature*. Cambridge, MA: Harvard University Asia Center, 2014.

Pines, Yuri. *Foundations of Confucian Thought*. Honolulu: University of Hawai'i Press, 2002.

——. "Zhou History and Historiography: Introducing the Bamboo *Xinian*." *T'oung Pao* 100, no. 4–5 (2014): 287–324.

Schaberg, David. *A Patterned Past: Form and Thought in Early Chinese Historiography*. Cambridge, MA: Harvard University Asia Center, 2001.

CHINESE

Feng Menglong 馮夢龍. *Xin lieguo zhi* 新列國志 (*A New Account of the Various States*). Later published as *Dong Zhou lieguo zhi* 東周列國志 (*Account of the Various States During Eastern Zhou*) with revisions by Cai Yuanfang 蔡元放. Edited by Liu Bendong 劉本棟. Taipei: Sanmin shuju, 1999.

Gu Donggao 顧棟高. *Chunqiu dashi biao* 春秋大事表 (*Tables of Major Events in the* Spring and Autumn Annals). Edited by Wu Shuping 吳樹平 and Li Jiemin 李解民. 3 vols. Beijing: Zhonghua shuju, 1995.

Gu Yanwu 顧炎武. *Rizhi lu jishi* 日知錄集釋 (*Records of Knowledge Daily Acquired, with Collected Annotations*). Compiled by Huang Rucheng 黃汝成. Zhengzhou: Zhongzhou guji chubanshe, [1936] 1990.

Guoyu 國語 (*Discourses of the States*). With commentaries by Wei Zhao 韋昭. Annotated by Shanghai shifan daxue guji zhengli yanjiu suo 上海師範大學古籍整理研究所. Shanghai: Shanghai guji chubanshe, 1988.

Hou Wenxue 侯文學 and Li Mingli 李明麗. *Qinghua jian "Xinian" yu "Zuozhuan" xushi bijiao yanjiu* 清華簡《繫年》與《左傳》比較研究 (*A Comparative Study of the Qinghua Bamboo Strips* Chronological Accounts *and* Zuo Commentary). Shanghai: Zhongxi shuju, 2015.

Li Disheng 李滌生, annot. *Xunzi jishi* 荀子集釋 (*Xunzi, with Collected Annotations*). Taipei: Xuesheng shuju, 1979.

Liu Xiang 劉向. *Shuoyuan jinzhu jinyi* 說苑今注今譯 (*Annotated and Translated* Garden of Anecdotes). Annotated and translated by Lu Yuanjun 盧元駿. Taipei: Shangwu yinshu guan, 1995.

Liu Xie 劉勰. *Wenxin diaolong yizheng* 文心雕龍義證 (*Annotated* Literary Mind and Carvings of Dragon). Compiled by Zhan Ying 詹鍈. Shanghai: Shanghai guji chubanshe, 1989.

Ma Su 馬驌. *Zuozhuan shi wei* 左傳事緯 (*Ordering of Events in the* Zuo Commentary). Jinan: Qi Lu shushe, 1992.

Sima Qian 司馬遷. *Shiji* 史記 (*Grand Scribe's Records*). Annotated by Pei Yin 裴駰, Sima Zhen 司馬貞, and Zhang Shoujie 張守節. 10 vols. Beijing: Zhonghua, 1959.

Su Jianzhou 蘇建州, Wu Wenwen 吳雯雯, and Lai Yixuan 賴怡璇, comps. *Qinghua er Xinian jijie* 清華二《繫年》集解 (*Annotations on* Chronological Accounts). Taipei: Wanjuanlou, 2013.

Wang Fuzhi 王夫之. *Chunqiu jia shuo* 春秋家說 (*The Wang Tradition on the* Spring and Autumn Annals). Vol. 5 of *Chuanshan quanshu* 船山全書 (*The Complete Works of Wang Fuzhi*). Edited by Chuanshan quanshu bianji weiyuan hui 船山全書編輯委員會. Changsha: Yuelu shushe, 1988.

Yang Bojun 楊伯峻, annot. *Mengzi yizhu* 孟子譯注 (*Translated and Annotated* Mengzi). Hong Kong: Zhonghua shuju, 2000.

Zhang Gaoping 張高評. *Zuozhuan zhi wenxue jiazhi* 左傳之文學價值 (*Literary Value of the* Zuo Commentary). Taipei: Wen shi zhe, 1982.

Zhu Xi 朱熹. *Zhuzi yulei* 朱子語類 (*Classified Conversations of Zhu Xi*). Compiled by Li Jingde 黎靖德. Edited by Wang Xingxian 王星賢. Beijing: Zhonghua shuju, 1994.

3

Pre-Qin Philosophical Prose

Recorded Conversations and Argumentative Essays

So far as we know, Confucius (Kongzi; 551–479 BCE) never authored any philosophical writings of his own. His wisdom was preserved for later generations only through the efforts of his disciples, who assiduously took notes of any important statements they heard their master utter, along with brief question-and-answer dialogues he had both with them and, occasionally, other noteworthy figures. Our main source for these utterances and conversations is the *Analects of Confucius* (*Lunyu*), a compilation likely initiated by either first- or second-generation disciples, but which did not take its final form until the early Han dynasty and thus may well contain some later accretions beyond an authentic core of original utterances. The *Analects*, however, is far from being the only early work that purports to record statements of and dialogues involving Confucius, as numerous instances of both can be found in pre-imperial chapters of the *Book of Rites* (*Li Ji*) and *Elder Dai's Book of Rites* (*Da Dai Li Ji*), and even among recently excavated Warring States manuscripts. Some of these latter dialogues involve Confucius in conversation with rulers or high ministers of his home state of Lu and often are more sustained than the brief exchanges we find in the *Lunyu*; it goes without saying that many of these dialogues may have been literary recreations of imagined conversations rather than genuine records of actual dialogues.

While such recorded conversations and pronouncements historically preceded the essay—a form that held great advantages when it came to the clear and coherent exposition of philosophical arguments—they by their very nature retained an air of authoritative wisdom that the essay could never quite duplicate. They thus remained a staple of Confucian philosophical writing throughout the Warring States and well beyond. The *Mencius*, which Mencius (Mengzi; ca. 385–305 BCE) himself may have had a hand in compiling, is essentially a collection of dialogues between Mencius and disciples, heads of state, philosophical rivals, and other figures, along with a few individual statements citing him as the speaker. Although some of the dialogues are rather lengthy and occasionally contain embedded parables and other narrative details the likes of which are not seen in the *Lunyu*, the basic form of the *Mencius* can nonetheless be thought to have derived from that of passages recorded in the former work. Xunzi (ca. 298–ca. 238 BCE), the third philosopher treated here, largely departed from this practice and instead adopted the essay form from rival schools (e.g., the Mohist; ☞ chap. 5), taking it to new heights in the process, but even the work under his name does not completely exclude texts that adhere to the form of recorded dialogue and debate. The genre of recorded conversations would prove to have remarkable staying power among Confucian philosophers in later ages. In the Han, Yang Xiong wrote his *Model Sayings* (*Fayan*) in direct imitation of the *Lunyu*, and over a millennium later, in the Song, our largest source for the thought of the great Neo-Confucian philosopher Zhu Xi (1130–1200) took the form of disciples' records of his answers to their questions, compiled and edited, much like the *Lunyu*, into a single work in the years and decades following the philosopher's death. At the same time, however, recorded conversations are by no means unique to the Confucians, as ruler-minister, minister-minister, and diplomatic dialogues were clearly central to such early historiographical works as the *Zuo Tradition* (*Zuozhuan*, ☞ chap. 2) and *Discourses of the States* (*Guoyu*), not to mention closely related philosophical texts associated with early major statesmen, such as the *Springs and Autumns of Master* Yan (*Yanzi chunqiu*).

This chapter focuses on passages from the three main works of pre-imperial Confucian thought—the *Lunyu*, the *Mencius*, and the *Xunzi*—and also includes a brief example from the Han compilation *Garden of Persuasions* (*Shuoyuan*). While they by no means constitute a comprehensive survey of early Confucian thought, these texts should serve to illuminate the development of recorded conversations and argumentative essays among the early Confucians by concentrating on a couple of issues of central concern to the three main philosophers in question: musical education and the nature of human nature, the latter of which was a matter of intense debate for both Mencius and Xunzi. Confucian thought and its early lineage as encapsulated in these seminal works would remain at the core of China's long literary and philosophical traditions for at least the next two millennia, and their influence can be seen in many of the texts discussed in subsequent chapters of this volume.

ANALECTS OF CONFUCIUS (*LUNYU*)

Whether there is any definite order to be discerned in the arrangement of passages in the *Analects* is a matter of debate, but it is in any case clear that one must read each passage against all others speaking to similar notions in order to interpret it judiciously, as quotations are usually provided without context and often stand ambiguous on their own. Consider the following two aphoristic statements attributed directly to Master Kong (Confucius):

論語・泰伯

C3.1 *Analects of Confucius*, "Tai Bo" 8.8

The Master said: "Arise through the Odes, become established through Ritual, and achieve completion through Music."

子曰：〝興於詩，立於禮，成於樂。〞

[*LYJZ* 104–105]

論語・雍也

子曰："知 之者不
如 好 之者，好 之者不
如 樂之者。"

[*LYJZ* 89]

N.B. Straight underline
indicates the use of repetitive
patterning; wavy underline
indicates the use of parallel
phrasing therein. For a
discussion on repetitive and
parallel patterning, ☛ C1.1–4
and C1.6–7.

論語・子罕

子曰："吾未見好德如
好色者也。"

[*LYJZ* 114]

論語・述而

子在齊聞韶，三月不知
肉味。曰："不圖為樂
之至於斯也！"

[*LYJZ* 96]

論語・為政

子曰："吾十有五而志
于學，三十而立，四十
而不惑，五十而知天
命，六十而耳順，七
十而從心所欲，不踰
矩。"

[*LYJZ* 54–55]

C3.2 *Analects of Confucius*, "Yong ye" 6.18

The Master said: "Those who know it (i.e., the proper way) are no match for those who have fondness for it, [while] those who have fondness for it are no match for those who find happiness in it."

Aside from their shared tripartite form, these two statements might not initially appear to have much in common. The astute reader, however, will notice that they both conclude with the same term, *yue/le* ("music/happiness," both of which are written with the same character and essentially the same word in different connotations), to represent the highest stage of attainment. Taken together, the passages thus point to a state of perfected virtue at once both joyous and musical in character, one that likely entails achieving a kind of harmony of distinct (and potentially conflicting) virtues kept in orchestrated balance. Much like the tones of a multistringed zither or an ensemble of diverse instruments, these virtues are cultivated to the point at which they all flow forth spontaneously like a well-rehearsed, perfectly executed, and rapturous musical composition. Now compare the following two passages:

C3.3 *Analects of Confucius*, "Zi han" 9.17

The Master said: "I have never seen anyone as fond of virtue as he is of sensual beauty (/sex)." (see also *Analects of Confucius*, 15.12)

C3.4 *Analects of Confucius*, "Shu er" 7.13

The Master heard [a performance of the sagely composition] Shao while in Qi and was for several months unaware of the taste of meat. He said: "I never imagined the making of music could reach such heights!"

If "fondness for it" is the stage that, through further effort, ultimately leads one to "find happiness in it," it is natural to suppose Confucius in fact intends to suggest that one ideally *should* hold fondness for virtue in precisely the way one does for sex, which is to say, come to take a quasi-visceral delight in it and become almost instinctually driven toward it in no less forceful a manner. Fully embodied, this fondness turns into a kind of contentment or "musical happiness" in virtuous action—precisely the state captured in the Shao music of the former sage-king Shun, a composition so sublime that it immediately caused Confucius to forget all his baser desires, now sublimated into blissful delight in the musical expression of virtue.

By comparing these passages, we also come to better appreciate the final stage of Confucius's life as he described it in this famous passage:

C3.5 *Analects of Confucius*, "Wei zheng" 2.4

The Master said: "At the age of fifteen my mind was intent on learning; at thirty I became established; at forty I was no longer perplexed; at fifty I understood Heaven's mandate; at sixty my ears were favorably receptive; and at seventy I could follow whatever my heart desired without transgressing the proper standards."

Assuming Confucius was able to successfully follow his own program of moral self-cultivation, he surely must have achieved in his own lifetime something akin to the "musical completion" to which one should aspire. And indeed, although the term itself is not used here, Confucius's capacity at age seventy as characterized here is precisely that: a state of attainment wherein he does not simply always do the right thing, but does so spontaneously, effortlessly, and happily, because his desires and virtue have become one and the same.

We could go on to find any number of examples from elsewhere in the *Analects* that would help us to better comprehend the other two lines of passage 8.8, but let us conclude this brief exercise with just one passage that may speak to the call to "Arise through the Odes," our first example of an exchange between master and disciple:

C3.6 *Analects of Confucius*, "Xue er" 1.15

論語・學而

Zigong said: "To be poor yet not obsequious, or wealthy yet not arrogant—how would that be?"

The Master said: "That would be acceptable, but it would not be as good as one who is poor yet happy, or wealthy yet fond of ritual."

Zigong said: "The ode says: 'Like cutting, like scraping, like carving, like polishing'—does it not refer to just that?"

The Master said: "Si![1] One may now discuss the Odes with you! Told of what has gone forth, you know what is coming."

子貢曰：“貧而無諂，富而無驕，何如？”子曰：“可也。未若貧而樂，富而好禮者也。”子貢曰：“詩云：‘如切如磋，如琢如磨。’斯之謂與？”子曰：“賜也，始可與言詩已矣！告諸往而知來者。”

[*LYJZ* 52–53]

To get at the notion of how one moves beyond the stage of simply behaving morally to a state in which, once again, one fully embodies virtue and finds in it one's source of lasting contentment, Zigong extracts, out of context, a line from the ode "Qi ao" ("The Banks of Qi") to suggest that it involves an arduous and unrelenting project of self-cultivation, akin to the process of cutting and scraping a raw stone and carving and polishing it into a precious gem. Presumably, it was through analogy to that concrete image that Zigong was first made to comprehend the true nature of moral training. This serves as an example of how Confucius utilized the Odes in his instruction of disciples to first "give rise" to their understanding of less tangible ethical principles.

For Confucius, of course, the goals of moral cultivation were not limited to the individual, but rather were to serve as the foundations for governance and the benefit of society at large. An exchange with another disciple, Zizhang, speaks to these larger aspects:

C3.7 *Analects of Confucius*, "Yao yue" 20.2

論語・堯曰

Zizhang asked Confucius: "In what manner may one [properly] engage in governance?"

The Master said: "Honor the five excellences and ward off the four iniquities, and you will thereby be able to engage in governance."

子張問於孔子曰：“何如斯可以從政矣？”子曰：“尊五美，屏四惡，斯可以從政矣。”子張曰：“何謂五美？”子曰：

---

[1] Si was Zigong's given name. His full name was Duanmu Si; Zigong was his secondary name.

"君子惠而不費，
勞而不怨，欲而
不貪，泰而不驕，
威而不猛。"子張
曰："何謂惠而不
費？"子曰："因民之
所利而利之，斯不亦惠
而不費乎？擇可勞而
勞之，又誰怨？欲仁
而得仁，又焉貪？君
子無眾寡，無小大，
無敢慢，斯不亦泰而
不驕乎？君子正其
衣冠，尊其瞻視，儼
然人望而畏之，斯不
亦威而不猛乎？"子
張曰："何謂四惡？"
子曰："不教而殺謂
之虐；不戒視成謂
之暴；慢令致期謂
之賊；猶之與人也，出
納之吝，謂之有司。"

[*LYJZ* 194–195]

Zizhang said: "What are the five excellences?"

The Master said: "The noble man bestows favors, but is not wasteful in them; he causes [people] toil, but garners no resentment for it; he desires, but holds no avarice; he achieves prominence, but exhibits no arrogance; and he strikes awe, but is never vicious."

Zizhang said: "To what do 'bestowing favors, but not being wasteful in them' [and so on] refer?"

The Master said: "To profit the people on the basis of where they find their own source of profit—is this not indeed to bestow favors but not be wasteful in them? Causing them toil by selecting what is worth toiling over—who will bear resentment? Desiring benevolence, he attains benevolence—wherein would he hold avarice? The noble man, regardless of his numbers [of people] or size [of power], never dares to be negligent—is this not indeed to achieve prominence yet exhibit no arrogance? The noble man straightens his clothing and cap and holds a respectful gaze, so solemn that the people look up to him and hold him in awe—is this not indeed to strike awe without being vicious?"

Zizhang said: "To what do the 'four iniquities' refer?"

The Master said: "To kill without having instructed we refer to as being 'abusive'; to look for results without having informed in advance we refer to as being 'impetuous'; to be negligent in issuing commands yet stringent in setting deadlines we refer to as being 'villainous'; and to intend to give something to others yet be stingy when it comes to parting with it we refer to as being 'officious.'"

One engaged in governance of necessity directs and employs the people, and rewards, punishes, and commands subordinates, but if that person is to govern virtuously, he is to do all this with benevolent care and a sense of fairness, justice, and august solemnity. The passage is typical of Confucius's thought in advocating a positive program of charismatic leadership that avoids all excesses and extremes, and while its paired enumeration of "five excellences" and "four iniquities" is somewhat atypical for the *Lunyu*, the work does contain a few other passages that specifically quantify a determinate set of either virtues or vices. In any case, that at least the content of this exchange had a long and prominent history in early Confucian thought is beyond doubt, as it is also seen, with some variation (and there not specifically attributed to Confucius), in a recently excavated Warring States bamboo manuscript.[1]

Let us conclude this selection of *Analects* passages with one further interesting exchange between master and disciple, this time Ziyou:

C3.8 *Analects of Confucius*, "Yang Huo" 17.4

論語•陽貨

子之武城，聞弦歌之
聲。夫子莞爾而笑，
曰："割雞焉用牛
刀？"子游對曰：

The Master went to Wucheng,[1] where he heard the sounds of zithers accompanying singing. The Master cracked a smile and said: "Why must you use an ox-carving knife to slaughter a chicken?"

---

[1] Wucheng was a small city in Confucius's home state of Lu where Ziyou was, at the time, serving as chief officer. As is clear from the context, other disciples accompanied Confucius on his visit there.

Ziyou replied: "Formerly I heard it from you, master: 'When the noble man studies the Way, he cares for others; when the lesser man studies the Way, he is easy to direct.' "

The Master said: "My disciples, Yan's[2] words are correct! When I spoke just now, I was merely teasing him."

"昔者偃也聞諸夫子曰：'君子學道則愛人，小人學道則易使也。' "子曰："二三子！偃之言是也。前言戲之耳。"

[*LYJZ* 176]

Musical education may be essential training for the noble man, who has the capacity and educational opportunities necessary to the serious pursuit of moral self-cultivation, but education in the proper Way is indeed for everyone, and all stand to benefit from such musical and ritual training in accordance with their potential. So, as the disciple astutely reminds his master, the utilization of such an "ox-carving knife" can never be considered an act of overreach. Whether Confucius was truly speaking in jest or simply got caught up in a moment of unreflective, playful chiding, he was quick to stand corrected once his disciple deftly turned his own words against him. This exchange gives us a good glimpse into the occasionally lighthearted give-and-take that characterized Confucius's interactions with his disciples.

Before turning to the *Mencius*, let us briefly observe an example of a narrative involving Confucius that appears in a later text, in this case showing how a brief excerpt found in the *Analects* likely evolved over time to become enriched with narrative detail. The passage is found in the "Cultivating Refinement" ("Xiu wen") chapter of the *Garden of Persuasions* (*Shuoyuan*), a Han compilation that drew generously upon Warring States materials. Although we cannot date the passage with precision, it appears all but certain that it derived from the same *Analects* episode. It reads as follows:

Confucius arrived just outside the external city wall of [the] Qi [capital], where he came across a toddler carrying a pitcher and who proceeded to walk alongside [Confucius's carriage], his gaze refined, his mind upright, and his gait proper. Confucius told his driver: "Drive on quickly! Drive on quickly! The Shao music (of sage-king Shun) is being performed!" Confucius arrived [at the capital] and heard the Shao, and for three months was unaware of the taste of meat.

Thus music is not only for entertaining (*le*) oneself, but also for entertaining others; it is not only for rectifying oneself, but also for rectifying others. How great it is! Those who delight (*le*) in it could never imagine the making of music could reach such heights.

孔子至齊郭門之外，遇一嬰兒挈一壺，相與俱行，其視精，其心正，其行端。孔子謂御曰："趣驅之，趣驅之！韶樂方作！"孔子至彼聞韶，三月不知肉味。故樂非獨以自樂也，又以樂人；非獨以自正也，又以正人。大矣哉！於此樂者，不圖為樂至於此。

[*SYJZ* 499]

---

[2] Yan was Ziyou's given name. His full name was Yan Yan; Ziyou was his secondary name.

Upon observing the upright toddler, Confucius correctly surmised that his deportment must have been the result of having just recently heard the sublime music of Shao being performed. The introduction of this brief narrative frame serves to effectively drive home a greater philosophical point: not only is the sage-philosopher Confucius susceptible to the profound sway of supremely virtuous music, but so too is one at the opposite end of the spectrum of self-cultivation, a mere toddler, who, while no doubt highly impressionable, is also inherently tied more deeply to his basest desires. If the same music is equally able to transform those at both extremes so thoroughly, the implication is that there is surely no one upon whom it would not hold such sway.

MENCIUS

The dialogues included in the *Mencius* tend to be much more elaborate than anything we find in the *Analects*. Included here are two examples: one is a relatively lengthy exchange between Mengzi (Master Meng, a.k.a. Mencius) and his disciple Gongsun Chou, and the other is a brief exchange between Mengzi and his philosophical rival Gaozi.

C3.9 *Mencius*, "Gongsun Chou, Part A" 2A.2

Gongsun Chou asked: "Were you, my master, to be granted the position of high minister in Qi and able to implement the proper way there, it would be nothing to marvel at even should [its ruler] thereby achieve the status of overlord or [true] king. Were this to transpire, would your mind be agitated by it?"

Mencius replied: "No. My mind has not been agitated since I turned forty."

"If that is the case, then my master has far surpassed Meng Ben [in courage]."[1]

"That is nothing difficult. [Even] Gaozi preceded me in achieving non-agitation of mind."

"Is there a proper way to not have the mind agitated?"

"There is. Beigong You's[2] cultivation of courage was such that his skin would not wince and his eyes would not flinch; he thought that to receive the slightest insult from another would be like getting whipped in the marketplace. He would not take anything from a coarsely-garbed commoner, and neither would he take it from the ruler of a state of 10,000 chariots; he viewed stabbing the ruler of such a state the same as he would stabbing the commoner. There were no feudal lords whom he held in awe. If an unpleasant remark came his way, he would invariably react against it.

"Meng shi She's[3] cultivation of courage was such that he would say: '[I] view not gaining victory as [I] would being victorious. To advance only after

孟子・公孫丑上

公孫丑問曰：「夫子加齊之卿相，得行道焉，雖由此霸王不異矣。如此，則動心否乎？」

孟子曰：「否。我四十不動心。」

曰：「若是，則夫子過孟賁遠矣。」

曰：「是不難，告子先我不動心。」

曰：「不動心有道乎？」

曰：「有。北宮黝之養勇也，不膚撓，不目逃，思以一豪挫於人，若撻之於市朝。不受於褐寬博，亦不受於萬乘之君。視刺萬乘之君，若刺褐夫。無嚴諸侯。惡聲至，必反之。孟施舍之所養勇也，曰：『視不勝猶勝也。量敵而後進，慮勝而後會，是畏三軍者也。舍豈能為必勝哉？能無懼而已矣。』孟施舍似曾子，北宮黝似子夏。夫二子之勇，未知其孰賢，然而

[1] Meng Ben was a famous Warring States–era warrior renowned for his strength and courage.
[2] Beigong You is a figure of uncertain identity; the name, at least as written here, appears only in this passage.
[3] Meng shi She is also a figure otherwise unknown outside of this passage.

sizing up the enemy, to meet [in battle] only after considering the prospects of victory—these are [the actions of] someone who lies in fear of armed forces. How could I guarantee victory? I can merely be without fear, and that is all.'

"Meng shi She resembled Zengzi, and Beigong You resembled Zixia.[4] Now I cannot ascertain which of the two gentlemen was more worthy; however, Meng shi She held guard [over his *qi*] more firmly.

"Formerly, Zengzi stated to Zixiang[5]: 'Are you fond of courage? I once heard of great courage from the Master: if I reflect upon myself and [find] I am not upright, then although it be a coarsely-garbed commoner, I will not intimidate him; if I reflect upon myself and [find] I am upright, then though they number in the thousands, I will go off [to confront them].' Meng shi She did not, in turn, hold guard over his *qi* (vital energy) as firmly as did Zengzi."

"Might I be so bold as to ask about [the difference] between my master's non-agitation of mind and that of Gaozi?"

"Gaozi has said: 'If you cannot attain it through discourse, do not seek it in your mind; if you cannot attain it in your mind, do not seek it in your *qi* (vital energy).' It is permissible to not seek in your *qi* what you cannot attain in your mind, but it is not permissible to not seek in your mind what you cannot attain through discourse. For the mind's intent (*zhi*) is the commander of the *qi*, whereas the *qi* is what infuses the body. Wherever the mind's intent arrives, the *qi* is to set up camp there.[6] Thus we say: 'maintain your mind's intent; do not allow your *qi* to erupt forth.'"

"What do you mean by saying both 'wherever the mind's intent arrives, the *qi* is to set up camp there' and 'maintain your mind's intent; do not allow your *qi* to erupt forth'?"

"When the mind's intent is concentrated, it mobilizes the *qi*; when the *qi* is concentrated, it mobilizes the mind's intent. Now in the case of someone who stumbles while running, this is a matter of the *qi*, conversely, mobilizing the mind."

"May I be so bold as to ask wherein my master excels?"

"I understand discourse, and I am skilled at cultivating my full-flowing *qi*."

"May I be so bold as to ask to what 'full-flowing *qi*' refers?"

"It is hard to describe. As a form of *qi*, it is the greatest and strongest of all, and if cultivated steadily and without harm, it fills the expanse between Heaven and Earth. As a form of *qi*, it pairs up with righteousness and the proper way;

---

[4] Zengzi and Zixia were two of Confucius's more prominent disciples. As Zhu Xi describes them, "Zixia held earnest trust in the sages, whereas Zengzi turned inward to seek things in himself"—characteristics that in some ways roughly map onto the descriptions of Beigong You and Meng shi She, respectively.

[5] Zixiang is identified as one of Zengzi's disciples. "The Master" referred to in Zengzi's answer is of course his own master, Confucius.

[6] Interpreting the sense of *zhi* and *ci* differently here, an alternative reading of this line would be "The mind's intent is the ultimate, and the *qi* is secondary to it."

孟施舍守約也。昔者曾子謂子襄曰：'子好勇乎？吾嘗聞大勇於夫子矣：自反而不縮，雖褐寬博，吾不惴焉；自反而縮，雖千萬人，吾往矣。'孟施舍之守氣，又不如曾子之守約也。"

N.B. Straight underline indicates the use of repetitive patterning; wavy underline the use of parallel phrasing therein. For a discussion on repetitive and parallel patterning, ☛ C1.1–4 and C1.6–7.

曰："敢問夫子之不動心，與告子之不動心，可得聞與？"

"告子曰：'不得於言，勿求於心；不得於心，勿求於氣。'不得於心，勿求於氣，可；不得於言，勿求於心，不可。夫志，氣之帥也；氣，體之充也。夫志至焉，氣次焉。故曰：'持其志，無暴其氣。'"

"既曰'志至焉，氣次焉'，又曰'持其志無暴其氣'者，何也？"

曰："志壹則動氣，氣壹則動志也。今夫蹶者趨者，是氣也，而反動其心。"

"敢問夫子惡乎長？"

曰："我知言，我善養吾浩然之氣。"

"敢問何謂浩然之氣？"

曰：“難言也。其
為氣也，至大至剛，以
直養而無害，則塞于天
地之閒。其為氣也，配
義與道；無是，餒也。
是集義所生者，非義襲
而取之也。行有不慊於
心，則餒矣。我故曰，
告子未嘗知義，以其外
之也。必有事焉而勿
正，心勿忘，勿助長
也。無若宋人然：宋人
有閔其苗之不長而揠之
者。芒芒然歸，謂其人
曰：‘今日病矣，予助
苗長矣。’其子趨而往
視之，苗則槁矣。天下
之不助苗長者寡矣。以
為無益而舍之者，不耘
苗者也；助之長者，揠
苗者也。非徒無益，而
又害之。”

“何謂知言？”

曰：“詖辭知其所
蔽，淫辭知其所陷，邪
辭知其所離，遁辭知其
所窮。生於其心，害於
其政；發於其政，害於
其事。聖人復起，必從
吾言矣。”

“宰我、子貢 善 為說
辭，冉牛、閔子、顏
淵 善 言德行。孔子兼
之，曰：‘我於辭命則
不能也。’然則夫子既
聖矣乎？”

曰：“惡！是 何
言也？昔者子貢問於
孔子曰：‘夫子聖矣
乎？’孔子曰：‘聖
則吾不能，我學不厭而
教不倦也。’子貢曰：

without these, it is famished. It is something born of accumulated righteousness, not captured through the sudden seizure of righteousness. Should one's conduct yield dissatisfaction in one's heart, it will starve. Thus I say: Gaozi has never understood righteousness, because he treats it as external.

"You must attend to it, but not [forcibly] rectify it; your mind must not forget it, but must also not 'help it grow.' Do not be like the man of [the state of] Song.[7] There once was a man of Song who, worried that his sprouts were not growing, pulled upon them. Oblivious [to what he had done], he returned home and told his family: 'Today I'm exhausted; I helped the sprouts to grow.' By the time his son rushed over to have a look at the sprouts, they had already withered.

"There are few in the world who do not 'help [their] sprouts to grow.' Those who find [cultivation] useless and forsake it [altogether] are those who do not weed [their] sprouts, [whereas] those who help them to grow are those who pull upon [their] sprouts—which is not only useless, but moreover harmful."

"What does it mean to 'understand discourse'?"

"With biased utterances, it is knowing what they obscure; with excessive utterances, it is knowing what traps they lead into; with heretical utterances, it is knowing the locus of their deviation; and with evasive utterances, it is knowing the place of their impoverishment. Arising from one's mind, [such words] are harmful to one's governance; applied to one's governance, they are harmful to one's affairs. Should a sage once again arise, he will certainly heed my words."

"Zai Wo and Zigong were skilled at persuasive rhetoric, [whereas] Ran Niu, Minzi, and Yan Yuan were skilled at discussing virtuous conduct.[8] Confucius possessed both [sets of skills], [though] he would say: 'As for the language of discourse, I am incapable.' This being the case, are you, my master, already a sage?"[9]

"Oh no! What kind of talk is this? Formerly, Zigong asked Confucius: 'Are you, my master, a sage?' Confucius replied: 'As for sagacity, I am incapable. I am [merely one who] never grows averse to learning and never grows tired of teaching.' Zigong said: 'To never grow averse to learning is wisdom; to never tire of teaching is benevolence. Being both benevolent and wise, my master is already a sage!' For sagacity is [a label] to which [even] Confucius would not accede—what kind of talk is this?"

---

[7] People from the state of Song were conventionally stereotyped as ignorant fools.

[8] Zai Wo, Zigong, Ran Niu, Minzi, and Yan Yuan, along with the aforementioned Zixia, Ziyou, Zizhang, and You Ruo cited again in the next section, were all disciples of Confucius. Similar attributions pertaining to these first five disciples are to be found in the second half of passage 11.2 in the *Lunyu*.

[9] Gongsun Chou asks this because Mencius claims to both understand discourse and be skilled at cultivating his full-flowing *qi*, two capacities that roughly correspond to the rhetorical talents and virtuous conduct that Confucius, alone, possesses simultaneously.

"Formerly I happened to hear the following: Zixia, Ziyou, and Zizhang each possessed one part of the body of the sage, whereas Ran Niu, Minzi, and Yan Yuan possessed the entire body, but only incipiently. May I be so bold as to ask where you stand [in relation to this]?"

"Enough of this [topic] for now."

"How would you characterize Boyi and Yi Yin?"[10]

"The ways they took were different. To not serve anyone other than one's own ruler, or to direct anyone other than one's own people, and to advance in times of order, but retire in times of chaos—this was Boyi. To [consider that] anyone [worth] serving is one's ruler, and all [worth] directing are one's people, and [thus] to advance in times of both order and chaos—this was Yi Yin. To enter service when it was permissible to enter, but to cease when it was permissible to cease, and to remain long when it was permissible to remain long, but to make haste when it was permissible to make haste—this was Confucius. They were all sages of antiquity, whose conduct I am in no case able to match, but in terms of my aspiration, I wish to emulate Confucius."

"Were Boyi and Yi Yin on a par with Confucius?"

"No. Ever since there have been living people, there has never been another Confucius."

"That being so, were there similarities?"

"There were. Were they able to attain rule over a territory of a [mere] hundred li,[11] each of them would have been able to possess the world and have the regional lords pay court. [But] if they could attain the world by means of practicing a single act of unrighteousness or killing a single innocent, none of them would have done so. In this they were the same."

"May I be so bold as to ask wherein they diverged?"

"Zai Wo, Zigong, and You Ruo all had knowledge sufficient to recognize a sage, and they would never degrade themselves to the point of showing partiality toward those they liked. Zai Wo said: 'In my observation of Confucius, I find him far more worthy than [even] Yao and Shun.'[12] Zigong said: 'Seeing their rituals, [he] would know their governance, and hearing their music, [he] would know their virtue. From [a vantage point of] a hundred ages hence, [he] could rank the kings of a hundred ages, and none would be able to defy [his

---

[10] Boyi was a legendary paragon of virtue who, along with his younger brother, went to serve the Zhou after declining the throne of his own state, but subsequently refused to serve the Zhou and went into reclusion following the Zhou's military conquest of the Shang. Yi Yin was a legendary Shang minister who supposedly rose from indentured servitude to serve the founding king of the Shang dynasty along with the Shang's subsequent three kings, the last of whom was characterized as cruel and lawless.

[11] One li was roughly a third of a mile.

[12] Yao and Shun were both legendary sage kings of antiquity. Yao abdicated the throne to Shun, and Shun, in turn, to his successor, Yu.

'學不厭，智也；教不倦，仁也。仁且智，夫子既聖矣！'夫聖，孔子不居，是何言也？"

"昔者竊聞之：子夏、子游、子張皆有聖人之一體，冉牛、閔子、顏淵則具體而微。敢問所安。"

曰："姑舍是。"

曰："伯夷、伊尹何如？"

曰："不同道。非其君不事，非其民不使；治則進，亂則退，伯夷也。何事非君，何使非民；治亦進，亂亦進，伊尹也。可以仕則仕，可以止則止，可以久則久，可以速則速，孔子也。皆古聖人也，吾未能有行焉；乃所願，則學孔子也。"

"伯夷、伊尹於孔子，若是班乎？"

曰："否。自有生民以來，未有孔子也。"

曰："然則有同與？"

曰："有。得百里之地而君之，皆能以朝諸侯有天下。行一不義、殺一不辜而得天下，皆不為也。是則同。"

曰："敢問其所以異？"

曰："宰我、子貢、有若智足以知聖人。汙，不至阿其所好。宰

我曰：'以予觀於夫
子，賢於堯舜遠矣。'
子貢曰：'見其禮而
知其政，聞其樂而知
其德。由百世之後，
等百世之王，莫之能
違也。自生民以來，未
有夫子也。'有若曰：
'豈惟民哉？麒麟之
於走獸，鳳凰之於飛
鳥，太山之於丘垤，河
海之於行潦，類也。聖
人之於民，亦類也。出
於其類，拔乎其萃，
自生民以來，未有盛於
孔子也。'"

[*MZJZ* 229–235]

recognition].[13] Ever since there have been living people, there has never been [such a one as] our master.' You Ruo said: 'Is it only so amongst the people? The *qilin* unicorn amongst all running beasts, the phoenixes amongst all flying birds, Mt. Tai amongst all hills and mounds, and the Yellow River and the Sea amongst all streams and puddles—they are all of a kind. The sage amongst the people—he is also of a kind. Emerging from his kind and rising high above the masses—no one has ever done this more abundantly than Confucius."

Through interlocution with his disciple, Mencius here expresses one of the core tenets of his philosophy: the primacy of the mind in determining the proper course of action. We all, from birth, possess the capacity for and, indeed, inclination toward virtue, and the "sprouts" from which each of our individual virtues grow are all innately present in our mind (*xin*; alternately, "heart-and-mind"). Thus, for example, the natural capacity to judge right and wrong, when properly tended, will ultimately develop into the virtue of wisdom (*zhi*). The key to successful cultivation of these virtues (also including benevolence [*ren*], righteousness [*yi*], and ritual propriety [*li*]) lies in utilizing the inherent ability of the mind to deliberate and reflect and thus not get beguiled by misleading and corrupting external influences.

It is against such a philosophical background that this dialogue unfolds. The central concern that ties all the various parts of the conversation together is the proper relationship between the mind, the *qi* (vital energy), and external discourse (*yan*, "words," "speech"), with Mencius steadfastly maintaining that the mind must take charge of the latter two. The first half of the exchange, set up by the disciple's question pertaining to a hypothetical scenario in which Mencius is able to fulfill his wildest political ambitions, focuses on the relationship between the mind and *qi*. The discussion of courage, in which three figures are compared, highlights both the moral dimension of true courage and the role of the mind in tightly "holding guard" (*shou*) in order to achieve it.

The wording here presents an interesting illustrative case of the ambiguities involved in interpretation and the clues we may avail ourselves of to resolve them. In the phrase stating that Meng shi She "held guard [more] firmly" (*shou yue*), traditional Chinese commentators are unanimous in understanding *yue* adverbially (or, more precisely, as the predicative adjective of the nominalized verb *shou*), along the lines of "essentially" (here "firmly"). That *yue* indeed predicates *shou* rather than serves as its nominal object is not only demanded by the nature of the sentence as a comparison, but is also largely demonstrated by comparison with the similar wording of passage 7.32, where the same phrase *shou yue* is syntactically parallel to *yan jin*, "[when] words are near." Nonetheless, the *seeming* parallel later in our present passage between verb-object *shou qi* and the phrase *shou yue*— in the sentence describing the manner in which Meng shi She's courage was, in

---

[13] Both the subject of these lines and the referent of their possessive pronouns (here rendered "their") are ambiguous, and alternate interpretations have been put forward. It may also be possible to understand the last line in the sense that no ruler has ever been able to defy Kongzi's "way."

turn, inferior to that of Zengzi—has proven a source of confusion for translators, who have consistently rendered the phrase *shou yue* along the lines of "preserved what is essential." It is the same confusion that befell the disciples of Song dynasty Neo-Confucian scholar Zhu Xi, and their questioning of the phrase prompted Zhu to correctively stress that "it is not a matter of preserving that '*yue*,' but that what is preserved is [described as] '*yue*'" (*ZZYL*, 1234–1235). Interpreting *yue* nominally, in fact, renders nonsense of the text, as it requires that what Meng shi She "preserves" or "guards over" randomly change: from "what is essential" in the first instance to *qi* in the next. Once we understand that, in the phrase describing how Meng shi She's holding guard over his *qi* did not match up to that of Zengzi, the phrase *shou yue* is simply an abbreviation of *shou [qi] yue*—the *qi* understood from the context of the comparison—all confusion disappears: in both cases, what is at issue is simply the "guarding over" or "preservation" of *qi* and the degree of firmness with which such guard is held.

This interpretive point is worth highlighting because it is difficult to make much coherent sense of the passage as a whole without first clarifying the fact that the focal point of the "courage" comparisons falls precisely on how the mind must hold guard over the *qi*. And this is the one point on which Mencius and his philosophical rival Gaozi agree: that one must not allow one's *qi* to agitate one's mind. For Mencius, the mind is to take command of the body's *qi* in the way a military commander leads his troops: harnessing its power with training and discipline in pursuit of a strategic objective, never allowing it to simply "erupt forth" and run amok of its own accord.

Gongsun Chou's question of "wherein" Mencius "excels" should be understood as his seeking clarification on how his master's own cultivation of a non-agitated mind surpasses that of Gaozi, and here the passage arrives at the central point of disagreement between the two philosophers: whether it is the mind's inner reflection or external verbal discourse that should take precedence. Gaozi prized debate and conclusions derived from verbal disputation and, moreover, adopted a view of morality that conceived of benevolence (*ren*) as internally derived but righteousness (*yi*) as a form of ethical conduct determined solely by circumstances external to the self. For Mencius, all truly virtuous action must take shape from within and be the outcome of a long and gradual process of organic cultivation, and the idea that one could be virtuous simply by conforming at any moment to some external norm was to him an anathema. That is why "discourse" can never take primacy over the reflection of one's own mind, the seat of the incipient moral sprouts that must be nurtured and grown but never forced—a point driven home by Mencius's vivid analogy of the "farmer of Song" foolishly tugging at his sprouts. The power of one's *qi* is limitless so long as the mind takes charge and cultivates it with moral training, but it becomes starved and feeble once that is forsaken in favor of immediate appeal to external norms.

This leads to the second area wherein Mencius excels: his ability to "understand discourse," to not be perplexed by the trappings of verbal disputation. A mind that too readily assents to crafty arguments without duly reflecting on them with its own intuitive moral compass can only be led astray, whereas the deliberative mind, bolstered by its own long-term cultivation, comes to have the ability to see through the biases, excesses, and pitfalls of all such specious arguments.

With Mencius having effectively claimed superiority in both virtuous self-cultivation and rhetorical acumen, Gongsun Chou hazards to further inflate his master's ego by asking whether he is, in fact, a sage. By implicitly comparing himself to Confucius—the best of all "sages of antiquity" and himself the subject of his own disciples' similar queries—Mencius finds a clever way indeed of feigning humility on this point: how could he ever dare accept such a label? But the astute disciple is expected, obviously, to see through such humility and recognize a sage for what he truly is.

The entire conversation thus works like a Socratic dialogue in reverse: it is not Mencius who asks leading questions to an unwitting straw-man interlocutor, but rather the disciple who tosses up softball questions for his master to hit out of the park. In either case, the rhetorical effect is an impression that the master has spontaneously and effortlessly managed to persuade his interlocutor of the validity of his own point of view, one to which we, the readers, should naturally also assent. The same applies to other dialogues in the *Mencius* where Mencius is seen, alternatively, persuading kings or besting philosophical rivals. Such dialogues may well have been genuine, but we should not be surprised if they also gave generous rein to literary license when they came to be written down for posterity. Our next passage is an example of Mencius sparring directly with Gaozi:

孟子 • 告子上

告子曰：" 性猶湍水也，決諸東方則東流，決諸西方則西流。人性之無分於善不善也，猶水之無分於東西也。"

孟子曰：" 水信無分於東西。無分於上下乎？人性之善也，猶水之就下也。人無有不善，水無有不下。今夫水，搏而躍之，可使過顙；激而行之，可使在山。是豈水之性哉？其勢則然也。人之可使為不善，其性亦猶是也。"

[*MZJZ* 325–326]

C3.10 *Mencius*, "Gaozi, Part A" 6A.2

Gaozi said: "Human nature is like water rushing down rapids: if you dredge a channel to the east, it flows eastward; if you dredge a channel to the west, it flows westward. That human nature has no inherent allotment pertaining to good or bad is comparable to water having no inherent allotment pertaining to east or west."

Mencius said: "Water truly has no inherent allotment pertaining to east or west, but does it have no allotment pertaining to up or down? The goodness of human nature is like water's flowing downward. There is no human who is not [inherently] good, and no water that does not [inherently] flow downward. Now as for water, you can make it splash up over your forehead if you strike it, and you can conduct it up a mountain if you dam its flow—but how could this lie in the inherent nature of water? It is rather the circumstances that make it thus. That humans can be made to do ill [does not change the fact that] their nature remains the same."

In addition to its insight into his view of human nature, this passage illustrates well the manner in which Mencius was adept at both using analogies and—if this account of the exchange is to be believed—at turning others' analogies against them.

XUNZI

A couple of generations after Mencius, the next famous philosopher of Confucian thought, Xunzi (ca. 340–245 BCE), was no less skillful in the art of analogy and the crafting of persuasive argument. Unlike Mencius, however, Xunzi's preferred form of written argumentation was the essay, which afforded better opportunities for intricately articulated persuasion. The essays found in the *Xunzi* count among the best examples of the genre in Warring States literature. Space here will allow for only excerpts; let us begin with the opening of the essay that heads the work:

C3.11 *Xunzi*, "Exhortation to Learning" (excerpt)

The noble man says: learning may never be halted. The color of deep blue is extracted from the indigo plant, but it is bluer than the indigo; ice is made from water, but it is colder than water. A piece of wood straight as a plumb line may be bent over fire to make a wheel, such that its curve would conform to the turn of a compass, never to stand straight again even if left to dry out in the sun—it is the bending over fire that makes it so. Truly, a piece of wood is made straight when subjected to the plumb line, metal is sharpened when brought to the whetstone, and the noble man becomes enlightened in knowledge and unerring in action when he learns widely and examines himself thrice daily.

Thus if you do not climb a high mountain, you will never know the heights of Heaven; if you do not overlook a deep valley, you will never know the depths of Earth; and if you do not hear the words bequeathed by the former kings, you will never know the greatness of learning and inquiry. The children of the Gan, Yue, Yi, and Mo peoples[1] all make the same cries at birth, but they grow to have different customs—it is education that makes this so. The Ode says: "Ah, you noble men, do not long feel secure in your repose! Earnestly fulfill your positions, and hold fondness for the correct and upright. The spirits, upon examining this, will assist you with radiant blessings."[2] There is nothing more "spiritual" than transformation through the Way, and no "blessings" more enduring than avoidance of error.[3]

I once contemplated for an entire day, but it was no match for what I learned through a single instant of study;[4] I once gazed into the distance standing on tiptoe, but it was no match for the breadth of what I observed upon ascending to a high place. When one beckons people having ascended to a high place, though one's arms have not grown longer, one can be seen far in the distance;

---

[1] These referred to indigenous peoples of the southeastern and northeastern extremities of the Chinese world.

[2] This line is from the ode "Xiao ming" in the "Xiao ya" section of the *Book of Poetry* (*Shijing*), in which an officer toiling away on service distantly addresses his colleagues back at court.

[3] The text here actually reads *huo* ("calamities"), but it makes better sense to see this as a phonetic loan for *guo* ("error"), referring back to how the noble man is "unerring in action."

[4] A similar sentiment is expressed in passage 15.30 of the *Analects*.

荀子・勸學 （摘錄）

君子曰：學不可以已。
青，取之於藍而青於
藍；冰，水為之而寒
於水。木直中繩，輮以
為輪，其曲中規，雖有
槁暴，不復挺者，輮使
之然也。故木受繩則
直，金就礪則利，君子
博學而日參省乎己，
則知明而行無過矣。
故不登高山，不知天之
高也；不臨深谿，不
知地之厚也；不聞
先王之遺言，不知學
問之大也。干、越、
夷、貉之子，生而同
聲，長而異俗，教使之
然也。詩曰："嗟爾
君子，無恆安息。靖
共爾位，好是正直。
神之聽之，介爾景
福。"神莫大於化道，
福莫長於無禍（過）。
吾嘗終日而思矣，不
如須臾之所學也；吾
嘗跂而望矣，不如登
高之博見也。登高
而招，臂非加長也，
而見者遠；順風而
呼，聲非加疾也，而聞
者彰。假輿馬者，非
利足也，而致千里；

假舟檝者，非能水也，
而　絕江河。君子生
非異也，　善假於物
也。......

[*XZJJ* 1–4]

N.B. Straight underline indicates the use of repetitive patterning; wavy underline the use of parallel phrasing therein. For a discussion on repetitive and parallel patterning, ☛ C1.1–4 and C1.6–7.

when one cries out in the direction of the wind, though one's voice has not itself quickened, one can be heard quite clearly. Those who make use of carriages and horses, though themselves not fleet of foot, are able to reach distances of a thousand *li*; those who make use of boats and oars, though themselves unable to swim, are able to traverse great rivers. It is not that the noble man is born different from others, but that he is skillful at making use of things. . . .

The essay begins with analogies, each showing how things may, through effort, be refined or improved beyond their inherent nature. The "bending of wood" example is particularly noteworthy, because Mencius (6A.1), in refuting an analogy put forth by Gaozi, had emphasized the fact that wood cannot be reshaped into drinking vessels without violating its original nature. Because Xunzi fundamentally disagreed with Mencius's assertion that human nature is inherently good, he felt free to embrace the point of the original analogy: nature must indeed be worked upon—brought to the fire or whetstone, as it were—for it to achieve its full potential. Thus, the learning of received wisdom plays a pivotal role in properly molding human nature, and we realize the full potential of our humanity not through simply cultivating what lies deep within us, but rather by crafting it artfully with the proper tools: the Odes and Documents of the former kings, and the institutions of ritual and music they have handed down to us. Following a pattern found throughout his writings—and reflecting a practice often observed in Confucian texts more generally—Xunzi concludes this first section of thought precisely with an appeal to a canonical ode. But the ode's words are to be understood in a manner that goes far beyond their original context, and Xunzi in fact provides them with new context by redefining two of the key terms from the final cited couple—"spirits" and "blessings"—along more broadly humanistic lines.

Many of Xunzi's writings take criticisms of other thinkers as a point of departure, and in this next essay, he takes on Mencius more directly:

C3.12 *Xunzi*, "Human Nature Is Deplorable" (excerpt)

荀子・性惡（摘錄）

人之性惡，　其善者偽
也。今人之性，生而
有好利焉，順是，故
爭奪生而辭
讓　亡焉；　生
而有疾惡焉，順是，
故殘賊生而忠信亡
焉；生而有耳目之
欲，有好聲色焉，順
是，故淫亂生而禮義
文理亡焉。然則從人
之性，順人之情，必出
於爭奪，合於犯分亂理
而歸於暴。故必將有師

Human nature is deplorable, and what is good in it is due to purposeful action. Now human nature is such that at birth it holds fondness for profit, and because we go along with this fondness, struggle and seizure arise and politeness and yielding are lost; at birth it holds hatred and spite, and because we go along with this, cruelty and villainy arise and loyalty and trust are lost; at birth it holds the desires of the ears and the eyes and a fondness for [pleasing] sounds and [beautiful] looks, and because we go along with this, transgression and disorder arise and ritual propriety and refined order are lost. It thus follows that going along with human nature and its affections invariably brings about struggle and seizure, coincides with the violation of divisions and destruction of organization, and ultimately results in violence. Thus [human nature] requires the transformative influence of teachers and standards and the guiding ways of ritual and propriety before it can be made to bring about politeness and yielding, coincide with refinement and organization, and ultimately result in order. Viewed in this way, it is clear that human nature is deplorable, and that what is good in it is due to purposeful action.

Thus a piece of curved wood must await the straightening machine and molding over fire before it will become straight, and dull metal must await the honing of the whetstone before it will become sharp. Now as human nature is deplorable, it [likewise] must await teachers and standards before it will become proper and must obtain rituals and propriety before it will become ordered . . .

Mencius said: "Now what one learns is [a development of] the goodness of one's own nature."

[I] say: That is not so. This is a case of failure to achieve an understanding of human nature and to thoroughly examine the distinction between human nature and purposeful action. Generally speaking, one's nature is that which is brought about by Heaven: it cannot be learned, and it cannot be worked upon. Rituals and propriety are what the sages gave rise to—that which humans become capable of through study and can achieve by working upon them. That part of humans that cannot be learned or worked upon we call nature; that part of humans that one can become capable of through study and can achieve by working upon we call purposeful action. This is the distinction between human nature and purposeful action. . . .

Xunzi does not initially head straight into his attack on Mencius's ideas, but puts forward his argument in his own terms before engaging directly with the main target of the essay. The same tactic can be seen in our final example, wherein Mozi (☞ chap. 5) is clearly the principal opponent, but which first and foremost offers a grand vision of musical education that stands on its own:

C3.13 *Xunzi*, "Discourse on Music" (excerpt)

"Music" is "merriment" (*le*, "happiness"): something to which human affections are unavoidably bound. Thus mankind cannot be without merriment, and merriment will invariably be expressed through song and music and take form [in dance] through movement and rest. And in the way (*dao*) of mankind, it is in these things—song and music, movement and rest—that variations in the pathways of human nature reach their limit.

Thus human beings cannot but make merry, and such merriment (or "happiness") cannot but take external form. If such forms do not move along proper channels (*dao*), it will be impossible to avoid disorder. The former kings detested such disorder and thus crafted the tones of the "Elegentiae" (*Ya*) and "Hymns" (*Song*)[1] to channel these musical forms. They made their sounds sufficient to take delight in (*le*) without getting carried away; made their lyrics sufficient to yield discernment without leading thoughts astray; made their

---

[1] These were the two major genres of courtly odes—all set to music—which also form distinct sections of the *Book of Poetry* (*Shijing*).

法之化，禮義之道，然後出於辭讓，合於文理，而歸於治。用此觀之，人之性惡明矣，其善者偽也。

故枸木 必將待 檃栝、烝、矯然後直；鈍金必將待礱、厲然後利。今人之性惡，必將待 師法然後正，得 禮義 然後治。……孟子曰："今之學者，其性善。"曰：是不然。是不及知人之性，而不察乎人之性、偽之分者也。凡性者，天之就也，不可學，不可事；禮義者，聖人之所生也，人之所學而能，所事而成者也。不可學、不可事而 在人者謂之 性，可學而能、可事而成之 在人者謂之 偽。是性、偽之分也。……

[*XZJJ* 434–436]

荀子 樂論(摘錄)

夫樂者，樂也，人情之所必不免也。故人不能 無 樂，樂則必發於聲音，形於動靜，而人之道，聲音、動靜，性術之變盡是矣。故人不能 不 樂，樂則 不能無形，形而不為道，則不能無亂。先王惡其亂也，故制雅、頌之聲以道之，使其聲 足以樂而

不流，使其文足
以辨而不諰，使其曲
直、繁省、廉肉、節
奏，足以感動人之善
心，使夫邪污之氣無由
得接焉。是先王立樂
之方也，而墨子非之，
奈何！

故樂在宗廟之中，君
臣上下同聽之，則莫不
和敬；閨門之內，父
子兄弟同聽之，則
莫不和親；鄉里族
長之中，長少同聽
之，則莫不和順。故樂
者，審一以定和者也，
比物以飾節者也，合奏
以成文者也，足以率一
道，足以治萬變。是先
王立樂之術也，而墨子
非之，奈何！

故聽其雅、頌之
聲，而志意得廣焉；
執其干戚，習其俯仰屈
伸，而容貌得莊焉；
行其綴兆，要其節
奏，而行列得正焉，
進退得齊焉。故樂
者，出所以征誅也，入
所以揖讓也。征誅揖
讓，其義一也。出所
以征誅，則莫不聽
從；入所以揖讓，則
莫不從服。故樂者，
天下之大齊也，中和
之紀也，人情之所必
不免也。是先王立樂
之術也，而墨子
非之，奈何！

且樂者，先王之所以
飾喜也；軍旅鈇鉞
者，先王之所以飾怒

[variations in terms of] winding or straight, intricate or sparse, acute or robust, and restrained or progressive sufficient to set into motion people's good-natured minds (*shanxin*), so that deviant and dirty energy (*qi*) would have no means by which to attach itself therein. This is the direction by which the former kings established Music. And yet Mozi denounced it—what can one do!

Thus when music is [performed] within the ancestral temple, and the ruler and his ministers, superiors and subordinates, listen to it together, there are none who are not harmonious in their respect. When it is [performed] within the chamber doors, and fathers and sons and elder and younger brothers listen to it together, there are none who are not harmonious in their affection. When it is [performed] in the midst of towns, villages, and hamlets, and the old and young listen to it together, there are none who are not harmonious in their accord.

Thus music is that wherein unity is manifested so as to establish harmony, that wherein materials are aligned so as to lend adornment to rhythmic regularity, and that which is performed in concert so as to bring fruition to patterns. It is sufficient to lead down a single way (*dao*), and sufficient to bring order to myriad changes. This is the path through which the former kings established music. And yet Mozi denounced it—what can one do!

Thus when one listens to the sounds of the *Ya* and the *Song*, the aspirations and ideals of one's mind may thereby be widened. When one grasps the shields and axes [of dance] and practices the [movements of] bowing and reclining, contracting and extending, one's countenance and demeanor may thereby achieve solemnity. When [the dancers] move along marked positions and boundaries, and keep in tandem with the halts and advances [of the music], the rows may thereby attain their proper alignment, and the advances and retreats may thus attain to an even uniformity.

Thus music is that by which, abroad, to engage in punitive expeditions and, in [court], to perform [the rituals of] hand-folding and bowing. Punitive expeditions and hand-folding and bowing [rituals]—their significance is the same. If [music] is that by which punitive expeditions are carried out, there will be no one who does not follow along obediently; if it is that by which hand-folding and bowing [rituals] are performed, there will be no one who does not yield in submission.

Thus music is the great unifier of all under Heaven; it is the ordering of centrality and harmony; and it is that to which human affections are unavoidably bound. This is the path by which the former kings established music. And yet Mozi denounced it—what can one do!

Music is, moreover, that through which the former kings lent adornment to their joy. Military troops and executioner axes are that by which the former kings lent adornment to their anger. The joy and the anger of the former kings were thereby both able to attain [a state of] even uniformity. Thus when joyous, all under Heaven would join them in harmony; when angry, [those prone to] violence and chaos would be in fear of them. In the ways of the former kings, ritual and music were precisely the most magnificent of things. And yet Mozi denounced them.

Thus [I] say: Mozi's relationship to the Way was like that of a blind person toward black and white, like that of a deaf person toward high and low pitch, or like wanting to go to Chu[2] and yet seeking for it in the north!

For music enters into people deeply and transforms people quickly. The former kings were thus cautious in making patterns for it. When music is central and balanced, the people will be harmonious and not indulgent; when music is solemn and stately, the people will be uniform and not chaotic. If the people are harmonious and uniform, the military will be strong and the city walls secure, and enemy states will not dare to make encroachments. If things are thus, there will not be anyone amongst the masses who is not at ease in his dwelling, happy in his village, and thus fully satisfied with his ruler. Only at this point will [the ruler] have a renown that is manifest and a radiance that is magnificent, and there will be none amongst all the people within the four seas who would not wish to make him their teacher (/leader). This is the beginning of [true] kingship. . . .

Music was of course central to the Confucian vision of education through moral suasion and charismatic political control, and for Xunzi as for Confucius before him (if less so for Mencius), the specific forms musical expression took were of crucial importance. Although this passage may read like a diatribe against Mozi's denunciation of music, that its message was in fact central to Xunzi's own program may be seen from the fact that the chapter's opening closely parallels that of its sister chapter, "Li lun" ("Discourse on Ritual"). The "Li lun" similarly describes the disorder that would result if inherent human desires were left unchecked, and how the former kings "detested such disorder" and thus created ritual to provide humankind with divisions, boundaries, and proper measures.

In this essay, Xunzi describes music as something that humans by nature cannot do without. Musical expression is just as natural a part of human life as the enjoyment of food and drink or engagement in sexual activity. And yet, just like food, drink, and sex, and often in tandem with them, music too is something that can easily lead to shameless indulgence if taken to excess. Therein lies the dilemma, for, as Xunzi emphasized, humans cannot but "make merry"—man is by nature a "party animal." Our own nature and affections are precisely what lead us astray, but we by definition cannot disown our nature, and so the key lies in finding some means to guide its expressions down productive channels and keep it from going astray. Prohibition is useless, as one can never control the floods of

也。先王喜怒皆得其齊焉。是故喜而天下和之，怒而暴亂畏之。先王之道，禮樂正其盛者也，而墨子非之。故曰：墨子之於道也，猶瞽之於白黑也，猶聾之於清濁也，猶欲之楚而北求之也。

夫聲樂之入人也深，其化人也速，故先王謹為之文。樂中平則民和而不流，樂肅莊則民齊而不亂。民和齊則兵勁城固，敵國不敢嬰也。如是，則百姓莫不安其處，樂其鄉，以至足其上矣。然後名聲於是白，光輝於是大，四海之民莫不願得以為師，是王者之始也。……

[*XZJJ* 379–380]

---

[2] Chu was a large state on the southern periphery of the Chinese world.

excess by simply damning up the rivers of thirst, desire, and joyous expression. No philosopher ever thought to prohibit sexual activity, only to normalize it and define its proper scope through the institution of marriage. Xunzi felt the same way about music, berating the Mohists for failing to recognize the fact that humans cannot meaningfully exist without musical expression. To denounce music outright is ridiculous, and the key is to guide it toward constructive ends that will serve the goals of social order and stability.

Xunzi never explicitly mentions Mozi's arguments against state expenditures on music, but he manages to effectively rebuke them nonetheless. Mozi contended, somewhat reasonably, that musical performances and the manufacturing of instruments constituted a large drain on both material and human resources while contributing nothing by way of positive economic return. Xunzi addresses this head-on by detailing precisely what music—the proper kind of music—achieves: nothing less than an orderly, harmonious, and politically stable society that may be effectively harnessed toward achieving precisely the sorts of goals of which even the Mohists themselves could hardly disapprove. But rather than deconstructing their argument step-by-step, Xunzi uses the essay form to merely lay out his own vision of a musically and ritually enriched society, and then tacks on a series of one-line rebukes of Mozi's untenable denunciation of music as a repetitive after-thought—and effectively belittling such denunciation in the process. The sharply critical comparison of Mozi to a blind or deaf person is in fact a playful mockery of the very types of analogies frequently employed in the *Mozi* itself to describe those who do not act in accord with Mohist standards of "benefit" (*li*). In the competitive world of late–Warring States philosophy, philosophical rivals were never very far from the forefront of one's discourse.

One of the central themes running throughout the whole of early Confucian discourse is the call for authenticity in everything one does, the idea that even the most venerated of external forms are entirely bereft of meaning if performed without genuine sincerity of intent—an idea expressed most succinctly in *Analects*:

子曰：“禮云禮云，玉帛云乎哉？樂云樂云，鐘鼓云乎哉？”（陽貨）

[*LYJZ* 176]

C3.14 *Analects of Confucius*, "Yang Huo" 17.11

The Master said: "Ritual, ritual—is it merely jades and silks? Music, music—is it merely bells and drums?"

This can and should be read against the themes of self-interest and manipulation that surface in the writings explored elsewhere in this volume by Paul R. Goldin (☞ chap. 5).

It must also be noted that, over the course of the Warring States, Confucius would become as much a literary figure as he was a philosopher in his own right, and nowhere is he utilized more artfully and playfully than in the *Zhuangzi*. There, the genre of recorded conversations takes a decidedly more imaginative turn, with Confucius found in frequent dialogue as either a foil or advocate for Zhuangzi's own philosophy—as Shuen-fu Lin examines in further detail in chapter 4.

Scott Bradley Cook

NOTE

1. The parallels are to be found in the Shanghai Museum manuscript "Cong zheng," strips A15–A5–A6+7. For photographs of the strips and Cheung Kwong Yue's transcription of this manuscript (originally mistakenly separated into two distinct manuscripts), see *SBCZCZS* 6–7, 57–84, and 211–238.

SUGGESTED READING

ENGLISH

Ames, Roger T., and Henry Rosemont, Jr., trans. *The Analects of Confucius: A Philosophical Translation.* New York: Ballantine, 1998.

Knoblock, John. *Xunzi: A Translation and Study of the Complete Works.* 3 vols. Stanford, CA: Stanford University Press, 1988, 1990, and 1994.

Lau, D. C., trans. *Confucius: The Analects.* London: Penguin, 1979.

Lau, D. C., trans. *Mencius.* London: Penguin, 1970.

Slingerland, Edward, trans. *Confucius: Analects.* Indianapolis: Hackett, 2003.

Van Norden, Bryan W., trans. *Mengzi: With Selections from Traditional Commentaries.* Indianapolis: Hackett, 2008.

Watson, Burton, trans. *Hsün Tzu: Basic Writings.* New York: Columbia University Press, 1963.

Waley, Arthur, trans. *The Analects of Confucius.* New York: Vintage, [1938] 1989.

CHINESE

Cheng Shude 程樹德 (1877–1944). *Lunyu jishi* 論語集釋 (*Collected Explanations of the* Analects). Edited by Cheng Junying 程俊英 and Jiang Jianyuan 蔣見元. Beijing: Zhonghua shuju, 1990.

Jiao Xun 焦循 (1763–1820). *Mengzi zhengyi* 孟子正義 (*Correct Meaning of the* Mencius). Edited by Shen Wenzhuo 沈文倬. Beijing: Zhonghua shuju, 1987.

Liu Baonan 劉寶楠 (1791–1855). *Lunyu zhengyi* 論語正義 (*Correct Meaning of the* Analects). Edited by Gao Liushui 高流水. Beijing: Zhonghua shuju, 1990.

Yang Bojun 楊伯峻. *Mengzi yizhu* 孟子譯注 (*An Annotated Translation of the* Mencius). Beijing: Zhonghua shuju, 1960.

Yang Bojun 楊伯峻. *Lunyu yizhu* 論語譯注 (*An Annotated Translation of the* Analects). Beijing: Zhonghua shuju, 1980.

✿ 4 ✿

Pre-Qin Philosophical Prose

The Inner Chapters of the *Zhuangzi*

The *Analects of Confucius* and the *Mencius* contain mostly aphorisms, sayings, dialogues, and, exclusively in the *Mencius*, debates, as we have seen in the discussion in chapter 3. These texts are not collections of "essays" per se. The earliest portions of the *Mozi* (*The Works of Master Mo*) written by followers of Mo Di (ca. 478–ca. 393 BCE) possibly during the late fifth and early fourth centuries BCE include longer "essays," each of which focuses on a special topic. Dialogues and anecdotes still figure prominently in these early examples of the ancient essay because philosophical discourse was primarily oral. Significantly, the writers of these essays also began to pay attention to the logical method of developing an argument. In terms of the evolution of early philosophical prose, the Inner Chapters of the *Zhuangzi* represents an important transition from these early works to the formal essays of Xunzi (Master Xun, ca. 298–238 BCE).

The *Zhuangzi* (*Master Zhuang*) is one of the principal texts of early Daoist philosophy, along with the *Laozi* or the *Book of the Way and Its Power* (*Daodejing*, traditionally attributed to a certain Laozi, or Master Lao, of the sixth century BCE). The original *Zhuangzi* was supposed to contain fifty-two chapters, but our modern received text, derived from the Guo Xiang (fl. third century CE) edition completed around 300 CE, contains only thirty-three chapters divided into three parts: the Inner Chapters (1–7), the Outer Chapters (8–22), and the Mixed Chapters (23–33). Modern scholarship has established that the *Zhuangzi* is not, as traditionally believed, exclusively the work of Zhuang Zhou (also called Zhuangzi or Master Zhuang), a brilliant iconoclastic thinker and writer who lived circa 369–286 BCE, but rather is a collection of writings from the fourth and third centuries BCE. With the exception of a few questionable sections, the Inner Chapters exhibit a remarkable unity and homogeneity in thought and writing style largely absent from the rest of the book. These chapters are generally accepted by modern scholars as the earliest and core segments of the text written by Zhuangzi, while the Outer and Mixed Chapters are regarded as the work of later followers.

Not much is known about the life of Zhuangzi. In a brief biographical note in his *Grand Scribe's Records* (*Shiji*), Sima Qian (ca. 145–ca.86 BCE) says that Zhuangzi was a native of Meng (in modern Henan Province) and once held a minor post in the Lacquer Garden (Qiyuan) there. He places Zhuangzi in the late fourth to early third centuries BCE, at the height of the Golden Age of ancient Chinese philosophy.

For more than two millennia, this text has had a profound influence on Chinese thought, literature, art, aesthetics, and religion. Although one can think of other works, such as the *Book of Changes* (*Yijing*), *Analects of Confucius* (*Lunyu*), the *Daodejing*, and the *Mencius* (*Master Meng*), that have exerted an equal or greater influence on Chinese culture, the *Zhuangzi* is unique in being both a great philosophical text and work of prose literature.

Zhuangzi's achievement as a writer is already recognized within the *Zhuangzi* text. Chapter 33, "The World" ("Tianxia"), is an extraordinary essay by a later follower that offers a critique of the major intellectual trends in ancient China, especially of the Warring States period (475–221 BCE), largely in terse descriptive and discursive language combined with some direct quotations from the representative thinkers. The only exception to this approach is the passage about Zhuangzi who is portrayed not only as a profound thinker but more important as a poet of unbridled imagination. The passage begins with nine four-character lines, five of which are cast in the interrogative form (a syntactic form frequently found in the Inner Chapters). The shift from an essentially discursive to a highly literary, or even poetic, style of language (obviously in imitation of the language of Zhuangzi's works) seems to be a deliberate attempt to do justice to the uniqueness of the life, thought, and writings of this thinker. It continues:

C4.1 Chapter 33, "The World" (excerpt)

He thought the world had sunk into turbidness and could not be spoken to in serious language. So he used "goblet words" for unfixed rambling, "weighty words" to give a ring of truth, and "metaphorical words" to widen the range. . . . Although his writings are extraordinary, they are subtle and tactful and will do no one any harm. Although his words are irregular, they are so crafty they deserve to be appreciated.

[*CWZ* 296, modified]

The distinctiveness of Zhuangzi's writings is described as embodied in three modes of discourse closely related to his ideas about language, life, and the world he lived in. Although the author of "The World" may be the first to recognize the literary merit of Zhuangzi's writings, he is not the only early writer to discuss the rhetorical devices found in them. In fact, the concepts for these three rhetorical modes may originate in the opening passage of chapter 27, entitled "Metaphorical Words" ("Yuyan"):

C4.2 Chapter 27, "Metaphorical Words" (excerpt)

Metaphorical words make up nine-tenths of it; weighty words make up seven-tenths of it; goblet words come forth day after day, harmonizing things in the heavenly distinctions. These metaphorical words which make up nine-tenths of it are things brought in from outside for the purpose of exposition. . . . These weighty words which make up seven-tenths of it are intended

莊子•天下（摘錄）

以天下為沈濁，不可與莊語，以巵言為曼衍，以重言為真，以寓言為廣。......其書雖瑰瑋而連犿无傷也。其辭雖參差而諔詭可觀。......

[*JZZZJS* 1098–1099]

N.B. Straight underline indicates the use of repetitive patterning; wavy underline the use of parallel phrasing therein. For a discussion on repetitive and parallel patterning, ☛ C1.1–4 and C1.6–7.

莊子•寓言（摘錄）

寓言十九，重言十七，巵言日出，和以天倪。寓言十九，藉外論之。......重言十七，所以已言也，是為

耆艾。．．．．．厄言日出，
和以天倪，因以曼衍，
所以窮年。．．．．．．

[*JZZZJS* 947–949]

to put an end to argument. They can do this because they are the words of the elders. . . . . With goblet words that come forth day after day, I harmonize all things in the heavenly distinctions, ramble freely and without any limit, and so live out my years.

[*CWZ* 234, modified]

The author acknowledges Zhuangzi's reliance on these three literary modes and explains their rationale. But he does not fully define them. Nonetheless, these modes observed by early writers are perceptive and useful in helping the reader appreciate Zhuangzi's art of discourse and disputation. I hope to arrive at a deeper understanding of both Zhuangzi's style and his thought through an analysis of his rhetorical devices and how he used them.

METAPHORICAL WORDS

Said to make up nine-tenths of Zhuangzi's writings, *yuyan* literally means "words that contain an implied meaning" (*jiyu zhi yan*). The author of chapter 27 goes on to say that "these words are like things borrowed from outside for the purpose of discussing my own ideas." We can see that the term "metaphorical words" is used to refer to the device of putting one's ideas into words that describe things existing outside of one's mind, instead of expressing them in straightforward language. Combining these two senses, metaphorical words can be understood first and foremost as a device for expressing ideas in imagistic and metaphorical language.

The term *yuyan* has most often been taken by Chinese scholars in the past as "putting one's own words into the mouths of other people" (*ji zhi taren zhi yan*). In this sense, it is a "parable." Because many of the stories in the *Zhuangzi* involve animal characters, the term also refers to what we usually regard as a "fable" in English.

I believe that *yuyan* in the *Zhuangzi* involves both senses of "metaphorical language" and "fable" or "parable" because the latter actually are extended versions of the former. Metaphors in Zhuangzi's writings usually operate on the level of discourse and narrative rather than of individual terms. The Inner Chapters are full of metaphors ranging from terms to extended stories. For instance, "free and easy wandering" (*xiaoyao you*) is metaphorical for "absolute spiritual freedom;" "the big tree with a gnarled and bumpy trunk" and such variations as the "deformed people" is used for "the great use of the useless"; "Zhuang Zhou dreams that he is a butterfly" for "the reversibility of subject and object" and for "the dissolution of the distinction between reality and illusion"; "butchering an ox" is used for "the principle of caring for life"; the humans who can fly without wings is used for "the persons of the highest spiritual attainment"; the Great Thoroughfare (*datong*) is used for "the Way"; and, finally, the "boring of seven holes in the primordial blob Hundun" stands for the "destruction of primordial oneness and harmony." Indeed, examined carefully, at least nine-tenths of the Inner Chapters are composed of highly imagistic and metaphorical language like these. As all good metaphors must by nature imply an intuitive perception of "similarity in dissimilars," Zhuangzi's metaphorical words have the power to broaden the reader's scope of vision and understanding.

The device of "putting one's ideas into the mouths of other people" brings to mind the notion of a "literary mask" widely discussed in modern literary criticism in the West. Not every story in the Inner Chapters involves the use of a "mask," however. Many are simply metaphorical of the author's particular ideas. The mask is found only in those stories in which a specific character is selected to serve as the author's mouthpiece. Both the story of the Peng Bird and that of Zhuang Zhou dreaming he is a butterfly are metaphorical; in the story about "butchering an ox," the cook is used as a mask.

Why does Zhuangzi prefer metaphorical language, fables, parables, and masks to straightforward discursive language for expression of his ideas and experiences? The metaphorical words Zhuangzi employs all contain images of things or animal and human characters that exist in the external world. They direct listeners or readers toward a seemingly objective world they can readily observe or identify. Thus, metaphorical words constitute a rhetorical device for the purpose of persuasion, for making the author's argument appear more objective and hence more compelling.

Let us turn to examine a fable, an example of metaphorical words involving animal characters that opens the entire *Zhuangzi* text:

C4.3 Chapter 1, "Free and Easy Wandering" (excerpt)

In the northern darkness there is a fish and his name is Kun. The Kun is so huge no one knows how many thousand *li* he measures. He transforms into a bird whose name is Peng. The back of the Peng measures no one knows how many thousand *li* across. When he rouses himself and flies off, his wings are like clouds hanging from the sky. When the sea begins to move, this bird sets off for the southern darkness, which is the Lake of Heaven.

The *Universal Harmony* records various wonders, and it says: "When the Peng journeys to the southern darkness, the waters are roiled for three thousand *li*. He spirals up ninety thousand *li* in the whirlwind, and is gone six months before he rests."[1] Heat hazes wavering like galloping wild horses, bits of dust, the breath living things blow at each other. The sky looks very blue. Is that its true color, or is it because it is so far away and has no end? When the bird looks down, all he sees is blue, too.

If water is not piled up deep enough, it won't have the strength to bear up a big boat. Overturn a cup of water into a hollow in the hall, and bits of grass will sail on it like boats. But set the cup there, and it will stick fast, for the water is too shallow and the boat too large. If the wind is not piled up deep enough, it won't have the strength to bear up great wings. Therefore, when the Peng rises ninety thousand *li*, he must have the wind under him like that. Only then can he mount on the back of the wind, shoulder the blue sky, and nothing can hinder or block him. Only then can he set his course for the south.

莊子・逍遙遊（摘錄）

北冥有魚，其名為鯤。鯤之大，不知其幾千里也。化而為鳥，其名為鵬。鵬之背，不知其幾千里也；怒而飛，其翼若垂天之雲。是鳥也，海運則將徙於南冥。南冥者，天池也。

齊諧者，志怪者也。諧之言曰："鵬之徙於南冥也，水擊三千里，搏扶搖而上者九萬里，去以六月息者也。"野馬也，塵埃也，生物之以息相吹也。天之蒼蒼，其正色邪？其遠而無所至極邪？其視下也，亦若是則已矣。

且夫水之積也不厚，則其負大舟也無力。覆

杯水於坳堂之上，則芥
為之舟；置杯焉則膠，
水淺而舟大也。風之積
也不厚，則其負大翼也
無力。故九萬里，則風
斯在下矣，而後乃今培
風；背負青天而莫之夭
閼者，而後乃今將圖
南。

蜩與學鳩笑之曰：
"我決起而飛，搶榆
枋，時則不至而控於地
而已矣，奚以之九萬里
而南為？"

適莽蒼者，三湌而
反，腹猶果然；適百里
者，宿舂糧；適千里
者，三月聚糧。之二
蟲又何知？小 知 不及
大知，小年不及大年。

[*JZZZJS* 2–11]

The cicada and the little dove laugh at this, saying, "When we swiftly rise up and fly off, we can get as far as the elm or the sapanwood tree, but sometimes we don't make it and just fall down on the ground. Now how is anyone going to go ninety thousand *li* to the south!"

If you go off to the green woods nearby, you can take along food for three meals and come back with your stomach as full as ever. If you are going a hundred *li*, you must grind your grain the night before, and if you are going a thousand *li*, you must start getting the provisions together three months in advance. What do these two creatures understand? Little understanding cannot come up to great understanding; the short-lived cannot come up to the long-lived.

[*CWZ* 1–2, modified]

Composed of seemingly disjointed sections all on the theme of unrestricted roaming, chapter 1, "Free and Easy Wandering" begins with a story about the Peng's amazing power to roam. Although the reader may assume the Peng acts as a metaphor for freedom, Zhuangzi is quick to remind us that space and time still impose boundaries and conditions of relativity on things. Peng's distant journey depends on enormous conditions, while the limited flying of the cicada and the dove requires little effort. In subsequent passages including even a variation of this story, Zhuangzi turns from these animals to talk about humans and concludes that, just like the Peng and the little birds, Song Rongzi and Liezi may ride the wind and soar through the air, yet they are incapable of the "free and easy wandering" of the Perfect Person (*zhiren*), the Spirit Person (*shenren*), and the Sage (*shengren*). Only at the end of this first long section in chapter 1, do we realize that the kind of "roaming" (metaphorical for "spiritual freedom") Zhuangzi advocates is of an absolute sort that relies on nothing, transcending all restrictions and boundaries.

It may seem natural for modern readers to view this story simply as a "fable" because it involves animal characters. Zhuangzi, however, does not just add a moral at the end, but rather he makes extensive comments and observations as he goes along. These somewhat ad hoc comments, constituting much of this entire section, belong to the "goblet words" mode to be discussed later. Suffice it to say for now that they illustrate the natural flow of the author's ideas as they emerge in his heart. A most interesting example of these goblet words are the lines: "Heat hazes wavering like galloping wild horses, bits of dust, the breath living things blow at each other. The sky looks very blue. Is that its true color, or is it because it is so far away and has no end? When the bird looks down, all it sees is blue, too." Zhuangzi first describes a view from above as if he is the Peng, then returns to being himself to ask the question about the color of the sky, and ends with the remark that

---

[1] This last phrase also can be read "setting off on the sixth-month gale," as Burton Watson has it. I think both meanings may be implied by Zhuangzi, even though it is impossible to do so in English translation. See Burton Watson, trans., *The Complete Works of Zhuangzi* (New York: Columbia University Press, 2013).

when the Peng "looks down, all it sees is blue, too." Thus the paragraph concludes with the implication that the Peng is really as limited in perception as we are on the ground.

WEIGHTY WORDS

The term *zhongyan* for the second mode of language literally means "weighty words." The term has also been read as *chongyan*, meaning "repeated words" or "passages quoted from other writers." The purpose of *zhongyan* is to "bring an end to an argument" by borrowing the weight or authority of "elders." In the Inner Chapters, "authority figures" refer not only to the wise men of the past but also to a wide range of personages, including the cook, Carpenter Shi, and cripples who may not be old but have the experience and understanding expected of the elderly. *Zhongyan* refers to stories in which wise persons—legendary heroes, ancient emperors, sages, and people from all walks of life who have achieved a high spirituality—are used as the author's masks so that his own words, so disguised, carry more authority and thus may "give a ring of truth."

Quotations from past wise men and historical anecdotes abound in writings from other schools of thought in the Warring States period, and for the same rhetorical purpose. But Zhuangzi's brilliant use of this mode displays his special characteristics. Compared with plants, animals, mythical or legendary personages, and other fictitious characters, the wise men of the past are rare in the Inner Chapters. The Yellow Emperor, Yao, Xu You, Confucius, and his disciples Yan Hui and Zi Gong constitute the main historical characters in the stories—sometimes used as masks and sometimes as contrasts to other idealized characters. In the stories involving Confucius and his disciples, parody and satire are often present. It is here that Zhuangzi shows himself to be a shrewd critic of Confucianism as he uses these respected people simultaneously as masks and targets of ridicule. Through fabricated conversations between Confucius and his disciples, Zhuangzi presents his own philosophy in a more persuasive way, thus undercutting his rival school through a caricature of its founder and some of his most famous disciples. On the whole, the fables and parables in the Inner Chapters are quite different from those found in other pre-Qin philosophical and narrative texts. Before Zhuangzi, fables and parables usually appear separately in prose and are used essentially as illustrative materials. A good example is Mengzi's "farmer of Song" analogy discussed in the previous chapter. In the Inner Chapters, they occupy the central position in the artistic design of the essays. Moreover, in suggestive power and comic exuberance, Zhuangzi's stories far surpass those found in other texts.

One of the splendid instances of Zhuangzi's weighty words is found in the following parable from chapter 6, "The Great Source as Teacher" ("Da Zongshi"):

C4.4 Chapter 6, "The Great Source as Teacher" (excerpt)

Yan Hui said, "I've made progress."

　　Confucius said, "What do you mean?"

　　"I've forgotten benevolence and righteousness."

莊子・大宗師（摘錄）

顏回曰：　"回益矣。"

仲尼曰：" 何 謂
也？ "

曰： " 回 忘 仁 義
矣。"

曰： " 可 矣，猶 未
也。"

他 日，復 見，曰：
" 回 益 矣。"

曰： " 何 謂 也？ "

曰 ： " 回 忘 禮 樂
矣。"

曰： " 可 矣，猶 未
也。"

他 日，復 見，曰：
" 回 益 矣。"

曰： " 何 謂 也？ "

曰： " 回 坐 忘 矣。"

仲尼 蹵 然 曰： " 何 謂
坐 忘？ "

顏回曰： " 墮 肢 體，
黜 聰 明，離 形 去 知，同
於 大 通，此 謂 坐 忘。 "

仲尼曰： " 同 則 无
好 也，化 則 无 常 也。
而 果 其 賢 乎！丘 也 請 從
而 後 也。"

[JZZZJS 282–285]

"That's good. But you still have not attained your goal yet."

Another day, the two met again and Yan Hui said, "I've made progress."

"What do you mean?"

"I've forgotten rites and music."

"That's good. But you still have not attained your goal yet."

Another day, the two met again and Yan Hui said, "I've made progress."

"What do you mean?"

"I'm able just to sit and forget."

Greatly taken aback, Confucius said, "What do you mean by sit and forget?"

Yan Hui said, "I let my limbs and organs drop away, expel my hearing and eyesight, detach from my physical form, cast off knowledge, and become identical with the Great Thoroughfare. This is what I mean by 'sit and forget'."

Confucius said, "If you are identical with it, you have no more partiality, and if you let yourself transform, you have no more rigid norms. You really are that worthy! May I, Qiu, ask to follow behind you as your disciple?"

[*CWZ* 52–53, modified]

This story is found only in the *Zhuangzi*, not in any other early text. Without doubt, it was invented by Zhuangzi as a way to use the authority of Confucius to voice his own philosophy. It illustrates metaphorically the process of attaining what Zhuangzi regards as the highest level of spiritual development, which is very different from the process of self-cultivation advocated in Confucianism. An example of metaphorical words at the same time, it also presents a sophisticated example of weighty words.

It starts off as a parody of the standard apprenticeship as recorded in the *Analects of Confucius*, in which students come to report to their teacher on their progress, ask questions, and seek further guidance. As the story proceeds, the tone becomes increasingly ironic. In Confucian self-cultivation, students are expected to internalize the ethical tenets until these become part of their personality so their actions are automatically guided by them. In this story, Yan Hui, Confucius's most talented disciple, reports that he has forgotten benevolence, righteousness, rites, and music—the four cardinal principles in Confucian ethics. For Zhuangzi, the process of learning—one that emphasizes internalizing ethics and acquiring new knowledge—becomes a process of un-learning as the disciple is praised for being able to cast away what he has learned previously. This "un-learning" process forms the core of Daoist spiritual cultivation. In Daoism, the touchstone of values is Nature and not humans, and therefore, all artificial knowledge and values must be abandoned. The irony culminates in Yan Hui's attainment of sagehood not by embodying all ethical principles in his person, but rather by having forgotten everything and thereby transcending his limited self to become identical with the Way. "Limbs and organs" refer to the physical body that is transformable, and "hearing and eyesight" refer to our sense perception that enables us to discriminate things.

Knowledge becomes the sum of what is perceived by the heart and senses. Only by forgetting the bodily self, the opposition of this self to other things, and all knowledge is one able to enter the spiritual wholeness of the Way. Zhuangzi does not end his story here. However highly the historical Confucius regarded Yan Hui, it would be ludicrous for the teacher to ask his student, to accept him as a disciple. In an entertaining way, Zhuangzi successfully uses Confucius and Yan Hui as masks and victims of his ridicule.

GOBLET WORDS

According to the author of chapter 27, the first two rhetorical modes focus on practical aspects of expression and winning an argument in debate or disputation, although both have some broader implications as well. The third mode, goblet words, however, is more directly related to the philosophical aspects of Zhuangzi's theory of language and self-expression.

The original term for goblet words (*zhiyan*) has been taken to mean a number of things. I am persuaded by the widely accepted view to read the *zhi* in *zhiyan* as "a goblet for urging wine on a guest." This object is apparently an unusual vessel designed to remain upright when empty and overturn when full, thus illustrating the property of emptiness, a core value in Daoism. The goblet seems to have been chosen as a Daoist metaphor for the ideal use of the heart in relation to speech. It is important for a Daoist to keep his heart empty of all preconceived ideas and values until the occasion for speech arises and, at the end of a discourse, empty out the ideas and values that he has taken in from outside. The point to be stressed is that the goblet—metaphor for the heart—is originally empty and gets filled with liquid from a larger container only as required by the occasion. Goblet words, then, refer to speech that is natural, unpremeditated, always responding to changes in the flow of discourse, and always returning the heart to its original state of emptiness as soon as speech is completed.

In chapter 7, "Responding to Being an Emperor or a King" ("Ying di wang"), it is said:

C4.5 Chapter 7, "Responding to Being an Emperor or a King" (excerpt)

莊子•應帝王（摘錄）

The Perfect Person uses his heart[1] like a mirror. He does not escort things as they go or welcome them as they come; he responds but does not store. Therefore, he can win over things without harming himself.

[CWZ 59, modified]

至人之用心若鏡，不將不迎，應而不藏，故能勝物而不傷。

[JZZZJS 307]

In chapter 2, "Making All Things, and the Discussions on Them, Equal" ("Qi wu lun"), it is said:

---

[1] In ancient Chinese philosophical texts, although the word *xin* (literally "heart") sometimes refers to the physical organ, it usually denotes a person's faculty that thinks, feels, and makes judgments, decisions, and plans.

莊子•齊物論（摘錄）

是以聖人和之以是非而
休乎天鈞，是之謂兩
行。

[JZZZJS 70]

C4.6a Chapter 2, "Making All Things, and the Discussions on Them, Equal" (excerpt)

The Sage harmonizes with both right and wrong and rests in the heavenly equality. This is called "walking two roads simultaneously."

[CWZ 11, modified]

The phrase "walking two roads simultaneously" refers to the skill to even out right and wrong, allowable and unallowable, this and that, self and other, dreaming and waking consciousness, illusion and reality, beauty and ugliness, even life and death—the endless sequence of dualities—in the expanded unifying vision of the Sage.

Goblet words signify the verbal acts in keeping with this balance within the heart. A good Daoist is expected to engage in natural, free, spontaneous, nonjudgmental, and nondiscriminatory speech, so that his heart can always return to its pristine state of naturalness, harmony, transparency, and emptiness. Those who have attained this will never run into conflict with things; nor will they ever make their hearts dull and weary. Thus no harm can come their way.

The discursive passages presenting the narrator's seemingly random comments on the stories are the most obvious examples of goblet words. In the stories themselves, such passages should be seen as goblet words as well. Goblet words are within metaphorical words and weighty words. In other words, they are not conceived as three rigidly distinct, but overlapping, rhetorical modes. Just like the note in chapter 1 on "heat hazes and bits of dust" or the story in chapter 6 of Yan Hui and Confucius, Yan Hui's "sit and forget everything" and Confucius's response present such embedded goblet words. Lacking any clearly observable rule of overall structure, these passages appear flexible, haphazard, and irregular.

I would like to take up one more parable which differs from the story of Yan Hui and Confucius in that it does not involve traditional authority figures and constitutes in itself a fantastic instantiation of the mode of goblet words.

莊子•齊物論（摘錄）

南郭子綦隱机而坐，仰
天而噓，荅焉似喪其
耦。顏成子游立侍乎
前，曰：「何居乎？形
固可使如槁木，而心固
可使如死灰乎？今之隱
机者，非昔之隱机者
也。」

　子綦曰：「偃，不
亦善乎，而問之也！今
者吾喪我，汝知之乎？

C4.6b Chapter 2, "Making All Things, and the Discussions on Them, Equal" (excerpt)

Ziqi of South Wall sat leaning on his armrest, staring up at the sky and breathing—in a trance as though he'd lost his partner. Yancheng Ziyou, who was standing before him in attendance, said, "What is this? Can you really make the body like a withered tree and the heart like dead ashes? The man leaning on the armrest now is not the one who leaned on it before!"

Ziqi said, "You've asked a great question, Yan.[1] Is it not so? Now I have lost my own self. Do you know it? You hear the piping of humans, but you haven't heard the piping of earth. Or if you've heard the piping of earth, you haven't heard the piping of Heaven!"

---

[1] "Yan" is Yancheng's given name and "Ziyou" is his courtesy name.

Ziyou said, "May I ask what this means?"

Ziqi said, "The Great Clod belches out breath and its name is wind. So long as it doesn't start up, nothing happens. But when it does, ten thousand hollows begin howling furiously.

Can't you hear them, long drawn out? [In] the towering heights of the mountains,[2] [there are] huge trees a hundred spans around with hollows and crevices, like nostrils, like mouths, like ears, like jugs, like cups, like mortars, like pools, like puddles. They roar like waves, whistle like arrows, scold gruffly, breathe gently, shout loudly, cry bitterly, squeak like door hinges, and trill like birds, those in the lead singing out *yeee!*, those behind singing out *yuuu!* A gentle breeze brings forth a small harmony, and a full gale a mighty symphony. And when the fierce wind has passed on, all the hollows are empty again. Can't you see the tossing and trembling that goes on?"

Ziyou said, "So the piping of earth simply means the sound of these hollows, and the piping of humans the sound of bamboo panpipes. May I ask about the piping of Heaven?"

Ziqi said, "Blowing on the ten thousand things in a different way, so that each[3] can be itself—each takes what it wants for itself, but who could be the rouser of all this sounding?"

[*CWZ* 7–8, modified]

This passage opens chapter 2, which bears the title that is often read either as "Discussion on Making All Things Equal" ("Qiwu lun") or as "Making the Discussions on All Things Equal" ("Qi wulun"). In fact, both readings are implied by Zhuangzi. The overall theme of "Qi wu lun" is the affirmation of the significance and value of all things, and it is made in a Zhuangzian Daoist way: things are equal precisely in their natural difference from one another, in each being uniquely itself. Evening out all the discussions humans made is thus a necessary step toward comprehending the "heavenly" (i.e., natural) equality of all things. To capture both implications, I shall translate the chapter's title "Making All Things, and the Discussions on Them, Equal."

Zhuangzi opens this long, complex, and marvelous chapter not with a direct exposition of its theme but with a parable about a sage person who has just gone through an extraordinary experience while sitting in meditation in the presence of a student. Just like the story about Confucius and Yan Hui, this parable consists of a dialogue between a teacher and his student. Although the device of weighty words is obvious, its use of goblet words and "metaphorical words" are not as apparent and need to be examined more closely.

[2] Following some commentators, I read *shanling* (towering mountains) in place of *shanlin* (mountain forests).

[3] In the Chinese text, Ziqi's final reply contains three instances of the character *qi*. In the first two, it is used as a pronoun, rendered here as "each." In the third occurrence, it functions as an adverb in a rhetorical question, with a meaning similar to *qi* (who could?).

女聞人籟而未聞地籟，女聞地籟而未聞天籟乎！"

子游曰："敢問其方。"

子綦曰："夫大塊噫氣，其名為風。是唯无作，作則萬竅怒呺。而獨不聞之翏翏乎？山林之畏佳，大木百圍之竅穴，似鼻，似口，似耳，似枅，似圈，似臼，似洼者，似污者；激者，謞者，叱者，吸者，叫者，譹者，宎者，咬者，前者唱于而隨者唱喁。泠風則小和，飄風則大和，厲風濟則眾竅為虛。而獨不見之調調，之刁刁［刀刀］乎？"

子游曰："地籟則眾竅是已，人籟則比竹是已。敢問天籟。"

子綦曰："夫吹萬不同，而使其自己也，咸其自取，怒者其誰邪！"

[*JZZZJS* 43–50]

Ziyou remarks on Ziqi's extraordinary experience with a curious question: "Can you really make the body like a withered tree and the heart like dead ashes?" In response, Ziqi first praises Ziyou for having asked a great question, and then inquires whether his student knows that he has just "lost his own self." Ziqi does not, of course, equate "losing his self" to a loss of physical vitality. Rather his "loss of self" is a metaphorical instantiation of the idea that the "Perfect Person has no self" (*zhiren wuji*) (*CWZ* 3; *JZZZJS* 17), a key idea first stated in chapter 1. Variations of this state appear later in the Inner Chapters, notably in chapter 4 in passages about "the fasting of the heart" (*xinzhai*) (*CWZ* 25; *JZZZJS* 147) and in chapter 6 in the already discussed Yan Hui's "sit and forget everything." Although difficult to discern, other variations can be found, such as the parable with Zhuangzi dreaming he is a butterfly that closes chapter 2, and the story about the cook in chapter 3 in which we find the line "My perception and understanding have come to a stop" (*guan zhi zhi*) (*CWZ* 19; *JZZZJS* 119).

The reason Zhuangzi does not simply have Ziqi explain what constitutes "the loss of self" is obviously that doing so would run counter to his ideal of "rambling freely without any limit." He continues to use his flexible, interrogative, and metaphorical strategy in the unfolding of the story with a focus on the theme of music. Ziqi queries whether Ziyou has heard the pipings of humans, earth, and Heaven. Undoubtedly baffled, Ziyou asks what his teacher means by this enigmatic reply. Again Ziqi responds not with a straight answer but with a depiction of what appears to be the piping of earth, along with a new question: has Ziyou heard the kind of music he is describing? Ziyou says that he knows the pipings of humans and earth but not that of Heaven. Ziqi's final response seems to suggest that "Heaven is not something distinct from earth and [hu]man[s], but a name applied to the natural and spontaneous functioning of the two" (*CWZ* 8), and yet leaves us with an unanswered question which may not be rhetorical at all: "Who could be the rouser of all this sounding?"

We can see that a real contrast is drawn between the natural piping of earth and the artificial piping of humans, with the former given a full description, whereas the latter is only mentioned. Furthermore, the unanswered question serves a significant purpose. In a chapter that argues for the natural uniqueness and equality of all things by evening out human opinions on them, the interrogative form is especially effective because it frees the speaker from imposing his own views and values while forcing the listener to probe the subject under discussion himself. A quick account of such a conversation between teacher and student reveals the potential randomness of the goblet words device.

Not to be ignored are two words denoting wind instruments and the passage about the earth's piping because all showcase Zhuangzi's care over word choice and his genius for descriptive writing. The word *lai* (rendered "piping") refers to the ancient instrument *yue*, "pipes." Zhuangzi then provides a gloss on *renlai* (human-made pipes) in Ziyou's comment: *bizhu*, literally "bamboo pipes (of varying lengths) arranged (in a sequence) side by side," can be rendered "panpipes." In *xiaohe* and *dahe* (rendered "small harmony" and "mighty symphony"), the character *he* is an old name for the small *sheng* (known in the West as "the Chinese mouth organ"), one of the oldest instruments in continuous usage down to the present day. The "Chinese mouth organ" is an instrument capable of producing a harmony of several notes simultaneously while the *panpipe* can produce only one note at a time.

Zhuangzi uses *lai* in terms referring to three kinds of music, and *he* in depicting music that involves the simultaneous sounding of numerous notes.. In Ziqi's final reply, "each" refers to "blowing" and "the ten-thousand things" to both "the hollows and crevices" of the mountain trees and to the hollows in the panpipes. Because the hollows are either naturally different as in the former or made different by humans as in the latter, blowing on them produces a myriad of distinct sounds. The simultaneous sounding of so many distinct tones in a harmonic state happens only when the wind blows through the hollows and crevices all at once. The mouth organ can produce a harmony of only a few notes at a time. Nonetheless, the idea of harmony derived from it is significant as it helps humans appreciate the power of harmony expressed in the music of nature.

The passage about the piping of earth in which the notion of harmony appears has been admired by readers throughout history. I wish to highlight a few of its artistic features. First, almost the entire section is framed between the two questions, "Can't you hear them, long drawn out?" and "Can't you see the tossing and trembling that goes on?" with the former alluding to the sense of hearing and the latter to that of sight. Second, within this frame, the original lines in Chinese are cast in discernibly parallel forms. Third, although Ziqi begins his reply to Ziyou with the howling of myriad hollows, he gets surprisingly animated in his delineation of the shapes of these hollows and the sounds they make. Fourth, Zhuangzi uses eight terms to describe shapes and another eight to describe sounds, with similarities and differences among them. Of the terms depicting shapes, three refer to three of the five organs on an animal's face, three to objects made by people, and two to things in nature. Of the terms depicting sounds, two refer to sounds in nature, four to sounds made by the human mouth, and two to sounds made by artificial objects. Thus, the two sets roughly parallel each other because they refer to the same three categories of things. Yet the terms in them are organized in different ways: the first set consists of six two-word and two three-word phrases, uniformly beginning with *si* (meaning "like"), and the second set consists of eight two-word phrases, uniformly ending with *zhe* (meaning "one who"). Cast in the form of "*si-x-zhe*," the two three-word phrases come at the end of the first set, serving as the link and transition to the second set. The phrases are patterned to reveal that the piping of earth produces a harmony, not a cacophony, of diverse sounds. Last, these qualities of similarity, variety, and regularity seamlessly lead to the author's somewhat off-the-cuff general remarks about chorus and harmony, grand and small. The last two lines of Ziqi's reply bring closure to the whole amazing passage. The first line harks back to the moment before the wind blows when the hollows are empty, and the final line, which is cast as a rhetorical question, entails an image of the trembling tree branches as the wind has already passed on, reminding us of the powerful music of earth that has just ended. Despite the part on the music of earth that exhibits some measure of regularity, the overall progression of the parable is flexible, adapting to changing circumstances in discourse. Moreover, it returns to the state of emptiness at the end. May we not suggest that the whole parable exhibits the quality of Zhuangzi's ideal speech embodied through the use of goblet words?

We have seen goblet words embedded in a fable and a parable, with their naturalness and randomness embodied in the parable with nontraditional authority figures as its main characters. Let us now examine a passage that consists entirely of goblet words, a passage cast entirely in the discursive mode.

Human values are most clearly and completely embodied in people's language. It is fitting then for Zhuangzi to bring his discussion to focus on language in the section following the Ziqi parable. He begins the third section of chapter 2:

莊子・齊物論（摘錄）

夫言非吹也，言者有言，其所言者特未定也。果有言邪？其未嘗有言邪？其以為異於鷇音，亦有辯乎，其無辯乎？　道惡乎隱而有真偽？言惡乎隱而有是非？道惡乎往而不存？言惡乎存而不可？道隱於小成，言隱於榮華。故有儒墨之是非，以是其所非而非其所是。欲是其所非而非其所是，則莫若以明。

[JZZZJS 63]

C4.6c Chapter 2, "Making All Things, and the Discussions on Them, Equal" (excerpt)

Words are not just the blowing of air. Words have something to say, but what they have to say is never fixed. So do they really say something, or do they never say anything? People suppose that words are different from the peeps of baby birds, but is there any difference, or isn't there? What is the Way hidden by [such] that we have true and false? What are words hidden by that we have right and wrong? How can the Way go away and not exist? How can words exist and not be acceptable? When the Way is hidden by little accomplishments and words by vain show, then we have the rights and wrongs of the Confucians and the Mohists. What one calls right, the other calls wrong, what one calls wrong, the other calls right. If we want to right their wrongs and wrong their rights, the best thing to use is clarity.

[CWZ 9–10, modified]

In C4.6c, Zhuangzi mixes declarative statements with interrogative sentences. He first asserts that "words are not just the blowing of air" because "words have something to say." The word *chui* ("the blowing [of air]") takes us back to Ziqi's final reply to Ziyou in which the blowing of air through the hollows in wind instruments and mountain trees produces a myriad of different sounds. Zhuangzi's assertion, then, is that words are not the same as the pipings of humans and of earth. We can cite some of the observations of American philosopher Susanne Langer (1895–1985) about language and music to illuminate Zhuangzi's insight. Langer writes, "In language, which is the most amazing symbolic system humanity has invented, separate words are assigned to separately conceived items in experience on a basis of simple, one-to-one correlation."[1] On music, she says, "since there is no meaning assigned to any of its parts, it lacks one of the basic characteristics of language—fixed association, and therewith a single, unequivocal reference."[2] Because words carry meanings that have distinct references to experience, they are not the same as the sounds made by blowing air through hollows in trees or in musical instruments.

Zhuangzi goes a step further than Langer by adding a qualifying comment: "what words have to say is never fixed." Then, without any elaboration, he poses a series of eight questions. We can understand the remark "what words have to say is never fixed" in this way: the meanings assigned to words can change over time and also can vary from speaker to speaker and from context to context. Because what words say is thus never truly fixed, can anyone still claim they have ever said anything, or that their words are "different from the peeps of baby birds?" By casting his utterance in the interrogative, Zhuangzi seems to encourage us to see that, ultimately, words are no different from the peeps of baby birds. After asking the initial four questions, Zhuangzi brings his discussion into focus on four other points concerning what hides both the Way and the words, giving rise in discourses on them to distinctions made by humans between true and false, right and wrong, acceptable and unacceptable. To close the section, he changes the narrator's voice from interrogative back to declarative, and from that of an ordinary person to a sage.

The narrator says that distinctions between true and false and so on arise because the Way is hidden by "little [i.e., partial] accomplishments" and words or speech by "vain show." During the mid–Warring States period, Confucians and Mohists formed the most prominent schools of thought, but they were far from alone. From whatever camp or conviction, each individual thinker claimed that his exposition of the Way was right while other expositions were all wrong. Zhuangzi asks from his Daoist perspective, because there is only one and the same all-inclusive Way, how can this be possible? He concludes by suggesting: "to right their wrongs and wrong their rights, the best thing to use is clarity." Although "clarity" would seem to appeal more to our visual than auditory sense, the ability to use it obviously relies on the same "loss of self" that allows Ziqi to hear the piping of Heaven. Similarly, in subsequent sections, the ability to see that "the Way runs through all, making them into one" (*CWZ* 11), to practice "walking two roads at the same time" (touched upon previously), and to understand that "Heaven and earth were born together with me and the ten-thousand things are one with me" (*CWZ* 13, modified) are all the result of "having lost one's self." And these important ideas seem to come forth not rigidly planned, but somewhat haphazardly.

I have spent considerable space discussing metaphorical words, weighty words, and goblet words because together they constitute the key to an appreciation of the rhetorical art of the Inner Chapters. Also crucial, though, is Zhuangzi's avoidance of a rigid structure in the composition of his essays. We have examined how he overlaps complex rhetorical modes in individual passages, but his use of metaphorical language, literary mask, and random ad hoc comments goes still further to permeate the entire work. Each of the Inner Chapters is composed of a series of stories—fables, brief anecdotes, and parables—intermixed with passages of discursive prose. When we read it, we seem to be going through a sequence of rambling, disconnected stories and discursive passages. If we are reading it for the first time, we are likely dazzled or bewildered by the images, ideas, and fantastic anecdotes that seem to come forth at random, or as the author of "The World" puts it, "[Zhuangzi's] words are irregular." The ideas and stories are indeed like wine flowing from the goblet, of a drinker who eschews all rigidly fixed rules. Together, these strange strings of story constitute a powerful illustration of the Inner Chapters' distinctive mode of writing and the philosophy that underpins it.

THE PRINCIPLE OF NURTURING LIFE

The remaining pages of this chapter will be devoted to a close reading of chapter 3, "The Principle of Nurturing Life." Although my focus is on chapter 3, I will have to cite numerous passages from other parts of the *Zhuangzi*, especially the Inner Chapters, to illuminate the terse text under scrutiny.

Despite its brevity, this Inner Chapter is an invaluable piece of writing from ancient China. It contains one of the earliest uses of the term *yangsheng* (the nurture of life) in received literature. Although the term does not even occur in the early medical manuscripts that have been excavated since the 1970s, the tradition of "nurturing life"—an essential part of ancient Chinese medicine—does exist in China in the fourth and third centuries BCE. Encompassing "dietetics, breath cultivation, exercise, and sexual cultivation," this tradition has been summarily called "macrobiotic hygiene" by Donald Harper.[3] Chapter 3 in the *Zhuangzi* represents a Daoist philosopher's response to this medical tradition. It does not share macrobiotic hygiene's goals of physical well-being and longevity but instead expresses Zhuangzi's outlook on life. It exhibits a discernible structure and some of Zhuangzi's central ideas.

Just like "Qi wu lun," the chapter title "Yang sheng zhu" has been read reversibly, either as "Yangsheng zhu" ("The Principle of Nurturing Life") or "Yang sheng-zhu" ("Nurturing the Principle of Life") and, again, both readings are implied by Zhuangzi. For simplicity's sake, I shall translate the title "The Principle of Nurturing Life."

This brief Inner Chapter consists of six sections of which two are cast completely in goblet words and four in the forms of parable and fable. Following is the complete text of the chapter:

莊子•養生主

吾生也有涯，而知也無涯。以有涯隨無涯，殆已；已而為知者，殆而已矣。為善无近名，為惡无近刑。緣督以為經，可以保身，可以全生，可以養親，可以盡年。

庖丁為文惠君解牛，手之所觸，肩之所倚，

C4.7 Chapter 3, "The Principle of Nurturing Life"

Our life has a boundary, but knowledge has none. If we use what has a boundary to pursue what has none, we will be in danger. If we understand this and still strive for knowledge, we will be in danger for certain! If we do good, don't go near fame. If we do bad, don't go near punishments. Follow the middle to be what is constant and we can stay in one piece, keep our life whole, nurture our own persons,[1] and live out our years.

---

[1] I follow the good sense of a few scholars who take the word *qin* to mean "one's own person" (*zishen*) rather than "parents." Examples of such usage can be found in ancient Chinese texts. In classical Chinese, *shen* can mean "body" and "self or person," the latter as in "self-cultivation." Because *shen* has already been used in a previous line, Zhuangzi uses *qin* in this line instead.

A cook[2] was cutting up an ox for Lord Wenhui:[3] wherever his hand touched, wherever his shoulder leaned, wherever his foot stepped, wherever his knee pressed[4]—zip! whoosh! the knife being played making a zing—all fell in with the perfect tone, in accord with the dance of the Mulberry Grove, and keeping time to the Jingshou music![5]

"Ah, this is marvelous!" said Lord Wenhui. "Imagine skill reaching such heights!"

The cook laid down his knife and replied, "What I care about is the Way, which goes beyond skill. When I first began cutting up oxen, all I could see was the ox itself. After three years I no longer see the whole ox. And now—now I go at it by spirit and don't look with my eyes. Perception and understanding have come to a stop, and spirit moves where it wants. I go along with the natural makeup, strike in the big hollows, guide the knife through the big openings, and follow things as they are. My skill is such that (my knife) never even passes through where flesh connects to the bones,[6] much less the big bones themselves.

"A good cook changes his knife once a year—because he cuts. A mediocre cook changes his knife once a month—because he hacks. I've had this knife of mine for nineteen years and I've cut up several thousand oxen with it, and yet the blade is as good as if it had just come from the whetstone. There are spaces between the joints, and the blade of the knife has really no thickness. If you insert what has no thickness into such spaces, then there's plenty of room—more than enough for the blade of the knife to roam about in. That's why after nineteen years, the blade of my knife is still as when it first came from the grindstone.

"However, whenever I come to a complicated place and know that it will be hard to handle, I become fearfully cautious, keep my eyes on what I'm doing, work very slowly and move the knife with the greatest subtlety, until—flop! the whole thing comes apart like a clod of earth crumbling to the ground. I stand there holding the knife and look all around me, completely satisfied and reluctant to move on, and then I wipe off the knife and put it away."

"Marvelous!" said Lord Wenhui. "I have heard the words of the cook and learned how to nurture life!"

---

[2] "Paoding" has also been read as "Cook Ding," treating "Ding" as the cook's surname. But "ding" is also a common word meaning a "male servant" or simply a "man." In ancient China, a cook also carried out the task of a butcher.

[3] Nobody knows who "Lord Wenhui" really was. Some say that he was "King Hui of Liang" (r. 369–319 BCE), a senior contemporary of Zhuangzi and Mencius, because the two share the same character "Hui" in them. No evidence supports that the two were indeed the same person.

[4] These four lines are modified from Brook Ziporyn's translation, 22.

[5] Mulberry Grove and the Jingshou music are names of music of the ancient sage-kings.

[6] I follow the suggestion of some scholars that this line in Chinese involves an inversion of word order. Normally the line reads *ji zhi wei chang jing ken qing* rather than *ji jing ken qing zhi wei chang* as it appears here in the chapter.

足之所履，膝之所踦，砉然響然，奏刀騞然，莫不中音，合於桑林之舞，乃中經首之會。

文惠君曰："譆，善哉！技蓋至此乎？"

庖丁釋刀對曰："臣之所好者道也，進乎技矣。始臣之解牛之時，所見无非牛者。三年之後，未嘗見全牛也。方今之時，臣以神遇而不以目視，官知止而神欲行。依乎天理，批大卻，導大窾，因其固然。技經肯綮之未嘗，而況大軱乎！良庖歲更刀，割也；族庖月更刀，折也。今臣之刀十九年矣，所解數千牛矣，而刀刃若新發於硎。彼節者有閒，而刀刃者无厚，以无厚入有閒，恢恢乎其於游刃必有餘地矣，是以十九年而刀刃若新發於硎。雖然，每至於族，吾見其難為，怵然為戒，視為止，行為遲，動刀甚微，謋然已解，如土委地。提刀而立，為之四顧，為之躊躇滿志，善刀而藏之。"

文惠君曰："善哉！吾聞庖丁之言，得養生焉。"

公文軒見右師而驚曰："是何人也？惡乎介也？天與，其人與？"曰："天也，非人也。天之生是使獨也，人之貌有與也。以是知其天也，非人也。"

澤雉十步一啄，百步
一飲，不蘄畜乎樊中。
神雖王，不善也。

老聃死，秦失弔之，
三號而出。

弟子曰：「非夫子之
友邪？」

曰：「然。」

「然則弔焉若此，可
乎？」

曰：「然。始也吾
以為其人也，而今非
也。向吾入而弔焉，
有老者哭之，如哭
其子；少者哭之，如哭
其母。彼其所以會之，
必有不蘄言而言，不
蘄哭而哭者。是遁天倍
情，忘其所受，古者謂
之遁天之刑。適來，夫
子時也；適去，夫
子順也。安時而處順，
哀樂不能入也，古者謂
是帝之縣解。」

指窮於為薪，火傳
也，不知其盡也。

[*JZZZJS* 115–129]

When Gongwen Xuan saw the Commander of the Right, he was startled and said, "What kind of man is this? How could he have but one foot? Was it Heaven? Or was it human?"

"It was Heaven, not human," said the Commander. "When Heaven gave me life, it saw to it that I would be one-footed. Human appearances are given. So I know this was the work of Heaven and not of human."

The swamp pheasant has to walk ten paces for one peck and a hundred paces for one drink, but it does not want to be kept in a cage. Even if its spirit appears exuberant,[7] this is not good.

When Lao Dan died, Qin Yi went to mourn for him, but after giving three cries, he left the room.

"Weren't you a friend of the Master?" asked Laozi's disciples.

"Yes."

"And you think it's all right to mourn him this way?"

"Yes," said Qin Yi. "At first I took him for a person, but now I know he wasn't. A little while ago, when I went in to mourn, I found old people weeping for him as though they were weeping for a son, and young people weeping for him as though they were weeping for a mother. To have these people gathered, he must have done something to make them talk about him, though he didn't ask them to talk, or make them weep for him, though he didn't ask them to weep. This is to escape from Heaven, turn one's back on the true state of affairs, and forget what one has received. In the old days, this was called the punishment for escaping from Heaven. The master happened to come because it was his time, and he happened to leave because he follows along (the course of things). If one is content with the time and willing to follow along, then grief and joy have no way to enter. In the old days, this was called being released from the Lord's[8] bonds."

Though the grease burns out of the torch, the fire passes on, and no one knows where it ends.

[*CWZ* 19–21, modified]

Of the seven Inner Chapters, only this one and chapter 6 open with the discursive mode of language or goblet words, whereas the others begin with fables or parables. Such discursive statements serve as a general introduction to the main ideas of knowledge, ethics, and the course of action that will bring good results to nurturing life.

The extreme laconic manner in which these ideas are brought forth in the opening section merits close attention. The word *ya*, rendered "boundary" here, literally

---

[7] I follow the reading of "wang" (meaning "king") as a loan word for "wang" (meaning "exuberant," "flourishing").

[8] "Di" (the Lord) refers to the Deified Ancestor, the Supreme Ruler of the cosmos in the remote ancient times. In the philosophical texts, the word "Di" has been replaced by, or used to refer to, "Tian" (Heaven or Nature).

means "edge or shore of water." Because life is being compared to a vast body of water enclosed within shores, we cannot view it as something bound only by the linear limits of time. The human heart, with the ideas, biases, and values it produces and holds, also imposes limits on our life. So "to use what has a boundary to go after what does not" necessarily results in turning the latter into something like the former. The pursuer of knowledge can no longer roam freely in a realm without bounds.

The word *dai* (which means "danger," "almost," "I am afraid," or "remiss" when used as a loan word for another *dai*) often has been erroneously taken to mean "exhaustion" (*pikun*). Zhuangzi obviously thinks that to pursue knowledge in the wrong way is serious because he devotes another sentence to reinforce the point. The second time *dai* is used, he qualifies it with the phrase *eryi*, meaning "that's all." The sentence literally reads: "If we already understand this and still strive for knowledge, there will certainly be danger and nothing else!"

After making this emphatic remark, Zhuangzi turns to the theme of ethics with two imperative sentences, literally: "If we do good, don't go near fame. If we do bad, don't go near punishments." On the surface, these sentences seem to suggest Zhuangzi condones what is ordinarily considered "immoral." But a conventional yardstick should never be applied to an iconoclastic Daoist thinker. Comments on the themes of "knowledge," "fame," and "punishment" elsewhere in the Inner Chapters can help us here. In chapter 4, "The World of Humans" ("Renjian shi"), Zhuangzi says: "Fame is something people use to crush each other, and knowledge is a device for wrangling. Both are evil weapons—not the sort of thing to bring perfection to your conduct" (*CWZ* 22, modified). Contrasting this negative notion of knowledge, he says at the beginning of chapter 6, "The Great Source as Teacher":

C4.8 Chapter 6, "The Great Source as Teacher" (excerpt)

莊子•大宗師 (摘錄)

He who knows what it is that Heaven does, and knows what it is that humans do, has reached the peak. Knowing what it is that Heaven does, he lives with Heaven. Knowing what it is that humans do, he uses the knowledge of what he knows to nurture the knowledge of what he doesn't know and lives out the years that Heaven gave him without being cut off midway—this is the exuberance of knowledge . . . There must first be an Authentic Person before there can be authentic knowledge.

[*CWZ* 42, modified]

知天之所為，知人之所為者，至矣。知天之所為者，天而生也；知人之所為者，以其知之所知，以養其知之所不知，終其天年而不中道夭者，是知之盛也。. . . . . .且有真人，而後有真知。

[*JZZZJS* 224–226]

Zhuangzi clearly distinguishes between knowledge in the ordinary sense and knowledge as possessed only by the Authentic Person (*zhenren*), a term he uses (along with the Sage, the Perfect Person, and the Spirit Person) to denote the ideal human of highest spiritual attainment. Because the Authentic Person knows the workings of Nature and lives with it, the knowledge he possesses is exuberant, free from the restrictions of the ordinary human heart. The Authentic Person is like

Ziqi of South Wall who has lost his self and thus the knowledge he possesses is like Nature itself without any boundaries.

When it comes to fame, Zhuangzi does not discern a positive category for it. In chapter 1, he unequivocally says that "the Sage has no fame" (*CWZ* 3). We have also just seen that Zhuangzi lumps fame and ordinary knowledge together as instruments of evil. As for punishments, Zhuangzi speaks of penalties inflicted on both the body and the heart or spirit, with the former referring to corporeal punishments (e.g., including death, mutilation, tattoos on a criminal's face, shackles) that also are used metaphorically to describe the latter. In one parable in chapter 4, for instance, Zhuangzi uses Confucius as a mask to tell Yan Hui not to go recklessly to a state in chaos where he would certainly get himself punished. That chapter closes with another parable in which the madman of Chu sings a song by Confucius's gate that contains the statement: "In times like the present, we do well to escape penalty" (*CWZ* 32). And in chapter 6, we read that someone has been "tattooed with benevolence and righteousness, and has had his nose cut off with right and wrong" (*CWZ* 52, modified).

The most telling account of Zhuangzi's view on fame and punishment is found in the parable of a certain Shushan No-Toes in chapter 5, "The Sign of Virtue Complete" ("De chong fu"). Stumping along on his heels, this No-Toes (so named after his toes were mutilated for a "wrongdoing") went to see Confucius who immediately reprimands him for coming too late, after he has already gotten himself into trouble with the law. No-Toes responds first by admitting that he lost his toes for being too careless, and then retorts that he had come to someone he thought was like the all-inclusive Heaven-and-Earth because he still had something more precious than his toes he wished to keep intact. After expressing his dismay at Confucius's unseemly behavior, he left to tell the story to Laozi:

莊子·德充符(摘錄)

"孔丘之於至人，其未邪？彼何賓賓以學子為？彼且蘄以諔詭幻怪之名聞，不知至人之以是為己桎梏邪？"

老耼曰："胡不直使彼以死生為一條，以可不可為一貫者，解其桎梏，其可乎？"

无趾曰："天刑之，安可解？"

[*JZZZJS* 204–205]

C4.9 Chapter 5, "The Sign of Virtue Complete" (excerpt)

"Confucius certainly hasn't reached the stage of a Perfect Person, has he? What does he mean coming around so often to study with you?[1] He is after the sham illusion of fame and expectation. Doesn't he know that the Perfect Person looks on these as handcuffs and fetters for himself?"

Lao Dan (i.e., Laozi) said, "Why don't you just make him see life and death as one strand, and acceptable and unacceptable as one string? Wouldn't it be good to free him from his handcuffs and fetters?"

No-Toes said, "When Heaven has punished him, how can you set him free?"

[*CWZ* 37, modified]

The put-down by No-Toes is echoed by Confucius's own self-reference in a parable in chapter 6: "I am one of those men punished by Heaven" (*CWZ* 50). It is clear from the quoted passages that Zhuangzi regards fame and ordinary knowledge as

---

[1] Tradition has it that Confucius visited Laozi to learn about ritual.

instruments of evil, and the relentless pursuit of them dangerous, inevitably harming one's life, whether physically or spiritually.

Returning now to the two sentences about doing good or bad, we cannot say that Zhuangzi has ever indicated that he condones what people ordinarily consider "bad." No-Toes was once careless, got into trouble with the law, and was duly punished for the "bad" he had done. What he has tried to "stay away from" since is forever "shackled" in his heart by the loss of his toes due to an unfortunate (although by no means deliberate) action.

The comments on knowledge and ethics are succeeded by the key line in the entire chapter: "follow the middle to be what is constant" (*yuan du yi wei jing*). Since the Southern Song period (1127–1279), the Chinese word for "the middle" (*du*) in this line has been read by many scholars to refer to the "Supervisor Vessel" (*dumai*) or a major pathway for the breath (*qi*) to pass through in a central line from the base of the spine to the head. The problem with this reading is that the term "Supervisor Vessel" first appears only in the received medical text *The Yellow Emperor's Inner Classic* (*Huangdi neijing*), roughly first century BCE, but not in any of the earlier excavated medical manuscripts. It is significant to note, however, that the traditional reading of the line as "follow the middle to be what is constant" has never been rejected by these scholars who equate *du* with *dumai*. So, if *du* (roughly "supervise," "oversee," or "be in charge") in Zhuangzi's line does not come from *dumai*, how can it mean "the middle"? Perhaps some traditional commentators were right to suggest that Zhuangzi uses *du* (supervise, oversee, be in charge) as a loan word for another character *du* that means "the central seam at the back of a coat."

Regarding the idea of the middle, Zhuangzi says in chapter 2:

C4.10 Chapter 2, "Making All Things, and the Discussions on Them, Equal" (excerpt)

A state in which "this" and "that" no longer find their counterparts is called the pivot of the Way. Once the pivot is found at the center of the circle, it can respond endlessly. Its right, then, is a single endlessness, and its wrong, too, is a single endlessness. So, I say, the best thing to use is clarity.

[*CWZ* 10, modified]

莊子•齊物論（摘錄）

彼是不得其偶，謂之道
樞。樞始得其環中，以
應无窮。是亦一无窮，
非亦一无窮也。故曰莫
若以明。

[*JZZZJS* 66]

The notion of the pivot of the Way adds an important dimension to the knowledge, spiritual attainment, and behavior of the Authentic Person or ideal figures like Yan Hui and Ziqi we have been discussing. Recall that Ziqi's loss of self is described as "having lost the partner of himself." Taking together all of the quoted comments Zhuangzi has made in different contexts, we can say that having transcended their limited selves, Authentic Persons know and accept the workings of Nature, in such a way that the bifurcated human values of this and that, right and wrong, acceptable and unacceptable, even life and death no longer form opposites. They can do this because they are able to hold fast to the middle course, the pivot of the Way, in whatever they do.

Placed in the center of the introductory section of chapter, "Follow the middle to be what is constant" offers a way to resolve the fundamental problems one encounters in the nurture of life as well as a recommended course of action that will produce the positive results of "keeping one's body in one piece, keeping one's life whole, nurturing one's own person, and living out the years one receives from Nature." Zhuangzi mentions these four positive results before illustrating them each through a parable or fable in the remainder of the chapter.

The second section of chapter 3 is composed of a parable. This parable, describing Lord Wenhui's cook, may be a parody of the story in the *Mencius* of an ox sacrificed to consecrate a bell with its blood in the context of a discussion on compassion. Although we can find no factual evidence to support this interpretation, we still admire Zhuangzi's audacity in using butchery as a metaphor for the ideal way to avoid one's body from harm.

The parable has two parts and features two characters, an aristocrat and his servant cook, who engage in a dialogue, much like the characters in the other parables we have examined. The cook does most of the talking, and the lord speaks only briefly at the end of each part.

The first part is an account of the cook's extraordinary skill. It consists of eleven lines, with the first providing the narrative context, the last giving the observer's admiration, and the nine in between, arranged in regulated forms, comparing the cook's feat to a performance of dance and music. A close look at the nine core lines will reveal their complex structure. Cast in the four-character pattern of "noun + *zhi* ('s, of) + *suo* (the place where) + verb," the first four lines depict the cook holding down the ox with his hand, shoulder, foot, and knee, while carrying out his butchering task. Lines 2 and 4 end with two rhyming words, "lean" (*yi*) and "press" (*ji* or *yi*). Because these identically structured lines only say, "Wherever his hand touched," they remain mere phrases. Are there other words connected with these phrases to form a sentence?

With the next three lines, Zhuangzi turns to describe sound, and changes the line format accordingly. Of the eight words in the first two lines, the adverbial marker *ran* occurs in three phrases uniformly cast in the "x+*ran*" pattern. The three adverbial phrases can be said to modify the verb phrase "the knife being played" (*zou dao*). "Being played" (*zou*) has been defined by commentators as "put forward" (*jin*). Undoubtedly Zhuangzi uses "*zou*" because it is a common word used to describe the playing of musical instruments. Although the word *xiang* in *xiangran* can be used as a verb meaning "to make a sound," it is probably meant here to indicate sound itself. The bona fide "sound" words are *xu* and *huo*, rendered "zip" and "zing" in my translation. These two basically onomatopoeia words are hapax legomena in pre-Qin literature, found only in the *Zhuangzi*, and have been pronounced differently. Followed by the adverbial marker *ran*, these two onomatopoeic words function like verbs as well. Zhuangzi concludes the two lines depicting sounds with "All fell in with the (perfect) tone." In the context of the passage, the sounds of "zip, whoosh, and zing" come from "where" the butcher places "his hand, shoulder, foot, and knee." Zhuangzi brings together the seven four-character lines with the seven-character couplet "in accord with the dance of the Mulberry Grove, / and keeping time to the Jingshou music," the first half of which harks back to the lines describing actions and the second half to those describing sounds. In its original Chinese construction, then, the whole nine-line passage constitutes one complex syntactical unit, likening the cutting up of an ox to the performance of dance and music. The cook's impressive feat calls forth his lord's effusive admiration of his superb skill.

In the second part of the parable, the cook first sets his lord straight by saying what he cares about is the Way. With his heart set on the Way, he gradually moves beyond skill, allows his spirit to take over the role of the eye, and attains the ability to "go along with the natural makeup, strike in the big hollows, guide the knife through the big openings, and follow things as they are." The cook's comment reminds us of Yan Hui's ability to "expel my hearing and eyesight, detach from my physical form, and cast off knowledge" in becoming "identical with the Great Thoroughfare." Just like Yan Hui (and Ziqi of South Wall), the cook is able to hold fast to the middle course, the pivot of the Way, in his work as a butcher. Although Zhuangzi does not make it obvious, the "spirit" (*shen*) seems to be another name for the invisible True Lord (*zhenzai* or *zhenjun*) mentioned in chapter 2, which we do not have space to discuss here. With this True Lord inside him freed from all restrictions, the cook can keep his knife as sharp as if it had "just come from the whetstone," after nineteen years of use, cutting up several thousand oxen. Zhuangzi describes its action curiously: "the blade of the knife to roam about" for its resonance with the theme of spiritual freedom, thus hinting at the metaphorical relation between the knife and a person's life.

Before concluding the parable, Zhuangzi adds a long passage about complicated spots difficult even for the master butcher to handle. As depicted in chapter 4, "the world of humans" is an extremely hazardous place, especially in an age of great social disorder like Zhuangzi's when mere preservation of life became all important. The ox serves as a metaphor for the complex situations that need to be dealt with carefully. Even the cook has to resort to using his eyes again to avoid damage to his knife. Butchering as a metaphor for the art of preserving or nurturing life is finally made explicit in Lord Wenhui's closing comment.

In the third section of the chapter, Zhuangzi uses a brief parable to discuss the sense of wholeness in human life. The one-footed Commander of the Right's reply to Gongwen Xuan's question is not a simple "I was born with one foot." It seems that he must have had one foot mutilated as punishment for some careless "wrongdoing," not unlike what happened to Shushan No-Toes. Ordinarily, people would consider the life of someone who has lost a foot "not whole." By relegating the loss of his foot to "the work of Heaven" (i.e., fate), the Commander avoids further psychological injury and keeps "his life whole." In chapter 5, the one-footed Shentu Jia talks about his loss: "To know what one can't do anything about and to be content with it as one would with fate—only a person of virtue can do that" (*CWZ* 36, modified). Both the Commander and Shentu Jia have kept their life whole despite the physical mutilation done to them.

The fourth section entails an even briefer fable to illustrate the nurturing of one's own person, specifically the inner spirit, or as suggested earlier, the True Lord immanent within. Brief as it is, this fable embodies a viable reading of the chapter's title. The cook's parable has already illustrated how, when freed from all restrictions, the spirit can roam about in a perilous world without encountering obstruction or harm. In the current story, a swamp pheasant prefers not to be put in a cage, even if it could thereby be spared the exhaustion of searching for food and water. The moral of the fable is that the best way for a person to nurture the True Lord within is to do it in a totally free, natural, and unbound environment.

In the fifth section consisting of the last parable of the chapter, Laozi has died, and a friend named Qin Yi comes to pay his last respects. Two details need to be clarified before we relate the passage to the chapter's subject. First, the line "after giving three cries, he left" (*san hao er chu*) describing Qin Yi's bizarre behavior appears to be a parody of "after performing three rounds of foot-stomping, one left" (*san yong er chu*), a custom often mentioned along with wailing (and sometimes also wearing proper attire, standing on the right spot, and facing the right direction) in ancient texts when a scene of mourning is recorded. The highly ritualized actions of wailing and foot-stomping are used by mourners to express grief and respect for the dead. Obviously, Qin Yi's "leaving after giving three cries" deviates from the social norm. Second, the word "person" in "At first I took him for a person" has been read by some as an error for "Perfect Person." I do not agree with this reading because I do not believe the iconoclastic Zhuangzi would have Qin Yi justify his behavior for simply realizing that his friend was not a Perfect Person. Other passages in the *Zhuangzi* can help us understand this cryptic sentence.

In chapter 6, there are three parables similar to this one. In one, two people about to die show no fear of death and welcome the opportunity to have their bodies transformed by Nature into other things; in another, two friends of a dead man are found "playing or singing beside his corpse"; and in the third, someone who has lost his mother "wails without shedding tears" and experiences no grief in his heart. In my view, the shocking parable from chapter 18, "Supreme Happiness" ("Zhi le"), best illuminates the Qin Yi story:

C4.11 Chapter 18, "Supreme Happiness" (excerpt)

莊子•至樂（摘錄）

莊子妻死，惠子弔之，莊子則方箕踞鼓盆而歌。惠子曰：“與人居長子，老身死，不哭亦足矣，又鼓盆而歌，不亦甚乎！”

莊子曰：“不然。是其始死也，我獨何能无概然！察其始而本无生，非徒无生也而本无形，非徒无形也而

Zhuangzi's wife died. When Huizi[1] went to convey his condolences, he found Zhuangzi sitting with his legs sprawled out, pounding on a tub and singing. "You lived with her, she brought up your children and grew old," said Huizi. "It should be enough simply not to weep at her death. But pounding on a tub and singing—this is going too far, isn't it?"

Zhuangzi said, "You're wrong. When she first died, do you think I didn't grieve like anyone else? But I looked back to her beginning and the time before she was born. Not only the time before she was born, but the time before she had a body. Not only the time before she had a body, but the time before she had

---

[1] Also known as Hui Shi (ca. 380–305 BCE), Huizi (Master Hui) is one of the best known logicians in the mid–Warring States period. He was a friend of Zhuangzi.

breath. In the midst of the jumble of wonder and mystery, a change took place and she had breath. Another change and she had a body. Another change and she was born. Now there's been another change and she's dead. It's just like the progression of the four seasons: spring, summer, fall, winter. Now she's going to lie down peacefully in a vast room. If I were to follow after her bawling and sobbing, it would show that I don't understand anything about fate. So I stopped."

[*CWZ* 140–141, modified]

本无氣。雜乎芒芴之
間，變而有氣，氣變而
有形，形變而有生，
今又變而之死，是相與
為春秋冬夏四時行也。
人且偃然寢於巨室，而
我噭噭然隨而哭之，自
以為不通乎命，故止
也。 ”

[*JZZZJS* 614–615]

Perhaps the author of this Outer Chapter merely uses Zhuangzi as a mask for his own philosophy on life, death, and mourning practices. Nevertheless, the philosophy expressed in this chapter aligns closely with that of the four parables in the Inner Chapters.

Regarding the part "breath" plays in the process of life and death, the following passage from chapter 22, "Knowledge Wandered North" ("Zhi bei you") is instructive:

C4.12 Chapter 22, "Knowledge Wandered North" (excerpt)

莊子·知北遊（摘錄）

Life is the companion of death; death is the beginning of life. Who understands their workings? Human life is a coming-together of breath. If it comes together there is life; if it scatters, there is death. And if life and death are companions to each other, then what is there for us to be anxious about?

[*CWZ* 177, slightly modified]

生也死之徒，死也生之
始，孰知其紀！人之
生，氣之聚也；聚則為
生，散則為死。若死生
為徒，吾又何患！

[*JZZZJS* 733]

We now can take a closer look at the Qin Yi story. Both Qin Yi and Zhuangzi seem to have felt grief before they grasped that life and death are but the coming-together and the scattering of breath, a process as natural as the progression of the seasons. When Laozi and Zhuangzi's wife are no longer humans, the breath, the stuff of which they were formed, goes back to the cosmos, that "vast room" where they "lie down peacefully." Thus, it violates "the true (i.e., natural) state of affairs" to mourn Laozi as if one has lost a son or a mother. Echoing the theme of punishment from the beginning of the chapter, Qin Yi calls this act "the punishment for escaping from Heaven." The way to stay free from such punishment is "to be content with the time (of birth) and to follow along (when one dies)," without experiencing any joy, anxiety, or sorrow. This Daoist attitude of complying with the process of nature matches that of the dying person in chapter 6:

C4.13 Chapter 6, "The Great Source as Teacher" (excerpt)

莊子·大宗師（摘錄）

I received life because the time had come; I will lose it because the order of things passes on. Be content with this time and dwell in this order, and then neither sorrow nor joy can touch you. In ancient times this was called the "freeing of the bound."

[*CWZ* 48]

且夫得者時也，失者
順也，安時而處順，哀
樂不能入也。此古之所
謂縣解也。

[*JZZZJS* 160]

In chapter 3, the parable of Laozi's death illustrates the theme of "living out the years one receives from Nature." Laozi did not, in other words, allow them to be cut short by any human punishment for wrongdoing. From the perspective of Nature, grief and joy have no place in a life that follows the Way of Nature. Furthermore, these ordinary human emotions can become a punishment, fettering human life unnecessarily. The best nurture of life thus must take into consideration attitudes toward life, death, and human emotions.

"Though the grease burns out of the torch, the fire passes on, and no one knows where it ends." So Zhuangzi concludes chapter 3 and although this brief sixth section may be read as part of Qin Yi's comment, it is preferable to take it as a final ad hoc comment from the author. Subject to various interpretations, I think the best reading starts with the torch as metaphor for a person's body, the grease for the physical aspect of life, and the fire for the spirit (i.e., the True Lord) within. It is important not to confuse this spirit with the immortal soul in Christianity, even as Zhuangzi seems to suggest that a person's spirit does not cease to exist when his or her body dies. Perhaps the spirit returns to the boundless cosmic flux, along with the breath, and nobody knows where (or when) it ends. Although the Laozi parable is focused on the corporeal aspect of human life, this concluding statement emphasizes the importance of the spirit. Since death does not mean total extinction, one need not fear its arrival for oneself or bemoan the passing of a friend or relative. The final words "no one knows where it ends" look back to the beginning of the chapter to suggest that life may have no boundaries after all.

CONCLUSION

Zhuangzi's "The Principle of Nurturing Life" may have been inspired by the ancient medical tradition of "nurturing life," but a closer reading reveals a very original philosopher's reflection on the subject. Cultivation of physical well-being and longevity, the core obsession of the medical tradition, is prominently absent in Zhuangzi's chapter. Moreover, as a prime example of Zhuangzi's prose art, it consists mainly of the three rhetorical devices of metaphorical words, weighty words, and goblet words. The integration of these literary modes into an organic whole through a network of images and ideas between the parts of the chapter (as well as the Inner Chapters as a whole) is Zhuangzi's remarkable contribution to the development of the philosophical essay in ancient China.

Shuen-fu Lin

NOTES

1. Susanne K. Langer, *Feeling and Form: A Theory of Art* (New York: Scribner, 1953), 30.
2. Langer, *Feeling and Form*, 31.
3. Donald J. Harper, *Early Chinese Medical Literature: The Mawangdui Medical Manuscripts. Translation and Study* (New York: Routledge, 2009), 6.

SECONDARY SOURCES

Feng Guansheng, "Four: Winds." In *Music in the Age of Confucius*, edited by Jenny F. So, 87–99. Washington, DC: Freer Gallery of Art and Arthur M. Sackler Gallery, 2000.

Harper, Donald J. *Early Chinese Medical Literature: The Mawangdui Medical Manuscripts. Translation and Study.* New York: Routledge, 2009.

Langer, Susanne K. *Feeling and Form: A Theory of Art.* New York: Scribner, 1953.

Lau, D. C. "On *Ch'ih Ying* 持盈 and the Story Concerning the So-called 'Tilting Vessel (*Ch'i Ch'i* 欹器).'" In *Symposium on Chinese Studies: Commemorating the Golden Jubilee of the University of Hong Kong, 1911–1961,* vol. 3, 18–33. Hong Kong: University of Hong Kong, 1968.

Mote, Frederick W. *Intellectual Foundations of China.* 2nd ed. New York: McGraw-Hill, 1989.

Thrasher, Alan R. "The Chinese *Sheng*: Emblem of the Phoenix." In *ACRM* (Journal of the Association for Chinese Music Research) 9, no. 1 (1996): 3–4.

SUGGESTED READING

ENGLISH

Berkson, Mark. "Death in the *Zhuangzi*: Mind, Nature, and the Art of Forgetting." In *Mortality in Traditional Chinese Thought,* edited by Amy Olberding and Philip J. Ivanhoe, 191–224. Albany: State University of New York Press, 2011.

Graham, A. C., trans. *Chuang-tzu: The Inner Chapters.* London: Mandala, 1991.

Ivanhoe, Philip J., and Bryan W. Van Norden, eds. *Readings in Classical Chinese Philosophy.* 2nd ed. Indianapolis: Hackett, 2005.

Lin, Shuen-fu. "Transforming the Dao: A Critique of A. C. Graham's Translation of the Inner Chapters of the *Zhuangzi*." In *Hiding the World in the World: Uneven Discourses on the Zhuangzi,* edited by Scott Cook, 263–290. Albany: State University of New York Press, 2003.

Savage, William E., trans. *Classifying the Zhuangzi Chapters.* Ann Arbor: University of Michigan Center for Chinese Studies, 1994.

Watson, Burton, trans. *The Complete Works of Zhuangzi.* New York: Columbia University Press, 2013.

Wu, Kuang-ming. *The Butterfly as Companion: Meditations on the First Three Chapters of the Chuang Tzu.* Albany: State University of New York Press, 1990.

Ziporyn, Brook A., trans. *Zhuangzi: The Essential Writings with Selections from Traditional Commentaries.* Indianapolis: Hackett, 2009.

CHINESE

Chen Guying 陳鼓應. *Zhuangzi jinzhu jinyi* 莊子今注今譯 (*Zhuangzi: A Modern Commentary and Translation*). Beijing: Zhonghua shuju, 1983.

Chow Tse-tsung 周策縱. "*Zhuangzi 'Yang sheng zhu' pian benyi fuyuan*" 《莊子·養生主》篇本義復原 (*Recovering the Original Meaning of the "Yang Sheng Chu" Chapter in* Chuang-tzu). *Zhongguo wenzhe yanjiu jikan* 中國文哲研究集刊 (*Bulletin of the Institute of Chinese Literature and Philosophy*) 2 (1992): 13–50.

Jiang Menma 蔣門馬. *Zhuangzi huijiao kaoding* 莊子彙校考訂 (*Zhuangzi: A Collection of Textual Collations, Examinations, and Corrections*). 2 vols. Chengdu: Bashu shushe, 2019.

Liu Xiaogan 劉笑敢. *Zhuangzi zhexue ji qi yanbian (xiuding ban)* 莊子哲學及其演變(修訂版) (*The Philosophy of* Zhuangzi *and Its Evolution* [Revised Edition]). Beijing: Zhongguo renmin daxue chubanshe, 2010.

Liu Zhengguo 劉正國. "Di hu chou hu yue hu–wei Jiahu yizhi chutude guzhi xiechuiguan kao ming" 笛乎 篙乎 籥乎—為賈湖遺址出土的骨質斜吹樂管考名 (*Di* Pipes? *Chou* Pipes? Or *Yue* Pipes?—An Examination of the Naming of the Obliquely Played Bone Pipes Unearthed in the Archaeological Site in Jiahu). *Yinyue yanjiu* 音樂研究 (*Studies on Music*) 3 (September 1996): 74–75.

Wang Shumin 王叔岷. *Zhuangzi jiaoquan* 莊子校詮 (*Zhuangzi: Collation and Interpretation*). 3 vols. Taipei: Institute of History and Linguistics, Academia Sinica, 1988.

Pre-Qin and Han Philosophical and Historical Prose

Self-Interest, Manipulation, and the Philosophical Marketplace

Readers may wonder why China's first philosophical burgeoning took place during a singularly chaotic period, the aptly named Warring States (*Zhanguo*). Would people really have taken a break from killing each other to engage in refined philosophical debate? The truth is that the people who were doing the refined philosophizing were not the people doing the killing: they were *advising* the people doing the killing, and usually for a good salary. We may like to think of ancient Chinese philosophers as high-minded gentlemen rather than venal careerists, but even high-minded gentlemen need to eat, and the necessities of life were most readily obtained by serving a ruler who wished to profit from their expertise.

The conventions of the Bronze Age, which had long held society together, were manifestly collapsing, and anyone with ideas about how to prosper in the tumultuous new world was bound to get a hearing at court. Philosophers chafed at being categorized with strategists, accountants, even jesters and jugglers—in short, anyone with specialized skills that might appeal to a lordly employer—but the records suggest they were treated with exceptional deference, receiving honorific phrases that dukes and magnates would not have used with ordinary subjects. This makes sense if we think of the Warring States as a great philosophical marketplace: rulers who attained a reputation for mistreating retainers would soon discover that no one wished to serve them. A ruler bereft of competent advisors soon became a ruler bereft of his throne.

We know from Adam Smith (1723–1790) that markets are driven by self-interest,[1] and Warring States China was no different. Moreover, the most cunning participants in that market showed little compunction about manipulating gullible victims, especially rulers and others with enough clout to make the deception worthwhile. Thus, the themes of self-interest and manipulation frequently went hand in hand, and any account of early Chinese philosophical prose would be incomplete without attention to them.

"TANG JU JIAN CHUNSHEN JUN" ("TANG JU HAD AN AUDIENCE WITH LORD CHUNSHEN")

"Tang Ju Had an Audience with Lord Chunshen" is a brief item in a large and diverse anthology called *Zhanguo ce* (*Stratagems of the Warring States*). This collection of ideologically indifferent anecdotes was compiled by Liu Xiang (77–6 BCE), a redactor who organized thousands of short bamboo texts in the palace library (as well as some private collections), producing many of the classical texts that survive to this day. Although *Zhanguo ce* is sometimes characterized as a handbook of rhetoric, Liu's own preface discloses a different purpose: to preserve the deeds of lords and ministers who hatched ingenious plans in their struggle for survival. These stratagems, he says, are "worth beholding" (*ke guan*) even though they do not necessarily accord with mainstream morality (*ZGCJZ* 1–3).

"Tang Ju Had an Audience with Lord Chunshen" might not seem noteworthy when taken out of context, but reading it against the known background reveals more layers than initially meet the eye. First, a complete translation:

C5.1 *Stratagems of the Warring States*, "Tang Ju Had an Audience with Lord Chunshen"

Tang Ju[1] had an audience with Lord Chunshen,[2] where he said: "The men of Qi[3] adorn themselves and cultivate their conduct in order to obtain lucrative employment, but I, your servant, would be ashamed [to act like this] and will not emulate them. I did not shirk crossing the Yangzi and Yellow Rivers, traveling more than a thousand *li*, in order to come here, because I secretly admired your purpose, Great Lord, and [wish] to abet your enterprise. I have heard that the world would consider Ben and Zhu[4] brave even if they hid their blades in their breast; the world would deem Shi of the West[5] beautiful even if her clothes were shabby. Now, Milord, you are the Prime Minister of the myriad-chariot state of Chu. In defending the Central States against turmoil, you have unfulfilled desires and unattained goals because your servitors' ranks are few. The Owl is able to act because of the assistance of its Pawns.[6] It is clear that one Owl is no match for five Pawns. Now, Milord, why not become the Owl of the world, and let us, your servitors, be your Pawns?"

On the surface, this is a straightforward example of a productive theme in early Chinese writing: a successful lord needs capable ministers. Tang Ju, an obscure adventurer, has traveled all the way from the north to visit Lord Chunshen, prime minister of the great southern state of Chu (this is why he claims to have crossed both the Yellow and Yangzi Rivers), to offer his services. Lord Chunshen, sometimes known as one of the "Four Princes of the Warring States" (*Zhanguo si gongzi*), was famous for recruiting talented retainers. We do not know whether Tang Ju's

戰國策•唐且見春申君

唐且見春申君曰："齊人飾身修行得為益，然臣羞而不學也。不避絕江河，行千餘里來，竊慕大君之義，而善君之業。臣聞之，賁、諸懷錐刃而天下為勇，西施衣褐而天下稱美。今君相萬乘之楚，禦中國之難，所欲者不成，所求者不得，臣等少也。夫梟棊之所以能為者，以散棊佐之也。夫一梟之不如不勝五散，亦明矣。今君何不為天下梟，而令臣等為散乎？"

[*ZGCJZ* 861–62]

---

[1] This name will be discussed later in this chapter.

[2] Huang Xie (d. 238 BCE), one of the leading statesmen of Chu.

[3] A great state in the northeast, known for its scholars.

[4] Meng Ben (dates unknown), from Qi, was known for his physical strength; Zhuan Zhu (d. 515 BCE), from Wu, was a famous assassin. Tang Ju deftly chooses examples from both the North and the South.

[5] A beautiful woman from Yue who was presented to the King of Wu—hence a paradigmatic beauty.

[6] The Owl and Pawns are pieces in the imperfectly understood board game called *liubo*. The Owl is much stronger than the Pawns, but evidently still requires their assistance.

effort was successful because Lord Chunshen's response is not recorded. That, in itself, is telling: for if Tang Ju were as talented as he suggests, we should already know of him as one of Lord Chunshen's followers. Since we do not, we must suspect that he was a charlatan.

A review of other references to Tang Ju, as well as the meaning of his name, adds to the reader's doubts. In a different anecdote in *Zhanguo ce*, Tang Ju is employed by the prime minister of Qin to bribe potential enemies in Zhao (*ZGCJZ* 343); in another, he appears to be in the service of Wei, for he beseeches the King of Qin to assist that beleaguered state (*ZGCJZ* 1450–51); and in the most famous story, he threatens to assassinate the King of Qin (the future First Emperor, r. 221–210 BCE), who has been bullying the Lord of Anling, a paltry principality (*ZGCJZ* 1467–68). As all of these stories are set in the third century BCE, it is conceivable these stories refer to the same person. He would have to be interpreted, however, as a faithless agent for different kingdoms at different times, now working for Qin, now against it.

The Chinese scholar Huang Xinguang has argued that Tang Ju was not a real person, and the name was simply invented for its meaning: "exaggerated proposals," a fine epithet for a cozener. If Huang is right, whenever we encounter the name Tang Ju, we should not trust anything that comes out of his mouth. To use a deprecating term from this period, Tang Ju is a *youshui*: an "itinerant persuader."

Some information about Lord Chunshen sheds even further light. As mentioned earlier, he is best known today for his retinue, which included a man who was at least as famous as he was: Xun Kuang (d. after 238 BCE), variously known as Xunzi (Master Xun) and Sun Qingzi (Master Chamberlain Sun). Xunzi is now considered one of China's greatest philosophers; even in his own day, he was known as "the most revered of teachers" (*zui wei laoshi*). Consequently, Tang Ju's assertion that Lord Chunshen has failed to achieve his ambitions because his "servitors are few" has to be interpreted as an oblique indictment of Xunzi's competence. Just imagine Merlin's reaction if some parvenu announced to King Arthur that he lacked satisfactory advisors.

Thus, "Tang Ju Had an Audience with Lord Chunshen" must be read in conjunction with a nearby story in *Zhanguo ce* (*ZGCJZ* 892–894), which relates how an unnamed "client" (*ke*) persuaded Lord Chunshen to dismiss Xunzi. Lord Chunshen immediately regrets heeding this advice, but when he tries to recall Xunzi, the latter sends him an outspoken letter that begins with the sentence: "The leper pities the King" (*Lairen lian wang*)—because no one tries to assassinate a leper.[2] Since Lord Chunshen was, in fact, assassinated in 238 BCE, any ancient reader would have understood Xunzi's words as a sage premonition, and a discerning reader might suspect that the unidentified retainer responsible for ousting Xunzi was none other than Tang Ju.

If *that* was the case, Tang Ju might best be understood as an agent sent by an enemy who perceived the first step toward assassinating Lord Chunshen was to remove the wise Xunzi from his side. What better method than to trick Lord Chunshen into dismissing Xunzi himself? *Cui bono?* Lord Chunshen's assassin was Li Yuan (d. 228 BCE), another one of his retainers (and, like Xunzi, an expatriate from

Zhao). With Lord Chunshen out of the way, Li Yuan became the prime minister, and his nephews would go on to ascend the throne as King You (r. 237–228 BCE) and King Ai of Chu (r. 228 BCE). (Much of this is related in *ZGCJZ* 914–916.) Li Yuan and his whole family perished just ten years later at the hands of yet another assassin, who became King Fuchu (r. 228–223 BCE). Soon Fuchu was killed when Qin conquered Chu. It was a violent age.

How much of this is true? That is precisely the wrong question. Readers of *Zhanguo ce* certainly knew that Lord Chunshen was assassinated soon after he dismissed Xunzi. That much was common knowledge. If Huang Xinguang is right that Tang Ju is an invented name, then the anecdote has to be interpreted as a fictitious but instructive story relating to these momentous events. What is more important than the veracity of the tale is its moral: do not heed the unsolicited counsel of people you do not know and cannot trust, especially if you are a juicy target. They might have unpleasant plans for you.

CHUNYU KUN AND THE VERTICAL AND HORIZONTAL ALLIANCES IN *LÜSHI CHUNQIU*

A common example illustrating the untrustworthiness of such itinerant persuaders is their advocacy of the so-called Vertical and Horizontal Alliances (*zongheng*). By the middle of the third century BCE, it was apparent to all observers that the state of Qin was at least as powerful as all the others combined. Accordingly, representatives of Qin's chief rivals attempted to unite under a Vertical Alliance, but Qin's counselors shrewdly recruited desperate states to its own league, known as the Horizontal Alliance. It is difficult to say more than this because almost all relevant information comes from literary sources that focus on the rhetorical strategies employed by self-interested speakers at court rather than the practical details of how the alliances were negotiated, sustained, and invoked. For diplomatic historians, the sources are frustratingly incomplete.

In philosophical and anecdotal literature, the stance toward these alliances is usually disparaging, as in the following anecdote from *Lüshi chunqiu* (*Springs and Autumns of Mr. Lü*),[3] an encyclopedic text compiled under the auspices of Lü Buwei (d. 235 BCE), a former chief minister of Qin and renowned patron like Lord Chunshen.

C5.2 *Springs and Autumns of Mr. Lü* (excerpt)

Among the men of Qi there was one Chunyu Kun, who persuaded the King of Wei [to join] the Vertical Alliance. The King of Wei, finding him cogent, furnished him with ten chariots and was about to dispatch him as an ambassador to Chu. As he was taking his leave,[1] he persuaded the King of Wei[2] [to join] the Horizontal Alliance, whereupon the King of Wei called off the expedition. He failed not only in his intention [of having the King join] the Vertical

呂氏春秋・離謂（摘錄）

齊人有淳于髡者，以從說魏王。魏王辯之，約車十乘，將使之荊。辭而行，有以橫說魏王，魏王乃止其行。失從之意，又失橫之事。夫其多能不若寡能，其有辯

---

[1] I suspect that this *you* 有 should be read *you* 又, with the sense of "not content with this much."

[2] Perhaps King Hui (r. 370–319 BCE).

不若無辯。周鼎著倕而
齕其指，先王有以見大
巧之不可為也。

[*LSCQXJS* 1188]

Alliance, but also in the matter [of having the King join] the Horizontal Alliance. Too much ability is worse than too little ability; an abundance of cogency is worse than a lack of it. Zhou cauldrons depict Chui[3] gnawing on his finger; by this means, the Former Kings demonstrated that great skill should not be practiced.

By referring to Chui, the venerable artisan who would rather bite his finger than allow it to mar his work, the anecdote makes use of another early commonplace: too much of a good thing can undo one's entire achievement. One of the most famous examples is the "Adding Feet to the Snake" story in *Zhanguo ce*: during a contest to see who can draw a snake the fastest, the presumptive winner shows off by adding feet to his snake while he waits for the others to finish—thereby ruining it and losing his prize (*ZGCJZ* 565). In the same vein, Chunyu Kun should be content with his reward of ten chariots and a royal commission, but instead he loses everything because he cannot resist the urge to display his silver tongue.

The very first word, "Qi," warns readers that the commonplace of the itinerant persuader is at work as well. The locus is the court of Wei, but Chunyu is not from Wei; he is an adventurer from Qi who has come to Wei to parlay his forensic skills into wealth and status. One can only surmise that Chunyu must have worn out his welcome in his home state if he is now trying his luck in Wei. In *ZGCJZ* 1382–1383, for example, he is accused of taking bribes to dissuade the King of Qi from attacking Wei; perhaps such chicanery led to his expulsion. At any rate, in the present story, the King of Wei is initially foolish enough to suppose that Chunyu's support for the Vertical Alliance is sincere, but as soon as he shows that he can just as easily argue for the Horizontal Alliance, the king grasps that he cannot be trusted.

HAN FEIZI

The theme of the self-interested, unscrupulous minister, whose attempts at persuasion must be resisted, is a major focus of *Han Feizi*, a collection of essays attributed to the brilliant writer and political philosopher Han Fei (d. 233 BCE). No one diagnosed more insightfully the interplay of conflicting interests at court. Ironically, he succumbed to the same forces he described so memorably in his writings: he was imprisoned on trumped-up charges and then talked into committing suicide by his main rival, Li Si (280–208 BCE). In the following excerpt from "Wudu" ("The Five Kinds of Vermin"), Han Fei explains how rulers go astray by failing to recognize that ministers make proposals to further their own interests, not those of the sovereign.

韓非子・五蠹（摘錄）

C5.3 *Han Feizi*, "The Five Kinds of Vermin" (excerpt)

故群臣之言外事者，非
有分於從衡之黨，則有
仇讎之忠，而借力於國
也。從者，合眾弱以

The thronging ministers who speak of foreign affairs either are members of the Vertical or Horizontal parties or are attempting to appropriate the strength of the state for the sake of some [personal] vendetta. The Vertical Alliance

---

[3] A legendary craftsman.

unites many weak [states] in order to attack one strong one; the Horizontal Alliance serves one strong [state] in order to attack many weak ones. Neither is a means to sustain one's own state.

Ministers who speak in favor of the Horizontal Alliance all say: "If you do not serve the great [state, i.e., Qin], when you come into conflict with an enemy, you will endure calamity." When you serve the great [state], though it is uncertain that [the strategy] will bear fruit, you must gather maps [of your domain] and submit them,[1] and present your seals [of state] when you request military assistance. If you offer such maps, your territory will be whittled away; if you present your seals, your reputation will be debased. If your territory is whittled away, your state is whittled away; if your reputation is debased, your government will be in disorder. Before you have seen any benefit from serving the great [state] and engaging in the Horizontal Alliance, you will lose your territory and your government will be in disorder.

Ministers who speak in favor of the Vertical Alliance all say: "If you do not rescue small [states] and attack the great one, the world will be lost; if the world is lost, your own state will be imperiled; if your state is imperiled, you, the ruler, will be debased." When you rescue small [states], though it is uncertain that [the strategy] will bear fruit, you must raise troops and become the enemy of the great [state]. When you rescue small [states], it is uncertain that they can be preserved, and when you attack the great [state], it is uncertain that there will be no dissension [among your allies]. If there is dissension, you will be controlled by the mighty state [you attacked]. If you send out your troops, your army will be defeated; if you withdraw in defense, your cities will be captured. Before you have seen any benefit from rescuing small [states] and engaging in the Vertical Alliance, you will lose your territory and your army will be defeated.

For these reasons, if you serve the mighty [state], it will use its influence to employ officials within [your administration]; if you rescue small [states], powerbrokers within [your administration] will seek profit abroad. Before any benefit has been established for the state, lands and generous remuneration will accrue [to such ministers]. The sovereign will be debased, yet ministers will be honored; the state's territory will be whittled away, yet private households will be enriched. If their affairs succeed, they will use their influence to extend their power; if their affairs fail, they will retire with their riches. When the ruler listens to such persuasions and deals with his ministers, he honors them with rank and remuneration even before their affairs have succeeded, nor does he punish them when their affairs fail. Why would itinerant persuaders not employ some "tethered-arrow" scheme and trust in a lucky outcome?[2]

---

[1] Offering maps of one's territory is a standard trope of submission because it allows the other country to invade more easily.

[2] A tethered arrow is used to hunt birds; here, presumably, it refers to a moon-shot scheme with little chance of success. Itinerant persuaders will not be reluctant to propose "tethered-arrow schemes" if they know there will be no consequences for failure.

攻一強也；而衡者，事一強以攻眾弱也；皆非所以持國也。今人臣之言衡者皆曰："不事大則遇敵受禍矣。"事大未必有實，則舉圖而委，效璽而請兵矣。獻圖則地削，效璽則名卑，地削則國削，名卑則政亂矣。事大為衡未見其利也，而亡地亂政矣。人臣之言從者皆曰："不救小而伐大則失天下，失天下則國危，國危而主卑。"救小未必有實，則起兵而敵大矣。救小未必能存，而交大未必不有疏，有疏則為強國制矣。出兵則軍敗，退守則城拔，救小為從未見其利，而亡地敗軍矣。是故事強則以外權士 [=仕] 官於內，救小則以內重求利於外，國利未立，封土厚祿至矣；主上雖卑，人臣尊矣；國地雖削，私家富矣。事成則以權長重，事敗則以富退處。人主之於其聽說也，於其臣，事未成則爵祿已尊矣；事敗而弗誅，則游說之士，孰不為用矰繳之說而徼倖其後？故破國亡主以聽言談者之浮說，此其故何也？是人君不明乎公私之利，不察當否之言，而誅罰不必其後也。

[*HFZXJZ* 1114]

N.B. Straight underline indicates the use of repetitive

patterning; wavy underline the
use of parallel patterning. For
a discussion on repetitive and
parallel patterning, ☛ C1.1–4
and C1.6–7.

Why, then, do the doomed rulers of broken states listen to the fanciful per-suasions of speechifiers? It is because such rulers are not clear-sighted about profit for *gong* and *si*,[3] do not investigate whether [ministers'] words are suit-able, and do not necessarily punish them for [disappointing] outcomes.

The key to understanding this passage comes toward the end, in the reference to *gong* and *si*. *Si* is the easier of the two terms to translate: it means "private," especially in the senses of "private interest" or "judgments reached by private, and hence arbitrary, criteria." Ministers who make proposals always do so out of *si*, in expectation of some private benefit. *Gong* is derived from the old word mean-ing "patriarch" or "duke"; by Han Fei's time, it had come to refer more broadly to the interests of the ruler. In modern writing, *gong* is often translated as "public," but this is misleading. (A phrase like *gongyong che* means "vehicle for public use" in modern Chinese, but would have meant "vehicle for the [exclusive] use of the Duke" in the classical language.) Occasionally *gong* is interpreted as something like "the general interests of the state as opposed to the private interests of its minis-ters." Although this might be defensible for other early Chinese texts (such as *Lüshi chunqiu*), it is still questionable in the context of *Han Feizi*, which acknowledges that the interests of a particular ruler—even long-term, prudential interests—are not necessarily identical to those of the abstract state.

Earlier in "Wudu," *gong* is defined straightforwardly as "that which opposes *si*" (*HFZXJZ* 1105). In *Han Feizi*, rulers are counseled not to trust anyone, not even their kin and bedfellows, but ministers are regarded as the party most likely to cause harm because they are indispensable: by Han Fei's time, states were already so large that a ruler could not hope to oversee the administration personally (cf. *HFZXJZ* 107, 1109, and 1141–42).[4] Relying on ministers is dangerous, however, because they act in their own interest (*si*), not that of their employer and certainly not that of the kingdom they represent (*gong*). Rulers who fail to distinguish between *gong* and *si* when they hear ministers' proposals will inevitably come to grief.

This passage illustrates this tension through the example of the Horizontal and Vertical Alliances. The addressee of "Wudu" is evidently the ruler of a state other than Qin, for he is advised to join neither party for two important reasons: the obli-gations will only weaken him, and the alliances are promoted by ministers with ulterior motives. The text does not specify the right strategy—a ruler worth his salt will have to analyze that for himself—but its advice is very similar to that of "Tang Ju jian Chunshen jun": do not blindly follow your ministers' proposals, because you cannot be sure of their designs. Above all, be aware that your demise may be all too convenient for them.[5]

A passage in a different chapter, "Zhudao" ("The Way of the Ruler"), illustrates a related point: in the face of all this duplicity, the ruler ought not to reveal his inner thoughts or even to try to outwit his underlings by dissembling (for dissembling

---

[3] *Si* means "private," especially in the sense of "private interest." *Gong* is derived from the old word meaning "patriarch" or "duke." These terms will be discussed further in the following section.

too can be detected); instead, he should present a blank poker-face to the outside world, leaving his enemies without any toehold whatsoever.

C5.4 *Han Feizi*, "The Way of the Ruler" (excerpt)

Thus it is said: The lord ought not to make his desires apparent. If the lord's desires are apparent, the ministers will carve and polish themselves [to his liking]. The lord ought not to make his intentions apparent. If the lord's intentions are apparent, the ministers will display themselves falsely. Thus it is said: Eliminate likes; eliminate dislikes. Then the ministers will appear plainly. Eliminate tradition; eliminate wisdom. Then the ministers will prepare themselves.

The ruler must "eliminate wisdom" because the wisest policy of all is to come across as a blockhead, all the while carefully observing and assessing everyone else. Such phrases evoke *Laozi*, although they are not direct quotes (at least not to any known edition of that text). *Han Feizi* contains many such allusions, including two complete chapters (of disputed authorship) offering direct interpretations of *Laozi* from the perspective of statecraft.

SUNZI

Whereas Han Fei was a real person and may have been the author of at least some chapters in *Han Feizi* (including "Wudu"), the military strategist Sun Wu is a less credible figure for several reasons. First, his given name (Warlike) seems too good to be true.[6] Second, the only biographical information about him is a patently romanticized story in *Shiji* (*Records of the Historian*) that relates how he trained the harem of King Helu of Wu (r. 514–496 BCE) to become a fearsome battalion. Third, and most important, the text of *Sunzi* bears hallmarks of a period much later than the turn of the sixth century BCE, when he must have been active if he really served King Helu. Consequently, we must treat it as an anonymous work that was proleptically attributed to a legendary figure of the past. This was a common practice at the time; another example is *Guanzi*, a collection attributed to Guan Zhong (d. 645 BCE), who probably did not write a single word of it.

The following excerpt from the "Mougong" ("Attacking Strategically") chapter of *Sunzi* stresses that warfare is a matter of rational self-interest rather than valor or bloodlust. Because the fundamental purpose of a military campaign is to increase the state's power, a commander must weigh the strategies that do and do not produce tangible results.

C5.5 *Sunzi*, "Attacking Strategically" (excerpt)

Master Sun said: According to the method of using troops, [capturing] a state intact is always best; destroying it is inferior. [Capturing] an army intact is best; destroying it is inferior. [Capturing] a battalion intact is best; destroying it is inferior. [Capturing] a company intact is best; destroying it is inferior. [Capturing] a squad intact is best; destroying it is inferior. For this reason, [one who

韓非子‧主道（摘錄）

故曰：君無見其所欲，君見其所欲，臣自將雕琢。君無見其意，君見其意，臣將自表異。故曰：去好去惡，臣乃見素，去舊去智，臣乃自備。

[HFZXJZ 66]

孫子‧謀攻（摘錄）

孫子曰：凡用兵之法，全國為上，破國次之；全軍為上，破軍次之；全旅為上，破旅次之；全卒為上，破卒次之；全伍為上，破伍次之。是故百戰百勝，非善之善者也；不戰而屈人之兵，善之善者也。

故上兵伐謀，其次伐交，其次伐兵，其下攻城。攻城之法，為不得已，修 [=脩] 櫓轒轀，具器械，三月而後成；距闉，又三月而後已。將不勝其忿而蟻附之，殺士三分之一，而城不拔者，此攻之災也。

故善用兵者，屈人之兵而非戰也；拔人之城而非攻也；毀人之國而非久也。必以全爭於天下，故兵不頓 [=鈍] 而利可全，此謀攻之法也。

[*SYJZSZJL* 44–52]

N.B. Straight underline indicates the use of repetitive patterning; wavy underline the use of parallel phrasing therein. For a discussion on repetitive and parallel patterning, ☞ C1.1–4 and C1.6–7.

孫子・虛實 （摘錄）

故策之而知得失之計，作之而知動靜之理，形之而知死生之地，角之而知有餘不足之處。故形兵之極，至於無形；無形，則深間不能窺，知者不能謀。因形而錯勝於眾，眾不能知。人皆知我所以勝之形，而莫知吾所以制勝

attains] a hundred victories in a hundred battles is not the most adept of the adept. One who subdues the enemy's troops without a battle is the most adept of the adept.

Thus the best military [strategy] is to attack [the enemy's] strategy; next comes attacking his alliances; next comes attacking his troops; last comes attacking cities. The method of attacking cities is to do so only when there is no alternative. Armored siege vehicles and other machinery take three months to complete; the earthworks take another three months to finish. If the commander cannot overcome his frustration and has [his troops] climb the walls like ants, one in three of his warriors will be killed and the city still not be seized. This would be a disastrous attack.

Thus one who is adept at using troops subdues the enemy's troops, but not through battle; he seizes the enemy's cities, but not by attacking; he annihilates the enemy's state, but not through protracted [campaigns]. [One's goal] must be to contend with the rest of the world by [capturing enemy targets] intact; thereby one's troops will not be depleted, but one's gains can be kept intact. This is the method of attacking strategically.

Contemporary literature frequently delights in the exploits of legendary or semi-legendary heroes (like the aforementioned Meng Ben), but *Sunzi* reminds its reader—who is evidently envisioned as a lord or strategist with national interests to consider—that although military glory may inspire encomiasts, it does not necessarily benefit the state. "Protracted campaigns," in particular, are unlikely to yield enough spoils to compensate for draining the state's coffers. Thus, the best battlefield strategy is often the one that *avoids* confrontation on the battlefield. Decisive action, especially when attacking cities, is inadvisable unless "there is no alternative" (*de bu yi*).

As in *Han Feizi*, one of the best techniques is to manipulate the enemy into committing first.

C5.6 *Sunzi*, "Weak Points and Strong" (excerpt)

Therefore, make [the enemy] formulate a strategy so as to calculate his strengths and weaknesses. Make him act so as to know the pattern of his movement and stillness. Make him assume a form so as to know whether his territory will [mean] life or death [for him]. Probe him so as to know the points where he has excess and deficiency.

Thus the supreme [object] in forming one's troops is to be without form. If we are without form, then even those under deep cover will not be able to spy us out, and those who are wise will not be able to plan for us. By adjusting to forms, one provides victories for one's army, but the army is unable to know this. Everyone will know the form that we use for victory, but no one will know the form that we used to determine victory. Thus when we are victorious in battle, we do not repeat ourselves, but respond to forms inexhaustibly.

"Formlessness" (*wuxing*)—another term that resonates with the philosophy of *Laozi* and allied traditions—is a byword for avoiding any type of committed formation until the enemy has already disclosed his intentions. It is the enemy who determines how he is to be destroyed: for every situation and for every enemy tactic, a shrewd commander will know the appropriate response. (Similarly, in games like curling and *bocce*, whoever throws last ought to win.) The strategy by which one attains victory can never be reused, because never again will precisely the same situation obtain.

The allusions to and evocations of *Laozi* are too pervasive to be accidental. The opening of *Laozi* 68 must have been written by someone familiar with these military traditions: "One who is adept at using warriors does not fight; one who is adept at battle does not rage; one who is adept at defeating the enemy does not engage him." (*LDJZJS* 17–172)

MOZI

Not all voices were pleased to see the pursuit of self-interest elevated to an art form, and the annexation of weaker kingdoms, which is presumed in *Sunzi* to be the very purpose of warfare, elsewhere elicited dismay. Nor did Confucians (☛ chap. 3) have a monopoly on moralizing critique. In a famous passage in *Mozi*, conquerors are compared with criminals such as thieves, kidnappers, and murderers: whereas everyone agrees that the latter should be punished forthwith, bellicose kings shamelessly declare themselves "righteous" (*yi*) merely because they despoil neighboring countries rather than their own.

Mozi is a collection of essays, anecdotes, logical exercises, and treatises on defensive warfare that seems to have served as a school text. Clearly, it is not the work of its putative author, Mo Di (ca. 478–ca. 393 BCE), because the text often quotes him as though he were a long-dead authority. Mo Di may have been a real person and may have established a functioning school, where documents like the received *Mozi* were used in instruction.

Mozi is notoriously repetitive, and the following selection from "Tianzhi xia" ("The Will of Heaven, Part C")[7] is no exception. Nevertheless, the concrete examples are effectively deployed to convey the *a fortiori* nature of the argument: if filching a neighbor's melons and ginger warrants punishment, how much more so does destroying a kingdom?

C5.7 *Mozi*, "The Will of Heaven, Part C" (excerpt)

Suppose there is someone who enters other people's gardens and takes their peaches, plums, melons, and ginger. If his superiors apprehend him, they will punish him; if the multitudes hear of [his conduct], they will decry him. Why? One would say it was because he reaped the fruit without engaging in the labor and took what was not his. How much more does this apply to one who climbs over other people's walls and kidnaps their sons and daughters? Or one who drills into other people's treasuries and steals their gold, gems, and silk

之形。故其戰勝不復，
而應形於無窮。

[*SYJZSZJL* 120–23]

墨子・天志下（摘錄）

若今有人於此，入人之
場園，取人之桃李瓜薑
者，上得且罰之，眾聞
則非之。是何也？曰：
不與其勞，獲其實，已
非其有所取之故。而況
有踰於人之牆垣，担格

人之子女者乎？與角人
之府庫，竊人之金玉蚤
絭 ［＝蠶絮］ 者乎？與
踰人之欄牢，竊人之牛
馬者乎？而況有殺一不
辜人乎？今王公大人之
為政也，自殺一不辜人
者，踰人之牆垣，担格
人之子女者；與角人之
府庫，竊人之金玉蚤絭
［＝蠶絮］者；與踰人之欄
牢，竊人牛馬者；與入
人之場園，竊人之桃李
瓜薑者。今王公大人之
加罰此也，雖古之堯、
舜、禹、湯、文、武之
為政，亦無以異此矣。
今天下之諸侯，將猶皆
侵凌攻伐兼并，此為殺
一不辜人者數千萬矣！
此為 踰人之牆垣，格
人之子女者，與角人
府庫，竊人金玉蚤絭
［＝蠶絮］者，數千萬矣！
踰人之欄牢，竊人之牛
馬者，與入人之場園，
竊人之桃李瓜薑者，數
千萬矣！而自曰義也。
故子墨子言曰：是蕡
我 ［＝紛義］ 者，則豈
有以異是蕡 ［＝紛］ 者
黑白甘苦之辯者哉！今
有人於此，少 而示之
黑 謂 之 黑，多 示 之 黑
謂白，必曰吾 目 亂，
不知黑白之別。今有
人 於 此，能 少 嘗 之
甘，謂甘，多嘗謂苦，
必曰吾 口 亂，不知其
甘苦之味。今王公大人
之政也，或殺人其 ［＝
于］ 國家，禁之此蚤越
［＝以斧鉞］，有能多殺
其鄰國之人，因以為文

fibers?[1] Or one who climbs into other people's fenced ranches and steals their oxen and horses? How much more does this apply to one who kills an innocent person? In the government of today's kings, lords, and grandees, one who kills an innocent person, climbs over other people's walls and kidnaps their sons and daughters, or drills into other people's treasuries and steals their gold, gems, and silk fibers, or climbs into other people's fenced ranches and steals their oxen and horses, or enters other people's gardens and takes their peaches, plums, melons, and ginger—today's kings, lords, and grandees punish such people just as Yao, Shun, Yu, Tang, and Kings Wen and Wu would have done in their own government.

When the territorial lords of the world today all invade, attack, and conquer one another, this is tens of millions of times worse than killing an innocent person. It is tens of millions of times worse than climbing over other people's walls and kidnapping their sons and daughters, or boring into other people's treasuries and stealing their gold, gems, and silk fibers. It is tens of millions of times worse than climbing into other people's fenced ranches and stealing their oxen and horses, or entering other people's gardens and taking their peaches, plums, melons, and ginger. Yet they all call themselves righteous.

Thus Master Mozi said: This is obscuring righteousness; how is it different from obscuring the distinction between black and white or sweet and bitter? Suppose there is someone who, having been shown a bit of black, calls it black, but having been shown a lot of black, calls it white. He would have to say: My eyes are defective; I cannot tell the difference between black and white. Suppose there is someone who, having tasted a bit of something sweet, calls it sweet, but having tasted a lot of it, calls it bitter. He would have to say: My mouth is defective; I cannot tell whether something tastes sweet or bitter. In the government of today's kings, lords, and grandees, killing people within the state is prohibited by means of the executioner's axe, but one who is able to kill many people in neighboring states is, for that reason, deemed praiseworthy and righteous. How is this different from obscuring the difference between black and white or sweet and bitter?

The complaint is reminiscent of Augustine's (354–430 CE) observation that a predator who plies the seas with one vessel is called a pirate, while one who does so with a whole fleet is called an emperor (*City of God* 4.4). Because they had few useful recommendations to offer would-be emperors, Mohists fell out of favor; eventually, the whole philosophy became a relic. The philosophical marketplace was a marketplace, after all.

---

[1] Although there is little doubt that the phrase *zaolei* must refer to precious silk, commentators do not agree on the precise meaning. I follow the emendation suggested in *MZJG*, even though the basis seems flimsy, because the overall meaning is not affected.

FALSE VIRTUE, TRUE REWARDS

Another story about Chunyu Kun exemplifies a final commonplace to be discussed: as "men-of-service" (*shi*) became known as a greedy and mendacious lot, feigning extraordinary honesty emerged as yet another profitable strategy.

C5.8 *Grand Scribe's Records*, "Biographies of Amusing Figures" (excerpt)

In the past, the King of Qi sent Chunyu Kun to offer a crane to [the King of] Chu. He set off through the gates of the city, and, on the road, the crane flew away. Bearing only an empty cage, he invented a fraudulent excuse. When he went to his audience with the King of Chu, he said: "The King of Qi sent me to offer you a crane, but, as I was crossing the river, the crane's thirst was too much for me to bear. When I let it out to drink, it left me and flew away. I wished to die by stabbing myself in the gut or hanging myself by the neck, but I was afraid that people would criticize my king for making his man-of-service kill himself for the sake of a bird. A crane is a feathered creature; there are many [other animals] of the same type. I wished to buy one in place [of the missing crane], but this would have been untrustworthy and deceptive toward my king. I wished to flee to another kingdom, but it pained me that this would cause a breach between the two rulers. Thus I have come here to admit my transgression; kowtowing, I shall accept your punishment, Great King."

The King of Chu said: "It is very good that the King of Qi has such trustworthy men-of-service!" He rewarded [Chunyu] generously, with riches several times greater than if the crane had still been with him.

This vignette appears in *Shiji* (☛ chap. 6), but was probably inserted by Chu Shaosun (104?–30? BCE), a scholar who has been criticized for having dared to add his words to Sima Qian's masterpiece. Regardless of its origin, the literary effect of this piece lies in its modulation of prior tales. The theme of the crane lost on the road is attested in a variety of early Chinese sources, but in earlier versions, the hapless emissary is someone other than Chunyu Kun; moreover, he is spared because he confesses *sincerely*.[8] Good things come to those who freely admit their guilt. The present text, however, reconfigures the dynamics by inserting the shifty Chunyu Kun as the protagonist and having the narrator state explicitly that he "invented a fraudulent excuse" (*zaozha chengci*). Now the moral is quite different: do not to be a dupe like the King of Chu, who not only rewards Chunyu richly, but also pronounces him "trustworthy" (*xin*)—precisely what a man-of-service *should* be, and the very opposite of what he is.

In later centuries, such themes were expanded into what Alan J. Berkowitz has called "reclusion as a ruse"—that is, conspicuously declining offers of employment to raise one's market value.[9] The more such men pretended not to be motivated by rank and salary, the more mercenary they really were. Even Confucius is said to have held out for the right price (*Analects* 9.13). To be sure, he is usually

義，此豈有異黃白黑、甘苦之別者哉？

[*MZJG* 711–718]

N.B. Straight underline indicates the use of repetitive patterning; wavy underline the use of parallel phrasing therein. For a discussion on repetitive and parallel patterning, ☛ C1.1–4 and C1.6–7.

史記•滑稽列傳（摘錄）

昔者，齊王使淳于髡獻鵠於楚。出邑門，道飛其鵠，徒揭空籠，造詐成辭，往見楚王曰："齊王使臣來獻鵠，過於水上，不忍鵠之渴，出而飲之，去我飛亡。吾欲刺腹絞頸而死。恐人之議吾王以鳥獸之故令士自傷殺也。鵠，毛物，多相類者，吾欲買而代之，是不信而欺吾王也。欲赴佗國奔亡，痛吾兩主使不通。故來服過，叩頭受罪大王。"

楚王曰："善，齊王有信士若此哉！"厚賜之，財倍鵠在也。

[*SKK* 126.25]

thought to have meant this metaphorically, but not all men-of-service were so pure and incorrupt.

Paul R. Goldin

NOTES

1. "It is not from the benevolence of the butcher, the brewer, or the baker that we expect our dinner, but from their regard to their own interest" (*An Inquiry into the Nature and Causes of the Wealth of Nations*, I.2). Similar observations can be found in *Shenzi* and *Han Feizi*.

2. This view does not cohere with what we know of Xunzi's philosophy from the extant text attributed to him; rather, it sounds like Han Fei, whom we will meet in the next section.

3. A parallel account appears in *Huainanzi* (*HNZJS* 1313).

4. The story of Yan Chu (late-fourth century BCE) in *Zhanguo ce* (*ZGCJZ* 639–641) is another famous text highlighting the need for competent ministers.

5. This is not the only criticism of the Vertical and Horizontal Alliances in *Han Feizi*. In a different chapter, the objection is that "mere words are not the means to achieve order" (*HFZXJZ* 1159).

6. Cf. Jens Østergård Petersen, "What's in a Name? On the Sources Concerning Sun Wu," *Asia Major* (3rd series) 5, no. 1 (1992): 28.

7. The core essays in *Mozi* are each presented in three distinct versions. This is the third of the three essays titled "The Will of Heaven."

8. See Giulia Baccini, "Narrative Variation and Motif Adaptation in Ancient Anecdotal Lore: A Perspective on the Bird-Gift Story in Early and Early Medieval Chinese Sources," *Archiv Orientální* 82, no. 2 (2014): esp. 299–305.

9. Alan J. Berkowitz, *Patterns of Disengagement: The Practice and Portrayal of Reclusion in Early Medieval China* (Stanford, CA: Stanford University Press, 2000), 118 and 136–138.

SUGGESTED READING

ENGLISH

Baccini, Giulia. "Narrative Variation and Motif Adaptation in Ancient Anecdotal Lore: A Perspective on the Bird-Gift Story in Early and Early Medieval Chinese Sources." *Archiv Orientální* 82, no. 2 (2014): 297–315.

Berkowitz, Alan J. *Patterns of Disengagement: The Practice and Portrayal of Reclusion in Early Medieval China*. Stanford, CA: Stanford University Press, 2000.

Crump, J. I., trans., *Chan-kuo ts'e*. Rev. ed. Ann Arbor: Center for Chinese Studies, University of Michigan, 1996.

Goldin, Paul R., ed. *Dao Companion to the Philosophy of Han Fei*. Dordrecht, Netherlands: Springer, 2013.

Meyer, Andrew. "Reading 'Sunzi' as a Master." *Asia Major* (3rd series) 30, no. 1 (2017): 1–24.

Petersen, Jens Østergård. "What's in a Name? On the Sources Concerning Sun Wu." *Asia Major* (3rd series) 5, no. 1 (1992): 1–31.

Pines, Yuri. *Envisioning Eternal Empire: Chinese Political Thought of the Warring States Era*. Honolulu: University of Hawai'i Press, 2009.

Weingarten, Oliver. "Chunyu Kun: Motifs, Narratives, and Personas in Early Chinese Anecdotal Literature." *Journal of the Royal Asiatic Society* 27, no. 3 (2017): 501–521.

CHINESE

He Jin 何晉. *Zhanguo ce yanjiu* 戰國策研究 (*Studies on* Stratagems of the Warring States). Beijing: Beijing daxue chubanshe, 2001.

Huang Xinguang 黃新光. "Tang Ju qiren kaobian" 唐雎其人考辨 ("An Examination of the Personage Tang Ju"). *Jiangxi daxue xuebao (Zhexue shehui kexue ban)* 江西大學學報 (哲學社

會科學版) (*Journal of Jiangxi University: Philosophy and Social Sciences Edition*), no. 3 (1985): 76–78.

Li Ling 李零. Sunzi *shisan pian zonghe yanjiu* 《孫子》十三篇綜合研究 (*An Integrated Study of the Thirteen Chapters of* Sunzi). Beijing: Zhonghua shuju, 2006.

Meng Xiangcai 孟祥才. *Guji dashi Chunyu Kun yu Dongfang Shuo* 滑稽大師淳于髡與東方朔 (*The Master Jesters Chunyu Kun and Dongfang Shuo*). Qilu lishi wenhua congshu. Ji'nan: Shandong wenyi chubanshe, 2004.

Zheng Jiewen 鄭傑文. *Zhongguo Moxue tongshi* 中國墨學通史 (*A Comprehensive History of Chinese Studies on Mozi*). Beijing: Renmin chubanshe, 2006.

PART II

The Han Dynasty and the Six Dynasties

Han Historical Prose

Sima Qian and the *Grand Scribe's Records* (*Shiji*)

The Han dynasty (206 BCE–220 CE) marks the beginning of an emphasis on the literary in the writing of history. It is the era in which the art of storytelling played a major role in how Chinese histories were conceived and written, as well as how we understand that early history today. The two major historical works of the period—Sima Qian's (ca. 145–ca. 86 BCE) *Grand Scribe's Records* (*Shiji*; hereafter *Records*) and Ban Gu's (32–92) *History of the Han* (*Han shu*)—are among the largest texts in early Chinese historiography, with the *Records* containing 526,500 characters and the *History of the Han* containing roughly 800,000. Spanning 2,500 years from the legendary Yellow Emperor through Emperor Wu of the Han (r. 141–87 BCE), the *Records* presented a general history that incorporated portions of many earlier texts, such as the *Book of Documents* (*Shangshu*), *Zuo Tradition* (*Zuozhuan*), and *Discourses of the States* (*Guoyu*) (☞ chap. 1, 2). With his powerful style and skillful narration, Sima Qian's version of these borrowed texts came to eclipse their sources. Called "the Yellow River of books" by Wang Chong (27–ca. 97), the *Records* still flows in our own times, a living source across China as one of the most popular works among Chinese readers of all ages and levels of education. It remains one of the two most important universal Chinese histories (along with Sima Guang's [1019–1086] *Zizhi tongjian*) and, through the fourteen chapters selected for the influential anthology *The Essential Collection of Ancient-Style Prose* (*Guwen guanzhi*, 1695 CE), it continues to shape modern thinking about classical Chinese prose.

Although clear traces of biographical writing appear in earlier works like the *Zuo Tradition* (☞chap. 2), the biographical genre formally began with Sima Qian's *liezhuan*, or "arranged traditions." The popularity of these biographies was enhanced by the inclusion of colorful subjects—knights-errant, ruthless officials, and assassin-retainers—in chapters that Sima Qian called "categorical biographies" or "prosopographies" (*leizhuan*). Although Ban Gu's *History of the Han* (posthumously completed with the help of several family members about 100 CE) took the *Records* as its major source for the early Han, Ban Gu deplored the repetition and loose liveliness of the *Records'* accounts and aimed for compactness and structure in his own writing. Ban Gu reorganized much of the material he borrowed from Sima Qian, adding original material from documents apparently not available to Sima Qian. The two works differ as well in their conception of history, especially as it pertains to Han rulers: Sima Qian is much more critical than

Ban Gu not only of his own ruler, Emperor Wu, but also of earlier Han emperors and kings. While Ban Gu's *History of the Han* became the model for the twenty-some dynastic histories that would follow over the next two millennia, Sima Qian's text imposed a perspective on historical events through 100 BCE that in large part still holds today. Moreover, the *Records'* prose style that so troubled Ban Gu, would go on to have a profound influence on subsequent biographical writings, both historical and literary (☞ chap. 13).

The *Records* was actually conceived by Sima Qian's father, Sima Tan (d. 110 BCE), during the last decades of the second century BCE and was finished by Sima Qian (145–ca. 87 BCE) during the first decade of the first century BCE.[1] Sima Qian was born in Hancheng roughly 130 miles northeast of the Han capital at Xi'an. Although there is no detailed account of his life, he probably spent his childhood and youth at home before moving to the capital. There, he continued his studies and would go on to travel extensively in his twenties and thirties. During this period, he became a palace gentleman (*langzhong*) serving Emperor Wu. In 111 BCE, he was sent as imperial envoy to inspect and pacify local tribes in what is now Sichuan and Yunnan. All of these experiences would influence his later work on the *Records*.

Upon Sima Tan's death in 110 BCE, Sima Qian became the "prefect of the grand scribes" (*taishiling*) and was entrusted with his father's project to complete an extensive history. Over the following decade, this became the *Grand Scribe's Records*—despite the tragedy of his later years. When Sima Qian defended a young general named Li Ling who had surrendered to the Xiongnu (Han arch-enemy), Emperor Wu believed Sima Qian was merely backing a friend and gave him over to the legal authorities. First sentenced to death, the decision was commuted, and he eventually was castrated and allowed to recover and to complete his work on the *Records*.

The *Records* consists of 130 chapters divided into five sections: twelve annals (*benji*), tracing in chronological order the rulers from earliest antiquity down to Sima Qian's time; eight chronological tables (*nianbiao*) that display events of each year across the various political entities that made up China throughout this early period, thereby juxtaposing events occurring in more than one state; ten treatises (*shu*), historical accounts of subjects such as "music," "ritual," or "geography"; thirty hereditary houses (*shijia*), illustrating the development of important families and states; and seventy memoirs or biographies (*liezhuan*, literally "arranged traditions"), presenting interpretive accounts of more than one hundred individuals often in pairs or groups. It is these seventy chapters, because of their style as well as their structure, which would become the model for later biographical writing (☞ chap. 13). The *Records* drew on both the oral tradition and more than one hundred known written sources. Sima Qian selected passages from his written sources carefully, rewriting narratives to suit his purposes. Because composition of the *Records* was not part of Sima Qian's official duties and thus the time he had to devote to it was limited, the chapters that adhere more closely to earlier sources may have been drafted in part by assistants.

The following selections, from one of the most popular biographical chapters, the "assassin-retainers" (*Cike liezhuan*), demonstrate some of the narrative strengths of the *Records* that have made it such an enduring and relevant feature of Chinese culture: namely, its use of dialogue to augment the narrative and bring individuals to life, and its interspersing of vivid scenes that slow the narrative pace and allow readers to visualize key events. In addition to ranking among the most famous, this chapter is also one of the most controversial. The controversy extends to the provenance of three biographies in this chapter—those of Bi Yurang, Nie Zheng, and Jing Ke. All three were until recent times presumed to have been based on parallel accounts in an early version of the text known today as the *Stratagems of the Warring States* (*Zhanguoce*; hereafter *Stratagems*; ☛ chap. 5). Modern scholars believe, however, that the relationship between the *Stratagems* and the *Records* is more complicated and that at the very least this account of Jing Ke in the *Records* is primary. A second point of controversy was the subject matter of these biographies. Beginning with Ban Gu, later scholars would criticize Sima Qian for focusing attention on a group of men they felt deserved only criticism and condemnation. Yet the fame and popularity of these narratives of the five assassin-retainers persist because they are among the best constructed and most compelling stories in the *Records*. Sima Qian explains why he compiled the chapter by highlighting the achievements of two of his subjects:

> Lu captured its lands with Caozi's sword,
> [Duke Jing of Qi] understood to keep his word;
> Yurang bound by duty could not act disloyally,
> Thus, I composed the "Biographies of the Assassin-Retainers, Number 26"

曹子匕首，魯獲其田，齊明其信；豫讓義不為二心。作刺客列傳第二十六。

[*SJ* 10:130.3315]

The biographies of these two, along with that of Jing Ke, will serve as exemplary narratives to demonstrate Sima Qian's literary skill.[2] The account of Cao Mo opens the chapter:

C6.1 *Grand Scribe's Records*, "Biographies of the Assassin-Retainers, Cao Mo"

史記・刺客列傳・曹沫

Cao Mo was a native of Lu. By means of his courage and strength he gained service with Duke Zhuang of Lu (r. 693–662 BCE). Duke Zhuang was fond of displays of strength. Cao Mo became a commander of Lu and fought against Qi, three times retreating in defeat. Duke Zhuang of Lu was afraid and then offered the territory of Suiyi to make peace, but he again allowed Cao Mo to be a commander.

曹沫者，魯人也，以勇力事魯莊公。莊公好力。曹沫為魯將，與齊戰，三敗北。魯莊公懼，乃獻遂邑之地以和。猶復以為將。

Duke Huan of Qi consented to meet with Lu at Ke and make an oath of alliance. When Duke Huan and Duke Zhuang had sworn the oath on the altar mound, Cao Mo, sword in hand, moved to threaten Duke Huan of Qi. When none of the duke's attendants dared move, [Duke Huan's adviser]

齊桓公許與魯會于柯而盟。桓公與莊公既盟於壇上，曹沫執匕首

劫齊桓公，桓公左右莫
敢動，而問曰：「子將
何欲？」曹沫曰：「齊
強魯弱，而大國侵魯亦
甚矣。今魯城壞即壓齊
境，君其圖之。」公乃
許盡歸魯之侵地. 既已
言，曹沫投其匕首，下
壇，北面就群臣之位，
顏色不變，辭令如故.
桓公怒，欲倍其約。管
仲曰：「不可。夫貪小
利以自快，棄信於諸
侯，失天下之援，不如
與之。」於是桓公乃遂
割魯侵地，曹沫三戰所
亡地盡復予魯。

[SJ 8:86.2515–2516]

Guan Zhong asked, "What do you want?"[1] Cao Mo said, "Qi is strong and Lu is weak, but your great state has gone too far in invading Lu! If the walls of Lu's capital were now to fall, they would fall on our border with Qi. Would that My Lord consider that!" Duke Huan then promised to return all the territory he had invaded to Lu. When the duke had finished speaking, Cao Mo threw his sword aside, came down from the mound, faced north, and took his place among the assembled vassals. His expression did not change and his speech was as before.

Duke Huan was angry and wanted to break the agreement. Guan Zhong said, "That is not permissible. If in your greed you find delight in small profit, you will cast away the trust of the other lords and lose the support of the world. It would be better to give it to them."

Only at this point did Duke Huan finally cede to Lu the territory he had invaded, returning to Lu all the territory Cao Mo had lost in three battles.

The basic structural element used here is the anecdote relating how Cao Mo regains the territory he had previously lost through poor tactics and excessive bravado. The narrative begins, however, with the backstory of how Cao Mo came to serve Duke Zhuang and how the lands were lost. The main text focuses on the "covenant" (*meng*) in which an agreement is made on a new allocation of territory followed by both dukes swearing an oath in confirmation. The Han-dynasty reader would know that Duke Huan was at this time considered the hegemon or overlord (*ba*) and that he and his state of Qi were recognized by other state rulers as the most powerful. Guan Zhong was his main adviser and was credited with much of Duke Huan's success. Cao Mo is portrayed not only as a man of daring, but also as a strategist who seized the moment to alter the history of Lu. In other early texts, Cao Mo (also known as Cao Gui) advises Duke Zhuang on battle strategy. Here his eloquence can be seen in his hyperbolic depiction of Qi's borders as virtually under the walls of the capital city of Lu. His courage is also on display when, after throwing away his sword and facing possible execution by Duke Huan's entourage, his expression and speech remain unchanged. The entire story in turn prefigures a narrative told in Sima Qian's biography of Confucius in which a minister of Qi tries unsuccessfully to coerce Duke Ding of Lu but is thwarted by Confucius who then also regains lost territory from Qi. Cao Mo's threatening Duke Huan is not the result of an assassination plot, but rather is a spontaneous reaction to the situation, and this has led some traditional scholars to decry Sima Qian's decision to place Cao Mo in this chapter.

Another of the five men depicted in this chapter is Bi Yurang who had served several of the powerful Jin clans but wound up a favorite retainer of the earl of Zhi. A leader of other clans against the Zhaos, the earl, in a drunken state, had even

---

[1] The speaker could also be Duke Huan, but another early text (*Gongyang Tradition* [*Gongyang zhuan*]) suggests it was Guan Zhong who spoke.

poured wine onto the head of the viscount of Zhao. The *Records'* account begins after the viscount defeats the earl in 455 BCE, killing him in battle:

C6.2 *Grand Scribe's Records*, "Biographies of the Assassin-Retainers, Yurang"

Yurang was a native of Jin.[1] Formerly he had served the Fan and Zhonghang clans,[2] but found no means to gain recognition. He left and served the Earl of Zhi.[3] The Earl of Zhi treated him with respect and favor. When the Earl of Zhi attacked Viscount Xiang of Zhao,[4] Viscount Xiang plotted together with Han and Wei to destroy the Earl of Zhi. After they had destroyed the Earl of Zhi, they divided his land three ways.[5] Viscount Xiang bore great resentment for the Earl of Zhi, lacquered his skull and used it as a drinking vessel.

Yurang escaped into the mountains and said, "Alas, a knight will die for one who recognizes his worth, a woman will make herself beautiful for one who delights in her. Now the Earl of Zhi recognized me and I must seek revenge on his enemy for him before I die. In this way after I die my soul will not suffer from shame." Then he changed his name, passed himself off as a convict-laborer, and entered the [viscount's] residence to plaster the privy. Under his sleeve he carried a sword, intending to use it to stab Viscount Xiang. When Viscount Xiang went to the privy, he felt uneasy and when he had the person who was plastering the privy seized and questioned, it turned out to be Yurang, carrying a sword within his clothes. He said, "I intended to avenge the Earl of Zhi's enemy." The viscount's attendants wanted to execute him, but Viscount Xiang said, "This is a righteous warrior. I will simply be careful to avoid him. Moreover, when the Earl of Zhi perished he had no descendants, yet his vassal intends to avenge his enemy. This is one of the worthiest men in the world!" In the end, he released Yurang and sent him away.

After a short while Yurang lacquered his body so as to produce carbuncles on his skin and swallowed charcoal to hoarsen his voice. Having rendered his appearance unrecognizable, he went begging in the marketplace. His wife did not recognize him. Along the way he saw his friend and his friend recognized him: "Aren't you Yurang?" "I am."

His friend wept for him and said, "With your talent, sir, you could have pledged yourself and served Viscount Xiang. Viscount Xiang would indeed have become a close favorite. Once you were a close favorite, then you could have done as you wished. Wouldn't [that] have been easy? Then why have you crippled your body and afflicted your frame? Isn't it more difficult to seek revenge through these means?" Yurang replied, "Once one has pledged

---

[1] Although in the *Records* he is known simply as Yurang, according to the account of Yurang in the *Stratagems of the Warring States* (*Zhanguoce*), Yurang had the lineage name (*shi*) Bi and he was the grandson of Bi Yang.

[2] Two of the six powerful clans who were the de facto rules of Jin in the early fifth century BCE.

[3] This was Xun Yao, a descendent of the founder of the Zhi Clan, Xun Shou.

[4] This was Zhao Wuxu, the leader of the Zhao Clan from 475–425 BCE.

[5] Thus the states of Zhao, Han and Wei were established.

史記・刺客列傳・豫讓

豫讓者，晉人也，故嘗事范氏及中行氏，而無所知名。去而事智伯，智伯甚尊寵之。及智伯伐趙襄子，趙襄子與韓、魏合謀滅智伯，滅智伯之後而三分其地。趙襄子最怨智伯，漆其頭以為飲器。豫讓遁逃山中，曰："嗟乎！士為知己者死，女為說己者容。今智伯知我，我必為報讎而死，以報智伯，則吾魂魄不愧矣。"乃變名姓為刑人，入宮塗廁，中挾匕首，欲以刺襄子。襄子如廁，心動，執問塗廁之刑人，則豫讓，內持刀兵，曰："欲為智伯報仇！"左右欲誅之。襄子曰："彼義人也，吾謹避之耳。且智伯亡無後，而其臣欲為報仇，此天下之賢人也。"卒釋去之。

居頃之，豫讓又漆身為厲，吞炭為啞，使形狀不可知，行乞於市。其妻不識也。行見其友，其友識之，曰："汝非豫讓邪？"曰："我是也。"其友為泣曰："以子之才，委質而臣事襄子，襄子必近幸子。近幸子，乃為所欲，顧不易邪？何乃殘身苦形，欲以求報襄子，不亦難乎！"豫讓曰："既已委質臣事人，而求殺之，是懷二心以事其君也。且吾所

為者極難耳！然所以為
此者，將以愧天下後世
之為人臣懷二心以事其
君者也。”

　　既去，頃之，襄子
當出，豫讓伏於所當過
之橋下。襄子至橋，馬
驚，襄子曰："此必是
豫讓也。”使人間之，
果豫讓也。於是襄子乃
數豫讓曰："子不嘗事
范、中行氏乎？智伯盡
滅之，而子不為報讎，
而反委質臣於智伯。智
伯亦已死矣，而子獨何
以為之報讎之深也？”
豫讓曰："臣事范、中
行氏，范、中行氏皆眾
人遇我，我故眾人報
之。至於智伯，國士遇
我，我故國士報之。”
襄子喟然歎息而泣
曰："嗟乎豫子！子之
為智伯，名既成矣，而
寡人赦子，亦已足矣。
子其自為計，寡人不復
釋子！”使兵圍之。豫
讓曰："臣聞明主不掩
人之美，而忠臣有死名
之義。前君已寬赦臣，
天下莫不稱君之賢。今
日之事，臣固伏誅，然
願請君之衣而擊之，焉
以致報讎之意，則雖死
不恨。非所敢望也，敢
布腹心！”於是襄子大
義之，乃使使持衣與豫
讓。豫讓拔劍三躍而擊
之，曰："吾可以下報
智伯矣！”遂伏劍自
殺。死之日，趙國志士
聞之，皆為涕泣。

[*SJ* 8:86.2519–2521]

oneself and served someone as a vassal, if one seeks to kill him, this would be serving one lord with loyalty to another.[6] What I have done was most difficult! But the reason I have done it is to shame those of later generations who serve as vassals to one lord but with loyalty to another."

A short while after his friend left, Viscount Xiang was about to leave his residence. Yurang hid under the bridge he would cross. When Viscount Xiang reached the bridge, his horse shied and Viscount Xiang said, "This must be Yurang." He sent someone to question him and it was as he expected Yurang. Only then did enumerate Yurang's faults: "Didn't you serve the Fan and Zhonghang clans? The Earl of Zhi wiped them completely out. Yet you did not seek revenge on his enemies. On the contrary, you pledged yourself as a vassal to the Earl of Zhi. Now the Earl of Zhi has also died. Why are you so determined to only seek revenge on *his* enemy?"

Yurang said, "I served the Fan and Zhonghang as a vassal and the Fan and Zhonghan treated me as an ordinary man. Thus I repaid them as an ordinary man would. As for the Earl of Zhi, he treated me as one of the knights of his state. Thus I repay him as a knight of the state would."

Viscount Xiang heaved a deep sigh, wept, and said: "Ah, Master Yu, in what you have done for the Earl of Zhi you have already made your name! But when I pardoned you before, that was indeed enough. Plan how you wish to die—I will not release you again." He had his soldiers surround him. Yurang said, "Your servant has heard that an enlightened ruler does not obscure the good deeds of a man and a loyal vassal has a duty to die for his good name. My Lord has already generously pardoned me before and the world praised you as a worthy man. For today's affair, I naturally accept the punishment of death, but I would request to stab at your coat to satisfy my desire to seek revenge on my enemy in this way. Then even though I die, I will have no regrets. I don't dare to hope for this, but only to lay out my innermost desire."

At this Viscount Xiang saw him as a greatly righteous man and had a man take his coat and give it to Yurang. Yurang drew his sword and leapt three times,[7] striking the coat, and said, "I can now go down [to the Yellow Springs] and report to the Earl of Zhi!" In the end he fell on his sword and died. On the day he died, when the men of high ideals of the state of Zhao heard of it they all wept for him.

Bi Yurang is mentioned in a number of pre-Qin and Han texts, but Sima Qian's presumed source for this tale was the *Stratagems* (➤ chap. 5), despite several differences between the accounts. Sima Qian neglects to mention Yurang's lineage name (Bi) and depicts his self-mutilation differently (in the *Stratagems*, he obliterates his hair and eyebrows). The *Stratagems* narrative has Yurang eating charcoal only after

---

[6] In other words, he could not pledge himself to Viscount Xiang and then kill him.

[7] Leaping into the air was a part of the traditional funeral ritual: "Beating the breast (by women) and leaping (by men) are extreme expressions of grief" ("Tangong, xia," *Liji*).

his wife comments that she still recognizes his voice through his changed appearance—this detection is not in the *Records* account. Finally, Yurang's response to his friend is so abbreviated in the *Records* that the logic of his argument becomes difficult to follow. Such abridgment is not infrequent in Sima Qian's borrowings from earlier texts and has been pointed out by traditional scholars such as Fang Bao (1668–1749; in his "Shu 'Cike liezhuan' hou"). These minor variations, and passages like the following from the preface of the *Spring and Autumn Annals of Master Lü* (*Lüshi chunqiu*), suggest that oral versions of the story were widely circulated and freely modified by the tellers:

> Once when Viscount Xiang of Zhao was roaming through his park, as he reached the bridge his horses stopped and would not proceed. Qing Ping inspected the chariot. Viscount Xiang said, "Go look under the bridge. Perhaps there is a man there." Qing Ping went to look under the bridge and found Yurang bent down and drenched, looking like a dead man. Cursing Qing Ping he said, "Be gone! It is your leader with whom I have business!" Qing Ping said, "When young, we were friends. But now you have embarked on this great task; were I to discuss it, I would be forsaking the Dao of mutual friendship. You intend to prey on my lord. Were I to say nothing, I would be forsaking the Dao of the vassal. In my situation only death is possible." With that he left and committed suicide.

> [*LSCQXJS* 655]

What are we to make of such extreme behavior? Did Sima Qian condone Yurang's actions? Regardless of his attitude toward Yurang or the nature of his sources, Sima Qian crafted his story in such a way that we can understand—or at least to recognize—Yurang's motivation through his own words: "A knight will die for one who recognized his worth." This recognition (*zhi*) is indeed a leitmotif running through the chapter's five biographies.

We turn now to the biography of Jing Ke, which begins:

C6.3 *Grand Scribe's Records*, "Biographies of the Assassin-Retainers, Jing Ke"

史記•刺客列傳•荊軻

This Jing Ke was a native of Wei. His ancestors were natives of Qi, then moved to Wei. The natives of Wei referred to him as Excellency Qing. Then he went to Yan and the natives of Yan referred to him as Excellency Jing.

荊軻者，衛人也。其先乃齊人，徙於衛，衛人謂之慶卿。而之燕，燕人謂之荊卿。

This account of Jing Ke has three major sections not found in the *Stratagems*: (1) the background of Jing Ke at the start of the text; (2) the three anecdotes describing Jing Ke's meetings with Ge Nie, Lu Goujian, and Gao Jianli; and (3) the final section in which Gao Jianli attempts to kill the first emperor of Qin. Sima Qian may have learned about Jing Ke's ancestry during his travels as a young man, perhaps hearing versions of the story in what was formerly Wei and Yan—where Jing Ke's name would have varied because of differences in dialect.

荊卿好讀書擊劍，以
術說衛元君，衛元君
不用。其後秦伐魏，
置東郡，徙衛元君之
支屬於野王。　荊軻嘗
游過榆次，與蓋聶論
劍，蓋聶怒而目之。荊
軻出，人或言復召荊
卿。蓋聶曰：「曩者吾
與論劍有不稱者，吾目
之；試往，是宜去，不
敢留。」　使使往之主
人，荊卿則已駕而去榆
次矣。使者還報，蓋聶
曰：」固去也，吾曩者
目攝之！」

Excellency Jing loved reading documents and swordplay.[1] He tried to persuade before Lord Yuan of Wei[2] on the art [of politics], but Lord Yuan did not use [his ideas]. Later, Qin attacked Wei, established its Eastern Commandery, and moved the subordinates of Lord Yuan of Wei to Yewang.

During his wanderings,[3] Jing Ke once stopped in Yuci [in Zhao]. He discussed swordsmanship with Ge Nie. Ge Nie became angry and glared at him. Jing Ke went out. Among the people someone suggested summoning His Excellency Jing again. Ge Nie said, "When I debated swordsmanship with him just now, there were some things that displeased me and I glared at him. Try to go after him; in this situation he must have left. He wouldn't have dared stay!" He sent a messenger to go to [Jing Ke's] host, but Excellency Jing had already harnessed his horses and left Yuci. When the messenger returned to report, Ge Nie said, "Of course he left. I stared him down just now."

Ge Nie whom Jing Ke met in Zhao, is probably Kuaikui—that is, Sima Qian's ancestor Sima Kuaikui—as argued in the commentary on the name Kuaikui in Sima Qian's "Postface by the Grand Scribe." The ancient pronunciations of the characters for Ge Nie and Kuaikui were similar. This reading well suits a chapter in which changing appearances (Yurang and Gao Jianli when he was in Songzi) and names (Jing Ke and Gao Jianli) feature prominently.

荊軻游於邯鄲，魯句踐
與荊軻博，爭道，魯句
踐怒而叱之，荊軻嘿而
逃去，遂不復會。

　荊軻既至燕，愛燕
之狗屠及善擊筑者高漸
離。荊軻嗜酒，日與
狗屠及高漸離飲於燕
市，酒酣以往，高漸離
擊筑，荊軻和而歌於市
中，相樂也，已而相
泣，旁若無人者。荊軻
雖游於酒人乎，然其為
人沈深好書；其所游諸
侯，盡與其賢豪長者相
結。其之燕，燕之處士
田光先生亦善待之，知
其非庸人也。

Jing Ke traveled to the city of Handan. Lu Goujian played *liubo*[4] with Jing Ke and contended for lanes [on the board]. Lu Goujian became angry and shouted at him. Jing Ke without saying a word then slipped away and never met with him again.

Having reached Yan, Jing Ke became fond of Gao Jianli, a dog butcher and a skilled *zhu* player. Jing Ke indulged himself in drink, everyday drinking with the dog butchers and Gao Jianli in the marketplace of Yan. After they were well into their cups, Gao Jianli would strike his *zhu* and Jing Ke would sing in harmony in the midst of the marketplace, enjoying themselves. After a while they wept together as if there was no one around.[5] Although Jing Ke associated with drinkers, he was by nature contemplative and fond of documents. Among those [states of the] feudal lords with whom he associated, he established ties to all the worthy, powerful and respected men. When he went to

---

[1] The language here is almost the same used to depict Sima Xiangru in his biography (*SJ* 117.2999).

[2] Lord Yuan (r. 252–230 BCE) was the son-in-law of King Anxi of Wei (r. 276–243 BCE). At this time, Wei was a satellite of Wei and had sent him to reside in Puyang (the Wei capital) calling him a "lord." When Qin took the eastern part of Wei in 241 BCE, they moved Lord Yuan to Yewang County (thirty miles northeast of modern Luoyang).

[3] *You*, "wanderings," could suggest that he was looking for a patron (as in *congyou*).

[4] *Liubo* was a game like chess played on a board resembling a sundial and containing many astrological symbols; see Armin Selbitschka, "A Tricky Game: A Re-evalution of Liubo 六博 Based on Archaeological and Textual Evidence," *Oriens extremus* 55 (2016): 105–66.

[5] Perhaps the singing and weeping were intended to draw attention.

Yan, Venerable Tian Guang, an untried scholar of Yan, also treated him well, recognizing that he was not an ordinary fellow.

These anecdotes and another on Gao Jianli toward the end of the chapter do not appear in any other early text and resemble other early short narratives that all probably derive from oral sources. Jing Ke appears, but he is not really the protagonist in any of these scenes. Aside from their narrative appeal, the practice of stringing anecdotes together, especially at the beginning of a chapter, was one of Sima Qian's standard methods in constructing a biography. These three vignettes of Jing Ke's encounters lend a shading to his character that have puzzled later readers, because they seem to portray him as lacking courage. Yet Sima Qian also depicts a famous Han general, Han Xin, as one who avoided conflict in his youth, but by biding his time later won many battles. Sima Qian shows both men to be conflicted. Jing Ke was, after all, someone who was fond of both books and swords.

After some time had passed, it happened that Dan, the Heir of Yan who had been a hostage in Qin, fled back to Yan.[6] Dan, the Heir of Yan, had [also] once been a hostage in Zhao. Zheng, the King of Qin,[7] was born in Zhao, and in his youth had been very friendly with Dan. When Zheng was enthroned as king, Dan was a hostage in Qin. But the King of Qin treated him badly, [and] thus he bore resentment and fled [Qin], returning home. After his return, he sought a way to retaliate against the King of Qin, but his state was small and his strength insufficient. After this, Qin daily sent troops east of the mountains, attacking Qi, Chu, and Three Jin, gradually nibbling away at the feudal lords. When they were about to reach Yan, the Lord of Yan and his vassals all feared the arrival of disaster. The Heir Dan was dismayed and questioned his tutor Ju Wu.[8]

Wu replied, "Qin's lands cover the world and its majesty threatens the clans of Han, Wei, and Zhao. To the north it has the strongholds of Ganquan and Gukou, to the south the fertility of the Jing and Wei [river valleys]; it wields the wealth of Ba and Han; to the right[9] it has the mountains of Long and Shu, and to the left the redoubts of the Pass and Xiao [Mountain]. Its people are numerous, its knights fierce, and it has a surplus of weapons and armor. Should an opportunity for its ambitions arise, there would be no secure place south of the Long Wall or north of the Yi River. How could you wish to rub its dragon-like scales the wrong way just because of your resentment at being humiliated?"

"Then what other way is there?" said Dan. 'Let me withdraw and consider it," he replied.

[6] He returned to Yan in 232 BCE. This passage marks the beginning of the *Stratagems* parallel narrative.

[7] That is, the future First Emperor of Qin.

[8] The *Stratagems* parallel text takes up the narrative from here.

[9] At this time Chinese maps were oriented with South on top, so that "right" referred to the West.

居頃之，會燕太子丹質秦亡歸燕。燕太子丹者，故嘗質於趙，而秦王政生於趙，其少時與丹驩。及政立為秦王，而丹質於秦。秦王之遇燕太子丹不善，故丹怨而亡歸。歸而求為報秦王者，國小，力不能。其後秦日出兵山東以伐齊、楚、三晉，稍蠶食諸侯，且至於燕，燕君臣皆恐禍之至。太子丹患之，問其傅鞠武。

武對曰：「秦地遍天下，威脅韓、魏、趙氏，北有甘泉、谷口之固，南有涇、渭之沃，擅巴、漢之饒，右隴、蜀之山，左關、殽之險，民眾而士厲，兵革有餘。意有所出，則長城之南，易水以北，未有所定也。奈何以見陵之怨，欲批其逆鱗哉！」丹曰：「然則何由？」對曰：「請入圖之。」

居有閒，秦將樊於期得
罪於秦王，亡之燕，
太子受而舍之。鞠武諫
曰：「不可。夫以秦王
之暴而積怒於燕，足為
寒心，又況聞樊將軍之
所在乎？是謂'委肉當
餓虎之蹊'也，禍必不
振矣！雖有管、晏，不
能為之謀也。願太子疾
遣樊將軍入匈奴以滅
口。請西約三晉，南連
齊、楚，北購於單于，
其後迺可圖也。」

太子曰：「太傅之計，
曠日彌久，心惽然，恐
不能須臾。且非獨於此
也，夫樊將軍窮困於天
下，歸身於丹，丹終不
以迫於彊秦而棄所哀憐
之交，置之匈奴，是
固丹命卒之時也。願太
傅更慮之。」鞠武曰：
「夫行危欲求安，造
禍而求福，計淺而怨
深，連結一人之後交，
不顧國家之大害，此
所謂'資怨而助禍'
矣。夫以鴻毛燎於爐炭
之上，必無事矣。且
以鵰鷙之秦，行怨暴之
怒，豈足道哉！燕有田
光先生，其為人智深而
勇沈，可與謀。」太子
曰：「願因太傅而得交
於田先生，可乎？」鞠
武曰：「敬諾。」出見
田先生，道「太子願圖
國事於先生也」。田
光曰：「敬奉教。」
乃造焉。

After some time had passed, the Qin general Fan Wuji offended the King of Qin and fled to Yan. The Heir took him in and put him in a guesthouse. Ju Wu admonished the Heir:

"This won't do! The King of Qin's tyranny and accumulated anger toward Yan are enough to chill the heart. How much more will this be so when he hears where General Fan is? This is called "throwing down meat to block a hungry tiger's path." Such a disaster would be beyond remedy. Even if you had Guan Zhong and Yan Ying,[10] they could devise no plans for you! I beg you, Heir, quickly dispatch General Fan to the Xiongnu to eliminate any pretexts [for Qin to attack]. I ask you to form an alliance with the Three Jin to the west, join in coalition with Qi and Chu to the south, and come to terms with the Chanyu[11] in the north; only after this can plans be laid."

The Heir said, "The Grand Tutor's plan would take much time. My mind is confused and, I cannot wait even a moment. But the problem does not lie only in this. Now, General Fan, finding himself in dire straits throughout the entire world, has turned to me. I will never abandon an acquaintance whom I love and pity because I am pressed by mighty Qin. The day I settle him among the Xiongnu, this is surely the day I die. I hope that you might consider this once more, Grand Tutor."

Ju Wu said, "To risk hazard in pursuit of safety, to invite disaster in pursuit of good fortune, to make shallow plans yet harbor profound resentment, to maintain a newly formed friendship with a single man yet ignore a great threat to the royal family and state, this is what is known as 'feeding resentment and aiding disaster'! If you heat a swan feather over stove coals, it will surely soon disappear. Moreover, [what would happen] if you allow that bird of prey, Qin, to vent its cruel and resentful anger [on us]. Yan has a Venerable Tian Guang, a man of deep wisdom and profound courage. You can make plans with him."

The Heir said, "I hope I might make the acquaintance of the Venerable Tian through you, Grand Tutor. Is this possible?"

Ju Wu replied, "I shall respectfully comply." He left and met with the Venerable Tian, telling him, "The Heir hopes to plan affairs of state with you, Venerable Sir."

"I respectfully receive your instructions," said Tian Guang, and then paid a visit to him [the Heir].

The Heir welcomed him, and, walking backward,[12] led him [to his place], knelt down and dusted off the mat.

When Tian Guang had seated himself and there were no attendants present, the Heir politely moved forward off his mat, stood up, and made his request. "Yan and Qin cannot both exist! I hope you might consider this."

---

[10] Two ancient advisers who were known for their guidance of rulers in the state of Qi.

[11] The title of the leader of the Xiongnu.

[12] So as not to turn his back on him; a sign of respect.

Tian Guang replied, "Your servant has heard that a black stallion can gallop a thousand *li* in one day in its prime, but a nag can pass it when it is old and feeble. Now, the Heir has heard of my prime and does not realize that my vigor has withered. Things being like this, I would not dare to allow myself to plan affairs of state. [But] my friend, Excellency Jing, could be of use."

The Heir said, "I hope that I might make the acquaintance of His Excellency Jing through you, Venerable Sir. Is this possible?" Tian Guang said, "I should respectfully comply." He rose immediately and hastened out. The Heir escorted him to the gate and cautioned him, "What I have reported to you and what you have spoken of are grand affairs of state, Venerable Sir. I beg you not to divulge them." Tian Guang looked down and laughed. "I shall comply."

Bowed with age, he went to see Excellency Jing. "My friendship with you is known to all in the state of Yan, Sir. Now, the Heir having heard of my prime, did not realize my body is not up to this and favored me by instructing me saying 'Yan and Qin cannot both survive, I would hope that you might consider this, Venerable Sir.' Presuming upon our friendship, I spoke of you to the Heir, Honorable Sir. I hope you might call on him at the palace."

"I shall carefully follow your instructions," replied Jing Ke.

Tian Guang said, "I have heard that a man of honor in his actions does not allow others to doubt him. Today the Heir told me 'What we have spoken of are great affairs of state, I beg you not to divulge them, Venerable Sir.' In this [it can be seen that] the Heir doubts me. When one's actions cause other men to doubt him, he is a knight-errant with no principles."

Having decided to move Jing Ke by killing himself, Tian Guang said, "I hope you will hasten to call on the Heir, Honorable Sir, and tell him that Guang has already died to ensure his silence." He then slit his throat and died.

Jing Ke then met with the Heir, told him that Tian Guang had died, and conveyed Guang's words. The Heir knelt and bowed twice, raised on his haunches and crawled forward on his knees, weeping profusely. He spoke only after some time. "The reason I warned Venerable Tian not to speak was because I hoped our great plan might thus succeed. Now Venerable Tian by dying had made clear that he will not speak [of it]. He has ensured his silence with death; how could this have been my intention!"

After Jing Ke was seated, the Heir moved off his mat, and knocked his forehead against the ground: "Venerable Tian, not recognizing my unworthiness, has made it possible for me to come before you and venture an opinion. It is in this way that Heaven takes pity on Yan, refusing to abandon its orphan. Now Qin has a heart greedy for profit, its desires can never be satisfied. Not until it has all the world's territory and made subjects of all the world's kings within the seas will it be satisfied. Now Qin has already captured the King of Han and accepted every inch of his territory. Further, it has raised troops and attacked Chu in the south and confronted Zhao in the north. Wang Jian[13] leading a

太子逢迎，卻行為導，跪而蔽席。田光坐定，左右無人，太子避席而請曰："燕秦不兩立，願先生留意也。"田光曰："臣聞騏驥盛壯之時，一日而馳千里；至其衰老，駑馬先之。今太子聞光盛壯之時，不知臣精已消亡矣。雖然，光不敢以圖國事，所善荊卿可使也。"太子曰："願因先生得結交於荊卿，可乎？"田光曰："敬諾。"即起，趨出。太子送至門，戒曰："丹所報，先生所言者，國之大事也，願先生勿泄也！"田光俛而笑曰："諾。"僂行見荊卿，曰："光與子相善，燕國莫不知。今太子聞光壯盛之時，不知吾形已不逮也，幸而教之曰'燕秦不兩立，願先生留意也'。光竊不自外，言足下於太子也，願足下過太子於宮。"荊軻曰："謹奉教。"田光曰："吾聞之，長者為行，不使人疑之。今太子告光曰：'所言者，國之大事也，願先生勿泄'，是太子疑光也。夫為行而使人疑之，非節俠也。"欲自殺以激荊卿，曰："願足下急過太子，言光已死，明不言也。"因遂自刎而死。

---

[13] Wang Jian and Li Xin were Qin military commanders. The Zhang probably marked the westernmost holdings of Zhao at this time.

荊軻遂見太子，言田光
已死，致光之言。太
子再拜而跪，膝行流
涕，有頃而後言曰：
「丹所以誠田先生毋言
者，欲以成大事之謀
也。今田先生以死明不
言，豈丹之心哉！」荊
軻坐定，太子避席頓首
曰：「田先生不知丹之
不肖，使得至前，敢有
所道，此天之所以哀燕
而不棄其孤也。今秦有
貪利之心，而欲不可足
也。非盡天下之地，臣
海內之王者，其意不
厭。今秦已虜韓王，盡
納其地。又舉兵南伐
楚，北臨趙；王翦將數
十萬之眾距漳、鄴，而
李信出太原、雲中。趙
不能支秦，必入臣，入
臣則禍至燕。燕小弱，
數困於兵，今計舉國不
足以當秦。諸侯服秦，
莫敢合從。丹之私計
愚，以為誠得天下之勇
士使於秦，闕以重利；
秦王貪，其勢必得所願
矣。誠得劫秦王，使悉
反諸侯侵地，若曹沫之
與齊桓公，則大善矣；
則不可，因而刺殺之。
彼秦大將擅兵於外而內
有亂，則君臣相疑，以
其閒諸侯得合從，其破
秦必矣。此丹之上願，
而不知所委命，唯荊卿
留意焉。」久之，荊
軻曰：「此國之大事
也，臣駑下，恐不足任
使。」太子前頓首，固
請毋讓，然後許諾。於
是尊荊卿為上卿，舍上

host of hundreds of thousands has arrived at the Zhang [River] and Ye, and Li Xin has come out through Taiyuan and Yunzhong. Zhao is unable to hold off Qin, and is sure to submit as a subject. When it submits as a subject, disaster is sure to strike Yan.

"Yan is small and weak and has frequently been hard pressed by troops. Now I calculate that mobilizing the entire state would still be insufficient to withstand Qin; the feudal lords have submitted to Qin and none dare to join an alliance. By my own calculations I foolishly suggested we secure one of the world's brave knights for a mission to Qin, and tempt Qin with some great profit, the King of Qin being greedy, under the circumstances we should be able to obtain what we desire. If he is then able to seize the King of Qin and have him return to the feudal lords all the lands he invaded, as Cao Mo did with Duke Huan of Qi, this would be best of all. If this is not possible, he might seize the opportunity to assassinate him. Those great commanders of Qin have taken command of their troops abroad and, when there is chaos at home, ruler and subjects will doubt each other, allowing the feudal lords in the meantime to join in alliance so that the defeat of Qin will be certain. This is my greatest hope, but I do not know to whom I might entrust such a mission. May I ask that you consider this, Excellency Jing?"

After a long pause Jing Ke replied, "This is a vital matter of state. Your servant is worn out and inferior and he fears he would be inadequate to take on such a task."

The Heir moved forward and knocked his forehead on the ground, strongly imploring him not to decline, and in the end he [Jing Ke] agreed. At this point [the Heir] honored Excellency Jing as a Senior Excellency and lodged him in the upper lodge. The Heir daily called at his gate, supplied him with the finest dishes,[14] drinks, and rare objects, frequently presenting carriages, horses, and beautiful women, indulging Jing Ke's every wish, all in order to meet his expectations.[15]

After some time, Jing Ke still showed no signs of setting out. Qin's general Wang Jian defeated Zhao, captured its king, and seized his entire territory, advancing his troops north, overrunning the territory up to the southern border of Yan. Heir Dan was terrified and only then did he implore Jing Ke: "The troops of Qin will cross the Yi River any day. And when they do, even though I might wish to continue waiting upon you, Honorable Sir, how would I be able to."

Jing Ke said, "Even had you not spoken, My Prince, your servant would have requested an audience with you. If I set off today, without a token of trust, I will

---

[14] Literally supplied with *tailao*, which included three kinds of meat: beef, mutton, and pork. As a sacrifice, it was offered exclusively to rulers. It demonstrates the respect with which Jing Ke was treated.

[15] The version of Jing Ke's life in the *Heir Dan of Yan* (*Yan Danzi*), a text that was compiled later than the *Records*, provides a lively description of the lengths to which the Heir went to please Jing Ke. For example, when Jing Ke admired the hands of a young girl, at Jing Ke's insistence, the Heir presented him only with her severed hands.

be unable to get close to [the King of] Qin. As for that General Fan, the King of Qin has offered a thousand catties of gold and a fief of ten-thousand households [for him]. If I could obtain General Fan's head and a map of Dukang in Yan to offer to the King of Qin, the King of Qin is sure to be pleased to see Your Servant and I will then in this way have an opportunity to repay you."

The Heir replied, "General Fan came in dire straits to give his allegiance to me. I could not bear the idea of harming an honorable man for my own selfish desires. I urge you to reconsider, Honorable Sir!"

Only when Jing Ke recognized that the Heir could not bear [to accept his plan], did he finally meet with Fan Wuji in private. "Qin's treatment of you may be called harsh indeed, General! Your parents and clansmen have all been slain or enslaved. Now I hear he would buy your head for a thousand *Jin* of gold and a manor of ten-thousand households. What will you do?" Fan Wuji raised his face to the sky, gave a deep sigh, and with tears running down his face, said, "Each time I think of it, the pain cuts to my marrow! But I do not know any way to manage this." Jing Ke said, "Now, General, what if a single sentence could free the state of Yan from its troubles and gain revenge on your foe?" Fan Wuji moved forward [off his mat? Or leant forward] and said, "How would it work?" Jing Ke said, "I wish to have the General's head to present to the King of Qin. The King of Qin is sure to be pleased and grant Your Subject an audience. With my left hand I will seize his sleeve, with my right hand I will stab his chest; in this way the General's foe will be avenged and the insults Yan has received will be erased! Do you have such resolve, General?" Fan Wuji bared one shoulder, gripped his wrist, and stepped forward.[16] "Day and night I have gnashed my teeth and seared my heart for such a plan. At last I have been able to hear of it." Then he slit his throat. When the Heir heard of it, he rushed in, leaned over the corpse, and wailed in the utmost sorrow. Only then, since nothing more could be done, did he have Fan Wuji's head put in a box and sealed it.

At this point, the Heir having earlier searched for the sharpest dagger that could be found, obtained one from a man of Zhao named Xu Furen for a hundred catties of gold, ordered his artisans to coat the blade with poison and try it out on some men; though the blood [shed] would stain only a thread, there was none who did not die immediately. Only then did he make preparations for sending off Excellency Jing. There was a brave man of the state of Yan named Qin Wuyang who at the age of thirteen had killed someone, and no one dared even to look him straight in the face. This man he then ordered to act as a second to Jing Ke. There was a man Jing Ke was waiting for, intending to go together with him. Though this person lived at a distance and had not yet arrived, [Jing Ke] made preparations for him in their journey. Some time passed, but still he did not set off. Only when the Heir saw that Jing Ke delayed

[16] To suggest his sincerity and determination.

舍。太子日造門下，供太牢具，異物間進，車騎美女恣荊軻所欲，以順適其意。

久之，荊軻未有行意。秦將王翦破趙，虜趙王，盡收入其地，進兵北略地至燕南界。太子丹恐懼，乃請荊軻曰：「秦兵旦暮渡易水，則雖欲長侍足下，豈可得哉！」荊軻曰：「微太子言，臣願謁之。今行而毋信，則秦未可親也。夫樊將軍，秦王購之金千斤，邑萬家。誠得樊將軍首與燕督亢之地圖，奉獻秦王，秦王必說見臣，臣乃得有以報。」太子曰：「樊將軍窮困來歸丹，丹不忍以己之私而傷長者之意，願足下更慮之！」

荊軻知太子不忍，乃遂私見樊於期曰：「秦之遇將軍可謂深矣，父母宗族皆為戮沒。今聞購將軍首金千斤，邑萬家，將奈何？」於期仰天太息流涕曰：「於期每念之，常痛於骨髓，顧計不知所出耳！」荊軻曰：「今有一言可以解燕國之患，報將軍之仇者，何如？」於期乃前曰：「為之奈何？」荊軻曰：「願得將軍之首以獻秦王，秦王必喜而見臣，臣左手把其袖，右手揕其匈，然則將軍之仇報而燕見陵之愧除矣。將軍豈有意

乎？"樊於期偏袒搤捥
而進曰："此臣之日夜切
齒腐心也，乃今得聞
教！"遂自剄。太子聞之，
馳往，伏屍而哭，極
哀。既已不可奈何，乃
遂盛樊於期首函封之。

於是太子豫求天下之利
匕首，得趙人徐夫人匕
首，取之百金，使工
以藥焠之，以試人，血
濡縷，人無不立死者。
乃裝為遣荊卿。燕國有
勇士秦舞陽，年十三，
殺人，人不敢忤視。乃
令秦舞陽為副。荊軻有
所待，欲與俱；其人居
遠未來，而為治行。頃
之，未發，太子遲之，
疑其改悔，乃復請曰：
"日已盡矣，荊卿豈有
意哉？丹請得先遣秦舞
陽。"荊軻怒，叱太子
曰："何太子之遣？往
而不返者，豎子也！且
提一匕首入不測之彊
秦，僕所以留者，待吾
客與俱。今太子遲之，
請辭決矣！"遂發。

太子及賓客知其事者，
皆白衣冠以送之。至易
水之上，既祖，取道，
高漸離擊筑　，荊軻和
而歌，為變徵之聲，士
皆垂淚涕泣。又前而為
歌曰："風蕭蕭兮易水
寒，壯士一去兮不復
還！"復為羽聲忼慨，
士皆瞋目，髮盡上指
冠。於是荊軻就車而
去，終已不顧。

and suspecting he had misgivings did he go again to inquire: "There is no time left. Does His Excellency Jing still have his mind set on this? I would like to be able to send Qin Wuyang on ahead." Jing Ke was angered and roared back at the Heir: "What is this about the Heir sending him [Qin Wuyang ahead]? The one who will go and not return would be this whelp! Moreover, the reason I am delayed in carrying a single dagger into the unfathomable might of Qin is I am waiting for my attendant who will go along. Now, since Your Majesty thinks I have been delaying, I beg permission to take my leave." And finally he set out.

Throughout the narrative, Jing Ke and others have waited for the proper time to act. This passage shows that Jing Ke hurried into action before he would have wished, perhaps foreshadowing his failure, and through the dialogue, also reveals a side of Jing Ke not evident earlier in the text.

The Heir and those of his retainers who learned of [Jing Ke's] affair all wore white robes and caps to see them off.[17] When they reached the banks of the Yi River, after sacrificing [to the god of the roads] and moving onto the road, Gao Jianli played the dulcimer and Jing Ke accompanied him in a song in the mournful key of *zhi*.[18] The knights all wept profusely. When they had advanced a little further [Jing Ke] sang:

The wind soughs and sighs, the Yi River cold.
Once we hearties leave, we'll never return to our fold!

Shifting to the martial key of *yu*[19] he roused himself, the eyes of the knights glared and their hair bristled beneath their caps. At this Jing Ke mounted his carriage and left, never once looking back.

Finally he arrived in Qin, presented gifts worth a thousand catties to the Palace Cadet, Meng Jia. Jia [then] spoke first on their behalf to the King of Qin: "The King of Yan, trembling and awed by you, Great King, has not dared to raise troops to oppose our armies and officers, wishing the whole state would become an interior vassal, aligned with the ranks the of other feudal lords, presenting tribute and corvée labor like your commanderies and counties, and able to present sacrifices and maintain the ancestral temple of the former kings [of Yan]. In his trepidation he has not dared to speak in person, but has taken the precaution of cutting off Fan Wuji's head, and presented it with a map of the territory of Dukang in Yan, sealed in a box.[20] The King of Yan respectfully saw them off from his court, causing his envoys to report [these things] to you, Great

---

[17] Dressed as if for a funeral.

[18] Similar to the key of F.

[19] Similar to the key of A.

King; I hope you will command them to do so, Great King." When the King of Qin heard this, he was greatly pleased, and only then put on his court robes and had the nine levels of officials arrayed to receive the envoys of Yan in the Xianyang Palace. Jing Ke carried the box with Fan Wuji's head respectfully with both hands, while Qin Wuyang bore a case with the map, advancing one after the other. When they reached the steps of the throne, Qin Wuyang turned pale and began to tremble, and the assembled vassals felt it strange. Jing Ke turned to Wuyang and laughed, then stepped forward to apologize: "This bumpkin from a northern barbarian tribe has never before seen the Son of Heaven, thus he is quaking. I ask that you, Great King, be a little tolerant of him and allow him to fulfill his mission before you." The King of Qin said to Jing Ke: "Get the map Wuyang is carrying!" When Jing Ke took the map and presented it, the King of Qin unrolled the map and at the end the dagger appeared. Jing Ke took advantage [of this] to seize the king's sleeve with his left hand, and with his right he picked up the dagger and thrust it at him. Before [the dagger] reached his body, the King of Qin started, pulled back, and stood up, his sleeve tearing away. He tried to draw his sword, but since it was too long, he [could only] grasp its scabbard. Since he was hurried at the time and the sword fit tightly [in its scabbard], he was not able to draw it immediately. As Jing Ke pursued the King of Qin, the king went running around the pillars. The assembled vassals were all startled, since this was sudden and unexpected, and completely lost their composure. According to Qin law, none of the assembled vassals waiting upon the king in the hall was allowed to carry even the smallest weapon. All the palace attendants who carried arms were arrayed below the hall, and without a royal command they were not able to ascend. In the press of the moment the king had no chance to summon the soldiers below and for this reason Jing Ke was then able to pursue him. Panic-stricken, [the assembled vassals] had nothing with which to attack Jing Ke, so together they beat him with their bare fists. At this time the attending physician, Xia Wuju, threw the bag of medicine he was carrying at Jing Ke. The king had just been circling the pillars and in his panic, did not know what to do. His attendants then said: "Put the sword on your back, Your Majesty!" When he had put the sword on his back, he then drew it and used it to attack Jing Ke, breaking his left leg at the thigh. Jing Ke, now crippled, raised his dagger and threw it at the King of Qin but missed, hitting a paulownia-wood roof pillar. The King of Qin attacked Jing Ke again and Jing Ke suffered eight wounds. Jing Ke, realizing the failure of his mission, leaned against a pillar, laughed, and with his legs spread apart before him, cursed [the King]. "The reason my task was not successful is because I tried to keep you [the King] alive, tried to convince you to conclude an agreement to repay the Heir!"

The popularity of this chapter over the centuries is surely not due to the long speeches that tend to lull the reader, but to Sima Qian's conclusion offering an

---

[20] Signifying that Yan is ceding this area to Qin.

遂至秦，持千金之資幣物，厚遺秦王寵臣中庶子蒙嘉。嘉為先言於秦王曰："燕王誠振怖大王之威，不敢舉兵以逆軍吏，願舉國為內臣，比諸侯之列，給貢職如郡縣，而得奉守先王之宗廟。恐懼不敢自陳，謹斬樊於期之頭，及獻燕督亢之地圖，函封，燕王拜送于庭，使使以聞大王，唯大王命之。"秦王聞之，大喜，乃朝服，設九賓，見燕使者咸陽宮。荊軻奉樊於期頭函，而秦舞陽奉地圖柙，以次進。至陛，秦舞陽色變振恐，群臣怪之。荊軻顧笑舞陽，前謝曰："北蕃蠻夷之鄙人，未嘗見天子，故振慴。願大王少假借之，使得畢使於前。"秦王謂軻曰："取舞陽所持地圖。"軻既取圖奏之，秦王發圖，圖窮而匕首見。因左手把秦王之袖，而右手持匕首揕之。未至身，秦王驚，自引而起，袖絕。拔劍，劍長，操其室。時惶急，劍堅，故不可立拔。荊軻逐秦王，秦王環柱而走。群臣皆愕，卒起不意，盡失其度。而秦法，群臣侍殿上者不得持尺寸之兵；諸郎中執兵皆陳殿下，非有詔召不得上。方急時，不及召下兵，以故荊軻乃逐秦王。而卒惶急，無以擊軻，而以手共搏之。

是時侍醫夏無且以其所
奉藥囊提荊軻也。秦王
方環柱走，卒惶急，不
知所為，左右乃曰：
"王負劍！"負劍，遂
拔以擊荊軻，斷其左
股。荊軻廢，乃引其
匕首以擿秦王，不中，
中桐柱。秦王復擊軻，
軻被八創。軻自知事不
就，倚柱而笑，箕踞以
罵曰："事所以不成
者，以欲生劫之，必得
約契以報太子也。"

於是左右既前殺軻，秦
王不怡者良久。已而
論功，賞群臣及當坐者
各有差，而賜夏無且黃
金二百溢，曰："無且
愛我，乃以藥囊提荊軻
也。"

於是秦王大怒，益發兵
詣趙，詔王翦軍以伐
燕。十月而拔薊城。
燕王喜、太子丹等盡率
其精兵東保於遼東。秦
將李信追擊燕王急，
代王嘉乃遺燕王喜書
曰："秦所以尤追燕急
者，以太子丹故也。今
王誠殺丹獻之秦王，秦
王必解，而社稷幸得血
食。"其後李信追丹，
丹匿衍水中，燕王乃使
使斬太子丹，欲獻之
秦。秦復進兵攻之。後

example of ekphrastic writing at its best. Jing Ke's concern over the suitability of Qin Wuyang for the mission is borne out when he young companion blanches at the sight of the King of Qin—unlike Cao Mo whose expression never changed when he coerced Duke Huan into returning territory to Lu.

The dramatic scene at the Qin court has a cinematic scope, as if a camera in the rafters had captured the king's clumsy attempts to draw his sword and then escape. The king runs around pillars, Jing Ke flings his dagger in desperation, and finally Jing Ke speaks his bitter last words to the king. The reader is also treated to Jing Ke's assessment of what went wrong: he was too indulgent in trying to take the king alive. As before when Jing Ke met extreme danger, he tried to bide his time. Although timing is a factor in the failure of the mission—all originating from the Heir's impatience—this final scene allows the reader to form a more complete understanding of Jing Ke: a courageous but phlegmatic and ultimately unsuccessful hero. This chapter thus works chiasmatically, beginning with Cao Mo's holding Duke Huan until he gives in and moving toward closure as the King of Qin eludes the grasp of Jing Ke.

> By this point the attendants had come forward to kill Jing Ke, but the King of Qin was unsettled for some time. After a little while, when evaluating [who had won] merit, he made a distinction between those among the assembled ministers [who tried to aide him] and those should be tried [for not helping], then presented Xia Wuju with two hundred *yi* of gold,[21] saying "Wuju cares for me, so he threw his bag of medicine at Jing Ke."

This account of the King of Qin also paints a unique, intimate portrait of his personality and thought processes, naturally absent from the basic annals Sima Qian devoted to his reign.

After this, the King of Qin, in great rage, sent more troops to go to Zhao and issued an edict for Wang Jian's army to attack Yan with them. In the tenth month (of 226 BCE), they seized Jicheng (Yan's capital). Xi, the King of Yan (r. 254–222 BC), Heir Dan, and others led their finest troops east to defend Liaodong. Qin's general Li Xin pursued them and pressed his attack on the King of Yan. Only then did Jia, the King of Dai,[22] send a letter to Xi, King of Yan[,] which read:

> The reason Qin presses the pursuit of Yan so hard is because of Heir Dan. Now if Your Majesty were really to kill Dan and present [his head] to the King of Qin, the King of Qin is sure to disengage, and your altars of soil and grain may be fortunate to continue to receive their blood sacrifices.

Afterwards, when Li Xin was in pursuit of Dan, Dan hid in the Yan River region.[23] The King of Yan then sent an envoy to cut off Heir Dan's head, intending to present it to Qin. [But] Qin again dispatched troops to attack it [Yan]. Five years later [222 BC], Qin finally destroyed Yan and captured Xi, the King of Yan.

---

[21] One *yi* is equal to about three hundred grams.

[22] After Wang Jian took Handan in 228 BCE and captured the King of Zhao, one of the King's sons set himself up as the King of Dai.

In this passage, Gao Jianli suddenly reappears, suggesting part of the narrative may have been lost.

> The next year [221 BC], [the King of] Qin annexed all under heaven and established himself as the August Emperor. At this point Qin began to pursue the retainers of Heir Dan and Jing Ke [but] they had all escaped. Gao Jianli changed his surname and given name and became a hired laborer for a man, hiding and working in Songzi. After some time he grew tired of working and whenever he heard a retainer play the dulcimer in the hall of their house, he would linger, unable to leave. He would often say[,] "That person does this well but does that poorly." A servant told the master, "That hired laborer is one who understands music. He privately speaks to what [the musicians] do correctly or incorrectly!" The lady of the house summoned him and had him come forward and play the dulcimer. Everyone seated there praised his skill, and they offered him wine. Only then did Gao Jianli, mindful of his long hiding and dreading the endless privations that lay ahead, retire, take out his dulcimer and his finest clothing from the case which held them, change his appearance and come forward with a solemn expression on his face. The seated guests were astounded, left their seats, and treated him as their equal, placing him in the seat of honor. They had him play the dulcimer and sing and there was no guest who left without weeping. The people of Songzi took turns hosting him and the First Emperor of Qin heard of this. The First Emperor of Qin summoned him to an audience where someone recognized him and said, "It's Gao Jianli!" The Emperor of Qin cherished his skill with the dulcimer and made an exception to pardon him but had him blinded. He had him play the dulcimer and not once did he [the Emperor] not praise his skill. Only when he was gradually allowed to draw closer and closer to [the Emperor] did Gao Jianli put a piece of lead in his dulcimer. When he was presented again and was able to draw close, he lifted his dulcimer and struck at the Emperor of Qin but missed him. Then [the Emperor] finally had Gao Jianli executed and for the rest of his life never again allowed the men from the [former] feudal lords to come close to him.

> Lu Goujian having heard of Jing Ke's [attempt] to assassinate the King of Qin, said to himself, "Alas, what a pity he did not study carefully the methods of assassination with a sword! How greatly did I fail to understand that man! When I cursed before, he must have thought I was not his kind of man!"[24]

The account of Gao Jianli is appended to the chapter possibly as a result of the stories that Dong Zhongshu and Gongsun Jigong told Sima Qian (see the historian's comment in the next section). This structure is not without parallel in other

---

[23] According to the "Basic Annals of the First Emperor of Qin" ("Qin Shihuang benji"), Heir Dan died in 226 BCE, when Qin general Wang Jian took the Yan capital of Ji.

[24] Or "he must have thought I was hardly human." Note that Jing Ke spoke of swordsmanship with Ge Nie, not Gao Jianli. Sima Qian nods here.

五年，秦卒滅燕，虜燕王喜。

其明年，秦并天下，立號為皇帝。於是秦逐太子丹、荊軻之客，皆亡。高漸離變名姓為人庸保，匿作於宋子。久之，作苦，聞其家堂上客擊筑，傍偟不能去。每出言曰："彼有善有不善。"從者以告其主，曰："彼庸乃知音，竊言是非。"家丈人召使前擊筑，一坐稱善，賜酒。而高漸離念久隱畏約無窮時，乃退，出其裝匣中筑與其善衣，更容貌而前。舉坐客皆驚，下與抗禮，以為上客。使擊筑而歌，客無不流涕而去者。宋子傳客之，聞於秦始皇。秦始皇召見，人有識者，乃曰："高漸離也。"秦皇帝惜其善擊筑，重赦之，乃矐其目。使擊筑，未嘗不稱善。稍益近之，高漸離乃以鉛置筑中，復進得近，舉筑朴秦皇帝，不中。於是遂誅高漸離，終身不復近諸侯之人。

魯句踐已聞荊軻之刺秦王，私曰："嗟乎，惜哉其不講於刺劍之術也！甚矣吾不知人也！曩者吾叱之，彼乃以我為非人也！"

biographies, such as the stories relating to Zhao general Li Mu that were appended to the biographies of Lian Po and Lin Xiangru or the notice on Yue Jian appended to the biography of his father, Yue Yi (see *SJ*, chap. 80–81).[4]

太史公曰：世言荊軻，
其稱太子丹之命，"天
雨粟，馬生角"也，太
過。又言荊軻傷秦王，
皆非也。始公孫季功、
董生與夏無且游，具知
其事，為余道之如是。
自曹沫至荊軻五人，此
其義或成或不成，然其
立意較然，不欺其志，
名垂後世，豈妄也哉！

[*SJ* 8:86.2527–2538]

His Honor the Grand Scribe says: "When the world speaks of Jing Ke, they claim that the fate of Heir Dan was [a matter of] "heaven raining grain and horses growing horns."[25] This is going too far! They also say that Jing Ke wounded the King of Qin, which is equally false. At the beginning [of the Han], Gongsun Jigong, Scholar Dong,[26] and Xia Wuju were friends and they all knew the details of these events; what they told me was like this [the previous account]. From Cao Mo down to Jing Ke, some of these five men were successful and some of them not in their righteous endeavors, but what they fixed their minds on was perfectly clear [to them]. They did not sell their goals short so how could it be presumptuous to think their fame would spread to later generations?"

In the final analysis, Sima Qian depicts Jing Ke more as a loyal, patient retainer than as an accomplished assassin. The famous poet Tao Yuanming (ca. 352–427) in a poem devoted to Jing Ke claims his failure was due to deficient skill with the sword. A better example of a killer would have been Yao Li of Wu, whom Sima Qian chose to ignore in this chapter. The emphasis on the retainer (*ke*) aspect is vital to Sima Qian's purpose because, as noted earlier, the overall theme of the chapter remains that recognition by a superior is paramount and must be repaid—if necessary, with one's life. The character *zhi* ("recognize") appears repeatedly in the text, perhaps reflecting Sima Qian's concern for his position. The irony is that Emperor Wu of the Han failed to recognize Sima Qian's worthiness and sentenced the historian who dared to argue against his ruler to death. The relationship between lord and retainer undergirds, often subtly, many chapters of the *Records*, and suggests Sima Qian's sublimated personal frustrations in establishing a satisfactory engagement with his own lord.

Conversely, Jing Ke was recognized (*zhi*) by both Tian Guang and Heir Dan who "indulged his every wish" and honored him as a senior excellency. Thus, he was bound to try to fulfill the heir's wish to assassinate the King of Qin. Like Cao Mo and Bi Yurang, however, in the end, Jing Ke kills no one. As portrayed in *Cike liezhuan*, because these retainers (*ke*) were recognized and well treated by their rulers, they were willing to attempt assassinations (*ci*) in good faith. The traditions surrounding these men (*zhuan*), both written and oral, were arranged (*lie*) by Sima

---

[25] This quotation was part of a prediction that claimed the Heir Dan would not escape his captivity in Qin until "heaven rained grain and horses grew horns." It is recorded in the *Yan Danzi* (*Heir Dan of Yan*) account of Jing Ke, a work generally considered to have been written after Sima Qian's death. This reference suggests a version of the *Yan Danxi* existed in Sima Qian's time or that it was part of the oral tradition of Jing Ke stories. The Sima's ability to accept or reject such material is verified by this claim that it "is going too far!"

[26] Gongsun Jigong is otherwise unknown. Dong Zhongshu (180–115 BCE) was a scholar with whom Sima Qian may have studied. But since Xia Wuju and Dong Zhongshu belong to a generation before Sima Qian, many scholars think Sima Tan was the author of this comment and possibly of the entire chapter.

Qian's compelling prose into one of the most memorable chapters in early Chinese narrative, one that continues to play out across China's literary genres today.

William H. Nienhauser, Jr.

NOTES

1. Although certain chapters, including that of the "assassin-retainers" (*Cike liezhuan*) presented here, are thought to have been compiled by Sima Tan, we do not know this for certain. Following convention, however, this chapter will refer to Sima Qian as the author.

2. The biographies of Zhuan Zhu and Nie Zheng are the other two assassin-retainers whose biographies are found in this chapter. An account of Yao Li, another well-known assassin of antiquity, does not appear in the *Records* at all. In Zou Yang's lengthy memorial submitted from prison, he links Jing Ke and Yao Li (*SJ* 8:86.2475).

3. Many well-known traditional scholars of the Ming and Qing such as Deng Yizan (1542–1599) and Fang Bao have suggested that the *Intrigues* version of the Jing Ke narrative could have been taken from the *Records*, and modern scholars suggest that Sima Qian and the compilers of the materials Liu Xiang (77–6 BCE) later edited into the *Intrigues* took their material from some earlier common source.

SUGGESTED READING

WESTERN LANGUAGES

Liu, James J. Y. *The Chinese Knight-Errant*. Chicago: University of Chicago Press, 1967.

Nienhauser, William H., Jr., ed. and trans. *The Grand Scribe's Records*. Vol. 7, *The Memoirs of Pre-Han China*. Rev. vol. Bloomington: Indiana University Press, 2021.

Pines, Yuri. "A Hero Terrorist: Adoration of Jing Ke Revisited." *Asia Major* (3rd Series), no. 21 (2008): 1–34.

Schaab-Hanke, Dorothee. "Bluträcher: Warum hat das *Shiji* ein 'Attentäterkapitel'?" ("Blood Avengers: Why Does the *Grand Scribe's Records* Have an 'Assassin Chapter'?"). *Oriens Extremus* 47 (2008): 177–191.

CHINESE

Han Zhaoqi 韓兆琦. *Shiji jianzheng* 史記箋證 (*Commentary and Supporting Evidence on the* Grand Scribe's Records). 10 vols. Nanchang: Jiangxi renmin chubanshe, 2004.

Li Shaoyong 李少勇. *Sima Qian zhuanji wenxue lungao* 司馬遷傳記文學論稿 (*A Draft Discussion of Sima Qian's Biographical Literature*). Chongqing: Chongqing chubanshe, 1987.

Shiji 史記 (*Grand Scribe's Records*). Edited by Zhao Shengqun 趙生群 et al. 10 vols. Beijing: Zhonghua shuju, 2014.

Zhang Haiming 張海明. "*Shiji* 'Jing Ke zhuan' yu *Zhanguoce* 'Yan Taizi, Dan, zhi yu Qin' guanxi kaolun" 史記荊軻傳與戰國策燕太子丹質于秦關係考論 ("A Study and Evaluation of the Relationship Between the 'Account of Jing Ke' in the *Grand Scribe's Records* and 'Heir Dan of Yan as Hostage in Qin' in the *Stratagems of the Warring States*"). *Qinghua Daxue xuebao (Zhexue shehui kexue ban)* 清華大學學報 (哲學社會科學版) (*Journal of Tsinghua University: Philosophy and Social Sciences Edition*) 28, no. 1 (2013): 94–113.

Zhanguoce jizhu huikao 戰國策集注匯考 (*A Variorum Study of the Collected Notes on the Stratagems of the Warring States*). Edited by Chu Zugeng 儲祖耿. 3 vols. Nanjing: Jiangsu guji chubanshe, 1985.

Zhanguoce zhushi 戰國策注釋 (*Explanatory Notes on the* Stratagems of the Warring States). Edited by He Jianzhang 何建章. 3 vols. Beijing: Zhonghua shuju, 1990.

Zhao Shengqun 趙生群. "Lun *Shiji* yu *Zhanguoce* de guanxi" 論史記與戰國策的關係 ("On the Relationship Between the *Grand Scribe's Records* and the *Stratagems of the Warring States*"). *Nanjing shida xuebao (Shehui kexue ban)* 南京師大學報(社會科學版) (*Journal of Nanjing Normal University: Social Sciences Edition*), no. 1 (1990): 42–48.

✿ 7 ✿

Han and Six Dynasties Epistolary Prose

Memorials and Letters

Letters have been an important means of communication since humans first began manipulating written language to record events. The earliest functions of letter writing can be traced back to the need to record changes in both terrestrial and celestial realms, the administrative affairs in human society, and the lessons or admonitions exchanged between teachers and students. From these early precedents, letters gradually developed into a general tool for conveying information between individuals. In premodern China, the general term for this prose genre was *shu* and for the sake of convenience in this chapter, I will use the broad, encompassing term "letter genre" (*shu wenti*).

There are different theories about the earliest origins of letters in premodern China. Qing dynasty (1644–1911) scholar Yao Nai (1732–1815), argued that the letter genre can be traced back to the "Jun Shi" chapter of the *Book of Documents* (*Shangshu*). This chapter records the words of the Duke of Zhou exhorting the Duke of Shao to loyally support feudal rule of the Zhou (1046–256 BCE) and to heed the errors of the preceding Shang dynasty (ca. 1600–1046 BCE). Given that the content of "Jun Shi" is derived from the spoken words of the Duke of Zhou, recorded and likely edited by court historians, this work is better understood as a form of oral admonition. During the Spring and Autumn (771–476 BCE) and Warring States (475–221 BCE) eras, when the numerous kingdoms of the Chinese ecumene competed with one another, letters were carried by envoys to transmit diplomatic exchanges and information between rulers. Several important examples are recorded in the historical chronicle, the *Zuo Tradition Commentary on the Spring and Autumn Annals* (*Chunqiu Zuozhuan*).[1] Although these more clearly take the form of full-length letters, they retain many qualities of oral spoken language found in recorded official diplomatic dialogues and stress persuasion and argumentation more than structural ingenuity and literary crafting. In this regard, Yue Yi's "Letter in Report to King Hui of Yan" ("Bao Yan Huiwang shu") from the Warring States period appears to be a transitional work. In this letter, Yue Yi's impassioned praise of the accomplishments of the sage kings of antiquity and his vigorous self-justification for his decision to abandon the state of Yan to support the state of Zhao reveal three qualities typically found in the later development of the letter genre: the expression of feelings, attention to literary crafting, and the trend toward using letters not only for official communication but also to explore personal life.

I argue, however, that the history of the letter genre fundamentally begins during the Han dynasty (221 BCE–206 CE) when it underwent a process of standardization and refinement. During this time, the functions of official and personal documents began to diverge from each other, with the letter emerging as a medium for establishing and maintaining personal relationships between individuals. In pre-imperial China, the bureaucratic nomenclature for genres was not yet well established and regardless of the relative status of the writer or addressee, documents exchanged between ministers and rulers often were referred to as "letters" (*shu*), even though these documents were unrelated to personal matters. By the Han, documents submitted by a minister to a ruler, moving up the social hierarchy came to be called "letters of submission" or "memorials" (*shangshu*) and were distinguished from letters addressed to friends or relatives.[2] These "letters of submission" represent a standardized form for these kind of official documents and are quite different in nature from the comparatively free form toward which personal letters would later develop.

To illustrate the full range and diversity of the letter genre in the Chinese literary tradition, this chapter presents and analyzes representative examples of memorials addressed to rulers and letters addressed to colleagues and family members from the second to sixth centuries.

MEMORIALS

The landmark work of Six Dynasties literary criticism and genre theory, *The Literary Mind and Carving of Dragons* (*Wenxin diaolong*) by Liu Xie (ca. 465–ca. 522) contains the earliest systematic discussion of "letters of submissions" or "memorials."[3] For our purposes, the most important part of Liu Xie's genre theory is his discussion of the memorial found in chapter 22 on "declarations and petitions" (*zhangbiao*). Liu Xie described two types of memorials: *zhang* or pieces used to express a writer's gratitude (*xie en*) and *biao* or pieces used to set forth a request (*chen qing*). The defining criterion of both types of memorials is that they were used exclusively to communicate with the throne. By at least the third century, memorials of personal expression began to appear. The conscious literary crafting and lyrical expression found in such memorials differentiate them from the straightforward bureaucratic language of other administrative documents. For this reason, Liu Xie states, "The function of *zhang* and *biao* are, respectively, to praise royal virtues and to express one's own opinion before the imperial court. They are both the ornaments of the person responsible for them and the flowers of the state."[4] Because memorials directly concerned governmental affairs, by necessity, they adhered to the facts of events and put forth arguments using rigorous logic and clear and concise language. Many memorials have been preserved from the second to sixth centuries, with the influential anthology *Selections of Refined Literature* (*Wen Xuan*) containing nineteen examples. Among these are some of the most famous pieces in this genre. Their content touches upon a broad range of rhetorical situations, including writers making recommendations for promotion, humbly withdrawing, actively seeking assistance, expressing gratitude, describing events, encouraging a ruler to advance a policy, or defending one's own errors or faults. Liu Xie stated that "declarations, petitions, presentations, and opinions are all crucial in the conduct of government," and Cao Pi (187–226) held that "literary works are the supreme achievement in the business of the state, a splendor that does not decay."[5] From this it can be seen that medieval Chinese literary critics emphasized the importance of memorials to the concrete details of governing the realm.

The memorial "Memorial on Deploying the Army" ("Chushi biao") was a report written by the famous minister-general Zhuge Liang (181–234) to his ruler, the young Liu Shan (207–271), on the eve of setting out on a military campaign. After the collapse of the Han dynasty in 220 CE, China split into the competing states of Wei (220–265), Wu (222–280), and Shu Han (221–263). Liu Bei (161–223) was the ruler of the Shu Han kingdom and claimed to be the legitimate successor of the Han emperors by virtue of having the surname Liu. Although Liu Bei proclaimed himself emperor and is naturally referred to as the "late emperor" in the following letter, neither he nor his son were so recognized by later historians. Zhuge Liang is remembered as the loyal chief-minister and strategist by whose sagacity and military skill Liu Bei was successful in establishing himself upon the throne. In this memorial, Zhuge fondly recalls the famous story of how Liu Bei's paid "three visits to the thatched hut" (sangu caolu) where Zhuge lived in reclusion to convince him to support the Shu cause. From this we can see the close bond of trust and mutual reliance that this ruler and his minister enjoyed.

Zhuge Liang would not have the same relationship with Liu Shan. Unlike memorials offering advice to a ruler that are packed with empty flattery, Zhuge's piece instead employs a sincere tone and straightforward language, unburdened by allusions or excessive literary tropes, to earnestly and tirelessly instruct Liu Shan on the best way to prepare Shu for war. In fact, while Zhuge's aim clearly is to persuade the young Liu Shan, Zhuge goes beyond the purely argumentative functions of the memorial and invests his work with the classic traits of lyrical prose. Again, as the chief minister, the goal of Zhuge's memorial is to illuminate matters of state, yet his work is pervaded by personal feelings, his remembrance of Liu Bei's past favor, and Zhuge's willingness to spare no efforts in the performance of his duties. This corresponds to the intention of memorials to illuminate the thoughts and intentions of its author and to advance the moral cultivation of its addressee. Zhuge's addressee was, however, a rather weak and feckless young emperor. Therefore, it was essential for Zhuge to convey the principles of governing and to explain the state of affairs in Shu clearly. At the same time, his memorial had to maintain the proper status and tone of a subordinate minister toward the ruler. Zhuge's "Memorial on Deploying the Army" has long been admired by Chinese writers for both the integrity of its author and for the artistic balance it struck in making its arguments. The words of Southern Song poet Lu You (1125–1209) in his couplet, "With his single memorial on Deploying the Army / Across a thousand years who has been able to match him?" capture well the enduring impact of Zhuge Liang's work.[6]

C7.1 Zhuge Liang, "Memorial on Deploying the Army"

諸葛亮 出師表

Your servant Liang states:

The late emperor (Liu Bei) died before his work of restoring the Han was half done. Now the land is divided into three parts, and our people here in Yizhou are worn and tired. This, indeed, is a critical time on which hangs our survival. Yet the officials of the imperial guard persevere at court, and loyal and noble-minded soldiers are selfless in the field. This presumably is because they recall the late emperor's remarkable solicitude and wish to repay it through Your Majesty. To be sure, you should lend a sage ear to a broader range of opinions so as to bring further glory to the virtue of the late emperor and enhance the morale of those patriots in the field. You should not be excessively modest or go wrong in following advice lest you block the channels of loyal criticism.

Those in the palace and the bureaucracy are all one body. They should not be treated differently with regard to promotions, punishments, praise, or censure. People who do evil and break the law and people who are loyal and good should all be turned over to the proper authorities to determine their respective punishments and rewards, thereby demonstrating the fairness and wisdom of Your Majesty's administration. You should not be biased and allow different standards to be applied within and without the palace.

Palace Attendants Guo Youzhi and Fei Hui and Attendant Gentleman Dong Yun are all able and honest. Their aims and ideas are loyal and true, so the late emperor picked them to serve Your Majesty after his death. In my opinion, if you always consult them before taking action on palace matters, no matter how important or trivial, they will surely be able to help remedy errors and omissions and be of vast benefit. General Xiang Chong's character and behavior are exemplary and just, and he is a master of military matters. The late emperor employed him in the past and praised him as capable, so one and all discussed making Chong commander-in-chief. In my opinion, if you always consult him on military strategy, he will surely be able to harmonize the armed forces and properly position the stronger and weaker units.

The Former Han flourished because it favored worthy subjects and kept disreputable people at a distance. The Later Han fell because it favored disreputable people and kept worthy subjects at a distance. Whenever the late emperor and I discussed these concerns, he always sighed with bitter regret over the reigns of Emperors Huan (reigned 147–167) and Ling (reigned 168–188). Palace Attendants Guo Youzhi and Fei Hui, Imperial Secretary Chen Zhen, Administrator Zhang Yi, and Adjutant Jiang Wan are all staunch and trustworthy subjects willing to dies for their integrity. I hope that Your Majesty will be on close terms with them and trust in them, for then the ascendancy of Shu Han will be just around the corner.

I was originally a commoner and farmed in Nanyang. I did whatever it took to save my skin in a turbulent world and did not seek celebrity among the nobles. The late emperor did not consider me contemptible, but rather was

先帝創業未半而中道崩殂，今天下三分，⁴益州疲弊，此誠危急存亡之秋也。然侍衛之臣不懈於內，忠志之士忘身於外者，蓋追先帝之殊遇，⁶⁺¹欲報之於陛下／也。⁶誠宜開張聖聽，⁶以光先帝遺德，⁶恢弘志士之氣，⁶不宜妄自菲薄，⁴引喻失義，⁶⁺¹以塞忠諫之路／也。

⁴宮中府中，⁴俱為一體，⁴陟罰臧否，⁴不宜異同。若有作姦犯科及為忠善者，宜付有司論其刑賞，以昭陛下平明之理，⁴不宜偏私，使內外異法也。　侍中、侍郎郭攸之、費禕、董允等，⁴此皆良實，⁴志慮忠純，是以先帝簡拔以遺陛下。愚以為宮中之事，⁴事無大小，⁴悉以咨之，⁴然後施行，⁶必能裨補闕漏，⁴有所廣益。⁴將軍向寵，⁴性行淑均，⁴曉暢軍事，試用於昔日，⁶先帝稱之曰能，是以眾議舉寵為督。愚以為營中之事，⁴悉以咨之，必能使行陳和睦，⁴優劣得所。親賢臣，遠小人，此先漢所以興隆也；親小人，遠賢臣，此後漢所以傾頹也。⁴先帝在時，⁶每與臣論此事，未嘗不歎息痛恨於桓、靈也。侍中、尚書、長

史、參軍，此悉貞良死
節之臣，願陛下親之信
之，則漢室之隆，　可
計日而待也。

⁴臣本布衣，躬耕於
南陽，苟全性命於亂
世，不求聞達於諸侯。
先帝不以臣卑鄙，⁴猥
自枉屈，三顧臣於草
廬之中，諮臣以當世之
事，⁴由是感激，遂許
先帝以驅馳。⁴後值傾
覆，受任於敗軍之際，
奉命於危難之間，爾
來二十有一年矣。⁶先
帝知臣謹慎，故臨崩
寄臣以大事也。⁴受
命以來，⁴夙夜憂歎，
恐託付不效，⁶以傷
先帝之明。故五月渡
瀘，⁴深入不毛。今南
方已定，⁴兵甲已足，
當獎率三軍，⁴北定中
原，⁴庶竭駑鈍，⁴攘除
姦凶，⁴興復漢室，⁴還
于舊都，此臣所以報
先帝而忠陛下之職
分也。⁶至於斟酌損
益，⁴進盡忠言，則攸
之、禕、允之任也。

願陛下託臣以討賊
興復之效；不效，則治
臣之罪，以告先帝之
靈。⁶若無興德之言，
則責攸之、禕、允等之
慢，⁴以彰其咎。⁶陛下
亦宜自謀，⁴⁺¹以/諮諏善
道，⁴察納雅言，⁶深追
先帝遺詔。臣不勝受恩
感激。⁴今當遠離，⁴臨
表涕零，⁴不知所言。

[*SGZ* 919–920]

kind enough to call on me three times in my thatched hut and consult me about current events. I was moved by this and gave my assent to him, serving at his beck and call. Later, we met a serious defeat, and for twenty-one years I accepted assignments amidst a beaten army and was entrusted with missions at a crucial and difficult time. The late emperor knew that I am cautious and prudent, so on his deathbed he charged me with the great affairs of state. Ever since I received his command, I have sighed in distress day and night, fearing that I would fail in my commission and thereby impugn his wisdom. Therefore, in the fifth month we crossed the Lu River and penetrated deep into the desert. Now, while the South is already pacified and our weapons and armor are in good supply, we should encourage the troops and lead them north to pacify the Central Plain. I yearn to use every bit of my limited ability to expel our arch-enemy, restore the house of Han, and return us to the old capital. In this way, I might repay the late emperor and demonstrate my loyalty to Your Majesty.

It is the duty of Guo, Fei, and Dong to offer honest advice in assessing government policies. But I pray that Your Majesty will entrust the job of suppressing the enemy and restoring the dynasty to me. If I fail, then punish me for my transgression in order to mollify the soul of the late emperor. If Guo, Fei, [and] Dong have no advice for enhancing your virtue, then rebuke them for their mistakes and expose their dereliction. Your Majesty should also seek solutions on your own, taking counsel and selecting wise policies, weighing and adopting appropriate advice, and bearing very much in mind the last wishes of the late emperor. I am deeply grateful for having received so much favor. Now I must go far away. I weep over this memorial, unaware of what I have said.[7]

The next work is a memorial composed by the Western Jin (256–316) official Li Mi (ca. 225–ca. 290) explaining his reasons for declining office, which later was given the title "Memorial Expressing My Feelings" ("Chenqing biao"). In contrast to Zhuge Liang's memorial that poured out his feelings as a loyal minister to persuade his ruler to pursue the right course on matters of state, Li Mi's work lays out an argument centered on familial ethics, the demands of filial piety, and the bond between grandson and grandmother. Li's narrative focuses on how a "grandmother and grandson relied on each other for their very lives," recounting how Li Mi was orphaned at a young age, explaining the way he was raised to adulthood by his grandmother, and expressing that now that she was ill, infirm, and without support, he ardently desired to repay his debt of gratitude by caring for her in her old age. The language of his memorial is somber, yet sincere, moving the reader naturally. Describing the unique combination of deeply held feelings and literary crafting in Li Mi's memorial, Song dynasty (960–1279) scholar-official Li Geifei (late eleventh–early twelfth centuries) stated, "powerfully flowing from the depths of his heart, yet surprisingly one sees no traces of the hatchet's cuts."[8] Li's memorial is replete with images and metaphors. It also makes frequent use of reduplication (*diezi*) and parallel passages (*paibi*) to enhance its emotive and persuasive power, such as "I am so miserable and alone, my body and shadow console each other" and "Grandmother Liu is nearing the sunset of her years, and with faint and weakened breath, her life has reached a precarious, delicate state. One cannot predict in the morning what will happen in the evening." Because of the way Li Mi combined vigorous expression with the artistry of parallelism, his piece was included in both anthologies that favored parallel prose as well as those that emphasized the freer rhythms of ancient-style prose and therefore continued to be read by generations of later readers.

C7.2 Li Mi, "Memorial Expressing My Feelings"

Your servant Mi states:

Because of a parlous fate, I early encountered grief and misfortune. When I was an infant of only six months my loving father passed away. When I was four my mother's brother forced my mother to remarry against her will. Grandmother Liu took pity on this weak orphan and personally cared for me. When young, I was often so sick that even at the age of nine I could not walk. Solitary and alone I suffered until I reached adulthood. I had neither uncles nor brothers, and my family was so destitute and devoid of good fortune that only late in life did I have offspring. Outside the household, I have no close relatives whom I can mourn; inside, I have not even a boy servant to watch the gate. I am so miserable and alone, my body and shadow console each other. Grandmother Liu long has been ill and is constantly bedridden. I serve her medicinal brews, and I have never abandoned her or left her side.

When I came into the service of this Sage dynasty, I bathed in Your pure transforming influence. First Governor Kui sponsored me as Filial and Pure. Later Inspector Rong recommended me as a Flourishing Talent. But because there was no one to care for grandmother, I declined and did not take up the appointment. An edict was especially issued appointing me Palace Gentleman. Not long thereafter I received imperial favor and was newly appointed Aide to the Crown Prince. I humbly believe that for a man as lowly and insignificant as I to be deemed worthy of serving in the Eastern Palace is an honor I could never requite you for even by giving my life. I informed you of all the circumstances in a memorial, and I again declined and did not go to my post. Your edict was insistent and stern, accusing me of being dilatory and disrespectful. The commandery and prefectural authorities tried to pressure me and urged me to take the road up to the capital. The local officials approached my door swifter than shooting stars. I wanted to comply with your edict and dash off to my post, but Grandmother Liu's illness daily became more grave. I wished temporarily to follow my personal desires, but my plea was not granted. Whether to serve or retire truly was a great dilemma!

I humbly believe that this Sage dynasty governs the empire by means of filial piety, and that all among the aged and elderly still receive compassion and care. How much more needful am I whose solitary suffering has been especially severe! Moreover, when young I served the false dynasty, and I have moved through the various gentleman posts. I originally planned to become

N.B. Straight underline indicates the use of repetitive patterning; wavy underline the use of parallel patterning. For a discussion on repetitive and parallel patterning,
➥ C1.1–4 and C1.6–7.

李密 陳情表

臣密言： ⁴臣以險
釁， ⁴夙遭閔凶。⁴生孩
六月， ⁴慈父見背； ⁴行
年四歲， ⁴舅奪母志。
祖母劉愍臣孤弱， ⁴躬
親撫養。 臣少多疾
病， ⁴九歲不行， ⁴零丁
孤苦， ⁴至於成立。⁴既
無伯叔， ⁴終鮮兄
弟， ⁴門衰祚薄， ⁴晚
有兒息。外無期功強
近之親， 內無應門
五尺之僮。⁴煢煢獨
立， ⁴形影相弔。而劉
夙嬰疾病， ⁴常在床
蓐。⁴臣侍湯藥， ⁴未曾
廢離。

⁴逮奉聖朝， ⁴沐浴
清化。 前太守臣逵
察臣孝廉，後刺史臣
榮舉臣秀才。臣以
供養無主， ⁴辭不赴
命。⁴詔書特下， ⁴拜臣
郎中， ⁴尋蒙國恩， ⁴除
臣洗馬。 ⁴猥以微
賤， ⁴當侍東宮，非臣
隕首所能上報。臣具以
表聞， ⁴辭不就職。⁴詔
書切峻， ⁴責臣逋
慢。⁴郡縣逼迫， ⁴催臣
上道；⁴州司臨門， ⁴急
於星火。 ⁶臣欲 奉
詔奔馳， ⁴⁺¹則／劉
病日篤； ⁴⁺¹欲／苟順
私情， ⁴⁺¹則／告訴不

許。⁴臣之進退，⁴實為
狼狽。

　伏惟聖朝以孝治天
下，⁴凡在故老，⁴猶蒙
矜育，⁴況臣孤苦，⁴特
為尤甚。⁶且臣少仕偽
朝，⁴歷職郎署，⁴本圖
宦達，⁴不矜名節。⁶今
臣亡國賤俘，⁴至微至
陋，⁴過蒙拔擢，⁴寵命
優渥，豈敢盤桓有所
希冀。但以劉日薄西
山，⁴氣息奄奄，⁴人命
危淺，⁴朝不慮夕。⁴臣
無祖母，無以至今日；
⁴祖母無臣，無以終餘
年。母孫二人更相為
命，是以區區不能廢
遠。

　臣密　今年　四
十有四，祖母劉今
年九十有六，是臣盡
節於陛下之日長，⁶⁺¹報
養劉之日短/也。⁴烏鳥
私情，⁴願乞終養。⁴臣
之辛苦，非獨蜀之人
士及二州牧伯所見明
知，⁴皇天后土，⁴實所
共鑒。願陛下矜愍愚
誠，⁴聽臣微志，庶劉
僥倖保卒餘年。臣生當
隕首，⁴死當結草。臣
不勝犬馬怖懼之情，謹
拜表以聞。

[WX 1694–1696]

N.B. Straight underline
indicates the use of repetitive
patterning; wavy underline the
use of parallel patterning. For
a discussion on repetitive and
parallel patterning, ☛ C1.1–4
and C1.6–7.

illustrious as an official, but I never cared about my reputation and character. Now I am a humble captive of a fallen state. I am utterly insignificant and unimportant, but I have received more promotions than I deserve, and your gracious charge is both liberal and generous. How would I dare demur, with the hope of receiving something better? However, I believe that Grandmother Liu is nearing the sunset of her years, and with faint and weakened breath, her life has reached a precarious, delicate stage. One cannot predict in the morning what will happen in the evening. Without grandmother I would not be alive today. Without me grandmother would not have been able to live out her remaining years. Grandmother and grandson have depended upon one another for life. Thus, simply because of my own small, selfish desires I cannot abandon or leave her. I am now in my forty-fourth year, and Grandmother Liu is now ninety-six. Thus, I have a long time in which to fulfill my duty to Your Majesty, and only a short time in which to repay Grandmother Liu for raising me. I am like the crow that feeds its mother, and I beg to be allowed to care for her to her final days. My suffering and misery are not only clearly known by the men of Shu and the governors of the two provinces (of Liang and Yi), they have been perceived by August Heaven and Sovereign Earth. I hope your majesty will take pity on my naïve sincerity and will grant my humble wish, so that Grandmother Liu will have the good fortune to preserve the remaining years of her life. While I am alive, I shall offer my life in your service. When dead, I shall "knot a clump of grass" for you.

　　With unbearable apprehension, like a loyal dog or horse, I respectfully present this memorial to inform you of my feelings.⁹

Li Mi's memorial can be productively compared with the letter written by late-imperial scholar-official Fang Bao (1668–1749) to examine how each author draws on Confucian familial-based ethics to justify different courses of action that contravened state authority, such as Li Mi's defense of his right to withdraw from office or Fang Bao's bearing witness to the unjustified imprisonment and torture of a beloved teacher (☛ C15.2).

Following the end of the Wei (220–265) and Jin (265–420) dynasties, political authority in medieval China was divided between kingdoms in the north and south with frequent usurpations of imperial power. Both the scope and number of memorials with lyrical content rapidly expanded during these turbulent centuries. With the rise of self-conscious literary creation and awareness of generic distinctions and decorum, writers paid greater attention to linguistic and rhetorical crafting in their pursuit of elegance and beauty. In his chapter on "Memorials," Liu Xie stated his standard for the genre as follows: "The *biao* must have intellectual delicacy in order to ensure that its influence will prevail, and purity of style to drive home the effect of beauty."¹⁰ Liu Xie reserved special distinction for the memorials of Cao Zhi (192–232), stating, "The memorials of Cao Zhi stand alone as the best among these talents. Just observe how his style was rich and his prosody harmonious, his words lucid and his intentions manifest. Responding to externals, he fashioned artistry; in accord with change, he generated delight. His control of the reins was superlative, so whether slow or fast, he adapted to the rhythm."[11]

The third example from the memorial genre is Cao Zhi's "Memorial Seeking to Prove Myself" ("Qiu zi shi biao"). Cao Zhi harbored high political ambitions as a youth and, with his literary talent, once enjoyed the favor of his father, Cao Cao (155–220). But when power passed first into the hands of his elder brother, Cao Pi, and later to his nephew Cao Rui (204–239), Cao Zhi became the object of suspicion at court. Increasingly marginalized from the center of power at the Wei dynasty court, Cao Zhi turned to literature as a means to express his discontent and frustrated ambition and as a persuasive tool to argue for his rightful return to positions of authority and influence. Cao Zhi's "Memorial Seeking to Prove Myself" addressed to Cao Rui as Emperor Ming of the Wei in the form of a self-recommendation to office. In this memorial, Cao Zhi assumes the self-deprecating tone of a disgraced minister who seeks not to enjoy high rank or salary, but rather to prove himself by serving in a military position, showing his willingness to die in support of his kingdom without regrets. The theme of "seeking to prove myself" is common to the memorial genre. Cao Zhi's work is remarkable for its synthesis of literary craft, rational argumentation, narration, and self-expression. In its use of language, this work alternates between parallel and free prose, using the former to intensify the forcefulness and rhythm of the prose and the latter to express himself in a sincere and direct manner. His frequent use of allusions adds subtly and deeper meaning to his arguments. In sum, the broad array of literary techniques employed by Cao Zhi in this single memorial have made it a model for later readers as well as a landmark for the mature development of parallel prose in Chinese literary history.

C7.3 Cao Zhi, "Memorial Seeking to Prove Myself"

Your servant Zhi states:

I have heard that while a man is alive he serves his father within and his ruler without. The height of serving one's father lies in glorifying one's parents, and the epitome of serving one's ruler lies in making the state prosper. Therefore, an affectionate father cannot love a worthless son, and a benevolent ruler cannot cherish a useless subject. The ruler who evaluates character before conferring office is one who will succeed in his work. The subject who takes stock of his abilities before accepting a title is one who will fulfill his mandate. Therefore, a ruler should not groundlessly confer office, nor should a subject groundlessly accept it. One may refer to the groundless conferring of office as a reckless appointment. One may refer to the groundless acceptance of an office as salary for a corpse. Such are the origins of the expression "freeload" in the *Classic of Songs*.

In the past when the two Guos did not decline office in the two states, it was because their moral character was substantial. And when Dan and Shi did not refuse fiefs in Yan and Lu, it was because their merit was great. Now, I have received the manifold kindnesses of the state for three reigns up to now.

曹植 求自試表

臣植言：⁶臣聞士之生世，⁴入則事父，⁴出則事君。⁶事父尚於榮親，⁶事君貴於興國。故慈父不能愛無益之子，仁君不能畜無用之臣。⁶⁺¹夫／論德而授官者，⁴⁺¹成功之君／也；⁶量能而受爵者，⁴⁺¹畢命之臣/也。⁴⁺¹故/君無虛授，⁴臣無虛受。⁶虛授謂之謬舉，⁶虛受謂之尸祿。詩之素餐所由作也。昔二虢不辭兩國之任，⁴其德厚也；

旦、奭不讓燕、魯之
封，⁴其功大也。⁶今
臣蒙國重恩，三世於
今矣。正值陛下升平
之際，⁴沐浴聖澤，⁴潛
潤德教，⁴可謂厚
幸／矣。⁴⁺¹而／位竊東
藩，⁴爵在上列，⁴身被
輕煖，⁴口厭百味，⁴目
極華靡，⁴⁺¹耳倦絲
竹／者，⁶⁺¹爵重祿厚
之所致／也。退念古
之受爵祿者，⁴有異
於此，⁶皆以功勤濟
國，⁴輔主惠民。⁶今
臣無德可述，⁴無功可
紀，⁴若此終年，⁴無
益國朝，將挂風人彼
己之譏。⁶是以上慚玄
冕，⁴俯愧朱紱。

⁶方今天下一統，⁴九
州晏如。顧西尚有違
命之蜀，⁶東有不
臣之吳。⁶⁺¹使／邊境未
得稅甲，⁶⁺¹謀士未得高
枕／者，⁶誠欲混同宇
內，⁴以致太和／也。故
啟滅有扈而夏功昭，成
克商、奄而周德著。
今陛下以聖明統世，
將欲卒文、武之功，
繼成、康之隆，⁴簡良
授能，以方叔，邵虎之
臣，⁴鎮衛四境，⁴⁺¹為國
爪牙／者，⁴可謂當矣。
然而高鳥未挂於輕
繳，淵魚未懸於鉤
餌者，恐鉤射之術
或未盡也。昔耿弇
不俟光武，⁴亟擊張
步，言不以賊遺於君
父也。故車右伏劍於
明轂，雍門刎首於齊
境。⁴若此二子，⁶⁺¹豈

To happen to have encountered a time of ascendant peace under Your Majesty, to be steeped in Your sage benevolence and imbued with Your virtuous teachings can be said to be very good fortune indeed. I have been placed in my eastern fief, my title of nobility is one of highest rank, my body is clothed in clothing that is light, yet warm, my mouth is sated with every kind of good taste, my eyes take in all that is gorgeous, my ears are weary of music—such being the result of my important title and generous income. When I consider the bestowal of ranks and emoluments in antiquity, it was different from this. It was always for meritorious endeavors in rescuing the state or aiding the ruler in being kind to the people. Now I have no virtue worth mentioning, no deeds worth writing down. If I end my days like this without benefiting state or court, I will encounter the ridicule "that fellow," which is used to criticize someone. Therefore, I am ashamed of my black cap above, and, looking down, embarrassed of my vermilion belt.

At present the empire is under one ruler and the nine provinces are at peace. But looking to the west there is Shu, which ignores commands, and in the east is Wu, which has not submitted. What prevents our border lands from laying down their arms and the strategists from resting peacefully is that we want to unite the world to bring about the great peace. Thus, Qi vanquished Youhu and the achievements of Xia shone, Cheng overcame Shang and Yan and the virtue of Zhou was made known.

Now Your Majesty uses his sage wisdom to unite the world and is about to complete the prosperity of Kings Cheng and Kang; so to select the worthy and confer office on the able, to use officials like Fangshu and Hu of Shao to subdue and control the four borders and be the claws and teeth of the state, can be termed appropriate. But when the high-flying bird is not strung on the light arrowstring, and the deep-diving fish is not hung from the baited hook, perhaps it is because one's archery and angling techniques are not yet fully developed.

In former times Geng Yan did not wait for Guangwu, but instead urgently attacked Zhang Bu, saying he would not bequeath rebels to the emperor. Of old, a chariot soldier killed himself over a squeaky hub; so Yongmen cut his own throat over the borders of Qi. It is impossible that men such as these two despised life and prized death. Actually, they were indignant at the disrespect and insult to their rulers. As to the favorite subjects of a ruler, they want to get rid of misfortune and initiate what is beneficial. As to the way a subject serves his ruler, he must give his life to quell disorder and repay the ruler's kindness with meritorious service. In the past, when Jia Yi was a youth, he sought a chance to prove himself in a dependent state and asked permission to "tie a rope about the neck of the khan and control his fate." And in his youth Zhong Jun was sent to Yue and wanted to get some long hatstrings, seize its king, and bring him bound to the northern palace. It is impossible that these two subjects merely wished to brag before their rulers and dazzle the world. Perhaps their ambitions were stifled and they wanted to display their talents and offer their abilities to enlightened rulers

Formerly, Emperor Wu of Han built a mansion for Huo Qubing, but Huo declined, saying, "Since the Xiongnu have not yet been wiped out, I shall not consider my family." Now, to be concerned for the country and forget about one's family, to give up one's life for its difficulties, such are the ambitions of the loyal subject. At present I live away from the court. It's not that I am not well off, yet I don't sleep soundly and I don't indulge in tasty food. My only thought is that Shu and Wu are not yet conquered.

I respectfully note that of my father Emperor Wu's military officials and veteran generals, there is often word that they have grown old and died. Even if worthies are not lacking in the world, it is the old generals and former soldiers who are not yet familiar with warfare. I do not know my abilities, but my ambition is to offer my life, and I hope to establish even the slightest merit to repay the favor I have received. If Your Majesty issues some unusual order putting me to the most trifling use, if I am allowed in the West to be attached to the General-in-chief and take charge of a single regiment, or in the East to be attached to the Commander-in-chief and take command of an auxiliary boat, I won't fail to ride into danger and march into difficulty, to speed my boat and spur my black charger, to run against blades and rush upon lances, and to be the vanguard of the troops. I am not yet able to capture Quan or cut off the ear of Liang, but I hope to capture their brave generals and destroy their evil followers. I will certainly offer up a speedy victory and thereby wipe out a lifetime's shame, make my name hang from historians' pens and my deeds go down in the records of the court. Even if my body is rent on the borders of Shu or my head hung from the gate towers of Wu, I will count it as years of life.

If my meager talents are not tested, I will have no fame to the end of my days. For me merely to glorify my person and enrich my body would be to make no contributions to affairs in life and to have no harmful effect on the fortunes [of our house] in death. To receive high position for no good reason and be unworthy of high salary, to rest like a beast and watch like a bird until white-haired, such a man is but a penned creature, and this is not what I aspire to.[12]

Memorials were originally considered a purely utilitarian genre, but beginning with the works of Cao Zhi, the form both adopted the enumerative style of the Han rhapsody through the use of cascading lists and layered descriptive phrases and focused on greater literary crafting, leading to the practice of writing memorials in parallel prose. Specifically, the diction of memorials went from being simple and unadorned to elegant and ornate, while sentences shifted from a free prose arrangement to greater use of parallel constructions. In the hands of later writers, this often resulted in memorials in which form overwhelmed substance. But despite its great length, amounting to more than one thousand and five hundred characters, Cao Zhi's "A Memorial Proving Myself" still impresses the reader with its free-flowing arguments and emotive power.

惡生而尚死哉？誠忿其慢主而凌君也。[4+1]夫君之寵臣，[6]欲以除患興利；[4]臣之事君，[6]必以殺身靜亂，[4+1]以功報主／也。昔賈誼弱冠，[4]求試屬國，請係單于之頸而制其命。終軍以妙年使越，欲得長纓占其王，[4]羈致北闕。[4]此二臣者，豈好爲夸主而曜世俗哉？[4]志或鬱結，欲逞其才力，輸能於明君也。昔漢武爲霍去病治第，辭曰：[4]"匈奴未滅，臣無以家爲！"[4+1]夫／憂國忘家，[4]捐軀濟難，[4+1]忠臣之志／也。

[4]今臣居外，[4]非不厚也，[4+1]而／寢不安席，[4+1]食不遑味／者，以二方未尅爲念。伏見先帝武臣宿兵，年者即世者有聞矣，雖賢不乏世，宿將舊卒由習戰也。[4]竊不自量，[4]志在授命，[6]庶立毛髮之功，[6]以報所受之恩。若使陛下出不世之詔，[6]效臣錐刀之用，使得西屬大將軍，當一校之隊。若東屬大司馬，統偏師之任。必乘危蹈險，[4]騁舟奮驪，[4]突刃觸鋒，[4]爲士卒先。雖未能擒權馘亮，[6]庶將虜其雄率，[4]殲其醜類，[6]必效須臾之捷，[6]以滅終身之愧。使名掛史筆，[4]事列朝榮。[4+1]雖／身分蜀境，[4]首懸吳

闕，猶生之年也。如微
才弗試，⁴沒世無聞，
徒榮其軀而豐其體，
生無益於事，死無
損於數，虛荷上位而忝
重祿，⁴禽息鳥視，⁴終
於白首，此徒圈牢之養
物，非臣之所志也。

[*CZJJ* 3b–6b]

N.B. Straight underline
indicates the use of repetitive
patterning; wavy underline the
use of parallel patterning. For
a discussion on repetitive and
parallel patterning, ☞ C1.1–4
and C1.6–7.

LETTERS

In contrast to the official nature of memorials, letters were primarily written works exchanged among friends and relatives. In premodern times transportation was less convenient. A centralized official courier network and relay stations emerged in the Qin dynasty (221–207 BCE) and was perfected in the Han dynasty. The majority of transmitted personal letters from early medieval China were delivered by private messengers. Linguistically the word *xin* (originally meaning "to be trustworthy") took on the new meaning of "messenger" for the first time toward the end of the early medieval period, highlighting the degree to which delivery of letters relied on the good will of their carriers. The sometimes-problematic dependence on messengers even became a literary theme. For this reason, the delivery of letters could take weeks, months, or up to a year in time.[13] Letters were an essential means to transmit important information, solidify the links among members of a far-flung social network, and express one's innermost feelings to a letter's addressee. Letters were more personal in nature and therefore opened a window onto their writer's thoughts and state of mind. Letters were not bound to any set length and could be quite flexible in generic form. After the Han dynasty, the number of personal letters composed increased, and it soon became a standard part of a scholar-official's literary repertoire. Between the second and sixth centuries, the generic status of the letter was raised in the hands of talented writers, gaining full recognition when anthologies began to collect and separately categorize letters as a genre with unique characteristics and distinct intrageneric references.[14]

Among the letters transmitted from the Han dynasty, the "Letter to Ren An" ("Bao Ren Shaoqing shu") by the grand historian Sima Qian (ca. 145–ca. 86 BCE) has long been the most renowned. Given the complex history of this influential letter's transmission, scholarly debates recently have arisen about the letter's provenance. But no matter how the content of the letter may have been reshaped in transmission, scholars are united in their admiration of this letter ascribed to Sima Qian as a profound literary landmark.[15] Sima Qian's letter recounts his ill-fated defense of Li Ling (died 74 BCE), a military man he greatly admired who had led a force of five thousand men deep into nomadic Xiongnu territory. Unfortunately, outnumbered and poorly supplied, Li Ling was defeated and captured. While others at the Han court spoke out against Li Ling, Sima continued to support him. Emperor Wu of Han (reigned 140–87 BCE) was enraged that Li Ling had been captured alive and had Sima imprisoned for defending Li's military defeat. Not long afterward, Sima was found guilty of "defaming the emperor," a crime that carried a sentence of death. Although this sentence could be commuted by the payment of a large sum of money, Sima's family was poor and could not afford to do so. Under the circumstances, it was expected that a man of noble character would commit suicide. Instead, Sima agreed to undergo the humiliating punishment of castration in place of either suicide or execution. Sima's letter is addressed to Ren An, a colleague who wrote to Sima Qian to advise Sima to be circumspect in his social contacts and confine himself to recommending other persons of talent to office after his punishment. By the time Sima replied, Ren An was in prison and awaiting execution due to accusations of his involvement in a rebellion led by Prince Li.

These extraordinary circumstances can account in part for the breathtaking directness with which Sima's letter exposes his pain and sense of injustice. The literary style of Sima's letter alternates between penetrating argumentation and impassioned lyricism. The "Letter to Ren An" is simultaneously a confession of Sima Qian's errors and shame, a powerful expression of his anger at the injustice of his punishment, and a justification of his decision to live with this humiliation based on the greater goal to complete his historical masterpiece, *Grand Scribe's Records* (*Shiji*).[16]

C7.4 Sima Qian, "Letter to Ren An"

司馬遷 報任安書

Some time ago you deigned to send me a letter in which you advised me to be concerned for my social contacts and devote myself to the recommendation and advancement of qualified persons. You expressed yourself with considerable vigor, as though you expected I would not follow your advice but would be influenced by the words of the vulgar: I would hardly behave in such a way. I may be a broken hack, but I have still been exposed to the teachings handed down by my elders. However, I see myself as mutilated and disgraced: I am criticized if I act, and where I hope to be helpful I do harm instead. This causes me secret distress, but to whom can I unburden myself? As the proverb says, "For whom do you do it? Who are you going to get to listen to you?" Why was it that Boya never again played his lute after Zhong Ziqi died? A gentleman acts on behalf of an understanding friend, as a woman makes herself beautiful for her lover. Someone like me whose virility is lacking could never be a hero, even if he had the endowments of the pearl of Sui and the jade of Bianhe or conducted himself like Xu You and Bo Yi; he would only succeed in being laughed at and put to shame.

I should have answered your letter sooner, but when I got back from the East in the emperor's suite I was very busy. We were seldom together, and then I was so pressed that there was never a moment's time when I could speak my mind. Now you, Shaoqing, are under an accusation whose outcome is uncertain. Weeks and months have passed until we have now reached the end of winter, and I am going to have to accompany the emperor to Yong. I am afraid that that may come to pass which cannot be avoided, and as a result I will never have the chance to give expression to my grievance and explain myself to you. It would mean that the souls of the departed would carry a never-ending burden of secret resentment. Let me say what is on my mind; I hope you will not hold it against me that I have been negligent in leaving your letter so long unanswered. . . .

It has been twenty years since I inherited my father's office and entered the service of the emperor. It occurs to me that during that time I have not been able to demonstrate my loyalty and sincerity or win praise for good advice and outstanding abilities in the service of a wise ruler; nor have I been able to make

⁴少卿足下：曩者辱
賜書，⁶教以慎於接
物、⁶推賢進士爲
務，⁶意氣勤勤懇懇，
若望僕不相師用，⁶而
流俗人之言。⁶僕非敢
如此也。雖罷駑，亦嘗
側聞長者遺風矣。顧
自以爲身殘處穢，⁴動
而見尤，⁴欲益反損，
是以抑鬱而無誰語。
諺曰：⁴誰爲爲之？⁴孰
令聽之？⁴⁺¹蓋／鍾子期
死，伯牙終身不復鼓
琴。何則？⁶士爲知
己者用，⁶女爲説
己者容。若僕大質已
虧缺，⁴⁺¹雖／材懷隨
和，⁴行若由夷，⁶終不
可以爲榮，適足以發笑
而自點耳。

⁴書辭宜答，會東從
上來，⁴又迫賤事，⁴相
見日淺，卒卒無須臾
之間，⁴得竭指意。今
少卿抱不測之罪，涉旬
月，迫季冬，僕又薄從
上上雍，⁶恐卒然不可
諱。是僕終已不得舒憤
懣以曉左右，則長逝者
魂魄私恨無窮。請略陳

固陋。⁴闋然不報，幸
勿過。

　　· · · · · ·

　　⁶僕賴先人緒業，⁶得
待罪輦轂下，二十餘
年矣。⁴所以自惟：上
之，⁶不能納忠效信，
有奇策才力之譽，⁴自
結明主；次之，又不
能拾遺補闕，⁴招賢進
能，顯巖穴之士；外
之，又不能備行伍，攻
城野戰，有斬將搴旗之
功；下之，⁶不能累日
積勞，取尊官厚祿，
以爲宗族交遊光寵。
四者無一遂，⁴苟合取
容，⁶無所短長之效，
可見於此矣。鄉者，僕
亦嘗廁下大夫之列，陪
外廷末議，不以此時引
維綱，盡思慮，今已
虧形爲掃除之隸，在
闒茸之中，乃欲卬首
信眉，⁴論列是非，不
亦輕朝廷，⁶羞當世之
士邪！嗟乎！嗟乎！如
僕，⁴尚何言哉！⁴尚何
言哉！· · · · · ·
　　僕之先人非有剖符
丹書之功，文史星曆近
乎卜祝之間，固主上所
戲弄，⁴倡優畜之，流
俗之所輕也。假令僕伏
法受誅，⁶若九牛亡一
毛，與螻蟻何異？而世
又不與能死節者比，特
以爲智窮罪極，⁴不能自
免，⁴卒就死耳。何也？
素所自樹立使然。人固
有一死，⁶死有<u>重於泰
山</u>，或<u>輕於鴻毛</u>，用
之所趨異也。太上不辱
先，<u>其次不辱身</u>，⁶其

good defects or omissions, or advance the worthy and talented, or induce wise hermits to serve; nor have I been able to serve in the ranks of the army, attacking walled cities and fighting in the field to win merit by taking an enemy general's head or capturing his banners; nor have I been able to win merit through long and faithful service to rise to high office and handsome salary, to the glory of my family and the benefit of my friends. From my failure in all four of these endeavors it follows that I am prepared to compromise with the times and avoid giving offense, wholly ineffectual for good or ill. Formerly as Great Officer of the third grade I once had the chance to participate in deliberations in a minor capacity. Since I then offered no great plans nor expressed myself freely, would it not be an insult to the court and an affront to my colleagues if now, mutilated, a menial who sweeps the floor, a miserable wretch, I should raise my head and stretch my eyebrows to argue right and wrong? Alas, for one like me what is there left to say? What is there left to say? . . .

My father never earned tally and patent of nobility; as annalist and astrologer I was not far removed from the diviners and invokers, truly the plaything of the emperor, kept like any singing girl of jester, and despised by the world. Had I chosen to submit to the law and let myself be put to death, it would have been no more important than the loss of a single hair from nine oxen, no different from the crushing of an ant. No one would have credited me with dying for a principle; rather they would have thought that I had simply died because I was at my wit's end and my offense allowed no other way out. And why? They would think so because of the occupation in which I established myself.

A man can die only once, and whether death to him is as weighty as Mount Tai or as light as a feather depends on the reason for which he dies. The most important thing is not to disgrace one's ancestors, the next is to not to disgrace one's self, the next not to disgrace one's principles, the next not to disgrace one's manners. Next worse is the disgrace of being put in fetters, the next is to wear a prisoner's garb, the next is to be beaten in the stocks, the next is to have the head shaved and a metal chain fastened around the neck, the next is mutilation, and the very worst disgrace of all is castration. It is said that corporal punishments are not applied to the great officers, implying that an officer cannot but be careful of his integrity. When the fierce tiger is in the depths of the mountain, all animals hold him in fear, but when he falls into a trap he waves his tail and begs for food: this is the end result of curtailing his dignity. Hence if you draw the plan of a jail on the ground, a gentleman will not step inside the figure, nor will he address even the wooden image of a jailor. In this way he shows his determination never to find himself in such a position. But let him cross his hands and feet to receive the bonds, expose his back to receive the whip, and be incarcerated in the barred cell—by then when he sees the jailor[,] he bows his head to the ground and at the sight of his underlings he pants in terror. And why? It is the result of the gradual curtailment of his dignity. If he now claims there has been no disgrace, he is devoid of a sense of shame and wholly unworthy of respect.

Wen Wang was an earl, and yet he was held prisoner in Youli; Li Si was primer minister and yet was visited with all five punishments; Han Xin was a prince and yet he was put in the stocks in Chen; Peng Yue and Zhang Ao each sat on a throne and called himself king, and yet the one was fettered in prison, the other put to death. These were all men of high rank and office and widespread reputation, but when they got into trouble with the law[,] they were unable resolutely to put an end to themselves. It has always been the same: when one lies in the dirt there is no question of his not being disgraced. In the light of these examples, bravery and cowardice are a matter of circumstance, strength and weakness depend on conditions. Once this is understood, there is nothing to be surprised at in their behavior. If by failing to do away with himself before he is in the clutches of the law a man is degraded to the point of being flogged and then wishes to rescue his honor, has he not missed his chance? This is no doubt why the ancients were chary of applying corporal punishment to a great officer.

Now there is no man who does not naturally cling to life and avoid death, love his parents and cherish his wife and children. But the man who is devoted to the right sometimes has no choice but to behave otherwise. I early had the misfortune to lose my father and mother; I had no brother and was quite alone. You have seen how little my affection for my wife and children deterred me from speaking out. But a brave man will not always die for his honor, and what efforts will not even a coward make in a cause to which he is devoted? I may be a coward and wish to live at the expense of my honor, but I surely know how to act appropriately. Would I have abandoned myself to ignominy of being tied and bound? Even a miserable slavegirl is capable of putting an end to herself; could you expect less of me, when I had so little choice? If I concealed my feelings and clung to life, burying myself in filth without protest, it was because I could not bear to leave unfinished my deeply cherished project, because I rejected the idea of dying without leaving.

In the past there have been innumerable men of wealth and rank whose names died with them; only the outstanding and unusual are known today. It was when King Wen was in prison that he expanded the *Book of Changes*; when Confucius was in straits he wrote the *Spring and Autumn Annals*; when Qu Yuan was banished he composed "On Encountering Trouble"; Zuo Qiu lost his sight and so we have the *Conversations from the States*; Sunzi had his feet chopped off, and *The Art of War* was put together. The general purport of the three hundred poems of the *Book of Songs* is the indignation expressed by the sages. All of these men were oppressed in their minds, and, unable to put into action their principles, wrote of the past with their eyes on the future. For example, Zuo Qiu without sight and Sunzi with amputated feet were permanently disabled. They retired to write books in which they expressed their pent-up feelings, hoping to realize themselves in literature, since action was denied them.

I have ventured not to look for more recent models, but with what little literary ability I possess I have brought together the scattered fragments of ancient lore.

次不辱 理色，⁶其次不辱 辭令，⁶其次 詘體受辱，⁶其次 易服受辱，其次 關木索、被箠楚受辱，其次 鬄毛髮、嬰金鐵受辱，其次 毀肌膚、斷支體 受辱，⁴最下腐刑，極矣。傳曰"刑不上大夫"，此言士節不可不勉也。猛虎處深山，⁴百獸震恐，及其在穽檻之中，搖尾而求食，積威約之漸也。故士有畫地爲牢勢不入，削木爲吏議不對，定計於鮮也。⁴今交 手足，受 木索，暴 肌膚，受榜箠，⁶幽於圜牆之中。⁴當此之時，見獄吏 則頭槍地，視徒隸則心惕息。何者？積威約之勢也。⁴及已至此，⁴言不辱者，所謂彊顏耳，⁴曷足貴乎！且西伯，伯也，拘羑里；李斯，相也，具五刑；淮陰，王也，⁴受械於陳；彭越、張敖，⁴南鄉稱孤，⁴繫獄具罪；絳侯誅諸呂，⁴權傾五伯，⁴囚於請室；魏其，大將也，衣赭、關三木；季布爲朱家鉗奴；⁶灌夫受辱居室。此人皆身至王侯將相，⁴聲聞隣國，及罪至罔加，⁶不能引決自財。在塵埃之中，⁴古今一體，安在其不辱也！⁴由此言之，勇怯，勢也；彊弱，形也。審矣，⁴曷足怪乎！且人不能蚤自財繩墨之外，已稍陵夷至於鞭箠之間，⁴乃欲引節，⁴⁺¹斯不

亦遠／乎！古人所以重
施刑於大夫者，殆爲此
也。

　夫人情莫不貪生惡
死，念親戚，顧妻子。
至激於義理者不然，乃
有不得已也。⁴今僕不
幸，⁴蚤失二親，無兄弟
之親，⁴獨身孤立。少卿
視僕於妻子何如哉？且
勇者不必死節，⁴怯夫慕
義，⁴⁺¹何處不勉／焉。僕
雖怯耎欲苟活，亦頗識
去就之分矣，何至自湛
溺累紲之辱哉！且夫臧
獲婢妾猶能引決，況若
僕之不得已乎？⁶所以隱
忍苟活，　函糞土之中
而不辭者，恨私心有所
不盡，鄙沒世而文采不
表於後也。

　古者富貴而名摩
滅，⁴不可勝記，唯俶
儻非常之人稱焉。⁴蓋
西伯拘，⁴而演《周
易》；仲尼厄，⁴而
作《春秋》；⁴屈原放
逐，⁴乃賦《離騷》
；⁴左丘失明，⁴厥有
《國語》；⁴孫子臏
腳，⁴兵法脩列；⁴不韋
遷蜀，⁴世傳《呂覽》
；⁴韓非囚秦，⁴《說
難》、《孤憤》。⁴《
詩》三百篇，大氐聖賢
發憤之所爲作也。此人
皆意有所鬱結，不得
通其道，⁴故述往事，
思來者。及如左丘明無
目，⁴孫子斷足，⁴終不
可用，退論書策以舒
其憤，思垂空文以自
見。⁴僕竊不遜，近自
託於無能之辭，網羅
天下放失舊聞，⁴考之

I studied the events of history and set them down in significant order; I have written 130 chapters in which appears the record of the past—its periods of greatness and decline, of achievement and failure. Further it was my hope, by a thorough comprehension of the workings of affairs divine and human, and a knowledge of the historical process, to create a philosophy of my own. Before my draft was complete this disaster overtook me. It was my concern over my unfinished work that made me submit to the worst of all punishments without showing the rage I felt. When at last I shall have finished my book, I shall store it away in the archives to await the man who will understand it. When it finally becomes known in the world, I shall have paid the debt of my shame; nor will I regret a thousand deaths.

However, this is something I can confide only to a person of intelligence; it would not do to speak of it to the vulgar crowd. When one is in a compromising situation, it is not easy to justify oneself; the world is always ready to misrepresent one's motives. It was in consequence of my speaking out that I met disaster in the first place; were I to make myself doubly a laughingstock in my native place, to the disgrace of my forebears, how could I ever have the face again to visit the grave of my father and mother? Even after a hundred generations my shame will but be the more. This is what makes my bowels burn within me nine times a day, so that at home I sit in a daze and lost, abroad I know not where I am going. Whenever I think of this shame the sweat drenches the clothes on my back. I am fit only to be a slave guarding the women's apartments: better that I should hide away in the farthest depths of the mountains. Instead I go on as best I can, putting up with whatever treatment is meted out to me, and so complete my degradation.

And now you want me to recommend worthy men for advancement! Is this not rather the last thing in the world I would want to do? Even if I should want to deck myself out with fine words and elegant phrases, it would not help me any against the world's incredulity; it would only bring more shame on me. In short, I can hope for justification only after my death.

In a letter I cannot say everything. What I have written is a crude and general statement of my feelings. Respectfully I bow to you.[17]

Sima Qian accomplishes three rhetorical goals through his lengthy letter. First, he provides the only complete firsthand account of the reasons behind his extraordinary punishment. Second, Sima reveals his personal values, expounding on the meaning of life and death. Given his low social status within the Han dynasty court, as one "not far removed from the diviners and invokers," Sima Qian states that to have committed suicide would have meant no greater loss than that "of a single hair from nine oxen, no different from the crushing of an ant." Yet he declares, in what later became an oft-quoted passage, that "A man can die only once, and whether death to him is as weighty as Mount Tai or as light as a feather depends on the reason for which he dies." On first reading, Sima's letter may appear to be simply his confession of cowardice in the face of death and desire to cling to life. Yet, as his argument proceeds, he contends that a man of integrity may choose to endure humiliation to live for the sake of a greater cause. For him, this greater cause is to continue the work of the historian that he inherited from his father. This argument appeals both to his sense of filial piety toward the dead and his responsibility to transmit events to future readers. Third, Sima's letter conveys his views on literature. Sima Qian enumerates several examples of pre-Qin authors who suffered physical punishment or mutilation and turned to writing as a means of transmitting their ideas to future readers. Using these precedents, Sima Qian became the first writer in Chinese history to put forth his philosophy that literature arises from frustration and alienation from the society of one's era. At the same time, he also recognizes that literature has the power to transcend the present moment and reach like-minded readers in the future through the immortality of the written word.

Sima's views on life, death, and literature expressed in his "Letter to Ren An" would have a profound influence on later writers. For example, note the way that late-imperial writer Zhang Pu (1602–1641) borrowed the phrase "heavy and light" (*qing zhong*) from Sima Qian's "Letter to Ren An" in his "The Five Men's Grave Stele" to discuss the meaning of human life and the willingness to sacrifice it for a worthy cause (☛C15.3). Or, consider how Sima Qian's forthright account of his experience facing the possibility of execution in prison created new discursive space for the agonistic voice of the marginalized official in the letter genre that could be taken up again by later writers such as Xia Wanchun (1631–1647) in his "Letter to My Mother, From Prison" (☛C15.5).

The "Letter to Shan Tao Breaking Off Relations" ("Yu Shan Juyuan juejiao shu") written by Ji Kang (223–262) is another letter famous for the frank expression of its author's views and personality, sharing many similar traits with Sima Qian's "Letter to Ren An." As one of the "Seven Sages of the Bamboo Grove" during the Wei dynasty, Ji Kang describes himself as a follower of "Laozi and Zhuangzi" or the school of neo-Daoist thought popular among intellectuals of that era and a person of unrestrained temperament. Ji Kang's letter is a response to Shan Tao's recommendation that he take up public office as Shan's assistant. Although the two men were once friends, Ji Kang bluntly expresses his disappointment in his friend, vehemently declines to take up the office he recommended Ji for, and concludes by breaking off their friendship permanently.[18] Using an argument common to other nonconformist intellectuals of the Wei–Jin period, Ji Kang first declares that he can no longer consider Shan Tao a friend based on Shan's inability to recognize Ji's authentic self or his human nature (*xing*). Ji states that, "all the various modes of conduct of the gentleman take him to the same goal by different paths. He acts in accordance with his nature and rests where he finds his ease." Ji continues to argue that official service constitutes a distortion of his inner nature by society, stating, "One can be so constituted that there are things one cannot endure; honest endorsement cannot be forced. So it is perhaps idle to talk about the familiar 'man of understanding' who can put up with anything, who takes no exception to vulgarity around him but who still preserves his integrity within."

行事，稽其成敗興壞之理，凡百三十篇。亦欲以究天人之際，通古今之變，成一家之言。草創未就，適會此禍，惜其不成，是以就極刑而無慍色。僕誠已著此書，藏之名山，傳之其人通邑大都。則僕償前辱之責，雖萬被戮，豈有悔哉！然此可爲智者道，難爲俗人言也。

且負下未易居，上流多謗議。僕以口語遇遭此禍，重爲鄉黨戮笑，汙辱先人，亦何面目復上父母之丘墓乎？雖累百世，垢彌甚耳！是以腸一日而九回，居則忽忽若有所亡，出則不知所如往。每念斯恥，汗未嘗不發背霑衣也。身直爲閨閤之臣，寧得自引深藏於巖穴邪！故且從俗浮湛，與時俯仰以通其狂惑。今少卿乃教以推賢進士，無乃與僕之私指謬乎？今雖欲自彫瑑，曼辭以自解，無益，於俗不信，祗取辱耳。要之死日，然後是非乃定。書不能盡意，故略陳固陋。

[*HS* 2725–2736]

N.B. Straight underline indicates the use of repetitive patterning; wavy underline the use of parallel patterning. For a discussion on repetitive and parallel patterning, ☛ C1.1–4 and C1.6–7.

He fully describes what he saw as the distorting influence of the court and society in his times in a list of the "seven things I could never stand" and the "two things which would never be condoned." Finally, he appeals to Shan Tao to allow him to pursue Daoist techniques to extend his life so that he may enjoy a simple existence with family away from the world of politics.

稽康　與山巨源絕交書

康白：足下昔稱吾於潁川，⁶吾常謂之知言，然經怪此意尚未熟悉於足下，何從便得之也？⁶前年從河東還，顯宗、阿都說足下議以吾自代，⁴事雖不行，知足下故不知之。⁴足下傍通，多可而少怪。吾直性狹中，⁴多所不堪，⁶⁺¹偶與足下相知／耳。間聞足下遷，⁴愴然不喜，恐足下羞庖人之獨割，⁶引尸祝以自助，⁴手薦鸞刀，⁴漫之羶腥，故具為足下陳其可否。

⁴吾昔讀書，得並介之人，⁴或謂無之，今乃信其真有耳。性有所不堪，⁴真不可強。今空語同知有達人無所不堪，⁴外不殊俗，⁴⁺¹而／內不失正，與一世同其波流，而悔吝不生耳。⁴老子、莊周，⁴吾之師也，⁴親居賤職；柳下惠、東方朔，達人也，⁴安乎卑位，吾豈敢短之哉！⁴⁺¹又／仲尼兼愛，⁴不羞執鞭；⁶子文無欲卿相，⁴⁺¹而／三登令尹，是乃君子思濟物之意也。所謂達則兼善而不渝，窮則自得而無悶。⁴以此觀

C7.5 Ji Kang, "Letter to Shan Tao Breaking Off Relations"

Kang reports:

Some time ago you spoke to me to your uncle, the Prefect of Yingchuan, and I must say I found your estimate of me just. But I wondered how you could have come to so accurate an understanding without really knowing what my principles are. Last year when I came back from Hedong, Gongsun Chong and Lu An said you had proposed me as your successor in office. Nothing came of it, but your proposal made it obvious you really did not understand me at all.

You are versatile: you accept most things and are surprised by little. I, on the other hand, am by nature straightforward and narrow-minded: there are lots of things that I cannot put up with. It was only chance that made us friends. When recently I heard of your promotion in office, I was upset and unhappy, fearing that the cook would be shy of doing the carving himself and would call in the Impersonator of the Dead to help, handing over a kitchen knife soiled with rancid fat. Hence I am writing to make clear what may and may not be done.

It used to be that when in my reading I came across people resolutely above the world, I rather doubted their existence, but now I am convinced that they really do exist after all. One can be so constituted that there are things one cannot endure; honest endorsement cannot be forced. So it is perhaps idle to talk about the familiar "man of understanding" who can put up with anything, who takes no exception to vulgarity around him but who still preserves his integrity within; who goes along with the vacillations of the times without ever feeling a twinge of regret. Laozi and Zhuang Zhou are my masters: they held mean positions. I would hardly criticize *them*. And Confucius, out of his love for all, was ready to hold a coachman's whip; and Ziwen, with no desire for the job, was thrice prime minister: these were gentlemen whose minds were bent on saving the world. This is what is meant by "in success, he shares the benefits with all and does not vacillate; in obscurity, he is content and not depressed."

From this point of view, Yao and Shun's ruling the world, Xu You's retirement to the hills, Zifang's helping Han and Jieyu's singing as he walked all add up to the same thing. When you consider all these gentleman, they can be said to have succeeded in doing what they wanted. Hence all the various modes of conduct of the gentleman take him to the same goal by different paths. He acts in accordance with his nature and rests where he finds his ease. Thus there are those who stick to the court and never emerge, and those who enter the wilderness and never come back.

Moreover, I am filled with admiration when I read the biographies of the recluses Shang Ziping and Tai Xiaowei and can imagine what sort of men they were. Add to that the fact that I lost my father when young, was spoiled by mother and elder brother and never took up the study of the Classics. I was already wayward and lazy by nature, so that my muscles became weak and my flesh flabby. I would commonly go half a month without washing my face, and until the itching became a considerable annoyance, I would not wash my hair. When I had to urinate, if I could stand it[,] I would wait until my bladder cramped inside before I got up.

Further, I was long left to my own devices, and my disposition became arrogant and careless, my bluntness diametrically opposed to etiquette; laziness and rudeness reinforcing one another. But my friends were indulgent and did not attack me for my faults.

Besides, my taste for independence was aggravated by my reading of *Zhuangzi* and *Laozi*; as a result any desire for fame or success grew daily weaker, and my commitment to freedom increasingly firmer. In this I am like the wild deer, which captured young and reared in captivity will be docile and obedient. But if it be caught when full-grown, it will stare wildly and butt against its bonds, dashing into boiling water or fire to escape. You may dress it up with a golden bridle and feed it delicacies, and it will but long the more for its native woods and yearn for rich pasture.

Ruan Ji is not one to talk about people's faults, and I have tried to model myself after him, but in vain. He is a man of finer character than most, one who never injured another. Only in drinking does he go to excess. But even so the proper and correct gentlemen with their restrictions hate him as a mortal enemy, and it is only thanks to the protection of Generalissimo Sima Zhao that he survives. But I, without Ruan Ji's superiority, have the faults of being rude and unrestrained, ignorant of people's characters and blind to opportunity, not careful like Shi Fen, but driven to carry things to their end. The longer I were involved in affairs the more clearly would these defects show. I might want to stay out of trouble, but would it be possible?

Furthermore, in society there are prescribed courtesies, and the court has its rules. When I consider the matter carefully, there are seven things I could never stand and two things which would never be condoned. I am fond of lying late abed, and the herald at my door would not leave me in peace: this is the first thing I could not stand. I like to walk, singing, with my lute in my arms, or go fowling or fishing in the woods. But surrounded by subordinates, I would be unable to move freely—this is the second thing I could not stand. When I kneel for a while I become as though paralyzed and unable to move. Being infested with lice, I am always scratching. To have to bow and kowtow to my superiors while dressed up in formal clothes—this is the third thing I could not stand. I have never been a facile calligrapher and do not like to write letters. Business matters would pile up on my table and fill my desk. To fail to answer would be bad manners and a violation of duty, but I would not long be able to force myself to do it. This is the fourth thing I could not stand. I do not like funerals and mourning, but these are things people consider

之，⁶故堯舜之君世，許由之巖栖，子房之佐漢，接輿之行歌，其揆一也。⁴仰瞻數君，可謂能遂其志者也。故君子百行，殊塗而同致，⁴循性而動，⁴各附所安。故有處朝廷而不出，入山林而不返之論。且延陵高子臧之風，長卿慕相如之節，⁴志氣所託，⁴不可奪也。吾每讀尚子平、臺孝威傳，⁴慨然慕之，⁴想其為人。少加孤露，⁴母兄見驕，⁴不涉經學。⁴性復疏嬾，⁴筋駑肉緩，頭面常一月十五日不洗，⁴不大悶癢，不能沐也。⁴每常小便，⁴而忍不起，令胞中略轉乃起耳。⁴⁺¹又／縱逸來久，⁴情意傲散，簡與禮相背，與慢相成，而為儕類見寬，⁴不攻其過。⁴又讀莊、老，⁴重增其放。故使榮進之心日積，⁶任實之情轉篤。此猶禽鹿少見馴育，則服從教制，⁴長而見羈，⁴則／狂顧頓纓，⁴赴蹈湯火，⁴雖／飾以金鑣，⁴饗以嘉肴，逾思長林而志在豐草也。

阮嗣宗口不論人過，吾每師之而未能及。⁴至性過人，⁴與物無傷，唯飲酒過差耳。至為禮法之士所繩，⁴疾之如讎，幸賴大將軍保持之耳。吾不如嗣宗之資，⁶而有慢弛之闕；⁴⁺¹又／不識人情，⁴闇於機宜；無萬石之慎，⁶而有好盡之累。⁴久與事接，⁴疵釁日興，⁴雖欲無患，⁴其可得乎？

⁴⁺¹又/人倫有禮，⁴朝
廷有法，⁴自惟至
熟，⁶有必不堪者七，
甚不可者二：⁴臥
喜晚起，⁶⁺¹而/當關
呼之不置，⁴一不堪
也。⁴抱琴行吟，⁴弋
釣草野，⁴⁺¹而/吏卒守
之，⁴不得妄動，⁴二不
堪也。⁴危坐一時，⁴痺
不得搖，⁴性復多
蝨，⁴杷搔無已，⁶而
當裹以章服，⁴揖拜上
官，⁴三不堪也。⁴素
不便書，⁴⁺¹又/不喜
作書，⁴⁺¹而/人間多
事，⁴堆案盈机，⁴不
相酬答，⁴⁺¹則/犯教傷
義，⁴欲自勉強，⁴則不
能久，⁴四不堪也。⁴不
喜弔喪，⁶⁺¹而/人道
以此為重，已為未見
恕者所怨，⁶至欲見中
傷者。⁴⁺¹雖/懍然自
責，⁴⁺¹然/性不可化，
欲降心順俗，⁴⁺¹則/詭
故不情，亦終不能獲無
咎無譽，如此，⁴五不堪
也。⁴不喜俗人，⁶而當
與之共事，⁴⁺¹或/賓客盈
坐，⁴鳴聲聒耳，⁴囂塵
臭處，⁴千變百伎，⁴在
人目前，⁴六不堪
也。⁴心不耐煩，⁴⁺¹而/
官事鞅掌，機務纏其
心，世故煩其慮，⁴七不
堪也。又每非湯武而薄
周孔，在人間不止，⁴此
事會顯，世教所不容，
此甚不可一也。⁴剛腸疾
惡，⁴輕肆直言，⁴遇事
便發，此甚不可二也。
以促中小心之性，⁴統此
九患，⁴不有外難，⁴當

important. Far from forgiving my offense, their resentment would reach the point where they would like to seem me injured. Although in alarm I might make the effort, I still could not change my nature. If I were to bend my mind to the expectations of the crowd, it would be dissembling and dishonest, and even so I would not be sure to go unblamed—this is the fifth thing I could not stand. I do not care for the crowd and yet I would have to serve together with such people. Or on occasions when guests fill the table and their clamor deafens the ears, their noise and dirt contaminating the place, before my very eyes they would indulge in their double-dealings. This is the sixth thing I could not stand. My heart cannot bear troubles, and official life is full of it. One's mind is bound with a thousand cares, one's thoughts are involved with worldly affairs. This is the seventh thing I could not stand.

Further, I am always finding fault with Tang and Wu Wang, or running down the Duke of Zhou and Confucius. If I did not stop this in society, it is clear that the religion of the times would not put up with me. This is the first thing which would never be condoned. I am quite ruthless in my hatred of evil, and speak out without hesitation, whenever I have the occasion. This is the second thing which would never be condoned.

To try to control these nine weaknesses with a disposition as narrow and niggling as mine could only result in my falling ill, if indeed I were able to avoid trouble with the authorities. Would I be long in the world of men? Besides, I have studied in the esoteric lore of Taoist masters, where a man's life can be indefinitely prolonged through eating herbs, and I firmly believe this to be so. To wander among the hills and streams, observing fish and birds, is what gives my heart great pleasure. Once I embarked on an official career, this is something I would have to give up forthwith. Why should I relinquish what gives me pleasure for something that fills me with dread?

What is esteemed in human relationships is the just estimate of another's inborn nature and helping him to realize it. . . . When you see a straight piece of wood, you do not want to make it into a wheel, nor do you try to make a rafter of a crooked piece, and this is because you would not want to pervert its heaven-given quality, but rather see that it finds its proper place. Now all four classes of people have each their own occupation, in which each takes pleasure in fulfilling his own ambition. It is only the man of understanding who can comprehend all of them. In this you have only to seek within yourself to know that one may not, out of one's own preference for formal clothes, force the people of Yue to wear figured caps, or, because one has a taste for putrid meat, try to feed a phoenix a dead rat.

Of late I have been studying the techniques of prolonging one's life, casting out all ideas of fame and glory, eliminating tastes, and letting my mind wander in stillness: what is most worthwhile to me is Inaction. Even if there were not these nine concerns, I could still pay no attention to your wishes. But beyond this, my mind tends toward melancholy, increasingly so of late, and I am personally convinced that I would not be able to stand any occupation in which

I took no pleasure. I really know myself in this respect. If worse comes to worst and there is no way out, then I shall simply die. But you have no grudge against me that you should cause me to lie lifeless in the gutter.

I am continually unhappy over the recent loss of the company of my mother and elder brother. My daughter is thirteen, my son eight years old—neither grown to maturity, and I am in ill health. This is another fact that pains me so much I cannot bear to speak further of it.

Today I only wish to stay on in this out-of-the-way lane and bring up my children and grandchildren, on occasion relaxing and reminiscing with old friends—cup of unstrained wine, song to the lute: this is the sum of my desires and ambitions.

If you keep on relentlessly nagging me, it can only be because you are anxious to get someone for the post who will be of use to the world. But you have always known what an irresponsible, bungling sort of person I am, not at all up on current affairs. I know myself that I am in all respects inferior to our modern men of ability. If you think me unlike ordinary men in that I alone do not find pleasure in fame and distinction, this is closest to my true feelings and deserves to be considered. If a man of great ability and endowments, able to turn his hand to anything, were able to be without ambition, he would be worth your respect. But one like me, frequently ill, who wants to stay out of office so as to take care of himself for the remaining years of his life—in me it is rather a deficiency. There is not much point in praising a eunuch for his chastity. If you insist on my joining you in the king's service, expecting that we will rise together and will be a joy and help to one another, one fine day you will find that the pressure has driven me quite mad. Only my bitterest enemy would go so far. The rustic who took such pleasure in the warm sun on his back, or the one who so esteemed the flavor of celery that they wanted to bring these things to the attention of the Most High: this showed them to be well-meaning, but it also showed their complete ignorance. I hope you will not do as they did. This being the way I feel about it, I have written to explain it to you and at the same time to say farewell.[19]

Ji Kang's "Letter to Shan Tao Breaking Off Relations" fully expresses the author's iconoclastic stance toward the ritual norms of his times and his fiercely independent and unrestrained personality. These aspects of Ji Kang's personality are first presented through his frequent use of vivid and often grotesque descriptions of his body. For example, he notes his distaste for formal court apparel and disregard for bodily appearance, stating, "When I kneel for a while I become as though paralyzed and unable to move. Being infested with lice, I am always scratching. To have to bow and kowtow to my superiors while dressed up in formal clothes—this is the third thing I could not stand."

In addition to using his unkept body as an external manifestation for his unconventional inner nature, Ji Kang also employs lively extended metaphors, inspired by his readings of the *Zhuangzi* and other texts, to articulate his rejection of court

有內病，⁶⁺¹寧可久處人間/邪！⁶又聞道士遺言，⁴餌朮黃精，⁴令人久壽，⁴意甚信之；遊山澤，觀魚鳥，⁴心甚樂之。⁴一行作吏，⁴此事便廢，安能舍其所樂而從其所懼哉？

夫人之相知，貴識其天性，⁴因而濟之。禹不偪伯成子高，⁴全其節也．．．足下見直木，必不可以為輪，曲者不可以為桷，蓋不欲以枉其天才，令得其所也。故四民有業，各以得志為樂，唯達者為能通之，此足下度內耳。不可自見好章甫，⁶⁺¹強越人以文冕/也；⁴己嗜臭腐，⁶⁺¹養鴛雛以死鼠/也。吾頃學養生之術，⁴方外榮華，去滋味，游心於寂寞，以無為為貴。⁴縱無九患，尚不顧足下所好者，⁴⁺¹又/有心悶疾，⁴頃轉增篤，⁴私意自試，不能堪其所不樂。⁴自卜已審，若道盡塗窮則已耳，足下無事冤之，令轉於溝壑也。

吾新失母兄之歡，⁴意常悽切。⁴女年十三，⁴男年八歲，⁴未及成人，⁴況復多病。⁴顧此恨恨，⁴如何可言！⁶今但願守陋巷，⁴教養子孫，⁶時與親舊敘闊，⁴陳說平生，⁴濁酒一杯，⁴彈琴一曲，⁴志願畢矣。足下若嬲之不置，不過欲為官得人，以益時用

耳。足下舊知吾潦倒
麤疏，⁴不切事情，自
惟亦皆不如今日之賢能
也。若以俗人皆喜榮
華，⁴獨能離之，⁴以此
為快，⁴此最近之，⁴可
得言耳。⁶然使長才廣
度，⁴無所不淹，⁴而能
不營，⁴乃可貴耳。若
吾多病困，欲離事自
全，⁴以保餘年，此真
所乏耳，豈可見黃門而
稱貞哉？若趣欲共登
王塗，⁴期於相致，⁴時
為歡益，⁴一旦迫之，
必發其狂疾，⁴自非重
怨，⁴不至於此/也。野
人有快炙背而美芹子
者，欲獻之至尊，⁶雖
有區區之意，⁴亦已
疏矣，⁶願足下勿似
之。⁴其意如此，既以
解足下，⁴並以為別。
嵇康白。

[XKJ 195–199]

N.B. Straight underline
indicates the use of repetitive
patterning; wavy underline the
use of parallel patterning. For
a discussion on repetitive and
parallel patterning,
☛ C1.1–4 and C1.6–7.

life as represented by Shan Tao.²⁰ In the opening address of his letter to Shan Tao, Ji Kang writes, "When I recently heard of your promotion in office, I was upset and unhappy, fearing that the cook would be shy of doing the carving himself and would call in the Impersonator of the Dead to help, handing over a kitchen knife soiled with rancid fat." Here Ji Kang adapts a passage from the chapter on "Free and Easy Wandering" ("Xiaoyao you") in the *Zhuangzi*.²¹ The context for this extended metaphor is a ritual performance in which a ruler has food prepared by a cook to serve to the impersonator of the dead, a spirit-medium whose role is to stand in for the ancestors and accept the food on their behalf. Whereas the cook's role involves him directly in the profane world, represented by the kitchen knife soiled with rancid fat, the spirit-medium by contrast must be "silent, inactive, majestic, awe-inspiring, and sacred" to effectively carry out his sacred role in mediating between the living and the dead.²² Ji Kang compares himself to the spirit-medium and Shan Tao to the cook to show the inappropriateness of Shan's request for Ji to join him as an assistant in office. This action would violate the nature of their different roles. Ji Kang again combines two different passages from the *Zhuang Zi*, from the chapter on "Free and Easy Wandering" and on "Autumn Waters" (*Qiu shui*), in a second extended metaphor when he states, "In this you have only to seek within yourself to know that one may not out of one's own preference for formal clothes, force the people of Yue to wear figured caps, or, because one has a taste for putrid meat, try to feed a phoenix a dead rat."²³ Ji Kang quotes these two situations from the *Zhuangzi* to illustrate how Shan Tao's request transgresses Ji's deeply held principle—the most important thing in human relationships is "the just estimate of another's inborn nature and helping him to realize it." In this analogy, just as it goes against the customs of the Yue people to wear figured caps and the high culinary standards of the lofty phoenix to eat a dead rat, so too Ji Kang is disgusted by Shan's attempt to force Ji into an official position that would entirely contradict his values and inner nature. Ji Kang's direct and blunt break with Shan Tao in this letter can be fruitfully contrasted with the subtlety with which late-imperial writer Hou Fangyu (1618–1655) refused the friendship of Ruan Dacheng (1587–1646), an official whose collusion with a violent and dictatorial eunuch made Ruan's request a dangerous and morally compromising proposition (☛ C15.4).

The letter was a genre flexible not only in terms of literary style, often alternating from parallel to free prose, but also in content. As we have seen in lengthy letters like Sima Qian's "Letter to Ren An" and Ji Kang's "A Letter to Shan Tao Breaking Off Friendship" both responded to specific situations raised by their correspondents and conveyed their deeply held feelings, convictions, and personal philosophies. When we arrive at the Wei, Jin, and Northern and Southern dynasties (386–581) period, letters were employed to address an even greater range of rhetorical purposes. From recommending a scholar for office to calling for a general's surrender, from discussing learning to admonishing a student, from requesting assistance to responding to a call for help, from establishing new friendships to recalling past meetings, from describing landscapes to recording interesting observations, all these topics were addressed in letters from this period. The sheer number of letters recorded in individual writers' literary collections increased greatly, too, a phenomenon spurred on by the greater availability and use of paper during this time.[24] We next examine excerpts from a few of the most famous letters from the second to sixth centuries, remarkable for their literary craft and compelling messages.

During the Later Han dynasty (25–220), Kong Rong (153–208) composed his "Letter to Cao Cao on the matter of Sheng Xiaozhang." In this letter, Kong beseeches Cao Cao to rescue Sheng Xiaozhang, a mutual friend and scholar who had encountered the hostility of the ruling Sun family of the newly risen Wu kingdom, first Sun Ce (175–200) and later his younger brother Sun Quan (182–252). Kong Rong was known as one of the "Seven Masters of the Jian'an Reign Period" (196–220) (Jian'an qizi), which was a reference to a group of talented writers from that era. Kong's literary and persuasive skills are on full display in this short passage. He opens the letter with an emotive appeal to their common friendship with Sheng. He then expands on this theme, arguing that if Cao Cao recruits Sheng as an official in the Han court, not only can he help out a friend in need but also enhance his own status by showing himself to be a manganous leader who will promulgate "the way of friendship" (youdao) throughout the empire. Kong skillfully uses historical allusions to reinforce his argument and its urgency. His letter is a model of how concision in words can intensify an urgent appeal.

C7.6 Kong Rong, "Letter to Cao Cao on the Matter of Sheng Xiaozhang"

Days and months pass by unceasingly and the seasons flow by like a stream. Suddenly one's fiftieth year has already arrived. Your honor has just reached this age, while I have passed it by two years. Within the four seas our old acquaintances have nearly all withered and disappeared. Only Sheng Xiaozhang of Guiji still remains. Now he has met trouble with the Sun Family. His wife and children have perished and he stands alone. Imperiled by his isolation he grieves in sadness. If these anxieties were to harm him [further], then this man might not be able to live out his natural years!

The *Spring and Autumn Annals* state, "When among the feudal vassals there was one that was about to be destroyed by another, if Duke Huan [of Qi] was unable to save it, then the Duke would feel shame about this."[1] Now Xiaozhang is truly a great hero among men. The eloquent scholars of our age have relied on him to broadcast their fame far and wide. Yet, he himself could not avoid

孔融 論盛孝章書

⁴歲月不居，⁴時節如流。⁴五十之年，⁴忽焉已至。⁴公為始滿，⁴融又過二。⁴海內知識，⁴零落殆盡，惟會稽盛孝章尚存。⁶其人困於孫氏，⁴妻孥湮沒，⁴單子獨立，⁴孤危愁苦。⁶若使憂能傷人，此子不得復永年矣！

⁴《春秋傳》曰："諸侯有相滅亡者，桓公不能救，⁴⁺¹則／桓公恥之。"今孝章實丈夫之雄也，⁴天下談士，⁴依以揚聲，⁶⁺¹而／身不免於幽繫，⁶命不期於旦夕，是吾祖不當復論損益之友，而朱穆所

---

[1] Duke Huan of Qi was the first of five "hegemons" (ba) that arose following the disintegration of the power and authority of the Zhou kingdom in the feudal world of pre-imperial China. The *Zuo commentary* on the *Spring and Autumn Annals* depicts Duke Huan of Qi as a benevolent ruler who sought to bring order to the chaos after the decline of the Zhou. Considering that Cao Cao claimed to be ruling in the name of the Han court during a time of turmoil, but in fact personally controlled all the levers of power, Kong Rong's likening of Cao to Duke Huan of Qi is a flattering and crafty comparison. This quotation derives from the *Gongyang commentary* on the *Spring and Autumn Annals*. See Zhu Dongrun, ed., *Zhongguo lidai wenxue zuopin xuan* (*A Selection of Chinese Literary Works by Dynasty*) (Shanghai: Shanghai guji chubanshe, 1979), 2:395.

以絕交也 。 公誠能
馳一介之使，加恩
尺之書，⁴⁺¹則/孝章可
致，⁴⁺¹友道可弘/矣。

[*HWLC* I: 1943–1947]

N.B. Straight underline
indicates the use of repetitive
patterning; wavy underline the
use of parallel patterning. For
a discussion on repetitive and
parallel patterning,
☛ C1.1–4 and C1.6–7.

丘遲　與陳伯之書

遲頓首 。 陳將軍足
下：無恙，⁴幸甚幸
甚！⁶將軍勇冠三
軍，⁴才為世出，⁶棄
鷰雀之小志，⁶慕鴻鵠
以高翔。⁴⁺¹昔/因機變
化，⁴遭遇明主，⁴立功
立事，⁴開國稱孤，⁴朱
輪華轂，⁴擁旄萬里，
何其壯也！如何一旦
為奔亡之虜，⁶聞鳴鏑
而股戰，⁶對穹廬以屈
膝，⁴又何劣邪！⁶尋
君去就之際，⁴非有他
故，直以不能內審諸
己，⁴外受流言，⁴沈迷
猖獗，⁴以至於此。

being imprisoned in darkness and his fate could be sealed at any moment. For this reason, there is no need for my ancestor [Kongzi] to further discuss which friends are beneficial and which are harmful nor for Zhu Mu (100–163) to have cause to break off a friendship.[2] If your honor is able to hastily dispatch a messenger, entrusting him with a brief letter, then Xiaozhang could be reached [in time], and the way of friendship propagated.[3]

Sadly, history records that although Kong Rong persuaded Cao Cao to issue an edict in the name of the Han court for Sheng Xiaozhang's recruitment, even before the edict arrived, Sheng had already been executed by Sun Quan.

In contrast, the "Letter to Chen Bozhi" by Qiu Chi (464–508) fully achieved its goal of persuading an important general who had defected to the enemy to return home once again. Qiu Chi's letter was written at the command of Liang dynasty (502–557) prince of Linchuan, Xiaohong (473–526). Chen Bozhi had previously served the southern Qi dynasty, but strategically switched alliance to the Liang dynasty, which subsequently overthrew Qi. Then again, under the encouragement of subordinates and enticements from abroad, he later defected to the rival state of Northern Wei (386–534). In the year 505, Xiaohong led troops on an expedition against the Northern Wei and was met by Chen Bozhi's defensive forces. The two sides were evenly matched and a military resolution of the battle seemed remote. As a counselor adjunct and chief secretary to the Liang court, Qiu Chi was responsible for the drafting of memorials and letters. Qiu's letter targets Chen Bozhi's concrete circumstances and psychological state of mind. In effect, Qiu wrote to make Chen Bozhi aware of the material benefits and costs that weighed on his decision of whether to return to the Liang, while also appealing to his emotional connections to his homeland.

C7.7 Qiu Chi, "Letter to Chen Bozhi"

Chi bows his head to you, General Chen:

That you are in good health is fortunate indeed, fortunate indeed! The general once bravely led the army with talent outstanding in the realm. You abandoned the petty ambitions of swallows and sparrows in your admiration for the lofty soaring of swan and geese. Previously, following the times you changed [your loyalty from the Qi to the Liang dynasty]. Having encountered an enlightened ruler, you established merit and accomplished matters, founded a new kingdom and were proclaimed a lord. [Riding on] vermillion wheels with ornamented hubs and surrounded by fur topped banners for hundreds of miles,

[2] Kong Rong was the twentieth-generation descendant of Confucius. Here he refers to the well-known passage 16.4 from the *Analects* of Confucius in which the master distinguished three types of beneficial friendship and three types of harmful friendship. Zhu Mu was a scholar of the Eastern Han dynasty who composed a work entitled "On Dissolving Friendship" ("Juejiao lun"). The general import of these allusions is to suggest that for Cao Cao to demonstrate his friendship to Sheng, what is needed is not further debate, but rather immediate action. See Zhu Dongrun, *Zhongguo lidai wenxue zuopin xuan*, 396–397.
[3] My translation.

what a mighty scene that was! How is it then, that after you went scurrying off to [join] those caitiffs, your legs quaked at the sound of whistling arrows and you stood on bended knees before [their] yurts? How perfidious! In [your] search for a ruler, the balance between leaving and staying was determined by no other cause than your inability to reflect and examine yourself. To have been externally influenced by scurrilous rumors and intoxicated by wild arrogance, that is what led you to this state.

Still, this sagely court can forgive the transgressions of those who seek [to establish] merit, toss aside imperfections in order to employ those of worth, and thereby promote its sincere intentions throughout the world, bringing calm to the fearful among all creatures. All this is known by the general and there is no need for your servant to elaborate. Zhu Wei spilt the blood of an imperial brother and Zhang Xiu assassinated [Cao Cao's] own beloved son, but the ruler of the Han dynasty did not doubt [Zhu] and the lord of the Wei dynasty still treated [Zhang] like an old friend.[1] Moreover, the general has committed no crimes [as severe] as these past individuals and further possesses great achievements that are recognized by all contemporaries. Now, to lose one's way along the road yet still know how to return, this is what ancient worthies prized; to have not gone too far yet still turn back, this is what the *Classic of Changes* valued the most. The lord on high can bend the rules to extend his gratitude—[when a whale] swallows a boat, there are always those who slip out. The pine and cypress [on your ancestor's graves] have not been cut down, your relatives reside in peace, your great halls have not been overturned, and your beloved concubine is still here. If in your heart if you think long on it, what more is there for me to say? . . .

In the third month of late spring grasses grow thick in the southlands. All kinds of flowers flourish among the trees while flocks of birds flutter riotously. To see the banners flying above your homeland and enjoy the life of former times, to strum a zither and ascend the parapet on the city walls, how can one not regret missing these? The reason that Lian Po (died 243 BCE) pined to be a general of Zhao again and that Wu Qi (440–381 BCE) wept on the western

---

[1] Zhu Wei was an official during the reign of the usurper Prince Huaiyang (r. 23–24) of the Han dynasty who participated in the emperor's plot to assassinate the imperial brother Liu Yin. Later when Liu Xiu or the future emperor Guangwu (r. 25–57) attacked the capital of Luoyang to put down the insurrection, Zhu Wei was defending it. Emperor Guangwu convinced Zhu Wei to surrender the city by promising Zhu Wei that his spilling of imperial blood would be forgiven. Zhang Xiu was a general who in 197 fought against the warlord Cao Cao, but then surrendered to him. Later angered by the fact that Cao took the widow of his former political patron, Zhang Ji, as his concubine, Zhang Xiu launched a surprise attack on Cao Cao at the battle of Wancheng. During Cao Cao's retreat from this battle, his eldest son, Cao Ang was killed. During another confrontation in 200, Zhang Xiu surrendered to Cao Cao a second time. Despite Zhang's earlier betrayals, because of his admiration of Zhang's military talent, Cao forgave Zhang's transgressions and solidified their alliance by marrying another one of his sons to Zhang's daughter. See Zhu Dongrun, *Zhongguo lidai wenxue zuopin xuan*, 454–455.

⁶聖朝赦罪責功，⁴棄瑕錄用，⁶推赤心於天下，⁶安反側於物。將軍之所知，⁶不假僕一二談／也。朱鮪涉血於友于，張繡剚刃於愛子，⁶漢主不以為疑，⁶魏君待之若舊。況將軍無昔人之罪，而勳重於當世。⁴⁺¹夫／迷塗知返，⁴往哲是與；⁴不遠而復，⁴先典攸高。⁶主上屈法申恩，⁴吞舟是漏；⁶將軍松柏不翦，⁴親戚安居，⁴高臺未傾，⁴愛妾尚在。⁴悠悠爾心，⁴亦何可言！ . . . . . .

⁴暮春三月，⁴江南草長，⁴雜花生樹，⁴群鶯亂飛。⁶見故國之旗鼓，⁶感平生於疇日，⁴撫弦登陴，⁴豈不愴悢！⁶⁺²所以／廉公之思趙將，⁶吳子之泣西河，人之情也，⁶將軍獨無情哉？想早勵良規，⁴自求多福。

. . . . . .

[*WX* 1943–1947]

N.B. Straight underline indicates the use of repetitive patterning; wavy underline the use of parallel patterning. For a discussion on repetitive and parallel patterning,
☛ C1.1–4 and C1.6–7.

bank of the Yellow River is because they were people of feeling.[2] How can you alone, general, be without feeling? I exhort you to make your plans soon and seek a prosperous future for yourself.[3]

The tone of Qiu's letter alternates from praise for past service, to righteous condemnation for present betrayal, and finally to the potential for forgiveness and redemption should the general be persuaded to return. Like other letters from this period, Qiu's makes ample use of parallel phrasing, especially in its enumeration of historical allusions. These historical figures are all examples of violent conflicts that arose between military officials and their sovereigns but were eventually resolved through the renewal of their bond of loyalty. These historical figures serve as mirrors for Chen Bozhi to reflect on in making his own decision. Also noteworthy is Qiu's emphasis on the safety of Chen Bozhi's family members in the south and his description of the lush landscapes in the "southland" (*Jiangnan*) as further enticements to sway the general's decision. This rhetoric of longing for landscape shows the extent to which personal and familial identity came to be constructed in terms of place and geography during the Northern and Southern dynasties period.[25]

The following two excerpts concern a major motif in the letters written by Cao Pi and Cao Zhi, the royal brothers of the Wei dynasty—that is, meetings with like-minded friends, often in the setting of a banquet or literary salon, and the later recollection of those gatherings shared through letters. As previously stated, the Wei dynasty witnessed the rise of self-conscious literary creation and a greater awareness of generic distinctions and decorum. Both letters can be seen as attempts to create a more lyrical form of prose in the letter genre, but with very different results in terms of their signature styles. The letters are addressed to Wu Zhi (177–230), an important Wei dynasty official and friend to both brothers. First, let us examine Cao Pi's "Letter to Wu Zhi" written in 218. Cao Pi's reflections on the meaning of friendship and mortality and on the role of literature in this letter were prompted by a virulent outbreak of plague in 217 that in quick succession struck down four members of the young emperor's literary salon.[26]

---

[2] Lian Po was a military general of the Zhao state in the Warring States period. At the battle of Changping, the king of Zhao was convinced by his ministers to replace Lian Po's command with another general who they thought would have a better strategy. Insulted Lian Po defected to the Wei state and then again to the Chu state, but never again found a ruler who would trust him. He lived to see the collapse of the Zhao state and throughout his wanderings pined to return to serve as a Zhao general again. Wu Qi was a general and famous strategist of the Warring States period. While serving the Marquis Wu of the Wei State (r. 386–371 BCE), Wu Qi was put in charge of the commandery of Xihe (modern-day Shaanxi province along the banks of the Yellow River). Trusting the criticisms of his ministers, the Marquis Wu had Wu Qi recalled. Knowing that once his forces withdrew Xihe would be annexed by the Qin state, Wu Qi wept on the western bank of the Yellow River. As he foresaw, Xihe was occupied by the Qin. See Zhu Dongrun, *Zhongguo lidai wenxue zuopin xuan*, 457

[3] My translation.

C7.8 Cao Pi, "Letter to Wu Zhi"

曹丕 與吳質書

Second month, third day, Pi reporting:

Years and months are all too easy to come by, and it's now been four years since we parted. Three years without seeing his friends and already the poet of "Eastern Hill" was complaining of how long it had been. How much more, then, in my case, when the time has been even longer! How can I bear to think of it? Though we send letters back and forth, they're hardly enough to free me from this tangle of depression.

In the disease and contagion last year, so many of my kin and old friends met with misfortune—Xu (Gan), Chen (Lin), Ying (Yang), and Liu (Zhen)—all carried off at one time! What words can describe this sorrow? In the old days, whether on an outing or at home, we traveled in carriages following one another, rested on mats ranged side by side—when were we ever parted even for a moment? And whenever the wine cup was passed around and strings and wood-winds joined to serenade us, at the height of the drinking, when ears began to burn and we titled back our heads and intoned our poems—at such times, thoughtless as we were, did we even realize that we were happy? We supposed that each of us had been allotted a hundred years, that we would always be here to look out for one another. Who'd have guessed that in a few years almost all of us would have fallen by the way? It hurts just to speak of it.

Recently I have been gathering up the writings that these men left behind and putting them all together in one volume. Looking at the names, I know they're already logged in the ledgers of the dead, and yet, as I think back over the outings we used to have, I see these gentlemen still in my mind's eye. And now all have been transformed, changed into stinking dirt! How can I go on speaking of it?[27]

⁴二月三日，丕白：⁴歲月易得，⁶別來行復四年。⁴三年不見，⁶《東山》猶歎其遠，⁴況乃過之？⁴思何可支！⁴雖/書疏往返，⁶未足解其勞結。⁴昔年疾疫，⁶親故多離其災。⁴徐（干）、陳（琳）、應（瑒）、劉（楨），⁴一時俱逝，⁴痛可言邪？⁴昔日遊處，⁴行則連輿，⁴止則接席，⁶何曾須臾相失。⁶每至觴酌流行，⁴絲竹並奏，⁴酒酣耳熱，⁴仰而賦詩。⁴當此之時，⁶⁺¹忽然不自知樂/也。⁴謂/百年己分，⁴可/長共相保。⁶何圖數年之間，⁴零落略盡，⁴言之傷心！⁴頃/撰其遺文，⁴都為一集。⁴觀其姓名，⁴已為鬼錄。⁴追思昔遊，⁴猶在心目。⁴而此諸子，⁴化為糞壤，⁴可復道哉！

[*WX* 1896–1897]

N.B. Straight underline indicates the use of repetitive patterning; wavy underline the use of parallel patterning. For a discussion on repetitive and parallel patterning,
➳ C1.1–4 and C1.6–7.

In narrating this memory of a former literary banquet, the lyrical focus of Cao Pi's letter shifts from the joys of the past, to the sorrows of the present, and then to a lament of the life's ephemerality. Cao Pi's full letter is considered by many scholars to be an important document of literary criticism from the Wei dynasty.[28] In the conclusion to Cao Pi's letter, we see his concern with collecting and preserving the works of his deceased friends. This preoccupation again suggests the idea that through literature one can achieve a kind of immortality and that Cao Pi hopes that the works of his literary coterie will live on in the minds of future readers.

Turning to Cao Zhi's "Letter to Wu Jizhong," we see that while it also takes up the theme of recalling the scene of a literary banquet with friends, the style and personality conveyed in Cao Zhi's letter is completely different from his elder brother. Cao Zhi strives to create a prose style that is ornate and beautiful, while the temperament he displays at the banquet is heroic and unrestrained. Whereas Cao Pi seeks to respect the memory of lost literary companions by collecting and transmitting their literary works, Cao Zhi records and shares his exuberant enjoyment of friendship in the moment. Given the ephemeral nature of life, it is best, Cao Zhi contends, to enjoy the present to the utmost.

C7.9 Cao Zhi, "Letter to Wu Jizhong"

When with bowls and cups riding wavelets in front, pipes and flutes playing music behind, you held your body like a hawk in flight, sang like a phoenix and glared like a tiger. I daresay even Xiao and Cao could not have equaled you, Wei and Huo could not have matched you. You looked left and glanced right, acting as though no one else was about. Was this not due to your heroic aspirations? Like chomping away while passing a butcher shop, though I got no meat, I prized it and was blissfully happy. At that moment we wanted to lift Mount Tai to use as meat, drain the Eastern Sea to use as ale, cut the bamboo of Yunmeng to use for flutes, chop the catalpas on the banks of Si to use for zithers. We ate as though filling a great gorge, drank as though pouring into a leaky cup. Our joy was truly hard to estimate. Was this not the joy of real men?

But the days were not with us, and the radiant spirit [i.e., the sun] quickened its pace. Our encounters have a velocity faster than light; our partings the boundless space betwixt Orion and Scorpio. I long to hold back the heads of the six dragon steeds, stay the reins of Xihe, break off blossoms from the Ruo tree, block the valley of the Edge of the Meng. But the route to the heavens is high and distant; for a very long time it has not been taken. I toss and turn with nostalgic longing. What to do? What to do?[29]

A final important topic in letters from the Northern and Southern dynasties are descriptions of landscape and travel. In this category, we cannot ignore the "Letter to My Younger Sister Upon Ascending the Banks of Thunder Garrison" ("Deng dalei an yu mei shu") by Bao Zhao (414–466) written in 439. This letter was written when Bao Zhao was traveling to take up an official post in Jiangzhou (southwest of modern Jiujiang in Jiangxi province) and stopped at the banks of Thunder Garrison, an important defensive fort on the Yangzi River. Although the beginning of the letter expresses the difficulties and sorrows of Bao's long journey and his concern for the health and well-being of his younger sister, even more space is devoted to describing the landscape and objects he encountered along the way. He shares these scenes with his sister, who was also a poet, as a form of vicarious travel. The selected excerpt focuses on Bao's depiction of Mount Lu (located in modern-day Jiangxi province). Bao Zhao captures the effects of evening light shining on the mountain through the use of parallel prose, replete with carefully balanced four-character lines, antithesis, and ornate courtly diction. Bao Zhao's work exemplifies the pursuit of formalism, even in letters, that became the dominant trend in literature of the second to sixth centuries.[30]

曹植 與吳季重書

6+2 若夫 / 觴酌凌波 於 前，6蕭笳發音於後。6足下鷹揚其體，4鳳歎虎視，6謂蕭、曹不足儔，衛、霍不足侔也。4左顧右盼，4謂若無人，6+1豈非吾子壯志 / 哉！6過屠門而大嚼，4雖不得肉，4貴且快意。4當斯之時，6願 / 舉太山以為肉，6傾東海以為酒，伐雲夢之竹以為笛，斬泗濱之梓以為箏，食若填巨壑，飲若灌漏卮，其樂固難量，豈非大丈夫之樂哉！4+1然 / 日不我與，4曜靈急節，6面有逸景之速，6別有參商之闊。思欲抑六龍之首，頓羲和之轡，折若木之華，閉蒙汜之谷。4天路高邈，4良久無緣，4懷戀反側，4如何如何！

[*WX* 1905–1906]

N.B. Straight underline indicates the use of repetitive patterning; wavy underline the use of parallel patterning. For a discussion on repetitive and parallel patterning, ☛ C1.1–4 and C1.6–7.

C7.10 Bao Zhao, "Letter to My Younger Sister Upon Ascending the Banks of Thunder Garrison"

鮑照 登大雷岸與妹書

Looking southwest toward Mount Lu,	西南望廬山，
2 I was struck by its remarkable aspect.	4又特驚異。
Its base bears down on the river tide,	4基壓江潮，
4 Its peaks are joined with the Milky Way.	6峰與辰漢連接。
Often gathered above it are clouds and mists,	上常積雲霞，
6 That are carved into elaborate brocades.	雕錦縟。
They glowed like the blossom of the *Ruo* Tree in the dusk.[1]	4若華夕曜，
8 Vapors from cliff and lake merge and blend,	4巖澤氣通，
They emanate radiance, disperse a riot of color,	4傳明散彩，
10 Resplendent as the crimson sky.	4赫似絳天。
Left and right there is a blue haze,	4左右青靄，
12 Complementing the Peak of Purple Empyrean.	4表裏紫霄。
From the mountain ridge up,	4從嶺而上，
14 The haze is filled with golden rays.	4氣盡金光，
From halfway down the mountain,	4半山以下，
16 All is dusky blue.	4純為黛色。
Truly this is the dwelling place of the gods,	信可以神居帝郊，
18 Capable of guarding and commanding the Xiang and Han Rivers.[31]	鎮控湘漢者也。
	[*PZJ* 877–878]

N.B. Wavy underline the use of parallel patterning. For a discussion on repetitive and parallel patterning, ➻ C1.1–4 and C1.6–7.

A second example of the trend toward incorporating parallel prose landscape descriptions into letters is found in Wu Jun's (469–520) "Letter to Zhu Yuansi" ("Yu Zhu Yuansi shu"). In this excerpt, Wu Jun describes the landscape along a hundred-mile stretch of the Fuchun River as it flows from Fuyang to Tonglu (located in modern-day western Zhejiang province), creating one of the most famous landscape vignettes in early medieval literature.

C7.11 Wu Jun, "Letter to Zhu Yuansi"

吳均 與朱元思書

On lofty mountains along both banks,	4夾嶂高山，
2 Grow evergreens everywhere,	4皆生寒樹，
Mountains supported by their mass compete to rise higher,	4負勢競上，
4 Together, they soar into the distance,	4互相軒邈，
Struggling aloft, pointing straight up:	4爭高直指，

---

[1] According to the *Classic of Mountains and Seas* (*Shanhai jing*), the mythical Ruo Tree grows in the west where the sun sets.

6   Hundreds, thousands, have become high peaks.   ⁴千百成峰。

Waterfalls dash against the rocks,   ⁴泉水激石,

8   Emitting sounds of *"ling-ling"*;   ⁴泠泠作響;

Elegant birds call to each other,   ⁴好鳥相鳴,

10   In a poetry of *"ying-ying."*   ⁴嚶嚶成韻。

Cicadas buzz ceaselessly in a thousand ways,   ⁶蟬則千轉不窮,

12   As monkeys utter a hundred cries without end.[32]   ⁶猿則百叫無絕。

[*HWLC* 5: 67]

N.B. Wavy underline the use of parallel patterning. For a discussion on repetitive and parallel patterning, ➦ C1.1–4 and C1.6–7. Superscripted number indicates the number of characters in a line. Of the twelve lines in this text, ten (83 percent) are four-character lines and two (17 percent) are six-character lines. These paralleled parts make up 100 percent of the lines in this text.

In a mere twelve lines of balanced four or six-character couplets, Wu Jun not only visually depicts the shape and power of the mountainous riverside landscape, but further combines this with auditory effects achieved through contrasting reduplicated onomatopoeia words. Thus, what would otherwise be a static "painting" of the Fuchun River becomes a dynamic scene full of the sights and sounds of waves crashing, birds calling, the buzz of cicadas, and the cries of monkeys throughout Fu Jun's journey down the river.

Last but not least, let us examine the "Letter Replying to Secretary Xie" ("Da Xie zhongshu shu") written by Liang dynasty Daoist poet-recluse Tao Hongjing (456–536).

C7.12 Tao Hongjing, "Letter Replying to Secretary Xie"
陶弘景 答謝中書書

The beauty of hills and streams,   山川之美,

2   has been acknowledged from ancient times.   古來共談。

Here, high peaks rise above the clouds;   高峰入雲,

4   And a rivulet can be seen clear to its bottom,   清流見底。

Between these rocky banks,   兩岸石壁,

6   is a pageant of the five colors.   五色交輝。

Dark pine woods and the green bamboos,   青林翠竹,

8   flourish in all four seasons.   四時俱備。

As the mists lift at dawn,   曉霧將歇,

10   the monkeys and birds cry in loud dissonance.   猿鳥亂鳴;

And when the sun sets,   夕日欲頹,

12   the fish come out of hiding to chase one another.   沉鱗競躍。

This indeed is an immortal's paradise on earth.   實是欲界之仙都,

And yet since Xie Lingyun (385–433),   自康樂以來,

there has been no one capable of entering wholeheartedly into   未復有能與其奇

the wonders of these natural surroundings.[33]   者。

[*HWLC* 4: 587]

N.B. Wavy underline indicates the use of parallel patterning. Paralleled parts make up 67 percent of the lines in this text. For a discussion on repetitive and parallel patterning, ➦ C1.1–4 and C1.6–7.

In this letter, Tao Hongjing recorded his observations of Mao Mountain (in modern-day Jiangsu province) where he lived in reclusion, practiced Daoist alchemy, and gained close familiarity with the natural environment of the region. Again, Tao's use of four-character parallel couplets allows him to succinctly describe the mountain's natural landscape, including juxtapositions of high mountains with deep, clear streams; the variety of dazzling colors with the endurance of evergreens across all seasons; and the animals that emerge at different times of the day. In the closing, Tao returns to free prose and elevates the landscape to a kind of Daoist utopia.

The focus on exploring wild and mountainous landscapes described in the letters of Bao Zhao, Wu Jun, and Tao Hongjing can be compared and contrasted to the celebration of the fundamental role of the humble farmer in cultivated fields and gardens in the letter of Zheng Xie (1693–1765), both in terms of their common interest in landscape as a medium of expression and in their accounts of vastly different ecologies (☞ C15.6).

In premodern China, memorials and letters originally developed to serve the practical functions of petitioning a ruler, setting forth requests, and maintaining links of communication among colleagues, family, and friends. From the second to the sixth centuries, the place of the letter genre in the literary canon was affirmed and consolidated for the first time. In the same era when letters and memorials received unprecedented theoretical treatment in works such as Cao Pi's "Letter to Wu Zhi" and Liu Xie's comprehensive *Literary Mind and the Carving of Dragons*, they also were established as distinct categories through their collection and circulation in Xiao Tong's influential literary anthology *Selections of Refined Literature*. This genre's new independent status can be seen first and foremost in the standardization of its form and conventions, particularly in the case of memorials. But for letter writing to truly become a part of the standard repertoire of early medieval writers, however, it had to rely on its literary qualities. This era saw the rise of a consciousness of literary creation and an awareness of generic conventions among writers that further accelerated their elevation of memorials and letters to the status of literary works. This pursuit of literary perfection also led to a fashion for parallel prose, sometime resulting in works that are little more than empty formalism. From this point in Chinese literary history, writers composed letters in even greater numbers, producing many outstanding pieces as the genre became an essential part of an author's literary oeuvre.

Yucai Liu

Translated by Benjamin Ridgway

NOTES

1. For example, the *Zuozhuan* contains important letters like "Letter from Zijia of the State of Zhao to Xuanzi of the State of Zheng," "Letter from Zichan to Fan Xuanzi," and "Letter from Wuchen to Zifan." For English translations of these letters see Stephen Durrant, Wai-yee Li, and David Schaberg, trans., *Zuo Tradition, Commentary on the "Spring and Autumn Annals"* (Seattle: University of Washington Press, 2016), 561–563, 1127, and 1181.

2. See Antje Richter, *Letters and Epistolary Culture in Early Medieval China* (Seattle: University of Washington Press, 2013), 35; and Robert Joe Cutter, "Letters and Memorials in the Early Third Century: The Case of Cao Zhi," in *A History of Chinese Letters and Epistolary Culture*, edited by Antje Richter (Leiden: Brill, 2015), 308–309.

3. Liu Xie divides "letters of submission" into three types in his chapters on "Declarations and Petitions" (chap. 22, *Zhangbiao*), "Presentations and Communications" (chap. 23, *Zouqi*), and "Discussions and Answers" (chap. 24, *Yidui*). My translations of these six terms used by Liu Xie to designate different administrative documents follow David Knechtges. See David Knechtges, "The Rhetoric of Imperial Abdication and Accession in a Third-Century Chinese Court: The Case of Cao Pi's Accession as Emperor of the Wei Dynasty," in *Rhetoric and the Discourses of Power in Court Culture: China, Europe, and Japan*, edited by David R. Knechtges and Eugene Vance (Seattle: University of Washington Press, 2005), 5–6.

4. Liu Xie (465–522), Huang Shulin comt. *Expanded Commentaries on the Literary Mind and the Carving of Dragons* (*Zengding Wenxin diaolong jiaozhu*) (Beijing: Zhonghua shuju, 2012): 302.

5. Vincent Shih, trans., *The Literary Mind and the Carving of Dragons* (New York: Columbia University Press, 1959), 129.

6. For Lu You's poems "Writing My Indignation" (*shufen*) see Qian Zhonglian, *Complete Annotated Poems of Lu You* (*Lu You quanji jiaozhu*) (Hangzhou: Zhejiang jiaoyu chubanshe, 2011), 15:140.

7. Robert Joe Cutter, trans., "Zhuge Liang (181–234), On Deploying the Army," in *Classical Chinese Literature, An Anthology of Translations*, vol. 1, *Antiquity to the Tang Dynasty*, edited by John Minford and Joseph S. M. Lau (New York: Columbia University Press, 2000), 593–596.

8. Hui Hong 惠洪 (1071–1128), Chen Xin 陳新, comp. *Evening Chats in the Chilly Studio* (*Lengzhai yehua* 冷齋夜話) (Beijing: Zhonghua shuju, 1988): 26.

9. David Knechtges, trans., "Li Mi (ca. 225–ca. 290), Memorial Expressing My Feelings," in *Classical Chinese Literature, An Anthology of Translations*, vol. 1, *Antiquity to the Tang Dynasty*, 597–599.

10. Shih, *The Literary Mind and the Carving of Dragons*, 129.

11. Robert Joe Cutter, trans., "Personal Crisis and Communication in the Life of Cao Zhi," in *Rhetoric and the Discourses of Power in Court Culture: China, Europe, and Japan*, 149–168.

12. Robert Joe Cutter, trans., "Cao Zhi (192–232) and His Poetry" (PhD diss., University of Washington, 1983), 491–495.

13. See Richter, *Letters and Epistolary Culture in Early Medieval China*, 30–33.

14. For an in-depth anatomy of the different parts of personal letters and their rhetorical functions in the early medieval period with comparisons to letters in the European literary tradition, see Antje Richter, *Letters and Epistolary Culture in Early Medieval China*.

15. See Stephen Durrant, Wai-Yee Li, Michael Nylan, and Hans Van Ess, *The Letter to Ren An and Sima Qian's Legacy* (Seattle: University of Washington Press, 2018).

16. For an interpretation of Sima's letter as a form of self-justification and a sublimation of his sense of frustration into literary creation, see Stephen W. Durrant, *The Cloudy Mirror, Tension and Conflict in the Writings of Sima Qian* (Albany: State University of New York Press, 1995), 16–19.

17. J. R. Hightower, trans., "Sima Qian (c.145–c.85 B.C.), Letter to Ren An," in *Classical Chinese Literature, An Anthology of Translations*, vol. 1, *Antiquity to the Tang Dynasty*, 572–582.

18. For a discussion of Ji Kang's letter to Shan Tao in the context of the political conflicts between the Cao clan with which Ji Kang was affiliated by marriage and the ruling Sima clan during the Wei dynasty see the useful introduction in Robert Henrick, *Philosophy and Argumentation in Third-Century China, The Essays of Hsi K'ang* (Princeton, NJ: Princeton University Press, 1983), 3–18.

19. J. R. Hightower, trans., "Letter to Shan Tao," in *Classical Chinese Literature, An Anthology of Translations*, vol. 1, *Antiquity to the Tang Dynasty*, 463–467.

20. For a study of how Xi Kang's poetry similarly embodies a practice of patching together quotations from his readings of contemporary philosophical works in what she terms "bricolage," see Wendy Swartz, *Reading Philosophy, Writing Poetry, Intertextual Modes of Making Meaning in Early Medieval China* (Cambridge, MA: Harvard University Asia Center, 2018), 43–106.

21. Brook Ziporyn, trans., *Zhuangzi: The Essential Writings with Selections from Traditional Commentaries* (Indianapolis, IN: Hackett, 2009), 6.

22. I follow the interpretation of this passage by Ziporyn, *Zhuangzi: The Essential Writings*, 6.

23. Ziporyn, *Zhuangzi: The Essential Writings*, 7 and 76.

24. According to historian Tsien Tsuen-Hsuin, although the invention of paper is dated to the first century CE, traditionally attributed to Cai Lun, it was not until the third or fourth century that the use of paper gradually supplanted bamboo and wood tablets and that paper books came to be more freely duplicated and distributed. See Tsuen-Hsiun Tsien, *Written on Bamboo and Silk, The Beginnings of Chinese Books and Inscriptions*, 2nd ed. (Chicago: University of Chicago Press, 2004), 145–152.

25. Examining the cultural impact of the division of the Chinese ecumene into competing kingdoms during the second to sixth centuries and the corresponding migration of many elites from the north to the south, the construction of the geographic identity for "north" and "south" has become an important topic in recent scholarship on Medieval China. See Xiaofei Tian, "From the Eastern Jin Through the early Tang (317–649)," in *The Cambridge History of China, Chinese Literature*, vol. I, *To 1375*, edited by Kang-I Sun Chang and Stephen Owen (Cambridge: Cambridge University Press, 2010), 266–268; and Jessey Choo, "Part I: The North and the South," in *Early Medieval China, A Sourcebook*, edited by Wendy Swartz, Robert Ford Campany, Yang Lu, and Jessey, Jiun-Chyi Choo (New York: Columbia University Press, 2014), 11–88.

26. See Xiaofei Tian, *The Halberd at Red Cliff, Jian'an and the Three Kingdoms* (Cambridge, MA: Harvard University Asia Center, 2018), 13–30.

27. Burton Watson, trans., "Cao Pi: Two Letters to Wu Zhi, Magistrate of Zhaoge," *Renditions* 41–42 (1994): 7–11.

28. For a discussion of this letter as a document of literary history see Richter, *Letters and Epistolary Culture in Early Medieval China*, 64–68.

29. Robert Joe Cutter, trans., "Letters and Memorials in the Early Third Century: The Case of Cao Zhi," in *A History of Chinese Letters and Epistolary Culture*, edited by Antje Richter (Leiden: Brill, 2015), 312–313.

30. For an in-depth discussion of the ways in which both Bao Zhao's parallel prose used in this letter and in his pentasyllabic poetry drew on the technique of "concentrated elaboration" in the rhapsody (*fu*) genre, see Kang-I Sun Chang, *Six Dynasties Poetry* (Princeton, NJ: Princeton University Press, 1986), 88–94.

31. Jui-lung Su, trans., "Bao Zhao: Letter to My Younger Sister Upon Ascending the Bank of Thunder Lake." *Renditions* 41–42 (1994): 22.

32. Richard E. Strassberg, trans., "From a Letter to Song Yuan-szu," in *Inscribed Landscapes, Travel Writing from Imperial China* (Berkeley: University of California Press, 1994), 31–32.

33. H. C. Chang, trans., "From a Letter to Secretary Xie by Tao Hongjing," in *Chinese Literature 2, Nature Poetry* (New York: Columbia University Press, 1977), 12.

SUGGESTED READING

ENGLISH

Choo, Jessey, et al., eds., *Early Medieval China: A Sourcebook*. New York: Columbia University Press, 2014.

Chung, Eva Yuen-wah. "A Study of the Shu (Letters) of the Han Dynasty." 2 vols. PhD diss., University of Washington, 1982.

Eggert, Marion, et al., eds. *Die klassische chinesische Prosa: Essay, Reisebericht, Skizze, Brief. Vom Mittelalter bis zur Neuzeit* (*Classical Chinese Prose from the Middle Ages to Contemporary Times: Essays, Travel Records, Notebooks, and Letters*). Munich: Saur, 2003.

Richter, Antje. *Letters and Epistolary Culture in Early Medieval China*. Seattle: University of Washington Press, 2013

——, ed. *A History of Chinese Letters and Epistolary Culture*. Leiden: Brill, 2015.

Strassberg, Richard, trans. *Inscribed Landscapes, Travel Writing from Imperial China*. Berkeley: University of California Press, 1994.

CHINESE

Chu Binjie 褚斌杰. *Zhongguo gudai wenti gailun* 中國古代文體概論 (*An Overview of Premodern Chinese Genres*). Beijing: Beijing daxue chubanshe, 1992.

Gu Bin 顧彬 (Wolfang Kubin), et al., eds. *Zhongguo gudian sanwen: Cong zhongshiji dao jindai de sanwen, youji, biji, he shuxin.* 中國古典散文—從中世紀到近代的散文、游記、筆記和書信 (*Classical Chinese Prose from the Middle Ages to Contemporary Times: Essays, Travel Records, Notebooks, and Letters*). Translated by Zhou Kejun 周克駿 and Li Shuangzhi 李雙志. Shanghai: Huadong shifan daxue chubanshe, 2008.

Shanghai tushuguan 上海圖書館. *Zhongguo chidu wenxian* 中國尺牘文獻 (*Collected Letters of Premodern China*). 2 vols. Shanghai: Shanghai guji chubanshe, 2013.

Zhao Shugong 趙樹功. *Zhongguo chidu wenxue shi* 中國尺牘文學史 (*A Literary History of China's Letters*). Hebei: Renmin chubanshe, 1999.

Six Dynasties Informal Prose

A New Account of the Tales of the World (Shishuo xinyu)

·

A New Account of the Tales of the World (*Shishuo xinyu*) was compiled by Liu Yiqing (403–444), a member of the royal family of the Former Song (420–479), and his editorial staff around 430 CE. It consists of 1,130 anecdotes that offer character sketches of 626 literati and nobles active from the late Eastern Han (25–220) to the Wei–Jin (220–420) period, and through them, a vivid representation of the "air and spirit" (*fengdu*) of the time.

The "tales of the world" are organized into thirty-six chapters, each focusing on one aspect of human character as expressed through words and deeds. Some of the chapter titles look familiar. For example, the first four—"Virtuous Conduct," "Speech and Conversation," "Affairs of State," and "Letters and Scholarship"—trace back to the four classifications of Confucius's disciples (*kongmen sike*; *Analects* 11.3) (☞ chap. 3). Moving down the list, however, we find not only some "moral-blind" categories, such as "Appearance and Manner," "Technical Understanding," and "The Free and Unrestrained," but also a number of categories treating dubious or outright defamatory properties like "Extravagance and Ostentation," "Slander and Treachery," "Delusion and Infatuation," and "Hostility and Alienation." Following these chapter headings to specific anecdotes, we are surprised by the discrepancies between label and content. All those extolled in the "Virtuous Conduct" are not really virtuous by traditional standards, and the character traits thought to be detestable do not always offend one's moral sense as the judgmental titles promise. Apparently, this is a new kind of prose writing whose main concern deviates from that of the morally conscious Great Tradition, exemplified in the prose works about people and events discussed in previous chapters.

The origin of this new subgenre of prose can be found in the "appraisal of human character," a practice that started off in the Later Han as a means for the recognition and selection of candidates for office. As the sociopolitical situation changed with time, the judgmental appraisal of the integrity and ability of an individual was also used as a weapon for attacking the moral weaknesses of political enemies and an effective tool for promoting self-cultivation and mutual emulation in good conduct. Then, with the falling apart of the Eastern Han and the steady weakening of the controlling power of Confucian ideology in the final years of the dynasty and the beginning of the Wei–Jin period, when the chaotic situation called for political talents rather than pedantic moralists, the emphasis of the character appraisal shifted from moral probity to personal capability. Parallel with this complex evolution of the evaluation criteria driven by pragmatic purposes was the development of a growing interest in the discussion and investigation of human nature in general. The once-pragmatic activities of evaluating specific individuals found new functions in the nonutilitarian reflection and appreciation of the quintessential qualities and fascinating traits of human being.

With the popularization of this practice, notable examples of character appraisal, in the form of insightful observations, witty comments, or just interesting anecdotes and hearsays, began to circulate in the gentry communities and eventually found their way into anthologies of the kind of stories we now see in the *Shishuo xinyu*.

The unique nature of the *Shishuo* genre explains its distinctive thematic and stylistic features. Although the characters in the text bear the names of real people and most of the major events involved are confirmed by historical records, people find it hard to take *Shishuo* tales for history. Unlike standard histories, whose shapes are fixed by a temporal framework and whose color and tone are predicated on the grammar of a semiotic system of moral admonition earnestly presenting history as a "mirror," the *Shishuo* text is dictated by nothing but the inner logic of storytelling. In the selection of subject matter, the authors and compilers are not obligated to choose the "right" historical figures and events to fit in, substantiate, or lend meaning to a chronological timeline. In their treatment of the subject matter, the authors primarily focus on descriptive details with intensity and immediacy. As long as the traits of characters and events are elicited and the ethos of the time is revealed, whether a story is "true" or whether an insignificant figure is unjustifiably brought into disproportionate relief is not a concern.

To sustain this quasi-historical space, the *Shishuo* authors found it necessary to enliven their prose with a more colloquial tone to ensure a natural flow: hence, their borrowing from everyday speech such transitional elements and cohesive devices as "aid-words" rarely found in classical prose.

Partly because of the versatile nature of the textual sources (i.e., collections of character appraisal anecdotes of different types) from which the *Shishuo* draws, the messages conveyed by individual stories have inconsistencies. For example, it is not uncommon to see a master calligrapher appear airy and graceful in one chapter, and then petty and peevish in another, or to find virile heroism and cold-bloodedness juxtaposed in the word pictures of the same generalissimo. Surprisingly, the compilers make no effort to mitigate or rationalize these inconsistencies. The possibly accidental editorial choice, however, turns out to be serendipitous. What readers notice—through a multidimensional net of relationships that connects the characters—is the unadorned representation of different sides of the characters' personalities through their interactions with different people at different times and under different circumstances. The otherwise thin and fragmented character vignettes gain layers of new meanings when interwoven into an integral whole.

Another prominent feature of the text indicates conscious authorial choice: the creators of the *Shishuo* refrain from direct comments, even when the most outrageous human frailties exposed in their stories cry out for strong opinion. These stories do not feature a judicial "Grand Scribe" like Sima Qian in the *Shiji* (☞ chap. 6). Other than the general classification of stories under value-charged headings (a perfunctory salute to the established value system), criticism and praise are expressed indirectly through participants in the stories, certain "people of the world," or the faceless "someone." One might conjecture that the *Shishuo* authors find it more satisfactory to simply relish the full array of human traits displayed under their objective writing brush. Free from authorial interference, the *Shishuo* story develops a special flavor as readers are tantalized by a plurality of possible interpretations and are invited to participate in the creation of meaning.

To allow readers a peek into this voluminous collection of tales, several dozen entries have been selected in their entirety and arranged under five headings.[1] This chapter attempts to summarize the content of the text, which is too rich and multicolored to be strictly categorized. The distinctive thematic and artistic features of the *Shishuo* discussed in this chapter should reveal themselves to careful readers.

CAPACITY, CHARACTER, AND CHARISMA

Amid the chaos of social and political instability of the Wei–Jin period, the decline of the once-unquestionable authority of Confucian ideology coincided with a new self-awareness of the cultural and intellectual elite. Moral integrity was no longer held as the primary criterion for the judgment of human character. A more natural and individualized human experience, therefore, became the goal of personal pursuit and the object of public adoration. Even a quick look at the *Shishuo* will suggest that the most important selection standard is not an entry's degree of moral purity, but rather its extraordinariness. Being merely good or bad was not enough to secure a spot in the *Shishuo* cast of characters; one had to be good or bad with *style*. So, for example:

C8.1 "Blameworthiness and Remorse, No. 13"

As he was reclining on his bed Huan Wen [312–373] once said, "If I keep on like this doing nothing, I'll be the laughingstock of Emperors Wen and Jing (Sima Zhao [211–265] and Sima Shi [208–255])." Then, after crouching and getting up from his seat, he continued, "Even if I can't let my fragrance be wafted down to later generations, does that mean I'm incapable of leaving behind a stench for ten thousand years?"

[*NATW* 513]

世說新語 • 尤悔

桓公臥語曰："作此寂寂，將為文、景所笑！"既而屈起坐曰："既不能流芳後世，亦不足復遺臭萬載邪？"

[*SSXYJJ* 483 (33/13)]

Taking for his models the usurpers Sima Zhao and Sima Shi, who founded the Western Jin, Huan always had an eye on the throne. He knew clearly that what he attempted would not make his name "fragrant," but no matter; he just wanted it to "be wafted down to later generations." His body language (crouching and getting up from a lethargic reclining posture) resolutely declares his determination to leave his mark, albeit a distasteful one. In that, he obviously succeeded.

The following story is an example of letting his "fragrance be wafted down to later generations":

C8.2 "Cultivated Tolerance, No. 35"

世說新語 • 雅量

謝公與人圍棋，俄而謝
玄淮上信至，看書竟，
默然無言，徐向局。客
問淮上利害，答曰：
"小兒輩大破賊。"意
色舉止，不異於常。

[*SSXYJJ* 209 (6/35)]

Xie An [320–385] was playing encirclement chess with someone, when suddenly a messenger arrived from Xie Xuan [who was leading the defense against Fu Jian (338–385)] at the Huai River [in 383]. An read the letter to the end in silence, and without saying a word, calmly turned back to the playing board. When his guests asked whether the news from the Huai was good or bad, he replied, "My little boys [his nephew, Xuan (343–388), and his younger brother, Shi (327–389)] have inflicted a crushing defeat on the invader." As he spoke his mood and expression and demeanor were no different from usual.

[*NATW* 204]

The military conflict referred to in the story was not just another battle, but the Battle of the Fei River (383), one of the most consequential battles in the history of China. The contrast between the weight of the news and the lightness of Xie's response is echoed by two other binary antitheses, namely the guest's anxious inquiry about good (*li*) or bad (*hai*) news from the battlefield (implying the life and death of the conflicting forces involved), and the striking contrast between the smallness (*xiao*) of Xie's generals ("my little boys") and the largeness (*da*) of their "crushing defeat" of the invaders. Then, just as readers wonder why Xie would choose this particular moment to play chess, they realize that this particular setting is part of the author's plan to highlight the composure of a strategist under the pressure of a grim situation. The way Xie handled the small chess game at hand has much to do with how and why the big battle was won, hundreds of leagues away.

The composure Xie so gracefully maintained, although not without moral implication, is seen by the *Shishuo* compilers as an example of "cultivated tolerance" and, accordingly, is placed under the category of *yaliang* (literally "elegant capacity"). Xie's capacity to absorb emotional shocks and endure extreme situations demonstrated a level of mental and psychological strength far above that of ordinary people.

Not all characters in the *Shishuo* are like Xie An. The one depicted in the following story, though colorful and fascinating, had neither Xie's calm tolerance, nor his grace:

C8.3 "Appearance and Manner, No. 1"

世說新語 • 容止

魏武將見匈奴使，自以
形陋，不足雄遠國，使
崔季珪代，帝自捉刀立
床頭。既畢，令間諜問
曰："魏王何如？"匈

When Cao Cao [155–220][1] was about to give audience to a Xiongnu envoy, since he himself felt that his own figure was insignificant and inadequate to impress a distant state with its virility, he had Cui Yan [ca. 154–216] substitute for him on the throne, while Cao himself, gripping his sword, stood at the head

---

[1] See chap. 7; *HTRCPIC* chap. 6.

of the dais. When the audience was ended he ordered a spy to ask the envoy, "What was the Prince of Wei like?" The Xiongnu envoy replied, "The Prince of Wei was refined and prepossessing to an extraordinary degree. But the man at the head of the dais who was gripping his sword—this was the heroic and virile one." When Cao Cao heard this, he had someone overtake and kill this envoy.

[*NATW* 330]

奴使答曰："魏王雅望非常，然床頭捉刀人，此乃英雄也。"魏武聞之，追殺此使。

[*SSXYJJ* 333 (14/1)]

Although the narrator does not explicitly state anything about Cao's "heroic and virile" demeanor, readers are instantly aware how much more impressive the fake attendant must have been than the fake prince, himself "refined and prepossessing to an extraordinary degree." Cao's charisma was simply impossible to hide. Or rather, it is precisely the storyteller's design to allow this carefully wrought scheme of the ever-calculating Cao to reveal more than what he attempted to hide. The narrator's skill does not stop here: the bloody conclusion of the anecdote intentionally invites questions not to be answered.

Much as the *Shishuo* authors seem to enjoy ambiguity, the moral of the next story reads direct and clear, at least at first sight:

C8.4a "Virtuous Conduct, No. 11"

Guan Ning [158–241] and Hua Xin [157–231] were together in the garden hoeing vegetables when they spied a piece of gold in the earth. Guan went on plying his hoe as though it were no different from a tile or a stone. Hua, seizing it, threw it away. On another occasion they were sharing a mat reading when someone riding a splendid carriage and wearing a ceremonial cap passed by the gate. Guan continued to read as before; Hua, putting down his book, went out to look. Guan cut the mat in two and sat apart, saying, "You're no friend of mine."

[*NATW* 5]

世說新語 • 德行

管寧、華歆共園中鋤菜，見地有片金，管揮鋤與瓦石不異，華捉而擲去之。又嘗同席讀書，有乘軒冕過門者，寧讀如故，歆廢書出看。寧割席分坐，曰："子非吾友也！"

[*SSXYJJ* 7 (1/11)]

Despite the casual tone of the narrative, its symbolism impinges on the reflective mind of the reader. Such allegorical imagery recalls a familiar line from Confucius: "Wealth [gold] and rank [splendid carriage] gained through unrighteous means, I ignore them as clouds floating by" (*Analects* 7.16) (☞ chap. 3). The two characters' different reactions to temptations are also allegorically formulaic. Guan Ning proved himself to be an impeccable student of Confucius, whereas Hua Xin failed the test.

We become less sure about this, however, as we read on and find another story involving Hua Xin:

C8.4b "Virtuous Conduct, No. 13"

Hua Xin and Wang Lang [d. 228] were sailing together in a boat fleeing the troubles of war when someone wanted to join them. Hua, for his part, disapproved,

世說新語 • 德行

華歆、王朗俱乘船避難，有一人欲依附，歆

輒難之。朗曰：“幸尚
寬，何為不可？”後賊
追至，王欲舍所攜人。
歆曰：“本所以疑，
正為此耳。既已納其
自託，寧可以急相棄
邪？”遂攜拯如初。世
以此定華、王之優劣。

[*SSXYJJ* 8 (1/13)]

but Wang said, "Fortunately we still have room. Why isn't it all right?" Later, when the rebels were overtaking them, Wang wanted to get rid of the man they had taken along, but Hua said, "This was precisely the reason I hesitated in the first place. But since we've already accepted his request, how can we abandon him in an emergency?" So they took him along as before to safety. The world by this incident has determined the relative merits of Hua and Wang.

[*NATW* 6]

The Hua here bore some resemblance to the Hua in the previous story: he had to go through an inner struggle before he could make a good choice. Unlike Guan, he found it hard not to put down his book to cast a curious eye on the splendid carriage as it passed. Although he returned to his seat and resumed reading, this wavering of character offered Guan sufficient excuse for his grandiose gesture of cutting a morally defected classmate. Hua's reaction to the discovery of the piece of gold is even more interesting: he grabbed (*zhuo*) the gold piece before throwing (*zhi*) it away. The strong sense of volition conveyed in the two active verbs betrays his troubled hesitation in a moment of moral crisis.

This is the same kind of hesitation Hua, in the second story, confessed to have felt "in the first place." Although he wavered when confronted with difficult choices, the doubts (*yi*) that crossed his mind did not prevent him from eventually making the decision he deemed right. In both stories, a moment's faltering turned out to be a moment of productive inner searching and reflection. The hesitation in the second story is not meant to expose a moral weakness, but instead to foreground the good judgment and decency of a real person. Seen in this light, the intent of the first story becomes less certain.

More often, the true color of a character is clearly, even ostentatiously, displayed:

世說新語 • 豪爽

王大將軍年少時，舊有
田舍名，語音亦楚。武
帝喚時賢共言伎藝事，
人皆多有所知，唯王都
無所關，意色殊惡。自
言知打鼓吹，帝令取鼓
與之。於坐振袖而起，
揚槌奮擊，音節諧捷，
神氣豪上，傍若無人，
舉坐歎其雄爽。

[*SSXYJJ* 325 (13/1)]

C8.5 "Virility and Boldness, No. 1"

When Generalissimo Wang Dun [266–324] was young he used to have the reputation of being a country bumpkin, and his speech also sounded like that of Chu. Emperor Wu [Sima Yan, r. 265–290] once invited the worthies of the time for a gathering and they were discussing artistic matter. Most of those present had some knowledge of the subject; Wang alone was totally uninvolved in the conversation, and his mood and expression were extraordinarily grim. Since he claimed for himself the ability to play the drums and pipes, the emperor [immediately] had someone fetch a drum and offered it to him. Right where he was sitting Wang shook out his sleeves and got up. Lifting the drumsticks he beat furiously with them, and the sound and rhythm were harmonious and rapid. His spirit and energy mounted with virility, as though no other persons were present. The entire company praised his martial vigor.

[*NATW* 322]

The bumpkin-turned-generalissimo found himself an odd man out in a gathering of cultured worthies, and his host was none other than his father-in-law, Emperor Wu. Showing off his percussion feats to that bunch of elegant artists might not have been the best way to lift himself out of the awkward situation. Yet that was precisely what Wang asked to do. No onomatopoeia is used to simulate the "harmonious and rapid" drum; the poetic rhythm of words, with its parallel structure of five successive four-syllable phrases, is sufficient to convey the sound and heat of the effervescent scene.

"The entire company praised his martial vigor" thus ends the story, but the generalissimo did not even notice. Totally engrossed in drumming, he ignored the others' possible judgment on his rustic art, "as though no other persons were present" (*pang ruo wu ren*). Only moments before, he was the victim of the entire company's *pang ruo wu ren* negligence, but the spontaneous display of this unembellished skill recalled from his bumpkin past enabled him to overcome the snobbery of the cultured "worthies of the time."

The reaction of readers to the following story may not be unanimous, but, without exception, their impression of the Generalissimo Wang will surely change:

C8.6 "Extravagance and Ostentation, No. 1"

世說新語 · 汰侈

Every time Shi Chong [249–300] invited guests for banquet gatherings he always had beautiful girls serving the wine. If any guests failed to drain their cups, he would have an attendant decapitate the girls one after the other. Chancellor Wang Dao [276–339] and his cousin, the generalissimo, Wang Dun, both went on one occasion to visit Shi Chong. The chancellor had never been able to drink, but with every toast forced himself to do so until he was dead drunk. Each time it came the generalissimo's turn, however, he deliberately refused to drink, in order to observe what would happen. Even after they had already decapitated three girls his facial expression remained unchanged and he was still unwilling to drink. When the chancellor chided him for it, the generalissimo said, "If he kills somebody from his own household, what business is it of yours?"

石崇每要客燕集，常令美人行酒，客飲酒不盡者，使黃門交斬美人。王丞相與大將軍嘗共詣崇，丞相素不能飲，輒自勉彊，至於沈醉。每至大將軍，固不飲以觀其變，已斬三人，顏色如故，尚不肯飲。丞相讓之，大將軍曰："自殺伊家人，何預卿事！"

[*NATW* 493]

[*SSXYJJ* 467–468 (30/1)]

The author's severe sanction, necessarily appropriate here, is nowhere to be found, leaving only the kindly, drunken Chancellor Wang to try in vain to save those poor girls, and readers to wonder how to make sense of the two different generalissimos.

Candor and spontaneity, tinged with attitude, are enough to make a strong character stand out from a mediocre crowd, as exemplified in the following passage:

C8.7 "Speech and Conversation, No. 31"

世說新語 · 言語

Whenever the day was fair, those who had crossed the Yangzi River would always gather at Xinting to drink and feast on the grass. On one occasion Zhou Yi [269–322], who was among the company, sighed and said, "The scene is not

過江諸人，每至美日，輒相邀新亭，藉卉飲宴。周侯中坐而歎

曰：“風景不殊，正自
有山河之異！”皆相視
流淚。唯王丞相愀然變
色曰：“當共戮力王
室，克復神州，何至作
楚囚相對？”

[*SSXYJJ* 50 (2/31)]

dissimilar to the old days in the North; it's just that naturally there's a difference between these mountains and rivers and those." All those present looked
at each other and wept. It was only Chancellor Wang Dao, who, looking very
grave, remarked with deep emotion, "We should all unite our strength around
the royal house and recover the sacred provinces. To what end do we sit here
facing each other like so many 'captives of Chu'?"

[*NATW* 47]

Wang Dao's heroic declaration, in content and tone, and emphasized by his stern
expression, inspires awe. Yet one cannot truly understand his words without grasp-
ing the meaning of Zhou Yi's sentimental remarks, which triggered both his companions' tears and Wang's vehement response. Zhou lamented that even if the
scene (*fengjing*) was not unlike the old days in the North, the mountains and rivers
(*shanhe*)—that is, the country—they faced were so different in the South. Obviously, by *fengjing*, Zhou did not mean the usual landscape (as the mountains and
rivers were decidedly different), but the air (*feng*) and the scene (*jing*), or rather,
the unchanging ambiance of the nobility's elegant picnics "on the grass" on a fair
day, and their euphoric sensuous enjoyment. Something ironic was lurking in this
weirdly sentimental situation, but it took the harsh admonition of a personality like
Chancellor Wang to expose the sarcasm. After such a scene, one cannot but wonder what those gentry from the North would now do "whenever the day was fair."

The verve and energy of Wang's emotional expression is presented through
comparison. Indeed, comparison is the purpose of character appraisal discussed
at the beginning of this chapter. Characters from the *Shishuo* not only allow themselves to be compared with each other but also invite self-promoting comparisons
by presenting ideal images of themselves and even challenging others to participate in comparisons of this kind. When these comparisons are made, sparks of
genuine and sincere ego flash from the pages, capturing our attention:

C8.8 "Grading Excellence, No. 35"

世說新語 • 品藻

桓公少與殷侯齊名，
常有競心。桓問殷：
“卿何如我？”殷
云：“我與我周旋久，
寧作我。”

[*SSXYJJ* 284 (9/35)]

When Huan Wen was young, he and Yin Hao [306–356] were of equal reputation, and they constantly felt a spirit of mutual rivalry. Huan once asked Yin,
"How do you compare with me?" Yin replied, "I've been keeping company
with myself a long time; I'd rather just be me."

[*NATW* 277]

Biographies of Huan and Yin in *The History of the Jin Dynasty* (*Jinshu*) tell us that
Yin Hao was not the winner of this rivalry, at least in the political arena,[2] yet his
self-esteem was too deeply rooted and staunch—the result of "keeping company
with [him]self a long time"—to be swayed by trivial worldly success. The tenacity
conveyed in the word *ning* (would rather) not only makes clear his resolve to be
himself but also implies a contemptuous refutation of the different choice made

by his rival. Declaring the joy of being his true self, Yin Hao gave the best possible answer to Huan Wen's provocative question.

ECCENTRICITY, IDIOSYNCRASY, AND ABERRANCE

To live in the world of the *Shishuo*, then, a character has to be uniquely his- or herself, or *extra*ordinary. In this section, we will see that when a character is idiosyncratically different from others, "eccentricity" becomes both the synonym and antonym of "extraordinariness." The most fascinating characters are those not merely different, but aberrantly different, from the norm.

Ruan Ji (210–263), one of the "Seven Worthies of the Bamboo Grove" (*zhulin qixian*) (☞ *HTRCPIC* chap. 8), a group of unruly intellectuals in the Wei–Jin period known for their iconoclastic behavior, stood out as an eccentric even in such company:

C8.9a "The Free and Unrestrained, No. 7"

Ruan Ji's sister-in-law was once returning to her parents' home, and Ji went to see her to say good-bye. When someone chided him for this, Ji replied, "Were the rites established for people like me?"

[*NATW* 402]

世說新語 • 任誕

阮籍嫂嘗還家，籍見與別。或譏之，籍曰：
"禮豈為我輩設也！"

[*SSXYJJ* 393 (23/7)]

One might wonder whether the author does not purposely create a sister-in-law for Ruan just to comment on a moral lesson from Mencius (372–289 BCE) (☞ chap. 3) decreeing that, according to ritual, one should not touch the hand of even one's sister-in-law unless she is drowning and needs a helping hand (*Mencius* 4a.17). Here, not faced with an extreme situation compelling him to reach out to his female kin, Ruan willfully crossed the line. Retorting the defender of rites with a rhetorical question, he emphasized the exclusive privilege enjoyed by "people like me." The claim, however, concedes to the necessity of rules and regulations, if only for "people *un*like me." Ruan Ji's friend Ji Kang (223–262), another "Worthy of the Bamboo Grove," proposed a theory that could come to his aid. "A gentleman is called a gentleman," says Ji Kang, "because he does not set his mind on what is right or what is wrong, and yet his actions never go against the way."[3]

Truly, rites had no use for Ruan; the thought of right and wrong never crossed his mind:

C8.9b "The Free and Unrestrained, No. 8"

The wife of Ruan Ji's neighbor was very pretty. She worked as a barmaid tending the vats and selling wine. Ruan and Wang Rong frequently drank at her place, and after Ruan became drunk he would sleep by this woman's side. Her husband at first was extraordinarily suspicious of him, but after careful investigations he ceased after a while to think anything amiss.

[*NATW* 402]

世說新語 • 任誕

阮公鄰家婦，有美色，當壚酤酒。阮與王安豐常從婦飲酒，阮醉，便眠其婦側。夫始殊疑之，伺察，終無他意。

[*SSXYJJ* 393 (23/8)]

The passage is a complete narration, starting with an attractive beginning, which leads to a logical development of rising action; followed by a point of crisis; finally, the denouement defuses a potential conflict. The efficacy of the narrative owes a lot to several adverbs in key places. The word *chang* (often, frequently) not only informs us that Ruan's fondness for female beauty was habitual but also implies there was nothing wrong with the habit. Every time he got intoxicated by wine (and very possibly also by the beauty), he would—*bian* (then and there, without pre-meditation)—lie down and sleep by the pretty barmaid. The casual *bian* connotes spontaneity and naturalness. In comparison, the husband of the barmaid was not so easy and natural. Growing particularly (*shu*) suspicious, he started a pretty long and thorough process of investigation, which went from a serious beginning (*shi*) to an eventual relieving conclusion (*zhong*). When this *zhong* is tightly combined with *wu* (nothing) into one word *zhongwu* (eventually nothing) to wrap up the investigation, the finality of the conclusion and complete absence of wrongdoing are doubly emphasized.

More often, Ruan declared with his action that any normal or natural person, whether like him or not, did not need the bondage of rites. For instance, another tale in the *Shishuo* tells that, while in mourning for his mother, Ruan did not refrain from drinking wine and devouring meat even in public. This serious contempt of social mores arouses outcries to have him ostracized. And yet, Ruan Ji was too traumatized by his loss to pay heed to the threat (*SSXYJJ* 390–391 [23/1]).

世說新語 • 任誕

阮籍當葬母，蒸一肥
豚，飲酒二斗，然後臨
訣，直言“窮矣！”都
得一號，因吐血，廢頓
良久。

[*SSXYJJ* 393 (23/9)]

C8.9c "The Free and Unrestrained, No. 9"

When Ruan Ji was about to bury his mother, he steamed a fat suckling pig, drank two dipperfuls of wine, and after that attended the last rites. He did nothing but cry, "It's all over!" and gave himself to continuous wailing. As a result of this he spit up blood and wasted away for a long time.

[*NATW* 402–403]

No moral code can measure his filial love or regulate his bereavement. When one is true to oneself, any nod to rites is but an affected gesture.

When people like Ruan Ji and his fellow "Worthies of the Bamboo Grove" became tone setters of the cultural ethos of the day, imitators followed. A *Shishuo* tale quotes someone saying, "a famous gentleman (*mingshi*) doesn't necessarily have to possess remarkable talent. Merely let a man be perpetually idle and a heavy drinker, and whoever has read the poem, 'Encountering Sorrow' ("Lisao"), can then be called a 'famous gentleman' " (*SSXYJJ* 391 [23/53]). The trendy craving for the fame of a "famous gentleman" cannot be anything less than a conscious effort of calculation and scheming.

Sometimes, the gritty disposition of a character shamelessly expresses itself in a lackluster moment of mundane trivialities:

C8.10 "Anger and Irascibility, No. 2"

Wang Shu [303–368] was by nature short-tempered. Once, while he was attempting to eat an egg, he speared it with his chopstick, but could not get hold of it. Immediately flying into a great rage, he lifted it up and hurled it to the ground. The egg rolled around on the ground and had not yet come to rest when he got down on the ground and stamped on it with the teeth of his clogs, but again failed to get hold of it. Thoroughly infuriated, [he] picked it up from the ground and stuffed it in his mouth. After biting it to pieces he immediately spewed it out. When Wang Xizhi [303–361] heard about it he laughed aloud, saying, "If the father Wang Cheng had had a temper like this, even with his reputation there still wouldn't be the slightest thing about him worth discussing. How much less in the case of Wang Shu!"

[NATW 500]

世說新語 • 忿狷

王藍田性急。嘗食雞子，以筋刺之，不得，便大怒，舉以擲地。雞子於地圓轉未止，仍下地以屐齒碾之，又不得。瞋甚，復於地取內口中，齧破即吐之。王右軍聞而大笑曰：「使安期有此性，猶當無一豪可論，況藍田邪？」

[SSXYJJ 473–474 (31/2)]

Imagine a man of eminent social and political status, eventually rising to the position of Imperial Secretariat president, exercised his anger and vengeance on an egg, which was only passively dragged into this unprovoked conflict. Enlivened by Wang's sudden flare-up of rage, the egg became a tenacious adversary, with a personality nearly matching Wang's, only a bit more elusive and slick. Every advance from Wang led to the egg's resilient response, and every automatic reaction from the elastically bouncing and rolling egg only fueled Wang's anger further. The two were thus drawn deeper and deeper into an escalating war, vividly realized in a series of active verbs.

To see this amusing story as an example of the capricious folly typical of a decadent aristocratic class is to miss its point. The spontaneity (though not in the best sense of the word) in Wang's behavior deserves some admiration. Xie An, who impressed us with his graceful composure in the second story in this chapter (C8.2), made the following comment on Wang the egg-fighter:

C8.11 "Appreciation and Praise, No. 78"

Xie An once praised Wang Shu, saying, "Lift up his skin, and underneath it's all real."

[NATW 248]

世說新語 • 賞譽

謝公稱藍田掇皮皆真。

[SSXYJJ 256 (8/78)]

At the end of this story, a garrulous Wang Xizhi (☛ HTRCProse-CCC, L22), the great calligrapher, assumed the role of commentator. Gloating over the egg on Wang Shu's face might not be too terrible a sin, as the two Wangs had been friendly nemeses for years, but to deride Wang Shu with open loud laughter was too much. In his attempt to disparage Wang Shu, Wang Xizhi went so far as to drag down Wang Shu's father. In doing so, he might unwittingly have given people reason to suspect that the grudge he harbored was the main cause of the sour relationship between the two.

Compared with Wang Xizhi, the "Calligraphy-Sage" burdened with petty worldly sentiments, his fifth son Wang Huizhi (338–386) appeared unearthly and transcendent. Different from any norm, this wayward aberrant behaved as if he did not belong in this world:

世說新語 • 任誕

王子猷居山陰，夜大雪，眠覺，開室命酌酒，四望皎然。因起彷徨，詠左思《招隱詩》，忽憶戴安道。時戴在剡，即便夜乘小船就之。經宿方至，造門不前而返。人問其故，王曰：「吾本乘興而行，興盡而返，何必見戴！」

[SSXYJJ 408 (23/47)]

C8.12a "The Free and Unrestrained, No. 47"

While Wang Huizhi was living in Shanyin, one night there was a heavy fall of snow. Waking from sleep, he opened the panels of his room, and, ordering wine, drank to the shining whiteness all about him. Then he got up and started to pace back and forth, humming Zuo Si's [d. 306] poem, "Summons to a Retired Gentleman" ["Zhao yin shi"]. All at once he remembered Dai Kui [d. 396], who was living at the time in Shan. On the spur of the moment he set out by night in a small boat to visit him. The whole night had passed before he finally arrived. When he reached Dai's gate he turned back without going in. When someone asked his reason, Wang replied, "I originally went on the strength of an impulse, and when the impulse was spent I turned back. Why was it necessary to see Dai?"

[NATW 419]

Wang Huizhi's spontaneous response to the "spur of the moment" can be observed in a series of uninterrupted actions touched off by an unexpected night snow. One could say that up to the point at which his poem chanting reminded him of his friend, his reactions to outside stimuli were not outrageously abnormal. Only then did it begin to get out of bounds. Setting out for a friend's place instantly (ji), then and there (bian), in the middle of a snowy night was not something ordinary people tended to do. Although one is still puzzling over this hotheaded decision, he surprised readers' expectation further with the coup de grace of defeating the purpose of his trip. In a world in which norms and conventions are respected, who would to this? But it was precisely this norm that held no interest to Wang. Only the "spur of the moment" mattered. He did what he did by riding (cheng) the spur or impulse of the moment. Once the impulse was spent, it was time to return.

The xing Wang rode (cheng) is more than a spur or an impulse. It was an irrepressible urge inside him that had to be satisfied to the fullest, which often puzzled earthly wisdom.

C8.12b "The Free and Unrestrained, No. 46"

世說新語 • 任誕

王子猷嘗暫寄人空宅住，便令種竹。或問：「暫住何煩爾？」王嘯詠良久，直指竹曰：「何可一日無此君！」

[SSXYJJ 408 (23/46)]

Wang Huizhi was once temporarily lodging in another man's vacant house, and ordered bamboos planted. Someone asked, "Since you're only living here temporarily, why bother?" Wang whistled and chanted poems a good while; then abruptly pointing to the bamboos, replied, "How could I live a single day without these gentlemen?"

[NATW 418–419]

Wang Huizhi was not the first to use the word "bamboos" to describe gentlemen. But the numerous accounts of Wang suggest that this eccentric was not one to care about the moral qualities traditionally associated with bamboo. His penchant for the plant was but a gesture to show to what extent he could let himself be carried away by a hobby. In other words, the emphasis of Wang's witty answer to the "why bother" question lies less on "these gentlemen" (*cijun*) than on his urge to make the best of each and every "single day" (*yiri*).

The *carpe diem* sentiment, so characteristic of the period from the late Eastern Han through Wang's time, is undeniable. The mood of "seizing the day" permeated this dark age of disunity and chaos, during which the populace suffered from frequent changes of political power and incessant wars, and few people survived their prime years. Compared with the desperate solution offered by one of the anonymous authors of the "Nineteen Old Poems"—if the day is too short, why not prolong it by lighting a candle and go reveling? (☛ *HTRCP*, C5.3)—Wang Huizhi's approach was more sober: just treasure every day as it comes.

Had Wang planted bamboos in his "permanent" residence, no eyebrows would be raised. The problem was that Wang stayed in that house only temporarily and the house belonged to someone else. But Wang saw things in a totally different light. A day he did not live to the fullest could not be counted as his day, and he refused to accept those "temporary" days of making do without bamboos. As to the house, "mine" or "his" made no sense to him. Like so many things in the world, a house was to be enjoyed, not to be possessed.

WORDS, WIT, AND WISDOM

In the world of the *Shishuo*, "language" serves almost as a verb. Characters act through words, and in turn, words betray various aspects of personality of the characters, either because or in spite of these words. This comes as no surprise, particularly when considering the fact that the history of character appraisal and the ensuing cultural and literary practices it generated is a long and gradual process of a complicated interaction between spoken words and written words, and between appraisers and appraisees.

Even in its brevity, the words of the character in the following example carry more than what is heard:

C8.13 "Taunting and Teasing, No. 31"

On the seventh day of the seventh month Hao Long [mid-fourth century] went out in the sun and lay on his back. When people asked what he was doing, he replied, "I'm sunning my books."

[*NATW* 446]

世說新語 ‧ 排調

郝隆七月七日出日中
仰臥，人問其故，答
曰："我曬書。"

[*SSXYJJ* 430 (25/31)]

This anecdote recalls another story in the text about how Ruan Xian (Ruan Ji's nephew and another member of the "Seven Worthies of the Bamboo Grove") deliberately hung out a pair of loose cloth underpants to thumb his nose at his rich neighbors' showy display of silks and brocades on the annual "sunning day" (*SSXYJJ* 393 [23/10]). In this story, Hao went a step further. Gaudy displays of wardrobes were vulgar, beneath his contempt; he had a library to flaunt. He also might have, in the process, thrown a passing jab at fake bibliophiles—the seventh day of the seventh month was the day for phonies to show off their vanity collections.

The clever use of words in the following anecdote is another typical example of *Shishuo*-style wit:

C8.14 "Worthy Beauties, No. 5"

世說新語 • 賢媛

趙母嫁女，女臨去，敕
之曰：「慎勿為好！」
女曰：「不為好，可為
惡邪？」母曰：「好尚
不可為，其況惡乎？」

[*SSXYJJ* 365 (19/5)]

Mother Zhao [d. 243] once gave her daughter in marriage. When the daughter was about to depart for her husband's home, Mother Zhao admonished her, saying, "Be careful not to do any good." The daughter said, "If I don't do good, then may I do evil?" Her mother said, "If even good may not be done, how much less evil!"

[*NATW* 365]

It is refreshing to have the complexity of good and evil laid bare under the sharp blade of a relentless paradox. By setting this moral lesson in the context of a mother sharing her hard-earned wisdom with her daughter as part of the dowry she brings to her future family, the author injects a dull credo with real-life content. Yet the significance of the aphorism "not to do any good," so accentuated and then clarified, goes beyond the usual role-playing and maneuvering skill necessary in the male-dominant family politics. And no wonder: the mother was not just any mother. She is the author of a lost commentary on Liu Xiang's *Accounts of Notable Women* (*Lienü zhuan*), and after her husband's death, was summoned to the palace by the ruler of the State of Wu (222–280) during the Three Kingdom period (220–280). Whereas the daughter followed conventional thinking and took "good" for the opposite of "evil," Mother Zhao demonstrated a more sophisticated understanding of the Confucian moral principles, implying—implicitly, yet unequivocally—that the opposite of "good" was not "evil" but rather "overly good" or, to be exact, "pretended good." Confucius would smile to read this story, being a sincere and realistic moralist who considered hypocrites "thieves of virtue" (*Analects* 17.13) (☛ chap. 3).

At a time like Wei–Jin, when the Confucian establishment met with serious challenges, interest in Daoist thought rose, as it did in the newly imported foreign religion of Buddhism. References to Buddhist and Daoist texts are found in many anecdotes:

C8.15a "Speech and Conversation, No. 41"

世說新語 • 言語

庾公嘗入佛圖，見臥
佛，曰：「此子疲於津
梁。」於時以為名言。

[*SSXYJJ* 56 (2/41)]

Yu Liang [289–340] once entered a stupa, and seeing there a representation of the reclining Buddha, remarked, "This man's tired after all the ferrying and bridging of sentient beings to salvation." At the time it was considered a famous remark.

[*NATW* 53]

C8.15b "Speech and Conversation, No. 19"

When Emperor Wu [Sima Yan (236–290)] first ascended the throne, he drew a divining straw and obtained the number "one." The number of reigns in a dynasty depends upon whether the number drawn is large or small. Since the emperor was plainly dismayed, all his ministers turned pale, and there was no one who had anything to say. The personal attendant, Pei Kai, then stepped forward and said, "your servant has heard that 'Heaven by attaining the One is limpid; earth by attaining the One is calm . . . and nobles and kings by attaining the One become the standard for the realm.' " The emperor was pleased, and all the ministers sighed with admiration.[1]

[NATW 41]

世說新語 • 言語

晉武帝始登阼，探策得一。王者世數，繫此多少。帝既不說，群臣失色，莫能有言者。侍中裴楷進曰：「臣聞天得一以清，地得一以寧，侯王得一以為天下貞。」帝說，群臣歎服。

[SSXYJJ 44 (2/19)]

C8.16 "The Free and Unrestrained, No. 6"

On many occasions Liu Ling [ca. 221–300], under the influence of wine, would be completely free and uninhibited, sometimes taking off his clothes and sitting naked in his room. Once when some person saw him and chided him for it, Ling retorted, "I take heaven and earth for my pillars and roof, and the rooms of my house for my pants and coat. What are you gentlemen doing in my pants?"

[NATW 402]

世說新語 • 任誕

劉伶恆縱酒放達，或脫衣裸形在屋中，人見譏之。伶曰：「我以天地為棟宇，屋室為褌衣，諸君何為入我褌中？」

[SSXYJJ 392 (23/6)]

The first example is a witty parody of Buddhist teaching; the second a clever trick of language in the name of Daoism; the third a motto for human existence in the guise of a joke, forged out of Zhuangzi's language.

The *Zhuangzi* text (☞ chap. 4) figures among the favorite topics of the *qingtan* (pure conversation): witty conversations or debates about mataphysics popular among the elite of the time, the origin of which traces to the practice of character appraisal. The following is one of many lifelike records of the *qingtan* gathering:

C8.17a "Letters and Scholarship, No. 55"

Zhi Dun [314–366], Xu Xun [fl. ca. 358], Xie An, and others of outstanding virtue were gathered together at the home of Wang Meng [309–347]. Xie, looking all around, said to everyone, "Today's is what might be called a distinguished assembly. Since time may not be made to stand still, and this assembly as well, no doubt, would be hard to prolong, we should all speak, or intone poems, to express our feelings." Xu then asked the host, "Have you a copy of the *Zhuangzi*?" It so happened that he had the one chapter, "The Old Fisherman" ("Yufu"). Xie looked at the title and then asked everyone present to make an exposition of it. Zhi Dun was the first to do so, using seven hundred or more

世說新語 • 文學

支道林、許、謝盛德共集王家，謝顧謂諸人：「今日可謂彥會。時既不可留，此集固亦難常，當共言詠，以寫其懷。」許便問主人：「有莊子不？」正得漁父一篇。謝看題，便各使四坐通。支道

---

[1] Mather's translation is slightly adjusted here.

林<u>先</u>通，作七百許
語，敘致精麗，才藻
奇拔，眾咸稱善。<u>於</u>
<u>是</u>四坐<u>各</u>言懷<u>畢</u>。
謝問曰：" 卿等<u>盡</u>
不？"<u>皆</u>曰："今日
之言，<u>少</u>不自竭。"
謝後䲭難，<u>因自</u>敘其
意，作萬餘語，才峰秀
逸，<u>既自</u>難干，<u>加</u>意氣
擬託，蕭然<u>自</u>得，四
坐<u>莫</u>不厭心。支謂謝
曰："君一往奔詣，
故復<u>自</u>佳<u>耳</u>。"

[*SSXYJJ* 129–130 (4/55)]

words. The ideas of his exposition were intricate and graceful, the style of his eloquence wonderful and unique, and the whole company voiced his praises. After him each of those present told what was in his mind. When they had finished, Xie asked them, "Have you gentlemen fully expressed yourselves?" They all answered, "In what we've said today, few of us have not expressed ourselves fully." Xie then raised a few general objections, and on the basis of these set forth his own ideas in more than ten thousand words. The peak of his eloquence was far and away superior to any of the others. Not only was he unquestionably beyond comparison, but in addition he put his heart and soul into it, forthright and self-assured. There was no one present who was not satisfied in his mind. Zhi Dun said to Xie, "From beginning to end you rushed straight on; without any doubt you were the best."

[*NATW* 127–128]

The orderly progression of the conference is clearly registered in the use of cohesive devices, such as "first" (*xian*), "thereafter" (*yushi*), "once done" (*bi*), "finally" (*hou*), and "then and there" (*yin*), whereas the logical outcome of the conversation—its thoroughness, comprehensiveness, and sophistication achieved—is confirmed by a series of adverbs like "all" (*xian*), "each and every" (*ge*), "unanimous" (*jie*), "already certainly . . . , in addition" (*ji zi . . . jia*), and "none is not" (*mobu*).

These adverbial "transitional elements" help articulate the story-telling, and elucidate what is articulated. The disproportional frequency of the "aid-words"[4] is one of the distinctive generic features of *Shishuo*. If we left out the 32 aid-words (underlined in the text) from this passage of 162 words, it would still be intelligible, but it would read like a piece of classical Chinese prose from the Han dynasty (206 BCE–220 CE) and before (☛ chaps. 1–7), the kind of standard prose known for its classical beauty of terseness. Yet the business of the *Shishuo* authors is not to achieve the stately weight of the ancient style, but rather to promote fluent and effective storytelling. As described in the tale, the *qingtan* conversationalists sought to *tong* (to dwell on a philosophical topic) by thoroughly exploring it. The rich connotations of the verb-noun-adjective *tong* also suggest that the language used in this conversation should be fluent and unobstructed. If Zhi Dun's *tong* of seven hundred odd words were already "intricate" and "eloquent," and the *tong* of other participants left little unexhausted, just imagine what Xie An had to do with his concluding speech of more than ten thousand words. However pithy and powerful the language of ancient-style prose, it is not the best tool for *qingtan*. Such lively and exuberant pure conversation needs a language that not only can pick up subtle tones to reveal nuances in attitudes but also can ease the jolting and jerking between statements and smooth the twists and turns in an argument. The use of aid-words, with their agility and flexibility borrowed from everyday speech, contributes to the creation of a language with its distinct characteristics. Interestingly, this language of *tong* overflows from the pure conversation to all other aspects of the *Shishuo* and emerges as the most prominent stylistic feature of the text.[5]

The accounts of *qingtan* give detailed descriptions of how these pure conversations were carried out, but they seldom elaborate on what was actually said:

C8.17b "Letters and Scholarship, No. 40"

世說新語 • 文學

Zhi Dun, Xu Xun, and other persons were once gathered at the villa of the Prince of Kuaiji, Sima Yu. Zhi acted as dharma master and Xu as discussant. Whenever Zhi explained an interpretation there was no one present who was not completely satisfied, and whenever Xu delivered an objection everyone applauded and danced with delight. But in every case they were filled with admiration for the forensic skill of the two performers, without the slightest discrimination regarding the content of their respective arguments.

支道林、許掾諸人共在
會稽王齋頭，支為法
師，許為都講。支通一
義，四坐莫不厭心；許
送一難，眾人莫不抃
舞。但共嗟詠二家之
美，不辯其理之所在。

[NATW 120]

[SSXYJJ 123–124 (4/40)]

This passage leaves one with the impression that style could be more important than content in the high-sounding conversations of the intellectual elite of the time. If the rhetorical finesse and eloquence of two interlocutors are considered sufficient manifestation of their wisdom, there is no reason not to take the physical beauty and outward bearing of a person for the emanation of his inner quality.

APPEARANCE, DEMEANOR, AND AIR

The enthusiasm demonstrated in the *Shishuo* for beautiful physical appearance and distinctive mien is unprecedented, reflecting a totally new cultural and aesthetic attitude of the age. This rise of a new aesthetic ideal can never be overemphasized when trying to understand and appreciate the *Shishuo*, as well as the Wei–Jin ethos and the sociocultural milieu of the time. For a good example of this particular obsession with beauty, we turn to the following:

C8.18 "Appearance and Manner, No. 2"

世說新語 • 容止

Pei Kai [237–291] possessed outstanding beauty and manners. Even after removing his official cap, with coarse clothing and undressed hair, he was always attractive. Contemporaries felt him to be a man of jade. One who saw him remarked, "looking at Pei Kai is like walking on top of a jade mountain with the light reflected back at you."

裴令公有儁容儀，脫冠
冕，麤服亂頭皆好，時
人以為“玉人”。見者
曰：“見裴叔則，如玉
山上行，光映照人。”

[NATW 333]

[SSXYJJ 336 (14/2)]

The simple sketch at the beginning of the passage is enough to present the "beauty and manners" of the character, yet it is the image of jade in the metaphor that brings the lustrous physical beauty to another level. This picture of Pei Kai in words recalls another story in the *Shishuo*, in which the painting of Pei Kai becomes a thought-provoking topic in the Chinese art history:

世說新語 • 巧藝

顧長康畫裴叔則，頰上
益三毛。人問其故？顧
曰：「裴楷儁朗有識
具，正此是其識具。」
看畫者尋之，定覺益三
毛如有神明，殊勝未安
時。

[SSXYJJ 387(21/9)]

C8.19 "Skill and Art, No. 9"

When Gu Kaizhi [ca. 348–405] painted Pei Kai's portrait he added three hairs
to his cheek. When someone asked his reason, Gu said, "Pei Kai was an outstanding and transparent person who possessed a knowledge of human capabilities. It's precisely these hairs which represent his knowledge of human
capabilities." Those who looked at the painting searched for this, and actually did feel that the added three hairs seemed somehow to make it possess
spirit and intelligence to a far greater degree than at the time before they had
been applied.

[NATW 394]

What the "added three hairs" do for the painting, the image of jade does for the
word picture. As the metaphor's vehicle, the jade does not need to bear any superficial resemblance to Pei—at least no more than the three hairs. What matters is the
symbolism of the precious stone conjured up by the image. Notably, Gu Kaizhi was
the first proponent of "catching the essence, instead of the outward appearance"
in painting. This new principle of art reminds one of the shift of focus from the
concrete and specific to the more general and metaphenomenal that happened in
the later development of character appraisal. This approach to the study of human
characters extends to the field of aesthetics.

To capture the essence of a character that is difficult to pin down with direct
description, nothing is more effective than metaphor:

世說新語 • 容止

時人目王右軍「飄如遊
雲，矯若驚龍」。

[SSXYJJ 341 (14/30)]

C8.20 "Appearance and Manner, No. 30"

Contemporaries characterized Wang Xizhi as follows: "Now drifting like a
floating cloud; now rearing up like a startled dragon."

[NATW 338]

世說新語 • 賞譽

王戎云：「太尉神姿高
徹，如瑤林瓊樹，自然
是風塵外物。」

[SSXYJJ 233 (8/16)]

C8.21a "Appreciation and Praise, No. 16"

Wang Rong [234–305] said, "The spirit and manner of the grand marshal,
Wang Yan, are lofty and transcendent, like a jade forest or a jasper tree. He's
naturally a being who lives beyond the reach of the wind and dust of the world."

[NATW 228]

世說新語 • 賞譽

公孫度目邴原：「所謂
雲中白鶴，非燕雀之網
所能羅也。」

[SSXYJJ 228 (8/4)]

C8.21b "Appreciation and Praise, No. 4"

Gongsun Du [d. 204] characterized Bing Yuan [d. 211] as follows: "He's what
might be called a white crane among the clouds; not to be caught in a net set
for swallows and sparrows."

[NATW 225]

C8.22 "Appearance and Manner, No. 39"

Someone praised the splendor of Wang Gong's [d. 398] appearance with the words, "Sleek and shining as the willow in the months of spring."

[*NATW* 340]

世說新語 • 容止

有人歎王恭形茂者，云："濯濯如春月柳。"

[*SSXYJJ* 342 (14/39)]

These metaphors are all clichés. Nonetheless, the subtle overtones and inexplicably suggestive and allusive power condensed in them—especially in the ethereal images of the first three—enable the overused expressions to succeed in conveying the intended meaning. The willow in the last example, although also a cliché, deserves a closer look. The aural, visual, and tactile implications in the reduplicative onomatopoeia *zhuozhuo* (sleek and shining), added to all the sensuous associations of spring, make the "splendor" of the character's appearance nearly palpable. Trite as the clichés are, once summoned by a new situation and arranged in different combinations with other descriptive elements, their original evocative power can be rejuvenated.

This technique of using new, concrete details to reinvigorate hackneyed, sometimes vague, expressions is also seen in the next example:

C8.23 "Admiration and Emulation, No. 6"

Before Meng Chang [d. 420] had achieved recognition, his family lived in Jiangkou. Once he saw Wang Gong riding a high carriage and wearing a robe of crane's plumes. At the time there was a light snow on the ground. Stealing a glimpse of him through the fences, Chang sighed in admiration, saying, "This is truly a man from among the gods and immortals!"

[*NATW* 345]

世說新語 • 企羨

孟昶未達時，家在京口。嘗見王恭乘高輿，被鶴氅裘。于時微雪，昶於籬間窺之，歎曰："此真神仙中人！"

[*SSXYJJ* 347 (16/6)]

The high carriage, the crane's plume, and the thin layer of whiteness from the light but timely snow combine to make an otherwise airy immortal vividly within an admirer's reach. The extra information about Meng's humble state (before he was "recognized") and his eagerness (peeking "through the fences") create a dramatic situation in which the aesthetic experience of unearthly beauty is intensified.

When the *Shishuo* authors found new vehicles of their own for metaphor, the results were refreshing:

C8.24a "Appreciation and Praise, No. 56"

Contemporaries characterized Zhou Yi [269–322] as: "Unscalable as a sheer cliff."

[*NATW* 243]

世說新語 • 賞譽

世目周侯：嶷如斷山。

[*SSXYJJ* 249 (8/56)]

To use mountain imagery in a reverse personification is not uncommon, but to compare a person to a "vertically cut mountain cliff" (*duanshan*) is not the same.

Decidedly terse and pithy, this eight-ideograph entry—the shortest in the entire text—is right on target with visual and auditory force. According to *The Annals of Jin Dynasty* (*Jin Yangqiu*), "Zhou Yi was so aloofly square that even his peers dared not to get close to or be familiar with him" (*SSXYJJ* 249 [8/56]). The readers' own experience with the shapes, angles, even the sense of weight and suspended momentum of certain perpendicular cliffs is evoked to help them grasp Zhou's distinctive personality.

Sensuous interpretation also plays an important role in the following passage:

世說新語 • 賞譽

卞令目叔向："朗朗如百間屋。"

[*SSXYJJ* 347 (8/50)]

C8.24b "Appreciation and Praise, No. 50"

Bian Kun [281–328] characterized his uncle Bian Xiang [?] as "bright and resonant as a big house of a hundred rooms."

The terse comment on the character does not reveal specifics of his appearance, but the beaming brightness, open spaciousness, and echoing resonance suggested by the synesthesia *langlang* (another reduplicative attribute) make this Uncle Bian congenially accessible.

In some cases, appreciation of the outstanding deportment and manner of characters is expressed through the aura surrounding them:

世說新語 • 容止

海西時，諸公每朝，朝堂猶暗，唯會稽王來，軒軒如朝霞舉。

[*SSXYJJ* 342 (14/35)]

C8.25 "Appearance and Manner, No. 35"

During the reign of the Duke of Haixi [Sima Yi, r. 365–371], each morning as the courtiers gathered for the dawn audience, the audience hall would still be dark. It was only when the Prince of Kuaiji, Sima Yu [320–372], came that all become radiantly light, like dawn clouds rising.

[*NATW* 339]

The irresistible personal appeal of the prince is likened to the radiation of dawn clouds. The use of *xuanxuan* (yet another reduplicative word) lights up the atmosphere: it not only visualizes the luminous appearance and stately, graceful demeanor of the prince but also nearly mimics the passage of time. The readers' eyes are directed toward the gradual change of the audience hall from a gloomy chamber into an open space aglow with soothing light resulting from the prince's arrival.

The power of aura is even more strongly felt in the next two passages:

世說新語 • 賞譽

庾太尉少為王眉子所知，庾過江，嘆王曰："庇其宇下，使人忘寒暑。"

[*SSXYJJ* 242 (8/35)]

C8.26 "Appreciation and Praise, No. 35"

When Yu Liang was young, he was recognized by Wang Xuan [d. 313]. After Yu had crossed the Yangzi River, he praised Wang, saying, "Just to take shelter under his eaves enabled a person to forget the heat or cold.

[*NATW* 237]

C8.27 "Virtuous Conduct, No. 34"

Xie An had such a high opinion of Chu Pou [303–349] that he would often praise him, saying, "Although Chu Pou doesn't talk much, the vital forces of the four seasons are complete in him."

世說新語•德行

謝太傅絕重褚公，常稱 "褚季野雖不言，而四時之氣亦備。"

[*SSXYJJ* 20 (1/34)]

In the first of these two passages, the reassuring presence of Wang Xuan's personality caused one to forget the "heat or cold" of the extreme seasons in both the human and the natural realm, while in the second, a taciturn but spontaneous Chu Pou recalled to his character appraiser the natural rhythmic cadence of the four seasons.

In the following example, the atmosphere of "temple or hall" is set against that of any "hill" and valley "stream" to highlight two characters' different dispositions and aspirations.

C8.28 "Grading Excellence, No. 17"

Emperor Ming once asked Xie Kun [280–322], "how would you rate yourself in comparison with Yu Liang?" Xie replied, "As for 'sitting in ceremonial attire' in temple or hall, and making the hundred officials keep to the rules, I'm no match for Liang. But when it comes to '[living in seclusion on] a single hill,' or '[fishing in] a single stream,' I consider myself superior to him."

[*NATW* 272]

世說新語 • 品藻

明帝問謝鯤："君自謂何如庾亮？" 答曰："端委廟堂，使百僚準則，臣不如亮，一丘一壑，自謂過之。"

[*SSXYJJ* 280 (9/17)]

Comparison and contrast are used to the fullest extent in the next example:

C8.29a "Appearance and Manner, No. 11"

Someone once said to Wang Rong, "Xi Shao [253–304] stands out prominently like a wild crane in a flock of chickens." Wang replied, "You never saw his father, that's all."

[*NATW* 333]

世說新語 • 容止

有人語王戎曰："嵇延祖卓卓如野鶴之在雞群。" 答曰："君未見其父耳！"

[*SSXYJJ* 336 (14/11)]

This passage features multiple layers of metaphor. First, the ordinary many are compared to a flock of chickens, and the extraordinary few to a wild crane. Then the difference between the mediocre and the outstanding is conveyed in the simile of the wild crane standing out from that flock of birds. The comparison does not stop here. No sooner do we see how extraordinary Xi Shao is than we are surprised with the revelation that, by another comparison, someone else is still more so. The extraordinary father turns out to be Ji Kang, another member of the "Seven Worthies" mentioned earlier. The first thinker to promote "transcending the established moral doctrines and giving free rein to nature" (*yue mingjiao er ren ziran*),[6] the elder Xi was a paragon among men:

世說新語 • 容止

嵇康身長七尺八寸，風
姿特秀。見者嘆曰：
"蕭蕭肅肅，爽朗清
舉。"或云："肅肅如
松下風，高而徐引。"
山公曰："嵇叔夜之為
人也，巖巖若孤松之獨
立；其醉也，傀俄若玉
山之將崩。"

[*SSXYJJ* 335 (14/5)]

C8.29b "Appearance and Manner, No. 5"

Ji Kang's body was seven feet, eight inches tall and his manner and appearance conspicuously outstanding. Some who saw him sighed, saying, "Serene and sedate, fresh and transparent, pure and exalted!" Others would say, "soughing like the wind beneath the pines, high and gently blowing." Shan Tao said, "As a person Ji Kang is majestically towering, like a solitary pine tree standing alone. But when he's drunk he leans crazily like a jade mountain about to collapse."

[*NATW* 331]

All the rhetorical devices we have seen thus far are enlisted in this passage to present a beautiful human being. Following the simple introduction to his outward appearance, a series of metaphors are employed to project aspects of Ji's physique and manner beyond the grasp of concrete terms. To sustain the metaphor of the pine tree, we see the onomatopoeia of the reduplicative *xiaoxiao* sound of wind—also a pun on the serenity of a pine—and the repeated appearance of the adjective-adverbial *susu*, which not only mimics the stately posture of the tree but also is a pun on the sound of the wind. The effect of these two phrases (echoed by yet another—the fourth in this passage—reduplicative attribute *yanyan*, used to highlight the solitary pine) is visually doubled by the overlapping of the shape of the ideographs *xiao* and *su* (蕭蕭肅肅), each of which is also doubled. Finally, the passage ends with the image of Ji as a "jade mountain." But there is a problem: one can find another "jade mountain" in the anecdote that goes immediately before this one, and worse yet, it too is "about to collapse" (*SSXYJJ* 334 [14/4]). To appropriate the simile, Ji just has to get intoxicated: a drunken state not only grants him a carefree and spontaneous posture but also lends the imposing "jade mountain" momentum: he "leans crazily" as if "about to collapse." This state of inebriation, a status symbol for the "famous gentlemen," is beautiful. For the loss of conscious mind under influence, one is compensated with spontaneity, which allows body and spirit—in words of another of the "Worthies"—to be "intimate with each other" (*NATW* 421; *SHXYJJ* 410 [23/52]). Careful readers might still remember the role played by wine in the earlier caricature of Ruan Ji (C8.9a–C8.9b).

Unfortunately, Ji's defiant rejection of corrupt court politics and his undisguised contempt for vulgar careerists made him many enemies and eventually brought his life to an early end. When the time came for the "jade mountain" to collapse, it did so beautifully:

世說新語 • 雅量

嵇中散臨刑東市，神氣
不變。索琴彈之，奏廣
陵散。曲終曰："袁孝
尼嘗請學此散，吾靳

C8.30 "Cultivated Tolerance, No. 2"

On the eve of Ji Kang's execution in the Eastern Marketplace of Luoyang [in 262], his spirit and manner showed no change. Taking out his seven-stringed zither, he plucked the strings and played the "Melody of *Guangling*" ["*Guangling san*"]. When the song was ended, he said, "Yuan Zhun [fl. 265–274] once asked to learn this melody, but I remained firm in my stubbornness, and never gave it to him. From now on the 'Melody of *Guangling*' is no more!" Three thousand scholars of the Grand Academy sent up a petition requesting Ji's release to become their teacher, but it was not granted. Sima Zhao [211–265] (who had ordered the execution) himself later repented of it.

固不與，廣陵散於今絕矣！"太學生三千人上書，請以為師，不許。文王亦尋悔焉。

[*NATW* 190]   [*SSXYJJ* 194–195 (6/2)]

The abrupt and unnatural ending of this beautiful life was cruel, yet Ji Kang faced his death with style and dignity. The last thing he wanted to do was to play his zither. Lest the world miss the message of this symbolic gesture, he sighed that, with the end of his life, "the 'Melody of *Guangling*' is no more!" To fully understand the weight of Ji Kang's lament, however, it takes another examination of the man's mindset and outlook. Zither was the favorite of the "famous gentlemen" of the time, not really because it was an instrument through which one expressed one's heart's intent, but because it was almost an alter ego of one's essence and spirit. A *Shishuo* story tells that when Wang Huizhi tried to play his brother's zither after his death, the strings refused to be tuned. Saddened, Wang cried out bitterly, "you and your zither are both gone forever!" (*NATW* 351; *SSXYJJ* 353 17/16]). Therefore, when Ji Kang says in his "Rhapsody of Zither" ("Qin fu") that, compared with that of all the other instruments, the virtue of the zither is of the highest order, he is not repeating the traditional representation theory. In his thesis "In Music There Is No Sorrow or Joy" ("Sheng wu aile lun"), he declares his audacious departure from the didactic tradition of the Confucian poetics. Music is the sound of nature, he says, while sorrow or joy or any ideological interpretation of music has nothing to do with its innate nature. Quoting a line from Zhuangzi's "Making All Things, and the Discussions on Them, Equal" ("Qi wu lun") Chapter (☛ C4.6b), he proves that, however rich and varied an individual piece of "wind music" might be, it is nothing but a manifestation of the "blowing" of Heaven. In light of this, the *Guangling* melody and Ji Kang's beautiful "jade mountain" being "no more" can be interpreted in a different way from Wang Huizhi's cry over the "no more" of both his brother and his zither. Is it possible that Ji Kang eventually came to the realization that, by letting go his individual "possession" of the Melody of *Guangling*, he went along with "Heaven's music"? As Zhuangzi says, "though the grease burns out of the torch, the fire passes on, and no one knows where it ends" (*CWZ* 21) (☛ C4.7). Hence, we understand the serenity of his "spirit and manner" when he bade farewell to the world. It is not enough to say that, when he sighed about the "Melody of *Guangling*," he saw himself as the repertoire and transmitter of "Heaven's music." He *was* the music.

SENSITIVITY, SENTIMENT, AND INSIGHT

The new awakening of self-awareness in the Wei–Jin period led to an emancipation of feelings and emotions. Released from the emotion regulation prescribed by Confucian moralists, people began to follow their natural impulses and feelings more freely. The intensely sensitive souls who populate the *Shishuo* text firmly reject any application of "correctness" to their feelings. They heed no authority beyond their own heart, intuition, and senses.

世說新語 • 任誕

桓子野每聞清歌，輒
喚 "奈何！" 謝公聞
之，曰："子野可謂一
往有深情。"

[SSXYJJ 406 (23/42)]

C8.31 "The Free and Unrestrained, No. 42"

Whenever Huan Yi [d. ca. 392] listened to unaccompanied singing, he would always cry aloud, "Alas! What shall I do?" Xie An, hearing him, said, "Ziye, you're what might be called a man of deep feeling all the way through!"

[NATW 417]

Huan's susceptibility to the unaccompanied (qing) singing of man is matched by Xie's susceptibility to Huan's unaccompanied feelings. "A man of deep feeling all the way through" is one who can appreciate the feelings of others, human or otherwise:

世說新語 • 言語

簡文入華林園，顧謂左
右曰："會心處不必在
遠，翳然林水，便自有
濠、濮閒想也，覺鳥獸
禽魚自來親人。"

[SSXYJJ 67 (2/61)]

C8.32a "Speech and Conversation, No. 61"

On entering the Flowery Grove Park Emperor Jianwen [Sima Yu (320–372)] looked around and remarked to his attendants, "The spot which suits the mind isn't necessarily far away. By any shady grove or stream one may quite naturally have such thoughts as Zhuangzi had by the Rivers Hao and Pu, where unself-consciously birds and animals, fowls and fish, come of their own accord to be intimate with men."

[NATW 63]

Once upon a time, beside the River Pu, Zhuangzi turned down a job offer from a king and busied himself instead with his angling game with fish. Now, while an emperor tried to steal a moment's leisure from royal duties, he recalled that story and sympathized with Zhuangzi. The emperor also recalled how, by River Hao, Zhuangzi exclaimed "the fish are happy!" His friend Hui Shi refuted him, saying that humans had no way to feel fish. The emperor knew better than Hui Shi. By feeling fish himself, he agreed with Zhuangzi.

This empathetic understanding of other beings through vicarious experience was by no means fallacious. More than intellectual sympathy, the sensitivity of the Wei–Jin people to the natural environment bordered on sentient empathy. The following story offers a vivid example:

世說新語 • 言語

支公好鶴，住剡東岇
山。有人遺其雙鶴，少
時翅長欲飛，支意惜
之，乃鎩其翮。鶴軒翥
不復能飛，乃反顧翅垂

C8.32b "Speech and Conversation, No. 76"

The Monk Zhi Dun was fond of cranes. While he was living on Yang Mountain in the eastern part of Shan Prefecture, someone sent him a pair of cranes. After a short time their wings grew out and they were on the point of flying away. Reluctant to let them go, Zhi clipped their pinions. The cranes spread their wings to soar aloft, but found they could no longer fly, and turning back to observe their wings, hung their heads and looked at Zhi as if with reproach and disappointment. Zhi said, "Since they look as if they would soar up to the clouds, how could they be willing to become pets for the pleasure of human ear and eyes?" Whereupon he cared for them until their pinions had grown out again and then set them free so they could fly away.

[*NATW* 69–70]

頭，視之如有懊喪意。
林曰：「既有凌霄之
姿，何肯為人作耳目近
玩！」養令翮成，置使
飛去。

[*SSXYJJ* 75 (2/76)]

Zhi loved cranes for their unbridled free spirit. But once he held the elegant creatures in captivity, he lost the beauty he desired. The symbolic meaning of clipping the birds' wings is important: such sham fondness for his pets, in a moment of self-love gone awry, could lead to an act of violence against the will and body of another being. Zhi was a philosopher, but rational reasoning was not enough to overcome human fatuity. It was the despair in the cranes' eyes that shocked the monk into sudden and empathic enlightenment. In the end, he regained freedom by appreciating the freedom of the birds—the natural creatures born to do nothing but "soar aloft."

The following two examples show that sensitive hearts are susceptible not only to animate creatures but also to all kinds of inanimate objects, along with the unfathomable space that houses them:

C8.32c "Speech and Conversation, No. 32"

When Wei Jie [fl. 311] was about to cross the Yangzi River [in 311] his body and spirit were emaciated and depressed, and he remarked to his attendants, "As I view this desolate expanse of water, somehow without my being aware of it a hundred thoughts come crowding together. But as long as we can't avoid having feelings, who indeed can be free of this?"

[*NATW* 47]

世說新語 • 言語

衛洗馬初欲渡江，形神
慘顇，語左右云：「見
此芒芒，不覺百端交
集。苟未免有情，亦復
誰能遣此！」

[*SSXYJJ* 51 (2/32)]

Eight hundred years before Wei Jie, an old man did something similar—standing on the bank of a river, Confucius sighed, "Alas, it passes just like this, never ceasing day or night!" (*Analects* 9.16) (☞ chap. 3). Sagacious as he was, Confucius could not "avoid having feelings." Despite its pensive tone, the mood of Confucius's philosophical contemplation was vast and universal, calm and serene. Wei Jie's lament, by comparison, was keenly individual, tinged with the tragic tone characteristic of the general mood of the Wei–Jin period.

C8.32d "Speech and Conversation, No. 83"

Yuan Hong [328–376] was appointed sergeant-at-arms to Xie Feng [fl. 340–360], the General Pacifying the South. To see him off, his friends in the capital accompanied him all the way to Lai Village. Before bidding them farewell, overwhelmed by sadness and a sense of loss, Yuan sighed, "Far and desolate are the rivers and mountains, appearing to be stretching out ten thousand *li* beyond my eyes!"

世說新語 • 言語

袁彥伯為謝安南司馬，
都下諸人送至瀨鄉。
將別，既自悽惘，歎
曰：「江山遼落，居然
有萬里之勢！」

[*SSXYJJ* 78 (2/83)]

The traveler in this anecdote happens to be the author of *Annals of the Later Han* (*Hou Han ji*). With a historian's keen sense, he could turn a particular juncture of time and space into a vantage point from which to ruminate over the significance of a human being in this precise location and moment. Beyond this temporal point, parted from friends, he would be alone; beyond this spatial point, he would lose himself in a vast stretch of unfamiliar wild land, undulating downward until it merged with the hinterland of the deep South. Yuan sighed not because of what he saw, but because of the unseen suggested by the seen, signified by the character *shi* (situation) in the *wanli zhi shi* (literally "the situation of the ten thousand *li*"). Rather than a static and definitely visible situation, the *shi* of the mountains and rivers in view was more of a mobile propensity, imbued with the energy and momentum accumulated from human experience from other times and places. A sense of tragic grandeur thus set in.

Similar sentiment, but aroused more by elapsed time, is felt in the follow passage:

世說新語　•　言語

桓公北征，經金城，見
前為琅邪時種柳，皆已
十圍，慨然曰：“木猶
如此，人何以堪！”攀
枝執條，泫然流淚。

[*SSXYJJ* 64 (2/55)]

C8.32e "Speech and Conversation, No. 55"

When Huan Wen went on his northern expedition [in 369], as he passed by Jincheng[,] he observed that the willows he had planted there earlier [in 341] while governing Langya Principality had all of them already reached a girth of ten double spans. With deep feeling he said, "If mere trees have changed like this, how can a man endure it?" And pulling a branch toward him, he held in his hands a slender twig,[1] while his tears fell in a flood.

[*NATW* 60]

To induce a "flood" of tears in a fifty-seven-year-old grand marshal (*dasima*) would surely take some doing. The author needed to pick the right kind of tree for Huan to plant twenty-eight years earlier. While time turned the willow sapling's stem into a stiff, coarse trunk, the supple and tender tips of its branches would still carry the memory of a willow's younger years. The most touching moment came not when the old man noticed the trunk's "ten double spans" girth (*shiwei*), but when he held the slender twig (*tiao*) in his hands—an intuitive move full of empathic feeling—as if trying to hold on to his own green years, irrecoverably lost. The contrast between the *shiwei* and the *tiao* is too shocking to endure.

The memory of taste, especially when refreshed by autumn winds, proves no less powerful:

世說新語　•　識鑒

張季鷹辟齊王東曹掾，
在洛，見秋風起，因思
吳中菰菜羹、鱸魚膾，
曰：“人生貴得適意

C8.33 "Insight and Judgment, No. 10"

Zhang Han [fl. first quarter, fourth century] was summoned to serve as an aide in the administration of the Prince of Qi, Sima Jiong [d. 302] [in 301]. While he was in Luoyang, and saw the autumn winds rising, it was then that he longed

[1] Mather's translation is slightly adjusted here.

for the wild rice, the water-lily soup, and the sliced perch of his old home in Wu. He said, "What a man values in life is just to find what suits his fancy, and nothing more. How can he tie himself down to an official post several thousand *li* from home, in pursuit of fame and rank?" Whereupon he ordered his carriage and proceeded to return home. Shortly thereafter the Prince of Qi was defeated and killed [in 302]. His contemporaries all claimed Zhang was clairvoyant.

[*NATW* 201]

爾，何能羈宦數千里以
要名爵！」遂命駕便
歸。俄而齊王敗，時人
皆謂為見機。

[*SSXYJJ* 217 (7/10)]

Zhang Han's contemporaries praised his clairvoyance for a reason. According to his biography in the *Jinshu*, Zhang revealed in a conversation with a townsman his awareness of the perils of an unpredictable political situation and his wish to retreat to the "hills and forests." Yet in the previous story, it was less the acute sense of smell of a politician than the taste buds of a gourmand that drove him from danger. Zhang's keen senses recall another story about him from two decades before, also recorded in the *Shishuo*:

C8.34 "The Free and Unrestrained, No. 22"

When He Xun [260–319] was on his way up to Luoyang from Kuaiji to take up his post as chamberlain of the imperial grandson Sima Yu, his boat passed through the Glorious Gate of Wu Commandery. He Xun was sitting in the boat playing a seven-stringed zither. Zhang Han had never made his acquaintance before, but when he first heard from his position in the Pavilion of Golden Glory the notes of the zither sounding so clear and pure, he went down to the boat where He Xun was playing, and thereby got to converse with him. In this way they struck up a great friendship and liking for each other. Zhang asked, "Where are you bound for?" He replied, "Up to Luoyang to take up a post. I'm just on my way." Zhang said, "I have some business in the northern capital, too, so I'll travel with you on the way." Thereupon he and He Xun set out together. Zhang had not notified his family beforehand, and the family found out about it only after pursuing him with inquiries.

[*NATW* 407–408]

世說新語 • 任誕

賀司空入洛赴命，為太
孫舍人，經吳閶門，在
船中彈琴。張季鷹本不
相識，先在金閶亭，聞
絃甚清，下船就賀，因
共語，便大相知說。問
賀：「卿欲何之？」賀
曰：「入洛赴命，正爾
進路。」張曰：「吾
亦有事北京，因路寄
載。」便與賀同發。初
不告家，家追問，迺
知。

[*SSXYJJ* 397 (23/22)]

Leaving behind everything he had and sailing away with a stranger without a second thought (emphasized by an adverb *bian*, then and there) was not unlike giving up his official post, and "thereupon" (also accentuated by an adverb *sui*, then and there) he ordered his carriage and headed home. If the younger Zhang could fall so easily for the sound of a zither, his mature self could not resist the temptation of the tastes of home suggested by the rising autumn winds.

CODA

Some 563 years after the "Melody of *Guangling*" fell tragically silent, the Tang poet Liu Yuxi (772–842) wrote this well-known quatrain brooding over the vicissitudes of history:

> Wild flowers blossom among grass by the Red Sparrow Bridge
> The evening sun sinks down the Black Robe Lane
> The swallows that once nested under the eaves of the halls in the Wangs and
> 　the Xies
> Now fly into some commoners' houses[7]

The Wangs and Xies, and many other prominent names who once occupied the grand halls of the *Shishuo* text are no more, but the swallows remain. As their chirpings come and go, numerous imitations of the *Shishuo* come into being, residing comfortably in the lanes and alleys of commoners' cozy dwellings. Inspired and nourished by their *Shishuo* predecessors, many writers from the post-Wei–Jin all the way to the present day have turned out fresh and witty anecdotes about the extraordinary words and deeds of the ordinary people of their own times. These "accounts of the tales of the world," old and new, have survived in the annals of Chinese prose as a unique subcategory: the *Shishuo ti* genre.

Xinda Lian

NOTES

1. Unless indicated otherwise, translations of the *Shishuo xinyu* texts are by Richard B. Mather, *A New Account of Tales of the World* (Ann Arbor: University of Michigan Press, University of Michigan Center for Chinese Studies, 2002).
2. See Fang Xuanling, ed., *Jinshu* (*The History of the Jin Dynasty*), 10 vols. (Beijing: Zhonghua shuju, 1974), 7:2043-2047, 8:2569–2571.
3. Ibid., 5:1369.
4. This is the term Glen W. Baxter uses in his English translation of the Japanese scholar Yoshikawa Kōjirō's article "The *Shi-shuo hsin-yü* and Six Dynasties Prose Style" for the Chinese *zhuzi*, the kind of character that has "neither substantive, adjectival, nor verbal force, functioning only to supplement or 'aid' the essential characters or *shizi*." My discussion of "aid-words" is inspired by Yoshikawa's study, especially his identification of "aid-words" in *SSXYJJ* 1:13. See Yoshikawa Kōjirō, "The *Shi-shuo hsin-yü* and Six Dynasties Prose Style," trans. Glen W. Baxter, *Harvard Journal of Asiatic Studies* 18 (1955): 124–141.
5. As Yoshikawa observes, "One plausible explanation for the unprecedented number of particles in the *Shishuo* is that the text reflects *qingtan* diction." See Yoshikawa, "The *Shi-shuo hsin-yü* and Six Dynasties Prose Style," 136–137.
6. Fang Xuanling, *Jinshu*, 5:1369.
7. See Lin Geng and Feng Yuanjun, eds., *Zhongguo lidai shige xuan* (*Anthology of Chinese Poetry from All Ages*), 4 vols. (Beijing: Remin wenxue chubanshe, 1979), 2:468. Translation by Xinda Lian.

SUGGESTED READING

ENGLISH

Li, Wai-yee. "*Shishuo xinyu* and the Emergence of Aesthetic Self-Consciousness in the Chinese Tradition." In *Chinese Aesthetics: The Ordering of Literature, the Arts, and the Universe in the Six Dynasties*, edited by Zong-Qi Cai, 237–276. Honolulu: University of Hawai'i Press, 2004.

Mather, Richard, trans. *Shih-shuo Hsin-yü: A New Account of Tales of the World*. Ann Arbor: University of Michigan Press, University of Michigan Center for Chinese Studies, 2002.

Qian, Nanxiu. *Spirit and Self in Medieval China*. Honolulu: University of Hawai'i Press, 2001.

Yoshikawa Kōjirō. "The *Shi-shuo hsin-yü* and Six Dynasties Prose Style." Translated by Glen W. Baxter. *Harvard Journal of Asiatic Studies* 18 (1955): 124–141.

CHINESE

Liu Weisheng 劉偉生. *Shishuo xinyu yishu yanjiu* 世說新語藝術研究 (*The Art of the* Shishuo xinyu). Changsha: Hunan daxue chubanshe, 2008.

Ning Jiayu 寧稼雨. *Shishuo xinyu yu zhonggu wenhua* 世說新語與中古文化 (Shishuo xinyu *and Medieval Culture*). Shijiazhuang: Hebei jiaoyu chubanshe, 1994.

❀ 9 ❀

Six Dynasties Parallel Prose

Descriptive and Expository

In Chinese prose studies, "parallel prose" (*pianwen*), along with its appellation "Four-Six" (*siliu*), is the only form-based genre category, brought into use as late as the Qing dynasty. As a genre designation, it is so elastic that it has been applied broadly to all Han and post-Han prose works that employ a preponderance of four-and-six-character lines, *or* narrowly to Qi–Liang (479–557 CE) and later prose that meticulously couples four- and six-character lines in varying modules. This genre exploits correspondence between coupled lines on multiple levels—rhythmic, semantic, syntactic, allusive, and tonal correspondence—to increase descriptive or discursive power.

Interestingly, these two alternate uses of the term "parallel prose" each facilitate our examination of parallel prose. First, the broad definition of parallel prose enables us to expand the scope of investigation and begin by tracing the development of proto-parallel prose in the first two texts to be discussed in this chapter. Then, the narrow definition of parallel prose guides us to focus on examining the intricate, distinctive features of the Qi–Liang parallel prose, as manifested in the latter two texts to be examined.

In my view, the early proto-parallel prose and the Qi–Liang parallel prose feature a qualitative difference—that of patterning. The proto-parallel prose predominantly employs aggregative patterning. Aggregative patterning refers to an aggregation of binomes (bisyllabic words) to form recurrent lines of four or six characters. These lines of equal length typically entail a doubling or tripling of binomes, thus creating a distinct 2 + 2 or a 2 + 2 + 2 rhythm. The deployment of this aggregative patterning is a hallmark of Han and Wei–Jin prose (☛ chap. 7). Then, in most Qi–Liang prose, we see a complete transformation of this aggregative patterning into parallel patterning. With few exceptions, Qi–Liang prose writers spared no effort pairing four- and six-character lines in varying modules to fully exploit semantic, syntactic, allusive, and tonal correspondence between coupled lines.

Of course, there is no absolute division between these two kinds of patterning. Aggregative patterning sometimes does entail natural semantic and syntactic correspondence of one kind or another, but there is an important difference between a natural matching of common expressions and a conscious, contrived coupling of elegant words and phrases. There is also the difference between occasional versus consistent occurrences of semantic-syntactic matching in a composition (☛ compare C5.3 with C9.4). These differences should not be hard for readers of this book to discern thanks to the commentaries. In my opinion, it is this qualitative difference that has given rise to an unending debate on whether most, if any, of Han and Wei–Jin prose can count as parallel prose. In the four texts to be discussed, we will observe a steadily increased use of parallel patterning until it becomes almost the sole mode of presentation in a text.

AGGREGATIVE PATTERNING IN HAN AND WEI–JIN DISCURSIVE WRITINGS

Aggregative patterning differs from repetitive patterning in that it no longer yokes sentences together through the heavy use of verbatim repetitions (see "6.1 Repetitive Patterning" in the Thematic Table of Contents). This shift was made possible by the explosive growth of binomes during the Han. Thanks to this sudden overabundance of binomes, Han and Wei–Jin prose writers could not only easily pile them up into four-character or six-character lines but also exploit morphological and semantic correspondence between coupled lines for various purposes. To see this transition from repetitive to aggregative patterning, let us look at a short family letter written by Zhuge Liang (181–234), the famed strategist of the Shu of the Three Kingdoms.

C9.1 Zhuge Liang, "A Letter Admonishing My Son" 誡子書

1. 夫 君子/之行，靜以/修身，儉以/養德。
   This is how a superior man conducts himself: cultivating the self through mental tranquility and fostering morality through frugal living.

2. 非/澹泊/無以/明志，
   非/寧靜/無以/致遠。
   If one is not free of mundane desires, one cannot know what his true aspiration should be; if one's mind isn't tranquil and peaceful, one cannot achieve any far-reaching success.

3. 夫 學/須靜/也，
   　才/須學/也。
   Learning requires a peaceful mind; talents require constant learning.

4. 非學/無以/廣才，
   非志/無以/成學。
   Without learning, one cannot reach the fullest potential of one's talents; without aspiration, one cannot achieve goals of learning.

5. 淫慢/則/不能/勵精，
   險躁/則/不能/冶性。
   If one dawdles, one cannot invigorate one's spirit; if one acts impetuously, one cannot forge one's character.

6. 年/與時/馳，
   意/與日/去，
   遂成/枯落，多不/接世，悲守/窮廬，將復/何及！
   One's years gallop with time; one's aspiration dwindles with each passing day. As a result, like a leaf withering away, one becomes disengaged from the world and finds oneself pitifully trapped in a humble hut, lamenting the squandered time that will never come back.[1]

---

[1] See *ZGLJ* 28. My translation.

This family letter, among the best known of its kind in China, presents a to-do list along with how-to-do advice, all couched in pithy and memorable binomes. The to-do list consists of exhortations to cultivate oneself, foster one's morality, reach one's potential, and so on. These exhortations are all expressed with verbal binomes that are "bonded" (i.e., having fixed meanings) and display a verb + object combination: cultivate (*xiu*) + oneself (*shen*); foster (*yang*) + one's virtues (*de*); know (*ming*) + one's intent (*zhi*); reach (*zhi*) + a distant place/goal (*yuan*); broaden (*guang*) + one's talent (*cai*); complete (*cheng*) + one's learning (*xue*); invigorate (*li*) + one's spirit (*jing*); forge (*ye*) + one's character (*xing*). The how-to-do advice spells out the essential conditions required for achieving the exhorted goals: freedom from mundane desires (*danpo*), mental tranquility (*ningjing*), intellectual training (*xue*), and temperament flaws to be avoided (*taoman, xianzao*). To achieve the maximum impact, these conditions are twice stated, first in the emphatic double-negative form "If not . . . one cannot . . ." (*fei . . . wuyi . . .*) and then in plain supposition "[If] . . . then one cannot . . ." (*. . . ze . . .*). Ending this letter, Zhuge Liang warns his son of the pathetic consequences that will befall him should he not heed his father's admonition and squander his precious time.

With the Chinese text parsed with slashes, the preponderance of binomes becomes all the more conspicuous. Of the binomes marked out by slashes, those set in boldface have stable, fixed meanings, and those not set in boldface are not yet bonded but make sense contextually. Apparently, the bonded binomes have outnumbered the unbonded ones. By doubling binomes, the author constructs four-character lines for making declarative statements (segments 1, 3, 6). Alternately, by tripling binomes, he produces six-character lines to accommodate complex cause-effect suppositions cast in the double-negative form (segments 2 and 4) or the simple affirmative form (segment 5). This tendency of doubling and tripling binomes is a pronounced feature of prose written during the Han and Wei-Jin periods.

The dominance of four-character and, to a lesser extent, six-character lines in Han and Wei–Jin prose is a development of profound significance in the history of Chinese prose. These types of lines, respectively, are often coupled, inviting prose writers to exploit morphological and semantic correspondence between them as they did in poetry. Generally speaking, writers living in the Han and Wei–Jin periods were less preoccupied with morphological and semantic correspondence than those living closer to the Qi–Liang period. But Zhuge Liang seems an exception. In "A Letter Admonishing My Son," we can observe his persistent effort to establish morphological and semantic correspondence. Indeed, segments 2–5 are all coupled sentences, with morphological categories and semantic tenor neatly matched. For instance, in segment 5, *taoman* (dawdling and slow) and *xianzao* (reckless and impetuous) match each other perfectly, both being adjectival binomes and synonymous in meaning. The same could be said of the pairing of the verbal binomes *lijing* (invigorating one's spirit) and *yexing* (forging one's character). To accentuate such morphological and semantic correspondence, I have marked out all coupled lines by setting them in two lines in the Chinese text and by separating them with a semicolon in the English translation.

In many ways, aggregative patterning can be seen as a transitional form between pre-Qing repetitive patterning and the Qi–Liang parallel patterning. Zhuge Liang's letter seems on the cusp of morphing into the latter. In fact, if the alternate-line parallelism (the hallmark of parallel prose to be examined next) were employed as well, this letter could very well be taken as parallel prose composition. Indeed, it is well ahead of the curve in its experiment with parallel patterning, even if we compare it with Zong Bing's (375–443) famous essay on landscape painting composed about two hundred years after Zhuge Liang's letter.

TRANSITION FROM AGGREGATIVE TO PARALLEL PATTERNING

The transition from aggregative to parallel patterning can be clearly observed in many compositions of the [Liu] Song dynasty, a time immediately preceding the rise of Qi–Liang parallel prose. Zong Bing's essay on landscape painting is an excellent case in point. As we analyze it, section by section, we observe this transition in progress, reflected in both the ratios and the forms of parallel patterning. The growing preponderance of parallel couplets should be visually evident as I have marked them in the Chinese text by indentation. Their variations will be differentiated case by case.

Zong's "Introduction of the Painting of Landscape" is the first extant Chinese essay on landscape painting. Its main purpose is to valorize the art form by asserting its capacity to embody religious spirituality and enable viewers to commune with that spirituality through pleasurable visualization and supra-visualization. It begins by tracing the source of this spirituality and the means by which it is transmitted to landscape:

C9.2 Zong Bing, "Introduction to the Painting of Landscape" 畫山水序

§1

聖人　含道　應物，
賢者　澄懷　味像。

The sages contain the Dao and manifest themselves in things, while worthies purify their minds and savor iconic images.

至於山水質有而趣靈，
是以軒轅堯孔廣成大隗許由孤竹之流，
必有崆峒具茨藐姑箕首大蒙之遊焉。
又稱仁智之樂焉。

Regarding mountains and rivers, they have the substance of existence and tend toward the numinous. Therefore, the likes of Xuanyuan, Yao, Kong, Guangcheng, Dawei, Xu You, and [the brothers of Boyi and Shuqi of] Guzhu took to roaming in the mountains of Kongtong, Juci, Miaogu, Ji, Shou, and Taimeng. Their roaming has also been described as the delight of the virtuous and the wise.

夫 聖人 以神 法道 而賢者 通，
　山水 以形 媚道 而仁者 樂，
不亦幾乎？

The sages establish the Spirit as the law of the Dao, and so worthies can commune with it. Mountains and rivers beautify the Dao with their forms, and thus the virtuous can take delight in them. Aren't these two alike?

The opening statement, "The sages encompass the Dao and manifest themselves in things, while worthies purify their minds and savor iconic images" is cast in perfect parallel patterning: two six-character sentences neatly coupled through semantic correspondence, without repetition of a single character. Interpretively, however, this line has posed significant challenges for more than one and a half millennia. With the ensuing reference to legendary and historical figures variously lionized by Confucians and Daoists, the "sages" have been taken by many to be Confucian and Daoist sages. But this reading runs into trouble because no Confucian or Daoist sage has ever been described as "encompassing the Dao" in extant Confucian or Daoist texts. The remaining option is to identify the sages as Buddhas. This interpretation is validated by Zong Bing's repeated reference to Buddhas as sages and things being encompassed (han) by Buddhas in his treatise *Illuminating the Buddhas* (*Ming Fo lun*). The second verbal phrase, "manifest in things" (yingwu) also calls for a Buddhist reading as "[for Buddhas] to manifest in things" because Zong frequently employs the phrase in this sense rather than in the traditional sense of "respond to things" found in Confucian and Daoist texts. This Buddhist reading of the first line makes it easier to understand the phrase "savor iconic images": it most likely alludes to the account of the Buddha's shadows or images being imprinted on cave rocks and worshiped by Buddhist believers for generations.[1]

If Zong Bing does assert the Buddhist origin of spirituality in external things as we have assumed, why, in the next breath, does he introduce a host of Confucian and Daoist figures? This contradiction is a red herring that distracted many critics and led them to assume that Zong's essay presents a Confucian or Daoist (rather than Buddhist) view, or a syncretic Confucian-Daoist-Buddhist view of landscape painting. But this contradiction was found to be no contradiction at all upon discovery that Zong, in his *Illuminating the Buddhas*, explicitly talks about this cohort of Confucian and Daoist figures as possibly being various incarnations of Buddhas. In my view, Zong had two reasons to introduce this group of non-Buddhist figures: to validate the spiritualization of landscape by sagely figures of all persuasions and, more important, to accentuate the aesthetic pleasure in contemplating such spiritualized landscapes. This latter purpose becomes quote clear when Zong describes how landscape beautifies the Dao while alluding to Confucius's remark about the virtuous and the wise taking delight in mountains and rivers.

The second and third segments feature highly irregular parallel sentences. In the second segment, the two parallel lines are each an extended list of two-character names. In the third segment, the lines are long sentences with many verbatim repetitions. They seem to be a hybrid of repetitive and parallel patterning. Irregular parallel sentences like these will be phased out in fully developed parallel prose of the Qi–Liang period.

§2

余 眷戀 廬衡,
　契闊 荊巫,
不知老之將至。愧不能凝氣怡身, 傷
跕石門之流, 於是司畫象布色, 構茲
雲嶺。

I was so fond of the Lu and Heng mountains and so attached to the Jing and Wu peaks that I became unaware of the approach of my old age. I felt ashamed that I could not concentrate my vital breath and keep my health good enough to limp along with others at the Stone Gate. Therefore, I paint images and spread colors to construct these cloudy peaks.

This second section is a short informal narrative passage serving two functions: to shift the discussion from landscape to landscape painting as the locus of spiritualization, and to allow the author to enter the essay. The insertion of this personal narrative not only enlivens an otherwise formal exposition but also sets the stage for the author's account at the essay's end of his transcendental self-transformation from contemplating landscape painting.

§3

且 理絕 於中古 之上者, 可 意 求 於千載 之 下;
　旨微 於 言象 之外者, 可 心 取 於書策 之 內。
況乎 身所盤桓,
　　目所綢繆,
　　以形寫形,
　　以色貌色也。

Principles lost beyond middle antiquity can be sought through the conceptions of the mind; and the subtle meaning beyond words and images can be obtained within books by the mind.

This is to say nothing of what involves the movement of one's body and engagement of one's eyes, or where forms can be described with forms, and colors with colors!

This section, too, begins with a statement involving parallel patterning: "Principles lost beyond middle antiquity can be sought through the conceptions of the mind; and the subtle meaning beyond words and images can be obtained within books by the mind." But it is composed not of two standard six-character lines as in the essay's opening statement, but rather of two irregular sixteen-character lines. Because these lines are too long, they are broken up into two, giving rise to an alternate-line parallelism marked by a matching of line 1 with line 3 and line 2 with line 4. While irregular long lines and verbal repetitions reveal the lingering influence of ancient repetitive patterning, this alternate-line parallelism heralds a defining feature of Qi–Liang parallel prose. Exploiting the expository potential of alternate-line parallelism, Zong cogently sums up the traditional praise of writing's ability to carry the mind into a realm beyond words and images. What really surprises us is his following statement, led by "to say nothing of," to claim even more magical evocative power for painting. Grounded in the assumption of direct visual representation's superiority—forms described with forms, colors with colors—over the abstract symbolization of written graphs, this claim is nothing less than revolutionary. Pre-Buddhist philosophical texts had a practically universal tendency to valorize the symbolic trigrams and hexagrams of the *Book of Changes*, from which written graphs are believed to have evolved, as the embodiment of the cosmic Dao. Correspondingly, in the realm of literature and arts, written graphs are consistently privileged over visual representation of objects, thanks to the magical symbolic or supravisual potency attributed to the former. This reification of writing is clearly demonstrated in the much higher status conferred on calligraphy over painting. Zong's radical claim seeks to reverse this entrenched hierarchy. As he will explain, his belief in the superiority of visualization is grounded in Buddhist theories and practices of image worship.

§4

且夫 崑崙山之大，
瞳子之小，
迫目以寸，則其形莫睹，
迥以數里，則可圍於寸眸。
誠自去之稍闊，則其見彌小。

The Kunlun mountains are so large and the eye's pupils so small that if the former impress themselves upon the eye from a distance of inches, they cannot be seen. But if they are a few miles away, they can be encompassed by the inch-size eye. This is because the farther off they are, the smaller they appear.

今張絹素以遠映，則崑閬之形，可圍於方寸之內。
豎劃 三寸， 當千仞 之 高；
橫墨 數尺， 體百里 之 迥。

If we now spread the fine silk to reflect things afar, the contours of the Kunlun mountains and the Lang Peak can be encompassed within a square inch. A vertical stroke of three inches equals the height of a thousand feet; a horizontal ink-dab of several feet signifies a distance of several hundred miles.

是以觀畫圖者，徒患類之不巧，不以制小而累其似，
此自然之勢。如是則
嵩華之秀，
玄牝之靈，
皆可得之於一圖矣。

Therefore, the beholders of paintings worry only about awkwardness in correspondence with the original, and do not consider the diminutive scale an impediment to verisimilitude—this is the propensity of nature. Given this, the magnificence of the Song and Hua mountains and the numen of the mysterious valleys can all be captured in a painting.

To reinforce his claim for pictorial art's primacy, Zong expounds, in two alternate-line parallel constructions, the rules of proportion in visual perspective that govern the viewing and painting of landscape. The first represents a parallelism of contrast, explaining how we cannot see the Kunlun mountains when too close, whereas the other two-line segment shows how our field of vision expands in proportion to the increased distance from the mountains, so that all comes into view. Next, Zong argues that landscape paintings offer the same wonder to our eye, but only if they strictly follow the rules of visual perspective. To emphasize this point, he introduces the other alternate-line parallel construction, that of agreement: "A vertical stroke of three inches equals the height of a thousand feet; a horizontal ink-dab of several feet signifies a distance of several hundred miles." This construction presents the same idea twice in its two segments for the sake of amplification. To Zong, a landscape painting that has deftly achieved verisimilitude can reveal the indwelling spiritual force of landscape. In view of the traditional uncomplimentary view of verisimilitude in indigenous Chinese aesthetic thought, Zong's claim for its spirit-revealing power is undoubtedly revolutionary and, again, speaks to strong Buddhist influence.

§5

夫以應目會心為理者。類之成巧，
則 目 亦同應，
　心 亦 俱會。
應會感神， 神超理得， 雖復虛求幽巖， 何以
加焉？又神本亡端， 棲形感類， 理入影跡， 誠
能妙寫， 亦誠盡矣。

The [transcendent] principle in landscape is what we respond to with the eye and meet with the mind. If a painting has deftly achieved correspondence with a landscape, we can engage it with eye and mind in the same fashion. Through such a response, one communes with the Spirit, achieves a transcendence of one's own spirit, and attains the [absolute] principle. Even though one can again search for the invisible amongst remote rocks, what else can be found? Infinite as it is by nature, the Spirit dwells in forms and resonates with things by category, to the effect that the [transcendent] principle enters even reflections and traces. If a painting is miraculously done, the same will surely occur in it.

This section marks a turning point in the essay as Zong shifts his perspective from creation to reception. In explaining the aesthetic impact of spiritualized landscape painting, Zong advances two philosophical concepts unknown to pre-Buddhist China. The first involves the eye's and the mind's simultaneous encounter with the transcendent principle. As noted, this elevation of the eye goes directly against the traditional Daoist dismissal of visualization and speaks to the Buddhist emphasis on the eye in the worship of iconic images. Indeed, "reflections and traces" actually refer to the shadows or reflections of the Buddha mysteriously imprinted on cave rocks, as recounted by Zong's Buddhist teacher Hui Yuan (334–416), head monk of the Lushan Buddhist society. The other concept is that of the Spirit as an unchanging entity transcending all things, as opposed to the miraculous, immanent operation of the cosmic yin-yang principle of Confucian and Daoist thinkers. The capitalization of the term (Spirit) in my translation is meant to accentuate this essential difference. Here, Zong has obviously borrowed from Hui Yuan, who co-opted the Chinese term *shen* to denote the ultimate reality lying beyond the endless karmic cycles of life and death. Identifying the Buddhism behind this *shen*, we can now revisit and better grasp the Buddhist tenor in "The sages establish the Spirit (*shen*) as the law of the Dao" from the opening section. With Hui Yuan's sense of *shen* (Spirit) as the unchanging ultimate reality, Zong is able to posit it as something that supersedes and governs the Dao.

§6

於是閒居理氣， 拂觴鳴琴， 按圖幽
對， 坐究四荒，
不違 天勵 之 藂，
獨應 無人 之 野。
峰岫嶤嶷，
雲林森渺。

Therefore, I live a leisurely life, controlling my vital breath, waving my cup, and strumming my lute. As I unroll paintings and face them in solitude, I probe far into the four desolate corners, not avoiding the overgrowth at the world's fringes, and confront the uninhabited wilderness by myself. The peaks and grottoes soar high, and the cloudy forests stretch deep into the distance.

聖賢映於絕代，萬趣融其神思，余
復何為哉？ 暢神而已， 神之所暢，
孰有先焉！

The sages and worthies cast their reflections from time immemorial, and the myriad things of interest are infused with their spirit and thought. What then should I do? Nothing but let my spirit expand untrammeled. Speaking of the expansion of one's spirit, how could there be an order of who was before whom!

In this concluding section, Zong again enters the scene to describe how he contemplates landscape paintings and lets his mind roam the world to its fringes. To demonstrate the ultimate promise of such contemplation, he repeats what he said in the opening section about sages and worthies infusing landscapes with their spirit, but with an important addition: he now projects himself into the ranks of sages and worthies by virtue of a comparable spiritual engagement, if at second remove, with landscape. Perhaps no greater claim than this can be made for the transformative possibilities inherent in both the creation and the appreciation of landscape painting.

PARALLEL PATTERNING IN QI-LIANG DESCRIPTIVE AND EXPOSITORY WRITINGS

The Qi–Liang period is no doubt the golden age of parallel patterning. Literary achievement was then largely evaluated in terms of how skillfully a writer deployed parallel patterning in poetry and artistic as well as practical prose. Any writing devoid of parallel and other forms of patterning would be expunged from the garden of refined literature, as we see, for instance, when Xiao Tong (501–531) compiled his *Anthology of Refined Literature* (*Wen xuan*), the most famous and comprehensive anthology of belletristic poetry and prose in traditional China.

With the Qi–Liang period, parallel patterning practically became the standard for prose as well as poetry, at least as far as literati writings are concerned. Qi–Liang parallel prose may be divided into two broad types: the descriptive and the expository. The unique features of descriptive parallel prose are demonstrated in this famous landscape depiction by Wu Jun (469–520).

C9.3 Wu Jun, "A Letter to Zhu Yuansi" (excerpt) 朱元思書

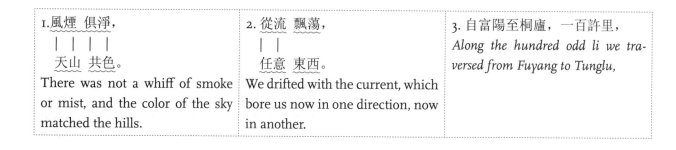

| 1. 風煙 俱淨，
　\| 　\| 　\| 　\|
　天山 共色。
There was not a whiff of smoke or mist, and the color of the sky matched the hills. | 2. 從流 飄蕩，
　\| 　\|
　任意 東西。
We drifted with the current, which bore us now in one direction, now in another. | 3. 自富陽至桐廬， 一百許里，
Along the hundred odd li we traversed from Fuyang to Tunglu, |

4. 奇山異水， 　天下獨絕。 There are spectacular mountains and water, unrivalled in the world.	5. 水皆縹碧，千丈見底； 　游魚細石，直視無礙。 The water was throughout a clear green, and over the deepest pools we fancied we saw to a depth of hundreds of feet; for we could see the fish swimming and the pebbles on the riverbed.	6. 急湍 甚箭， 　｜　｜　｜　｜ 　猛浪 若奔。 At times the current was swift as an arrow and angry waves surged forward.
7. 夾岸高山， 　皆生寒樹， The hills on either bank were planted with coniferous trees	8. 負勢 競上，互相 軒邈， 　｜　｜　｜　｜ 　爭高 直指，千百 成峯。 and rose to a great height, seeming to vie with one another in steepness or eminence. There were hundreds of jutting peaks.	9. 泉水 激石，泠泠 作響； 　｜　｜　　　｜　｜　｜　｜ 　好鳥 相鳴，嚶嚶 成韻。 The torrents dashed against the rocks as they came rushing down the hill-sides, humming and gurgling. The birds sang melodiously in chorus.
10. 蟬　則　千轉 不窮， 　｜　｜　｜　｜　｜　｜ 　猿　則　百叫 無絕。 The chirping of cicadas was interrupted now and then by the ape's shrill cries.	11. 鳶飛戾天者，望峯 息心； 　　　　　　　｜　｜　｜ 　經綸世務者，窺谷 忘 返。 Even as the eagle desists from its soaring flight when confronted with a massive mountain, so those engaged in governmental affairs would forgo their worldly ambitions if they set eyes on one of the mysterious ravines,	12. 橫柯　上蔽，在晝猶昏； 　｜　｜　　｜　｜ 　疏條　交映，有時見日。 shrouded in perpetual twilight by thick overhanging trees forming a screen through which the sun but seldom penetrates.[2]

This composition gives an account of the breathtaking scenes stretching over one hundred *li*, probably seen from a boat aimlessly drifting downstream. It is constituted of eleven units of coupled lines along with one uncoupled unit (the italicized third unit). The first four units are informational, telling us when, how, and where the boat journey took place and setting forth the topic of description: spectacular scenery of water and mountains. The next four units alternately present river and mountain scenes. The river and mountain scenes contain an alternation of contrasting subscenes. First, still and transparent pools (5) are set against swift rapids and surging waves (6); and then motionless mountains (7) are followed by the imagined soaring of the mountains (8). Then, units 9–10 turn from the world of sights to that of sounds: the bubbling of a spring, chirping of birds and cicadas, and cries of apes blending into perfect harmony. The final two units (11–12) return to the mountain view, but now are lifted skyward to where an eagle dares not soar and inspiring a wish to forgo worldly affairs and take refuge in these mountains.

This piece of descriptive parallel prose vividly reminds us of the landscape poetry written by Xie Lingyun (385–433) just decades earlier. Its salient formal features may be best demonstrated through a comparison of similarities and differences between the two. First, we should take note of their similar exploitation of morphological and semantic correspondence between coupled lines. In presenting the delightful sights and sounds of his excursion, Wu does exactly what Xie has done: casting them all in well-wrought parallel lines. In this prose piece, all the coupled lines entail morphological and semantic correspondence, and segments 1, 2, 6, 8, 9, 10, 11 contain the neatest kind of such correspondence. First, as indicated by wavy underlines, all binomes in these segments are *both* morphologically and semantically matched: nouns with nouns (e.g., "swift current" with "surging waves") and verbal phrase with verbal phrase (e.g., "seeing peaks" with "peeking into ravines"). Moreover, this matching penetrates to the level of single characters. In segment 11, for instance, the paralleled binomes *wangfeng* and *guigu* entail a matching of verbs (*wang* [look at] with *gui* [take a peek]) and a matching of object-nouns (*feng* [peak] with *gu* [valley]). Such character-to-character matching is indicated in the passage by vertical lines linking matched characters.

What, then, distinguishes Wu's prose landscape description from Xie's poetic counterpart? Well, the absence of rhyme is the most obvious difference that few fail to notice. The second most obvious is perhaps the change from Xie's five-character lines to Wu's four-character lines. The profound significance of this one-character reduction, however, is scarcely noted. In my view, this reduction leads to a fundamental change in the mode of authorial presentation and readerly reception. In a five-character line, the odd fifth character is often a verb that can be flexibly deployed in any position within a line. The positions in which it appears most frequently is the third character in a line. When appearing in the middle third-character position, it tends to have two noun binomes (mostly natural images) on both sides, and the author usually uses it to convey his perception of a dynamic interplay of two natural phenomena, grand or minuscule.[3] Often, two verbs are employed in a line, with one verb appearing in the first- or second-character position and the other verb in the third-, fourth-, or fifth-character position.[4] In such a two-verb line, two snapshots of nature's action are sequentially presented, often inviting us to perceive them in a cause-effect relationship. In these two types of lines, the lone verb-character enables Xie to convey his intense perception and, in some cases, imagination of the interplay of natural images or scenes. Similarly, it makes it possible for the reader to conjure up this interplay in a similar way.[5]

In Wu's piece, the disappearance of this free-floating one-verb character necessitates a fundamental change of presentation and reception. In a four-character line, a one-character verb almost invariably appears together with a noun character after it or with an adverb before it. This leaves only enough space for a noun binome. If a line can accommodate just one natural image, we cannot speak of any perceived interaction between natural phenomena. Consequently, Wu could resort only to reporting his sense impressions of nature in an aggregative fashion—one line for one impression, using as many lines as impressions.

To mitigate this lack of interplay of images, Wu and other parallel prose writers resurrected what is called "fan-like parallelism" (*shandui*), an ancient module of parallelism tracing back to the *Book of Poetry* (*Shijing*). This module can very well be considered to be an extension of a normal couplet. When each line of a couplet is extended to two lines to accommodate more content, we have a four-line parallel module, in which the first line is paralleled with the third and the second with the fourth. Thus, this module can be accurately called "alternate-line parallelism" (*geju dui*). While this module was used only sporadically in the *Book of Poetry* and dispensed with altogether in pentasyllabic poetry, it caught on in Six Dynasties parallel prose and became one of its defining features. In descriptive parallel prose like Wu's piece, it primarily functions to accommodate more images and set them in dynamic interplay. In segment 9, for instance, it is only through an alternate-line parallelism that Wu Jun managed to blend four delightfully heard sounds—those of a bubbling spring, chirping birds and cicadas, and crying apes—into perfect harmony or symphony. This newfound popularity of alternate-line parallelism also has much to do with its special usefulness for discursive writings, as shown by the next example.

In turning our attention to expository parallel prose, we examine the following excerpt from the "Spirit Thought" chapter ("Shensi") of *The Literary Mind and the Carving of Dragons* (*Wenxin diaolong*), where Liu Xie (ca. 465–522) analyses the dynamic interplay of transcendental roaming with physiological and linguistic intervention in the creative mind:

C9.4 Liu Xie, "Spirit Thought, from the *Literary Mind*" (excerpt) 文心雕龍・神思

1.　　　古人云：形 在 江海 之上，
　　　　　　　｜　｜　　｜　　｜
　　　　　　心 存 魏闕 之下。
　　　神思之謂也。文之思也，其神遠矣。

An ancient said, "while one's body is on the rivers and lakes, his mind remains at the foot of the high palace tower." This is what is called "spirit and thought." In the exercise of the literary mind, the spirit travels afar.

2.　故　　寂然 凝慮，思 接 千載；
　　　　　｜｜｜｜　｜　｜　｜｜
　　　　悄焉 動容，視 通 萬里。
　　　　吟詠 之間，吐納 珠玉 之聲；
　　　　｜｜｜｜　｜｜｜｜　　｜
　　　　眉睫 之前，卷舒 風雲 之色。

So quietly attaining concentration, his thinking may go through one thousand years; slightly stirring his countenance, his seeing may traverse ten thousand *li*.

In the midst of his chanting and singing, the sounds of pearls and jade issue forth. Right before his brows and lashes, the spectacle of windblown clouds spreads out.

3.   其思理之致乎！故思理為妙，神與物遊。

All this is made possible by the workings of the mind. With the workings of the mind at its most miraculous, the spirit wanders along with things.

4.   神 居 胸臆，而 志氣 統 其 關鍵；
　　　　│ │ │ │ 　　│ │ │ 　　│ │
　　　　物 沿 耳目，而 辭令 管 其 樞機。
　　　　樞機 方通，則 物 無 隱貌；
　　　　│ │ │ │ 　　│ │ │ │
　　　　關鍵 將塞，則 神 有 遯心。

The spirit dwells in the bosom, with intent (*zhi*) and vital breath (*qi*) being the pivot of its outlet. Things come to us through ear and eye, with words and phrases controlling the hinge and trigger [for their influx].

When the hinge and trigger allow passage, nothing can hide its appearance. When the pivot of its outlet is closed, the spirit is impeded.

5.   是以   陶鈞 文思，貴在虛靜；
　　　　　　│ │
　　　　　　疏瀹 五藏，澡雪精神。
　　　　　　積學 以 儲寶，酌理 以 富才，
　　　　　　│ │ 　　│ │ │ │ 　　　│ │
　　　　　　研閱 以 窮照，馴致 以 懌辭。

For this reason,   in shaping and developing literary thought, the greatest importance lies in "emptiness and stillness": so, remove obstructions in the five viscera and cleanse the spirit!

One must accumulate learning to store up treasures; one must contemplate the principles [of things] to enrich his talent; one must sharpen his perceptual power to bring things to the fullest light; one must master literary art to make his phrasing felicitous.

6.   然後使   玄解 之 宰，尋 聲律 而 定墨；
　　　　　　│ │ 　　│ 　│ │ │ 　　│ │
　　　　　　獨照 之 匠，闚 意象 而 運斤。

Only after all these   does one exercise the power of "the mysterious butcher" within him to search for metric patterns and set down words. Only then does he call up the "master wheelwright" within him to wield the axe [of phrasing] in accord with the image of his mind.

7.   此蓋   馭文 之 首術，
　　　　　│ │ 　　│ │
　　　　　謀篇 之 大端。

This, in short,   is the cardinal principle of writing and the primary guide for drafting a composition.[1]

---

[1] See *WXDLSY* 338. My translation.

Comparing this excerpt with Wu Jun's piece, we can discern two distinguishing features of expository parallel prose vis-à-vis descriptive parallel prose. The first is a more extensive use of unparallel sentences and connectives (indicated by italics). In segments 1 and 3, unparallel sentences set forth the two main topics of discussion: the mind's transcendental flight (*shen, shensi*) versus conscious thinking (*sili*). Placed at the head of other segments (second column), short connectives spell out the temporal or logical relationships between adjacent parallel blocks, thus effectively advancing a sustained linear expository process.

The second distinguishing feature is the use of a much richer variety of parallel patterning. In typical expository parallel prose, while unparallel sentences and connectives provide a global grid of organization, parallel patterning primarily serves as a means of local organization—that is, to provide an optimal structure, with which an author could present multiple concepts and statements and illuminate their intricate relationship. As expository contents vary greatly in degree of complexity, a corresponding repertoire of parallel forms are developed and deployed in Six Dynasties parallel prose. Liu is undoubtedly a superb master of these forms. In this excerpt, each choice of parallel form is best suited to a specific need in a given stage of exposition.

Segment 1 begins with a parallel form of the simplest kind: a coupling of two single lines. This parallelism is more sophisticated, however, than what was seen in Wu Jun's piece. It operates not through a double correspondence in morphology and semantics but rather a tension between morphological correspondence and semantic antithesis (shown by boldface). As shown by the vertical lines in the block citation, all corresponding characters have the same parts of speech. In meaning, however, all major characters are antithetically set (shown by boldface): the physical form versus the heart; rivers and lakes versus the Wei tower; above versus below. This simple antithetical parallelism serves Liu's purpose perfectly: to capture the transcendental flight of the mind unhindered by geographic separation.

In segment 2, Liu proceeds to provide a fuller description of this transcendental flight. For this purpose, he calls into use two units of alternate-line parallelism. In the first unit, the first and third lines contrast a cessation of thought with a stirring of one's countenance, whereas the second and fourth lines contrast between "one thousand years" and "ten thousand *li*." If the first unit introduces a new dimension of time, the second unit tells us that this transcendental flight is a two-way journey, eventually returning to appear right before the author, in the virtual form of sounds and sights.

Segment 4 turns to discuss physiological and linguistic mediation needed for launching transcendental flights of the mind. It is composed of two units of alternate-line parallelism. These two units consider some seemingly unnecessary repetitions and surely do not read as smoothly as other parallel units. Upon closer scrutiny, I discovered that these two units are actually constructed by breaking up this longer, four-line parallelism:

¹神居胸臆，²而志氣統其關鍵；³關鍵將塞，⁴則神有遯心。
⁵物沿耳目，⁶而辭令管其樞機。⁷樞機方通，⁸則物無隱貌。

The intended meaning comes through much more clearly in this extended parallelism. The first four lines explain three essential points regarding the spirit's outbound flight: (1) the spirit resides in the mind before its outbound flight; (2) the vital energy is the conduit of spirit; and (3) if the conduit is blocked, the transcendental flight will be thwarted. Similarly, the next four lines explain three essential points pertaining to the spirit's inbound flight: (1) spirit courses back with things (i.e., images) through the ears and eyes, to the author; (2) phrasing competence is the crucial medium through which this inbound flight must pass; and (3) if this medium is wide open, things will reveal their true form. But if Liu were to present his ideas in this way, he would be writing ancient-style prose rather than parallel prose. This is because parallel prose allows a maximum of four lines in an alternate-line parallelism. A seemingly simple solution would be just to break the eight lines in this way:

¹神居胸臆，²而志氣統其關鍵；
³關鍵將塞，⁴則神有遯心。
⁵物沿耳目，⁶而辭令管其樞機。
⁷樞機方通，⁸則物無隱貌。

But this would not work either, because all parallel lines must be of equal length. In this passage, the second and fourth lines and the sixth and eighth lines are of different lengths. So, the only solution left is to reposition the third and fourth lines after the seventh and eighth lines, as Liu has actually done. So, in this case, we seem to witness an uncommon instance of the required parallel form impeding the expository process.[6]

Segment 5 features yet another case of pigeonholing a long unparallel sentence into a parallel form. What Liu means to say is actually this:

陶鈞文思，貴在虛靜，[貴在]疏瀹五藏，[貴在]澡雪精神.

In other words, the last two lines are object clauses of the verbal phrase "the importance lies in" in the second line. But the rules of parallelism force Liu to break up this sentence and turn it into an imperfect alternate-line parallelism. This is followed by a "to-do" list for any writer who wishes to embark on the two-way flight of spirit and reach the optimal state for compositional execution, the final creative stage adumbrated in segment 6.

Having gone over the entire excerpt, we cannot but admire Liu's virtuosity in parallel patterning. Taking advantage of allowable expandability of line length, he masterfully varies it in ways that best advance his expository process. In this excerpt, he does not use any parallel form twice. When he has run out of choices toward the end, he unexpectedly employs enumerative cataloging, a device associated with the rhapsody (*fu*) genre, as he lists the writer's four tasks of learning. This constant length variation, slight though it is, effectively mitigates the boredom of recurrent textual patterning and injects cadence and energy into what could easily have been a monotonous exposition.

From these four texts, readers can perceive a steady trajectory from loose aggregative patterning to ever more complex parallel patterning. I have focused on the interplay of semantic and syntactic parallelism and have left out the discussion of the more complex allusive and tonal parallelism meticulously wrought by some Qi–Liang prose masters. Allusive parallelism refers to an embedding of historical events or texts in coupled phrases and sentences, primarily as a subtext that enhances lyrical tenor. Tonal parallelism refers to a conscious deployment of contrastive tones between coupled lines. Both allusive and tonal parallelism are left out of my discussion because they are too complex to explain in this general introduction to parallel prose.

After achieving absolute dominance during the Qi–Liang period, parallel prose could not maintain its glory for long. Qi–Liang parallel prose has an intrinsic vulnerability common to any extreme formalism: an obsession with form-crafting to the neglect of content. Indeed, all too soon this vulnerability became all the lightning rod of sustained blistering attacks. First, Sui and early Tang rulers banned florid phrasing and patterning in official documents, identifying them as a cause of moral decadence leading to the downfall of the Qi and Liang dynasties. Then, in the mid-Tang, parallel prose was singled out for castigation by exponents of ancient-style prose, its arch rival (☞ chap. 10–13). Although parallel prose was knocked from its pedestal of preeminence by Tang and Song practitioners of ancient-style prose, it was never out of fashion. In fact, it continued to grow, though in a more subdued fashion. Evolving within the parameters of the Qi–Liang model, Tang and Song parallel prose developed distinctive formal features: intricate tonal patterning in Tang parallel prose, and a prevalent use of alternate-line parallel constructions ([4 + 6] + [4 + 6] module) in the Song. The resurgence of parallel prose in the Ming and Qing followed a different path as it reverted to the less restrictive patterning of the Han and Wei–Jin style. With all its variations, the long, continuous growth of parallel prose is no doubt a testament to the unfading appeal of parallel patterning to Chinese literati, as a powerful tool in the crafting of descriptive, expository, and lyrical works.

Zong-qi Cai

NOTES

1. See Susan Bush, "Tsung Ping's Essay on Painting Landscape and the 'Landscape Buddhism' of Mount Lu," in *Theories of the Arts in China*, edited by Susan Bush and Christian Murck (Princeton, NJ: Princeton University Press, 1983), 132–164.

2. See *WJNBCWXSCKZL* 652; translated by H. C. Chang in John Minford and Joseph S. M. Lau, eds., *Classical Chinese Literature* (New York: Columbia University Press, 2002), 613–614. Moderately modified.

3. See, for instance, lines 6–7, 13–17 of "What I Observed as I Crossed the Lake on My Way from Southern Mountain to Northern Mountain," in *HTRCP* 133.

4. See, for instance, lines 2–4, 10–11, 17–20 of "What I Observed as I Crossed the Lake on My Way," in *HTRCP* 133.

5. See my comments on Xie's famous couplet (word-for-word translation: pond bank grow spring grass, garden willow change crying birds) in *HTRCP* 385–386.

6. On the constraints of the parallel form faced by Liu Xie, see Stephen Owen, "Liu Xie and the Discourse Machine," in *A Chinese Literary Mind: Culture, Creativity, and Rhetoric in Wenxin diaolong*, edited by Zong-qi Cai (Stanford, CA: Stanford University Press, 2001), 175–191.

SUGGESTED READING

ENGLISH

Cai, Zong-qi, ed. *A Chinese Literary Mind: Culture, Creativity, and Rhetoric in Wenxin diaolong*. Stanford, CA: Stanford University Press, 2001.

Hightower, James R. "Some Characteristics of Parallel Prose." In *Studies in Chinese Literature*, edited by John Bishop, 108–139. Cambridge, MA: Harvard University Press, 1965.

Langley, C. Bradford. "Pien wen" ["Parallel Prose"]. In *Indiana Companion to Traditional Chinese Literature*, edited by William H. Nienhauser, 656–660. Bloomington: Indiana University Press, 1986.

Nienhauser, William H. "Prose." In *Indiana Companion to Traditional Chinese Literature*, edited by William H. Nienhauser, 93–120. Bloomington: Indiana University Press, 1986.

Owen, Stephen. "Liu Xie and the Discourse Machine." In *A Chinese Literary Mind: Culture, Creativity, and Rhetoric in Wenxin diaolong*, edited by Zong-qi Cai, 175–191. Stanford, CA: Stanford University Press, 2001.

CHINESE

Jiang Shuge 姜書閣. *Pianwen shilun* 駢文史論 (*Discussions on the History of Parallel Prose*). Beijing: Renmin wenxue chubanshe, 1986.

Liu Linsheng 劉麟生. *Zhongguo pianwen shi* 中國駢文史 (*A History of Chinese Parallel Prose*). Beijing: Dongfang chubanshe, 1996.

Mo Daocai 莫道才. *Pianwen tonglun* 駢文通論 (*Comprehensive Studies on Parallel Prose*). Nanning: Guangxi jiaoyu chubanshe, 1994.

Yu Jingxiang 于景祥. *Tangdai pianwen shi* 唐代駢文史 (*History of Tang Parallel Prose*). Shenyang: Liaoning renmin chubanshe, 1991.

Xu Yimin 許逸民, comp. *Gudai pianwn jinghua* 古代駢文精華 (*Splendors of Ancient Parallel Prose*). Beijing: Renmin wenxue chubanshe, 1995.

Zhou Zhenfu 周振甫, comp. *Pianwen jingcui* 駢文精粹 (*Essentials of Parallel Prose*). Taiyuan: Shanxi guji chubanshe, 1996.

PART III

The Tang and Song Dynasties

Tang and Song Expository Prose

The Practice of Persuasion

The Tang and Song dynasties were periods of extraordinary creativity that gave rise to a number of significant developments in Chinese literary history: the perfection of regulated verse (*lüshi*) (☞ *HTRCP* chap. 8) and the quatrain (*jueju*) (☞ *HTRCP* chap. 10); the emergence and flourishing of the lyric (*ci*) (☞ *HTRCP* chap. 12); and the creation of new styles and forms of prose writing, many of which—for example, origins (*yuan*), theories (*shuo*), disquisitions (*lun*), records (*ji*), biographies (*zhuan*), prefaces (*xu*), and letters (*shu*)—are discussed in this volume (☞ chap. 11–13). The prose compositions of eight authors in particular—Han Yü (768–824) and Liu Zongyuan (773–819) from the Tang along with Ouyang Xiu (1007–1072), Su Xun (1009–1066), Su Shi (1037–1101), Su Zhe (1039–1112), Zeng Gong (1019–1112), and Wang Anshi (1021–1086) from the Song—have long been admired. Collectively called the "Eight Great Prose Masters of the Tang and Song" (*Tang Song ba da jia*), their writings have served as exemplary models since the twelfth century.[1] In this chapter, we will focus on the essays of Han Yu, Liu Zongyuan, and Su Xun; later chapters will discuss works by other of the Eight Masters (☞ chap. 11–13).

The artistic and intellectual creativity of Tang and Song prose literature, especially that of the Eight Masters, has conventionally been understood as part of the "classical prose movement" (*guwen yundong*) (☞ chap. 16). According to this paradigm, developments in style and form arose from a new ideology of textual practice that looked to classical Confucian writings for inspiration and moral guidance. The roots of this movement can be traced to early fifth-century dissatisfaction with the onerous conventions of parallel prose (*pianwen*), which required writers to produce works composed almost exclusively in verbally parallel four- or six-character phrases that were also densely allusive and adhered to specific patterns of tonal euphony (☞ chap. 9). This classical prose movement gained momentum in the mid-eighth century as part of a broader reevaluation of existing social and cultural institutions following the near-collapse of the Tang dynasty. Recent studies have identified additional factors that contributed to literary innovation in this era: the rise of the civil service examination (☞ chap. 14; *HTRCPIC* chap. 11), evolving complexity and interconnectedness of social and literary networks, growing commercialization of literacy and literary talent, development of new regional centers of literary culture, and changing circulation patterns of both texts and people.

This chapter focuses on three examples of "expository prose" from this extraordinary period of Chinese literary history. Expository prose, according to sixth-century literary theoretician Liu Xie (ca. 465–ca. 522), refers to compositions that "take into consideration a variety of statements for the purpose of examining minutely a specific idea."[2] As a category of writing, it encompassed several genres that, in practice, share two features: they were written as stand-alone compositions (as opposed to being part of longer book-length treatises) and their primary function was to present an argument—whether that be to distinguish truth from falsehood, to abstract broader principles from individual examples, or to probe difficult questions to advance understanding and interpretation in new directions. Stylistically, writers of expository prose essays strove to present their arguments clearly and logically, and at the same time be intellectually powerful, emotionally suasive, and, most of all, convincing.

From the Tang dynasty forward, the ability to convey arguments well in written form became an important skill for the educated elite, one used in a variety of contexts. Candidates for the civil service examination were tested on their competence in composing expository prose in different genres. Officials throughout the imperial bureaucracy were at times required to draft legal arguments for adjudications within their administrative districts or to advocate persuasively for their preferred policy positions at court. Expository prose played an important role in historical writing and in early fiction as well and was used for summary arguments preceding or following historical accounts or in storytellers' elucidation of a tale's moral. Essays such as the ones translated in this chapter were often included in prose anthologies and offered up as models for later students to emulate in their own writing. The study of expository prose thus offers readers today insight into how Tang and Song writers identified and analyzed social or intellectual problems, the range of theoretical approaches they used to resolve them, and the language and rhetoric they thought were the most effective for persuading contemporary and later audiences. As such, they form an invaluable resource for understanding both the ethos and thought processes of this period.

HAN YU AND "ON THE ORIGIN OF THE WAY"

Our first essay, Han Yu's "On the Origin of the Way" ("Yuandao"), occupies an especially important position in Chinese literary and intellectual history. Its definitions of key Confucian concepts and strategic intertwining of the history of Confucian thought with Chinese civilization played an important role in the development of neo-Confucian thought during the Song dynasty. Despite its significance, some basic questions about the composition, such as exactly when it was written (possibly between the early 800s and the early 820s), remain unresolved.

The *yuan* ("On the Origin of," also translated "On the Source of," "Original," or simply "On . . .") differentiates itself from other expository genres, according to Ming dynasty genre theorist Xu Shizeng (1517–1580), in that its arguments are structured around "tracing something back to its original source and exploring in detail its application in the immediate present."[3] Literary historians, in turn, trace the origin of the *yuan* as an expository prose genre to five compositions by Han Yu in the early ninth century: "On the Origin of the Way" ("Yuandao"), "On the Origin of Human Nature" ("Yuanxing"), "On the Origin of Slander" ("Yuanhui"), "On the Origin of People" ("Yuanren"), and "On the Origin of Ghosts" ("Yuangui"). Only after the appearance of "On the Origin of the Way" do we begin to find other writers, in the Tang and later, making use of the "Origin" genre to support their own arguments.

Han Yu, author of "On the Origins of the Way," was one of the most important literary figures of the ninth century, famous in his time as both a poet and essayist. By the Song dynasty, he was also considered to be one of the greatest Confucian polemicists of the medieval period. The prose genres in which Han was most renowned and where we find the theoretical underpinnings of the classical prose movement he advocated most clearly manifested—letter, prefaces on parting, expository essays, and fictional biography—are discussed in this and other chapters of this volume.

C10.1 Han Yu, "On the Origin of the Way" (*Yuan dao*)

韓愈　原道

1. Universal compassion is called "humaneness" (*ren*). Conduct that accords with it is called "righteousness" (*yi*).[1] What proceeds from here and goes to there is called "the Way" (*dao*). [What is] sufficient in oneself and dependent upon nothing outside is called "character" (*de*).[2] Humaneness and righteousness are fixed terms; the Way and character are potential positions.[3] Thus there is the Way of the cultivated gentleman and of the petty man, and character has that which is evil and that which is favorable.[4]

博愛之謂仁，行而宜之之謂義，由是而之焉之謂道，足乎己無待於外之謂德。仁與義為定名，道與德為虛位。故道有君子小人，而德有凶有吉。

Laozi's belittling of humaneness and righteousness does not mean they should actually be scorned; it is just that he had little understanding of them.[5] One who stays in the bottom of a well and contemplates the sky would say "the sky is little"; this does not mean that the sky is actually little.[6] He [i.e., Laozi] understood humaneness to mean small kindnesses and righteousness

老子之小仁義，非毀之也，其見者小也。坐井而觀天，曰天小者，非天小也。彼以煦煦為仁，孑孑為義，其小之也則宜。其所謂道，道其所道，非吾所謂道也；其所謂德，德其所德，非吾所謂德也。凡吾所謂道德云者，合仁與義言之也，天下之公言也；老子之所謂道德云者，去仁與義言之也，一人之私言也。

---

[1] "Humaneness" (*ren*, also translated as "benevolence) and "righteousness" (*yi*, also translated as "propriety" or "appropriateness") are two virtues central to Confucian thought.

[2] The terms "the Way" (*dao*) and "character" (*de*) are ubiquitous within many schools of early Chinese thought. The latter term, *de*, is also translated as "virtue" or "inner power."

[3] Han Yu is claiming that while "humaneness" and "righteousness" are terms whose meanings are concretely defined and commonly accepted, "the Way" and "character" are more abstract and without fixed content, and their meaning is contingent on their context.

[4] A passage in the *Zuo Tradition* (*Zuozhuan*) clarifies what Han Yu means: "Filial piety (*xiao*), respect (*jing*), loyalty (*zhong*), and good faith (*xin*) are favorable character traits (*de*); robbery (*dao*), rebellion (*zei*), conspiracy (*cang*), and usurpation (*jian*) are evil character traits."[4]

[5] Han Yu's critique is targeted against passages in the *Book of the Way and Its Power* (*Daodejing*) and the *Zhuangzi* that disparage humaneness and righteousness, and even character, as qualities that become pertinent only after the Way has been abandoned.

[6] Han Yu here dismissively compares Laozi to the well-dwelling frog of the *Zhuangzi*, a figure used allegorically to mock those who mistakenly believe their understanding of their limited environment allows them to discourse on the wider world.

to mean small favors. His belittling of them is in that case appropriate. But what he called the Way was simply taking what he thought was the Way as the Way; this is not what I call the Way. What he called character was simply taking what he thought was character as character; this is not what I call character.[7] In general when I discuss what I call the Way and character, I speak of them in conjunction with humaneness and righteousness. This is how they are commonly discussed in the world. When Laozi discussed what he called the Way and character, he spoke of them apart from humaneness and righteousness. This is his own idiosyncratic way of discussing them.[8]

周道衰，孔子沒，火于秦，黃老于漢，佛于晉魏梁隋之間。其言道德仁義者，不入于楊，則入于墨。不入于老，則入于佛。入于彼，必出于此。入者主之，出者奴之；入者附之，出者汙之。噫！後之人其欲聞仁義道德之說，孰從而聽之？老者曰：孔子，吾師之弟子也。佛者曰：孔子，吾師之弟子也。為孔子者習聞其說，樂其誕而自小也，亦曰：吾師亦嘗師之云爾。不惟舉之於其口，而又筆之於其書。噫！後之人雖欲聞仁義道德之說，其孰從而求之？甚矣，人之好怪也！不求其端，不訊其末，惟怪之欲聞。

2. The Way of the Zhou[1] declined. Confucius died. [The books] were burned in the Qin.[2] Huang-Lao[3] [arose] in the Han. Buddhism [appeared] during the Jin, Wei, Liang, and Sui.[4] As for those who discussed the Way, character, humaneness, and righteousness: if they had not accepted [the teachings of] Yang [Zhu],[5] then they had accepted [the teachings of] Mozi.[6] If they had not accepted [the teachings of] Laozi, they had accepted the [teachings of] Buddha. Accepting that one, they inevitably rejected this one. The one they accepted, they made dominant; the one they rejected, they made subordinate. The one they accepted, they embellished; the one they rejected, they smeared. Alas!

[7] Han Yu's phrasing subtly alludes to the "Webbed Toes" chapter of the *Zhuangzi*, in which similar phrasing ("is not what I would call") is used by Daoist philosopher Zhuangzi (ca. 369–ca. 286 BCE) to critique humaneness, righteousness, and other Confucian principles.

[8] Han Yu defines four key Confucian concepts—humaneness, righteousness, the Way, and character—and condemns the alternative understanding of them advocated within Daoist thought as flawed and idiosyncratic. The opening paragraph moreover displays Han's skill in modulating prose rhythm. The first four phrases are all of different length—five, seven, eight, and ten characters long respectively—and are followed immediately by two sets of parallel phrases each of which are six characters long. The asymmetry of the first four lines allows each definition to stand apart while also drawing the reader deeper with each adjacent phrase, before finally presenting a clear summation in memorable couplets.

[1] The Zhou, along with the Xia and Shang that preceded it, were the "Three Dynasties" (*san dai*) of Chinese antiquity.

[2] The burning of the books refers to the infamous destruction of books perpetuated by the first emperor of the Qin dynasty at the behest of his Legalist adviser, Li Si (280–208 BCE), in 213 BCE.

[3] "Huang-Lao" refers to a syncretic tradition of Daoist thought that flourished in the second century BCE. Named after the "Yellow Emperor" (Huangdi) and the "Old Master" (Laozi), it is often viewed as the beginning of religious Daoism.

[4] The Jin (265–420), Wei (220–65), Liang (502–87), and Sui (581–618) were all short-lived dynasties that existed between the Han dynasty (206 BCE–220) and the Tang. All had emperors who converted to Buddhism.

[5] Yang Zhu was a contemporary of Mencius (fourth century BCE). He argued that, given the brevity of human life, people should fully enjoy its various sensory pleasures while they could rather than struggle for wealth or status. He was often ridiculed by Confucians as a selfish, immoral hedonist.

[6] Mozi (ca. 468–376 BCE) was a contemporary of Confucius. His philosophy emphasized in part the idea of "universal love" (*boai*), defined as caring for others equally and impartially. His philosophy was criticized by Confucians for going against filial piety in that it advocated treating parents and family no differently from strangers.

Those people in later times who wished to hear an explanation of humaneness, righteousness, the Way, and character—from whom might they hear them? The followers of Laozi say, "Confucius was actually a disciple of our master." The followers of Buddha say, "Confucius was actually a disciple of our master."[7] Those one might consider followers of Confucius became used to hearing these claims. They actually indulged in these absurdities and so belittled themselves, saying as well, "Our master for his part indeed once regarded them as teachers," etc. They not only uttered these claims with their mouths, but moreover wrote them down in their books. Alas! Although those people in later times might long to hear explanations of humaneness, righteousness, the Way, and character, to whom might they go to seek this? Extreme indeed, people's fondness for the bizarre. They do not seek out where [these claims] began nor investigate where they end. They wish only to hear about the bizarre.[8]

3. In antiquity, the people were made up of four groups. Nowadays, the people are made up of six groups.[1] In antiquity, those who taught occupied one of those groups. Nowadays, those who teach occupy three of them. Households of farmers are found in only one [of these groups], but the households of those who consume their grains are found in all six. Households of craftsmen are found in only one [of these groups], but the households of those who use their products are found in all six. Households of merchants are found in only one [of these groups], but the households supplied by them are found in all six. No wonder the people cannot but be poor and thieving![2]

In the time of antiquity, there were many things that imperiled people. Later on, sages arose who taught them the Way of living together and taking care of one another. They served as their rulers and served as their teachers. Driving away the creepy-crawly vermin and the harmful beasts, they settled the people in the central lands. When cold, they taught them to make clothing. When hungry, they taught them to produce food. When they dwelt in trees and fell down or dwelt in the earth and fell ill, they taught them how to build houses and palaces. They taught them crafts so that tools and implements could be supplied. They taught them trade so that those with and those without could have free exchange. They taught them healing and

[7] Han Yu is attacking claims made within some Buddhist and Daoist writings that state that Confucius was, respectively, a bodhisattva or a disciple of Laozi.

[8] Han Yu outlines the challenges confronting his contemporaries who seek to correctly understand the true meaning of key Confucian concepts such as humaneness, righteousness, character, and the Way.

[1] The traditional four classes were scholar-officials (*shi*), farmers (*nong*), craftsmen (*gong*), and merchants (*shang*). Han Yu appends Daoists and Buddhists as two additional classes that increase that number to six. The expansion of "those who teach" (*jiaozhe*) from one to three categories reflects the addition of those latter two groups.

[2] Because of the imbalance between producers and consumers within society. Han Yu echoes a critique made by many of his predecessors and contemporaries in the Tang that Buddhist and Daoist clergy were freeloaders on the traditional economy, consuming goods but producing nothing of value.

古之為民者四，今之為民者六；古之教者處其一，今之教者處其三；農之家一，而食粟之家六；工之家一，而用器之家六；賈之家一，而資焉之家六。奈之何民不窮且盜也！

古之時人之害多矣。有聖人者立，然後教之以相生養之道。為之君，為之師，驅其蟲蛇禽獸而處之中土。寒然後為之衣，饑然後為之食。木處而顛，土處而病也，然後為之宮室。為之工以贍其器用，為之賈以通其有無，為之醫藥以濟其夭死，為之葬埋祭祀以長其恩愛，為之禮以次其先後，為之樂以宣其湮鬱，為之政以率其怠勤，為之刑以鋤其強梗。相欺也，為之符璽斗斛權衡以信之；相奪也，為之城郭甲兵以守之。害至而

為之備，患生而為之
防。今其言曰：聖人不
死，大盜不止；剖斗折
衡，而民不爭。嗚呼！
其亦不思而已矣！如古
之無聖人，人之類滅久
矣。何也？無羽毛鱗介
以居寒熱也，無爪牙以
爭食也。

medicine so that those who were dying prematurely could be saved. They taught them funerals and burials, sacrifices and offerings, so that [feelings of] kindness and love could be made eternal. They taught them ritual, so that superior and subordinate could be properly ranked. They taught them music, so that pent up and tangled [emotions] could be released. They taught them government so that the idle and indolent could be given direction. They taught them punishments so that the violent and the brutal could be weeded out. [The people] deceived one another, so they taught them tallies and seals, peck-measures and bushel-measures, balance-weights and scales, so they might trust [one another]. [The people] plundered one another, so they taught them to build inner walls and outer fortifications and to make armor and weaponry, so they might defend themselves. When perils arrived, they taught them to prepare [for them]. When calamities arose, they taught them to defend [against them].[3]

Now their [e.g., the Daoist] doctrine states that:

If the sages do not die
Great robbers will not stop coming . . .
Break the peck-measures and split the scales,
And the people will no longer bicker and fight.[4]

O woe! They are for their part simply not thinking. If there had been no sages in antiquity, human beings would have been eradicated long ago. Why? They lack the feathers, fur, scales, or shells for living in heat or cold. They lack the claws and teeth with which to fight for food.[5]

---

[3] Many earlier works, such as the Mozi, the "Commentary on the Appended Phrases" ("Xici zhuan") of the *Book of Changes* (*Yijing*), and the *Mencius*, included legendary accounts of the civilizing teachings of the mythical sages.

[4] Translation slightly modified from Brook Zipporyn, trans., *Zhuangzi: The Essential Writings with Selections from Traditional Commentaries* (Indianapolis: Hackett, 2009), 64. Han Yu is quoting from the tenth chapter of the *Zhuangzi*, in which the civilizing teaching of the sages is blamed for simultaneously bringing about the rise of various social ills. That chapter moreover advocates for a return to the simpler life of an earlier time in which people were guided by the Daoist principle of nonaction.

[5] Han Yu first places blame for the pervasiveness of poverty and crime on the addition of two parasitic social groups, Daoists and Buddhists, to the ancient four classes of Chinese society. He then attributes the development of Chinese civilization to the teachings of the Confucian sages. Finally, he draws a sharp contrast between these sages' tangible contributions and the shortsighted, potentially deadly, critiques of their teachings by Daoists.

The first paragraph of this section uses a straightforward and unambiguous structure to draw a clear contrast between past and present. The second paragraph once again shows Han Yu's skill with prose rhythm. He uses the phrase *wei zhi* X (translated as "served as X" and "taught them how to X") seventeen times but avoids tediousness by placing it variously at the beginning, middle, or end of phrases. The efficacy of his technique is poetically summed up by a later reader, who describes this passage as being "like layered peaks and folded ridges or leaping billows and giant waves that bring such delight to the reader's heart that one is unaware of the repetition of these characters."[5]

4. For these reasons, to be "a ruler" means to be the one who issues commands, to be "a minister" means to be the one who enacts the commands of the ruler so that they take effect among the people; and to be "the people" means to be the ones who produce grains, rice, hemp, and silk, who make tools and utensils, and who exchange commodities and cash, all so as to serve those who are their superiors. Should rulers not issue commands, they lose that which defines them as rulers. Should ministers not enact the commands of the ruler so that they take effect among the people, they lose that which defines them as ministers. Should the people not produce grains, rice, hemp, and silk, nor make tools and vessels, nor exchange commodities and cash so as to serve their superiors, they are punished.[1]

Now their dharma [e.g., Buddhist doctrine] states that "you must forsake your rulers and ministers, abandon your fathers and sons, and forbid the Way of living together and nurturing one another"—all in order to seek their so-called purity and nirvāna.[2] O woe! It is fortunate on the one hand that [the dharma] emerged only after the Three Dynasties and so could not be denounced by Yu, Tang, Wen and Wu, the Duke of Zhou, and Confucius.[3] It is unfortunate on the other hand that it did not emerge prior to the Three Dynasties and so could not be rectified by Yu, Tang, Wen and Wu, the Duke of Zhou, and Confucius.

[The Five] Emperors and [the Three] Kings[4]: though the titles differ, what made them sagely was the same. Wearing hemp in summer and fur-lined garments in winter, drinking when thirsty and eating when hungry: although the situations differ, what makes them rational is the same. Now their [Daoist] discourse states, "How come we do not practice non-action [in response to] situations as in remote antiquity?" This is the same as criticizing those who wear fur-lined clothing in the winter by saying, "How come you do not keep it simple by wearing hemp?" or criticizing those who eat when hungry by saying, "How come you do not keep it simple by drinking something?"[5]

是故君者，出令者也；臣者，行君之令而致之民者也；民者，出粟米麻絲，作器皿，通貨財，以事其上者也。君不出令，則失其所以為君；臣不行君之令而致之民，則失其所以為臣；民不出粟米麻絲，作器皿，通貨財，以事其上，則誅。今其法曰：必棄而君臣，去而父子，禁而相生養之道。以求其所謂清靜寂滅者。嗚呼！其亦幸而出於三代之後，不見黜於禹、湯、文、武、周公、孔子也。其亦不幸而不出於三代之前，不見正於禹、湯、文、武、周公、孔子也。

帝之與王，其號雖殊，其所以為聖一也；夏葛而冬裘，渴飲而飢食，其事雖殊，其所以為智一也。今其言曰：曷不為太古之無事？是亦責冬之裘者曰：曷不為葛之之易也？責飢之食者曰：曷不為飲之之易也？

[1] While most commentators interpret the term used by Han Yu here, *zhu*, as "punished," it could also mean "to censure" or "to execute."

[2] The extinguishing of desire.

[3] King Yu ruled during the Xia, King Tang during the Shang, and Kings Wen and Wu during the Zhou. All of them, along with the Duke of Zhou and Confucius (who lived during the Zhou) were considered by Confucians to be moral exemplars.

[4] The term "Five Emperors" is most commonly understood to refer to those listed in the "Five Emperors" chapter of the *Grand Scribe's Records* (*Shiji*): Huangdi, Zhuan Xu, Di Ku, Yao, and Shun. The "Three Kings" likely refers to King Yu, King Tang, and King Wen (see note 3). All were exemplary rulers.

[5] Han argues that social identity is intrinsically tied to social performance; failing to act in the manner appropriate to one's social identity results in punishment or the loss of that social identity. He critiques Buddhists for rejecting established social relationships and Daoists for their irrational adherence to the principle of nonaction regardless of circumstance.

《傳》曰：“古之欲明
明德於天下者，先治
其國；欲治其國者，
先齊其家；欲齊其
家者，先修其身；欲
修其身者，先正其
心；欲正其心者，
先誠其意。”然則
古之所謂正心而誠意
者，將以有為也。今也
欲治其心而外天下國
家，滅其天常，子焉
而不父其父，臣焉而
不君其君，民焉而
不事其事。孔子之作
《春秋》也，諸侯用夷
禮則夷之。夷而進於中
國則中國之。《經》
曰：“夷狄之有君，不
如諸夏之亡！”《詩》
曰：“戎狄是膺，荊舒
是懲。”今也舉夷狄之
法而加之先王之教之
上，幾何其不胥而為
夷也！

夫所謂先王之教者何
也？博愛之謂仁，行
而宜之之謂義，由是
而之焉之謂道，足乎
己無待於外之謂德。
其文：《詩》、《書》、
《易》、《春秋》；
其法：禮、樂、刑、
政；其民：士、農、
工、賈；其位：君臣、
父子、師友、賓主、
昆弟、夫婦；其服：
麻、絲；其居：宮室；
其食：粟米、果蔬、魚
肉。其為道易明，而其
為教易行也。是
故以之為己，則順

5. The *Traditions* state: "Those in antiquity who wished to illuminate luminous virtue throughout the world would first govern their states; wishing to govern their states, they would first bring order to their families; wishing to bring order to their families, they would first cultivate their own persons; wishing to cultivate their own persons, they would first rectify their minds; wishing to rectify their minds, they would first make their thoughts sincere."[1] Given this, one then [can understand] that what in antiquity was called "rectify the mind so as to make thoughts sincere" was something that required deliberate action.

Now however in desiring to govern their minds, they [the Buddhists] set themselves apart from their family, state, and the entire world, and extinguish the natural constants [of human relations]. How can one be a son yet not treat one's father as a father? How can one be a minister yet not treat one's ruler as a ruler? How can one be of the people yet not treat one's duties as duties?

When Confucius created the *Spring and Autumn Annals*, he identified as Yi-barbarians those feudal lords who used the rituals of Yi-barbarians, yet identified as Chinese those Yi-barbarians who had advanced to [using] Chinese [rituals]. The *Classic* states, "The Yi and Di barbarians, even with their rulers, are inferior to Chinese states without them."[2] The [*Book of*] *Poetry* states "[They] have faced the Rong and Di barbarians, have given pause to the Jing and Xu barbarians."[3] Now however the dharma of the Yi and Di barbarians is elevated, and put above the teachings of the former kings. How is this not having wholly become barbarians?[4]

6. What exactly is meant by the "teachings of the former kings"? Universal compassion is called humaneness. Conduct that accords with it is called righteousness. What proceeds from here and goes to there is called the Way. [What is] sufficient in oneself and dependent upon nothing outside is called character. Their texts: [*the Book of*] *Poetry* (*Shi*), [*the Book of*] *Documents* (*Shu*), [*the Book of*] *Changes* (*Yi*), and the *Spring and Autumn Annals* (*Chunqiu*). Their methods: ritual, music, punishments, and government. Their [classes of] the people: scholars, farmers, craftsmen, and merchants. Their [social] positions: ruler

---

[1] Wm. Theodore de Mary and Irene Bloom, comp., *Sources of Chinese Tradition* (New York: Columbia University Press, 1999), 1:330–331. For alternative translations of this passage, see Andrew H. Plaks, *Ta Hsüeh and Chung Yung* (New York: Penguin Books, 2003), 5; James Legge, *The Li Ki* (Delhi: Motilal Banarsidass, 1992), 411–412.

[2] Translation slightly modified from Edward Slingerland, trans., *Confucius Analects* (Indianapolis: Hackett, 2003), 18.

[3] Translation modified from Arthur Waley, *The Book of Songs* (New York: Grove Press, 1996), 315.

[4] The Yi, Di, and Rong were tribes living, respectively, to the east, north, and west of the central China plains during the time of Confucius. The Jing and Xu were tribes that dwelt to the south. The poem Han references describes various military conflicts between the Zhou dynasty and these tribes.

Han quotes a passage from the *Book of Rites* (*Li ji*) to clarify how Daoist and Buddhist understandings of self-cultivation undermine social order and, ultimately, run counter to the essence of what makes Chinese civilization Chinese.

and minister, father and son, teacher and friend, guest and host, older brother and younger brother, husband and wife. Their clothing: hemp and silk. Their dwellings: houses and palaces. Their food: grains and rice, fruits and vegetables, meat and fish. Theirs is a Way that is easy to understand and theirs are teachings that are easy to put into practice. This is why:

Use them in one's self-conduct and all will then be effortless and in your favor.
Use them in one's conduct with others and all will then be compassionate and fair.
Use them to conduct the heart-mind and all will then be harmonious and calm.
Use them to conduct the household, kingdom, and the entire world and there will be nothing that is where it shouldn't be.

This is why:

In life, realizing one's innate nature,
Dying only after having exhausted one's allotted lifespan.
At the suburban temples, heavenly divinities will attend;
At the ancestral shrine, human ghosts will be well-supplied.

Someone might say, "Which Way is this Way?" I would say, "This is what *I* call 'the Way.' It is not that so-called Way of the Daoists and Buddhists mentioned earlier." What Yao transmitted to Shun was this, what Shun transmitted to Yu was this, what Yu transmitted to Tang was this, what Tang transmitted to King Wen, King Wu, and the Duke of Zhou was this. King Wen, King Wu, and the Duke of Zhou transmitted it to Confucius, and Confucius transmitted it to Meng Ke. With [Meng] Ke's death, it did not get transmitted by him to anyone. As for Xun[zi] and Yang [Xiong], they excerpted from it but missed the essential ideas, talked about it but were not precise.[1] [Those who understood the Way, like] the Duke of Zhou and those before him rose up to serve as rulers and thus practiced it in their affairs. Following the Duke of Zhou, [those who understood the Way] came down to serve as ministers and so elaborated upon it in their discourse.

Given this then, what would make things right? [I] say, "No blocking, no flow; no stopping, no practicing."[2] Turn their personnel into [common] people.[3] Turn their books into bonfires. Turn their [monastic] residences into

而 祥；以 之 為 人，
則 愛 而 公；以 之 為
心，則 和 而 平；以
之 為 天下國家，無
所 處 而 不 當 。 是 故
生 則 得 其 情，死 則 盡
其 常，郊 焉 而 天神假，
廟 焉 而 人鬼饗。曰：
斯 道 也 ， 何 道 也 ？
曰：斯吾所謂道也，
非 向 所 謂 老 與 佛 之 道
也。堯 以 是 傳 之 舜，
舜 以 是 傳 之 禹，禹 以
是 傳 之 湯，湯 以 是 傳
之 文、武、周公，文、
武、周公 傳 之 孔子，
孔子 傳 之 孟軻。軻 之
死，不 得 其 傳 焉。荀 與
楊 也，擇 焉 而 不 精，
語 焉 而 不 詳。由 周公
而 上，上 而 為 君，故
其 事行；由 周公 而 下，
下 而 為臣，故 其 說長。
然 則 如 之 何 而 可 也？
曰：不塞不流，不止
不 行。人 其 人，火 其
書，盧 其 居，明 先王之
道 以 道 之，鰥寡孤獨廢
疾者有養也。其 亦 庶 乎
其 可 也。

[*HYWJHJJZ* 1:1–4]

N.B. Straight underline indicates the use of repetitive patterning; wavy underline the use of parallel phrasing therein. For a discussion on repetitive and parallel patterning,
☛ C1.1–4 and C1.6–7.

---

[1] Both Meng Ke (also known as Mencius, 372–289 BCE) and Xunzi (ca. 298–ca. 238 BCE) were the two most influential teachers and transmitters of Confucian thought in the fourth century BCE. Yang Xiong (53 BCE–18 CE) was an important philosopher of the Han dynasty, perhaps best known for his treatise, *Model Sayings (Fayan)*, which he wrote in imitation of the *Analects of Confucius*.

[2] Meaning that without "blocking" and "stopping" Buddhism and Daoism, Confucianism will not be able to "flow" (i.e., "be propagated") or be "practiced."

[3] Han is advocating the laicization of Buddhist and Daoist clergy.

farmhouses. Guide them by enlightening them to the Way of the former kings, and provide those who are widowers, widows, orphaned, bereft, disabled, or sick with what they need."[4] This in and of itself would make things right for the most part.[5]

Han Yu's "On the Origin of the Way" constitutes a rigorous defense of the value and significance of Confucian philosophy to Chinese society and culture. At its core, it is an argument that Han's way of understanding the Way is the right way. Reading carefully through the different sections of his essay, we discover Han's argument rests on a series of claims that link key concepts and conduct to social order and Chinese civilization—and in the end come full circle.

Han begins by defining four key terms: humaneness, righteousness, character, and the Way. His selection is strategic. In addition to being central to Confucian thought, these concepts also occupy important positions in Daoist and Buddhist discourses. Han's targeting of these terms—that is, "restoring" them to their original and commonly recognized Confucian meanings—thus represents the opening salvo in his broader assault on these alternative systems of thought.

Han's defining these terms in relation to one another is also strategic, firmly establishing the foundation for his arguments about the Way while simultaneously undermining alternative definitions and the thought systems that rely on them. For Han, humaneness defines a fundamental worldview that when enacted is called righteousness. The translation of that worldview into action is called the Way, and the capacity that individuals possess for adhering to the process of that translation (i.e., the Way) autonomously is called character. Properly understanding the Way thus involves, in part, acknowledging the inseparability of these concepts. That, Han claims, is where Daoism first fails. He suggests that Laozi viewed these four terms as mapping a movement away from the Way rather than as what they actually are—labels for different aspects of an integral whole. This, Han argues, is why Laozi's understanding is fundamentally flawed and arbitrarily idiosyncratic.

---

[4] Note the parallel that Han Yu is drawing between those who have suffered or who live with loss and those who are Buddhists. Both need to be provided with what they require: nurturing care or an education in the correct *dao*.

Han Yu likely alludes here to a passage in the *Mencius*: "These four [widowers, widows, bereft, and orphaned] are the most destitute and have no one to turn to for help. Whenever King Wen put humane measures into effect, he always gave them first consideration." (translation slightly modified from D. C. Lau, trans., *Mencius* [London: Penguin, 1970], 65).

[5] In this passage, Han Yu reiterates the definitions of key terms from his opening paragraph and elaborates on the content, value, and history of the Confucian Way. It concludes with Han advocating for the excision of Buddhism and Daoism from Chinese society. Throughout the passage, Han subtly modulates the length and pattern of phrases to underscore key points. His repetition of the phrase "*qi* X" ("their X") seven times before switching in the last two iterations to *qi wei* X (translated above as "theirs are X that are") sharpens the reader's focus on the final two lines and intimates their key significance. His phrasing in the passage delineating the transmission of the Way is similarly meaningful; the abrupt termination in its conclusion of the pattern of "what was transmitted" established in the six phrases immediately preceding mirrors the break in the transmission of the Way being described.

Han uses this critique in turn to query how faulty understandings of the Way have become the norm. He identifies three reasons. First, a series of calamities that have impeded the transmission of the correct Way. Second, the gradual perversion of Confucian concepts by exegetes seduced by rival schools of thought who seek to advance their own intellectual agendas at the expense of all others. Third, the widespread circulation of "alternative facts," which subordinate Confucius within the traditions of Daoism and Buddhism, that have been accepted and reproduced uncritically by those Han views as Confucians in name only.

Han addresses the unstated question at the end of the second section—what *is* the correct understanding of the Way?—in the third and fourth sections of his essay. He opens with a series of "that was then, this is now" comparisons that highlight how Chinese society was significantly better off before the advent of Daoism and Buddhism. Daoists and Buddhists, Han claims, are entirely parasitic, consuming what others produce while contributing, in the words of a slightly earlier contemporary, Peng Yan (fl. late-eighth century), nothing more than "dangerous teachings and deceitful words so as to befuddle the ignorant."[6] Han concludes the paragraph by claiming that the addition of Buddhists and Daoists to the traditional four social classes created an imbalance between producers and consumers. These Buddhists and Daoists, therefore, are to blame for the present ubiquity of poverty and larceny within Chinese society.

The Confucian sages by contrast taught the people the Way of living together and taking care of one another. In so doing, they ensured the survival of the people when they were in peril, and they were responsible for building Chinese society and culture—clothing, farming, architecture, tool-making, trade, medicine, burial practices, ritual, music, government, the judicial system, economics, military arts, and disaster management—from the ground up. Han's listing of the positive contributions of the sages highlights the ridiculousness of Daoist claims that blame the sages for social disorder. Without their teachings, Han responds, humans would have become extinct, lacking as they do the biological advantages (feathers, fur, scales, shells, claws, and teeth) of competing species. Han thus demonstrates the superiority of the Confucian Way over that of the Daoists and Buddhists in part by enumerating their respective positive and negative effects on Chinese civilization.

The civilization and society created by the sages, Han then claims, functions successfully because social identities correlate with social performance: rulers rule, ministers minister, farmers farm, craftsmen craft, and merchants trade (note that he makes no mention of Daoists and Buddhists, having already implied in the previous section that they add nothing constructive). Failure to fulfill the functions of one's identity has negative consequences: either loss of that identity or punishment. This highlights another problem with Daoists and Buddhists. Both Daoism and Buddhism, in Han's view, encourage their followers to abrogate their social responsibilities as part of their pursuit of self-cultivation. Han thus argues for the superiority of the Confucian Way as well by examining not just what the Way does for each person but also what the Way requires each person to do. The Confucian Way asks that individuals be responsible and contributing members of society. Buddhism by contrast encourages its followers to abandon family and friends while Daoism insists that its adherents fanatically adhere to the principle of simplicity rather than respond pragmatically to their circumstances.

The emphasis of Confucian self-cultivation on the interconnectedness between the moral life of the individual and the broader welfare of Chinese society further throws the iconoclasm of Buddhist and Daoist self-cultivation into sharp relief. Citing the *Book of Rites*, Han demonstrates that, for Confucians, the deep-rooted metamorphosis of the inner state of the individual is the foundation for family harmony, social order, and the moral transformation of the entire world. In so doing, Han draws a clear distinction between Confucian and Buddhist self-cultivation: the former strengthens social order, the latter destroys it. Han concludes this section by extending his "you are what you do" argument to culture: those who adhere to Chinese (i.e., Confucian) culture are Chinese, and those who do not are not. How then, Han asks, can those who elevate the foreign beliefs of Buddhism over the teachings of the former kings still be viewed as "Chinese"?

What are "the teachings of the former kings" anyway? Han asks exactly this question at the beginning of his concluding section. He answers immediately by repeating his definitions of humaneness, righteousness, the Way, and character verbatim, enumerating the many different places—including texts, methods, social organization and hierarchy, and material culture—where those teachings can be found, and stressing how they are comprehensible, doable, and beneficial to all aspects of one's life and afterlife.

If this Way is so easy to understand and its practice so salutary, why, one might ask, has it declined? In part, Han answers, it is because it was not (before Han Yu) transmitted after Mencius' death, and in part because those who understood it were no longer rulers who implemented its practice throughout society but rather were ministers who merely elaborated on its meaning. This latter reason is ultimately why the revitalization of Confucianism requires the purge of those other systems of thought from society. Only after their odious influence has been eliminated can Confucianism flourish once again.

In addition to being admired for its argument, Han's "On the Origin of the Way" was also revered as a masterwork of prose composition. His essay weaves together literary allusions and passages from the classics with colloquial speech and lively paralinguistic expressions ("Alas!") that render its complex, erudite, and powerful arguments readable and entertaining. Later critics especially singled out for praise the versatility and control Han Yu demonstrates over the rhythm of his prose and the overall clarity of the structure of this composition. Han deliberately employs phrases of different length to modulate the speed and force of his argument, moving from shorter to longer phrases in the beginning of sections and alternating between parallel and nonparallel clauses to both avoid repetition and underscore key arguments. His composition moreover has a clearly articulated structure, in which he lays out his thesis in the beginning, develops his argument along multiple avenues in the body, and ties everything together in a powerful concluding passage. For this reason, later critics viewed this work as a good model for aspiring students, in that its structure was entirely consistent with the principles of composition for the eight-legged essay (chap. 14).

LIU ZONGYUAN AND "DISCOURSE OF HEAVEN"

The innovative reinterpretation of the Confucian intellectual tradition demonstrated in Han Yu's "Origin of the Way" is characteristic of the mid-Tang period in which he lived and wrote. We see a similarly creative exploration of a classical concept in "Discourse of Heaven" ("Tianshuo"), an essay by Han's contemporary and colleague, Liu Zongyuan, that offers competing interpretations of how and why Heaven responds to the actions of human beings.

The genre Liu Zongyuan chose for his essay, the *shuo* ("discourse," also translated "theory," "persuasion," or simply "On . . ."), was characterized by Ming dynasty literary theorist Wu Na (1372–1457) very simply: "Discourse means . . . to lay out principles clearly and describe them in terms of your own ideas."[7] This genre existed quite early in Chinese literary history, but it became widely practiced as of the Tang, no doubt in part because of the positive reception of works such as Liu's.

Aside from Han Yu, Liu Zongyuan was the only other writer from the Tang to be included among the "Eight Great Prose Masters of the Tang and Song." As a young man, he had excellent career prospects: he came from an elite family with good connections in the capital, showed literary talent early on, passed the prestigious "Presented Scholar" (*jinshi*) examination at the tender age of twenty-one and the "Erudite Literatus" (*boxue hongci*) examination three years later. Because of his involvement with the wrong political faction, however, he was exiled in 805 and died fourteen years later in the remote southwestern city of Liuzhou, never able to return to official service in the capital. Many of his best-known writings, including records of travel and fictional biographies, were produced during his period of exile.

C10.2 Liu Zongyuan, "Discourse of Heaven" ("Tianshuo")

Han Yu spoke to Master Liu, and said, "Do you understand the Discourse of Heaven? Let me you tell you about the Discourse of Heaven. Nowadays whenever people experience an excessive degree of illness, pain, exhaustion, disgrace, hunger, or cold, they because of this look up and cry out to Heaven, saying, 'Harm the people and you thrive, help the people and you're deprived!' They then again look up and cry out to Heaven, saying, 'Why do you make me suffer to such an extreme?' Those who act like this cannot understand Heaven at all.

In general, when fruit or gourds or food or drink decay, bugs appear in it. When the vital energy (*qi*) and blood of a person declines, flows backwards, or becomes obstructed, it produces abscesses and ulcers, excrescences and bulges, fistulas and hemorrhoids, and likewise bugs appear in it. Trees[1] rot and then grubs appear inside them. Grasses[2] decompose and then fireflies fly

柳宗元 天說

韓愈謂柳子曰："若知天之說乎？吾為子言天之說。今夫人有疾痛、倦辱、饑寒甚者，因仰而呼天曰：'殘民者昌，佑民者殃。'又仰而呼天曰：'何為使至此極戾也？'若是者，舉不能知天。夫果蓏、飲食既壞，蟲生之。人之血氣敗逆壅底為癰瘍、疣贅、瘻痔，亦蟲生之。木朽而蠍中，草腐而螢飛，是豈不以壞而後出耶？物壞，蟲由

---

[1] Referring broadly to all kinds of woody plants.

[2] Referring to all varieties of herbaceous plants.

之生。元氣陰陽之壞，
人由之生。蟲之生而
物益壞，食齧之，攻
穴之，蟲之禍物也滋
甚。其有能去之者，有
功於物者也。繁而息之
者，物之讎也。人之
壞，元氣陰陽也亦滋
甚。墾原田，伐山林，
鑿泉以井飲，窾墓以送
死，而又穴為偃溲，築
為牆垣、城郭、臺榭、
觀游，疏為川瀆、溝
洫、陂池，燧木以燔，
革金以鎔，陶甄琢磨，
悴然使天地萬物不得其
情，倖倖衝衝，攻殘敗
撓而未嘗息。其為禍元
氣陰陽也，不甚於蟲之
所為乎？吾意有能殘斯
人使日薄歲削，禍元氣
陰陽者滋少，是則有功
於天地者也。蕃而息之
者，天地之讎也。今夫
人舉不能知天，故為是
呼且怨也。吾意天聞其
呼且怨，則有功者受賞
必大矣，其禍焉者受罰
亦大矣。子以吾言為何
如？」

forth from them. How is this not because things come forth only after decay takes place? Things decay and this is why bugs appear in them. The Primal Essence and Yin-and-Yang[3] decayed and this is why human beings appeared in them.

After bugs are produced, a thing decays even more as they eat it and gnaw it and dig into it and bore through it. Bugs indeed greatly exacerbate the calamity inflicted upon a thing. Whatever can get rid of them is performing meritorious service to that thing. Whatever causes them to prosper and multiply earns the enmity of that thing. Human beings similarly greatly exacerbate the decay suffered by the Primal Essence and Yin-and-Yang: plowing virgin plains and felling mountain forests, drilling underground springs in order to have wells and hollowing out tombs in order to send off the dead. Moreover: digging pits to make latrines, pounding earth to make residential walls, city fortifications, terraces, temples, and belvederes, clearing channels to make canals, irrigation ditches, ponds, and reservoirs, kindling wood to make fires, transforming metals to make molten ores for casting, firing and molding, grinding and polishing, exhausting everything, and allowing none of the myriad things of Heaven and Earth to remain true to their nature, raging and resentful, constantly charging ahead, assaulting and harming and ravaging and warping without cease. Is the calamity they inflict upon the Primal Essence and Yin-and-Yang not far greater than that done by bugs?

I imagine that if something could harm these human beings, and cause them to dwindle day by day and diminish year after year, the calamity inflicted upon the Primal Essence and Yin-and-Yang would be greatly reduced. This would then be something that is performing meritorious service for Heaven and Earth. Whatever caused human beings to prosper and multiply would earn the enmity of Heaven and Earth. Nowadays people cannot understand Heaven at all, and so they indeed do this kind of crying out and complaining. I imagine Heaven hears their cries and complaints, and then inevitably greatly rewards whatever has performed meritorious service for it, and also inevitably greatly punishes whatever has brought calamity upon it. What do you make of what I said?"

柳子曰：「子誠有激而
為是耶？則信辯且美
矣，吾能終其說。彼上
而玄者，世謂之天；下
而黃者，世謂之地。渾
然而中處者，世謂之元
氣；寒而暑者，世之謂
之陰陽。是雖大，無異
果蓏、癰痔、草木也。
假而有能去其攻穴者，
是物也，其能有報乎？

Master Liu said, "You surely came up with this after having been provoked, right? Rest assured that it is articulately argued and elegantly stated. But allow me to finish off your Discourse. The world calls that which is above and darkly mysterious "Heaven." The world calls that which is below and yellow "Earth." The world calls the undifferentiated primordial chaos that exists between them "Primal Essence." The world calls that alternation between cold and hot "Yin

---

[3] "Primal Essence" (*yuanqi*) refers to the fundamental material substance that makes up the universe and everything within it. "Yin-and-Yang" (*yin yang*) refers to the complementary but bipolar opposite positions that constitute the two extremes of any dynamic, oscillating, or cyclical process, such as growth and decay, rise and fall, heating and cooling, and so on.

and Yang." These, despite their enormity, are really no different from fruits or melons, abscesses or hemorrhoids, or grasses or trees. They are things. Even supposing there was something that could eliminate that which digs or bores [into them], how could they feel indebted? And [even supposing there was] something that could propagate and multiply them, how could they feel anger? Heaven and Earth are simply enormous fruits or melons. The Primal Essence is simply an enormous abscess or hemorrhoid, Yin and Yang are simply enormous grasses or trees. How could such things reward meritorious service or punish calamity?

Those who render meritorious service do so on their own, and those who inflict calamity do so on their own. To desire or expect to be rewarded or punished is ridiculous. Crying out and complaining out of a desire or expectation for sympathy or compassion is even more ridiculous. If you truly believe in your own sense of humaneness and righteousness, acting spontaneously in accordance with them throughout your life all the way to your death, how could you claim that life and death or success and failure are due to fruits and melons, abscesses and hemorrhoids, or grasses and trees?"

蕃而息之者，其能有怒乎？天地，大果蓏也；元氣，大癰痔也；陰陽，大草木也，其烏能賞功而罰禍乎？功者自功，禍者自禍，欲望其賞罰者，大謬矣。呼而怨，慾望其哀且仁者，愈大謬矣。子而信子之仁義以游其內，生而死爾，烏置存亡得喪於果蓏、癰痔、草木耶？"

[*LZYJJZ* 4:1089–1090]

Questions about Heaven—its origin, whether it has physical form, is bounded or limitless, and how its relation to human beings, if one exists, should be understood—have long been debated within Chinese philosophy, science, and religion. While Liu Zongyuan discusses them over the course of his various writings, his "Discourse on Heaven" focuses on this last question.

The positions taken by Han Yu and Liu Zongyuan in this essay reflect two distinct traditional conceptions of Heaven (*tian*). The first understands Heaven as a supreme power overseeing worldly affairs, one that evaluates human conduct as good or evil and dispenses reward or punishment accordingly. Han Yu twists this idea of a sentient and moral universe by redefining what constitutes "good" and "evil." From Heaven's perspective, Han argues, human beings are malevolent and destructive vermin. Moreover, those practices most closely associated with human civilization—farming and forestry, drilling and excavation, architecture and irrigation, and metallurgy and manufacture—only exacerbate the devastation humans wreak on the natural world. For Han, how Heaven responds to human beings is analogous to how human beings respond to vermin: they encourage whatever eradicates them and undermine whatever strengthens them. Given this analogy, Han concludes, appealing to Heaven to relieve one's suffering is pointless, and in fact, will only make things worse.

The second traditional conception of Heaven, and the one to which Liu Zongyuan seems to subscribe, understands Heaven as the natural order. Encompassing the myriad processes and phenomena of the physical world, this understanding views Heaven as fundamentally mechanistic; events occur spontaneously, beings act according to their respective natures, and individuals must determine for themselves whether their lives have been well lived.

Liu Zongyuan's "Discourse of Heaven" exemplifies many of the best qualities of expository prose. The two interlocutors' positions are developed clearly and logically from the opening lines through the conclusion, and shocking analogies (e.g., people as bugs in a rotting universe) are perfectly employed to both illustrate an argument and entertain the reader. Its presentation of ideas through dialogue not only makes the discussion more lively and engaging but also opens up space for its continuation (on dialogic aspects of prose, ☛ chap. 12). We see that invitation accepted by Liu Yuxi (772–842), a close friend of both Han Yu and Liu Zongyuan, in his elaborate and lengthy response, "A Disquisition on Heaven" (*Tian lun*), and by many later authors who draw on and respond to ideas expressed in "Discourse of Heaven."

SU XUN AND "DISQUISITION ON THE SIX STATES"

Finally, Su Xun's "Disquisition on the Six States" ("Liu guo lun") focuses on a historical event—that is, the destruction by the state of Qin of its six rival kingdoms at the end of the Warring States period (403–221 BCE) (☛ chap. 3, 5). This, Su argues, resulted from attempts to appease rather than resist Qin. His discussion is more than simply historical argument. Through analysis of past events, Su Xun makes a point about contemporary policies, namely that the most pragmatic response to the threat of powerful foreign neighbors is not tribute and trade, but rather the strategic and sustained use of military force.

Although the "disquisition" (*lun*) form Su employs shares many similarities with the "Discourse" genre, there are nonetheless some fundamental differences between them. Theories were comparatively unrestricted in terms of topic and style, relied on narration rather than analysis, and sought to persuade, at least in part, by eliciting a strong emotional response. Disquisitions, by contrast, stressed rational analysis and explanation, focused primarily on more "serious" topics, and sought to convince audiences through logic and the extrapolation of general principles from close study of specific cases.

Su Xun's later renown, both as the father of two of the most famous literary figures of the Song dynasty, Su Shi and Su Zhe, and as a literary giant in his own right, would have been difficult to anticipate from his early history. In his youth, he was not particularly studious, only buckling down in middle age after failing the civil service examination multiple times. After having accompanied his sons to the capital Kaifeng in 1056, the eminent literatus Ouyang Xiu personally submitted twenty-two of Su Xun's essays to the emperor to help him secure an official appointment without going through the examination system. "Disquisition on the Six States" was one of those essays.

蘇洵　六國論

六國破滅，非兵不利，
戰不善，弊在賂秦。
賂秦而力虧，破滅之道
也。

　或曰：「六國互
喪，率賂秦耶？」曰：

C10.3 Su Xun, "Disquisition on the Six States" ("Liu guo lun")

The ruination of the six states[1] was not caused by the dullness of their weapons nor their failures in battle. Their destruction lay in their appeasement of

---

[1] The six states refers to the Warring States period kingdoms of Yan (eleventh century–222 BCE), Zhao (403–228 BCE), Qi (11th eleventh –221 BCE), Chu (?–223 BCE), Han (403–230 BCE), and Wei (403–225 BCE).

Qin.[2] In appeasing Qin they diminished their strength; this was the Way of their ruination.

Someone said, "The six states were destroyed one after the other; was this entirely due to appeasing Qin?" [I] say, "Those that did not appease were destroyed by those who did appease—undoubtedly due to having lost powerful support and being incapable of remaining intact on their own. Thus I say, 'Their destruction lay in their appeasement of Qin.'" Through means other than seizure by conquest,[3] Qin at the very least would obtain towns and at most obtain cities. What Qin got [through appeasement] was a hundred-fold what it got through victory in battle, and what the feudal lords lost [through appeasement] was a hundred-fold what they lost through defeat in battle. Thus what was most desired by Qin and what was most calamitous to the feudal lords was most certainly not battle.

Now their founding forefathers endured frost and dew, and cleared brambles and brushwood to obtain a mere inch or foot of territory. Their descendants nevertheless didn't regard it as particularly worth preserving, and gave it all away to others as though they were discarding straw. This day they would carve off five cities, the next carve off ten cities, and for all that would get but a single evening of peaceful rest. When they next got up and looked to their four borders, the armies of Qin had arrived once again. It was like this because the territory possessed by the feudal lords had a limit while the desire of the rapacious Qin was insatiable. The greater the amount offered, the more pressing their aggression became, and thus [who was] powerful and weak and victor and vanquished was already settled without battle. All the way through the toppling of kingdoms, this principle remained consistent. The ancients had a saying: "Serving up land to Qin is like carrying firewood to go fight a fire; so long as the firewood doesn't run out, the fire will not be extinguished."[4] This saying gets it.

The people of Qi never tried to appease Qin, but in the end it followed the other five states in being extinguished. Why was this? Because it sided with Ying[1] and did not help the other five states. Once the five states had been destroyed, Qi for their part could not avoid it. From the start, the rulers of Yan and Zhao strategized for the long term. They were able to protect their lands and rightfully did not appease Qin. This is why Yan, despite being small, was lost only later. This is armies being used effectively. Coming to [Prince] Dan [of Yan], he

"不賂者以賂者喪，蓋失強援不能獨完，故曰‘弊在賂秦’也。"秦以攻取之外，小則獲邑，大則得城。較秦之所得，與戰勝而得者，其實百倍，諸侯之所亡，與戰敗而亡者，其實亦百倍。則秦之所大欲，諸侯之所大患，固不在戰矣。思厥先祖父，暴霜露，斬荊棘，以有尺寸之地。子孫視之不甚惜，舉以予人，如棄草芥。今日割五城，明日割十城，然後得一夕安寢。起視四境，而秦兵又至矣。然則諸侯之地有限，暴秦之欲無厭，奉之彌繁，侵之愈急，故不戰而強弱勝負已判矣。至于顛覆，理固宜然。古人云："以地事秦，猶抱薪救火，薪不盡，火不滅。"此言得之。

齊人未嘗賂秦，終繼五國遷滅，何哉？與嬴而不助五國也。五國既喪，齊亦不免矣。燕、趙之君，始有遠略，能守其土，義不賂秦。是故燕雖小國而後亡，斯用兵之效也。至丹，以荊卿為計，始速禍焉。趙嘗五戰於秦，二敗而三勝；後秦擊趙者再，李牧連卻之。洎牧以讒誅，邯鄲為郡；惜其用武而不終也。且燕、趙處秦革

---

[2] The kingdom of Qin founded the Qin dynasty (221 BCE–206 BCE) following the destruction of its rival kingdoms.

[3] In other words, through appeasement.

[4] Su is quoting from a passage in the "Hereditary House of Wei" ("Wei shijia") chapter of the *Grand's Scribes Records* (*Shiji*) in which an adviser, the wandering persuader Su Dai (third century BCE), warns the king of Wei not to give up territory to Qin.

---

[1] The surname of the Qin royal house was Ying. This refers to Qin.

滅殆盡之際，可謂智力孤危，戰敗而亡，誠不得已。向使三國各愛其地，齊人勿附於秦，刺客不行，良將猶在，則勝負之數，存亡之理，當與秦相較，或未易量。

plotted to use the assassin Jing Ke, which just hastened Yan's demise.[2] Zhao did battle with Qin five times, and was defeated twice but [was] victorious three times.[3] Afterwards Qin twice more struck against Zhao, but Li Mu over and over again forced them to retreat.[4] Later Mu was slandered and executed, and Handan became a commandery [of Qin].[5] What a pity that they used their military might but did not come to a better end.

What's more, Yan and Zhao were in a situation in which Qin was on the verge of almost completely destroying [the other states], and in terms of resources and military strength, were themselves cut off and in crisis. They were lost after their defeat in battle and truly there was nothing they could do. If earlier the three states[6] had each cherished their territory, and the people of Qi had not attached themselves to Qin, if assassins were not dispatched, and excellent generals were still present, then when they pitted their strength against Qin, the calculation of who would be victor or vanquished and the principle of who would survive or be destroyed would perhaps not have been so easily gauged.

嗚呼！以賂秦之地，封天下之謀臣；以事秦之心，禮天下之奇才，并力西嚮，則吾恐秦人食之不得下咽也。悲夫！有如此之勢，而為秦人積威之所劫，日削月割，以趨於亡，為國者無使為積威之所劫哉！

夫六國與秦皆諸侯，其勢弱於秦，而猶有可以不賂而勝之之勢；苟以天下之大，下而從六國破亡之故事，是又在六國下矣！

[JYJ 3.3B–4B]

Alas! If the territory used to appease Qin had instead been used to enfeoff the strategizing ministers of the world, and if the deferential attitude used to serve Qin was instead used to revere the extraordinary talents of the world, and if all had combined forces in opposition to the west, then I am afraid the people of Qin could not have swallowed them up. What a pity! The potential opposition [to Qin] was like this yet still [the six states] were dominated by the slowly accumulated might of the people of Qin. Pared down day after day and carved out month after month, and so tending inevitably to their own demise. Rulers, do not be intimidated by the accumulated might of others!

The [rulers of the] six states, like Qin, were all feudal lords. Their position was weaker than Qin, but they were still in a position to avoid appeasement

---

[2] In 227 BCE, Prince Dan (?–226 BCE) sent the assassin Jing Ke (227 BCE) to Qin under the pretense of surrendering territory. The assassination failed, Jing Ke was slain, and Qin launched a massive invasion of Yan in retaliation, resulting in its destruction.

[3] Su is paraphrasing the words of the wandering persuader Su Qin (?–284 BCE) as recorded in his biography in the *Grand Scribe's Records* (*Shiji*). Note that the numbers are rhetorical. The armies of Zhao and Qin engaged each other in battle far more than five times, and Zhao did not just lose twice in those engagements. The point Su is making is that victory can come about if one perseveres.

[4] Li Mu (?–229 BCE) was a skilled military commander and strategist of the state of Yan. According to the account of the "Hereditary House of Zhao" ("Zhao shijia") in the *Grand Scribe's Records*, in 233 and 234 BCE, the Qin attacked Zhao but were repeatedly defeated by Li Mu.

[5] According to the "Biography of Li Mu" in the *Grand Scribe's Records*, in 229 BCE, Qin general Wang Jian (third century BCE) was dispatched to attack Zhao, but defeated repeatedly by Li Mu. The Qin then bribed Zhao minister Guo Kai to accuse Li of plotting sedition. The king of Zhao believed Guo and sent an order relieving Li of command. Li refused to obey the order and was killed. In 228 BCE, three months after Li's death, Qin conquered Zhao, and made it into a commandery of Qin, Handan (named for the former capital of the Zhao).

[6] Referring to Han, Wei, and Chu.

and emerge victorious. Given that [our state] is as large as the world, proceeding by following the past examples that led to the destruction of the six states, is to end up being even lower than the six states.

Su Xun wrote "Disquisition of the Six States" when the Song had powerful foreign neighbors of its own—the Qidan of the Liao dynasty (907–1125) to the north and the Tanguts of the Western Xia (1038–1227) to the northwest. Both had negotiated treaties with the Song that resulted in their acquiring territory and annual "gifts" from the court. Su Xun disquisition is clearly about more than history—it is a policy paper based on insightful analysis of historical events that advocates against a practice of appeasement and for political solidarity, promotion of talented officials, and increased use of military might.

From the first paragraph, Su unequivocally places blame for the fall of the six kingdoms on the kingdoms, specifically on the policy of appeasement that three of them had pursued. He grounds his critique in a multivalent cost-benefit analysis of appeasement versus resistance, including the relative amount of territory acquired, the durability of the respite gained, whether appeasement strengthened or weakened a state over time, and the effects of one state's appeasement on another's survival. Touching on politics, economics, foreign relations, and military affairs over the course of his disquisition, his argument was viewed by contemporary and later readers as more nuanced, multifaceted, and ultimately convincing than earlier analyses.

Both of Su Xun's sons, Su Shi and Su Zhe, also wrote works titled "Disquisition on the Six States." Su Shi contended that the distinction between the longevity of the six states and the quick demise of the Qin dynasty was due to their differing treatment of talented scholar-officials (*shi*). Su Zhe argued that the six states were destroyed by Qin, despite possessing a combined territory and population several times larger, because they lacked solidarity in opposing Qin. Although aspects of these arguments can be found in Su Xun's essay, neither of the sons explicitly linked their arguments to the contemporary political scene. This is where Su Xun's essay is unique. His combination of forthrightness and penetrating analysis made Su Xun particularly acclaimed.

Roughly seven decades after the "Disquisition of the Six States" appeared in 1127, the Song capital of Bianjing (present-day Kaifeng) was ransacked by the army of the Jurchen Jin dynasty (1115–1234), which had ended the Liao dynasty the year before. Capturing Song emperor Qinzong and his son Huizong, this event marked the end of the Northern Song and the centuries-long loss of significant northern territories to non-Han rulers. Later readers are unanimous in seeing these events as confirmation of Su Xun's political acumen and prescience.

Alexei Kamran Ditter

NOTES

1. From the early Song, prose writings by these eight writers began to monopolize prose anthologies. Sixty of the sixty-two pieces included in Lü Zuqian's (1137–81) *Guwen guanjian* (*Key to Classical Prose*), for example, were written by seven of these eight authors (the exception

was Wang Anshi). The phrase "Eight Great Prose Masters of the Tang and Song" was first coined by Mao Kun (1512–1601) in his widely circulated prose anthology, *Tang Song ba da jia wen chao* (*Selected Writings of the Eight Great Prose Masters of the Tang and Song*). For a more detailed discussion of the canonization of these eight writers, see Takatsu Takashi, "The Selection of the 'Eight Great Prose Masters of the T'ang and Sung' and Chinese Society in the Sung and Later," *Acta Asiatica* 84 (2003): 1–19.

2. Vincent Shih, *The Literary Mind and the Carving of Dragons* (Hong Kong: Chinese University Press, 1983), 199–201.

3. "Prefatory Explanations to *Genres of Writing, Distinguished Clearly*," compiled by Xu Shizeng (Beijing: Renmin wenxue, 1962), 87.

4. Stephen Durrant, Wai-yee Li, and David Schaberg, trans., *Zuozhuan* (*Zuo Tradition*), 3 vols. (Seattle: University of Washington Press, 2016), 1:572–573.

5. Xie Fangde (1226–1289), *Wenzhang guifan* (*Models of Prose*), cited in *Han Yu guwen jiaozhu huiji* (*Comprehensive Collation and Annotation of the Classical Prose of Han Yu*), edited by Luo Liantian (Taibei: Guoli bianyi guan, 2003), I:1.79n67.

6. See "Biography of Peng Yan," in *Old History of the Tang* (Taipei: Dingwen, 1981), 127.3580.

7. Wu Na [1372–1457], *Wenzhang bianti xushuo* (*Explanatory Preface to Distinctions Between Genres of Writing*), edited by Guo Shaoyu (Beijing: Renmin wenxue chubanshe, 1962), 43.

SUGGESTED READING

ENGLISH

Chen, Yu-shih. *Images and Ideas in Chinese Classical Prose: Studies of Four Masters.* Stanford, CA: Stanford University Press, 1988.

Hartman, Charles. *Han Yü and the T'ang Search for Unity.* Princeton, NJ: Princeton University Press, 1986.

Hatch, George. "Su Hsun's Pragmatic Statecraft." In *Ordering the World: Approaches to State and Society in Sung Dynasty China*, edited by Robert P. Hymes and Conrad Schirokauer, 59–75. Berkeley: University of California Press, 1993.

Lamont, H. G. "An Early Ninth Century Debate on Heaven: Liu Tsung-yüan's T'ien Shuo and Liu Yü-hsi's T'ien Lun, An Annotated Translation and Introduction." *Asia Major*, n.s., Part I, 18, no. 2 (1973): 181–208; Part II, 19, no. 1 (1974): 37–85.

Liu, Shih Shun. *Chinese Classical Prose: The Eight Masters of the Tang-Song Period.* Hong Kong: Chinese University Press, 1979.

CHINESE

Feng Zhihong 馮志弘. *Bei Song guwen yundong de xingcheng* 北宋古文運動的形成 (*The Development of the Classical Prose Movement During the Northern Song*). Shanghai: Shanghai guji chubanshe, 2009.

He Jipeng 何寄澎. *Bei Song de guwen yundong* 北宋的古文運動 (*The Classical Prose Movement During the Northern Song*). Shanghai: Shanghai guji chubanshe, 2011.

Ge Xiaoyin 葛曉音. *Tang Song sanwen* 唐宋散文 (*Prose Literature of the Tang and Song*). Shanghai: Shanghai guji, 2011.

Niu Baotong 牛寶彤. *Tang Song ba da jia tonglun* 唐宋八大家通論 (*General Survey of the Eight Great Master of the Tang and Song*). Lanzhou: Gansu jiaoyu, 2016.

II

Tang and Song Occasional Prose

Accounts of Places, Things, and Events

In the Tang and Song dynasties, prose writing changed considerably from the parallel style discussed in chapter 9. It moved in the direction of becoming more flexible and personal and was less dominated by forms that tended toward the ritualistic (e.g., funerary writings) or bureaucratic (e.g., memorials, reports, drafts of decrees), although such forms and purposes continued to be used. Hand in hand with this change was a prosodic and stylistic change: parallel prose (*pianti, siliu wen, pianti wen*), that is, prose written in "couplets" of matching parallel lines, increasingly gave way to prose that did not use such parallel units as its fundamental building blocks. The alternative style was prosodically freer and less predictable, and thus it lent itself to argumentation or description that was not necessarily tied to parallel or antithetical phrases. This alternative style was often called *guwen* (ancient-style prose style) because it mimicked the prose of the Classics, the early philosophical texts, and the historiographical writing of the Han dynasty, all of which were produced before parallel prose became ascendant in the post-Han period. Naturally, parallel prose never disappeared—it was too decorous and satisfying to be abandoned. But what would come to be viewed as the mainstream of Tang and Song prose, and the style in which its signature works were cast, was that written in the *guwen* style.

This chapter focuses on the prose form named *ji* ("account" or "record"), but it also includes an example of the form *xu* ("preface"). This chapter should be read in conjunction with that by Anna Shields and Stephen H. West (☞ chap. 12) that deals with the Tang and Song letters and provides a fuller discussion of the varieties of the prefaces genre.

LIU ZONGYUAN AND THE RECORD OF OUTINGS

One of the primary prose genres of the Tang and Song is the *ji*. The basic meaning of the term, is "account" or "record," as in the *Shi ji*, the great Han dynasty *Grand Scribe's Records*. As the name of a literary genre, *ji* often designated a "record" of a building (e.g., a temple or government building) or some other monument. The *ji* would probably be engraved on stone or wood and actually be displayed somewhere in the building; in such cases, *ji* may be rendered "inscription." Typically, the composition would explain the purpose of the building and its history and give credit to the person or persons responsible for its construction, perhaps even list-ing donors, if there were any. In the hands of Tang literati, the *ji* became more per-sonal. It developed into a highly flexible form that could be used for a wide variety of intensely personal expression.

That development raises a question: how did writers' use of prose for personal rather than official or documentary purposes differ from their use of classical poetry (*shi*)? Poetry in China had always been the preeminent form for personal, lyrical expression. Prose meanwhile was rarely used in such a way, owing to its ancient roots in philosophical, ritualistic, and expository writing, and with the establishment of the empire, its use in bureaucratic and documentary forms. We know that poetry also underwent important changes in the Tang, as writ-ers "discovered" new evocative techniques that constituted what would, in time, come to be thought of as quintessential to China's poetic tradition. The personal turn of prose during the Tang is often overlooked, because the brilliance of Tang poetry tends to consume everyone's attention. Yet, as we will see in the follow-ing examples, writers did utilize prose to reflect on their personal situation and for intimate communication with friends, just the sort of purposes dominated by poetry. What prompted them to occasionally make the unexpected choice of prose over poetry, or what they could accomplish in prose form that perhaps they could not have captured in poetry, are issues that await further investigation and analysis.

Liu Zongyuan (773–819) is known in literary history as one of the eight prose masters of the Tang and Song dynasties. In his day, however, neither his stature nor his literary fame was nearly so eminent. As a young man, he had risen quickly in office at the court, but then became involved in a political faction of so-called reformers who tried to take advantage of a new emperor's ill health in 805 to assert their power and will. When this Wang Shuwen faction, named for its leader, lost its bid to seize control, its leaders, including Liu Zongyuan, were all sentenced to distant southern exiles. Liu's exile was to Yongzhou, in the southern extreme of the Tang Empire (south of modern Hunan), a land viewed at the time as semibarbar-ian. The ten years that Liu Zongyuan spent in this place marked a huge setback in his career, but the work he produced during the period ensured his later literary fame. After Yongzhou, Liu was briefly recalled to the capital, but was soon sent into an even more disagreeable exile in the distant southwest.

Liu Zongyuan's most celebrated works from Yongzhou are the eight prose pieces he wrote about his surroundings, in which he reflects on the strange land-scape and local customs he saw as he visited different landscape sites. In later cen-turies, a favorite subtype of the literary *ji* recorded such "outings" (usually just a day trip, but sometimes longer), and came to be called *youji* "record of an outing" (or excursion account). Even though most of Liu Zongyuan's eight compositions on sites in Yongzhou are not explicitly titled *youji* (only one of them is), retrospec-tively, the compositions came to be thought of as exemplars of the subgenre and inspired other writers through the centuries.

C11.1 Liu Zongyuan, "A Record of Little Stone Ramparts Hill"

柳宗元　小石城山記

Walking north from the start of West Mountain Road, after crossing Yellow Cogon Ridge, on the way down there are two paths. One goes west, but I have taken it and it leads nowhere. The other continues north and then turns slightly east. Before you go eighty meters the path ends in a stream, and at that endpoint there is an outcrop of rocks. On the top it looks like a rampart of stone, complete with pillars and beams, and to one side there is a fortification, with what looks like a doorway. I peered inside and it was completely black. I tossed a small stone in, and from the cavern came the sound of splashing water. The echoes of the splashing noise lasted several moments. Circling around, I climbed to the top, and from there could see afar. The top has no soil to speak of yet there are fine trees and lovely bamboos growing there, all unusually attractive and sturdy. The spacing and the height of the plants, which fit and complement each other so well, make it seem as if it were all planned and put there by a mind of great intelligence.

Ah! I have long wondered about the existence of the Creator. Seeing this, I was more inclined than ever to think that he must really exist. But then how to explain that he would not put such a fine spot in the central lands, but place it instead here in the barbarian borderlands, so that for thousands of years his ingenuity would never be manifest to anyone? How could he have wasted all his labor this way? If a god should not perform such useless acts, does that mean that he does not exist after all? Someone explained the matter this way: "The Creator put the hill here to console worthy gentlemen who were humiliated by being exiled to this place." Someone else had a different idea: "The divine power of the *qi* in this region does not produce great men but instead produces landscapes like this. That is why there are few noteworthy men in Chu[1] but many remarkable rock formations." But I cannot accept either of these explanations.

自西山道口徑北，踰黃
茅嶺而下，有二道，其
一西出，尋之無所得。
其一少北而東，不過四
十丈，土斷而川分，有
積石橫當其垠。其上爲
睥睨樑欐之形，其旁出
堡塢，有若門焉。窺之
正黑，投以小石，洞然
有水聲，其響之激越，
良久乃已。環之可上，
望甚遠，無土壤而生嘉
樹美箭，益奇而堅，
其疏數偃仰，類智者所
施設也。噫！吾疑造物
者之有無久矣。及是，
愈以爲誠有。又怪其不
爲之於中州，而列是夷
狄，更千百年不得一售
其伎，是固勞而無用。
神者儻不宜如是，則其
果無乎？或曰：以慰夫
賢而辱於此者。或曰：
其氣之靈，不爲偉人，
而獨爲是物，故楚之南
少人而多石。是二者，
余未信之。

[*LZYJJZ* 6.29.1934]

Liu Zongyuan proclaims himself pleased to find a delightful landscape spot hidden away but discoverable on a short walk. He then raises the question of why such a pleasant place would be located in the inhospitable and disagreeable locale of Yongzhou. This leads him to reflect on the question of the existence of the Creator—that is, a god or at least a divine power in ancient mythology. Behind the explicit meaning and driving the entire piece is the question of how Liu Zongyuan could have been exiled to such a place, and what that exile says about the existence (or nonexistence) of divine justice.

The opening paragraph is description of the spot the speaker finds unexpectedly. The various features of the landscape are found to be so "right," so aptly

---

[1] Chu is the name of the ancient southern state, and the name continued to be used in later times to designate the lands corresponding to modern Hunan.

coordinated and aptly spaced, that the speaker comes to the conclusion that such a layout of elements cannot be accidental but rather must be the result of intelligent design, that is, divine design. This leads to the reflections on the Creator that constitute the second section.

That section begins by acknowledging that the author has long had doubts about the existence of the Creator, spoken about in many ancient Chinese texts but not present in all origin stories of the universe. Thus, the author's doubts about the existence of such a god must have been widespread in his time. Why would the Creator put such a lovely place in such a remote and unattractive region? It makes no sense. If the existence of Little Stone Ramparts Hill is an argument in favor of a divine intelligence controlling the world, its location in a locale like Yongzhou is an argument against it. At this point, midway through the second paragraph, the existence of the Creator *seems* to be the main issue. But we soon understand that issue is not the author's primary concern.

Possible explanations of the contradiction are considered next and are presented as if Liu Zongyuan heard them from other people. But it seems more likely they are actually the author's attempt to settle the matter in his mind. Perhaps there really is a Creator after all, and he put this comely place here—where we would not expect to find it—to console worthy men (like himself) who do not deserve exile to such a vile region. This is one explanation that many exiles might indulge themselves imagining. It would mean that Heaven pitied such treatment by the emperor. There may be no justice in the human sphere, but there is divine commiseration and some degree of compensation. The second explanation considered is that the presence of Little Stone Ramparts Hill does *not* reflect the Creator's sympathy for virtuous exiles but instead is the result of cosmic forces. This possibility completes a dichotomy featuring two alternate visions of the cosmos: one positing a Creator, a willful yet sympathetic supreme being; while in the other, a cosmic, impersonal force (*qi*) governs the world, indifferent to humans and thus never arranging the physical world to suit their comfort or needs. In fact, it seems the cosmic forces in this strange semibarbarian land favor the creation of extraordinary rock formations over the nurturing of extraordinary men. By rejecting both explanations, Liu Zongyuan leaves his initial question unresolved. He rejects the consolation of divine commiseration (the easy answer), thereby showing his stoicism. Yet, by also rejecting the explanation of cosmic *qi*, he leaves some room for the possibility that a Creator exists after all, even if it is a Creator who does not necessarily side with worthy exiles.

The interest of the piece largely derives from how differently it may be interpreted, especially because the author is so noncommittal in the closing. But this much will probably be agreed upon by most readers: Liu is telling us that he does not understand the world or cosmos and cannot make up his mind about the existence of the Creator. He is pessimistic (almost nihilistic) about the possibility of finding answers to the question he raises. We are left with a nagging concern: if there really were a Creator, how could he have allowed Liu to be exiled to such a place? The thought that the Creator put a lovely place in a desolate region to console him or men like him is cold comfort. The composition, for all its exploratory gestures, conveys a clear sense of frustration and bitterness. The author ultimately rejects any consoling thought, and we are left with the feeling that Little Stone Ramparts Hill is being wasted in a land of such obscurity and meanness. In that sense, the lovely small haven that Liu Zongyuan has stumbled upon is an analogue for Liu. He should not find himself relegated to such a region, but he does.

HAN YU AND THE FAREWELL

A new, and interesting prose form that reached maturity during the Tang dynasty was the prose farewell (*songxu*). One example is presented and discussed here not only for its inherent fame and interest but also because it resonates with the themes of official service *versus* exile (or withdrawal), travel, and geographic displacement that are central to the *ji* writings discussed elsewhere in this chapter.

The older tradition of literary farewells involved the composition of farewell poems for a friend or relative on the eve of his departure for a journey. But many such poems required a prose preface to explain the reasons for the traveler's departure, where he was going, and in what state of mind. In time, these prose prefaces came to constitute a prose genre or subgenre in themselves, and by the High Tang no longer necessarily had a poem attached to them. Technically still called "preface" (*xu*), they now stood as an independent literary form (for a longer discussion of the *xu*, especially as preface, ☞ chap. 12). Eventually, the prose farewell took its place among the prose genres separately classified in a writer's collected writings (*wenji*). Han Yu (768–824) utilized the form quite frequently, leaving in all roughly thirty such compositions. The form would never become a major prose genre, never rival, for example, the *ji* (record), *shu* (letter), or *lun* (essay), much less the biographical-funerary form of *muzhiming*, yet its development and indeed persistence from the Tang onward attests to the niche it came to occupy in literary expression. Its development as an offshoot of the farewell poem also suggests something about the ways prose expression differs from poetry. Clearly, writers felt they could say things in prose on a friend's departure they would have found difficult to put into a farewell poem. Otherwise, how do we explain the prose "preface" to a farewell poem morphing into a form able to stand alone? The precise nature of such expressive content may be difficult to generalize today, but the following piece, with its density of meaning and unexpected twists and turns, gives a good example of the kind of statement difficult if not impossible to put in a poem.

A word about travel and parting in "middle ages" China is in order. It is not an accident that elite writing of the period is filled with farewell pieces (whether prose or poetry) and references to travel and longing for home. The educated class was very mobile, especially once they entered the imperial bureaucracy.[1] Official appointments typically consisted of two- or three-year assignments, and the majority of a dynasty's vast bureaucratic class was assigned somewhere in the provinces. That meant they not only had to leave the capital to journey to their provincial post, but also, at the end of each appointment, many had to return to the capital to await a new assignment. Moreover, some effort was made to avoid assignment to officials' native locales, to reduce nepotism and corruption in the discharging of duties. Other features of society and office-holding added to the frequency of travel, including the expectation that upon the death of one's parents one would return to the ancestral home to observe a protracted period of mourning, and the bureaucracy's custom of sending officials who had fallen out of favor or committed crimes in office into exile, sometimes to the empire's borderlands.

Han Yu, a leading figure of Tang literary and intellectual history who served in various high court positions, became a major voice in the political and intellectual debates of the day. Now remembered primarily as a poet and prose stylist, he championed a call for "return to antiquity" (fugu), a cause with both literary and ideological dimensions. One of the most visible and public manifestations of fugu values was the promotion of "ancient-style prose" writing. This meant rejecting the cultivation of a highly euphuistic prose style, often called "parallel prose," as mentioned earlier, because of its peculiar couplet structure and prosody. Han Yu's prose shuns such studied balance and elegance, prizing terseness over prolixity and abrupt, clipped phrases over florid and expansive presentations.

The following prose farewell was written for Dong Shaonan, a younger man Han Yu had gotten to know some years before, and whom Han Yu had written admiringly about. During the Yuanhe period (806–820), Dong Shaonan met Han Yu again, this time in the capital, where Dong tried unsuccessfully more than once to pass the examinations that would have allowed him to enter officialdom. At the time, men such as Dong who viewed themselves as rejected by capital elite often sought refuge with the military governors in the north, who maintained a quasi-independence from the central government. These generals welcomed to their staff disaffected men whom the central government had rebuffed. Han Yu was like many court officials eager to see the power of the northern military leaders curtailed. Dong Shaonan's decision to leave the capital for the north presented Han Yu with something of a dilemma. He sympathized with Dong Shaonan's sense of frustration, but he did not relish the prospect of seeing the younger man he admired pursue an alternative career in the northern military command. Han Yu thus uses the occasion of Dong Shaonan's departure to urge not only Dong but also other capable men like him in the north to reconsider their choices.

韓愈　送董邵南遊河北序

燕趙古稱多感慨悲歌之士。董生舉進士，連不得志於有司。懷抱利器，鬱鬱適茲土。吾知其必有合也。董生勉乎哉！夫以子之不遇時，苟慕義彊仁者皆愛惜焉。矧燕趙之士出乎其

C11.2 Han Yu, "A Prose Farewell to Dong Shaonan, Departing for North of the Yellow River"

Yan and Zhao[1] have since ancient times been known as regions where men with deep feelings express their frustrations in ardent song. Master Dong was recommended for the Presented Scholar degree[2] here in the capital. But the examining officials repeatedly prevented him from achieving his aims. Now, keeping his "sharpened blade" to himself, he is setting off for that region, filled

---

[1] Yan and Zhao were two ancient states in northern China.

[2] Presented Scholar is the name of the most prestigious degree of the civil examinations, for those "presented" to the emperor for consideration of official appointment.

with melancholy. I know he is sure to find patrons there who appreciate him. Do your best, Master Dong!

Since you have not met favor in your time, gentlemen who esteem what is right and strive to be humane will all cherish you. These traits, moreover, are inborn in the gentlemen of Yan and Zhao. Nevertheless, I have heard that local customs may change with the temper of the age. How can we be sure the region is the same today as it was in ancient times? Now that you are going there, please look into this for me. Do your best, Master Dong!

Your journey there has given me an idea: kindly go perform the mourning ritual on my behalf at the tomb of the lord of Wangzhu.[3] Go also to observe in the marketplace: is there still anyone there like the dog butcher of ancient times?[4] If so, please tell him this for me: "Today an enlightened Son of Heaven sits on the throne. You can come out of reclusion and serve!"

性者哉？然吾嘗聞：風
俗與化移易。吾惡知其
今不異於古所云邪？聊
以吾子之行卜之也。董
生勉乎哉！吾因子有所
感矣：為我弔望諸君之
墓。而觀於其市，復有
昔時屠狗者乎？為我謝
曰：明天子在上，可以
出而仕矣。

[*HYWJHJJZ* 3.10.1055]

The issue of official service—to serve or not to serve, to try to pass the civil examinations—hung over men in elite Chinese society to an extent difficult for us to appreciate today. Official service was *the* career for educated men in the Tang and other dynasties. Dong Shaonan tried and failed several times to pass the examination, the hurdle in his way to enter officialdom. One might think Han Yu, knowing Shaonan has taken the exams repeatedly without success, would accept what must have seemed obvious: that Shaonan, despite Han Yu's high opinion of him, was not fated to become an official. But Han Yu cannot let the issue rest. There was, after all, no limit to the number of times a person could sit for the exams, and other methods (e.g., recommendation, different exams) could lead to official appointment. Even older than the examination system was the imperative to enter the service of a ruler, dating at least to Confucius. Complementing that was the imperative to refuse an offer of service if it came from a ruler judged unworthy or worse. In the latter case, a good man would bide his time or even go into hiding (as a true recluse or one who "hides" himself in what was ordinarily considered an ignominious livelihood, like dog butcher). All these options, these conflicting courses and the judgments that lay behind them, were ever-present in the minds of educated men of Han Yu's time. Naturally, it was all too easy for men who failed in the examinations to console themselves with the thought that the examiners (and, by extension, the ruler who appointed them) were unworthy. Failure could readily be transformed into a self-perception of high worth—proof of merit by

---

[3] The lord of Wangzhu was the enfeoffment title of Yue Yi (third century BCE), a general of the state of Yan.

[4] "The dog butcher of ancient times" refers to Gao Jianli, another native of Yan who took up Jing Ke's cause of trying to assassinate the first emperor of Qin. He too, like Jing Ke, lost his life in the attempt. His failure in that quest is not the issue here, though. Han Yu is thinking of Gao's livelihood as a dog butcher in Yan. Gao Jianli epitomizes the man of great principles and ambitions who, unappreciated in his time, hides himself in menial life, biding his time until the opportunity to show his exceptional character presents itself.

those whose bruised egos needed such reassurance. Naturally, Han Yu was well aware of this ploy and tries to ensure that Dong Shaonan does not succumb to this temptation.

Brevity of language, an ancient prose style ideal, is taken in this passage to an extreme. The entire piece is less than two hundred characters, shorter by several times what would be expected. There is no real argumentation or reasoned exposition; reason and argument have been replaced by exhortation. Han Yu tells Shaonan: do this, do that. And he lets these injunctions concerning historical figures implicitly convey the message he wants to give: that Shaonan and others like him who have thrown their lot in with the military governors in the north have made the wrong decision. This is not an age in which withdrawal is the virtuous course. With an enlightened ruler on the throne (so Han Yu claims), this is an age in which withdrawal constitutes an unwise and even immoral decision. Reading this piece against Han Yu's "Letter in Reply to Li Yi" (☛ translated and discussed in chap. 12) suggests both certain stylistic consistencies in Han Yu's writing and shows how different the same writer may sound, in rhetorical tone and expository structure, in two different prose genres.

The piece is much admired for the cleverness with which commendation gives way to implicit but unmistakable disapproval. The opening paragraph provides the necessary background that readers, other than the recipient, would need to understand the circumstances of Shaonan's departure. With the thought that, after all, times change and local cultures along with them, the assumptions of the opening section are abruptly called into question. This is the first rhetorical sleight of hand. The implication is that the region known for producing men of valor in ancient times may not be such a land anymore. What follows is another surprise: the notion that even if principled recluses may still be found "hiding" in the north, they should be told that their reclusion is misguided in the present day. The present ruler's goodness invalidates any idea that reclusion is the only way to keep one's virtue intact. This is the second rhetorical sleight of hand. It derives from no less an authority than the Confucian *Analects*, which says that when the Way prevails in a state, a gentleman who is impoverished and lowly (because he has refused to enter the government) should be ashamed (*Analects* 8.13). With the last sentence, the turnaround from commiseration with Shaonan and approval of his decision to leave the capital to disagreement with that decision is complete. The reader, who may not have seen where the piece was going, finally understands and sees as well that Han Yu has not clearly shown his true intent until this very last sentence. To accomplish this reversal in such a short space is a *tour de force*.

FAN ZHONGYAN'S INSCRIPTION FOR YUEYANG TOWER

In the Song dynasty, prose writing of the kind examined in this chapter took a new turn. It became more personal and lyrical and was used to treat a wider range of topics and sentiments. This change is easier to notice than it is to account for. The conventional understanding is that this development is the "second act" of the ancient prose revival. It is true that Song prose masters looked back to the *fugu* prose masters of the Tang, especially Han Yu, and claimed it as their inspiration. But this alone is not a satisfactory explanation of the new modes of prose writing that were produced, because they have no real precedent in the actual ancient prose of classical times (the Warring States and Han dynasty) or in the "first act" of the ancient prose revival led by Tang writers. The innovations of the Song prose masters must be understood as being closely tied to the new language they developed, although even this is difficult to adequately pinpoint or describe. It is a language less consciously archaizing than that used by Han Yu and those he influenced. It is "toned down," less apt to call attention to itself, and consequently more supple, adaptable, and suited to a wide range of expressive purposes. A more precise and linguistic analysis of the shift from Tang to Song ancient prose in terms of vocabulary, syntax, rhythm, allusion, and other traits is a task that awaits future study and would be of great interest. To say even that Song prose is more "personal" than its counterpart in the Tang is already a tricky proposition. Personal in what way? We have seen that Liu Zongyuan could be deeply personal in his prose. Yet this impression abides, as illustrated in the following examples, especially in the last three.

Fan Zhongyan (989–1052) is known as a Northern Song dynasty official who was one of the leaders of the Qingli Reforms of the mid-1040s, an ambitious program that sought to restrict official favors and patronage but whose adoption was short-lived. Those reforms have a certain significance in Song political history. But in the larger arena of cultural history, Fan Zhongyan is remembered primarily for the next essay and, indeed, for the uplifting and powerful climactic sentence with which it concludes. This is of course something that happens in many times and cultures: a person somehow manages to come up with a single statement that captures deeply held cultural values and ideals, a statement so moving and perfectly formulated that it eclipses everything else that person ever said or, indeed, ever did. That is what happened with Fan Zhongyan and his statement about self-abnegation in the following prose piece, written in 1046.

The piece is a *ji* "inscription" written for a newly reconstructed tower on the shore of the enormous Dongting Lake in Hunan Province. To the north of the tower lies the Yangzi River and the lake stretches to the south. A tower had stood at the spot for several centuries, and the vista it provides had long attracted poets passing through Yueyang, on journeys up and down the Yangzi. (A modern reconstruction of the tower stands on the spot today, where it is still a popular tourist destination.) Fan Zhongyan's prose piece was written at the invitation of the governor of Baling, Teng Zongliang (Zijing). This man was an old friend of Fan's, someone who had passed the civil service exams with him in 1015. But Teng had run into trouble in his official career and was accused of misusing government funds, and in 1044, he was demoted and sent away from the capital to be governor of Yueyang. Fan's own reform program had been abandoned in 1045, and he too was sent off to a provincial assignment.

In other words, Teng's letter to Fan Zhongyan requesting a dedicatory inscription for the rebuilt tower was received at a time when both men were coping with setbacks in their careers and ambitions. The letter provided Fan with an opportunity to lend some encouragement to Teng in the midst of his disappointment. Yet the task also posed certain problems for Fan. Given the suspicions about Teng's misuse of government funds, Fan could hardly write about the grandeur of the building Teng had reconstructed at local government expense. Fan could have written about the grandeur of the natural setting, which is what Teng expected him to do as he implies in his letter (Teng's letter to Fan survives). Indeed, knowing that Fan had never been to Yueyang, Teng had enclosed a landscape painting with his letter of request, to help Fan envision the splendid natural setting there. But Fan chose not to write about the beauty of the landscape, or rather he chose to write about it in a way that gave it subordinate importance. This is the composition that Fan sent back to Teng:

范仲淹　岳陽樓記

慶曆四年春，滕子京謫守巴陵郡。越明年，政通人和，百廢具興，乃重修岳陽樓，增其舊制，刻唐賢今人詩賦於其上。屬予作文以記之。予觀夫巴陵勝狀，在洞庭一湖。銜遠山，吞長江，浩浩湯湯，橫無際涯，朝暉夕陰，氣象萬千，此則岳陽樓之大觀也，前人之述備矣。然則北通巫峽，南極瀟湘，遷客騷人，多會於此，覽物之情，得無異乎？　若夫霪雨霏霏，連月不開，陰風怒號，濁浪排空；日星隱耀，山岳潛形；商旅不行，檣傾楫摧；薄暮冥冥，虎嘯猿啼。登斯樓也，則有去國懷鄉，憂讒畏譏，滿目蕭然，感極而悲者矣。至若春和景明，波瀾不驚，上下天光，一碧萬頃；沙鷗翔集，錦鱗游泳；岸芷汀蘭，郁郁青青。而或

C11.3 Fan Zhongyan, "Yueyang Tower Inscription"

In the fourth year of the Qingli reign [1044], Teng Zijing was exiled as governor of Baling Prefecture. One year later, his administration was already functioning smoothly and the people were in harmony. Everything that had been abandoned was made anew. He then repaired and reconstructed Yueyang Tower, expanding the ancient structure, and engraved the poems composed there by Tang worthies and recent poets on the upper terrace. He asked me to write an inscription commemorating the new building.

The outstanding scenery of Baling is concentrated around Dongting Lake. The lake envelops distant mountains and swallows the Yangzi River. Stretching far and wide, it appears to have no shore. In the morning's sun and evening's shadows, the changing images it presents are innumerable. This is the grand view enjoyed from the top of Yueyang Tower, and it has been fully described by earlier writers. This is also a place that provides access northward to the Wu Gorges region and southward to the Xiaoxiang lands. Banished ministers and poets have often passed through this place. The sentiments they felt as they looked out over this landscape, in the midst of their distant journeys, how could they not have been exceptional?.

When heavy rains soak the land, lasting for months at a time, and dark winds howl angrily, making frothy waves reach to the skies, the sun and stars are no longer visible, and mountain peaks are obscured. Traveling merchants do not go forth, as masts are broken and oars snapped. Late in the day it is already dark, when tigers roar and gibbons cry out. Under such conditions, those who climb this tower, as they leave the capital and long for their homeland, worry about slander and fear vilification. As such a bleak and desolate landscape fills their eyes, they are overcome with emotion and truly dispirited!

When, however, spring is genial and the landscape bright, waves no longer interrupt travel, the sky and earth are awash with heavenly light, and the cyan-blue of the lake covers ten thousand hectares. Sand gulls circle in the sky, and brocaded fish dart through the waters. Angelica on the shores and thorough-wort on the islets are aromatic and deep green. Sometimes hovering mists completely vanish and bright moonlight fills a thousand miles. Moonbeams are dancing gold upon the rippled water or, when the water is still, the orb appears as a submerged jade disk. As fishermen's songs answer each other, the joy of the scene knows no bounds! Those who climb the tower under such conditions find their hearts put at ease and their spirits rejuvenated. They forget all about political favor and disgrace. As they hold the wine cup facing the breeze, their pleasure is overflowing.

Oh! I once investigated the heart of benevolent men of ancient times, and found that it differed from the two states of mind just described. How so? Benevolent men did not find pleasure in external circumstances, nor did they become dispirited over their own personal situation. When they occupied lofty positions at the court they were apprehensive about the welfare of the people; and when they resided on the banks of remote rivers and lakes they were apprehensive about the well-being of their ruler. Thus when they experienced official eminence they were apprehensive, and when they suffered demotion they were also apprehensive. When did they ever know joy? The maxim they lived by was this: "Be the first person to feel apprehension, before anyone else in the empire does; be the last person to feel joy, after everyone else in the empire does." Ah! Except for such a man, with whom could I associate?

· Written on the fifteenth day of the ninth month of the sixth year [1046].

長煙一空，皓月千里，浮光躍金，靜影沉璧，漁歌互答，此樂何極！登斯樓也，則有心曠神怡，寵辱偕忘，把酒臨風，其喜洋洋者矣。嗟夫！予嘗求古仁人之心，或異二者之爲，何哉？不以物喜，不以己悲；居廟堂之高，則憂其民；處江湖之遠，則憂其君。是進亦憂，退亦憂。然則何時而樂耶？其必曰：先天下之憂而憂，後天下之樂而樂乎。噫！微斯人，吾誰與歸？時六年九月十五日。

[FZYQJ 1.9.194–195]

A Song period source reports that when the reconstruction of the tower was finished, someone congratulated Teng Zongliang on the completion of the undertaking. Teng replied by asking what there was to congratulate. "All I want," he explained, "is to lean on the upper railing, look out, and heave a few great sighs!"[2] Whether or not this story is true, Fan Zhongyan would have known that such an emotional and self-pitying appropriation by the exiled governor of the new building he had constructed and the grand prospect it provided was all too predictable. Fan was certainly familiar with the venerable tradition of "climbing high and composing poetry," poetry that typically reflects on the grandness of the landscape and the viewer's own relative insignificance, especially during moments when his ambitions seemed to have gone awry. So Fan writes that reaction into his composition, along with its opposite, that of finding solace and joy in viewing the landscape under favorable conditions. Fan writes both of these conventional uses of the tower and its vista into his inscription, but does so only to call them both into question. What Fan advocates is an alternative to both conventional responses to the tower and its grand view. It is a response that transcends both self-pitying and self-indulgence. This must be intended as encouragement to his old friend, and a gentle admonishment to him not to be discouraged and lose sight of higher ideals. The piece may likewise be read as self-admonishment.

Just because the ending of Fan's composition undercuts the legitimacy of the two reactions previously described (being dispirited, feeling joy), one should not conclude that those sections of the essay are devoid of interest. Readers of the original will savor rich descriptions of the lake scene in rain-swept and clear weather conditions. Note that these passages are composed in "couplets" of matching lines. They might even be presented as verse:

When heavy rains soak the land,	若夫霪雨霏霏
lasting for months at a time,	連月不開
and dark winds howl angrily,	陰風怒號
making frothy waves reach to the skies,	濁浪排空
the sun and stars are no longer visible,	日星隱輝
and mountain peaks are obscured.	山岳潛形
Traveling merchants do not go forth,	商旅不行
as masts are broken and oars snapped.	檣傾楫摧
Late in the day it is already dark,	薄暮冥冥
when tigers roar and gibbons cry out.	虎嘯猿啼

It is relatively easy and hence natural to write literary Chinese in such units of metrically equivalent lines. This is true even in prose that is not written in the parallel prose style; that is, even so-called ancient-style prose sometimes slips into this mode of presentation, especially as in this descriptive passage. (Note, however, that the entire piece is not written this way, as it would be in parallel prose.) Sometimes the paired lines duplicate each other's grammar, as in the lines about the sun and stars and mountain peaks. In other places, the grammatical parallelism links couplets together, as in the line about tigers and gibbons that matches the line about masts and oars.

Readers may see an expository similarity between this composition and Han Yu's prose farewell. In both pieces, the argument turns back on itself, as the ending runs counter to what the writer seems to favor at the start. But Han Yu uses irony and indirection at his farewell's end to convey the point. There is nothing indirect or ironic about the way Fan Zhongyan undercuts the two moods atop the tower he has described. His is a disarmingly straightforward evocation of a noble transcendence of self-centeredness. This impossible-sounding ideal stands firmly in the Confucian tradition, but rarely had it been so succinctly and effectively articulated.

OUYANG XIU ON HIS ZITHERS

Ouyang Xiu (1007–1072) was a younger associate of Fan Zhongyan and would become more influential than Fan as a poet and literatus. He is known as a spokesman for the *fugu* cause of the Northern Song. But more important than any advocacy he engaged in is the large corpus of prose, in many different forms, he produced. Collectively, his writings had the effect of extending the topical range and uses of personal, even lyrical prose. A short example of his efforts is given next.

The *qin* (usually rendered as "zither" in English, or less accurately as "lute") was the most venerable of musical instruments, already associated in the time of Confucius with learning and refinement. Its sound is quiet, and it was often played alone or to an audience of a single friend. Ouyang Xiu lists the *qin* as one of his six possessions from which he took his sobriquet, the Retired Scholar of Six Solitary Things. The following account elaborates on the special affinity he has developed in his old age for one of his antique zithers.

C11.4 Ouyang Xiu, "Account of My Three Zithers"

歐陽修 三琴記

In my household there are three zithers. One is said to be a Zhang Yue zither, one a Lou Ze zither, and one a Lei family zither.[1] Their craftsmanship is excellent and their construction correct in every way, yet I cannot be sure about their reputed origins. Regardless, the important thing about a zither is how it sounds, not how old it is or who made it. The surface of my zithers all have transverse lines like those on the underside of snakes. People who know about zithers say such lines are the mark of antique zithers. It is because the lacquer only develops such lines after one hundred years, and so they are used to authenticate an instrument's age.

One of my zithers has gold inlaid studs, one has stone studs, and one has jade studs. The one with gold studs is the Zhang Yue zither, the one with stone studs the Lou Ze zither, and the one with jade studs the Lei family zither. The sound of the gold-studded instrument is full-toned and far-reaching, the sound of the stone-studded one is clear, firm, and soft, and the sound of the jade-studded one [is] harmonious and lingering. Today, anyone who owned a single one of these instruments would consider it a treasure and now I own all three of them. Nevertheless, it is only the stone-studded zither that is really suited for an old man like me. Nowadays people generally use gold, jade, or oyster shell for zither studs. When those materials are placed beside a candle at night they give a shimmering reflection. But an old man's eyes are weak, and he will find it hard to place his fingers exactly on the shimmering studs. It is only stone studs that do not reflect light, and so even when they are placed beside a candle the studs can be clearly seen against the black wood. That is why the stone-studded instrument is best for an old man like me.

Ever since I was young I disliked "the music of Zheng and Wei."[2] But I always liked zither music and am particularly fond of the minor piece "Flowing Water." Owing to the many hardships I have experienced, rushing about north and south, I have forgotten all the other zither pieces I used to know. Only "Flowing Water," that one piece, I have never forgotten, whether dreaming or

吾家三琴，其一傳為張越琴，其一傳為樓則琴，其一傳為雷氏琴。其製作皆精而有法，然不知是否。要在其聲如何，不問其古今何人作也。琴面皆有橫紋如蛇腹，世之識琴者以此為古琴，蓋其漆過百年始有斷文，用以為驗爾。其一金徽，其一石徽，其一玉徽。金徽者張越琴也，石徽者樓則琴也，玉徽者雷氏琴也。金徽其聲暢而遠，石徽其聲清實而緩，玉徽其聲和而有餘。今人有其一已足為寶，而余兼有之，然惟石徽者老人之所宜也。世人多用金玉蚌琴徽，此數物者，夜置之燭下，炫耀有光，老人目昏，視徽難準。惟石無光，置之燭下黑白分明，故為老者之所宜也。余自少不喜鄭衛，獨愛琴聲，尤愛小流水曲。平生患難，南北奔馳，琴曲率皆廢忘，獨流水一曲，夢寐不忘。今老矣，猶時時能作之。其他不過數小調弄，足以自娛。琴曲不必多學，要于自適。

---

[1] Zhang Yue, Lou Ze, and the Lei family were all famous zither makers of the Tang dynasty. In the Song dynasty, these were the Stradivarius of zither-makers, which may be why Ouyang later says he is not entirely confident about the instruments' supposed provenance.

[2] "The music of Zheng and Wei": music in the two ancient states, believed to have been licentious and immoral.

琴亦不必多藏，然業已
有之，亦不必患多而
棄也。

[*OYXQJ* 3.64.943–944]

awake. Today I am old, but am still able to play it from time to time. The other pieces I play are nothing more than little tunes. But even these are enough to give me pleasure. One need not learn a lot of zither pieces. The important thing is to enjoy what you know. One also need not possess many zithers. But since I already have these three, there is no need to worry about having too many and get rid of any of them.

The "studs" referred to in this passage are the small dots, usually twelve in number, inset on the face of a zither, marking the points along the strings the player depresses to change the musical note they produce. The studs thus function much like frets on a guitar. Naturally, the accuracy of a player's finger placement at the right spot on the strings corresponding to the spot marked by the studs is crucial to producing the exact required note.

The beauty of this piece lies in the subtlety with which Ouyang Xiu manages the transition from physical description of his three zithers to using the contrast between stone studs and those made of gold or jade to evoke different sets of priorities in life, implicitly contrasting youthful ambition and avarice with the preference for simplicity and "naturalness" that comes with old age and wisdom (here suggested by clear sightedness). Incidentally, readers of the eighteenth-century novel *The Story of the Stone* (*Honglou meng*, also known as *Dream of the Red Chamber*) will recognize this contrast. It anticipates the juxtaposition of the pairing of gold and jade with the stone and wood pairing crucial to the novel. The contrast is likewise rooted in material things, but is seamlessly extrapolated from them to more abstract qualities and human preferences.

A piece of writing like this one about a seemingly ordinary possession (but endowing it with special personal significance, even if only hinted at) anticipates in many ways the Ming and Qing period development of *xiaopin wen* (for a discussion by Yunte Huang, ☞ chap. 16). Ouyang's piece, unlike Fan Zhongyan's *ji*, is intensely personal, and that focus on the private life of the writer would become characteristic of later *xiaopin* literature.

SU SHI ON OUTINGS IN EXILE

In many people's estimate, Su Shi (Su Dongpo, 1037–1101) is the greatest writer of the Song dynasty, if not one of the premiere writers in all of Chinese history. He produced a large and varied collection of prose in addition to poetry, excelling in multiple prose genres, including the formal and informal, official and nonofficial, public and private, and on topics that are historical, philosophical, literary, and aesthetic. The sheet quantity of his prose writings is remarkable and fills eight thousand pages in a recent typeset edition. If it were all translated into English, it would easily fill twice as many pages. Aside from the more formal prose written on more conventional topics, some fifteen hundred personal letters written by him to friends and family members survive. These give unparalleled insight into his daily life and the kind of mundane circumstances we simply do not find in surviving works by earlier writers.

One kind of prose that Su Shi developed and explored is the informal account. Often called *ji* in their title, they tend to be more informal and personal than those from earlier writers. The piece translated next is an example:

C11.5 Su Shi, "Record of A Nighttime Outing to Chengtian Temple"

On the twelfth day of the tenth month of the sixth year of the Yuanfeng reign [1083], at night, I changed my clothes to get ready to sleep. Moonlight came in through my window. Delighted, I got up and walked outside. Thinking I had no one to share the pleasure with, I went to Chengtian Temple to look for Zhang Huaimin. Huaimin was also still awake, and together we strolled about in the temple's central courtyard. The ground in the courtyard looked like a pool of water, empty and bright. Aquatic grasses crisscrossed on the surface of the water. These were the shadows of the bamboo and cypress growing nearby. What night has no moon? What place has no bamboo and cypress? It's just that there are few people who have such leisure as the two of us.

Written by Su so-and-so, assistant military training commissioner of Huangzhou.

蘇軾 記承天夜遊

元豐六年十月十二日，夜，解衣欲睡，月色入戶，欣然起行。念無與樂者，遂至承天寺，尋張懷民。懷民亦未寢，相與步於中庭。庭下如積水空明，水中藻荇交橫，蓋竹柏影也。何夜無月？何處無竹柏？但少閑人如吾兩人耳！黃州團練副使蘇某書。

[*SSWJJZ* 19.71.8082]

Su Shi was in the third year of his Huangzhou exile when he wrote this. One would never guess from reading this piece the concerns Su had about his immediate and long-term future. In his third year as an exile, Su had already gone through all of the savings he had brought with him to Huangzhou (on the Yangzi River, in modern Hubei) and had begun planting rice and vegetables on an abandoned plot of land that a friend secured on his behalf. One of the most celebrated men of his time, a man who had performed brilliantly on the highest civil service exams, so brilliantly that the emperor gave him and his younger brother the honor of a special "above level" exam, it is safe to say that he never imagined he would be reduced in middle age to farming to keep himself and his family alive. Su's exile to Huangzhou was not for a set period. He had no idea when or even if he would be allowed to leave the backwater place and be restored to a position in the imperial bureaucracy. It turns out that the friend Su Shi goes to find in this prose piece, Zhang Huaimin, was also an exile to Huangzhou. This man is otherwise almost completely unknown. His only claim to fame is that Su Shi befriended him after meeting him in Huangzhou and mentioned him in this piece.

Zhang Huaimin was residing in the Chengtian Temple, where Su finds him in his nocturnal outing. In all likelihood, Huaimin was living in the Buddhist temple because it was the only place he could find temporary shelter. Political exiles often had this problem when they arrived at their place of confinement: no one wanted to be seen as befriending or helping them, because it might be politically risky to do so. Consequently, they often had difficulty finding a suitable place to live. In the year after Su Shi wrote this composition, Huaimin managed to build his own place, and Su Shi's brother, Su Zhe, wrote an inscription for it. Su Shi himself provided the name for this new residence, which may be translated as "How Joyful" (*kuaizai*).

Finding joy in the midst of exile and hardship is a major theme of Su Shi's writing during his Huangzhou and later exiles. The name that Su Shi gave to Zhang Huaimin's residence is no accident, nor is the pleasure he writes about in this short piece about a moonlit outing, when he goes to seek out his friend. There is no small irony in Su speaking of himself and Huaimin as men distinguished by their enjoyment of "leisure." Theirs was a forced leisure, the leisure of the exiled official who had been stripped of high office and responsibilities (and salary). The fact that Su signs the piece with his lowly but real official title in exile only adds to the irony of what he says about "leisure." Still, Su Shi was determined to show that he could turn the official disgrace into an occasion for personal contentment and growth.

That effort often involved a willful imagining of beauty and comfort amid what many men of his class would have considered disagreeable circumstances. A specific instance of such use of the imagination is featured in the previous piece. There is no pool of water in the temple courtyard: it is the moonlight cast on the ground (earthen or tiled) that makes it look like shimmering water. Nor is there any aquatic grass growing there: the crisscrossing pattern that Su Shi sees is, as he tells us, the moonlight shadows of the bamboo and cypress growing around the perimeter of the courtyard. Moreover, the claim that Su Shi goes on to make, that moonlit nights are *always* at hand, and that bamboo and cypress grow *everywhere* is of course not true. But in his state of mind, in which he is intent on stressing the ubiquitousness of phenomena that may be turned into simple pleasures, even in what are thought unpleasant places, if only we take the time to find the pleasures they hold, it seems plausible to him to make such claims.

Following is a second nighttime outing record by Su Shi, this one written toward the end of his life during his Hainan Island exile:

C11.6 Su Shi, "A Nighttime Outing on First Prime"

On the night of First Prime in the *jimao* year [1099], when I was at Dan'er, several old students came to visit me, saying, "On such a fine night with a bright moon, won't you, sir, come out with us for a while?" Delighted, I followed them out. We walked west of the city wall, went into monks' quarters, and then passed through small lanes. Han and tribesmen were all thrown together, and meat vendors and wine sellers were everywhere. When I got home it was already past midnight. My gate was closed and people inside were sound asleep, I could hear them snoring. I put down my walking stick and laughed. Who has gained and who has lost, after all? Someone came by and asked me what I was laughing at. I was laughing at myself. But I was also laughing at Han Yu, who said that if you do not catch a fish where you first cast a line, you should be willing to go far away to a larger body of water. He did not know that even someone who goes to the ocean need not catch a large fish.

蘇軾　書上元夜遊

己卯上元，予在儋州，有老書生數人來過，曰：「良月嘉夜，先生能一出乎？」予欣然從之，步城西，入僧舍，歷小巷，民夷雜糅，屠沽紛然。歸舍已三鼓矣。舍中掩關熟睡，已再鼾矣。放杖而笑，孰為得失？過問先生何笑，蓋自笑也。然亦笑韓退之釣魚無得，更欲遠去，不知走海者未必得大魚也。

[*SSWJJZ* 19.71.8127]

Su Shi was in his third year of exile to Hainan Island (south of the Leizhou Peninsula, off the coast of Vietnam), living in Dan'er, when he wrote this piece about a nighttime outing on First Prime (the Lantern Festival), the first full moon of the new year, in 1099. The description he gives of the outing could hardly be any more abbreviated. And yet the wording also makes it clear, terse as it is, that Su Shi was fascinated by what he saw. He calls attention to the ethnic mix of the population of Hainan ("Han and tribesmen"), but his mention of this fact carries nothing of the pejorative tone we would expect from an elite Han writer.

In fact, Su Shi makes it clear at the end of the short piece that the outing has been something of a revelation to him. He has new appreciation for what he has "gained" or "won" by being sentenced to this geographically extreme and harsh exile. And so he laughs at himself, realizing that whatever dread he had of this exile sentence was misplaced and unnecessary. But he also laughs at Han Yu, who had advised a friend that if he were unsatisfied with the "catch" he was getting when fishing locally (i.e., confined to his hometown), he should be more ambitious and go out into the world and try his luck in a larger body of water (i.e., seek to advance himself by befriending more powerful men elsewhere).[3] Su Shi had now come, through no choice of his own, to the southern ocean. But what he discovered on this night was that even there he could find satisfaction in simple and humble pleasures, such as walking through the lanes and alleys, observing the commoners enjoy themselves on a festival night.

No doubt, Su Shi had genuine admiration for the great Tang statesman and writer. But he was also fond of disagreeing with Han Yu, even gently mocking him, as we see in this passage. These two short pieces by Su Shi on nocturnal outings also make a nice contrast with the exile outing piece by Liu Zongyuan examined earlier. The reaction by Su Shi to his exile and his attitude toward the unfamiliar setting it situated him in could hardly be more different from that of the Tang literatus. That difference, given Su Shi's stature and influence, points to significant divergences between the Tang and Song periods in their literature and larger cultural history.

In their discovery of abundant interest and joy in seemingly mundane or even lowly settings, these two short records on outings by Su Shi anticipate some of the Ming–Qing writings on excursions that transform ordinary outings into accounts with great literary appeal (☞ chap. 16). It is no accident that the Ming–Qing *xiaopin wen* writers held Su Shi in such high regard: their approach to writing was informed and partly inspired by what he had done.

Ronald Egan

NOTES

1. For an excellent general study of the culture of travel in the Song dynasty, see Cong Ellen Zhang, *Transformative Journeys: Travel and Culture in Song China* (Honolulu: University of Hawai'i Press, 2011).
2. *QBZZ* 4.42.
3. "Zeng Hou Xi," in *HCLSXNJS* 1.2.141–142.

SUGGESTED READING

ENGLISH

Chen, Yu-shih. *Images and Ideas in Classical Chinese Prose: Studies of Four Masters*. Stanford, CA: Stanford University Press, 1988.

Egan, Ronald. *The Literary Works of Ou-yang Hsiu (1007–72)*. Cambridge: Cambridge University Press, 2009.

Owen, Stephen. *The End of the Chinese "Middle Ages": Essays in Mid-Tang Literary Culture*. Stanford, CA: Stanford University Press, 1996.

Zhang, Cong Ellen. *Transformative Journeys: Travel and Culture in Song China*. Honolulu: University of Hawai'i Press, 2011.

CHINESE

Chen Bixiang 陳必祥, ed. and annot. *Ouyang Xiu sanwen xuan* 歐陽修散文選 (*A Selection of Ouyang Xiu's Prose*). Hong Kong: Joint Publishing Company, 1990.

Gu Yisheng 顧易生 and Xu Cuiyu 徐粹育, ed. and annot. *Han Yu sanwen xuan* 韓愈散文選 (*A Selection of Han Yu's Prose*). Hong Kong: Joint Publishing Company, 1992.

Liu Naichang 劉乃昌 and Gao Hongkui 高洪奎, ed. and annot. *Su Shi sanwen xuan* 蘇軾散文選 (*A Selection of Su Shi's Prose*). Hong Kong: Joint Publishing Company, 1991.

12

Tang and Song Occasional Prose

Prefaces and Epistolary Writing

Among Tang and Song prose forms, prefaces (*xu*) and letters (*shu*) gave writers extraordinary stylistic and formal freedom to treat a wide range of occasions and topics. For sheer diversity, prefaces and letters reveal the inadequacy of the English term "prose" to encompass medieval Chinese literary genres: as we will see, such texts not were only profoundly lyrical in their expression and imagery but also employed a variety of metrical and rhythmic patterns. Prefaces and letters had important social dimensions as well and spoke to audiences varying in size and intimacy. Both forms became increasingly popular and influential among Tang and Song literati because of political and cultural changes, in particular the flourishing of the Chinese bureaucracy from the Tang onward and the accelerated spread of book culture and printing in the Northern Song.

Broadly speaking, the most common types of preface before the Tang were introductions or paratexts to literary works and pieces connected to celebrations, such as a banquet or farewell feast at which poems were often composed (for a discussion of this form, ☛ chap. 10). As we saw in the famous introduction for the poems of the Lanting Pavilion gathering, early medieval writers had long enjoyed crafting prefaces for small verse collections, in which they could describe a social event with its setting, participants, and individual contributions. Such texts tended to be brief and often circulated separately from the occasion's other compositions. Prefaces accompanying poetry collections, anthologies, or anecdote compilations commonly discussed the goals of the work, motives of its authors, the contents, and the principles of selection or organization. Although these prefaces to literary works could circulate separately (and often were preserved in a writer's collection), they also were attached to the larger work and became associated with it. Both types of prefaces so flourished and proliferated during the Tang dynasty that the early Northern Song literary anthology *Brilliant Blossoms from the Literary Garden* (*Wenyuan yinghua*) established seven "preface" subcategories for its more than six hundred selections. Thousands more survive in the *Complete Tang Prose* (*Quan Tang wen*). While imperial and princely courts remained the center of literary culture, banquet and farewell prefaces continued in popularity. But as collecting and circulating practices became decentralized in the second half of the Tang, shifting to smaller circles and more personal spaces, we begin to see more prefaces for literary works in writers' corpora, particularly prefaces composed for friends. With the blossoming of print culture in the Northern Song and a concomitant new interest in books as commodities and repositories of knowledge, writers became increasingly interested in creating new styles and forms of prefaces, postfaces, colophons, and other "notes" to works they had compiled, edited, and published.

Although from at least the Han dynasty onward letters had been an important genre of elite prose, used for communication, philosophical discourse, and personal expression, it was only in the Tang and Song dynasties that letter writing emerged as a prominent social, material, and literary practice. The communicative dimension of letters was essential to high officials whose careers took them all over China, to new posts and sometimes into exile. Letters were used to sustain social and political networks and offered literati a venue to explore challenging intellectual issues at length and in many different formal and informal registers. At the same time, letters allowed for self-expression and emotional dialogue, thus capturing a writer's intimate feelings. Because the letter was the medieval prose form with the greatest stylistic and formal latitude, innovative writers such as Han Yu, Liu Zongyuan, Su Shi, and Ouyang Xiu pushed its boundaries far beyond their predecessors. With the rise of printing in the Song, the letters of the most famous writers could now be regularly printed and sold. Moreover, writers began to draw finer distinctions between formal letters and private, informal communications (*shujian*) and published the two types separately. More than any other medieval prose form, the letter exploited an implicit awareness of public and private audiences, the sense that a writer was speaking directly to one addressee yet mindful of a wider reading public.

Prefaces and letters also explored the possibilities of self-representation in subtle ways. In prefaces to small verse collections or larger literary works, such as the two discussed next, the author had to explain the social event prompting the texts or their contents, the raison d'être of the work, the talents (or perhaps deficiencies) of the author or compiler, and the attractions the work might hold for future readers. Sometimes theoretical and lofty in tone, these explanations often revealed the author's personal relationship to the work as well. As we see in Li Qingzhao's preface, Song dynasty writers in particular expanded medieval conventions of the preface by incorporating more of their personal experiences and by reflecting on quotidian objects and practices, such as games. As dialogic texts, letters—even when ostensibly instructive—required the writer to disclose his or her own position on an issue, sometimes with passion. In two of the examples in this chapter, we also see how letters could be performative in nature: the letters by Han Yu and Su Zhe discussing language and its relationship to one's *qi* were written as demonstrations of powerful, supple writing to their recipients, not mere discourses on the topic. Finally, both prefaces and letters required the writer to simultaneously negotiate multiple social relationships: between writer and immediate addressee (whether another work's author or a letter's recipient), writer and text, and writer and the wider readership, present and future. Li Qingzhao's preface reveals how a writer could negotiate her gender identity in a preface by simultaneously explaining her relationship to the subject, a requirement of the preface form, and offering a learned, sophisticated overview of its history, presenting herself as an erudite in a traditionally masculine mode. Both prefaces and letters could be used for advertising: the preface vaunted the merits of its accompanying text as well as proving the author's own talent; letters showcased a writer's skill in self-presentation. These social dimensions of Tang and Song prefaces and letters lent them, at their best, a dynamic, compelling quality that endures today.

PREFACES FROM THE TANG AND SOUTHERN SONG

Although we usually translate the term for the literary genre *xu* as "preface" in English, the verbal meaning of the word is "to put in order" and from that a nominalized meaning of "in order of precedence"; another meaning, often used to gloss the term for the prose genre, is "recount" or "give an account of" (*xu*). Both are relevant to the scope of the prose preface: it preceded the main text or texts (postfaces, *houxu*, also became popular in the Song), and it provided an account of the circumstances of the main texts' composition. Prefaces created overlapping explanatory frames for the events they described or texts they accompanied, helping the reader appreciate the temporal, seasonal, historical, personal, and literary contexts in which a work was composed. Writers of prefaces also carefully positioned themselves in relation to the accompanying text. If they were not the principal authors, their role was to praise those who were and to promote the text to potential readers; if the preface-writers were the authors of the main text, they sought to explain their goals precisely but humbly, in a self-deprecatory manner that would provoke the reader's interest in the text. Prefaces could sometimes be polemical, taking a stance in a political or literary debate, for example, or offering a corrective to contemporary views. As noted, they could adopt any prose style, from elaborate parallel prose with ornamental, highly allusive language to unadorned, simple prose. In this respect, prefaces gave writers room to experiment and dazzle readers with their skill.

In 731, Tang writer Li Bai (701–762) went on a springtime outing with his younger cousins to "Peach Blossom Garden," in present-day Henan. Although he had already gained some recognition for a few of his daring, youthful works, he had not yet risen to the emperor's notice at the Tang capital of Chang'an, as he would a decade later. In this preface to the event and its poems (which no longer survive), Li Bai expresses the carpe diem sensibility of many similar compositions on banquets, from the Wei dynasty through the Southern dynasties, and updates them in his own style.

C12.1 Li Bai, "Preface to the Spring Feast at Peach Blossom Garden with My Younger Cousins"[1]

Heaven and earth are but the guesthouse for the myriad phenomena—the sun and moon, the passing travelers for hundreds of generations. Yet this floating life is like a dream; how long do we have to make merry? The ancients "seized

李白　春夜宴諸從弟桃
花園序

夫天地者，萬物之逆
旅也；光陰者，百

代之過客也。而浮生
若夢，為歡幾何？ 古人
秉燭夜游，良有以也。
況陽春召我以煙景，大
塊假 我以 文章。會桃
花之芳園，序天倫之樂
事！群季俊秀，皆為惠
連。吾人詠歌，獨慚康
樂。幽賞未已，高談轉
清。開瓊筵以坐花，飛
羽觴而醉月，不有詠，
何伸雅懷？ 如詩不成，
罰依金谷酒數。

[*LBQJJZHSJP* 8:4139]

N.B. Straight underline
indicates the use of repetitive
patterning; wavy underline the
use of parallel phrasing therein.
For a discussion on repetitive
and parallel patterning,
☛ C1.1–4 and C1.6–7. Of the
twenty four lines in this text,
eleven (46 percent) are four-
character lines and eight
(33 percent) are six-character
lines. An addition of one
extra character creates two
variants of the two basic line
types: five-character lines and
seven-character lines. These
paralleled parts make up
33 percent of the lines in
this text.

a candle to roam at night," and how right they were![1] The warm spring tempts me even more with misty scenes, and the Great Clod [of earth] provides me with literary composition. As we are gathered here in the fragrant garden of peach blossoms, I recount our shared familial delights. In the superbly flourishing talent of this group of younger cousins, each and every one is a Xie [Huilian]; in my songs and praise, I alone am shamed before the Duke of Kangle [Xie Lingyun].[2] My unseen admiration had yet to end, before our lofty discourses turned towards the pure. We unroll our jeweled mats to sit among flowers, let fly our feathered beakers to drink beneath the moon; if we did not have our compositions, how could we prolong our refined feelings? If the poems are not finished, the punishments shall be levied according to the number of cups in the Golden Valley.[3]

This "feast" was surely modest—the fact that the company included thirty-year-old Li Bai and his younger cousins, with apparently no patron present, suggests that it could not have been much more than a pleasant spring picnic. Yet the echoes of earlier texts on palatial banquets resound in almost every line, and Li Bai borrows them to glorify his account of their outing. He opens grandly, invoking the vastness of Heaven and earth and the passage of time marked by sun and moon as a frame for the inevitable realization of life's brevity. He then incorporates a series of famous reflections on this theme: alluding to letters by the first Wei emperor Cao Pi to his friend Wu Zhi reminiscing on their outings in the imperial gardens; quoting a phrase from one of the "Nineteen Old Poems" of the Han that urged readers to "seize a candle and go roaming at night" in the face of ephemeral human life; and referencing the fabled extravagant feasts at the estate of Western Jin magnate Shi Chong, at his Golden Valley Garden, for which Shi Chong had composed a preface that described the drinking penalties for failure to compose poems. Finally, Li Bai flatters his younger cousins by likening them to Eastern Jin poet Xie Huilian, known for his precocious talent. By self-deprecatingly balking at the comparison, he then assumes the mantle of the greater poet,

---

[1] Li Bai refers to "seizing a candle and roaming at night," a phrase from #15 of the "Nineteen Old Poems" and also quotes from a letter lamenting the passage of time by Cao Pi (187–226), Emperor Wen of the Wei, in his first "Letter to Wu Zhi."

[2] Xie Huilian (407–433) was the younger cousin of aristocratic poet Xie Lingyun (385–433), duke of Kangle. Both Xies were acclaimed for their poetry. Xie Huilian was known for his literary talent from his youth (*SS* 53.1525).

[3] Golden Valley Garden was the estate of Western Jin aristocrat Shi Chong (249–300), known for his extravagance, and the site of many elaborate gatherings at which literati would compose poems. Shi Chong composed a preface for a collection of such poems, which stated that the penalty for failing to compose a poem was to drink three *dou* (6.5 quarts) of wine. For a translation of Shi Chong's preface, see David Knechtges, "Estate Culture in Early Medieval China," in *Early Medieval China: A Sourcebook*, edited by Wendy Swartz, Robert Ford Campany, Yang Lu, and Jessey Jiun-Chyi Choo (New York: Columbia University Press, 2014), 530–537.

Xie Lingyun, Huilian's older cousin. Li Bai's rhetoric dresses the gathering in the finest of literary clothing.

In terms of mood, the "Peach Blossom Spring" in the title suggests to readers that it will be about the passage of time. As described in Jin dynasty poet Tao Qian's story, "Spring" was a place where entire generations of people had escaped the vicissitudes of war to live in perfect peace with an agricultural order based on the flow of nature, a utopia free from historical time. The opening of the preface sets the mechanism of the cosmological order in play: the constant disappearance and recreation of materiality ("the myriad phenomena") within the flux of time. Li Bai reminds us that humans, like other objects, are but temporary phenomena, shaped by the creator of things and passing through spaces of the material world like travelers lodging for a moment at the inn of the universe. In this life like a floating dream, pleasures are few and far between, but the best of all unite family and subject in a moment of literary expression. Each gathering is marked by specific seasonal conditions, as when springtime turns the world into a misty scene of beauty, thus awakening in the writer the pain that beauty and impermanence, coupled together, create in the receptive mind. But that "Great Clod," the unseen force behind the creation of matter, also tempts writers through their talent in *wenzhang* and makes them write. The writing then shifts back to the social world of the preface to recreate the context of communion with friends and family. To do so, it enlists stories of the past that mingle drinking, writing, and good cheer, and places the present moment back in time where its mirror image occurs. Li Bai suggests that these repetitions over historical time of such meetings and literary compositions give us a way to resist, through the endurance of writing, the inexorable flow of the cosmos.

As a demonstration of Li Bai's mastery of the literary tradition, the preface highlights his ability to synthesize images and phrases coherently, rather than merely inserting them into his prose. This work showcases Li Bai's metrical skills, alternating four-word phrases with longer six-word phrases in a balanced, supple flow. As a promising talent with great ambition, Li Bai would have seen this text as a prime addition to his literary portfolio, to be circulated among the wealthy and prominent men he hoped to cultivate. Without the poems other writers presumably composed on the occasion, we cannot know how well they achieved the elegant tone Li Bai summons, but the preface nonetheless remains intelligible as an independent work. In the case of prefaces to surviving volumes or collections, however, the relationship between a preface's rhetoric and that of its accompanying text could be more complex.

One example of this complexity can be found in the preface to a remembrance of the Northern Song capital Bianliang (modern Kaifeng), written by a northern writer, Meng Yuanlao, after he was driven to the southern city of Hangzhou. The text, *Dreaming a Dream of Splendors Past: The Eastern Capital* (*Dongjing meng Hua lu*), was written to unite the large expatriate community in Hangzhou, forced to emigrate by the Jurchen invasions of 1125–1126. It is the first of the so-called capital journals, descriptions of the large urban centers that served as capitals in the Northern and Southern Song, as well as those of later dynasties. The mood of earlier Song journals was always one of nostalgia, framing moments in the city as scenes interweaving the materiality of urban life, the myriad sensations evoked, and the activities of small social groups into a narrative not of linear flow, but like a series of *tableau vivant* distilling the impressions of that life. Overwhelming in the variety of foods, entertainment, social behavior, ritual, and mercantilism, each journal also captured the linguistic register and argot of place, a lexicon less of high culture than of a daily life marked by a fully developed system of excessive consumption and display of wealth in the material symbols of the good life: food, clothing, conveyances, gambling, theater, and other diversions.

The text was completed in 1147, when the knowledge collectively held by that community was disappearing along with the older generation. This was a gesture to recreate, through remembrance, the bond between all those who self-identified as "people of the capital" (*duren*) and to keep the memory of the city alive as well. The preface to *Dreaming a Dream of Splendors Past*, written in a mixture of demotic *guwen* and parallel prose, stays true to Meng's stated intention to keep it simple for "everyone, high or low, to understand."

孟元老　東京夢華錄序

僕從先人宦遊南北，崇
寧癸未到京師，卜居於
州西金梁橋西夾道之
南。漸次長立，正當輦
轂之下。太平日久，人
物繁阜。垂髫之童，但
習鼓舞；班白之老，不
識干戈。時節相次，各
有觀賞。燈宵月夕，雪
際花時，乞巧登高，教
池游苑。舉目則青樓畫
閣，繡戶珠簾。

雕車競駐於天街，
寶馬爭馳於御路，金翠
耀目，羅綺飄香。新聲
巧笑於柳陌花衢，按管
調弦於茶坊酒肆。八荒
爭湊，萬國咸通。集四
海之珍奇，皆歸市易；
會寰區之異味，悉在
庖厨。花光滿路，何限
春遊；簫鼓喧空，幾家

C12.2 Meng Yuanlao, Hermit of the Hidden Thoroughwort, "Preface to *A Record of Dreaming a Dream of Splendors Past in the Eastern Capital*"

I followed my late father[1] on his official travels north and south. In the year *guiwei* of the Chongning reign period [1103], we arrived at the capital city and sited our residence in the western part of the prefecture, west of the Jinliang Bridge and south of a road that ran along [the Bian River] where, by and by, I grew up,[2] right beneath the hub of the imperial chariot.

> Peace stretched on day after day,
> people were numerous, things abundant;
> youths with trailing locks
>   practiced naught but drumming and dancing,
> the aged with white speckled hair
>   knew neither shield nor spear.
> Season and festival followed one upon the other,
> each with its own sights to enjoy:
> lamplit nights there were and moonlit eves,
> intervals of snow and periods of blossoming,

[1] On Meng's father, see Kong Xianyi, "Meng Yuanlao qi ren," *Lishi yanjiu*, no. 4 (1980): 143–148; and Stephen H. West, "The Interpretation of a Dream: The Sources, Evaluation, and Influence of the *Dongjing meng Hua lu*," *T'oung Pao* 71 (1985): 63–108.

[2] Jinliang Bridge, the fourth bridge up the Bian River from the central Bridge of Dragon's Ford, which accommodated the Imperial Way.

times to seek skills or ascend heights,

    to roam in the training reservoir and garden.[3]

Raise the eyes and there were

    green bowers and painted chambers,

    embroidered gates and pearly shades.

Decorated chariots vied to park in the Heavenly Avenue,

bejeweled horses competed to spur through the Imperial Street.

Gold and kingfisher green dazzled the eye,

silky cloth and silken gauze let float their perfumes.

New songs and sly giggles were found in the willowy lanes and flowered paths,

pipes were played and strings were harmonized in the tea districts and wine wards.[4]

The eight wilds strived to assemble in Bianliang,

    the myriad states were all in communication.

Gathered were

the valued and the rare from the four seas—

    all found their way to market for trade.

Assembled were

extraordinary flavors of the whole world—

    all were in the kitchens of Bianliang.[5]

The radiance of flowers filled the roads—

    what limit to spring excursions?

Pipes and drums throbbed in the empty air—

    how many households held nighttime feasts?

The skills and crafts—

    they startled a person's eyes and ears;

The waste and extravagance—

    they prolonged a person's inner spirit.

---

[3] Lamplit nights refers to the Lantern Festival of the First Prime, the fifteenth day of the first civil month. The Mid-Autumn Festival of which moon viewing was part. "Twelfth Month" refers to feasts of the rich to celebrate snowfalls and hold competitions in which lions and other beasts were sculpted in snow and ice. "Times of blossom": spring tours through the famous gardens of Bianliang's suburbs to view flowering plants and trees. "Beseeching skills": the festival of the seventh day of the seventh month, when young women asked Heaven to grant them the distaff skills. "Climbing the heights": the festival of the ninth day of the ninth month, noted for its appreciation of chrysanthemums, wine, and picnic outings, part of which included ascending heights. "Training reservoir": festivals of the third month held at the Reservoir of Metal's Luster and the Garden of the Chalcedony Grove, where units of the imperial army put on an annual spectacle for the emperor to be shared with the citizens of Kaifeng.

[4] The pleasure precincts of Kaifeng: brothels, theaters, wine houses, and restaurants that were found scattered throughout the capital.

[5] A truly astounding array of foodstuffs is found in the text. Other works on the capital give extensive, if somewhat fanciful lists of goods, foodstuffs, and other items imported into the capital for luxury consumption.

夜宴。伎巧則驚人耳目，侈奢則長人精神。瞻天表則元夕教池，拜郊孟享。頻觀公主下降，皇子納妃。修造則創建明堂，冶鑄則立成鼎鼐。觀妓籍則府曹衙罷，內省宴回；看變化則舉子唱名，武人換授。僕數十年爛賞疊游，莫知厭足。一旦兵火，靖康丙午之明年，出京南來，避地江左。情緒牢落，漸入桑榆。暗想當年，節物風流，人情和美，但成悵恨。近與親戚會面，談及曩昔，後生往往妄生不然。僕恐浸久，論其風俗者，失於事實，成為可惜。謹省記編次成集，庶幾開卷得睹當時之盛。古人有夢遊華胥之國，其樂無涯者，僕今追念，回首悵然，豈非華胥之夢覺哉？目之曰《夢華錄》。然以京師之浩穰，及有未嘗經從處，得之於人，不無遺闕。倘遇鄉黨宿德，補綴周備，不勝幸甚。此錄語言鄙俚，不以文飾者，蓋欲上下通曉爾，觀者幸詳焉。紹興丁卯歲除日，幽蘭居士孟元老序。²

[*DJMHLJZ* 1:1–6]

N.B. Straight underline indicates the use of repetitive patterning; wavy underline the use of parallel phrasing therein. For a discussion on repetitive and parallel patterning, ☛ C1.1–4 and C1.6–7. Of the eighty-seven lines in this text, forty-eight (55 percent) are four-character lines and seven (8 percent) are six-character lines. An addition of one extra character creates two variants of the two basic line types: five-character lines and seven-character lines. Paralleled parts make up 41 percent of the lines in this text.

To look upon the Heavenly countenance there were

the events of Prime Eve and the training reservoir,[6]
the Suburban Sacrifices and the Ancestral Rites of the First [Days of the Quarters].[7]

Time after time we observed

imperial princesses being handed down in marriage
and august princes receiving their consorts.[8]

As for refurbishing and construction,

there was the raising of the Bright Hall;[9]

As for casting and molding,

there was the creation of the Great Cauldrons.[10]

As for observing the registry of the sing-song girls:

[they performed] on the days off of the sub-functionaries of [Kaifeng] Superior Prefecture
and at feasts in the Inner Councils.[11]

As for looking at changes and transformations,[12]

there were the calling out of names of recommended scholars[13]
and the evaluation of military men to receive a command.[14]

For ten years I thoroughly enjoyed [these sights] and roamed often [through the city], yet I never grew tired of it. Then one morning came the first of war

---

[6] The two major public appearances by the emperor, the first full moon of the year, Prime Eve, and the opening of the Reservoir of Metal's Luster in the third month.

[7] Ancestral sacrifices held in the first month of each quarter. These were performed at the Grand Temple (*Taimiao*) Eastern and Western Palaces of Grand Noumenality (*Jingling dong, xi gong*).

[8] Wedding ceremonies of princes and princesses.

[9] A site, near the emperor's residence, symbolic of dynastic legitimacy, and in which the emperor personally performed such ceremonies as the comprehensive sacrifice to the former kings (*daxiang*), symbolically implemented executive commands and moral teachings (*buzheng*), fêted officials, and performed seasonal sacrifices.

[10] Nine *ding* cast by Song emperor Huizong and placed in the Palace of Nine Completions, where they were filled with the "earth and water" (*shuitu*) of the eight directions, and then housed in separate enclosures.

[11] Entertainers were subject to a form of corveé, called "summons to official service" (*huan guan shen*), which took precedence over any other performance.

[12] "Changes and transformations" is adopted from the lexicon of Buddhism, where it is particularly used to describe the change from a prior form to a new one; it is frequently used for the avatars of Buddhas and bodhisattvas. Here it is used to refer to the sudden transformation, the "rags to riches" scenario of passing the examinations and being admitted to the fraternity of the elite.

[13] The practice of the emperor himself calling out the names of the successful candidates and awarding them their degree. According to the *Origin of Events and Things*, a Song text on the sources of institutions and names, the practice was begun by Song emperor Taizong.

[14] Literally "to exchange and bestow" positions (*huanshou*), a system of direct appointment in which a person's qualities were assessed by superiors to transfer them to a new position. It appears in the Song to have been used mainly for military persons, for bureaucratic ranks below the Nine Grade system, and for members of the imperial bureaucracy.

and in the next year, year *bingwu* of the Jiankang reign period [1126], I went out of the capital and came south to this haven on the left side of the Yangtze.

My emotions despondent and fallen,
by and by [the sun] sets into the mulberry and elm,
and as I silently recall those years—
the style and sophistication of seasonal things,
the gentleness and comeliness of human feelings—
they become only disconsolance and vexation.

In recent times, when meeting with kith and kin, as the discussions turned back to former days, the younger born constantly fancied what was never so. I feared that, as time went by, those who would discuss the customs and traditions [of the capital] would be at a loss for hard fact—and this was truly lamentable. I have carefully recalled [what I know] and put it all in order to make this collection. I would hope that, as soon as one opens a chapter, one can see the flourishing of that time.

Among the ancients was one who dreamed of roaming in the land of Hua Xu[15] where his pleasures knew no bounds. Now, when I trace my own thoughts back to that time and then turn my head back to the present in disappointment—is this not awakening from the dream of Hua Xu? I have entitled this work *A Record of Dreaming a Dream of Splendors Past*. But from all of that widespread bustle in the capital, of all those places I myself never ventured but only heard of from others, there cannot but be omissions. If an older, more virtuous man of my home village should be met who can supplement this record and thus bring it fullness and completeness, then that would be to my good fortune.

That the language of this record is coarse and vulgar and that it is not adorned by literary style is because I wanted everyone, high or low, to understand it. Reader, please take careful note of this!

Prefaced on the last day of the year *dingmao* of the Shaoxing reign period [February 1, 1147] by the Hermit of the Hidden Thoroughwort, Meng Yuanlao.

Meng Yuanlao's preface offers us a dazzling portal into the book that follows, not only explaining the context of its composition but also transporting us to the events of that time. He hints at how high ritual and imperial power are reduced to street theater and set against the pleasures of food, sex, and entertainment available to

---

[15] A reference to the dream journey of the mythical Yellow Emperor through the Land of Hua Xu, where there was no ruler and where people lived without desire, completely at ease with their lives. Because they did not fear death nor contend for things out of desire, they lived in a world where there was no hatred or struggle for self-benefit. When the Yellow Emperor awoke from his dream, he became aware that the Way could not be sought through passion. Hua Xu thus becomes a standard trope for a utopian paradise. See *Book of Lieh Tzu*, translated by A. C. Graham (London: Butler and Tanner, 1960), 34–35; and Zhou Shaoxian, *Liezi yaoyi* (Taipei: Zhonghua shuju, 1983), 158–159.

commoners with no hierarchy but material quality. As the first expression of an urban class of consumers focused on everyday pleasures, it is also recognizable as a portrait of a developing commercial, proto-capitalistic society.

Portions of this translation are set in poetic lines to reflect the careful prosody and tonal patterning of the four- and six-character lines of parallel prose. Contrasts in tonal pitch and rhyme or semi-rhyme make the lines read more like free verse than prose. Such lyric passages punctuate the otherwise descriptive portions of the text and mark emotional moments in the act of recollection. They reveal both Meng Yuanlao's inner state and his imagination as he summons these rich scenes to mind and reimagines them in his own writing. The first part of the parallel section functions as an expressive table of contents outlining the highlights of the ten chapters of *Dreaming a Dream of Splendors Past* while simultaneously emphasizing the exorbitant material splendor of a capital now under alien rule. Meng's own sense of loss is palpable in the last section of parallel prose, in which he laments not only the lost places and activities but also the sense of community and sociality that infused them.

This last section of subjective expression is foreshadowed by the rather subdued line, "I never grew tired of it." English translation is hard pressed to fully render *yanzu* ("get tired of") as it contains both a sense of insatiability (the impossibility of ever getting enough) and, at the same time, of never growing tired of something. This incisive reflection serves as a linguistic trip switch between the material splendor so fondly described—the colors, fragrances, clothing, foods—to the feelings of disconsolate loss and sadness that follow. In contrast to the lavish descriptions throughout the work, Meng expresses muted self-criticism, of himself as well as of his community, suggesting that material obsession, casually indulged, eventually brings tragedy. This old trope that desire must be contained, so central to Chinese writing, also allows us to read Meng's note of caution to later generations somewhat differently. It is not simply their lack of experience and consequent misunderstanding of an earlier time in the capital he sought to remedy; he wanted also to warn against the unbridled desire for material wealth and comfort, still so much a part of his generation's memory, he knew could only end badly.

The prefaces by Li Bai and Meng Yuanlao, though conceived for vastly different occasions and purposes, share some key themes and rhetorical techniques. Time and its passage are evident in both texts: Li Bai draws on layers of historical time to frame his simple gathering as a reenactment of a long and venerated literary tradition; Meng Yuanlao, hoping to preserve the splendors of the Northern Song capital for future readers, plumbs the recent past for vivid, meaningful detail to draw readers into the emotive power of his recollections. The two prefaces also share a delight in social gatherings and their literary commemoration. But what of the social life that occurred beyond the realm of public life or men's intimate circles—could those be documented in prefaces or other forms and be composed by women? We have few portraits of women's social and literary exchange from the Tang and Song dynasties, but the work of Song dynasty writer Li Qingzhao (1084– ca. 1155), the most famous woman author in Chinese history, preserves a few rare glimpses of pursuits elite women enjoyed outside the public realm, particularly in her "Preface to a Handbook for 'Capture the Horse'."[3] Although best known for her compositions in the "song lyric" (*ci*) form of poetry, Li Qingzhao's corpus preserves a few remarkable prose pieces, including her autobiographical postface (*houxu*) to the *Catalogue of Inscriptions on Metal and Stone* by her husband Zhao Mingcheng (1081–1129), an essay on song lyrics, a letter, and the "Preface to a Handbook." Like Meng Yuanlao, Li Qingzhao lived through the devastation of the Jurchen conquest of northern China, and she suffered painful financial and personal losses, including the death of her husband, in the flight south and its aftermath.

In her surviving prose pieces, Li Qingzhao reflects on the ongoing Song political crises, discusses book collecting and antiquarianism, and displays her formidable skills at literary composition and her knowledge of games. Each extant text reveals different facets of her erudition, mastery of literary style, and critical judgment. In addition to being one among few extant pieces of literary prose by Song women, the "Preface to a Handbook for 'Capture the Horse' " is unusual among Tang and Song prefaces for its subject matter—a game that was at the time played largely by women, in the "women's quarters" (*guifang*)—and for its technical expertise. Li Qingzhao revealed this expertise in other pieces on the same game, including the "Rhapsody on 'Capture the Horse' " and a series of thirteen brief poems on the game's different strategies and outcomes.

Games had long been serious business in China, the training ground for strategic thinking in warfare as well as a form of male social bonding and entertainment. Games played by women, however, left little trace in the literary record before the rise of women's writing in the late-imperial period. In Li Qingzhao's preface, written to accompany a handbook that is now lost (for a game we can reconstruct only in outline), Li Qingzhao launches a strong defense of "Capture the Horse" as an activity requiring "refined skill" and the "Resident Scholar of Yi'an" (her adopted sobriquet) as a consummate player.[4] Unlike the prefaces by Li Bai and Meng Yuanlao, which reinforce social bonds among living participants of a shared culture, Li Qingzhao's preface features only herself in conversation with the historical tradition and with the actual game. More personal details, such as when and where she played the game, and with whom, remain unstated.

C12.3 Li Qingzhao, "Preface to a Handbook for 'Capture the Horse' "

"Insight leads to penetrating understanding, and with penetrating understanding there is nothing to which the mind cannot reach";[1] concentration leads to refined skill, and with refined skill everything one does will be at a level of marvelous excellence. Therefore, whether it be Cook Ding's carving of oxen, the man of Ying's wielding of the ax, the hearing of Musician Kuang, the eyesight of Lilou, matters of such great import as the humaneness of Yao

李清照 打馬圖經序

慧則通，通即無所不達；專則精，精即無所不妙。故庖丁之解牛，郢人之運斤，師曠之聽，離婁之視，大至於堯舜之仁，桀紂之惡，小至於擲豆起蠅，巾角拂棋，皆臻至理者何？妙而已。後世之人，不

---

[1] Quoting from Ling Xuan's (first century BCE) preface to the unofficial biography of the Han empress Zhao Feiyan. Li Qingzhao is quoting from an early defense of male interest in a formidable (and beautiful) woman.

惟學聖人之道不到聖
處，雖嬉戲之事，亦不
得其依稀彷彿而遂止者
多矣。夫博者，無他，
爭先術耳，故專者能
之。予性喜博，凡所謂
博者皆耽之，晝夜每忘
寢食。且平生多寡未嘗
不進者何？精而已。

自南渡來，流離遷
徙，盡散博具，故罕為
之，然實未嘗忘於胸中
也。今年冬十月朔，聞
淮上警報，江浙之人，
自東走西，自南走北，
居山林者謀入城市，居
城市者謀入山林，旁午
絡繹，莫不失所。易安
居士亦自臨安泝流，涉
嚴灘之險，抵金華，卜
居陳氏第。乍釋舟楫而
見軒窗，意頗適然。更
長燭明，奈此良夜何。
於是博奕之事講矣。

且長行、葉子、博
塞、彈棋，近世無傳。
若打揭、大小豬窩、族
鬼、胡畫、數倉、賭快
之類，皆鄙俚不經見。
藏酒、摴蒲、雙蠻融，
近漸廢絕。選仙、加
減、插關火，質魯任
命，無所施人智巧。
大小象戲、奕棋，又
惟可容二人。獨采選、
打馬，特為閨房雅戲。
嘗恨采選叢繁，勞於檢
閱，故能通者少，難遇
勍敵。打馬簡要，而苦
無文采。

按打馬世有二種：一
種一將十馬者，謂之
"關西馬"；一種無將

and Shun or the wickedness of Jie and Zhou, or matters of such little import as throwing beans and catching flies or moving chess pieces with the corner of a handkerchief, they all arrived at the ultimate principle of things.[2] Why? Because each attained marvelous excellence at what he did. But as for people of later ages, not only did they fail to reach the level of the sages in their learning of the sagely Way, even in amusements and games, most of them gave up their cultivation before ever achieving even a semblance of what earlier men had achieved. Now, board games can be reduced to this: techniques for striving to win. Anyone who gives them his concentration can master them. By nature, I am fond of board games. I can lose myself in any of them so that I can play all night long without thought of food or sleep. My whole life I have won most of the contests I have played. Why? Because of level of refined skill.

Since crossing the Yangzi River southward, I have been separated from loved ones and forced to wander here and there. I have seen my board games lost and scattered, and so seldom have I had any chance to play. But in my heart I have never forgotten them. This year on the first day of the tenth month, winter, we heard that military emergencies were reported on the Huai River. Those who lived in the Yangzi River and Zhe River regions fled westward from the east and northward from the south. Those who live in the hills and forests made plans to flee into cities, while those who live in cities made plans to flee to hills and forests. In this protracted flight, with everyone hurrying this way and that, ultimately there was no one who was not displaced. I myself, the Resident Scholar of Yi'an, traveled upstream from Lin'an. I crossed the river amid the high terrain of Yan Rapids and proceeded to Jinhua, where I found a place to live in the home of the Chen family. Having recently exchanged the comforts of verandas and windows for the hardships of boat and oar, I feel quite content. But "the night watches are slow and the lamp burns bright"[3]—how can I pass the long night? So I resolved to write an account of board games.

Now, Long Walk, Leaves, Borderlands, and Pellets, these games are no longer known. Strike and Lift, Big and Little Pigpen, Ghost Clans, Barbarian Drawings, Storehouse of Numbers, and Fast Bets, these kinds of game are vulgar and not often seen. Storing Ale, Clutch the Reed, and Double Alert have been abandoned and forgotten in recent times. Pick the Immortal, Add and Take Away, and Insert the Flame are simple, dull games that depend on luck and leave no room for people to apply their knowledge or ingenuity. Large and Small Ivories and Weiqi can only be played by two persons at a time. It is only Selecting Colors and Capture the Horse that can be considered elegant games of the women's inner quarters. But I dislike how complicated Selecting Colors is, requiring so much looking up. Few people can really master it, and so it is

---

[2] The references are to legendary figures known for their mastery of crafts, or virtuous or benighted rulers. Cao Pi was said to have used his handkerchief to flip the playing pieces in the game Pellet Chess.

[3] The line quoted is from a poem by Du Fu.

difficult to find an able opponent. Capture the Horse, by contrast, is simple and straightforward, although it is somewhat lacking in color and style.

I note that there are two versions of Capture the Horse. One version uses one general and ten horses. It is known as Horses West of the Passes. The other version has no general but uses twenty horses. This one is known as Horses by the Handbook. Having been around for a long time, both versions have handbooks and rules that can be consulted. The two have some different moves, rewards, and punishments. There is also another version developed during the Xuanhe reign period [1119–1125] that uses two types of horses in different quantities. This version depends more on luck, and the ancient flavor of the game is completely lost. It is known as Xuanhe Horses. The version I like is Horses by the Handbook. Here, I have made estimates of some scenarios for reward and punishment, and have composed a few lines on each one, which are appended to each of the named arrangement of the pieces on the board. And I have had a youngster draw a diagram of each. This work may be transmitted not only to players of the game, but also to other interested persons so that a million generations hence everyone who hears of Capture the Horse will know that writings about the game began with the Resident Scholar Yi'an.

The twenty-fourth day of the eleventh month of the fourth year of the Shaoxing period [1134], by Lady Yi'an.

二十馬者，謂之"依經馬。"流行既久，各有圖經凡例可考；行移賞罰，互有同異。又宣和間人取二種馬，參雜加減，大約交加僥倖，古意盡矣。所謂"宣和馬"者是也。予獨愛"依經馬"因取其賞罰互度，每事作數語，隨事附見，使兒輩圖之。不獨施之博徒，實足貽諸好事，使千萬世後知命辭打馬，始自易安居士也。

時紹興四年十一月二十四日，易安室序。[5]

[*LQZJJZ* 366–381]

By opening with a history of "refined skills" attributed to famous figures of antiquity, Li Qingzhao makes her ambitions clear from the outset: although she later defines Capture the Horse modestly as an "elegant game of the women's quarters," over the course of the essay, she teases out multiple layers of meaning, depicting it as an index of cultural knowledge, an emblem of the many losses endured in the collapse of the Northern Song, and a test of her own intelligence and literary refinement. Capture the Horse becomes a world in miniature, and the "Resident Scholar of Yi'an"—a name that elides Li's sex—its master. As we saw in Li Bai's preface, the broad historical and cultural panorama that sets the stage slowly tightens to focus on Li as consummate player, although one bereft of worthy opponents, and finally to the game's rules and stratagems, which she apparently documented in the handbook.

Gender plays a significant if implicit role here: throughout the text, Li exploits the contrast between the martial, masculine character of Capture the Horse and its status as a women's game, and between her own skill as a combatant ("my whole life I have won most of the contests I have played") and the military defeat of the Song forces. But Li defines her identity through her cultural achievements rather than by gender. In fact, her closing claim—that she is the creator of a new literary topos for which she will be known to "other interested persons . . . a million generations hence"—is among the oldest in the Chinese literary tradition, the desire to have one's name live into the future through literary writing, one that Li Bai and Meng Yuanlao certainly shared. Even though Li Qingzhao is often prized as a "woman writer," her own stated ambitions echoed those of most writers, regardless of gender, in Chinese history. Each of these three prefaces stands as an independent, indelible portrait of a speaking subject grounded in a particular time and place.

LITERARY SELF-REPRESENTATION IN TANG AND SONG LETTERS

Letters that survive from the Han and early medieval period are generally formal rather than personal in nature (☛ chap. 6). Although extant Tang and Song letters retain something of that formality, we begin to discover a broader spectrum of style, tone, and register as intellectual and literary matters are deliberately interwoven with personal interests and feelings. Used to create and maintain social bonds over time and space, letters by nature also depict those bonds. As writers sought to communicate knowledge through letters, they also revealed much about themselves—both to their intended readers and to those with whom the letters were shared (or, by the Song, those who bought and read volumes of letters). This combination of instruction and self-disclosure could be intimate or showily formal, as the next three letters demonstrate. Whatever the tone or register, though, the first-person voice of letters created a rhetorical space of authenticity and trust, giving readers the sense of the writer's sincerity in expressing his or her mind. Nonetheless, social positioning remained extremely important in medieval Chinese letters: writers used specific terms of address, and formal or intimate references, to clearly define their relationship to the addressee. As we see in these letters, negotiating power in a social relationship—whether adopting a humble posture, creating an inviting, friendly tone, or even taking a bold stance before the mighty—was a central rather than peripheral goal of epistolary communication. Although Tang and Song letters were often preserved in literary collections without their social frames (the opening and closing remarks), these elements of the text often encoded essential information about the underlying social bond and the larger goals of the exchange.[6]

In a letter to his friend Pei Di, High Tang writer Wang Wei (699–761) writes with simple lyricism, enticing his friend to join him in the tranquil beauty of the mountains near his estate on the Wang River (roughly thirty miles south of the capital Chang'an), where they had once spent much time together, traveling the landscape and composing verse. The two men were already known for their matching poems, composed on Wang's estate, that circulated in a small compilation as the *Wang River Collection* (*Wang chuan ji*). In that collection, Wang and Pei matched quatrains on twenty specific sites. As Pauline Yu has noted, the set as a whole reveals consistent features of Wang's literary style and interests: "the same transcendence of temporal distinctions, the awareness of boundlessness, the emphasis on perceptual and cognitive limitations, and . . . a sense of the harmony of man and nature."[7] The same features can be seen in Wang's letter to Pei: the season is slowly turning to spring, and Wang evokes the transition from current chill to future warmth seamlessly in two sections of the letter. He roams the landscape and uses what he observes to bring even distant phenomena into view. He closes with an appeal to his friend's keen ability to comprehend such experiences, suggesting this pleasure can be fully realized only if shared.

C12.4 Wang Wei, "Letter Sent to Illustrious Talent Pei Di from Wang Wei in the Mountains"

王維　山中與裴秀才迪書

As we approach the end of the year, the air and scenery are mild and limpid, when the mountains are especially worth visiting. Right now you are studying, and I do not dare bother you. So I went off to the mountains, rested at Huagan Temple,[1] where I ate dinner with the monks and left. To the north I reached the dark waters of the Ba, where the clear moon shone on the walls. At night I climbed Huazi Ridge, and the ripples of the Wang River bobbed up and down with the moonlight. There were distant fires in the cold mountains that flickered beyond the woods; barking of cold dogs in the deep lanes sounded like panthers. In the deserted village, the nighttime pestle-pounding mixed with faint sounds of bells.

As I sat alone, the servant boys all still and silent, I reflected long on bygone days, when we clasped hands and composed poetry, treading the narrow paths, peering over the clear flows. Now I wait for spring, when grasses and trees will begin to sprout, and the spring mountains draw my gaze; silvery minnows will leap from the water, and white gulls spread their wings; dew will soak the green hillocks, and pheasants call from mounds of grain. Since spring is not very far off, perhaps you might come wander with me? If it weren't for your keen and subtle disposition, how could I invite you here for such an inconsequential matter? Yet there is a profound pleasure in all this that you should not miss. Because the cork-hauler is about to leave [with this letter], I do not say all here. Wang Wei from amid the mountains writes you.[2]

Wang Wei's letter resembles his poetry in its simple style and calm tone, transparent in every feature of the prose text. The vocabulary is plain and unadorned, no obvious allusions or historical references; the grammar is equally simple, with one direct question ("could you not join me?") and one gentle rhetorical question that also flatters his friend ("if you weren't the kind of person you are, why else would I invite you?") to close out the letter. Metrically, the pace is measured and even, dominated by four-word phrases describing the action and contemplation of the scenes—both those Wang has visited and recounts for his friend, and the anticipated scenes he imagines will tempt Pei Di's visit. The long phrases concluding the letter are intended as the closing arguments in Wang's strenuous appeal. Final lines explaining why a letter must end—in this case, because the carrier was about to leave—were standard epistolary convention. Here a letter between friends did not require elaborate rhetoric or an elevated style (often the case), but with the picturesque touch of cork-hauler packing up, Wang Wei recreates in the letter the very

近臘月下，景氣和暢，故山殊可過。足下方溫經，猥不敢相煩，輒便往山中，憩感配寺，與山僧飯訖而去。北涉玄灞，清月映郭。夜登華子岡，輞水淪漣，與月上下；寒山遠火，明滅林外；深巷寒犬，吠聲如豹‧；村墟夜春，復與疏鐘相間。此時獨坐，僮僕靜默，多思曩昔，攜手賦詩，步仄徑，臨清流也。當待春中，草木蔓發，春山可望，輕鰷出水，白鷗矯翼，露濕青皋，麥隴朝雊，斯之不遠，倘能從我遊乎？非子天機清妙者，豈能以此不急之務相邀，然是中有深趣矣，無忽。因馱黃蘗人往，不一。山中人王維白。8

[WWJJZ 3: 929–930]

---

[1] The original reads Ganpei Temple, but several commentators suggest that this should be Huagan Temple, close to Wang's estate, which he mentions in other poems.

[2] For an elegant translation of this letter, consulted here, see Paul Rouzer, *The Poetry and Prose of Wang Wei*, vol. 2 (Berlin: De Gruyter, 2020), 240—241.

atmosphere he hoped they would enjoy together. As an exchange between friends, the text's simplicity also hints at the depth and length of their friendship: Pei Di knew all these places well, and Wang Wei needed only mention details to prompt shared happy memories.

Wang Wei's letter shows us that the precise nature of the relationship between letter-writer and recipient influenced many literary choices within the text. The following example from mid-Tang writer Han Yu (768–824) to a student seeking his advice reflects an unequal, more distant and formal relationship, with its different style and register choices stemming from both the social relationship and the specific topic under discussion, namely, how to cultivate one's literary writing. The topic of literary composition had long been a prominent subject of learned letters in medieval China, and the formal and stylistic freedom of the letter gave writers room to self-consciously experiment while "writing about writing" as well as to expound on literary standards. The fundamental self-referentiality of epistolary writing was heightened in letters on literature: writers performed literary values as they described them. Han Yu acted as a teacher and mentor to many in his circle and was sought out by young men seeking to master the literary skills needed to pass the civil service examinations and gain office. In some letters to those supplicants, Han Yu was repressive and unrevealing, but in this reply to Li Yi, one of his most famous statements on writing, he decided to discuss his personal experience in cultivating his literary writing as a way to instruct the young man. Throughout his life, Han Yu was an innovative, pathbreaking writer who advocated a process of learning and self-cultivation to produce original work. As he describes it to Student Li, the challenge he personally struggled with was creating work that was powerful and original, grounded in the Way of the ancient sages yet not imitative or derivative. In his letter, Han Yu first assesses the sincerity of Li's motives; then describes the stages of his process of literary development; and, finally, reflects on whether, in the end, his process is of benefit to anyone but himself.

韓愈　答李翊書

六月二十六日，愈白。李生足下：生之書辭甚高，而其問何下而恭也。能如是，誰不欲告生以其道？道德之歸也有日矣，況其外之文乎？抑愈所謂望孔子之門墻而不入於其宮者，焉足以知是且非邪？雖然，不可不為生言之。

生所謂"立言"者，是也；生所為者與所期者，甚似而幾矣。抑不

C12.5 Han Yu, "Letter in Reply to Li Yi"

On the twenty-sixth of the sixth month [of 801], Han Yu writes to Master Li: The words you have written me are lofty, and how respectful is your inquiry! Since you can be like this, who could not wish to inform you of his Way? Your turning to the Way and virtue is imminent, and even more so its external manifestation in writing. Since I am like one who has gazed on Confucius's gate and walls but not entered into his hall,[1] how can I be sure I know what is correct and incorrect? And yet I must speak of these things for you.

What you said about "establishing oneself through words" is correct, and there is little gap between what you intended and what you achieved. Or perhaps I am not sure if your resolve is to seek to surpass others, or to be recognized by others [for your writing]? Or do you seek to emulate the ancients who established themselves through words? If you seek to surpass others and

[1] Referring to *Analects* 19.23.

be recognized, then you have certainly done so; but if you seek to emulate the ancients who established themselves through words, then you should not anticipate a quick completion or be tempted by power or profit. [As with a plant,] you should nourish its roots and wait for it to fruit; [or like a lamp,] add lard to it and wait for its glow. When the roots are strong, the fruit will follow; when the lard is rich, the flame's glow will be brilliant. The words of a humane and correct person are of gentle allure.

Or perhaps there are still other difficulties. In terms of what I have accomplished, I am not certain if I have attained it or not, yet I have studied it for more than twenty years. At the beginning, I did not dare to read anything that was not from the Xia, Shang, Zhou, or the two Han dynasties, nor did I keep anything that did not preserve the commitments of the sages. At home, it was as if I had forgotten something; when I went out, it was though I had lost something. I was serious as though I was constantly reflecting; I was dazed as though I had lost my way. But in what I seized from within and poured out through my brush, I labored only to eliminate stale words—the difficulty was indeed that challenging! When others looked at my work, I did not understand that their smiling criticism was actually mockery. I went on like this for years without change; only after a long time did I recognize the true and the false in the works of the ancients, as well as that which was correct but not perfect; in all these, the white luminously split from the black. And I worked to eliminate the false and imperfect, thus slowly making some progress.

And then what I took from my heart to pour out through my hands came like a gushing torrent. When I showed my work to others, if they laughed, I was pleased, and if they praised it, I was anxious, taking it to mean that there was something still there about which people could form differing opinions. Only after going on like this for years did it become a surging flood. Yet I feared there were still impurities in my work, so I took it up and examined it critically, scrutinizing it with a calm mind, and if it was pure in every sense, only then did I release it. And yet still I needed to nurture it, and enact it on the path of humaneness and rightness, letting it roam freely in the spring of the Classics, never confusing its path, never severing its sources to the end of my life.

Qi is water, and language is a floating thing. When water is full, things will float on it no matter how large or small. The relation between *qi* and language is the same: when *qi* is full within, then the length or brevity of one's words and the pitch of one's tones will all be fitting. Even though this is true, how could I dare claim to be close to completion? Even if I were close to completion, if my writings were to be recognized, what would others gain from it? However, is not waiting to be used like being a mere tool, where being used or not depends on others? The superior person is not like this. In settling his heart, he follows the Way, in his conduct, he has measure; when he is employed, he spreads this to others, and when not employed, he transmits it to his followers, handing it down through writing to become a model for later generations. But is

知生之志：蘄勝於人而取於人邪？將蘄至於古之立言者邪？蘄勝於人而取於人，則固勝於人而可取於人矣！將蘄至於古之立言者，則無望其速成，無誘於勢利，養其根而俟其實，加其膏而希其光。根之茂者其實遂，膏之沃者其光曄。仁義之人，其言藹如也。

抑又有難者。愈之所為，不自知其至猶未也；雖然，學之二十餘年矣。始者，非三代兩漢之書不敢觀，非聖人之志不敢存。處若忘，行若遺，儼乎其若思，茫乎其若迷。當其取於心而注於手也，惟陳言之務去，戛戛乎其難哉！其觀於人，不知其非笑之為非笑也。如是者亦有年，猶不改。然後識古書之正偽，與雖正而不至焉者，昭昭然白黑分矣，而務去之，乃徐有得也。

當其取於心而注於手也，汩汩然來矣。其觀於人也，笑之則以為喜，譽之則以為憂，以其猶有人之說者存也。如是者亦有年，然後浩乎其沛然矣。吾又懼其雜也，迎而距之，平心而察之，其皆醇也，然後肆焉。雖然，不可以不養也，行之乎仁義之途，游之乎詩書之源，無迷其途，無絕其源，終吾身而已矣。

氣，水也；言，浮
物也。水大而物之浮者
大小畢浮。氣之與言猶
是也，氣盛則言之短長
與聲之高下者皆宜。雖
如是，其敢自謂幾於成
乎？雖幾於成，其用於
人也奚取焉？雖然，待
用於人者，其肖於器
邪？用與舍屬諸人。君
子則不然。處心有道，
行己有方，用則施諸
人，舍則傳諸其徒，垂
諸文而為後世法。如是
者，其亦足樂乎？其無
足樂也？

有志乎古者希矣，志
乎古必遺乎今。吾誠樂
而悲之。亟稱其人，所
以勸之，非敢褒其可
褒而貶其可貶也。問於
愈者多矣，念生之言不
志乎利，聊相為言之。
愈白。

[*HYGWJZHJ* 1:712–727]

this something to delight in, or is it not? There are few whose resolve is set on antiquity, and those who set their resolve on antiquity are sure to be neglected in the present. I truly delight in and yet also grieve at this. I often praise such people to encourage them; it is not that I would dare just praise what is praiseworthy or fault what is worth faulting. There are indeed many who inquire of me, but because your words are not set on profit, I have tentatively spoken of this to you. Han Yu writes you.[9]

The social roles these two men occupied—Li Yi the aspiring examination candidate and Han Yu the sage (though still young) mentor—are essential to understanding some of the twists and turns of this letter. For Li to win high office, he had to be recognized for his literary talents in the civil service examination, particularly the *jinshi*, "Presented Scholar" examination. Han Yu by this time had served as an instructor in the College of the Four Gates at the Directorate of Education, the academy for training elites for the examinations in Chang'an, and he had become known as someone who could spot and promote talented young men. But Han Yu's letter to Li Yi quickly moves past the frames of their social relationship and the quest for office, redirecting the young man toward the true topic under discussion: how to cultivate one's literary writing. Unsurprisingly, Han Yu opens with a somewhat-skeptical tone about the young man's motives—one senses that he had been burned before by self-serving young men seeking his advice—asking him, in effect, "Are you seeking my advice for career advancement or are you willing to take the hard road?" The path Han Yu recommends has no sure profit (i.e., office) or a fixed duration, as he goes on to explain. But his metaphors of ripening fruit and overflowing oil in a lamp suggest the inevitability and also the brilliance of the transformation that will result from this training.

Han Yu's process of cultivating his literary talent is grounded in the foundational image of "full-flowing *qi*" from *Mencius* 2A.2. As in Mencius's case, for Han Yu, having this flood-like *qi* was a necessary part of being good at language (or "understanding discourse," *zhiyan*). But Han Yu does not begin by discussing *qi*; he begins by recounting his youthful efforts to read and internalize the work of the sages, by which he means the classics, the ancient histories, and the masters such as Confucius and Mencius. Internalizing these works cannot mean simply quoting them, and in fact, Han Yu describes one critical stage of this process as eliminating "stale words," or the repeated language of the past. "Establishing oneself through words" must involve original, creative composition. In Han Yu's account of his process, even with years of reading, good writing came slowly and painfully, each stage a constant struggle of production and revision. For Han Yu, producing good writing was not merely a skill, or an expedient way to a career—it meant creating work with moral and ethical power: "And yet still I needed to nurture it, and enact it on the path of humaneness and rightness, letting it roam freely in the spring of the Classics, never confusing its path, never severing its sources to the end of my life."

Han Yu's simplest, most powerful metaphor for writing describes the relationship between *qi* and language as comparable to water and things that float upon it.

One's *qi* has to be cultivated through reading and study to become "full," for only then will language float naturally and responsively upon it. But like Confucius, quoted in the Mencius discussion of "full-flowing *qi*," Han Yu refutes the notion that he has "achieved" or perfected himself. He also raises the question of the "use" of this talent, suggesting that even the framework of being used or employed is an inadequate conception of this process and its goals. The writing of a "superior person" (the *junzi*) should be morally transformative, not merely talented or showy: "In settling his heart, he follows the Way, in his conduct, he has measure; when he is employed, he spreads this to others, and when not employed, he transmits it to his followers, handing it down through writing to become a model for later generations." Perhaps somewhat unexpectedly, Han Yu ends with the possibility that those whose "resolve is set on antiquity" are doomed to be unemployed, because they do not merely seek to enrich themselves. The radical reorientation he lays out for Li Yi comes with neither timeline nor guarantees.

In terms of epistolary craft, Han Yu's letter demonstrates an extraordinary range of literary techniques. A master of the rhetorical question in his prose, Han often used it repeatedly to emphasize a point for his addressees—and sometimes to keep them in their place. He deploys rhetorical questions to probe the genuineness of Li Yi's motives at the outset; later in the letter, he uses another to set up his counterintuitive conclusion of the failure of those who love antiquity to find employment: "But is this something to delight in, or is it not?" Such questions keep the sense of dialogue alive in the letter, sustaining an ongoing debate. Han Yu also had a sensitive ear for sentence and paragraph structure, varying his long, hypotactic sentences with briefer phrases. His images of fruit, lamp, and *qi* as water are strengthened by their brevity—expressed in short, forceful sentences—and their simple familiarity. Although the Mencius passage is the obvious backdrop for the discussion of *qi* and language, Han Yu evokes it through phrases like "torrent" and "surging flood" rather than discussing or quoting it directly. In this way, he embodies the very method he is teaching Li Yi: he internalizes the works of antiquity through years of study, hones his craft through trial and error, and then produces new literary works. As advice from a mentor, it is challenging stuff. Han Yu depicts his progress in evocative but unspecific terms, and we can imagine that the recipient of this letter might have been confused about how to put it into practice. We do not know if Li Yi succeeded in the end according to Han Yu's standards, rather than the world's: Han Yu went on to recommend him along with nine other students to Lu San (748?–802), the assistant to the chief examiner Quan Deyu (759–818) in 802, and Li Yi passed the *jinshi* that year. Han's annoyed second letter to Li Yi (composed some months later), however, suggests that Li Yi was ultimately interested in self-advancement, and thereafter we hear no more of him. No record of Li Yi's response or his progress on this difficult path remains.

We have many more exchanges that survive from the Song dynasty, including letters between mentors and supplicating juniors. During this period, officials worked to reform the examination system and decrease its emphasis on literary craft as a criterion for success, but those reforms were only slowly adopted, and aspiring young men still tried to hone their literary skills for the examinations, and sought out influential mentors and patrons to assist them. The following letter is a bold, even audacious attempt by a young man to impress a superior. Su Zhe, the letter-writer, was a youth of nineteen *sui* from Sichuan who had recently arrived in the capital along with his brother Su Shi (☞ chap. 9, 10), where the two had passed the *jinshi* examination in 1057, with Su Shi at the top of the list, and Su Zhe just behind. But where Su Shi had been sponsored by the esteemed official Ouyang Xiu, Su Zhe had not made as great a splash. In the following letter, he writes to promote himself to Han Qi (1008–1075), then one of the three highest-ranked officials at the Song court, a renowned general in charge of the country's military affairs with long experience in the border regions. Although it had no immediate effect on Su Zhe's career (the mother of the Su brothers also passed away shortly after this letter was submitted, requiring them to return to Sichuan for two and a half years of mourning), the letter survives as a daring, imaginative gambit. It also reveals the influence of Han Yu's concept of the relation of *qi* to literary writing. Like other literati associated with the ancient-style prose movement of the mid-eleventh century, the Su brothers (and their father, Su Xun, 1009–1066), were great admirers of the mid-Tang writers associated with Han Yu and knew their works well. But where Han Yu explained his development as a writer to an aspiring student, Su Zhe reverses the roles and gives Han Qi an account of his explorations in the empire and in the capital that "broadened" his viewpoint and nourished his *qi* so that he could master literary composition in the manner of the ancients.

蘇轍　上樞密韓太尉書

太尉執事：轍生好為
文，思之至深，以為文
者氣之所形。然文不可
以學而　能，氣可以養
而致。孟子曰：「我善
養吾浩然之氣。」今觀
其文章，寬厚宏博，充
乎天地之間，稱其氣之
小大。太史公行天下，
周覽四海名山大川，與
燕、趙間豪俊交遊；故
其文疏蕩，頗有奇氣。
此二子者，豈嘗執筆學
為如此之文哉？其氣充
乎其中，而溢乎貌，動
乎其言，而見乎其文，
而不自知也。

　　轍生十有九年矣。其
居家所與游者，不過其
鄰里鄉黨之人，所見不

C12.6 Su Zhe, "Letter Presented to Military Affairs Commissioner and Defender-in-Chief Han Qi"

To the Defender-in-Chief: Since birth, I have liked composing *wen*; now that I have reflected deeply on it, I believe that writing is given form by *qi*. Although writing cannot be mastered through study, one's *qi* can be nourished in order to attain it. Mencius said, "I am good at nourishing my flood-like *qi*." Observing his compositions, [we see that they] are capacious and profound, vast and broad, filling up the space between Heaven and earth, matching the size of his *qi*. The Grand Scribe [Han historian Sima Qian] traveled the world, widely viewing the four seas, famous mountains, and great rivers, mingling with the men of surpassing wisdom and ability in Yan and Zhao. Therefore, his writing is bold and unrestrained, imbued with an extraordinary *qi*. How could these two have simply grasped the brush and studied to write like this? Their *qi* filled them within and overflowed in their mien; their *qi* stimulated their language and appeared in their writing; and yet they themselves were unaware of it.

I am now nineteen [*sui*]. Those I roamed with when I lived at home were no more than those of my neighborhood or village, and what I experienced did not exceed several hundred *li* in area—there were no high mountains or great wilds to climb and view from in order to broaden myself. Though there was not a book I did not read among the works of the hundred masters, they were all the traces left by ancient people and were not sufficient to stir up my aspirations or ambitions. I feared I would drown in this backwater, so I resolutely quitted my home to seek out the world's extraordinary stories and grand spectacles, in order to comprehend the breadth and grandeur of Heaven and earth.

I journeyed to the homelands of Qin and Han, unrestrainedly viewing the heights of Zhongnan Mountain and the Ranges of Song and Hua; to the north I looked upon the torrents of the Yellow River; stirred, I imagined seeing the renowned heroes of antiquity. When I arrived at the capital [of Bianjing], I looked up to view the might of the Son of Heaven's palaces and towers, along with the wealth and greatness of the imperial granaries, treasuries, city walls, moats, and gardens—and then I understood the tremendous beauty of all under Heaven. I saw the Hanlin Scholar Lord Ouyang, and listened to the magnificent disputations of his discourses, observed the refined stateliness of his visage and person, and went about with the worthy scholars among his retainers—and then I understood that the literary writing of all under Heaven was gathered there.

The Defender-in-Chief stands supreme in the world for his talents and stratagems, and the world, depending on him, has been without trouble, and the Four Barbarians, in fear of him, do not dare to rise up. At court, he is like the Duke of Zhou and the Duke of Shao; abroad, he is like generals Fang Shu and Shao Hu[1]—and yet I, Zhe, have not yet seen this. Yet in one's studies, if one does not resolve to see the *great*, then what use is it to see *more*? Since I set out, among mountains I have seen the heights of Zhongnan, Song, and Hua, among waters I have seen the breadth and depths of the Yellow River, and among people I have visited Lord Ouyang—yet I still have not seen the Defender-in-Chief! Therefore I wish to have the opportunity to observe the brilliant resplendence of your worthy person, hear one word to strengthen myself—and only then will I have thoroughly encountered the great sights of all under Heaven and have no regrets.

I am still a youth, and as yet have been unable to fully practice the work of an official. When I first arrived, it was not to seek a salary to support myself; unexpectedly I obtained that [by passing the *jinshi*], but it was not what pleased me. However, I was fortunate to be granted the opportunity to return home to await selection [for office],[2] allowing me the leisure to improve my control of writing and to study governance. If the Defender-in-Chief believes that I am worth instructing and so deigns to instruct me, I would be even more fortunate.

---

[1] The dukes of Zhou and Shao were revered noble rulers of the early Western Zhou; Fang Shu and Shao Hu (Shao Duke Mu) were successful generals of the Western Zhou.

[2] Su Shi and Su Zhe passed the *jinshi* examination in the third month of 1057, but before they could sit for the palace examination to be awarded an office, their mother died in the fourth month, which required them to return home to Sichuan for mourning.

過數百里之間，無高山大野，可登覽以自廣。百氏之書雖無所不讀，然皆古人之陳述，不足以激發其志氣。恐遂汩沒，故決然捨去，求天下奇聞壯觀，以知天地之廣大。

過秦漢之故鄉，恣觀終南、嵩、華之高；北顧黃河之奔流，慨然想見古之豪傑。至京師，仰觀天子宮闕之壯，與倉廩府庫、城池苑囿之富且大也，而後知天下之巨麗。見翰林歐陽公，聽其議論之宏辯，觀其容貌之秀偉，與其門人賢士大夫遊，而後知天下之文章聚乎此也。

太尉以才略冠天下，天下之所恃以無憂，四夷之所憚以不敢發。入則周公、召公，出則方叔、召虎，而轍也未之見焉。且夫人之學也，不志其大，雖多而何為？轍之來也，於山終南、嵩、華之高，於水見黃河之大且深，於人見歐陽公，而猶以為未見太尉也！故願得觀賢人之光耀，聞一言以自壯，然後可以盡天下之大觀而無憾者矣。

轍年少，未能通習吏事。嚮之來，非有取於升斗之祿；偶然得之，非其所樂。然幸得賜歸待選，使得優游數年之前，將歸益治其文，且學為政。太尉苟以為可教而辱教之，又幸矣。[10]

[*LCJ* 1:477–478]

Su Zhe's bold self-confidence leaps off the page of this letter—from his images of *qi* filling the vast space between Heaven and earth, to his narrative of seeing the great vistas of the empire, to his description of the glories of the capital, the language is strong, declarative, and deliberately "heroic" in tone. In this letter, we see *qi* as the source of Su Zhe's *wen*, writing, and indeed the thing that gives writing its form. But where Han Yu focused on reading and the mastery of the ancients before years of practicing his literary writing to perfect it, Su Zhe approaches the work of developing his *qi* after the model of historian Sima Qian. According to Su Zhe, it was extensive travel around the country that made Sima Qian's *qi* so vast and full, and his writing therefore "bold and unrestrained." Su Zhe set himself a plan of travel to similarly "broaden himself." This quest for experience, rather than reading and writing, as a means to develop his *qi* informs the rest of the letter.

Su Zhe depicts his youth in Meishan, Sichuan, as narrow, dull, and inadequate to properly stimulate his *qi*. His claim to not have enough "high mountains" (with Mount Emei, the highest sacred Buddhist mountain of China, around the corner) or books to inspire and educate him is perhaps disingenuous. But the characterization works to introduce the grand adventures that would truly cultivate and expand his *qi*. Images of looming grandeur abound in the letter. Where Han Yu's images emphasized flow, fullness, and brilliance, Su Zhe's vistas are all "vast and broad," "prodigious," and "tremendous." The sites he visits are also laden with ancient historical significance: the sacred mountains of the central plain, the capital regions of the Qin and Han dynasties, and the great Yellow River, all associated with Chinese antiquity. Moreover, an air of distinctly masculine, even martial heroism, runs through this letter that was surely intended to appeal to the great general. Su Zhe paints himself striding across the empire bravely and alone, arriving at the capital as an awestruck young man who nonetheless sought out the powerful Ouyang Xiu to be further awed at his "resplendence." Representing Ouyang Xiu as one of the "sights" to be viewed allows Su Zhe to return to the topic of writing. In Ouyang Xiu's presence, he sees how grandeur (of size and elegance) coincides with literary brilliance at the Song capital: "then I understood that the literary writing of all under Heaven was gathered there." Su Zhe's panoramic description of the glories at the Northern Song capital suggests that Meng Yuanlao's nostalgic portrait was no exaggeration.

After his evocation of the grandeur of the capital, Su Zhe cleverly pivots to what was often the most difficult and uncomfortable task of a letter to a prospective patron: how to flatter the high-ranking recipient without sounding unctuous or sycophantic. But the assertive voice he has adopted thus far helps Su Zhe introduce Han Qi's significant accomplishments as a military general and leader—not requiring him to stretch the truth too far—and also to naturally frame Han Qi as the "martial" complement to Ouyang Xiu's "literary brilliance." Furthermore, Su Zhe's self-representation to this point as a lone voyager seeking the inspiring sights of the empire makes his desire to see Han Qi only fitting, as Han becomes the inevitable final destination of his voyage. Su Zhe employs only one rhetorical question in the letter, and he uses it not only to flatter Han Qi's "greatness" but also to present himself as someone who truly understands how to "broaden oneself" and, by extension, expand his *qi* and his literary talent: "Yet in one's studies, if one does not resolve to see the *great*, then what use is it to see *more*?" In the end, rather than seeking an audience with Han Qi like other aspiring young men, Su Zhe suggests that Han is destined to complete Su's voyage of self-cultivation. How could Han Qi refuse to see such a persevering and perspicacious talent?

As the close of the letter explains, however, fate had already intervened in Su Zhe's quest for Han Qi's patronage, with the death of Su's mother in Sichuan. Su Zhe assures Han Qi he will continue to develop his skills in governance—of which he has none, at age nineteen—and further improve his writing, in the hope of gaining Han's instruction upon his return. Su Zhe's letter is both politically and rhetorically daring: although he had renown as one of the two brilliant Su brothers so successful in the examinations, he had no practical talents other than his writing. The letter therefore had to display that talent, along with his character, in the most brilliant light possible. Where Han Yu spoke in the voice of a master, demonstrating his literary skills while explaining to Li Yi how he should cultivate them, Su Zhe makes just one strong claim about his understanding of literary writing at the outset, and then uses the remainder of the letter to perform his knowledge—narrating the expansion of his *qi*—for Han Qi. Although Su Zhe went on to many high offices, Han Qi was never particularly instrumental in his career. The letter itself became famous, as much for the way it advertised Su Zhe's social boldness as for its display of his literary creativity.

More acutely than other forms of medieval Chinese prose, Tang and Song prefaces and letters reveal a deep awareness of their audiences—both their engaged contemporary readers and recipients, as well as readers far into the future. This social awareness shaped the texts' rhetoric, imagery, and voice and allows us to reimagine the contexts and relationships in which they were composed. The sociality of prefaces and letters also affected their treatment of time and temporality. Although prefaces needed to explain and recount, they also had to reflect self-consciously on the circumstances of their composition. This could lead writers like Li Bai to make connections to earlier medieval precedents such as the outings and feasts of the Wei and Jin courts, thus situating his familial, personal experience in historical time; likewise Meng Yuanlao, explaining the reasons for his work, could reach back nostalgically into personal memory to inscribe it into dynastic history. Li Qingzhao, too, drew on the long history of "refined skill" to frame her discussion of what some might regard as a trivial, contemporary women's pastime. In letters, gaps of time and sometimes distance between letter-writer and recipient often prompted anxiety about the passage of time and inspired autobiographical narratives of change over time. In the letters of this chapter, Wang Wei moves across past, present, and future to appeal to Pei Di; Han Yu uses personal recollection of the struggle to perfect his writing as a lesson for Li Yi, and wonders about his future; and Su Zhe offers an account of his voyages to impress his potential patron Han Qi, and then casts forward to a hoped-for future in his conclusion. Finally, prefaces and letters are particularly compelling because of their contingent nature. Whether composed for an occasion or an accompanying text, prefaces had to frame, explain, and convince readers of the significance of a moment or text. And letters, whether to close friends, supplicating students, or lofty officials, were meant to instruct, persuade, and sometimes challenge their recipient. Perhaps for these reasons the voices of the texts still resonate so clearly today.

Anna M. Shields and Stephen H. West

NOTES

1. Zhan Ying dates the preface to 731, when Li Bai was in Anlu (present-day Henan); the "younger cousins" he refers to were likely Li Youcheng and Li Lingwen. Zhan Ying, ed., *Li Bai quanji jiaozhu huishi jiping* (Beijing: Baihua wenyi chubanshe, 1996), 8:4139.

2. Meng Yuanlao, "Xu," in *Dongjing meng Hua lu jianzhu*, edited by Yi Yongwen (Beijing: Zhonghua shuju, 2007), 1:1–6.

3. For an important recent study of Li Qingzhao's life and work, see Ronald Egan, *The Burden of Female Talent: The Poet Li Qingzhao and Her History in China* (Cambridge, MA: Harvard Asia Center, 2013).

4. Translation and footnotes to the text by Ronald Egan, used with permission, from *The Works of Li Qingzhao*, translated by Ronald Egan, edited by Anna M. Shields (Berlin: De Gruyter, 2019), 86–91.

5. Xu Peijun, ed., *Li Qingzhao ji jianzhu (xiuding ben)* (Shanghai: Shanghai guji chubanshe 2018), 366–381.

6. For a discussion of the conventional structures of Chinese letters, with reference to the forms of medieval and early modern European epistolary literature, see Antje Richter, *Letters and Epistolary Culture in Early Medieval China* (Seattle: University of Washington Press, 2013), 75–116.

7. Pauline Yu, *The Poetry of Wang Wei* (Bloomington: Indiana University Press, 1980), 165.

8. Chen Tiemin, ed., *Wang Wei ji jiaozhu*, 4 vols. (Beijing: Zhonghua shuju, 1997), 3:929–930.

9. Luo Liantian, ed., *Han Yu guwen jiaozhu huiji* (Taipei: Dingwen shuju, 2003), 1:712–727.

10. Su Zhe, *Luancheng ji*, edited by Zeng Zaozhuang and Ma Defu (Shanghai: Shanghai guji chubanshe, 1987), 1:477–478.

SUGGESTED READING

ENGLISH

Egan, Ronald. *The Burden of Female Talent: The Poet Li Qingzhao and Her History in China.* Cambridge, MA: Harvard Asia Center, 2013.

Richter, Antje, ed. *A History of Chinese Letters and Epistolary Culture.* Leiden: Brill, 2015.

Rouzer, Paul. *The Poetry and Prose of Wang Wei.* 2 vols. Berlin: De Gruyter, 2019–2020.

Shields, Anna M. *One Who Knows Me: Friendship and Literary Culture in Mid-Tang China.* Cambridge, MA: Harvard Asia Center, 2015.

Warner, Ding Xiang. "The Two Voices of *Wangchuan ji*: Poetic Exchange Between Wang Wei and Pei Di." *Early Medieval China* 2 (2005): 57–72.

West, Stephen H. "The Interpretation of a Dream: The Sources, Evaluation, and Influence of the *Dongjing meng Hua lu*." *T'oung Pao* 71(1985): 63–108.

CHINESE

Gao Buying 高步瀛, ed. *Tang Song wen juyao* 唐宋文舉要 (*Essential Prose Works of the Tang and Song*). 3 vols. Beijing: Zhonghua shuju, 1963.

Huang Diming 黃滌明, Ye Guangda 葉光大, and Yuan Huazhong 袁華忠, eds. *Lidai mingzhu xuba xuanzhu* 歷代名著序跋選注 (*Selected and Annotated Famous Prefaces and Postfaces from Across the Dynasties*). Lanzhou: Gansu renmin chubanshe, 1986, 169–208.

Bei Yuanchen 貝遠辰, Huang Jun 黃鈞, and 葉幼明, eds. *Lidai shuxin xuan* 歷代書信選 (*Selected Letters from Across the Dynasties*). Changsha: Hunan renmin chubanshe, 1980.

13

Tang and Song Biographical Prose

Allegorical and Fictional

Interest in the lives and accomplishments of individual figures has a long history, dating back to the beginning of Chinese literature, and was interwoven with the tradition and conventions of historical writing. The purpose of such writings was not just to record what a person did but, more important, to illustrate the moral motives behind their actions and the lessons that might be extracted for later generations. Thus, we find a prominent didactic component in biographical writings, in the words of the protagonists themselves, and in the commentary provided by the author, often positioned at the end of the work.

Both content and form of the genre were heavily influenced by pre-Qin historical writings (☞ chap. 2) and by Han dynasty historian Sima Qian's the *Grand Scribe's Records* (*Shiji*) (☞ chap. 6). The *Grand Scribe's Records* played an especially important role in shaping the norms and standards of biographical writing as a form of history and a genre of literature in later periods; a considerable portion of it was devoted to the lives and deeds of important historical or legendary figures, from generals and high-ranking court officials to a variety of remarkable personalities, including scholars, warriors, wandering knights, even assassin-retainers who sacrificed their lives for their lords or the greater good (☞ chap. 6). By Tang and Song times, biographical writing had developed beyond the confines of official historical writing, establishing itself as an independent form of literary prose used by scholars and literati to serve a variety of political and cultural purposes. Presentation of historical facts and political and moral persuasion remained an important driving force in the new genre of literary biography, but writers now sought different means to achieve that goal, ushering in new rhetorical devices, new subject matter, and new levels of innovativeness. The subjects of these biographies are mostly common folks, both historical figures and figurative ones, whose actions and life stories the author considers worth telling for political advocacy, moral education, and other cultural purposes. Fictional construction plays as much a role as the presentation of historical facts.

The four authors discussed in this chapter—Han Yu (768–824), Liu Zongyuan (773–819), Wang Anshi (1021–1086), and Su Shi (1037–1101)—were well-known scholars and established writers of their times. Their writings were essential to the traditional historical biography's transformation into a prestigious form of literary and cultural expression that significantly shaped our knowledge and understanding of Tang and Song biographical prose. All four authors well earned their place among the elite group of prose writers known as the "Eight Prose Masters of the Tang and Song" (*Tang Song ba dajia*) (🕮 chap. 10).

These four authors also were the major figures behind the so-called ancient-style prose movement (*guwen yundong*) in the Tang and Song, creators and practitioners of a new prose style characterized by clarity and precision to counter the dominant influence of parallel prose (*pianti wen*) (🕮 chap. 9), a genre popular since the early medieval period, but criticized by the ancient-style prose advocates for its pursuit of ornate embellishment at the expense of content and meaning. Although the stated goal of the ancient-style prose movement was a return to the stylistically straightforward and morally robust writing of the pre-Qin classical period, the outcome was a refreshingly new style that laid the foundation of prose writing for the next millennium in Chinese literary history. For this reason, some modern scholars would call it by its alternative name "Tang and Song poetry and prose modernization movement" (*Tang Song shi wen gexin yundong*).

In this chapter, we translate and analyze six specimens of the new biographical prose by these four authors. We start with Tang writer Han Yu's "A Biography of Mao Ying." This is an extraordinary piece that showcases the formal features of the traditional biography at the same time it parodies it. The parody comes from the fact that the subject of the biography turns out not to be a real historical figure, but instead allegorically constructed.

韓愈　毛穎傳

毛穎者，中山人也。其先明視，佐禹治東方土。養萬物有功，因封於卯地，死為十二神。嘗曰：“吾子孫神明之後，不可與物同，當吐而生。”已而果然。明視八世孫䶄，世傳當殷時居中山，得神仙之術，能匿光使物。竊桓娥，騎蟾蜍入月。其後代遂隱不仕云。居東郭者曰䨓，狡而善走。與韓盧爭能，盧不及。盧怒，與宋鵲謀而殺之，醢其家。

C13.1 Han Yu, "A Biography of Mao Ying, Master Brush Tip" ("Mao Ying zhuan")

Mao Ying was a native of Zhongshan.[1] His ancestor Mingshi[2] assisted Yu[3] in governing the eastern land, and because of his accomplishments in nurturing the myriad things, was enfeoffed in Mao and after his death became one of the twelve zodiac gods.[4] He once said: "My children are descendants of gods and deities and must not be treated the same as other creatures. They shall be born from the mouth."[5] It turned out indeed to be like that. His eighth-generation descendant, Nou, was believed to have lived in Zhongshan during the Yin dynasty[6] and obtained the techniques of the immortals, able to make his body invisible and objects move. He was said to have had a secret affair with Heng E and together they rode to the moon on the back of a toad.[7] Since then, his

---

[1] Zhongshan was an ancient state in modern Hebei of north China known for its production of writing brushes.

[2] Mingshi was an abstruse reference to rabbits. The original Chinese text uses an archaic script for the character *shi*, which is replaced here with its standard form.

[3] Yu was the legendary ruler of Chinese antiquity remembered for his heroic deeds in controlling floods.

[4] Mao, here a different character from the subject's surname, is the fourth of the Twelve Earthly Branches, corresponding to rabbit in the Chinese zodiac. Combined with the Ten Heavenly Stems, the Twelve Earthly Branches were used to mark time and direction as well. Mao corresponds to the east.

[5] Legend has it that rabbits are born out of the mouth of their mothers; hence, the crack in their lips.

[6] Alternate name of the Shang dynasty, one of the "Three Dynasties" of Chinese antiquity.

[7] Heng E, better known as Chang E, the moon goddess who was banished to live there in the company of only a toad and a rabbit.

descendants have withdrawn from the world and have not taken office. One of them, living in East Suburb, was named Jun, who was clever and good at running. He once competed with Han Lu, who could not catch up with him. Han Lu was angry and colluded with Song Que[8] to have Jun murdered, annihilating his whole family, turning them into meat sauce.[9]

At the time of the first emperor of Qin, when General Meng Tian[10] was launching the southern campaign against Chu, he stationed his army at Zhongshan, planning to conduct a grand hunt to deter the enemy. He summoned his captains and lieutenants on the left and right, performed a divination using the Linked Mountains[11] method, and obtained a sign of both heavenly and human significance. The diviners congratulated him, prognosticating: "Today's captures will be something with no horns or teeth, wearing coarse garment, with a crack in the mouth and a long beard, having eight apertures[12] and sitting crossed-legged. Pluck its hair, use it for aid to the wooden tablets and bamboo strips,[13] and the world's writing will be unified. Isn't this a sign for the Qin's eventual victory over the various feudal lords?" Thereupon they started the hunt and surrounded the entire Mao clan. They pulled off their hair, and returned to Qin carrying Ying with them. The prisoners were presented to the emperor at Zhangtai Palace,[14] and Ying was ordered to live with his folks under surveillance. The emperor of Qin sent Tian to bestow on Ying hot water and a bath, and enfeoffed him at Guancheng, dubbing him Lord of Tube City.[15] He grew increasingly intimate with the emperor and was gradually charged with responsibilities.[16]

秦始皇時，蒙將軍恬南伐楚，次中山，將大獵以懼楚。召左右庶長與軍尉，以連山筮之，得天與人文之兆。筮者賀曰："今日之獲，不角不牙。衣褐之徒，缺口而長鬚，八竅而趺居。獨取其髦，簡牘是資，天下其同書。秦其遂兼諸侯乎！"遂獵圍毛氏之族，拔其毫，載穎而歸，獻俘于章臺宮，聚其族而加束縛焉。秦皇帝使恬賜之湯沐，而封諸管城，號管城子，日見親寵任事。

---

[8] Han Lu and Song Que were names of two legendary dogs from the Warring States period who excelled at running. The original Chinese text uses an archaic script for the character *que*, which is replaced here with its standard form.

[9] The paragraph mimics the standard beginning of official biographies in dynastic histories, providing key information about Mao Ying's ancestry and family history, from the time of the legendary Yu to the Shang dynasty, down to the Warring States period of the Eastern Zhou. Han Yu ingeniously incorporates a multitude of fantastic legends and popular lore about rabbits into his narrative, mapping them unnoticeably onto the timeline of established history. On the surface of the text, nothing shows that the biography is totally fabricated.

[10] Meng Tian was a famous general of Qin who was credited with the invention of the Chinese writing brush.

[11] Linked Mountains was one of the three ancient methods of divination.

[12] Humans have seven apertures (mouth, two eyes, two ears, and two nostrils). Rabbits were believed in traditional folklore to have eight.

[13] Material for writing before the invention of paper.

[14] A famous palace of Qin.

[15] Guancheng means Tube City, referring to the barrel of the writing brush.

[16] The narrative progresses to the period of the biography's subject, the time of the first emperor of Qin, and gives an account of Ying's capture and enfeoffment. Again, Han Yu skillfully weaves rabbit lore into concurrent events in the political theatre of the Qin's bloody conquest of the world. It centers on the popular belief that credited General Meng Tian with the invention of the Chinese writing brush. The passage also features a popular allusion in later literature referring to the writing brush as "Master Tube City" (*Guancheng zi*), a point that will be reintroduced later in the biography.

穎為人彊記而便敏，自
結繩之代以及秦事，無
不纂錄。陰陽、卜筮、
占相、醫方、族氏、山
經、地志、字書、圖
畫，九流百家天人之
書，及至浮屠老子外國
之說，皆所詳悉。又通
於當代之務，官府簿
書，市井貨錢注記，惟
上所使。自秦始皇帝及
太子扶蘇、胡亥，丞相
李斯、中車府令高，下
及國人，無不愛重。又
善隨人意，正直邪曲
巧拙，一隨其人。雖
後見廢棄，終默不洩。
惟不喜武士，然見請亦
時往。累拜中書令，與
上益狎，上嘗呼為中書
君。上親決事，以衡石
自程，雖宮人不得立左
右。獨穎與執燭者常
侍，上休乃罷。穎與絳
人陳玄、弘農陶泓及會
稽楮先生友善相推致，
其出處必偕。上召穎，
三人者不待詔輒俱往，
上未嘗怪焉。

As a person, Ying had a great memory and was facile and quick with factual information. From ancient records in knotted cords to the time of Qin, nothing was left unrecorded by him. He was fully conversant with books dealing with both comic and human matters, and nothing was left out—cosmology, divination, physiognomy, medicine, genealogy, geography, paleography, cartography, the Nine Streams and the Hundred Schools, even the teachings of Buddhism,[17] of Laozi, and doctrines from foreign lands. He was also skilled at contemporary affairs, from official registers and government documents to the lending and borrowing notes and accounts of merchants in the marketplace—he could be used as the emperor liked. From the emperor to the Crown Prince Fu Su and Hu Hai,[18] to Prime Minister Li Si, Captain of the Imperial Chariot Command Zhao Gao all the way to the common people, all loved and respected him. He was also good at following wholeheartedly the minds of people, be it the upright, uncorrupt type, or the crooked and the cunning—he was happy to go with all of them. Although he had seen his share of succession intrigues,[19] he would keep them to himself and did not divulge them. Only he did not like the martial type, but even so when he was invited he would sometimes also go. He rose ultimately to the position of Chief of the Palace Secretariat,[20] and got even more intimate with the emperor, who once called him affectionately "Lord Palace Secretariat."[21] When the emperor was deliberating on state affairs on his own, he would set a certain target for himself,[22] and even the palace attendants were not allowed to be around, Ying and a candle holder being the only exceptions. And he would retire only after the emperor had finished work. Ying got along very well with Chen Xuan of Jiang,[23] Tao Hong of Hongnong,[24] as well as Mr. Chu of Kuaiji.[25] They admired and often hung around with one another;

---

[17] Han Yu is being a bit anachronistic because Buddhism was not introduced into China until a few centuries after the first emperor of Qin's time.

[18] Hu Hai was the second and youngest son of the first emperor of Qin, who later succeeded his father as second emperor.

[19] I am interpreting the word *feiqi* ("abandonment and discard") in the Chinese text as referring to the succession intrigues Ying as a scribe had witnessed and recorded, not his own abandonment later in his career. The word *hou* in the Chinese text was, according to some commentators, added by later editors.

[20] The Secretariat (*zhongshu*), later a tripartite branch of the central government, was at this time charged mainly with taking care of the emperor's personal scribal and secretarial needs.

[21] The epithet shows the emperor's favor and affection toward Ying.

[22] The first emperor of Qin was known in history as a diligent, hardworking sovereign who set high and rigorous quotas for his daily work.

[23] The name Chen Xuan plays on its literal meaning of Old Black, referring to ink. Jiang of Shanxi in north China was noted for its production of ink.

[24] The name Tao Hong plays on its literal meaning of Pottery Pool, referring to the inkstone. Hongnong of modern Henan in central China was known for its pottery inkstones.

[25] Chu is a quick-growth, soft-wood tree whose bark was used in making paper (hence, its popular name "paper mulberry"). Kuaiji of modern Zhejiang was known for its paper products.

in repose or action, they would always go together. When the emperor summoned Ying, the other three would accompany him without being ordered, and the emperor never considered it strange.[26]

Later, at an audience, the emperor wanted to appoint Ying to an important position, bringing him out of obscurity,[27] and Ying took off his hat to thank His Majesty. Thereupon His Majesty saw Ying's bald head; in addition, something Ying had written[28] did not meet His Majesty's expectations. The emperor chuckled: "Lordy, Lordy, old and bald, you are no longer useful. I used to call you Lord Palace Secretariat. Haven't you not exhausted your usefulness as a companion of books?"[29] Ying replied: "Your servant has done his best." After that, he was no longer summoned by the emperor. He was asked to return to his enfeoffment in Tube City and lived the rest of his life there. His descendants were many and lived all across China as well as the barbarian lands. All of them considered Tube City their native place, but only those who lived in Zhongshan could match the accomplishments of their forebears.[30]

The Lord Grand Scribe says: There were two lineages of the Mao clan. One of them was surnamed Ji, whose founder was a son of King Wen[31] and was enfeoffed at Mao; the classical expression "[the four states of] Lu, Wei, Mao, Dan" is evidence.[32] During the Warring States period, there were Lord Mao and Mao Sui who came from this lineage.[33] Zhongshan was the other lineage. No one knows where they came from, but their descendants were most prosperous. After Confucius stopped writing the *Spring and Autumn Annals*,

後因進見，上將有任使，拂拭之，因免冠謝。上見其髮禿，又所摹書不能稱上意。上嘻笑曰：「中書君老而禿，不任吾用。吾嘗謂君中書，而今不中書耶？」對曰：「臣所謂盡心者。」因不復召，歸封邑，終於管城。其子孫甚多，散處中國夷狄，皆冒管城，惟居中山者能繼父祖業。

太史公曰：毛氏有兩族，其一姬姓，文王之子封於毛，所謂魯衛毛聃者也，戰國時有毛公、毛遂。獨中山之族不知其本所出，子孫最為蕃昌。《春秋》之成，見絕於孔子，而非其罪。及蒙將軍拔中山之毫，始皇封之管城，世遂有名，而姬姓之毛無聞。穎始以俘見，卒見任使，秦之滅諸侯，穎與有功。賞不酬勞，以老見疎，秦真少恩哉！

[HYWJHJJZ
6:2717–2718]

---

[26] This is the longest and most substantive paragraph of the biography. The qualities and functions of the writing brush, in the personified figure of Mao Ying, are given detailed and full representation. Its role as a medium for recording and for writing, illustrated in Ying's willingness to be used "as the emperor liked" (*wei shang suo shi*) and its adeptness at "following wholeheartedly the minds of people" (*yi sui qi ren*), having no subjectivity of its own, both explains the favor and affection he enjoys with the emperor and presages his fall and eventual demise (the topic of the next paragraph).

[27] There is some ambiguity in wording here, perhaps intended by Han Yu. *Fushi* could mean physical dusting or the figurative sense of bringing Ying out of his relative obscurity as a scribe.

[28] A variant reading has "painted" (*hua*) instead of "written" (*shu*).

[29] The Chinese word *zhong*, when used as a verb, also can mean "to hit the mark." The emperor obviously takes pleasure in his clever wordplay.

[30] As a worn-out brush can no longer fully perform its functions, Ying has also run out of favor with the emperor, who hastily abandons him and sends him away when his service is no longer desired. As his capture and entrance into imperial serve are incidental, his downfall, too, is presented as gratuitous, illustrated in His Majesty's insensitive jokes and giggles.

[31] King Wen and his son King Wu were founders of the Zhou dynasty. Ji was the surname of the royal family of Zhou.

[32] Lu, Wei, Mao, and Dan were names of the four enfeoffments to King Wen's sons.

[33] Lord Mao and Mao Sui were famous political advisors to the rulers of Wei and Zhao, respectively, during the Warring States period.

they were abandoned, but it was not their fault.[34] When General Meng Tian pulled off their hairs at Zhongshan, and the First Emperor enfeoffed Ying at Tube City, they started to be known in the world and those from the Ji-sur-named lineage went into obscurity. Ying first appeared as a captive but eventually got employment and charged with official responsibilities. He participated in Qin's conquest of the world and earned merits. That the reward he received did not match his labor, that in the end he was estranged due to old age was indeed evidence of Qin's lack of grace.[35]

Commentators rightly have had difficulty deciphering Han Yu's motive and intentions in writing "A Biography of Mao Ying." What is the message? What should the reader take away from a piece that, on the surface, recounts the rise and fall of the historical figure Mao Ying with all the formal and stylistic trappings of standard historical biography, but with the writing brush (the literal meaning of Mao Ying is "Brush Tip") as its real subject? Some found consolation in Han Yu's ending the piece with an explicit criticism of the fickleness of the first emperor of Qin (an easy target of such criticism) and read the Mao Ying biography as a veiled expression of Han's frustration with his own political career. Others recognized the playfulness of the work but found it hard to align it with the serious purpose the genre was supposed to serve, relegating it as a frivolous pastime Han Yu indulged for amusement.

Leaving judgment of interpretations aside, recognizing this layer of deliberate double-play is key to appreciating Han Yu's brilliance as a writer. The realization that the piece narrates the life of a writing brush should not reduce readers' satisfaction but rather encourage them to come back to the text and fully appreciate the author's ingenuity and enjoy the process of discovery. The deliberate and carefully maintained tension between the narrative's double layers of text and meaning and the ironic seriousness with which Han Yu tells the story lie at the core of the Mao Ying biography's everlasting appeal to both traditional and modern readers.

For a less allegorical biography, we next turn to Liu Zongyuan, a contemporary of Han Yu. The clarity of purpose and message in Liu's "A Discourse on the Snake Catcher" contrasts sharply with Han Yu's fictional biography for Mao Ying. The polemical nature of the work and its intended use for political and policy advocacy are illustrated in its writing style as well, nearly devoid of all the formal conventions we see in Han Yu's work. Liu Zongyuan makes liberal use of dialogue as a

---

[34] It was said that the reason Confucius ended the *Spring and Autumn Annals* in the year 481 BCE was that in that year a unicorn (*lin*) was captured, which Confucius considered to be a bad omen and therefore stopped writing. *Spring and Autumn Annals* is one of the Five Confucian Classics credited to Confucius.

[35] In obvious simulation of the Lord Grand Scribe (*Taishi gong*), Sima Qian's practice of issuing final judgements on his subjects at the end of the biographies (☛ chap. 6), Han Yu ends the piece conventionally by providing a quick summary of Ying's lineage and his personal achievements, placing the blame of his eventual downfall squarely on the first emperor of Qin.

device to not only advance the plot but capture the intense emotions and mood shifts of the story's protagonist. All these would become characteristic features of the new style of prose biography.

C13.2 Liu Zongyuan, "A Discourse of the Snake Catcher" ("Buzhe zhe shuo")

柳宗元 捕蛇者說

The wilds of Yongzhou[1] produces a rare kind of snake. It has a black body with white stripes. The grasses and plants it touches all die; if a person is bitten, there is no cure. When captured and dried, however, its meat can serve as a drug catalyst, and help cure leprosy, cramps, neck lumps, ulcers, get rid of dead muscles and kill the Three Worms.[2] At the beginning, the palace doctors used imperial order to collect it, twice every year; they recruited those who could catch it, allowing them to use it in lieu of taxes. People at Yongzhou vied with one another to try their luck.

永州之野產異蛇，黑質而白章。觸草木，盡死。以齧人，無禦之者。然得而腊之以為餌，可以已大風、攣踠、瘻癘，去死肌，殺三蟲。其始，太醫以王命聚之，歲賦其二。募有能捕之者，當其租入。永之人爭奔走焉。

There was a person with the surname of Jiang, whose family had monopolized the business for three generations. When asked, he said to me: "My grandfather died of this. My father died of this. Now I've been doing this for twelve years. Several times I almost died as well." After these words, he seemed to be overwhelmed with grief. I was saddened, and said: "Do you have grudges against this? I will bring it up to the administrators, asking them to change your labor and restore your taxes. What do you think of it?"

有蔣氏者，專其利三世矣。問之，則曰："吾祖死於是，吾父死於是，今吾嗣為之十二年，幾死者數矣。"言之，貌若甚戚者。余悲之，且曰："若毒之乎？余將告于蒞事者，更若役，復若賦，則何如？"

Jiang fell into great grief, his eyes brimming with tears, and said: "Do you, Sir, want to have pity on me and save my life? Then the misfortune of this labor is not as bad as that of restoring my taxes. Had I not taken on this business, I would have long been in dire straits. Since my family moved to this place, it has now been three generations and sixty years. Look at my neighbors—they are getting more impoverished by the day. They have exhausted what their lands can produce; whatever they can get their hands on is gone. Howling and crying, they migrate from one place to another; hungry and thirsty, they collapse to the ground. Weathering winds and rain, exposed to heat and cold, they breathe miasmal vapors, the bodies of their dead piling up one on top of the other. Those who used to live in the same village with my grandfather, now not one-tenth of their households are still here. Those who lived in the same village with my father, now not two- or three-tenths of their households are still here. Those who have lived in the same village with me over the past twelve years, now not four- or five-tenths of their households are still here. If not dead, they have moved elsewhere. But I alone have survived due to my skills catching the snakes. When fierce officers came to my village, they shouted east and west, chased around south and north; in the frightening chaos, even chickens and dogs could not rest but were

蔣氏大戚，汪然出涕曰："君將哀而生之乎？則吾斯役之不幸，未若復吾賦不幸之甚也。嚮吾不為斯役，則久已病矣。自吾氏三世居是鄉，積於今六十歲矣，而鄉鄰之生日蹙。殫其地之出，竭其廬之入，號呼而轉徙，飢渴而頓踣，觸風雨，犯寒暑，呼噓毒癘，往往而死者相藉也。曩與吾祖居者，今其室十無一焉。與吾父居者，今其室十無二三焉。與吾居

---

[1] Yongzhou was a small town in the mountainous area of southern Hunan.

[2] The Three Worms refer to the different types of parasites in the body.

十二年者，今其室十無
四五焉。非死即徙爾。
而吾以捕蛇獨存。悍吏
之來吾鄉，叫囂乎東
西，隳突乎南北，譁然
而駭者，雖雞狗不得寧
焉。吾恂恂而起，視其
缶，而吾蛇尚存，則弛
然而臥。謹食之，時而
獻焉。退而甘食其土之
有，以盡吾齒。蓋一歲
之犯死者二焉，其餘則
熙熙而樂，豈若吾鄉鄰
之旦旦有是哉？今雖死
乎此，比吾鄉鄰之死
則已後矣，又安敢毒
耶？"

余聞而愈悲。孔子
曰："苛政猛於虎
也。"吾嘗疑乎是。今
以蔣氏觀之，猶信。嗚
呼！孰知賦斂之毒，有
甚是蛇者乎！故為之
說，以俟夫觀人風者得
焉。

[*LZYJJZ* 4:1116–1117]

柳宗元 種樹郭橐駝傳

郭橐駝，不知始何名。
病僂，隆然伏行，有類
橐駝者，故鄉人號之
駝。駝聞之曰："甚
善，名我固當。"因
捨其名，亦自謂橐駝
云。其鄉曰豐樂鄉，

aroused. With anxious apprehension, I rose up, looked at the jar, and if my snakes were still there, I would relax and go back to sleep. I carefully feed them, waiting for the time to send them away. After that, I retreat and rely on what the lands have to offer, and live out my remaining years in contentment. There are only two times in a year when I have to risk my life, with the rest of the days spent in peace and enjoyment. How can you even think of comparing me to my neighbors who have to suffer every day! Now even if I end up dying of this, it will already be later than my neighbors. How dare I harbor grudges?"

I heard this and became even more saddened. Confucius said: "A tyrannical government is fiercer than tigers."[3] I had been skeptical of this. Now looking at it from Jiang's example, I was convinced. Alas! Who would think that the evil of exorbitant taxation is worse than a poisonous snake! I therefore made this discourse and hope those surveillance officials will get it.

The power of Liu Zongyuan's "A Discourse of the Snake Catcher" is achieved through several well-executed techniques and literary devices. First, Han Yu's Mao Ying biography is told from the third-person perspective of a faceless historian, whereas Liu Zongyuan tells Jiang's story from his personal experience, serving as both witness to Jiang's miseries and sympathetic listener and interlocutor whose questions not only advance the narrative but also enhance the emotional intensity of the story. Second, as befits the title (a *shuo* or "discourse") and the story's political purpose, Jiang's passionate defense of his life-endangering job constitutes the bulk of the text. His elaborate speech in the third paragraph carries the brunt of the argument and the core of the message. Finally, Jiang's speech is interspersed with several memorable literary descriptions, high points in the narrative that foreground his suffering and that of his neighbors.

This focused, exhaustive mode of presentation is also demonstrated in the next piece by Liu Zongyuan, this time through the words of a tree grower on his art of planting. Notice that Liu Zongyuan maintains the basic dialogue structure of the previous story but hides his identity behind an anonymous interlocutor (*wenzhe*).

C13.3 Liu Zongyuan, "An Account of Guo Hunchback, the Tree Grower" ("Zhongshu Guo Tuotuo zhuan")

Guo Tuotuo's original name was not known. He suffered from an illness in his back and had to hump up while walking, like a camel. For that reason, the folks just called him "Hunchback." When he heard of this, he said: "Very good! A name right for me." He thereupon disregarded his real name and

---

[3] This is a comment by Confucius recorded in the Tangong chapter of the *Book of Rites*.

called himself Hunchback as well. He lived in a village called Fengle,[1] just west of Chang'an.[2] Guo made his living by growing trees, and all the wealthy and powerful families in Chang'an who wanted to make a garden or those who made a living selling fruits, competed to hire him. The trees he planted, when moved to another place, would all live; and they all grew big and strong, bearing early and abundant fruit. Other growers tried to spy on and copy him, but no one was able to match what he did.

Someone asked him about this, and he replied: "It is not that I can make trees live long and thrive; it is that I follow their natural dispositions and extend their inherent qualities. That's all. There are a few basic rules in growing tress: the roots need to be relaxed, the mounding needs to be level, the soil needs to be old, the ramming needs to be tight. After that is finished, do not touch them again, do not worry about them. Leave and do not come back. If in planting you treat them as if they were your kids, and in maintenance you leave them alone as if abandoned, then their natural dispositions will be protected and their inherent qualities be obtained. Thus, I simply do not harm their growth—not that I can make them big and strong; I simply do not suppress or hamper their fruiting—not that I can make their fruit come early and abundant. Other growers are not like this. They twist their roots and change the soil; when mounding, they err in either being excessive or falling short. When there is someone who can reverse this tendency, they often love them too much, or worry about them too diligently. They go look at them in the morning and fondle them in the evening; after they leave, they come back. What's more, they scratch the barks to check if the trees are alive or dead, shake their roots to see if the soil is tight or loose. And the inherent qualities of the trees slip away day by day. Seemingly loving them, they actually harm them; seemingly concerned about them, they actually treat them as enemies. Therefore, they are not as good as me. What can I do about it?"

The inquirer said: "Is it alright to take your methods and apply them to the matter of government?" Hunchback said: "I know only how to grow trees. The matter of government is totally beyond me. However, when I was with my folks in the village, I saw that the administrators were fond of issuing orders. They seemed to love the people but in the end only harmed them. From morning to evening, officers came shouting: 'We are here by official order to encourage your plowing, admonish your planting, monitor your harvesting. Quicken your silk reeling, hasten your cloth weaving, nurture your kids, take care of your chickens and pigs!' They struck the drums and gathered the people, beat the wooden clappers and summoned them. The villagers even had no time

---

[1] Meaning, literally, "abundant joy."
[2] Capital city of the Tang, modern-day Xi'an, literally meaning "everlasting peace."

在長安西。駝業種樹，凡長安豪富人為觀游及賣果者，皆爭迎取養。視駝所種樹，或移徙，無不活，且碩茂，蚤實以蕃。他植者雖窺伺傚慕，莫能如也。

有問之，對曰："橐駝非能使木壽且孳也，能順木之天以致其性焉爾。凡植木之性，其本欲舒，其培欲平，其土欲故，其築欲密。既然已，勿動勿慮，去不復顧。其蒔也若子，其置也若棄，則其天者全而其性得矣。故吾不害其長而已，非有能碩茂之也；不抑耗其實而已，非有能蚤而蕃之也。他植者則不然。根拳而土易，其培之也，若不過焉則不及。苟有能反是者，則又愛之太殷，憂之太勤，且視而暮撫，已去而復顧。甚者，爪其膚以驗其生枯，搖其本以觀其疏密，而木之性日以離矣。雖曰愛之，其實害之；雖曰憂之，其實讎之，故不我若也。吾又何能為哉！"

問者曰："以子之道，移之官理，可乎？"駝曰："我知種樹而已。理，非吾業也。然吾居鄉，見長人者好煩其令，若甚憐焉，而卒以禍。旦暮吏來而呼曰：'官命促爾耕，勗

爾植，督爾獲。蚤繰而
緒，蚤織而縷，字而幼
孩，遂而雞豚。'鳴鼓
而聚之，擊木而召之。
吾小人輟飧饔以勞吏
者，且不得暇，又何以
蕃吾生而安吾性耶？故
病且怠。若是，則與吾
業者其亦有類乎？"

問者嘻曰："不亦善
夫！吾問養樹，得養人
術。"傳其事以為官
戒也。

[*LZYJJZ* 4:1172–1173]

to finish their breakfast or supper in order to receive the officers. How could they make their lives prosperous and have their natural dispositions nurtured? They only got sick and tired. If this is so, then I suppose there is something in common with my profession?"

The inquirer exclaimed: "Alas, isn't that great! I asked about growing trees and got techniques of nurturing people." He then passed down the story as an admonishment for the officials.

The story offers lessons in "the matter of government" (*guan li*) and "nurturing people" (*yang ren*) by way of the biographical subject Guo Tuotuo's lecture on the methods and principles of growing trees. "Is it alright to take your methods and apply them" to human governance, the unspecified interlocutor asks Guo after hearing his elaborate lecture given in the second paragraph. Guo first declines the question but then accepts its pertinence by describing the overbearing manners and insidious effects of the officials, in the same fashion as Jiang accused his oppressors in the previous story. Guo's message of naturalness and nonintervention is overtly endorsed by the author in the last paragraph, where he states the political purpose of the writing.

The force of the analogy depends on Guo's reputation and authority as a master tree grower, a fact that is carefully established in the first two paragraphs. While it gives ample space to describing Guo's skills, the text remains essentially silent on the origin of those skills, or how Guo came to possess them. In opening the biography with an explanation of Guo's nickname, the author seems to be suggesting a relation between Guo's hunchback and his extraordinary knack for tree growing. Liu Zongyuan could be tapping into a long tradition in Chinese literature of characters with physical deformations (*ji*) who have remarkable (*qi*) skills or techniques (e.g., Zhuangzi's cicada catcher), but he leaves us only to speculate.

If the element of remarkableness (*qi*) or strangeness (*guai*) in "An Account of Guo Tuotuo, the Tree Grower" plays only a peripheral role, it becomes a central feature in the third piece we discuss by Liu Zongyuan. The title describes it too as a *zhuan* or biographical account, but of the six texts we discuss in this chapter, "An Account of Li Chi" is the furthest, both stylistically and contentwise, from official historical biography. This account is rooted instead in the then-fashionable Tang short story (*Tang chuanqi*), tending more toward fiction than history.

柳宗元 李赤傳

李赤，江湖浪人也。嘗
曰："吾善為歌詩，詩
類李白。"故自號曰
李赤。遊宣州，州人館
之。其友與俱遊者有

C13.4 Liu Zongyuan, "An Account of Li Chi" ("Li Chi zhuan")

Li Chi was a vagabond scholar wandering among the rivers and lakes.[1] He once said: "I'm good at making songs and poems, and my poetry resembles

---

[1] "Rivers and lakes" (*jianghu*) is used in its figurative sense referring to the world outside of officialdom and court service, a way of life detached from politics.

that of Li Bai."[2] He thus named himself Li Chi.[3] He once traveled to Xuan-zhou,[4] and the locals there lodged him in an inn. A friend of his was a relative of the person traveling with him, and a few days later, followed him to the inn. Chi was found talking with a woman, and the friend joked about the relationship. Chi said: "By this you have made me a match. I am going to marry this woman." The friend was shocked, and said: "You, Sir, already have a wife who is in good health, and your mother is still alive. How can you do this? Is it that you are deluded and lost your mind?" He fetched a Crimson Snow[5] and asked Chi to take it, but Chi refused. After some time, the woman came and talked with Chi again. Thereupon she brought out a cloth and strangled his neck with it. Chi helped her with his own hands, to the point that his tongue was all out. His friend shouted, coming to rescue him. The woman untied the cloth and ran away. Chi angrily said to his friend: "You were being unreasonable! I was just going to follow my wife. Why did you do that?" Chi then went to beside the windows, wrote a letter, rolled it up and sealed it. Then, he wrote another one, and sealed it as well. When that was done, he went to the lavatory and did not return after a long while. The friend went over and saw Chi in the lavatory head down, hugging the receptacle with both arms, smiling eerily, glancing sideways, as if trying to get the whole body into it. The friend got him out by pulling backward. Chi was infuriated, saying: "I had already ascended the hall and seen my wife. My wife's beauty is unmatched in this world. The halls of her house are magnificent and gorgeously decorated, filled with all kinds of fragrance. Looking back, your world is just a dirty lavatory, and my wife's house is like the Ethereal Metropolis of the Heavenly Emperor.[6] Why do you want me to keep suffering like this?" Only after that did his friend realize that what Chi had met was a lavatory ghost.[7]

---

[2] A famous poet of the Tang, and a fellow freedom-seeking wanderer.

[3] This is an intentional word play, with Chi, meaning "red," matching up and contrasting with Bai, or "white," in Li Bai's name.

[4] Li Bai once visited the place and left behind famous poems.

[5] A legendary Daoist pill.

[6] Ethereal Metropolis (Qingdu) is where the Heavenly Emperor's palaces are located, at the center of the heavens.

[7] Unlike "A Discourse of the Snake Catcher" or "An Account of Guo Hunchback," where the main point is relatively easy to grasp from the start, reading the story of Li Chi requires the reader's constant attention to detail, how the plot unfolds step by step, especially the many instances of strangeness in Li Chi's behavior. He is determined to marry the woman he has spoken to simply because of a casual joke from his friend; he helps the woman in her attempt to strangle him; he calls the woman his wife even though he has been married to another one; and, finally, the bizarre jar hugging trying to get into the lavatory. All the suspense seems to be resolved when the paragraph ends and the woman's identity is revealed, except for the letters Li Chi has written, for which we have to wait until the end of the story.

The uncanny, macabre lavatory scene will recur as the story continues, but the reader begins by now to expect anything.

姻焉，間纍日，乃從之館。赤方與婦人言，其友戲之。赤曰："是媒我也，吾將娶乎是。"友大駭，曰："足下妻固無恙，太夫人在堂，安得有是？豈狂易病惑耶？"取絳雪餌之，赤不肯。有間，婦人至，又與赤言。即取巾經其脰，赤兩手助之，舌盡出。其友號而救之，婦人解其巾走去。赤怒曰："汝無道。吾將從吾妻，汝何為者？"赤乃就牖間為書，輾而圓封之。又為書，博封之。訖，如厠。久，其友從之，見赤軒厠抱甕，詭笑而側視，勢且下入。乃倒曳得之。又大怒曰："吾已升堂面吾妻。吾妻之容，世固無有。堂之飾，宏大富麗，椒蘭之氣，油然而起。顧視汝之世，猶溷厠也。而吾妻之居，與帝居鈞天清都無以異，若何苦余至此哉？"然後其友知赤之所遭，乃厠鬼也。

聚僕謀曰：“亟去是
厠。”遂行宿三十里。
夜，赤又如厠久，從
之，且復入矣。

The friend gathered the servants and discussed the matter with them, saying: "Get away from this lavatory real quick!" Thereupon they traveled thirty leagues and stopped for the night. During the night, Chi went to the lavatory and again did not come back after a long time. His friend went over and again saw Chi trying to get into it.

Though quick and decisive, his friend's efforts to protect Li Chi are destined to fail, not only because the lavatory ghost seems to be unrestricted to a particular place but more important, Li Chi's entrapment is such that he is determined to join his "wife" by whatever means. Nothing seems to work, as the next paragraph shows.

持出，洗其汙，眾環之
以至旦。去抵他縣，縣
之吏方宴，赤拜揖跪起
無異者。酒行，友未及
言，已飲而顧赤，則已
去矣。走從之。赤入
厠，舉其牀捍門，門堅
不可入，其友叫且言
之。眾發牆以入，赤之
面陷不潔者半矣。又出
洗之。縣之吏更召巫師
善呪術者守赤，赤自若
也。夜半，守者怠，皆
睡。及覺，更呼而求
之，見其足於厠外，赤
死久矣。獨得屍歸其
家。取其所為書讀之，
蓋與其母妻訣，其言辭
猶人也。

He grabbed him and pulled him out, had him washed up, and stayed with him and the others till dawn. They left the place and arrived at another county. The clerks of the county were just having a banquet, and Chi behaved normally, his greeting and saluting showing no signs of oddity. Then wine was served, and after the drinks, having not spoken to him, his friend looked around and found Chi already gone. He hustled over and followed Chi to the lavatory, but Chi had jammed the door with a chair, and he could not get in. His friend shouted and told the story. The crowd breached the wall and when they entered, Chi's face was already half buried in the dirty stuff. Again, they pulled him out and washed him clean. The clerks of the county then summoned wizards who were good with charms to guard him, but Chi acted as if nothing had happened. At midnight, the guards were tired and all fell asleep. When they awoke, they shouted and tried to find him and saw his feet outside the lavatory, but Chi was already long dead. They could do nothing but return his body to his home. When they read the letters he had sent home, he was bidding farewell to his mother and wife, and the words were no different from those of normal people.

By the end of this paragraph, all that can be told has been told, including revealing the content of the letters Li Chi had sent home. At the start of the paragraph, when Li Chi is pulled out of the lavatory for the second time, the reader can already surmise his inevitable death, which is then narrated through a quick succession of events leading to it.

The text ends with another paragraph in which the author steps out to reveal the intended moral of the story, now assuming the role of the traditional historian passing judgments on their subjects, to ensure his subtlety is not lost in the entertainment of reading.

柳先生曰：李赤之傳不
誣矣。是其病心而為是
耶？抑故有厠鬼耶？赤
之名聞江湖間，其始為
士，無以異於人也。一
惑於怪，而所為若是，

Mister Liu says: The account of Li Chi is not false. Was he sick in his mind and did this? Or were there indeed lavatory ghosts? Chi's name was known among the rivers and lakes; when he started out, he was no different from other scholars. Once he was deluded by the demons, however, his actions could go to such an extreme, considering the world, and the Ethereal Metropolis of the Heavenly Emperor, dirty places; his determination, however, was unmistakable.

Now people in the world all laugh at Chi's delusions, but how many of us are able to not act like him when faced with decisions of right and wrong, give and take, life and death? I will consider us lucky if we can go back to cultivating ourselves, not letting our minds be forever changed by desire, profits, love and hatred—how would we even have time to laugh at Chi?

乃反以世為溷，溷為帝居清都，其屬意明白。今世皆知笑赤之惑也，及至是非取與向背決不為赤者，幾何人耶？反修而身，無以欲利好惡遷其神而不返，則幸矣，又何暇赤之笑哉？

[*LZYJJZ* 4:1204–1205]

In his concluding comment, Liu Zongyuan justifies the story by attributing Li Chi's miserable demise to his "delusions" (*huo*). But he quickly shifts the emphasis to say the laugh is not really on Li Chi; it is a lesson for us all. The only safeguard against the allures of the strange (*guai*), he warns, is by constantly cultivating our mind, not letting it be influenced by external forces, a task that he suggests is much harder than we think.

In all three pieces, Liu Zongyuan remains both a clear-minded preacher of morality and an immersive storyteller carefully tending to his message as well as its delivery. This strong authorial control is pushed to another level in the two remaining texts we discuss, both of which are from his counterparts in the Northern Song.

C13.5 Wang Anshi, "A Lament for Zhongyong" ("Shang Zhongyong")

王安石　傷仲永

There was a commoner in Jinxi,[1] Fang Zhongyong, whose family had farmed there for generations. Until Zhongyong was five years old, he had never seen a writing instrument, but all of a sudden, he cried for them. His father considered it strange and borrowed them for him from the neighbors. He immediately wrote down a poem of four lines, and signed his name to it. The poem had taking care of one's parents and clan solidarity as its theme and was shown to all the talented writers in the district. Thereafter, he was able to compose poems on any topic at hand and finish them almost instantly, and the meaning and logic behind them were all worth noting. The local people marveled at it and gradually began to treat his father nicely, some even seeking to buy his poems with money. His father considered it a profitable business, and every day brought Zhongyong to make the rounds among the villagers, not asking him to study.

金谿民方仲永，世隸耕。仲永生五年，未嘗識書具，忽啼求之。父異焉，借旁近與之，即書詩四句，并自為其名。其詩以養父母、收族為意，傳一鄉秀才觀之。自是指物作詩立就，其文理皆有可觀者。邑人奇之，稍稍賓客其父，或以錢幣乞之。父利其然也，日扳仲永環謁於邑人，不使學。

I had heard of this for a while. During the Mingdao[2] period, I escorted my deceased father's coffin home for burial, and met him at my maternal uncle's house; he was then already twelve or thirteen. I asked him to compose poems but they could not match his previous fame. Another seven years later, I returned home from Yangzhou,[3] and again visited my uncle's house and asked about him. I was told: "He has disappeared into a nobody."

予聞之也久。明道中，從先人還家，於舅家見之，十二三矣。令作詩，不能稱前時之聞。又七年，還自揚州，復到舅家，問焉，曰："泯然眾人矣。"

---

[1] In modern Jiangxi, Wang Anshi's home province.

[2] Reign period of Renzong of the Northern Song, 1032–1033.

[3] In modern Jiangsu on the lower Yangtze River.

王子曰：仲永之通悟，
受之天也。其受之天
也，賢於材人遠矣，卒
之為眾人，則其受於人
者不至也。彼其受之天
也，如此其賢也，不受
之人，且為眾人。今夫
不受之天，固眾人，又
不受之人，得為眾人而
已邪？

[*WASQJ* 6:1277–1278]

Master Wang says: Zhongyong's intelligence was received from Heaven. What he received from Heaven far exceeded that of usual talents. That he ended up being an ordinary person was because what he should have received from people did not arrive. What he received from Heaven made him such an able kid; having not received from people made him just an ordinary person. Now, if one does not receive from Heaven, he surely is no more than an ordinary person; if he again does not receive from people, will he even be able to become an ordinary person?

In this short but famous piece, Wang Anshi keeps some of the formal features of the genre but shows a level of argumentative and structural efficiency not seen in the work of his Tang predecessors. Devoid of the dialogic framework of Liu Zongyuan's "A Discourse of the Snake Catcher" or the device of suspense in the narration of the strange events in "An Account of Li Chi," this language is plain, without any unusual characters, and the syntax is remarkably simple and straightforward, at times even colloquial. The argument, however, is powerfully presented, with a complexity of thought and idea that belies the text's simple, smooth language.

The author begins his lament over Zhongyong's fall into oblivion with a sentence that situates him in a web of relationships, suggesting that Zhongyong's fall is inexplicable except as a result of the material conditions and family circumstances that determine his fate. Zhongyong is being moved through the narrative, out of his control from the very beginning. Wang Anshi even withholds the word "person" (*ren*) to refer to Zhongyong, choosing instead "commoner" (*min*), to open the piece.

That such limiting circumstances determine the outcome is reinforced by the structure of the story. Unlike the previous pieces, Wang Anshi takes care, through details of his/the narrator's movements, to describe when, where, and how he gains information about Zhongyong, thus weaving himself into the narrative as witness to Zhongyong's rise and fall, and ultimately mourner of his fate. Wang Anshi does not simply tell Zhongyong's story, leaving interpretation to some overseeing "officials"; instead, by placing himself at the center of the story's narrative, Wang authorizes himself to shape and frame its message. He suggests through this consistent narrative intervention what he explicitly names in the thoughtful and carefully argued commentary: that without the arrival of what one "should receive from the people," even the greatest gifts fail to materialize. To avoid the fate of the Zhongyongs, Wang indirectly admonishes his readers to make whatever effort is necessary to fully develop what is "received from Heaven"—our own and others' natural endowments. This entreaty, a persistent message of the time, stands in contrast to Liu Zongyuan's advocacy of naturalness and nonintervention in, for example, the Guo Tuotuo story.

By exercising careful authorial control over both story and argument, Wang Anshi is no longer the traditional historian issuing general moral judgment over his protagonists' actions, but rather asserts his presence and viewpoint into the story. If he only gradually builds that role by easing himself into the narrative step by step, Su Shi, Wang's Northern Song contemporary and colleague, as in the following story, "An Account of Fang Shanzi," actively participates in the unfolding of the story and its intellectual and emotional agenda from the beginning. Indeed, one might argue that this author makes himself an equal participant in the story along with his biographical subject. As we will see, it is as much about Fang Shanzi as Su Shi himself. This sets it apart from all the previous five stories, in which the narrator assumes a strong interventionist stance but maintains his independence from his subject.

C13.6 Su Shi, "An Account of Fang Shanzi, Master Square Mountain" ("Fang Shanzi zhuan")

蘇軾　方山子傳

Fang Shanzi was a person living a reclusive life in the area between Guangzhou and Huangzhou.[1] When he was young he admired the heroisms of Zhu Jia and Guo Jie,[2] and the young dandies in the neighborhood all looked up to him. As he grew older, however, he changed his mind and committed to studying, hoping to gallop the world[3] by means of his scholarship, but ended up not meeting his time.[4] At old age, he hid himself in a place between Guangzhou and Huangzhou called Qiting.[5] He lived in a thatched house and ate coarse food, and did not have dealings with the outside world. He gave up his horses and carriages, destroyed his gorgeous garment, traveled in the mountains on foot, and no one recognized him. They saw that the hat he wore had a square top and was tall, and said: "Isn't this modeled on the old Square Mountain hat from antiquity?" Thus they called him "Master Square Mountain."[6]

方山子，光、黃間隱人也。少時慕朱家、郭解為人，閭里之俠皆宗之。稍壯，折節讀書，欲以此馳騁當世。然終不遇，晚乃遯於光、黃間曰歧亭。菴居蔬食，不與世相聞。棄車馬，毀冠服，徒步往來山中，人莫識也。見其所著帽，方屋而高，曰：“此豈古方山冠之遺像乎？”因謂之方山子。

When I was banished to Huangzhou,[7] I passed by Qiting one day,[8] and happened to run into him. I said: "Alas! Isn't this my old friend Chen Zao, Jichang?[9] What are you doing here?" Fang Shanzi was also surprised and asked me why I was there. I told him my story. He bent down his body and did not reply, and then straightening up, he laughed, and invited me to stay at his house. I looked around the interior of his house and it had a desolate look, but his wife, children, and servants all bore a calm expression of satisfaction.

余謫居于黃，過歧亭，適見焉。曰：“嗚呼！此吾故人陳慥季常也。何為而在此？”方山子亦矍然問余所以至此者。余告之故。俯而不答，仰而笑，呼余宿其家。環堵蕭然，而妻子奴婢皆有自得之意。

---

[1] Guangzhou and Huangzhou were bordering prefectures in modern Henan and Hubei, respectively. Note that Guangzhou here is not the city with the same spelling in modern Guangdong.

[2] Zhu Jia and Guo Jie were famous wandering knights during the Western Han.

[3] That is, to achieve fame and glory.

[4] That is, unsuccessful.

[5] The name of the place means literally "Crossroads Pavilion"; boundary crossing is a larger point suggested in the biography.

[6] Fang Shanzi means literally "Master Square Mountain."

[7] Su Shi was demoted and banished to Huangzhou at the end of 1079 as a result of the infamous Crow Terrace literary inquisition against him, accused of using poetry to criticize the New Policies. He stayed in Huangzhou until 1084.

[8] The text does not make clear whether he was on his way to Huangzhou via Qiting or whether he visited the place after his arrival in Huangzhou.

[9] Chen Zao, courtesy Jichang, whose exact dates are unknown, was the fourth son of Chen Xiliang (1002–1065), under whom Su Shi had served in Shaanxi at the start his career. Chen Xiliang was the great grandfather of late–Northern Song poet Chen Yuyi (1090–1139). The next paragraph features Su Shi's recollection of his first encounter with Chen Zao in Shaanxi.

余既聳然異之，獨念方
山子少時，使酒好劍，
用財如糞土。前十有九
年，余在岐下，見方山
子從兩騎，挾二矢，游
西山。鵲起于前，使騎
逐而射之，不獲。方山
子怒馬獨出，一發得
之。因與余馬上論用兵
及古今成敗，自謂一世
豪士。今幾日耳，精悍
之色猶見於眉間，而豈
山中之人哉！然方山子
世有勳閥，當得官，
使從事於其間，今已顯
聞。而其家在洛陽，園
宅壯麗與公侯等。河北
有田，歲得帛千匹，亦
足以富樂。皆棄不取，
獨來窮山中，此豈無得
而然哉！余聞光、黃間
多異人，往往陽狂垢
汙，不可得而見。方山
子儻見之歟？

[*SSWJ* 2:420–421]

Surprised by this, my thoughts then raced back to when Fang Shanzi was young and fond of drinking and swordsmanship, spending money like muck and dirt. Nineteen years earlier, I was at Qishan[10] and saw Fang Shanzi at the western mountains accompanied by two riders and with two arrows under his arm. A fowl flew up in front of them; he asked the riders to chase and shoot it, but they were unable to catch it. Fang Shanzi galloped his horse out and got it with a single shot. Still on his horseback, he thereupon talked about strategies of using troops and the glories and failures of past and present times with me, considering himself a proud knight of the world. Not so many days had passed now and the vigorous spirit was still there in his eyes—how can he be a man of the mountains? Fang Shanzi was from an eminent family with accumulated merits from generations of government service, and he could have easily gained office through that.[11] Had he taken that route, he would now have made a name for himself among the great statesmen. In addition, his home was in Luoyang and the magnificence of his family estates and gardens matched that of the noble lords and dukes. His family also owned land north of the Yellow River, which gave them an income of a thousand bolts of cloth every year, enough for an affluent and enjoyable life. All these he abandoned and had come here alone to the remote mountains—how can this be so without his deliberate thought? I have heard that there are many unusual people living in seclusion among the Guangzhou and Huangzhou mountains, and they often feign madness and intentionally smear their appearances, and cannot be seen. Will Fang Shanzi perhaps have a chance to meet them?

The two dramatic moments of encounter between author and biographical subject—the first told in the second paragraph relating Su Shi chancing upon Fang Shanzi in Qiting and recognizing the latter's real identity, and the second recollected in the last paragraph nineteen years earlier when both were young and had first met in Shaanxi—provide the account with emotional intensity and simultaneously cultural significance. These fondly narrated moments present a representation of Chen Zao's character as well as Su Shi's self-portrait. Su Shi's appreciation of Chen Zao's youthful ambition and heroics and his contentment with his way of life in old age comes from the depths of his heart. In emphasizing that Chen Zao's life of seclusion and withdrawal from politics is not driven by external circumstances but came from deliberate thought, Su Shi not only endorses the value inherent in Chen's action but also paves the way for his own transformation during his five-year Huangzhou exile. From this exile emerged a cultural personality described by his modern biographer Lin Yutang as "the gay genius," embodying a spirit that values self-fulfillment and satisfaction far above worldly achievements. This is the

---

[10] Su Shi was appointed assistant prefect of Fengxiang, of modern Shaanxi in the Mount Qi area, in 1061 after passing a prestigious special exam. Chen Zao's father Chen Xiliang, the prefect, was his supervisor.

[11] The hereditary "protection privileges" (*yin*) of high-ranking officials qualified their children for government service without taking the examinations.

message Su Shi powerfully delivers in his account of Fang Shanzi. In other words, Su Shi's biographical sketch of Chen Zao (*a.k.a.* Fang Shanzi, or "Master Square Mountain") is personally motivated as a manifesto of their shared way of life symbolized by the tall and archaic form of the hat, which is an indirect criticism of the contemporary status of things.

Walking through these six biographical works piece by piece ideally made them easy to grasp and clarified some of their literary devices and historical and cultural contexts. To conclude this chapter, a few key points made or suggested in this discussion are worth stressing. Historical and moral persuasion remains an important part of such biographical writings throughout the Tang and Song period, but we also witnessed the genre undergoing significant new development, becoming an independent form of literature for personal and cultural expression outside of official historiography. This is perhaps their most prominent new collective identity, shaped by both their prototypes in historical biography of earlier periods (☞ chap. 2, 6) and the emerging tendency in the Tang and Song toward individual and cultural expression. The increased use of colloquial expressions, attention to narrative and logical detail and clarity, and avoidance of ornate phrasing and parallel syntax structures demonstrated in these pieces illustrate how the new biographical writing was influenced, both stylistically and intellectually, by the generally reformed style of prose in the broader literary culture.

Also worth noting is an aspect of change that is only implied in these discussions. The biographical writings translated and analyzed in this chapter represent a new development against the genre's historical origins, but a simultaneous internal change occurred within the period. The two pieces by Wang Anshi and Su Shi from the Northern Song are much more intimately associated with the author's personal life experience as well as more rooted in the intellectual and cultural circumstances of the time than the works by their Tang counterparts. The messages of Han Yu and Liu Zongyuan are essentially politically and morally motivated, whereas those of Wang Anshi and Su Shi were more culturally based. What this cultural shift in biographical writing might mean for the development of Chinese literature and culture in general and for later periods, we leave the readers to ponder.

Notably, these writings are not only vehicles for understanding the cultural and historical contexts that inspired their creation but also specimens of the finest prose writing of the period and in Chinese literature as a whole. For both of these reasons, they are still widely read and diligently studied by students in contemporary China and around the world.

Yugen Wang

SUGGESTED READING

ENGLISH

Chen, Jo-shui. *Liu Zongyuan and Intellectual Change in Tang China, 773–819.* Cambridge: Cambridge University Press, 1992.

Egan, Ronald. *Word, Image, and Deed in the Life of Su Shi.* Cambridge, MA: Harvard University Press, 1994.

Hartman, Charles. "Alieniloquium: Liu Zongyuan's Other Voice." *Chinese Literature: Essays, Articles, Reviews* 4, no. 1 (1982): 23–73.

Hightower, James R. "Han Yu as a Humorist." *Harvard Journal of Asiatic Studies* 44 (1984): 5–27.

Liu, Shih Shun. *Chinese Classical Prose: The Eight Masters of the Tang-Song Period*. Hong Kong: Chinese University Press, 1979.

CHINESE

Han Zhaoqi 韓兆琦. *Zhongguo zhuanji yishu* 中國傳記藝術 (*The Art of Chinese Biographical Writing*). Hohhot: Neimenggu jiaoyu chubanshe, 1998.

Jiang Tao 姜濤 and Zhao Hua 趙華. *Gudai zhuanji wenxue shigao* 古代傳記文學史稿 (*A Draft History of Traditional Biographical Literature*). Shenyang: Liaoning daxue chubanshe, 1990.

Shi Suzhao 史素昭. *Tangdai zhuanji wenxue yanjiu* 唐代傳記文學研究 (*A Study of Tang Dynasty Biographical Literature*). Changsha: Yuelu shushe, 2009.

Yu Zhanghua 俞樟華. *Zhongguo zhuanji wenxue lilun yanjiu* 中國傳記文學理論研究 (*A Study of Theories of Chinese Biographical Literature*). Changsha: Hunan wenyi chubanshe, 2000.

PART IV

The Ming and Qing Dynasties

14

Ming and Qing Eight-Legged Essays

The "eight-legged essay" (*baguwen*) is the common name for the most stringent form of classical Chinese composition required in late-imperial civil service examinations. Civil service examinations had been a hallmark of the Chinese state bureaucracy from the tenth through the early twentieth century. Meritocratic at least in theory, it allowed the court to attract the service of educated men from a broader social base and enhanced the solidity between the rulers and the elite. Often referred to as the late-imperial period because they were the last two dynasties in Chinese history, the Ming (1368–1644) and the Qing (1644–1911), with one brief hiatus, adopted the eight-legged essay as the central requirement in their civil service examinations. This literary genre thus became the obsession of hundreds of thousands of educated men across the empire who spent long years preparing for the examinations and strived for the slim chance of success at different levels of the examination ladder. The essay gets its name from the two beginning, two middle, two penultimate, and two final parallel sets of sentences at its core in the standard form (its eight "legs"), which constitute the designated rhetorical structure for argumentation. Actual compositions, however, could be flexible, and there are six-, ten-, and even sixteen-legged examples. The many alternative names for the essay emphasize its other features, such as "contemporary-style essay" (*shiwen*), "formulated craft" (*zhiyi*), and "formulated exegesis [of Confucian Classics]" (*zhiyi*).

Late-imperial civil service examinations were built on a long legacy. Although evaluative mechanisms for officials can be traced to earlier periods, it was the Tang (618–907) system that provided the blueprint. While Tang bureaucracy relied heavily on family privileges and recommendations, a small portion (less than 10 percent) of its new officials was selected through examinations, allowing educated men with few or no court connections to earn entry through their talent. These examinations were mounted principally in two ways. First, the emperor could issue a decree to select special talents needed at court, and candidates would then come to the capital to take those irregularly set examinations. Second, each prefecture was required to annually send to the court, along with tribute goods, candidates with expertise in certain areas. Once in the capital, those candidates took examinations granting them degrees in mathematics, law, and other specialties. The most sought-after titles were Canonical Expert (*mingjing*) and Presented Scholar (*jinshi*), with the latter surpassing the former in prestige by the eighth century. The Canonical Expert examination emphasized candidates' memorization of the Confucian

Classics, whereas the main criterion for the Presented Scholar examination was poetic excellence. The prestige of the Presented Scholar examination had to do with its low success rate (5 percent or lower), passing only about twenty to thirty men a year, and its degree-holders tended to enjoy more successful careers than those from other types of examinations (☞ *HTRCPIC* chap. 11).

Although the Song dynasty (960–1279) still allowed family privileges and the emperors also held special examinations, regular recruitment examinations played a much bigger role. As of the 1060s, examinations were held every three years. Candidates had to first pass local examinations before they could participate in the metropolitan examination, and the emperor presided over the palace examination to rank graduates of the metropolitan examination. In contrast to their Tang counterparts, who earned only eligibility for office and had to wait for appointments, metropolitan-level graduates were appointed to office immediately. To ensure impartiality, the Song system blocked out the names of candidates or had answer sheets recopied. Although the Presented Scholar examination maintained its prominence, its criteria shifted as those who saw poetry as superficial and irrelevant to official recruitment gained more influence. In 1071, the statesman Wang Anshi (1021–1086) replaced the poetic composition with the classical essay and required candidates to articulate their understanding of the Confucian Classics.

The Yuan dynasty (1279–1368) largely abandoned civil service examinations, but the system was reinstated in the Ming to attract educated men to government service. Structurally, the Ming examinations were divided into four levels. County- and prefectural-level examinations were held annually by local officials. Successful candidates were eligible to take the provincial examinations, held every three years. Provincial graduates then congregated in the capital in the following year for the metropolitan examinations. Those who passed took the palace examination and were ranked, awarded a Presented Scholar degree, and usually assigned official posts. The Qing dynasty adopted the same system with minor modifications. The examinations were extremely competitive, and only the lucky few, ranging roughly from one hundred to four hundred men each time, were able to win the Presented Scholar degree. Candidates who passed the lower-level examinations, however, could earn various privileges as well as opportunities to serve in local governments. Many men spent most of their lives climbing the examination ladder. Famous writer and compiler Feng Menglong (1574–1646), for instance, was close to sixty years old when he finally acquired the status of an outstanding prefectural graduate and started his career as a local official. In light of such competitiveness, it is not surprising that when the twenty-three-year-old Yuan Mei (1716–1797) won his Presented Scholar degree, he instantly became a celebrity as an icon of youthful genius; he was able to retire from officialdom in his late thirties and lead a comfortable life by capitalizing on his fame and social connections.

The eight-legged essay constituted the most important part of the late-imperial (or Ming and Qing) civil service examinations. Candidates were required to compose in other genres as well, including policy questions, legal judgments, and edicts. The Chinese linguistic system at this time was defined by a bifurcation between the written classical language, a lingua franca similar to Latin, and spoken vernaculars, including provincial dialects and the capital dialect, generally adopted by officials. Although the examination system was meritocratic by design and supposedly open to all, its compositions had to be in classical Chinese. This excluded a large sector of the society unable to afford a lengthy classical education. In addition, the compositions had to be written out in acceptable calligraphic styles, follow designated formats, and be free of mistakes and smudges. It was the eight-legged essay, however, that was most difficult yet most crucial to a candidate's success.

Introduced in the Chenghua reign (1465–1487), the eight-legged essay established strict rules for the form and content of the composition. Its content should be devoted to the exegesis of Confucian Classics, specifically following the Learning of the Way (daoxue) interpretive tradition of Neo-Confucianism. Formulated by brothers Cheng Hao (1032–85) and Cheng Yi (1033–1107) and a few other thinkers, and later synthesized by Zhu Xi (1130–1200), the Learning of the Way advocated cultivating the heart and mind as the foundation for transcending selfish desires and comprehending the principles (li), or the Way (dao), inherent in human nature and the cosmos. The "investigation of things" (gewu) in the world was central to the program of self-cultivation, but emphasis was also placed on the Confucian Classics, which, if interpreted "correctly," offered guidance from the ancient sages. Zhu Xi in particular promoted the Four Books, namely, the *Great Learning* (*Daxue*), *Doctrine of the Mean* (*Zhongyong*), *Analects* (*Lunyu*), and *Mencius* (*Mengzi*). He tried to provide "correct" interpretations of the Four Books through his own commentaries and those that he approved. Zhu Xi and other like-minded scholars were successful in recruiting followers, and as a result of changing court politics and historical circumstances, their ideas eventually won the official support of the court toward the end of the Southern Song (1127–1279). When the early Ming rulers adopted the Learning of the Way as state orthodoxy, they made Cheng-Zhu interpretations of the Four Books as well as the Five Classics—namely, the *Book of Poetry* (*Shijing*), *Book of Documents* (*Shangshu*), *Book of Rites* (*Liji*), *Book of Changes* (*Yijing*), and *Spring and Autumn Annals* (*Chunqiu*)—the core of civil service examinations and educational curricula across the empire.

Although few candidates mastered the entire Five Classics, all were expected to memorize the Four Books and fully comprehend Zhu Xi's commentaries on them. Excelling in the eight-legged essay was essential as it was the first and most important part of the examinations at all three levels preceding the palace ranking. During the Ming, for example, the first session of the provincial and metropolitan examinations required candidates to compose three eight-legged essays on the Four Books and four on the Five Classics, with priority given to the former. During the Qing, the essays on the Four Books remained in the first session, but those on the Five Classics were moved to the second. Because of the supreme importance of the Four Books, the eight-legged essay is also referred to simply as the "essay on the Four Books" (*Sishu wen*).

Examiners selected quotations from those canonical texts as topics for the essay. Since both provincial and metropolitan examinations were held every three years, topic repetition was less likely than with annual local examinations. As a result, the higher-level examinations tended to quote more complete units of meaning (e.g., passages or lines), whereas the local examinations had more truncated selections (e.g., phrases). The greater difficulty of the latter also screened out less-competent candidates among the hundreds of thousands who sat for the local examinations across the empire. After identifying the quotations and their original context, a candidate was expected to explain their meanings without repeating either the classics or the approved exegeses. Meanwhile, the candidate was required to "speak on behalf of a sage" (*dai shengren liyan*). In other words, he had to fully internalize the moral teachings and demonstrate his ability to articulate and spread their message as a later-day embodiment of the original Confucian sage. This impersonation requirement suggested an affinity between the eight-legged essay and drama, and exclamatory particles and single-character conjunctions often were used to convey the manner of a speaking voice and enhance the essay's oratorical force. Meanwhile, the deployment of rhetorical argumentation could be linked to the tradition established in the expository prose of the Tang and Song (☛ chap. 10).

In addition to the constraints in content, the eight-legged essay was also distinguished by its strict formal requirements. It was limited to five hundred characters in late Ming, then seven hundred in mid-Qing. The standard structure contains these main parts:

> Breaking open the topic (*poti*) → Developing the topic (*chengti*) → Beginning discussion (*qijiang*) → Initial legs (*qigu*) → Middle legs (*zhonggu*) → Penultimate legs (*hougu*) → Last legs (*shugu*) → Grand conclusion (*dajie*)

The following sample essays illustrate the distinctive function of each part and how they work together. Note, however, that this standard structure is an idealized template rather than an inflexible grid. In actual compositions, a writer could vary the number of legs, as well as include transitional sentences, phrases, and particles to ensure the essay's rhetorical flow.

At the same time, the rule of parallelism in the legs remains constant. The hallmark of the most challenging forms of traditional Chinese poetry, parallelism refers to the construction of two phrases, lines, sentences, or sets of sentences that parallel each other in length, syntax, vocabulary, structure, and even tonal pattern. While parallel patterning was established in the "parallel prose" (*pianwen*) of the early medieval period (☛ chap. 9), it was during the Tang that it evolved into the rigid requirement that the "regulated verse" (*lüshi*) was famous for (☛ *HTRCP* chap. 8). A regulated verse must include parallel couplets. Take for instance a couplet by Tang poet Du Fu (712–770), a master in the art:

Two yellow orioles sing among green willows;	兩個黃鸝鳴翠柳，
	＼ ＼ － － － ＼ ＼，
A trail of white egrets flies up to the blue sky.	一行白鷺上青天。
	－ － － ＼ ＼ － －.

[*DSXZ* 13.1143]

The seven-character lines follow the same structure: subject (i.e., number + noun) action (i.e., verb) location (i.e., adjective + noun). Meanwhile, the words in the same positions in the two lines form a series of contrasts in meaning and image: two single birds versus a trail of birds, yellow orioles versus white egrets, sitting and singing (horizontal motion, sound) versus flying up (vertical motion, silence), and green willows (Earth) versus the blue sky (Heaven). Although Chinese languages, including dialects, are characterized by their varied number of tones (e.g., modern Mandarin has four tones), traditional poetry divides the tones of Chinese characters into two groups, the level (*pingsheng*, now marked by "—") and the oblique tone (*zesheng*, now marked by "\") (➥ *HTRCP* chap. 8). The tonal patterns of Du Fu's couplet establish similarities and differences that produce the nice musicality of the couplet when it is read aloud. Parallelism thus creates sophisticated syntactical, semantic, and tonal contrasts, similarities, and complements. For the poet, however, it greatly limits the word choices. For example, "green" (*cui*, oblique tone) in the first line would require the match of another color word with a level tone in the sixth-character position of the second line, "blue" (*qing*) in this case. In contrast to Du Fu's seven-character couplet, the legs of the eight-legged essay do not have any set length or designated tonal patterns, and word repetitions are allowed. Nevertheless, a leg can include multiple sentences, each of which requires a corresponding parallel in the following leg. In the first sample essay, for instance, the last legs contain twenty sentences in total (ten in each leg). The parallelism in the eight legs (or as many as sixteen legs) also has to serve the function of coherent, layered argumentation. Given the scale and complexity of the challenge of parallelism in the legs, the reputation of the eight-legged essay as the most difficult kind of literary composition in late-imperial China is no exaggeration. It has been portrayed as "dancing with shackles."

With such stringent requirements, training for the eight-legged essay started early and became central to the lives of millions of educated men in late-imperial China. Once school children finished their primers, they began to study and memorize the Four Books and attempt the eight-legged essay. Under a teacher's guidance, they first would practice "breaking open the topic," before gradually expanding to other parts of the essay. They also would study sample essays by well-known writers, most of whom were successful graduates, whereas some were recognized masters of the form despite not having achieved high-level examination success. The publishing industry was more than happy to cater to the needs of so many candidates, printing collections of sample essays along with other study guides. Successful examples from provincial and metropolitan examinations were often anthologized, while individual compilers also tried to sway literary trends by putting out collections in line with their tastes. Even the court saw the need to step in and offer its own authoritative edition, as the Qianlong emperor (r. 1735–1796) of the Qing commissioned his official Fang Bao (1668–1749) to compile the *Imperially Authorized Essays on the Four Books* (*Qinding Sishu wen*). Highly influential, the collection featured sample essays from different time periods and established a canonical tradition for the genre.

We examine one essay by Chen Zilong (1608–1647) from this collection as an example. A talented writer and scholar from Songjiang (today's Shanghai), Chen was already active in the local literary circles as a young man. He published his eight-legged essays along with other core members of a literary society in a collected anthology, thereby gaining wider recognition for his talent. In 1637, he passed the metropolitan examination and became a Presented Scholar degree holder. But his official career was delayed by mourning for his stepmother and then thwarted by the fall of the Ming in 1644 as the Manchus began their takeover of China. Although Chen joined the fallback Southern Ming court in Jiangnan, he quickly became disillusioned and returned home. Despite a brief stint as a Buddhist monk, he became heavily involved in the anti-Qing resistance and was later captured by Qing forces. As he was being transported to the regional capital Nanjing, he committed suicide by throwing himself into a river.

The topic of the essay in the *Imperially Authorized Essays on the Four Books* by Chen Zilong was taken from the *Analects*. It is a one-line quotation from Confucius (ca. 551–ca. 479 BCE): "The Master said, 'A superior man detests dying without achieving renown.'" In the *Collected Commentaries on the* Analects (*Lunyu jizhu*), however, Zhu Xi does not provide an explanation of his own for this particular quote but instead cites the commentary of the historian and scholar Fan Zuyu (1041–98): "Mr. Fan said, 'A superior man studies only for his own sake and does not seek to be known by others. If he dies without achieving renown, however, one can tell that he has not done any good.'" (*LYJZ* 8.165). Therein, Fan tries to reconcile the apparent contradiction between this assertion by Confucius and the immediately preceding one, to wit, that a superior man should not worry about being unknown. Fan bridges these statements by arguing that self-cultivation should not have any ulterior motive, such as fame, which can be achieved posthumously through the good that one did for the world while alive. Conversely, Chen Zilong tries in his essay to fully explore the tensions between intention and result, self and others, and short- and long-term reputation.

C14.1 Chen Zilong, "A Superior Man Detests Dying Without Achieving Renown"

陳子龍　君子疾沒世而名不稱焉

1.	破題	無後世之名，聖人之所憂也。
	Breaking open the topic	That he will lack renown in posterity, this is what worries the sage.

This first section identifies the meaning of the designated topic, thereby demonstrating that the writer has an accurate understanding of its original context and approved interpretation. He is expected to not repeat the topic verbatim but to paraphrase it. Chen Zilong fulfills this requirement by skillfully substituting "the sage" for "a superior man" in the topic, "worry" with "detest," and "renown in posterity" for "dying without achieving renown."

2.	承題 Developing the topic	夫 一時 之名 不必有也，後世 之名 不可無也。故君子不求名，而又不得不疾乎此。 Indeed, short-lived renown is dispensable; renown in later times is requisite. Therefore, the superior man does not seek renown, yet he cannot but suffer concern about it.

The function of this second section is to supplement the first by further explaining the thesis. Chen Zilong breaks down the superior man's worry into two contrasting sets of choices he confronts: the short-lived versus the long-lasting renown, and the pursuit of renown versus the concern about it. The superior man's seemingly paradoxical preferences for not pursuing renown and for being concerned about it warrant an in-depth explanation, thus opening up room for subsequent discussion and analysis.

3.	起講 Beginning discussion	夫子若曰：好名者，人之恒情也，故下士求名，人亦不得以為躁，但我恨其急一時之名，而非千秋萬世之名耳，若君子則知所以審處於此矣。 The Master [Confucius] would say: To love renown is people's normal inclination. Thus, when a low-status gentleman seeks renown, people should not regard him as impetuous. I would just regret his hastening after short-lived renown, rather than the renown of ten-thousand generations. A superior man would reflect seriously in managing this.

The third section requires the writer to step into the persona of the ancient sage and start speaking in his voice. In addition, the section usually lays out the issues to be elaborated on later and sets the stage for the core, namely, the eight-legged section. Because Chen Zilong's topic is drawn from the *Analects*, he assumes the voice of Confucius. Consistent with the traditional image of Confucius as a wise, humane teacher, Chen's version of the Master recognizes that love for renown is part of human nature and is not morally wrong in itself. Just like a civil man who rises above his natural appetites for food and sex to reach a moral state of being, a superior man is careful about what kind of renown he pursues. This part adds a new contrast, the superior man versus his inferiors, including ordinary people who follow their inclinations and a low-status gentleman who has not yet set his priorities straight. Subtly, Chen Zilong replaces "renown in later times" from the previous section with "renown of ten-thousand generations," suggesting that the posthumous renown is immortal and thereby giving it more weight than "short-lived renown."

4. 起股
Initial legs

4a.以為一時之名，自我為之，而其權在人，苟我之聰明才力，注乎名則有名，而皆倚人以為重，盛與衰我不得而知之，此名而名者也。

Speaking more specifically, while short-lived renown is shaped by oneself, the ultimate power lies with others. If I pour my wisdom and talent into pursuing such renown, I will attain it. But that [kind of] renown relies heavily on others, and I cannot know whether it will rise or fall. This is renown in name only.

4b.千秋萬世之名，自人為之，而其權在我，苟我之聰明才力，注乎名未必有名，而常修己以自立，高與下我將得而定之，此名而實者也。

Though renown that lasts ten-thousand generations is shaped by others, the ultimate power lies in oneself. If I pour my wisdom and talent into pursuing such renown, I will not necessarily attain it. But with regular self-cultivation to establish myself, I get to determine whether it is lofty or lowly. This is renown with substance.

This fourth section consists of the initial legs, which usually focus on one aspect of the central thesis onto which the subsequent legs can be built. Chen Zilong uses the initial legs to present the first pair of extended contrasting arguments. He elaborates on the contrast between short-lived and the long-lasting renown in terms of attainability, one's control, and the nature of the end result, detailed in the two legs, respectively. Although one can try hard to attain short-lived renown, it is in name only because it depends on others' assessment. In stark contrast, despite personal efforts, one may not attain long-lasting renown; however, such renown has more substance because the kind of posthumous reputation one leaves is determined by oneself. These comparisons shore up the superiority of long-lasting over short-lived renown.

5. 中股
Middle legs

5a.名而名者，無之在於未沒世之前，君子豈可以徒疾乎？

Renown in name only: lacking it before death, how could a superior man disapprove of this?

5b.名而實者，無之在於既沒世之後，君子豈得而不疾乎？

Renown with substance: lacking it after death, how could a superior man not be distressed by this?

The fifth section, the middle legs, bridges the initial and penultimate legs. Chen Zilong builds on the previous section to extend the argument. Using rhetorical questions instead of plain statements, Chen makes it seem obvious that a superior man would choose long-lasting renown and become distressed if he fails to achieve his objective. The questions also serve to connect with the reader by conveying an assumption of shared logic. By making clear distinctions between short-lived and long-lasting renown and separating them into two parallel legs in both the initial and the middle legs, Chen splits the arguments into two neat, contrasting parts, an effective strategy for privileging one over the other.

6.	後股 Penultimate legs	6a.人之生也有愛有憎，故有幸而有名者，有不幸而無名者，至於身沒之後，與其人不相接，則不可曰愛憎之所為也，而寂寂者竟如斯，則將何以自異於里巷之子耶？	6b.人之生也有失勢有得勢，故有幸而無名者，又有不幸而有名者，至於身沒之後，與其時不相及，則又有非得勢失勢之可論矣，而泯泯者遂如斯，則又何以自別於草木之儔耶？
		In life people have their loves and hates. [Accordingly] the fortunate become famous, and the unfortunate become obscure. After death, they have no contact with people [of later times], so [their reputations] cannot be said to result from [latter-day people's] loves or hates. In a situation like this, if one becomes forgotten [posthumously], how can he distinguish himself from the riffraff of alleys and lanes?	In life people can hit or miss the trend of the times. So some have luck but not renown, while others have no luck but do gain renown. After death, they become irrelevant to contemporary times, so there is no matter of hitting or missing the trend to discuss. In a situation like this, if one becomes obscure [posthumously], how can he distinguish himself from the common run of folk?

This sixth section is long because the penultimate legs carry the most substantial portion of the argument. Chen Zilong expands on the main themes of previous sections by further explaining why posthumous renown is long-lasting and the superior man is concerned about it. Unlike the initial and middle legs, both of which separate the different arguments about short-lived versus long-lasting renown in two respective legs, the two legs in this section make the same argument but with different emphases. The first points out that renown in life is short-lived because it is determined by other people's subjective judgments, whereas the second contends that it also can be due to one's luck in matching contemporary trends, with posthumous renown in both cases immune to such variations. Posthumous renown thus becomes the true indicator of one's worthiness, obscurity an indictment of one's lack of it. Whereas the latter fate often befalls ordinary people, it is what the superior man tries to avoid. The parallel arguments in the penultimate legs thus effectively echo and reinforce each other to drive home the point. Although Chen's reasoning certainly betrays his elitist bias, we should keep in mind that the Confucian definition of a "superior man" is predicated on his moral and intellectual superiority to the common folk.

7.   束股   **7a.** 人之貴乎榮名者，貴其有<u>益生</u>之樂   **7b.** 人之以為沒世之名者，是我<u>身後</u>之<u>計</u>
     Last legs   也；君子之貴榮名者，貴其有不死之業   也；君子以為沒世之名者，是我大生之事
       也。死而無聞，則其死<u>可悲</u>矣；死而可   也。死而無聞，則其死 <u>不及憂</u> 矣；死不
       悲，則其生<u>更可悲</u>矣。是以君子<u>抗節礪</u>   及憂，則其生大可憂矣。是以君子 <u>趨事赴</u>
       <u>行</u>，惟恐<u>不及</u>耳。   功，惟日不足耳。

An [ordinary] man, in valuing great renown, is valuing its increase to life's enjoyment. A superior man, in valuing great renown, is valuing its [mark of] immortal accomplishment. A death in obscurity is a lamentable death. If one's death is lamentable, then one's life is even more lamentable. So a superior man upholds principles and refines his conduct, fearing only that [renown] may not be reached.	To an [ordinary] man, posthumous renown concerns one's plan for what happens after one dies. To a superior man, posthumous renown constitutes the challenge of one's whole life. A death in obscurity is a death not worth concern. If one's death is not worth concern, then one's life is greatly concerning. So a superior man hastens to [handle] affairs and strives for success, [worrying] only that there is not sufficient time.

This seventh section, the last legs, is often substantial because it typically serves to extend the reasoning of the penultimate legs or bring in new strands central to the thesis. Chen Zilong elaborates on the superiority of a superior man to an ordinary one, as illustrated by their different approaches to renown in this life and posthumous renown. In terms of rhetorical structure, it is more complex because it combines the split arguments of the initial and middle legs and the parallel arguments of the penultimate legs. The first leg starts with the value of renown in this life for the ordinary man and the superior man, whereas the second leg treats the relative value of posthumous renown. Both the first leg and the second one, however, end with the same argument: a death in obscurity is not acceptable to the superior man because it indicates a lack of accomplishment in life—his real motivation in pursuing self-cultivation and worldly success. The last legs reiterate the gist of Fan Zuyu's commentary, thus demonstrating Chen's accurate understanding of the orthodox interpretation of Confucius's statement.

8.   大結   人但見君子之為人也，譽之而不喜，毀之而不懼，<u>以為君子之忘名也如此</u>，<u>而不知有所甚不忘</u>
     Grand   <u>也</u>；不大言以欺人，不奇行以駭俗，<u>以為君子之遠名也如此</u>，<u>而不知有所甚不遠也</u>。蓋<u>有大於</u>
     conclusion   此者而已，有久於此者而已。若夫營營於旦夕之間，是求速盡者也，好名者豈如是乎？

People merely observe a superior man's behavior: He is neither happy when praised nor scared when maligned. So people take this to be his indifference to renown, not knowing what it is that he never forgets. He does not exaggerate to deceive others nor act strangely to astound the world. So people take this to be his distancing himself from renown, not knowing that from which he never is distant. There simply is something greater than [what they perceive], and more lasting as well. If one bustles about from dawn to dusk [hoping to gain a short-term reputation], it is simply the pursuit of a quick demise. How could one who loves [true] renown be like that?

[*QDSSW* 14:5.3a–4b]

[☛ HTRCProse-CCC, L31]

N.B. Straight underline indicates the use of repetitive patterning; wavy underline the use of parallel patterning. For a discussion on repetitive and parallel patterning, ☛ C1.1–4 and C1.6–7.

This eighth section sums up previous analysis and offers a broad perspective that both reiterates and elevates the central argument. Chen again underscores the superiority of the superior man over ordinary folk by pointing out their common misunderstanding of his true intentions, a misunderstanding that stems from his moral principles and refusal to cater to the world for short-term renown in life. His seeming indifference to this kind of renown is a deliberate moral choice, for he sets his heart on more meaningful, long-lasting posthumous renown. The conclusion thus returns to the larger context of Confucius's statement within the *Analects* and sums up the essay's skillful resolution of that statement's seeming contradiction with his preceding assertion that a superior man should not be worried about being unknown to others. Thus, the superior man can fulfill both teachings by caring not about renown in life but about posthumous renown.

Chen Zilong's work embodies the standard structure of the eight-legged essay and the sophisticated argumentation it requires. From "breaking open the topic" to the "grand conclusion," the essay unpacks the nuanced meanings of Confucius's statement and resolves any implicit contradictions through a disciplined rhetorical analysis. The eight legs, constituting the central part of the essay, use parallelism to establish a series of contrasts and build a layered argument. A good essay like Chen Zilong's thus demonstrates the writer's strong command of classical Chinese, his literary talent, his impressive analytical skills, and his deep grasp of Confucian orthodoxy. These indications of his outstanding literary, moral, and intellectual capacities would qualify him for official positions. Advocates of the eight-legged essay often touted it as the most demanding, and hence the highest, form of literary art to distinguish the masterful from the mediocre. For examiners, the essay provided a more-or-less standardized grid on which to grade large numbers of test papers efficiently and expeditiously.

Although the stringent requirements of the eight-legged essay made it arguably the most constrained literary form, writers still found creative ways to play with it—thus the birth of the "playful eight-legged essay" (*youxi baguwen*). This alternative, produced as a literary pastime outside the official spheres of examinations and court services, is characterized by its appropriation of the examination genre for jesting and humor. Instead of "speaking on behalf of a sage," the writer impersonates a fictive character from some famous drama. Rather than the ideology of the Learning of the Way with its emphasis on self-control and social propriety, he articulates the dramatic character's private thoughts and desires, such as love-sickness, which was disapproved by Confucian thinkers. Writers who chose phrases or lines from the Four Books as their topics deviated from the orthodox interpretation to offer their own light-hearted, ingenious spins. Others picked unconventional subjects like popular sayings, life events, and typological characters for topics. The playful eight-legged essay fit into a longstanding literary tradition of jesting and parody. Scorned by stern moralists, this tradition remained vibrant as even famous writers sometimes engaged in such playful compositions. By jesting with the court-determined examination genre in particular, writers of the playful eight-legged essay could subvert the seriousness of the form and the orthodoxy of its content. Yet the audacity of such challenges was veiled by a light-heartedness that implied no serious intent.

The best-known playful eight-legged essays were those devoted to the drama *Story of the Western Wing* (*Xixiang ji*) by Wang Shifu (1260–1316). Based on a Tang dynasty short story, the play focuses on the love affair between a young examination candidate Student Zhang and a beautiful girl from an official family named Cui Yingying. After chancing upon Yingying in a Buddhist monastery, Zhang falls in love with her and they begin to communicate through poetry. When a rebel general wants to take Yingying by force, her mother promises her to anyone who can resolve the crisis, to which Student Zhang responds by enlisting the help of a friend. When the mother goes back on her word, the lovers secretly meet with the help of Yingying's maid. But their affair is exposed, and Zhang is forced to leave for the capital to sit for the examinations. There, he meets success, wins the title of the top graduate, and returns to marry Yingying. The drama was highly popular in the late-imperial period: many editions, some with exquisite illustrations, were printed and circulated, and it was also performed in different operatic styles. In a social milieu in which arranged marriage was the norm and young people's romantic liaisons were considered immoral, the story of a couple's transgressions had appeal in theatrical form. For educated men in particular, the figure of Student Zhang reinforced gender norms and affirmed their shared belief in literary talent as well as their fantasy of sexual and social success. In addition, the play was a literary masterpiece marked by elegant poetry and sentimental aesthetics. As a drama extolling romantic love, its popularity in the late-imperial period also had to do with the rise of cultural trends promoting the spontaneity and authenticity of *qing* (sentiment, passion, feelings).

The first playful eight-legged essay on the *Story of the Western Wing* was written by the literatus You Tong (1618–1704), a prolific writer of poems, plays, and other works. His playful eight-legged essay "How Irresistible That Parting Glance of Her [Eyes, Like] Autumn Ripples" was one of his many tongue-in-cheek compositions, reflecting his lively and humorous personality. Although essays discussing the main characters and plot of the *Story of the Western Wing* appeared as early as the late-fifteenth-century in a print edition of the play, You Tong's was different because it strictly followed the formal requirements of the examination genre. According to his own account, he composed the piece impromptu, just for fun at a banquet with friends. This playful eight-legged essay, however, enjoyed wide circulation, reaching even the Shunzhi emperor (r. 1643–61), who praised You Tong's talent. Royal endorsement enhanced his reputation still further and although he was unsuccessful at provincial examinations, You Tong later passed a special palace examination held by the Kangxi emperor (1661–1722), and came into prestigious appointments.

The topic of "How Irresistible That Parting Glance of Her [Eyes, Like] Autumn Ripples?" is taken from the first act of the *Story of the Western Wing*. Student Zhang visits the Buddhist monastery where Yingying is staying and sees her out taking a stroll. Realizing that a male visitor is nearby, she immediately retires as required by social etiquette, but not before she casts a glance at him. Completely stunned by Yingying's beauty, Zhang is left to lament the devastating effect of her glance, singing, "My hungry eyes keep gazing until they are strained, / My ravenous mouth in vain swallows saliva. / To no avail, I am infected by a love-sickness that pierces my bone marrow; / How irresistible that parting glance of her [eyes, like] autumn ripples" (*XXJ* 9). You Tong's playful eight-legged essay adopts the persona of Zhang to articulate his feelings and desires at this love-struck moment.

C14.2 You Tong, "How Irresistible That Parting Glance of Her [Eyes, Like] Autumn Ripples?"

尤侗　怎當他臨去秋波那一轉

1.	破題 Breaking open the topic	想雙文之目成，情以轉而通焉。 One reckons that Shuangwen's eyes cast [a glance], which, in turning, conveyed her passion.

"Autumn ripples" is a traditional metaphor for a woman's beautiful eyes, pictured as clear, lively, and potentially seductive. In breaking open the topic, You Tong substitutes this key term in the original with the alternative phrase "Shuangwen's eyes" to avoid repetition, as required by the generic convention. Instead of evoking her given name Yingying directly, however, You Tong uses her nickname Shuangwen. This nickname had been attached to Yingying since the Song, when literati started to accept the belief that Tang poet Yuan Zhen (779–831), who is mentioned in the original short story, was Student Zhang in real life and that the story was Yuan's autobiographical account. In several poems, Yuan wrote in the first-person voice of a man reminiscing about his encounter with a girl named Shuangwen (literally "double elegance" or "double graphs"). These poems are taken as the evidence of Yuan's own love affair, and Shuangwen is seen as his code name for Yingying (the name repeats or doubles the character *ying*, literally "oriole"). By referring to the heroine as Shuangwen throughout the essay, You Tong not only underscores the story's alleged real-life origin but also assumes a readership that shares this understanding. In addition, he introduces the key term "passion," which is central to his argument and will be the main focus of his essay.

2.	承題 Developing the topic	蓋秋波非能轉，情轉之也，然則雙文雖去，其猶有未去者存哉！ Her [eyes, like] autumn ripples, could not have glanced back by themselves; it was her passion that turned them. Although Shuangwen was departing, something remained behind.

In developing the topic, You Tong reiterates his thesis that Yingying's glance was motivated by her passion. Since he did not address another keyword, "parting," in the opening of the topic earlier, he links it to his thesis here by pointing out that

Yingying's departure was not the end of the story. She left something behind, presumably a sign of her passion.

3.	起講 Beginning discussion	張生若曰：世之好色者，吾知之。來相憐，去相捐也。此無他，情動而來，情盡而去耳。鍾情者正於將盡之時，露其微動之色，故足致人思焉。有如雙文者乎？ Student Zhang would say: The world's lustful people—I know them [well]. They come in affection toward the other, and depart in rejection of the other. This is naught but: coming when passion rises, and leaving when passion is spent. The truly passionate who, when desire is almost spent, disclose their [still] fluttering heart enough to extend [the paramour's] longing. Is there any like Shuangwen?

You Tong takes on the voice of Student Zhang to offer a theoretical reflection on what counts as true, hence legitimate, passion. Because sexual desires and romantic liaisons are condemned in Confucian Classics, they require justification. You Tong's Student Zhang makes a distinction between the "lustful" and the "truly passionate." The passion of the former is transient because it is nothing but carnal desire and entails no serious commitment, whereas with the latter, passion is enduring and thus entails devotion. The attribution of positive meaning to true passion is in line with other works, both earlier and contemporaneous, advocating valorization of *qing*. Zhang is imagining Yingying's passion for him in her parting glance; thus, his placing her in the category of the "truly passionate" circumvents any potential negative judgment of her as an immoral, lustful woman. Most important, the imagination and legitimation of Yingying's passion justify Zhang's desire and pursuit, for he is simply responding to her initiative. The subtle shift of moral responsibility to Yingying reveals Zhang's self-centered perspective, which dovetails with the traditional misogynism that faults women for men's inability to control their sexual desires.

4.	起股 Initial legs	4a.最可念者，囀鶯聲於花外，半晌方言，而今餘音歇矣，乃口不能傳者，目若傳之。 Most memorable was her voice, like an oriole singing beyond the flowers, so reticent was she to speak. Now as [even] that sound is trailing off, her eyes seem to convey what her mouth cannot.	4b.更可戀者，襯玉趾於殘紅，一步漸遠，而今香塵滅矣，乃足不能停者，目若停之。 Even more endearing were her feet, the jade-like toes covered with fallen blossoms as she walked, step by step, slowly away. Now that the fragrance of her movement is ceasing, her eyes seem to halt when her feet cannot.

In these initial legs, You Tong elaborates on Zhang's observations of Yingying's departure. As her elegant voice and movements make a strong impression on

Zhang, he wishfully tries to put a positive spin on her departure by assuming her interest in him. The description of her voice and her movements in the separate legs creates a contrast and a parallel that highlight Zhang's desire for her and his efforts to construe meaning from her parting glance.

| 5. | 過接
Transition | 唯見瀠瀠者，波也；脈脈者，秋波也，乍離乍合者，秋波之一轉也。吾向未之見也，不意於臨去遇之。 |

One only sees: ripples—all swirly; autumn ripples—so tender; one moment parting, one moment rejoining, [her eyes make a] turn like autumn ripples. Having never seen its like before, I did not expect to encounter it as she left.

Instead of the parallelism of another pair of legs, You Tong uses the technique of extension to make the transition from Yingying's "eyes" in the previous section to her "autumn ripples" here. Evoking "ripples" in the natural world first and then expanding it into a metaphor for her beautiful eyes, the progression underscores her natural beauty. To connect this text to the next section, You Tong shifts the focus to Student Zhang and describes his surprise discovery at the moment of her departure.

| 6. | 中股
Middle
legs | **6a.** 吾不知未去之前，秋波何屬？或者垂眺於庭軒，縱觀於花柳，不過良辰美景，偶爾相遭耳。獨是庭軒已隔，花柳方移，而婉兮清揚，忽徘徊其如送者奚爲乎？所云含睇宜笑，轉正有轉於笑之中者，雖使靚修矑於覿面，不若此際之銷魂矣！ | **6b.** 吾不知既去之後，秋波何往？意者凝眸於深院，掩淚於珠簾，不過怨粉愁香，淒其獨對耳。惟是深院將歸，珠簾半閉，而嫣然美盼，似恍惚其欲接者奚爲乎？所云眇眇愁予，轉[正]有轉於愁之中者，雖使開羞目於燈前，不若此時之心蕩矣！ |

6a. I do not know, before she left, what her "autumn ripples" fixed upon. Perhaps her gaze fell afar on the halls and verandas, or swept across the flowers and willows. On that fine day in that beautiful scene, it was by mere chance that we met. But just as she was taking leave of those halls and verandas, flowers and willows, with her lovely eyes so genial, how was it that she, delicate and elegant, unexpectedly lingered as if to see me off? It is called "holding a nice smile in a casual glance": Her turning indeed was a turn within a smile. Even if I could behold her fine eyes face to face, I could not be more enraptured than in that moment.

6b. I do not know, after she left, what her "autumn ripples" pursued. Presumably she stared into the deep cloister, and covered her tears behind pearl curtains. Naught but grief's powder and melancholy's perfume did she face, chillingly alone. But just as she began returning to the deep cloister and the pearl curtains were half closed, how was it that she, with a beguiling look, in a [slight] daze seemed desirous to meet me? It is said, "not seeing [one's beloved] makes one sad": Her turning [indeed] was a turn within sorrow. Even if she were to open her shy eyes directly in the lamplight, my heart could not be more overwhelmed than in that moment.

In these middle legs, You Tong elaborates on Zhang's imagination of Yingying's actions and sentiments before and after their encounter. With the repeated use of indeterminate phrases and words such as "I do not know" and "perhaps" as well as rhetorical questions, You Tong calls attention to the imaginative nature of Zhang's vision. The two expressions, "holding a nice smile in a casual glance" and "not seeing [one's beloved] makes one sad," are quoted from one of the earliest poetic anthologies *The Songs of Chu* (*Chu ci*) and refer to a mountain spirit and the Goddess of Xiang, respectively. The quotations emphasize Zhang's presumed familiarity with the literary canon, consistent with his identity as an educated man and examination candidate. Moreover, evoking the encounter with a goddess as a euphemism for that with a mortal woman is a longstanding poetic tradition, for the goddess from the higher realm would not be subject to the ethical constraints of this world like her mortal counterpart. In the original Tang short story, we are told that Student Zhang writes precisely such a poem to commemorate his first night with Yingying and that his friend Yuan Zhen is later inspired to compose a poem on the same topic. You Tong's portrayal of Zhang's vision of Yingying as a goddess also emphasizes her elusiveness to him, revealing the wishful nature of his imagination at the moment of being overwhelmed by her beauty.

7.	束股 Last legs	**7a.**此一轉也，以爲無情耶？轉之不能忘情，可知也！以爲有情耶？轉之不爲情滯，又可知也！人見爲秋波轉，而不見彼之心思有與爲轉者。吾即欲流睞相迎，其如一轉之不易受何？	**7b.**此一轉也，以爲情多耶？吾惜其止此一轉也。以爲情少耶？吾又恨其餘此一轉也。彼知爲秋波一轉，而不知吾之魂夢有與爲千萬轉者。吾即欲閉目不窺，其如一轉之不可却何。
		That one turn—should it be seen as lacking passion? Surely she turned out of unforgettable passion. Was it possessed of passion? Surely that turn was unimpeded by her passion. People only see the turning of her "autumn ripples," but do not see that the turning was imparted by her heart. Even if I had wished to move my eyes to meet [hers], how hard any contact would have been!	That one turn—should it be seen as a surfeit of passion? I regret that she turned but that once. Should it be seen as a deficit of passion? I also hate that she went so far as to turn that once. She knew that her "autumn ripples" made that one turn, but not that they caused my dreaming soul to make ten-thousand turns. Even if I had wished to close my eyes and not peer, how unlikely it would have been to resist that one turn!

In the last legs, You Tong's Student Zhang further contemplates the potential meanings of Yingying's one glance. The questions Zhang poses about whether to take it as an indication of her passion, the lack of it, too much of it, or too little of it, capture his sense of uncertainty. Yet with his own reassuring answers, he persuades himself of her interest in him. The two legs end with contrasting exclamations: the first on the fleeting nature of her glance and his frustration over the dim prospects for further interactions, the second on the overwhelming power of her glance and his feigned protest against its irresistibility. The contrast well conveys his anxiety and exhilaration over his newfound love.

8.　大結　　　噫嘻！
　Grand　　　招楚客於三年，似曾相識；
　conclusion　傾漢宮於一顧，無可奈何。
　　　　　　　有雙文之秋波一轉，宜小生之眼花繚亂也哉！抑老僧四壁，畫西廂而悟禪，恰在個
　　　　　　　中。蓋一轉者，情禪也。參學人試於此下一轉語。

Alas!

A Chu man's [soul] summoned three years [after his death]—this seems familiar;

A Han palace toppled by [a woman's] one backward look—nothing to be done.

How fitting that one turn of Shuangwen's "autumn ripples" completely dazzled a young scholar's eyes. Or, [also fitting] would be an old monk painting the Story of the Western Wing on his four walls, to therein achieve Chan awakening. Yes, one glance is a meditation through passion. Practitioners [of this], try turning a phrase on this [paradox].

[YTJ 122–123]

N.B. Straight underline indicates the use of repetitive patterning; wavy underline the use of parallel patterning. For a discussion on repetitive and parallel patterning, ☛ C1.1–4 and C1.6–7.

In the grand conclusion, You Tong moves into a broader reflection on the implications of love and passion. The parallel lines about a Chu man's soul and a Han palace, respectively, make a connection between male death and female beauty. The first alludes to "Summoning a Soul" from the *Songs of Chu*, which features the postmortem ritual of calling back a deceased man's spirit. The second evokes the story of how Lady Li was selected to become a favorite concubine of Emperor Wu of the Han dynasty (r. 141–87 BCE). Her brother Li Yannian, a court musician, is said to have sung a song about a woman who is so beautiful that her first backward glance topples a city and her second topples a state. He recommended his sister when the emperor's interest was piqued. By juxtaposing the allusions, You Tong suggests that the captivating effect of female beauty is as inescapable as death for men. So it is fitting that Student Zhang would find himself dazzled by Yingying's one glance. Meanwhile, the connection between male death and female beauty also evokes the traditional misogynistic view of beautiful women as a threat to men, seducing them into sexual indulgence that destroys their health by exhausting their life force, and leads them to forsake their moral and social responsibilities. For You Tong, this is the very reason the *Story of the Western Wing* is an appropriate subject of meditation for an old monk. The goal of Chan awakening is to transcend one's worldly entanglements, whereas Yingying's one glance, with its irresistible power to arouse a man's passion for sex and pleasure, epitomizes the obstacle to Buddhist enlightenment. You Tong's concluding invitation to practitioners to convey their understanding of the issue extends the challenge to his male readers: would you become Student Zhang, head over heels in love with Yingying, or the old monk who can contemplate and transcend his sexual passion?

You Tong's work illustrates important dynamics of the playful eight-legged essay as an elite literary game. Its rigid formal constraints make it an ideal form for the demonstration of writing skills and literary talent. By adopting the fictive persona of a dramatic character, however, the writer breaks through the ideological constraints of the eight-legged essay. His parody of the examination genre wins him an alternative form of success outside the examination system: the applause and laughter of his readers. In addition, such literary role-playing becomes theatrical in nature as he enacts his hero's monologue full of inner thoughts and feelings, thereby expanding the dramatic space and the character's psychic dimensions. In this regard, the playful essay also conveys the writer's nuanced understanding of character and constitutes a sort of commentary on the play. Furthermore, by offering a broader perspective on the topic at the end, the author also demonstrates his own philosophical depth and connects his discussion to the intellectual and moral discourses of his time. Through humor and parody, the playful eight-legged essay thus not only showcases the writer's erudition and dexterity but also effectively elicits a wide range of knowledge and caters to the cultured tastes of its elite readers.

These appealing qualities help to explain the popularity of the playful eight-legged essay in general and those on the *Story of the Western Wing* in particular. Inspired by You Tong, his friend Huang Zhouxing (1611–80) composed six similar essays on lines drawn from the drama, and there were many other enthusiasts as well. Later, a scholar named Qian Shu (fl. early eighteenth century) compiled *A Collection for Elegant Tastes* (*Yaqu cangshu*) or *Illustrated Contemporary Literary Art on The Western Wing* (*Xiuxiang Xixiang shiyi*). Printed in 1703, it included twenty-eight playful eight-legged essays devoted to each act of the drama and was the model for at least four other collections. These collections were later incorporated into the *Sixth Book of Genius* (*Di liu caizi shu*), the most popular editions of the *Story of the Western Wing* with commentaries by the famous critic Jin Shengtan (1608–1661). In other words, the playful eight-legged essay on this drama became a subgenre in its own right, so much so that publishers included them in the appendices to increase the appeal of their editions to readers. A parallel case occurred with the *Story of the Lute* (*Pipa ji*), a drama that portrays an examination candidate's journey to and success in the capital as well as his devoted wife's efforts to take care of his family and eventually to find and reunite with him. Playful eight-legged essays devoted to this play were reprinted along with it as a major attraction of its editions.

Despite its subversive nature, the playful eight-legged essay was not meant as a serious challenge to the examination genre, for its popularity rested on the genre's prestige. Readers, including the Shunzhi emperor, appreciated the writers' ingenuity and humor. The examination genre, however, was also criticized for a range of reasons. The Four Books were a relatively small body of texts and examination topics based on them were bound to be repetitious. Candidates could memorize sample essays and get lucky if the topics happened to be repeated. Some resorted to cheating by sneaking texts into the examination halls. Examiners who tried to vary topics sometimes went so far as to put different halves of sentences together or even phrases from different parts of the text, creating truncated, difficult topics. Accusations of bias and corruption were leveled at examiners believed to have acted unethically. Critics also questioned whether the eight-legged essay was an effective way to select officials given that it had little pragmatic use in terms of governance.

As the Qing government suffered repeated defeat by colonial powers, including Great Britain, France, and Japan, in the nineteenth century, criticisms of the eight-legged essay took on new urgency and momentum. To many, China faced a national crisis, lagging dangerously behind in technology, military power, and other aspects of modernization. Critics blamed China's backwardness on the eight-legged essay, maintaining that its narrow focus on the Confucian Classics had shaped candidates and officials into men who were ignorant of other fields of knowledge. These critics eventually prevailed, and in 1901, the first and second sessions of the provincial and metropolitan examinations required essays on Chinese political history and foreign political systems, respectively. Not long after, in 1905, the whole civil service examination system was abolished as advocates of Western learning and modernization pushed for greater measures of political and social reform. With the fall of the Qing in 1911, and with the advent of the New Culture movement in 1919, Chinese intellectuals eagerly repudiated traditional culture as outdated and even reactionary in their effort to modernize and strengthen the nation. The eight-legged essay, defined by its adherence to classical language and Confucian orthodoxy, was seen as epitomizing the negative aspects of imperial autocracy and Confucian indoctrination. Condemned and vilified, it completely receded from the cultural scene, despite its earlier glory as the most studied and prized literary form in the realm.

Because of its cultural stigma, modern literary historians have tended to ignore the eight-legged essay in their accounts of literary history. Those who have covered it often have adopted an apologetic tone, admitting its formulaic nature and its constraints on writers' creativity. Such marginalization also has led to the rapid disappearance of once-voluminous publications of sample eight-legged essays and relevant materials. Recently, however, interest has been renewed in the eight-legged essay, perhaps because historical distance diminishes the need to politicize it and increases the essay's appeal as a little understood, even exotic, subject. More than twenty books devoted to the history, analysis, and translation of eight-legged essays, including playful eight-legged essays, have been published in the past two decades. These works allow us to understand and appreciate the genre beyond twentieth-century stereotypes. Such reengagement with the genre not only restore its rightful place in Chinese literary history but also enable a more accurate understanding of late-imperial Chinese intellectual and sociopolitical life.

Manling Luo

SUGGESTED READING

ENGLISH

De Weerdt, Hilde. *Competition Over Content: Negotiating Standards for the Civil Service Examinations in Imperial China (1127–1279)*. Cambridge, MA: Harvard University Asia Center, 2007.

Elman, Benjamin A. *A Cultural History of Civil Examinations in Late Imperial China*. Berkeley: University of California Press, 2000.

Luo, Manling. "Tang Civil Service Examinations." In *How to Read Chinese Poetry in Context: Poetic Culture from Antiquity Through the Tang*, edited by Zong-qi Cai, 173–184. New York: Columbia University Press, 2017.

Moore, Oliver. *Rituals of Recruitment in Tang China: Reading an Annual Programme in the Collected Statements by Wang Dingbao (870–940)*. Leiden: Brill, 2004.

Wu, Yinghui. "Constructing a Playful Space: Eight-Legged Essays on *Xixiang ji* and *Pipa ji*." *T'oung Pao: International Journal of Chinese Studies* 102 (2016): 503–545.

CHINESE

Gong Duqing 龔篤清, ed. *Baguwen jianshang* 八股文鑒賞 (*Appreciating the Eight-Legged Essay*). Changsha: Yuelu shushe, 2006.

Huang Qiang 黃強, and Wang Ying 王穎. *Youxi baguwen yanjiu* 遊戲八股文研究 (*A Study of the Playful Eight-Legged Essay*). Wuhan: Wuhan daxue chubanshe, 2015.

Li Shu 李樹. *Zhongguo keju shihua* 中國科舉史話 (*A History of Chinese Civil Service Examinations*). Jinan: Qilu shushe, 2004.

Wang Kaifu 王凱符. *Baguwen gaishuo* 八股文概說 (*A Brief Account of the Eight-Legged Essay*). Beijing: Zhonghua shuju, 2002.

Zhao Jiyao 趙基耀, ed. *Qingdai baguwen yizhu* 清代八股文譯註 (*Translations and Annotations of Eight-Legged Essays of the Qing Dynasty*). Shanghai: Shanghai guji chubanshe, 2011.

15

Ming and Qing Occasional Prose

Letters and Funerary Inscriptions

Perhaps more than ever before in China's history, the art of letter writing flourished in late-imperial times. Improved transportation networks connected commercialized cities and towns, facilitating travel throughout the empire. Letters enabled those suffering the dislocations of the Ming–Qing transition to share experiences, communicate their hopes and fears, and strategize about the future of the country. Like the occasional essay (*xiaopin*), which also flourished in this period (☞ chap. 16), the epistolary genre appealed to scholars for its seeming spontaneity and authenticity as well as its flexible form. Thus, the letter became a suitable medium for recording details of everyday life and debating weighty topics of personal and national import. Thanks to the expansion of print culture during the Ming dynasty, more letters—and more letters by women—survive from the Ming–Qing than from earlier periods. The widespread publication of letters fundamentally changed the practice of reading and composing in this genre. Since at least the Western Jin dynasty (266–316), writing and receiving personal letters had been viewed as intimate acts: authors expressed nuances of feeling through their choice of paper, ink, and calligraphic style. But widespread print publication threatened this sense of intimacy. To be sure, premodern letter-writers had always been aware that "private" letters might be intercepted or clandestinely perused by nosy messengers. But these indiscretions paled beside the wide publicity facilitated by mass publication in print: a letter initially intended for a single recipient could now be read by anyone. This raised the specter of misunderstanding—and even embarrassment—if confidences meant to be shared exclusively among trusted friends were exposed to an anonymous public. Nonetheless, although some authors may have found the publication of their letters awkward, many more seem to have celebrated the possibilities such publicity brought. Savvy and self-promoting letter-writers crafted epistles with a double audience in mind, cognizant that the missive's first reader would often not be its last.

The presence of a double audience accentuated the element of performance implicit in writing letters. Writers who hoped or suspected their letters would attain a wide contemporary readership—or better yet, be passed down to posterity—took pains to present themselves in the best possible light. Letters thus became vehicles of self-fashioning, as authors strove to promote an exemplary Confucian image of themselves: the filial son, the devoted husband or faithful wife, loyal subject or friend. These Confucian themes assumed heightened importance during the violent upheavals that accompanied the Ming–Qing transition.

In crafting these images, editors also took an active role. In this period, letters were published not only in individuals' collected writings (*wenji*) but also in anthologies of essays, letters, poems, and other short pieces (*xiaopin ji* and *congshu*). Most important, the turn of the seventeenth century witnessed the growing popularity and commercial success of anthologies of historical and especially contemporary letters. The compilers of these anthologies took many editorial liberties: in addition to excising any parts of a letter they deemed superfluous—notably greetings, closings, and dates—some contrived to merge two or more letters, presenting them as a single text.[1] The effect was to diminish the particularity of a letter's original recipient, rendering texts more open and accessible to print readership. These editorial practices also blurred the boundaries between letters and other short prose forms. The affinity between letters and prefaces (☞ chap. 12), led many compilers of letter anthologies to adopt an expansive view: rather than distinguish rigorously among prose genres, they sprinkled truncated or otherwise-altered prefaces and other short prose works in among personal letters (*chidu* or *shujian*) and more formal epistles (*shu*). For instance, in an editorial preface to the seventeenth-century collection *Complete Letters Ancient and Modern* (*Gujin chidu daquan* 古今尺牘大全), the compiler, Li Yu, states that he included "anything . . . of benefit to body and soul, family and state."[2] Eager to produce books that would edify readers by providing examples of upright Confucian conduct, while at the same time entertaining readers with accounts of recent events, editors included widely diverse materials. The large numbers of such collections and the commercial success they garnered attest to the popularity of the epistolary genre during this tumultuous time.

In the final years of the Ming dynasty, eunuchs dominated court politics, bandits ransacked the countryside, and foreign armies made incursions along the northern frontier. Deeply distressed, Confucian scholars across China sought strategies to save the country from ruin. By the 1620s, the Donglin (Eastern Grove) faction had emerged as the most powerful such group: its members, from all corners of the empire, aspired to restore functional government based on core Confucian ethics. As part of this program, they opposed the cruel and mercurial eunuch Wei Zhongxian who, by 1626, had assumed nearly absolute power. Wei retaliated with an inquisition against Donglin members, murdering and imprisoning many. When Wei was finally ousted in 1627, Donglin sympathizers regrouped, forming several similar organizations, most notably the Fushe (Restoration Society). As its name suggests, this organization looked to the Confucian past for models of just government. Society members' widely disseminated letters obsessively ruminate on Confucian scholars' duties to family and state. They glorify the heroic acts of some and expose the complacency—or worse, the venality—of others. In so doing, these letters exhibit their authors' moral reflections on contemporary events and provide readers with examples of both upright and disgraceful behavior.

Like letters, grave stele inscriptions encouraged reflection on contemporary events. But where letters freely depicted daily activities and casual interactions, grave steles addressed a more limited subject matter. Composed in formal language, these inscriptions traditionally focused on peak events in the life of the deceased: they praised the accomplishments of the dead and narrated the circumstances of his or her death. Thus, tomb inscriptions provided a ready-made platform for recording the deaths of Ming loyalists, while extolling their courage and presenting them as paragons of Confucian ethics. During the Ming–Qing transition, tomb stele inscriptions often employed highly stylized, emotional language to report the gruesome deaths of Ming martyrs. Through publication, these sensational accounts reached a wide audience and frequently influenced public opinion. The following translations represent both the epistolary and grave stele inscription genres; they are arranged in roughly chronological order according to the events described.

EDUCATING HERSELF WHILE NURTURING HER SONS: GU RUOPU'S STRUGGLES AS A LOYAL WIDOW, DEVOTED MOTHER, AND SELF-EFFACING SCHOLAR

Gu Ruopu (1592–ca. 1681) was one of the most influential female teachers and women of letters in her generation. She grew up in the bustling cultural center of Hangzhou, where her father, vice-director of the Office of Imperial Parks, saw to her basic education and secured a good match for her. After thirteen years of marriage, her husband, Huang Maowu, died. For the next six decades, Gu Ruopu lived as a chaste widow and blossomed into an acclaimed writer and beloved teacher. She owed her literary success in part to the mentorship of her father-in-law, the Ming loyalist Huang Ruheng (1558–1598). Recognizing Gu Ruopu's prodigious literary gifts, Huang Ruheng provided her with a complete education in the Confucian Classics (usually reserved for men), personally commented on her poems, and entrusted to her the education of her four children, two boys and two girls. In championing Gu's intellectual pursuits, Huang Ruheng participated in a small but growing trend among forward-thinking male scholars who dared to imagine that a woman's erudition might not compromise her virtue. Some local gazetteers even boasted of the accomplishments of local women. Gu herself went one step further: she regarded book learning as essential for strengthening a girl's virtue and bolstering her qualifications to nurture the next generation.[3]

The following passage was one of only a few works by women included in two of the most influential seventeenth-century letter anthologies compiled by Ming loyalists, Zhou Lianggong's *New Collection of Modern Letters* (*Chidu xinchao*, preface dated 1662) and Wang Qi's 1663 *New Account of Modern Letters* (*Chidu xinyu*). Although presented in these anthologies as a letter to Gu's younger brother, the text appears to have been lifted verbatim from the middle of Gu's 1626 authorial preface to her poetry collection *Drafts from the Studio for Reclining in the Moonlight* (*Woyue xuangao*), published in 1651.[4] The title "Letter to My Younger Brother" seems to have been added later and indeed makes little sense, as the letter refers to Gu's brothers in the third person. The fact that this text circulated as both a preface and a letter, however, underscores the fluidity of prose genres in this period.

Composed in elegant classical Chinese and replete with erudite allusions, the piece poignantly portrays Gu's tribulations as a widowed mother steadfastly overseeing her sons' education. By contrast, the text presents her own education as merely a by-product of her efforts to instruct them. Other sources attest that Gu received daily tutoring from her father-in-law, but this text glosses over his role in her education, focusing instead on Gu's tenacity, indomitable spirit, and insatiable thirst for knowledge not only of traditionally "feminine" genres, such as poetry, but also of history, classics, and politics.[5] It seems that this zeal for learning enabled her to endure the loss of her husband.

She faced many challenges, among them the practical difficulty of carving out time for study while also fulfilling her domestic duties. This problem, shared by so many women, was also described by Wang Duanshu: "Alas, it is only after the intricate labors of our sex—embroidery, the reeling of silk, and all our other tasks—have been completed that we women are able to borrow from the Classics to complete the patterns of our writing."[6] Gu also confronted psychological challenges: several times in the text she refers to gnawing self-doubt, fear of failure, and a pervasive sense of inadequacy even with respect to other female writers. These self-effacing statements carry an air of conventionality, however, and Dorothy Ko has suggested that they may even be read as strategic: by presenting herself as a demure, traditional woman, not an outspoken opponent of patriarchal values, Gu Ruopu assumed an unthreatening position from which she was able to secure the resources needed to educate not only her sons and herself but also her daughters and countless other young women.[7]

顧若璞　與弟

夫溘云逝，骨爍魂銷，惟殯而哭。不如死之久矣。豈能視息人世，復有所謂緣情靡麗之作邪。徒以死節易，守節難。有藐諸孤在。不敢不學古丸熊畫荻者。以俟其成。於是時君舅方督學西江。余復遠我父母兄弟。念不稍涉經史。奚以課藐諸而俟之成。　余日惴惴。懼終負初志。以不得從夫子於九京也。於是酒漿組紃之暇。陳發所藏書。自四子經傳以及古史監、皇明通紀、大政紀之屬。日夜披覽如不及。二子者從外傅入。

C15.1 Gu Ruopu, "Letter to My Younger Brother"

When my husband suddenly passed away, I felt as if my bones had melted and my spirit dissolved. I wept over his coffin wishing I had died long ago.[1] How could I linger pointlessly in this world, let alone express my feelings in elegant poetry? Committing suicide as a loyal wife would have been easier; maintaining my widow chastity has been more difficult. I had to think of my orphaned children. When I considered how they would grow up, I had no choice but to emulate those virtuous women of the past who fed their children pills of bear gall [to fortify their diligence] and wrote characters in the sand with reeds [to teach them to read].[2] At that time, my father-in-law [Huang Ruheng] had just become superintendent of education for Jiangxi Province [so he was extremely busy], and I was living far away from my parents and brothers [so they too could not assist in educating my children].[3] My father-in-law, [occupied with

---

[1] Allusion to the poem "Lu'e," Mao no. 202, in *The Book of Songs* (*Shijing*).

[2] Allegedly, the mother of the great Song dynasty statesman Ouyang Xiu taught him to read by writing characters in the sand and the mother of the Tang dynasty official Liu Zhongying concocted pills of bear gall to help him concentrate on his studies late into the night.

[3] The version of the text reprinted in Wang Xiuqin's *Lidai mingyuan shujian* uses the character 為, but the character in Gu Ruopu's 1651 *Woyue xuangao* is 遠. The latter makes more sense.

official duties], gave no thought to classics or histories. [So the task fell to me.] But how could I presume to instruct my children and see them to maturity? Every day I was anxious, fearful that in the end I might fail in my original resolve and not succeed in following my husband into the afterworld. So, in breaks from my domestic chores of brewing and weaving,[4] I would spread out my books, beginning with the *Four Books*, and the *Five Classics*, and moving on to other texts like *The Mirror of Ancient History*, *The Continuous Chronicle of the August Ming*, and *The Record of Great Administration*. Day and night I would pore over these books as if worried I might fall behind. When my two sons returned home from sessions with their tutor, I would have them light the lamp as I sat in the corner recounting to them what I had understood. And I would have them take turns reciting aloud to me.[5] We would not leave off until midnight, but how we enjoyed ourselves! I did not even notice how exhausted I was. As the days and months passed, I gradually accumulated more knowledge. The sages and worthies, classics and commentaries nourished my virtue and purified my heart. And on the side, I browsed at leisure through "Encountering Sorrow" and the "Elegantiae" of *The Book of Songs*, as well as lyrics and rhapsodies.[6] I yearned to use these works to express my own melancholy and disconsolate feelings. Thankfully, I did not fall ill from dark brooding. Instead, just as spring birds and autumn insects chirp and warble, moved by the season, so did I too make some offhanded jottings, which I sequestered in bamboo boxes, since they scarcely count as examples of "crying out against injustice."[7] How dare I incur blame for "imitating the Handan walk"[8] by comparing my [paltry] writings to those by Ban Zhao, Zuo Fen, or other virtuous women of antiquity?[9]

輒令籌燈坐隅為陳說吾
所明。更相率呷吾。至
丙夜乃罷。顧復樂之。
誠不自知其瘁也。日月
漸多。聞見與積。聖賢
經傳。育德洗心。旁及
騷雅詞賦。遊焉息焉。
冀以自發其哀思，舒其
憤悶。幸不底於幽憂之
疾。而春鳥秋蟲。感時
流響。率爾操觚。藏諸
笥篋。雖然。亦不平鳴
耳。詎敢方古班左諸淑
媛取邯鄲學步之誚耶。

[*LDMYSJ* 2:3]

---

[4] These are among the duties of a Confucian woman, as prescribed by the "Pattern of the Family" (Neize) chapter of *The Book of Rites* (*Liji*).

[5] I interpret 呷吾 as 咿唔, the sound of reading aloud.

[6] In the "Record on the Subject of Education," the *Book or Rites* (*Liji*) stipulates that scholars should not only study diligently but also "browse at leisure."

[7] This passage alludes playfully to Sima Qian's "Letter to Ren'an" (➤ C7.4), which states that writings of lasting value are produced when men of lofty aspirations cry out against injustice, "hoping to realize themselves in literature, since action was denied them." In the same letter, Sima Qian, fearing that no one of his own generation will possesses the requisite insight and compassion to appreciate his writings, vows to "sequester them in a famous mountain" to await an appreciative reader (for translation and analysis of this letter, ➤ chap. 7).

[8] This is an allusion to the "Autumn Floods" (Qiushui) chapter of the *Zhuangzi*: "Perhaps you've never heard about the boy of Shouling who went to learn the Handan Walk. He hadn't mastered what the Handan people had to teach him when he forgot about his old way of walking, so he had to crawl all the way back home." Watson, *The Complete Works of Chuang Tzu*, 187. Romanization has been changed from Wade-Giles to pinyin.

[9] The historian Ban Zhao (45–114 CE) and the poet Zuo Fen (255?–300) were among the most celebrated female writers in Chinese literary history.

HONORING AN INSPIRING TEACHER AND A LOYAL DISCIPLE:
FANG BAO'S ACCOUNT OF ZUO GUANGDOU AND SHI KEFA

The next letter further explores the theme of education, introduced in the previous selection, but from the perspective of neither teacher nor student. Instead, Fang Bao describes an intense emotional bond between two heroes of the Ming resistance, a teacher and a student, Zuo Guangdou (1575–1625) and his disciple, Shi Kefa (1601–1645), both of whom died before Fang was born. Born into the Qing dynasty, which he loyally served, rising to the position of vice minister of rites, Fang Bao (1668–1749) grappled in his writings with the aftershocks of the Ming dynastic collapse. He felt a strong affinity for the loyalist martyr Zuo Guangdou, a leader of the Donglin faction and fellow native of his ancestral hometown, Tongcheng, in Anhui province.

Early in his career, while serving as a supervisor for education in the capital district, Zuo encountered the young Shi Kefa, whose heroic military actions, especially in the Battle of Yangzhou, would later earn him a reputation as one of the greatest martyrs of the Ming. Shi's military valor was inspired by the deeds of his fearless mentor, Zuo Guangdou. In 1625, Zuo, along with other prominent members of the Donglin faction, ran afoul of Wei Zhongxian, the eunuch who by that time had arrogated to himself nearly supreme power. The previous year, another leader of the Donglin faction had submitted a memorial accusing Wei of twenty-four "great crimes" against the state. These included falsifying examination results, usurping imperial authority, and ruthlessly murdering his opponents. In reprisal, Wei moved to purge members of the Donglin faction: many were removed from office, stripped of honors, beaten in court, tortured in prison, and even killed. Zuo Guangdou was among those seized. Although he died a grisly death in prison, he tenaciously defended his principles to the end. With Wei Zhongxian's fall from power, Zuo's bravery was recognized in his posthumous titles, "Junior Guardian to the Heir Apparent" and "Zuo the Loyal and Steadfast." These are the appellations by which Fang Bao respectfully refers to him.

The powerful, unadorned style, honest emotions, and hard-hitting Confucian message of Fang's letter are characteristic of the Tongcheng school, which he helped found. This movement would exert a profound influence on literary aesthetics throughout the Qing dynasty. An avid student of the Classics and admirer of Tang and Song prose masters, Fang drew inspiration as well from late-Ming notions that writing should express the author's genuine feelings. His literary style thus sought to unite moral substance (*yi*) with method (*fa*) and to fuse personal self-expression with core Confucian principles.

As such, the letter conveys emotions with almost novelistic craftsmanship. Using rich descriptors that draw on a wide array of sensory perception, Fang portrays the chill in the wintry air, the textures of garments worn by Zuo and Shi, the fiery glare in Zuo's eye, and the crashing sounds of ice as it falls from Shi's armor. Still more striking, Fang's detailed observations of physical postures throughout the letter subtly analogize the master–student bond to officially sanctioned

Confucian relationships between parents and children, and between rulers and subjects. In the men's first encounter, Zuo, undetected, comes upon the young Shi, a student who has fallen asleep over a composition. Reading Shi's essay, Zuo marvels at its literary skill, removes his own coat, and places it over the shoulders of the sleeping scholar. Shi's slumped posture and Zuo's kind, protective gesture in this scene echo an incident described later in the letter. When Zuo is imprisoned, Shi visits him to revive his spirits. There he finds Zuo sprawled on the floor of his prison cell, his body almost unrecognizably mangled by torture. Aghast, Shi sinks to the ground and wraps his suffering teacher in an embrace. The compassion Shi reflexively displays toward his vulnerable teacher mirrors Zuo's initial empathy for Shi, highlighting the reciprocity between master and disciple. Further, in exemplary Confucian fashion, Shi extends his reverence for his teacher to other relationships: after Zuo's demise, Shi expresses loyalty and dedication both to Zuo's family and to the fallen Ming dynasty, which his teacher so passionately defended.

The letter pairs exquisite literary patterning with credible claims to veracity. It both opens and closes with references to men who knew Zuo personally and whose accounts therefore hold weight. Thus, although Fang was born too late to know Zuo and Shi, his letter nonetheless purports to convey privileged, eye-witness information.

C15.2 Fang Bao, "An Anecdote Concerning Zuo the Loyal and Steadfast"

方苞　左忠毅公逸事

My father told me that Zuo the Loyal and Steadfast, from our county [of Tongcheng, in Anhui], served as supervisor of education for the capital district. One windy, bitter cold, winter day, dressed in unofficial garb, he set out on horseback along with several companions to visit an old temple. In a side room, they came upon a student slumped over on his desk having just completed a draft of an essay. No sooner had Zuo read it than he removed the ermine cloak he had been wearing and placed it over the student's shoulders. Shutting the door, he inquired of a monk at the temple who the student might be. It turned out to be Shi Kefa.

先君子嘗言，鄉先輩左忠毅公視學京畿，一日，風雪嚴寒，從數騎出，微行入古寺。廡下一生伏案臥，文方成草。公閱畢，即解貂覆生，爲掩戶。叩之寺僧，則史公可法也。

At the next examination, when the official calling the roll spoke Shi Kefa's name, Zuo stared in astonishment. The papers were submitted, and as soon as he read Shi Kefa's exam, he assigned it the highest mark. He then summoned Shi Kefa to his home to pay respects to his wife, saying "Our sons are all quite mediocre. Someday this student alone will carry on my legacy."

及試，吏呼名至史公，公瞿然注視，呈卷，即面署第一。召入，使拜夫人，曰：「吾諸兒碌碌，他日繼吾志事，惟此生耳。」

When Zuo Guangdou was imprisoned by the [eunuch's] secret police, Shi Kefa kept watch by the [prison] door day and night. But the tyrannical eunuch's guards were extremely vigilant; not even a servant from Zuo's own household could sneak past them. After a long time, Shi Kefa heard that Zuo Guangdou had been tortured with a branding iron and might die any day. In tears, and offering 50 taels of silver, Shi Kefa approached a guard.

及左公下廠獄，史朝夕獄門外。逆閹防伺甚嚴，雖家僕不得近。久之，聞左公被炮烙，旦夕且死，持五十金涕泣謀於禁卒。卒感焉；一日，使

史更敝衣，草屨，背筐，
手長鑱，爲除不潔者，引
入，微指左公處。則席地
倚牆而坐，面額焦爛不
可辨，左膝以下筋骨盡脫
矣。史前跪，抱公膝而
嗚咽。

公辨其聲，而目不可開，
乃奮臂以指撥眥，目光如
炬。怒曰：「庸奴！此
何地也！而汝來前？國家
之事糜爛至此。老夫已
矣，汝復輕身而昧大義，
天下事誰可支拄者！不速
去，無俟姦人構陷，吾今
即撲殺汝！」 因摸地上
刑械作投擊勢。史噤不敢
發聲，趨而出。後常流涕
述其事以語人，曰：「吾
師肺肝，皆鐵石所鑄造
也。」

崇禎末，流賊張獻忠出
沒蘄、黃、潛、桐間，
史公以鳳廬道奉檄守
禦。每有警，輒數月不
就寢，使將士更休，而
自坐幄幕外。擇健卒十
人，令二人蹲踞而背倚
之，漏鼓移則番代。每
寒夜起立，振衣裳，甲
上冰霜迸落，鏗然有
聲。或勸以少休，公
曰：「吾上恐負朝廷，
下恐媿吾師也。」

史公治兵，往來桐城，
必躬造左公第，候太
公、太母起居，拜夫人
於堂上。

余宗老塗山，左公甥
也，與先君子善，謂獄
中語乃親得之于史公云。

[*MQSWX* 269–272]

The guard was moved [and relented]: one day he instructed Shi Kefa to put on a tattered coat and straw sandals. Dressed like a janitor, carrying a large bamboo basket on his back and a spade in his hands, Shi Kefa was led into the prison. The guard indicated where Zuo Guangdou was sitting on the floor, leaning propped up against the wall; his face was singed beyond recognition and the flesh below his left knee had been completely torn from the bone. Shi Kefa knelt before him and, clasping him by the knees, wept bitterly.

Zuo Guangdou recognized Shi Kefa's voice, but was unable to open his eyes. So he raised his arm and, using his fingers, pried his eyelid open. Then, with a fiery glare, he barked: "Imbecile! What are you doing here?! Our country is putrefying before our very eyes. I'm an old man whose life is already over. But look at you—risking your life [by coming here], while neglecting what really matters. Who will support the world?! If you don't get out of here immediately, those bastards won't have time to bring charges against you; I'll kill you myself—right now!" So saying, he groped his way on the ground until he found an instrument of torture and flung it at Shi Kefa. Shi Kefa fled, not daring to make a sound. Later, he often shed tears as he recounted these events, saying, "My teacher's conviction was rock solid; he had an iron will."

In the final years of the Chongzhen reign [1627–1644], the roving bandit Zhang Xianzhong preyed on the regions of Qichun and Huanggang [in modern-day Hubei province], as well as Qianshan and Tongcheng [in modern-day Anhui province]. Shi Kefa, as Military Circuit Intendant of Fengyang and Lujiang [in modern-day Anhui], was ordered to defend these areas. Whenever an incident was reported, he would not go to bed for several months. He instructed his men to rest in shifts, and he himself sat outside the tent. He would choose ten strong men and make two of them kneel on the ground; he would lean against them until the drum sounding the hour was struck. Then two more men would take their place. On cold nights, he would stand and shake his cloak, and the frost and ice that had accumulated on his armor would fall to the ground with a crash. If anyone urged him to rest, he would reply: "I fear betraying my country and disgracing my teacher."

When Shi Kefa led an army through Tongcheng, he insisted on visiting Zuo's home, personally inquiring into the well-being of his parents, and paying respects to Zuo's widow in the formal hall. My senior kinsman [Fang] Tushan, Zuo's son-in-law, maintained cordial relations with my late father, and told me that Shi had personally related to him what happened in prison.

COMMEMORATING FIVE MING MARTYRS AND THE SUZHOU RIOT OF 1626: ZHANG PU'S GRAVE STELE INSCRIPTION

Like the previous letter, this tomb stele honors martyrs to the fallen Ming. Written by the founder of the Restoration Society, Zhang Pu (1602–1641), the text commemorates five bold commoners—Yan Peiwei, Yang Nianru, Ma Jie, Shen Yang, and Zhou Wenyuan—who lost their lives in the Suzhou riot of 1626. The incident was recorded in several historical accounts and inspired Li Yu's play, *A Composition on Uprightness and Loyalty* (*Qingzhong pu*), which in turn spawned further adaptations. This well-documented uprising broke out after the arrest of Zhou Shunchang (1584–1626), a high-ranking official in the Ministry of Personnel, whose moral character, incorruptibility, and staunch defense of the people's plight were well-known. Politically sympathetic to the Donglin faction, and, by the mid-1620s living in retirement in Suzhou, Zhou courageously criticized the eunuch Wei Zhongxian, who by then was flagrantly abusing power and grandiosely ordering that shrines be erected in his honor. Zhou's criticism stung the megalomaniacal eunuch, who promptly called for his arrest.

Although the text of the grave stele minimizes the extent of the chaos and violence that ensued, other contemporary sources provide greater detail: Imperial guards came to arrest Zhou, but he only piled curses on Wei Zhongxian. His fearlessness inspired bystanders' awe and amazement. News of Zhou's arrest—and his audacious defiance of the authorities—provoked mass demonstrations: thousands of people swarmed the streets of Suzhou, blocking the progress of the imperial guards and calling for justice and clemency. Attempts by local officials to restore order failed. The five men whose grave stele the inscription adorns led the crowd in demanding that the agents of the state disclose whether it was the court or the eunuch-led secret police that had issued Zhou's arrest warrant. Under pressure, the guards confessed that the secret police, not the court, had issued the warrant. This revelation infuriated the crowd: it surged forward flinging tiles, stones, and verbal abuse. Several imperial guards were killed, and the censor-in-chief of Suzhou, Mao Yilu, had to take cover in some bushes by a latrine. The riot shook Wei Zhongxian's confidence, for it signaled the people's determined opposition to his reign of terror. Eager to assert dominance, yet fearful of provoking further backlash, he ordered only the five principal instigators rounded up and executed as examples. Others were flogged, and then the matter was dropped.

The text of the grave stele hinges on the theme of exemplarity: facing death, the five martyrs model their behavior on the example of their leader, Zhou Shunchang. Just as Zhou, upon his arrest, hurled insults at Wei Zhongxian, so, too, do the men fling accusations at the censor-in-chief, Mao Yilu, who ordered their execution. More important, the text invites readers to regard the five men as examples of Confucian deportment. Yet for a grave inscription, Zhang's text provides remarkably little information on them as individuals. This lack of specificity encourages readers to regard them as representative of universal Confucian values—models of selflessness, righteousness, and loyalty, yardsticks for measuring one's own moral achievement. Zhang especially stresses the men's status as commoners. Building on the mid-Ming philosopher Wang Yangming's idea that every human being possesses innate ethical faculties and therefore the potential to become a sage, Zhang emphasizes that the lack of formal education did not hinder the men from taking decisive moral action. By contrasting their humble origins with their extraordinary valor, the text raises the following question: if men unschooled in the Classics are capable of such heroic deeds, why do so many eminent scholars fail to live up to Confucian ideals?

The stele inscription ends abruptly by invoking three "righteous gentlemen," prominent members of the Donglin faction whose names were likely known to readers: Wu Mo (1554–1640), Wen Zhenmeng (1574–1636), and Yao Ximeng (1579–1636). This use of the phrase "righteous gentlemen" recalls a line earlier in the inscription: "Some righteous gentlemen paid fifty taels of silver to buy the five [martyrs'] heads, which they placed in boxes and . . . reunited with the men's bodies. Thus the bodies in the grave are [once again] whole." Repetition of this phrase at the end of the inscription suggests that Wu, Wen, and Yao may be precisely the "righteous gentlemen" mentioned earlier. But even if they played no role in the reburial, at least two of them drew inspiration from the martyrs' virtuous actions: Wen wrote a long, vituperative memorial denouncing Wei Zhongxian; and Yao, a close friend of Zhou Shunchang, published an exposé of the events surrounding Zhou's arrest. The stele inscription's praise of these righteous gentlemen encourages readers to take inspiration from their deeds as well as from the courage of Zhou and the five martyrs.

張溥　五人墓碑記

五人者，蓋當蓼洲周公
之被逮，激於義而死焉
者也。至於今，郡之賢
士大夫，請於當道，即
除魏閹廢祠之址以葬
之，且立石於其墓之
門，以旌其所爲。嗚
呼，亦盛矣哉！

夫五人之死，去今之墓
而葬焉，其爲時止十有
一月爾。夫十有一月之
中，凡富貴之子，慷慨
得志之徒，其疾病而
死，死而湮沒不足道
者，亦已衆矣；況草野
之無聞者歟？獨五人之
皦皦，何也？

C15.3 Zhang Pu, "The Five Men's Grave Stele"

When Mr. Zhou [Shunchang] of Liaozhou [Suzhou] was seized, the five men laid down their lives for righteousness. To this day, honorable scholars of Suzhou have been requesting that the authorities tear down the abandoned shrine to Wei Zhongxian, that the five men be buried there, and that a stone stele be erected at the gate to commemorate their deeds. Oh how magnificent that would be!

Only eleven months have passed since the five men who are receiving [proper] burial here died. In these eleven months, a great number of illustrious scions of well-to-do families and passionate, successful men have died of illness and fallen into oblivion. Not to mention the countless men of humble origin [who have also died without leaving a name]. So why do these five men shine brighter than the rest?

I still remember when Mr. Zhou was captured on the fifteenth day of the third month of the year *dingmao*.[1] Exemplary members of the [Restoration] Society

---

[1] All scholarly works I have consulted agree that the event took place in 1626; however, the text says *dingmao*, which was 1627. I have not been able to resolve this discrepancy.

spoke out for justice on his behalf and collected money to send him off.[2] Our cries shook heaven and earth. But the imperial guards advanced holding swords and demanded, "Who are you so upset about?" The people could not bear [the guards' insolence]. So they beat them up and left them flat on their faces.

At that time, the Censor-in-Chief of Suzhou [Mao Yilu] was a member of Wei Zhongxian's clique. It was he who ordered Zhou's arrest. The common people were overcome with grief, so when he was haranguing them [and urging them to disperse], they made a great clamor and chased after him. He hid in the hedges by an outhouse to avoid being caught.

Subsequently, the Censor-in-Chief had an audience at court to discuss the Suzhou riot, and the five men were executed accordingly. Their names were Yan Peiwei, Yang Nianru, Ma Jie, Shen Yang, and Zhou Wenyuan. These are the five who lie side by side in the grave before us. The five men faced torture with an indomitable will: cursing the censor-in-chief by name, they went to their deaths laughing. Their severed heads were displayed above the city gate, but their complexions scarcely changed. Some righteous gentlemen paid fifty taels of silver to buy the five men's heads, which they placed in boxes and, at long last, reunited with the men's bodies. Thus the bodies in the grave are [once again] whole.

Alas! How many officials in this world are capable of remaining true to their ideals even in the face of the havoc wrought by powerful eunuchs? And yet these five men were of humble origin; they had never been instructed in the Classics. How then could they, impassioned and righteous, have regarded death so lightly? What's more, [at that time] the world was awash in falsified imperial orders and [members of the Donglin] faction were being implicated and arrested everywhere. But in the end, because of our fervent attack in Suzhou, the eunuch clique did not dare to draw anyone else into the controversy. [Quite the contrary:] Wei Zhongxian's cronies became hesitant and fearful, for their unsavory schemes had become difficult to implement. As soon as a sage emperor [Chongzhen (r. 1627–1644)] ascended the throne, Wei Zhongxian hanged himself by the side of the road. Surely, the determination of these five men played a part in bringing about this dénouement.

By contrast, nobles and officials today who face punishment for a crime either flee, not daring to show their face at home or abroad, or shave their head and go into reclusion [as monks], or, feigning madness, disappear without a trace. How could such disgraceful behavior compare to the [righteous] deaths of these five men? Which course of action is the weightier? When Mr. Zhou's loyal and virtuous conduct was reported at court he was rewarded with

[2] The money may have been raised to bribe agents of the state to spare Zhou from unnecessary torture and to provide him with adequate food during his time in prison.

予猶記周公之被逮，在丁卯三月之望。吾社之行爲士先者，爲之聲義，斂貲財以送其行，哭聲震動天地。緹騎按劍而前，問誰爲哀者？衆不能堪，抶而仆之。是時以大中丞撫吳者，爲魏之私人，周公之逮所由使也。吳之民方痛心焉，於是乘其厲聲以呵，則噪而相逐。中丞匿於溷藩以免。

既而以吳民之亂請於朝，按誅五人，曰：顏佩韋、楊念如、馬傑、沈揚、周文元，即今之傫然在墓者也。然五人之當刑也，意氣揚揚，呼中丞之名而詈之；談笑以死。斷頭置城上，顏色不少變。有賢士大夫發五十金，買五人之脰而函之，卒與屍合。故今之墓中，全乎爲五人也。

嗟乎！大閹之亂，縉紳而能不易其志者，四海之大，有幾人歟？而五人生於編伍之間，素不聞詩書之訓，激昂大義，蹈死不顧，亦曷故哉？且矯詔紛出，鈎黨之捕，徧於天下，卒以吾郡之發憤一擊，不敢復有株治。大閹亦逡巡畏義，非常之謀，難於猝發。待聖人之出，而投繯道路，不可謂非五人之力也。

由是觀之，則今之高爵
顯位，一旦抵罪，或脫
身以逃，不能容於遠
近，而又有剪髮杜門，
佯狂不知所之者，其辱
人賤行，視五人之死，
輕重固何如哉？是以蓼
洲周公，忠義暴於朝
廷，贈諡美顯，榮於身
後。而五人亦得以加其
土封，列其姓名於大堤
之上，凡四方之士，無
有不過而拜且泣者，斯
固百世之遇也。

不然，令五人者保其首
領，以老於戶牖之下，
則盡其天年，人皆得以
隸使之，安能屈豪傑之
流，扼腕墓道，發其
志士之悲哉？故予與
同社諸君子，哀斯墓
之徒有其石也，而爲
之記。亦以明死生之
大，匹夫之有重於社
稷也。

　賢士大夫者，冏卿
因之吳公、太史文起文
公、孟長姚公也。

[*MQSWJX* 139–144]

a glorious posthumous title, honored in death. The five men's burial mounds too were raised higher; their names are displayed on this great embankment. Scholars from every direction come here, shed tears, and pay respects. Thus, the five men's fame will be passed down for a hundred generations.

But if the five men had kept their heads on their necks, growing old by the window and living out their natural span of years, everyone would have walked all over them. How could they have inspired the respect of outstanding, heroic, and principled men, causing them to wring their hands and express anguish [as they approached the gravesite along the ceremonial] spirit path? For this reason, I was pained, as were several other members of the [Restoration] Society, that this grave was marked with nothing more than a stone. I have written this record for it, to shed light on the magnitude of life and death and the profound service that ordinary people can render to the state.

The Chief Minister of the Court of the Imperial Stud Wu Mo, the Hanlin Academician Wen Zhenmeng, and Yao Ximeng are righteous gentlemen.

EXONERATING ONESELF AND EXPOSING A HYPOCRITE: HOU FANGYU'S DENUNCIATION OF RUAN DACHENG

In contrast to the grave stele inscription above, the following letter illustrates a less dramatic, though equally impassioned, response to the political intrigues of the day. The author, Hou Fangyu (1618–1655), was a close friend of Zhang Pu and shared Zhang's conviction that literature should express its author's genuine convictions in clear, precise language. Celebrated as one of the most accomplished writers of his day, Hou came from a long line of dedicated reformers: his grandfather, father, and uncle were all members of the Donglin faction, and his father zealously opposed the eunuch Wei Zhongxian. For his own part, Hou joined the Restoration Society and strongly advocated a return to Confucian ethics. The next letter embodies this ideal. In unvarnished prose, Hou sternly takes the letter's recipient, Ruan Dacheng (1587–1646), to task; he points out Ruan's errors and earnestly entreats him to reform.

Yet, as Hou knew well, Ruan was unlikely to change—by the time the letter was composed, Ruan had earned a reputation for vindictive, calculating, and relentlessly self-serving behavior. Early in his career, when the Donglin faction still had influence at court, Ruan had made overtures to members of this group. But once the Donglin faction endorsed someone other than Ruan for promotion, Ruan switched his alliance to Wei Zhongxian's eunuch clique. From that point on, Ruan actively persecuted members of the Donglin faction and even falsely boasted that he had personally brought about Zuo Guangdou's death. After Wei Zhongxian's fall from power, Ruan again reversed himself. Fearful of reprisals against those who had collaborated with the depraved eunuch, Ruan endeavored to hide his role in Wei Zhongxian's government. His efforts failed, and he was removed from office. Nonetheless, living in retirement in Nanjing, he deployed all his ingenuity to worm his way back into the good graces of the reformers, especially Hou Fangyu. At first Ruan tried using gifts and bribes to win over Hou. But when these failed, he resorted to more desperate tactics, including an attempt to frame Hou as a traitor and collaborator with General Zuo Liangyu (1599–1645), whose army was advancing ominously toward Nanjing. Ruan's fabricated charges forced Hou to flee the city. Yet before he fled, he jotted down the following letter. In this missive, Hou remonstrates with Ruan, urging him to repent for his past actions, and promising redemption if he does. Hou's belief that even a villain may reform demonstrates his commitment to the Mencian idea that human beings are fundamentally good.

The audience for the letter is somewhat ambiguous: unquestionably, it was intended for Ruan's eyes. But did Hou also anticipate that it would garner a wider readership in print? Hou's indirect references to Ruan's most heinous acts of collusion with Wei Zhongxian could suggest that the letter was meant for Ruan alone. Twice Hou states, "Surely you recall . . . ; I need not rehearse [the matter] here" and "I need not spell [things] out." These veiled allusions, which draw on a fund of knowledge shared between author and recipient, suggest that perhaps Hou intended the letter for Ruan alone. This preterition, however, may be better interpreted as a rhetorical ploy designed to create a false sense of intimacy between the author and his print readership. After all, the details of the case were well known to many. Additionally, Hou's letter supplies information that would have seemed superfluous to Ruan. For instance, Hou reminds Ruan that his own father was roughly the same age as Ruan and served with him in the court of Ming emperor Shenzong [Wanli]. Surely Ruan would not have required such a reminder. Did Hou then intend the letter for a wider audience? Was he merely using the epistolary genre as a platform from which to publicly exonerate himself from the charge of treason Ruan leveled against him?

This interpretation seems plausible. Either way, the letter succeeds rhetorically as a powerful work of self-fashioning. It alternates between explicit exposure of Ruan's misdeeds and cryptic hints, culminating in the enigmatic, if formulaic, final words: "much more could be said." By providing only partial information and leaving much to the fertile imagination of his readers, Hou effectively casts Ruan as a villain and himself as a righteous and hapless victim. History suggests that Hou's letter did indeed circulate widely, generating intense public interest in and sympathy for its author. More than fifty years later, the popular historical opera *The Peach Blossom Fan* (*Taohua shan*) dramatized the relationship between Ruan and Hou, casting Hou, of course, as the hero.

C15.4 Hou Fangyu, "Letter to Ruan Dacheng, Written in 1643 on the Day of My Departure from Jinling [Nanjing]"

I have heard that gentlemen comport themselves thus: they do not seek to make excuses for themselves while blaming others, for doing so would violate the Way. Your Excellency, however, has not treated me in this manner. I wish to provide some examples.

侯方域　癸未去金陵日
與阮光祿書

僕竊聞，君子處己，不
欲自恕，而苛責他人以
非其道。今執事之於
僕，乃有不然者，願爲
執事陳之。

執事，僕之父行也。神
宗之末，與大人同朝，
相得甚歡。其後乃有欲
終事執事而不能者。執
事當自追憶其故，不必
僕言之也。

大人削官歸，僕時方
少。每侍，未嘗不念執
事之才，而嗟惜者彌
日。及僕稍長，知讀
書，求友金陵，將戒
途，而大人送之曰：
「金陵有御史成公勇
者，雖於我爲後進，我
常心重之；汝至，當以
爲師。又有老友方公孔
炤，汝當持刺拜於床
下。」語不及執事。

及至金陵，則成公已得
罪去，僅見方公；而其
子以智者，余之夙交
也，以此晨夕過從。執
事與方公同爲父行，理
當謁；然而不敢者，
執事當自追憶其故，
不必僕言之也。今執
事乃責僕與方公厚，
而與執事薄，噫！亦
過矣。

忽一日，有王將軍過
僕，甚恭。每一至，必
邀僕爲詩歌，既得之，
必喜。而爲僕貰酒奏
伎，招遊舫，攜山屐，
殷殷積句不倦。僕初不
解，既而疑，以問將
軍。將軍乃屏人以告僕
曰：「是皆阮光祿所願
納交於君者也。光祿方
爲諸君訴。願更以道之
君之友陳君定生、吳君
次尾，庶稍湔乎。」

Your excellency is of the same generation as my father. In the final years of Emperor Shenzong's [Wanli's] reign [1572–1620], the two of you served together at court and got along well with one another. My father ardently wished to be of service to Your Excellency, but he was unable to do so. Surely Your Excellency recalls the reason why;[1] I need not rehearse it here.

When my father was dismissed from office, I was quite young. Yet whenever I waited upon him he lost no opportunity to mention Your Excellency's abilities with sorrowful sighs.

As I grew older and began to study, I set out for Jinling [Nanjing] in search of companions. Seeing me off, my father said, "The imperial censor Cheng Yong lives in Jinling.[2] Although he is my junior, I have abiding respect for him. When you arrive, you must honor him as your teacher. My old friend Fang Kongzhao also lives in Jinling. You should pay a call on him and leave your card." He said nothing about Your Excellency.

When I reached Jinling, Cheng Yong had already left the city, having been accused of a crime, so I was only able to see Fang Kongzhao and his son Fang Yizhi; they became my inseparable friends. Since Your Excellency and Fang Kongzhao were both of my father's generation, I ought to have paid a formal visit to Your Excellency, but I dared not. Your Excellency surely recalls the reason why. I need not spell it out. Now Your Excellency is blaming me for solidifying my relations with Fang Kongzhao while attenuating my relations with Your Excellency. Ai! It's too much!

One day, quite unexpectedly, General Wang came to visit me and treated me with great courtesy.[3] From then on, whenever he visited, he would request that I compose poetry for him, which he received with delight. And he would entertain me with wine and sing-song girls, inviting me on boating trips and excursions in the mountains. Week after week he ardently sought me out and seemed never to tire of my company. At first I did not understand his motivation. But later I became somewhat wary and asked why he was behaving like this. Dismissing everyone else from our presence, the general informed me, "This is all because Grand Master Ruan Dacheng wants to develop a close relationship with you. Recently, many officials have heaped abuse on him.

---

[1] The reason was that Ruan Dacheng supported the powerful eunuch Wei Zhongxian, whom Hou Fangyu's father, Hou Xun (1590–1659), vehemently opposed.

[2] Hou Fangyu's father respected Cheng Yong (d. 1658) and Fang Kongzhao (1591–1655) because of their staunch opposition to Wei Zhongxian. Fang Kongzhao, father of Hou Fangyu's "inseparable friend," the polymath and renowned Revival Society member Fang Yizhi (d. 1671), spoke out vehemently against Wei Zhongxian. Cheng Yong similarly refused to associate with Wei Zhongxian's cronies and was eventually demoted for daring to criticize one of Emperor Chongzhen's favorites, Yang Sichang (1588–1641). This appears to be Cheng Yong's "crime" mentioned in the next section.

[3] General Wang's identity is not known.

Furthermore, he would like to discuss this matter with your friends Chen Zhenhui and Wu Yingji so as to clean up his reputation.[4]

With a serious expression, I bade farewell to the general, saying: "The Grand Master is a high official who does not lack well-placed connections or avenues for amusement. Why would he need to call upon a few students? If I were to raise the issue with the two others [Chen and Wu], I know they would vehemently refuse [to associate with Ruan]. And I fear it would be of no use to His Excellency if I alone were to establish friendly relations with him. Unworthy though I am, he has, with magnanimous intentions, extended his hospitality to me for eight days. But I must reject this solicitation." Having weighed the matter seriously in my mind, I determined that my reply was not excessive. Yet Your Excellency remains implacably resentful, and I truly have no way to escape your accusations.

Last night just as I was going to bed, County Magistrate Yang Wencong [a painter friendly with several members of the Restoration Society], came knocking on my door. He said, "General Zuo [Liangyu] is approaching with his army. The people in the capital are panicking. Grand Master Ruan is spreading it about in the Hall for Upright Discussion that you and [the general] are old friends and that you stand ready to assist him [if he attacks the city]. Why have you not fled?" It was then that I realized Your Excellency was not merely angry; you loathed me and would not be satisfied until my entire family had been exterminated.

Indeed, I have known General Zuo [Liangyu] for a long time. I obeyed Minister Xiong [Mingyu]'s command and dashed off a letter telling [General Zuo] to stay put, but I did not know his intentions. If he intended to rebel [by attacking the city], he was a criminal, and I too would be a criminal if I assisted him. But how could any scholar with the slightest understanding of ritual propriety willingly commit such a crime? Even if there were such a person, he would have to have "traveled the path [of iniquity] for so long that [he dared not] turn back," just like all those so-called "sons and grandsons" [of Wei Zhongxian] who, finding themselves in dire circumstances, permitted themselves to behave this way.[5] But how could I resemble such people?! And how could Your Excellency entangle me with this yarn of yours!?

僕斂容謝之曰：“光祿身爲貴卿，又不少佳賓客，足自娛；安用此二三書生爲哉？僕道之兩君，必重爲兩君所絕；若僕獨私從光祿遊，又竊恐無益光祿。辱相款八日，意良厚，然不得不絕矣。” 凡此皆僕平心稱量，自以爲未甚太過，而執事顧含怒不已，僕誠無所逃罪矣。

昨夜方寢，而楊令君文聰叩門過僕曰：“左將軍兵且來，都人洶洶，阮光祿颺言於清議堂云：‘子與有舊，且應之於內。’子盍行乎？” 僕乃知執事不獨見怒，且恨之，欲置之族滅而後快也。

僕與左誠有舊，亦已奉熊尚書之教，馳書止之。其心事尚不可知。若其犯順，則賊也；僕誠應之於內，亦賊也。士君子稍知禮義，何至甘心作賊？萬一有焉，此必日暮途窮倒行而逆施，若昔日乾兒、義孫之徒，計無復之，容出於此；而僕豈其人耶？何執事文織之深也。

---

[4] Chen Zhenhui (1604–1656) and Wu Yingji (1594–1645) were close friends of Hou's and active members of the Restoration Society. Like Hou, they strongly condemned Ruan's duplicity, and in 1538 the three men, along with several other members of the Restoration Society, submitted a memorial exposing Ruan's crimes of bribery and treason.

[5] The phrase "traveled the path [of iniquity] for so long that [he dared not] turn back," is a quotation from Sima Qian's "Biography of Wu Zixu." In that work, the title character exhumes and brutally flogs the corpse of a king he formerly served. When reprimanded for this behavior, Wu Zixu offers this phrase as explanation (☛ SJ, j. 66). Wei Zhongxian was known for nepotism, so certain unscrupulous individuals sought to advance their careers by pretending to be his relatives. These are the so-called sons and grandsons to whom the text refers.

竊怪執事常願下交天下
士，而展轉蹉跎，乃至
嫁禍而滅人之族，亦甚
違其本念。倘一旦追憶
天下士所以相遠之故，
未必不悔；悔，未必不
改；果悔且改，靜待之
數年，心事未必不暴
白；心事果暴白，天下
士未必不接踵而至執
事之門；僕果見天下
之士，接踵而至執事
之門，亦必且隨屬其
後，長揖謝過，　豈爲
晚乎？

而奈何陰毒左計，一至
於此！僕今已遭亂無
家，扁舟短棹，措此身
甚易。獨惜執事忮機一
動，長伏草莽則已，萬
一復得志，必至殺盡天
下士，以酬其宿所不
快；則是使天下士終不
復至執事之門，而後世
操簡書以議執事者，
不能如僕之詞微而義
婉也。

僕且去，可以不言；然
恐執事不察，終謂僕於
長者傲，故敢述其區
區，不宣。

[*MQSWX* 170–172]

I take umbrage at the fact that Your Excellency always [claims] you want to befriend scholars from all over. Yet you vacillate, falter, and cast blame on others, even to the point of having their entire families exterminated! This behavior violates your own core beliefs. If someday you think back on the reasons why scholars from all over have distanced themselves from you, you cannot fail to regret your actions. And having experienced regret, you cannot fail to change your behavior. Since you will have experienced regret and mended your ways, if you wait patiently for a few years, your true intentions will become known. And when this happens, there is no reason for scholars from all over not to flock to Your Excellency's door. When I see them flocking to Your Excellency's door, I will follow them, bow deeply to you, and apologize for my wrongdoings. It won't be too late.

What am I to do in the face of these diabolical and sinister plans of yours?! I have already met with disaster and lost my home, yet I can easily manage living in a small boat. I am just concerned that Your Excellency's rancor may be stirred. If you were to lie low in the hinterlands [as a recluse], fine. But if one day you should attain your ambition [and return to court], you would take revenge on the scholars of the world, annihilating them all to vent your own pent-up frustrations. And if this were to happen, they would not come flocking to Your Excellency's door! What's more, commentators in the future would not judge Your Excellency as gently and leniently as I have done.

I am about to leave. I need not have said any of this. But I feared that unless Your Excellency examined the issues I raised, you might claim that I acted arrogantly toward my elders. This is why I have dared to record these minor details. Much more could be said.[8]

CHOREOGRAPHING ONE'S OWN EXIT: XIA WANCHUN'S DYING WORDS

If the previous letter concludes with a form of leave-taking as Hou Fangyu prepares to flee by boat to Henan and Zhejiang, the next letter exemplifies a far more final farewell. Writing in 1647 from inside a Qing prison in Nanjing, the sixteen-year-old Ming loyalist soldier and literary prodigy Xia Wanchun (1631–1647) pours out his heart in elegantly paired four- and five-character phrases as he prepares for imminent death. With exquisite poise and self-control, he commends his final thoughts to his two mothers: his birth mother, a concubine surnamed Lu, and his official mother, his father's legal wife, née Sheng.

This epistle, the last he would write, swells with passionate declarations of Confucian filiality and loyalty, expressed as ardent patriotism. Steeped in the Confucian Classics since his earliest childhood, Xia, whose style name was "Preserving Antiquity" (*cungu*), prided himself on embodying the ideal of the gentleman who willingly lays down his life for his country. His sense of mission was amplified by the fact that his father, a distinguished scholar, had committed suicide two years earlier, after having been defeated in battle against the Qing. Outraged by the tragedy of his father's death and filled with admiration for his courage, Xia consecrates his own death to the same principles that motivated his father.

Yet despite Xia's fierce determination, the letter seems to reveal an embattled psyche and gnawing self-doubt. Is it really ethical, he wonders, to die for one's country when doing so means leaving behind vulnerable mothers and sisters, not to mention a defenseless wife? After he is gone, on whom will these bereft women rely and how will they survive? Reflecting nostalgically on his official mother's tender treatment of him and the care she took in his education, Xia exclaims, "her loving kindness was unmatched in all history!" This hyperbolic language conveys the depth of Xia's emotion and his grief that he will not live to repay the love she lavished on him in childhood.

No less disturbing is the fact that he has failed in his most sacred Confucian duty to produce an heir. Xia several times reproaches himself for his lack of filiality. As if to assuage his overwhelming guilt, he arrogantly boasts of the family's achievements: "How many people could rival the integrity, righteousness, and literary accomplishments of my father or myself?" He also invokes an even worse scenario: Zhang Pu, who died without an heir, and later the renowned poet and scholar Qian Qianyi (1582–1664) led the effort to appoint one. However, Qian also disgraced the Zhang family by surrendering to the Qing. In this letter, Xia insinuates that no matter how shameful and regrettable it may be for him to die without an heir, his misdeed pales beside the humiliation of allowing a traitor to appoint one's heir.

Alternating between overconfident declarations of his own moral rectitude and harrowing expressions of remorse, the letter suggests that Xia may be trying to convince himself that his death will not be in vain. This sense of desperation comes through all the more poignantly in Xia's fervent pleas that his family be taken care of and his exaggerated promises that everything will someday turn out all right.

C15.5 Xia Wanchun, "Letter to My Mothers, From Prison"

夏完淳　獄中上母書

Today I, the unworthy Wanchun, will die. In sacrificing my life to honor my father, I will not have the opportunity to repay my mothers. I grieve that two years have passed since my father's death. With cruelty increasing day by day, I have undergone countless hardships. At first I tried to restore the clear skies of the Ming, take revenge on our great enemy, and ensure that the dead not have perished in vain and the living receive honor.

不孝完淳，今日死矣。以身殉父，不得以身報母矣。痛自嚴君見背，兩易春秋，冤酷日深，艱辛歷盡。本圖復見天日，以報大仇，邮死榮生，告成黃土。

Alas! Heaven did not help me. Disaster befell the Ming, and no sooner had a battalion been raised than it was smashed to pieces. The following year in battle, I sensed that I was fated to die. Who would have suspected that my life would be extended and I would die today? But despite this two-year reprieve, I still have not been able to repay even a single day of the care my parents lavished on me in childhood. Things have come to the point that my official mother has taken refuge in Buddhism while my birth mother has entrusted

奈天不佑我，鍾虐先朝，一旅才興，便成齏粉。去年之舉，淳已自分必死，誰知不死，死於今日也。斤斤延此

二年之命，菽水之養，
無一日焉。致慈君托迹
於空門，生母寄生於別
姓。一門漂泊，生不得
相依，死不得相問。淳
今日又溘然先從九京，
不孝之罪，上通於天。

嗚呼！雙慈在堂，下有
妹女，門祚衰薄，終鮮
兄弟。淳一死不足惜，
哀哀八口，何以爲生？
雖然已矣，淳之身，父
之所遺，淳之身，君之
所用。爲父爲君，死亦
何負於雙慈？但慈君推
乾就濕，教禮習詩，十
五年如一日；嫡母慈
惠，千古所難。大恩未
酬，令人痛絕。慈君託
之義融女兄，生母托之
昭南女弟。　　　　·

淳死之後，新婦遺腹得
雄，便以爲家門之幸；
如其不然，萬勿置後！
會稽大望，至今而零極
矣。節義文章，如我父
子者幾人哉！立一不肖
後，如西銘先生，爲人
所訕笑，何如不立之爲
愈耶！嗚呼！大造茫
茫，總歸無後，有一日
中興再造，則廟食千
秋，豈止麥飯豚蹄，不
爲餒鬼而已哉！若有妄
言立後者，淳且與先文
忠在冥冥誅殛頑嚚，決
不肯捨！

兵戈天地，淳死後，亂
且未有定期。雙慈善保
玉體，無以淳爲念。二
十年後，淳且與先文忠

her life to relatives bearing a different surname. We who once formed a single household have drifted apart. In life we could not rely on one another, nor in death will we be able to communicate with one another. I am preceding the others in death, and, unfilial that I am, my crime is known even in heaven.

Alas! Both of my mothers are alive, as is my younger sister. Our family's fortune is waning, for I have no brothers. My own death is not worth lamenting, but I grieve for all the others. How will they get by? So be it! This body of mine was bequeathed to me by my father and employed in the service of my lord. In dying to honor my father and my lord, could it be that I have failed to live up to my mothers' expectations? It's just that my official mother [was so kind that when I wet the bed as a child, she] would move me to a dry place and sleep on the wet [bed] herself. She instructed me in the rites and taught me poetry. Under her tutelage, fifteen years sped by like a single day. Her loving kindness was unmatched in all of history. That I have not been able to recompense her for her great compassion pains me no end. Entrust her to my older sister Yirong, and commend my birth mother to my younger sister Zhaonan.

After I die, it would be a great boon if my bride should turn out to be pregnant with a son. But if she is not, by no means should you allow anyone else to inherit. We the Xias of Kuaiji [in Zhejiang province] are a distinguished family, even though there are now very few of us. How many people could rival the integrity, righteousness, and literary accomplishments of my father or myself? Installing some ne'er-do-well to inherit, as happened in the case of Zhang Pu, would invite ridicule. It would be preferable to have no successor at all! Alas! The whole of creation is vast. After things have returned to nothingness, the day will come when [our family] will flourish again. Then sacrifices will be restored, and our sacrifices will be far more sumptuous than mere grain and pigs' feet. We will certainly not be hungry ghosts! If anyone should rashly suggest that any successor other than a blood relative be established, my late father, [who bore the posthumous title of] Faithful Civil Servant, and I will, from the grave, punish that person with death. We will never let the matter rest!

Armed conflicts fill the world. After my death, who knows how long this chaos will continue? Oh mothers, take good care of your health and do not miss me too much. Twenty years from now, the Faithful Civil Servant [i.e., my father] and I will return upon the Northern frontier. Do not grieve. Do not grieve. Take care to abide by these words, which I have entrusted to you. My nephew Wugong [official name Hou Qing] has great potential; entrust all family matters to him. On the Cold Food Festival and the Ghost Festival, set out a cup of clear wine and a dim lamp so that I need not become a hungry ghost. This is all I could wish for. My bride and I have been married for two years; her virtue and filiality are evident. Wugong, my nephew, please take good care of her, since you and I have always enjoyed the close relationship befitting an uncle and a nephew.

My words pour out in disarray. [It is said that] those who are about to die speak frankly. Oh woe. Oh woe. Who can escape death? I value the opportunity to die for a purpose. My father died a loyal minister, and I am dying a filial son. Willingly, I return to the Great Void, having fulfilled my mission. The great Dao admits neither life nor death, so I regard this body of mine as a worn-out shoe. Only because I was infused with the spirit of integrity was I able to comprehend the principles of Heaven and man. This nightmare having lasted for seventeen years, I will be avenged in the next life. When my spirit roams between heaven and earth, I will have no regrets.[9]

ENJOYING THE RUSTIC LIFE: ZHENG XIE'S FAMILY PRECEPTS FROM PLANK BRIDGE

The theme of providing for one's kin, introduced in the previous letter, receives further elaboration in the next selection. This letter appears in a series of sixteen notes written by the accomplished painter, poet, and calligrapher Zheng Xie (1693–1765) to his younger cousin Zheng Mo. While serving as district magistrate of Fan County (in current-day Henan province), Zheng wrote frequently to his young cousin and provided him with both practical guidance and material support. In this letter, Zheng Xie expresses his aspiration to grant Mo a modest piece of farmland to cultivate. He also passes on to his cousin the family's ethical principles of hard work, respect for people of all social classes, and the ability to derive satisfaction from simple pleasures. Zheng's appreciation of rustic life finds further expression in his humble sobriquet, "Plank Bridge" (*Banqiao*).

Steeped in the Confucian Classics since his earliest childhood, Zheng strongly embraced integrity and tenacity, moral values he expressed symbolically in paintings of bamboo, rocks, and orchids. As an official, he attempted to live up to these ideals and earned a reputation for compassionate, ethical administration. Yet he ultimately became an outspoken critic of Confucian officialdom for its conformism, rigidity, and careerism. Best known as an experimental visual artist and one of the "eight eccentrics of Yangzhou," Zheng boldly voiced unconventional opinions, especially when his views were rooted in ethical conviction. In this letter, he upends the traditional Confucian hierarchy of the four classes of persons (*si min*) by elevating farmers, craftsmen, and merchants over scholars. His inversion of this well-established order rests on honoring farmers' fundamental contribution to society, namely food. Throughout this letter, Zheng emphasizes the importance of recognizing farmers' hard work and treating even the lowliest members of society with dignity. These ringing endorsements of egalitarianism resonate with his own experiences. As the letter displays, he possessed detailed knowledge of agricultural tools used for harvesting and processing grain and enjoyed dining on rustic fare. Clearly, Zheng was a district magistrate intimately familiar with the lives of those under his jurisdiction.

為北塞之舉矣。勿悲，勿悲。相托之言，慎勿相負！武功甥將來大器，家事盡以委之。寒食盂蘭，一杯清酒，一盞寒燈，不至作若敖之鬼，則吾願畢矣。新婦結褵二年，賢孝素著，武功甥好為我善待之。亦武功渭陽情也。

語無倫次，將死言善。痛哉，痛哉！人生孰無死？貴得死所耳。父得為忠臣，子得為孝子，含笑歸太虛，了我分內事。大道本無生，視身若敝屣，但為氣所激，緣悟天人理。惡夢十七年，報仇在來世。神游天地間，可以無愧矣！

[*XWCJJJ* 413–414]

The unadorned style of the letter corresponds to its quotidian subject matter. Zheng employs clear diction and eschews recondite classical allusions. He refers only to the popular legend of the Shepherd Boy and Weaving Girl. These features lend the letter a down-to-earth air. The exclamatory particles *jiehu* (translated here as "Mmm! ahh!") further add to this impression, endowing the letter with a sense of immediacy and authenticity characteristic of Zheng's paintings and calligraphy. In fact, unlike the other works translated in this chapter, which illustrate the tendency of much late-imperial epistolary prose to address matters of serious national import or to discourse on life and death, this letter may seem more accessible to modern readers on account of its homier scope and more intimate, personal tone.

鄭燮　范縣署中寄舍弟
墨第四書

十月二十六日得家書，
知新置田穫秋稼五百
斛，甚喜。而今而後，
堪爲農夫以沒世矣。要
須制碓、制磨、制篩羅
簸箕、制大小掃帚、制
升斗斛。家中婦女，率
諸婢妾，皆令習舂揄蹂
簸之事，便是一種靠田
園長子孫氣象。天寒冰
凍時，窮親戚朋友到
門，先泡一大碗炒米送
手中，佐以醬姜一小
碟，最是暖老溫貧之
具。暇日咽碎米餅，煮
糊塗粥，雙手捧碗，縮
頸而啜之，霜晨雪早，
得此周身俱暖。嗟乎！
嗟乎！吾其長爲農夫以
沒世乎！

我想天地間第一等人，
只有農夫，而士爲四民
之末。農夫上者種地百
畝，其次七八十畝，其
次五六十畝，皆苦其
身，勤其力，耕種收
穫，以養天下之人。使

C15.6 Zheng Xie, "Fourth Letter to My Younger Cousin Mo, Written from My Official Residence in Fan County"

On the twenty-sixth day of the tenth month I received a letter from home and was immensely pleased to learn that five hundred *hu* of grain had been harvested from the fields we recently bought. From now on, we can spend our lives as farmers! We'll need to make a millstone and a hammer for hulling rice, sifters and winnowing fans, as well as large and small brooms and *sheng* and *dou* measures.[1] The women of our family will set an example for the serving girls and concubines and instruct them to practice pounding and winnowing. In this atmosphere, we'll raise our sons and grandsons to rely for their livelihood on the fields and orchards. On freezing, wintry days, when poor relatives and friends call on us, we'll offer them a big bowl of steeped, puffed rice, along with a small dish of ginger sauce; this is the best comfort food for the poor and the elderly. On idle days, we'll guzzle down crushed rice cakes and bowls of sticky rice gruel. Holding the bowls in both hands, we'll throw back our heads and slurp it down. On frosty mornings, it will warm us from head to toe. Mmm! Ah! To be a farmer till the end of my days!

In my opinion the best people in the world are farmers; of the four classes of persons [scholars, farmers, artisans, and merchants], scholars are the worst. The most prosperous farmers cultivate 100 *mu* of land; the next most prosperous cultivate 70 or 80 *mu*, and the ones after them cultivate 50 or 60 *mu*.[2] But all of them toil diligently, exerting their strength in ploughing and reaping so as to feed the people of the world. If there were no farmers, we would all starve to death. We scholars are considered superior to farmers because we exhibit filial piety and brotherly affection at home and abroad, displaying respect for our elders and looking after the next generation. If we are recognized for our

---

[1] *Sheng, dou*, and *hu* are all measures of volume. There are ten *sheng* in a *dou*. The number of *dou* per *hu* is more difficult to state with accuracy because it varied over time.

[2] A *mu* is one fifteenth of a hectare.

abilities and selected for government service, we extend favor to the people. If not, we cultivate ourselves and set an example for others. This is why we're ranked one grade higher than farmers.

But scholars these days don't behave this way. No sooner do they pick up a book than they start thinking about passing the provincial and national examinations and becoming officials; they start scheming about how to make money, build big houses, and acquire large tracts of land. No sooner have they begun than they head down the wrong path, and the farther they go, the worse they become; things scarcely ever turn out well for such people. Those who don't succeed [on the exams] go to the countryside where they behave reprehensibly, wheedling and currying favor, which is even more inappropriate. There are, of course, some who possess a sense of self-restraint. Many discipline and restrain themselves to resist their passions and follow the ancients. But the good are ensnared by the bad, and there's nothing people like us can say about it. If we were to open our mouths, we would immediately become a laughingstock. People would say, "You scholars sure can talk! But then when you become officials you change your tune." So we must hold our tongues and keep our own counsel as we endure their taunts. Craftsmen make useful tools. Merchants transport goods to where they're needed. Both bring advantage to the people. Only scholars seriously disadvantage the people. It's no wonder they rank lowest among the four classes. In fact, they don't even deserve to rank at all!

I have always thought extremely highly of farmers. We must treat the newly-arrived tenant farmers with courtesy. They should call us "hosts" and we should refer to them as "guests." The guest-host relationship has always been grounded in reciprocity: surely we are no more honorable than they, nor they any less honorable than we! We must be polite to them and treat them with compassion. If they [ask to] borrow something, we should help them out, and if they cannot repay us, we must forgive their debts. I once noted with amusement that Tang poetry about the Qixi Festival invokes the Shepherd Boy and Weaving Girl's sorrow at parting, but neglects to comment on the root meanings of their names: "Weaving Girl" refers to the origin of clothing and "Shepherd Boy" refers to the source of food. These are the most honored stars in heaven. So if heaven regards them so highly, how come human beings don't? Hardworking farmers, who dedicate their lives to providing the necessities of life, shine brightly, reflecting [the principles contained in these stars' names].

The women in our village do not know how to weave bolts of cloth, but they do manage the cooking and practice needlework, so they cannot be deemed neglectful of their duties. [However,] they've recently become fond of listening to drum-songs and holding card tournaments. You must warn them at once against such laxity in their customs!

天下無農夫，舉世皆餓死矣。吾輩讀書人，入則孝，出則弟，守先待後，得志澤加於民，不得志修身見於世，所以又高於農夫一等。

今則不然，一捧書本，便想中舉、中進士、作官，如何攫取金錢、造大房屋、置多田產。起手便錯走了路頭，後來越做越壞，總沒有一個好結果。其不能發達者，鄉裏作惡，小頭銳面，更不可當。夫束修自好者，豈無其人。經濟自期，抗懷千古者，亦所在多有。而好人爲壞人所累，遂令我輩開不得口，一開口，人便笑曰：汝輩書生，總是會說，他日居官，便不如此說了。所以忍氣吞聲，只得捱人笑罵。工人制器利用，賈人搬有運無，皆有便民之處。而士獨於民大不便，無怪乎居四民之末也！且求居四民之末而亦不可得也！

愚兄平生最重農夫，新招佃地人，必須待之以禮。彼稱我為主人，我稱彼為客戶，主客原是對待之義，我何貴而彼何賤乎？要體貌他，要憐憫他。有所借貸，要周全他。不能償還，要寬讓他。嘗笑唐人七夕詩，詠牛郎織女，皆作會別可憐之語，殊失命名本旨。織女，衣之源

也，牽牛，食之本也，
在天星為最貴。天顧重
之，而人反不重乎！其
務本勤民，呈象昭昭可
鑒矣。

　吾邑婦人，不能織紬
織布，然而主中饋，習
針線，猶不失為勤謹。
近日頗有聽鼓兒詞，以
斗葉為戲者，風俗蕩
軼，亟宜戒之。

　吾家業地雖有三百畝，
總是典產，不可久恃。
將來須買田二百畝，予
兄弟二人，各得百畝足
矣，亦古者一夫受田百
畝之義也。若再求多，
便是占人產業，莫大罪
過。天下無田無業者多
矣，我獨何人，貪求無
厭，窮民將何所措足
乎！或曰：世上連阡越
陌，數百頃有余者，子
將奈何？應之曰：他自
做他家事，我自做我家
事，世道盛則一德遵
王，風俗偷則不同為
惡，亦板橋之家法也。
哥哥字。

[*ZBQQJ* 186–188]

Although our family possesses 300 *mu* of land, it is all mortgaged property on which we cannot rely permanently. In the future, we should buy 200 *mu* of land to divide between us cousins. One hundred *mu* will be enough for each of us, for, according to ancient custom, each man should receive a hundred *mu*. Seeking to acquire more would mean seizing other people's property, and there is no greater crime than this. Many people in the world have no property or livelihood at all. If we were greedy, what would become of the poor people? If anyone were to ask what I think of the fact that some people possess several thousand *mu* of adjacent rice paddy fields, I would reply: what others do is their family's concern; what we do is our family's concern. When the Way flourishes, we unite in serving the ruler virtuously; but when customs degenerate, we refrain from following others' evil ways. These are the family principles of Plank Bridge. Your older cousin.[10]

LEANING DEJECTEDLY ON HER ARMREST: WANG DUANSHU'S MULTIFACETED SELF-PORTRAYAL

In contrast to the previous letter, in which Zheng Xie describes with delight the simple life of the countryside but criticizes illiterate village women for indulging in idle pleasures like playing cards and listening to drum songs, this final selection by the brilliant female writer Wang Duanshu (1621–ca. 1706) invokes a far more urbane and refined lifestyle. As a girl, Wang Duanshu studied alongside her brothers, distinguishing herself for her prodigious memory and literary ability. In fact her father, the Ming loyalist Wang Siren (1575–1646), considered her to be the most capable scholar of all his children, including his eight sons! In adulthood, Wang Duanshu shuttled among several bustling cultural centers: Beijing, where her husband's family lived; her natal home of Shaoxing, where the couple fled after the fall of Beijing; and the cultural and artistic mecca of Hangzhou. An accomplished painter and calligrapher, prolific author, and editor of at least ten volumes, Wang Duanshu is perhaps best known for *Writings of the Fall* (*Yinhong ji*), a collection of her own poetry and prose that departed from traditionally "feminine" topics like love and instead addressed the national calamity of the fall of the Ming. Her works brought her into contact with leading cultural figures, many of whom petitioned her to contribute poetry and prefaces for their works.[11] Although circumstances forced her to relocate several times, she maintained a robust social life through her correspondence.

This brief letter provides an artfully framed glimpse into Wang Duanshu's aesthetic and emotional life; we see her laboring on her poetry late into the night and gazing sadly into the mirror in the morning, seemingly afflicted by both illness and success. The date of this letter has not been preserved, and we cannot be sure of the identity of the recipient, a certain Madame Feng. Yet the two women clearly enjoyed a cordial friendship and, like many educated women of their social class, viewed letters not merely as practical means of communication but as important vehicles for literary and visual self-fashioning and self-expression.

The letter closes with Wang mentioning a fan, originally a gift from Madame Feng, which Wang has decorated and is now returning. On the fan, Wang has painted an image from the theater, a *dan* or "leading lady," the role type associated with women of noble character, often damsels in distress. The theme is significant for, like her reflection in the mirror, the painted *dan* symbolizes Wang's own sense of suffering and loss following the dynastic collapse. In the unfolding drama of her life, Wang was unquestionably a leading lady, and her studied self-description in this letter evokes an almost theatrical self-consciousness. Thus like the image painted on the fan and the likeness reflected in the mirror, Wang's verbal self-portrayal may be understood as an artfully constructed record of the author's melancholy.

C15.7 Wang Duanshu, "Letter to Madame Feng"

王端淑　柬馮夫人

Since I fell ill I've scarcely had sufficient energy [to pick up my brush]. Leaning dejectedly on my armrest, I see incoming letters piled up so high they bury my ink stone.[1] Every day I receive at least ten more requests for my writings. But I am not able to write much; too much writing makes my head hurt. In my spare time, I compose poems orally. Unable to complete them swiftly, I agonize over them, sometimes all night. The next morning, when I take out my mirror to look at myself, I see several more strands of white hair at my temples. On the fan you sent, I have painted a *dan*. Please take a look.[12]

病後心氣苦不足。來書
韜硯嗒然隱几。徵書者
日十數至。亦不能多作
書。多書，頭岑岑也。
間有吟咏。苦索不夙
就。或至竟夜。明日抽
鏡視之。鬢髮又添數莖
白矣。　來扇附青衣呈
鑒。

[*LDMYSJ* 2:8]

Whether in elegant, formal diction or in seemingly casual prose, the documents translated in this chapter illustrate the wide range of literary styles employed in late-imperial epistolary prose and funerary writings. Furthermore, they attest to the central importance of loyal patriotism; personal self-sacrifice; and ardent devotion to parents and children, spouses, teachers, and friends during a period of chaos and dynastic upheaval. The prominence of these themes finds expression in the authors' attempts to portray themselves favorably, as upright members of society. But the texts are not merely exercises in flattering self-fashioning; they also offer glimpses of the authors' intimate thoughts—their inner struggles and self-doubts. These self-reflexive explorations and eye-witness accounts furnish moving testimony of the very real moral and practical predicaments facing individuals at all levels of society during the Ming–Qing transition. By exhibiting an array of ethical positions and literary styles, these documents exemplify the diversity of lived experience and provide a compelling counterpoint to more staid official histories.

Rivi Handler-Spitz

---

[1] The phrase "leaning dejectedly on my armrest" is borrowed from the opening passage of Zhuangzi's "Discussion on Making Things Equal" (*Qi wu lun*).

NOTES

1. On the practice of editing letters in the Ming, see Timothy Brook, "The Public of Letters: The Correspondence of Li Zhi and Geng Dingxiang," in *The Objectionable Li Zhi: Fiction, Criticism, and Dissent in Late-Ming China*, edited by Rivi Handler-Spitz, Pauline C. Lee, and Haun Saussy (Seattle: University of Washington Press, 2021), 75–91.

2. Li Yu in *Complete Letters Ancient and Modern* (*Gujin chidu daquan*), cited in David Pattinson, "The Market for Letter Collections in Seventeenth-Century China," *Chinese Literature: Essays, Articles, Reviews* 28 (December 2006): 146. Compilers Zhou Lianggong and Wang Shizhen made similar statements; see David John Pattinson, *The Chidu in Late Ming and Early Qing China* (PhD diss., Australian National University, 1997), 65, 103.

3. Dorothy Ko, *Teachers of the Inner Chambers: Women and Culture in Seventeenth Century China* (Stanford, CA: Stanford University Press, 1994), 238–239. See also Gu's poem, "Purposely Written as a 'Rebuttal of Ridicule' After Having Been Criticized for Hiring a Teacher to Instruct My Daughters," translated in Wilt Idema and Beata Grant, *The Red Brush: Writing Women of Imperial China* (Cambridge, MA: Harvard University Asia Center, 2004), 418–419.

4. This preface is translated in Idema and Grant, *The Red Brush*, 415–418.

5. *Renhe xianzhi*, 20.51b, cited in Ko, *Teachers of the Inner Chambers*, 238 n44.

6. Wang Duanshu, "Preface to Mingyuan shiwei," translated by Haun Saussy in *Women Writers of Traditional China: An Anthology of Poetry and Criticism*, edited by Kang-i Sun Chang, and Haun Saussy (Stanford, CA: Stanford University Press, 1999), 692.

7. Ko, *Teachers of the Inner Chambers*, 246.

8. For an alternative translation of this text, see "To Ruan Dacheng on Leaving Nanjing, 1643," translated by David E. Pollard in *Renditions* 41–42 (1994), 106–109.

9. For an alternative translation, see "From the Death Cell to his Mother," translated by David E. Pollard in *Renditions* 41–42 (1994), 110–113.

10. For an alternative translation of portions of this letter, see "Fourth Letter to Brother Mo from the Magistrate's Residence at Fanhsien," translated by Lin Yutang " in Lin Yutang 林語堂. *Lin Yutang Zhong Ying duizhao Banqiao jia shu* 林語堂中英對照板橋家書 (*Lin Yutang's Chinese-English Bilingual Edition of Banqiao's Letters to His Family*). Edited by Li Ming 黎明 (Taipei: Zhongzheng shuju, 2009), 52–61.

11. For instance, she contributed a preface to Li Yu's *Sole Mates*. Ellen Widmer, "The Epistolary World of Female Talent in Seventeenth-Century China," *Late Imperial China* 10, no. 2 (December 1989): 11.

12. For an alternative translation of this letter, see "To Madame Feng," translated by Ellen Widmer in "Selected Short Works of Wang Duanshu," in *Under Confucian Eyes: Writings on Gender in Chinese History*, edited by Susan Mann and Yu-Yin Cheng (Berkeley: University of California Press, 2001), 188.

SUGGESTED READINGS

ENGLISH

Cheng, Yu-Yin. "Letters by Women of the Ming-Qing Period." In *Under Confucian Eyes: Writings on Gender in Chinese History*, edited by Susan Mann and Yu-Yin Cheng, 169–178. Berkeley: University of California Press, 2001.

Dardess, John. W. *Blood and History: The Donglin Faction and Its Repression 1620–1627*. Honolulu: University of Hawai'i Press, 2002.

Elman, Benjamin. "Imperial Politics and Confucian Societies in Late Imperial China: The Hanlin and Donglin Academies." *Modern China* 15, no. 14 (October 1999): 379–418.

Hucker, Charles O. "Su-chow and the Agents of Wei Chung-hsien, 1626." In *Two Studies on Ming History*, 41–83. Ann Arbor: University of Michigan Papers in Chinese Studies, 1971.

Idema, Wilt, and Beata Grant. *The Red Brush: Writing Women of Imperial China*. Cambridge, MA: Harvard University Asia Center, 2004.

Ko, Dorothy. *Teachers of the Inner Chambers: Women and Culture in Seventeenth Century China*. Stanford, CA: Stanford University Press, 1994.

Pattinson, David John. "Zhou Lianggong and *Chidu Xinchao*: Genre and Political Marginalization in the Ming-Qing Transition." *East Asian History* 20 (December 2000): 60–82.

Widmer, Ellen. "The Epistolary World of Female Talent in Seventeenth-Century China." *Late Imperial China* 10, no. 2 (December 1989): 1–43.

CHINESE

Gu Ruopu 顧若璞. *Huang Furen Woyue xuangao* 黃夫人臥月軒稿 (*Madame Huang's* Drafts from the Studio for Reclining in the Moonlight). Shunzhi ben 順治本, 1651.

Liao Kebin 廖可斌. *Mingdai wenxue fugu yundong yanjiu* 明代文學復古運動研究 (*Studies on the Literary Antiquarian Movement in the Ming Dynasty*). Beijing: Shangwu yinshuguan, 2008.

Lin Yutang 林語堂. *Lin Yutang Zhong Ying duizhao Banqiao jia shu* 林語堂中英對照板橋家書 (*Lin Yutang's Chinese-English Bilingual Edition of Banqiao's Letters to His Family*). Edited by Li Ming 黎明. Taipei: Zhongzheng shuju, 2009.

Shi Shouqian 石守謙 and Yang Rubin 楊儒賓, eds. *Mingdai mingxian chidu ji* 明代明賢尺牘集 (*Collected Letters of Eminent Ming Scholars*). Taipei: Hechuangshi shufa yishu wenjiao jijinhui, 2013.

Wang Xiuqin 王秀琴. *Lidai mingyuan shujian* 歷代名媛書簡 (*Letters by Literary Ladies of China*). Changsha: Shangwu yinshuguan, 1950.

Zhao Shugong 趙樹功. *Zhongguo chidu wenxueshi* 中國尺牘文學史 (*A History of Chinese Epistolarity*). Shijiazhuang: Hebei renmin chubanshe, 1999.

Wu Guoping 吳國平. *Mingqing wenxue lunsou* 明清文學論藪 (*Collected Essays on Ming Qing Literature*). Beijing: Fenghuang chubanshe, 2011.

Zhang Xiuling 張修齡. *Qingchu sanwen lungao* 清初散文論稿 (*On Early Qing Essays*). Shanghai: Fudan daxue chubanshe, 2010.

16

Ming and Qing Occasional Prose

Accounts of Places and People

Compared with the canonical "Eight Prose Masters of the Tang and Song" (*Tang Song ba dajia*) discussed in part III (☞ chap. 10–13), the essayists of the Ming and Qing we encounter here might seem like dabblers in a genre mired in the trivial and mundane. Already, the term *xiaopin wen* suggests an earthy quality that could easily have consigned the genre to the margins of literary history. Variously translated as occasional essays, informal essays, familiar essays, or more literally, lesser works or minor pieces, *xiaopin wen* is a form of belles lettres that provides a writer with great—almost too great—flexibility in subject matter. In the words of Lin Yutang, one of the foremost advocates of the genre in the modern era, *xiaopin wen* can treat a topic "as great as the universe or as tiny as a fly."[1] The subject matter of the six essays discussed in this chapter falls somewhere in between: ranging from an anecdotal account of a scholar's studio to a bibliophile's remarks on book borrowing, descriptions of a suburban excursion, a night of moon watching, a mountain hike, and a museum visit.

Despite its putative triviality, *xiaopin wen* occupies a unique place in Chinese literary history. In fact, according to Lin Yutang, Zhou Zuoren, and other modernists who retrospectively canonized the genre, it is in the gems of Ming and Qing *xiaopin*, those occasional essays about cricket raising, ant fighting, and such, that we find the origins of modern Chinese literature. Perhaps, as some scholars have pointed out, these leaders of the New Culture movement in the 1920s were looking for something from the past to justify their impulse toward literary reform or revolution. Literary history is littered with examples of forgotten works being resurrected and enshrined as classics by later generations. Without the efforts by Carl van Doren and other critics and writers in the early twentieth century, Herman Melville would have remained an obscure author whose all-embracing novel, *Moby-Dick*, hardly a success on publication, would have sunk to the pelagic bottom of American literature like the *Pequod*. Or, closer to our subject, the canon of the Eight Masters of Tang and Song, still the benchmark for ancient prose, was in fact established retrospectively by writers of the mid-Ming, including Gui Youguang, whom we will read in this chapter. Mindful of the whimsical nature of literary fame, the unpredictable rise and fall of authors and schools, we nonetheless can describe the essential characteristics of *xiaopin wen*, especially those that served in its resurrection, and the cultural and historical milieu in which this boutique genre of Chinese prose flourished in the Ming and Qing dynasties.

As Ronald Egan points out in his discussion of Tang and Song occasional prose (👉 chap. 11), Chinese prose in those two earlier dynasties had already experienced a shift from the ritualistic and bureaucratic parallel prose to the more flexible and personal essays. When we arrived at the early and mid-Ming, we found that the literary scene was dominated by the so-called Former Seven Masters and Later Seven Masters, all archaists who championed formal correctness and moral earnestness modeled on the ancient masters. Native to a literary culture suffering from recurrent bouts of antiquarianism, these worshippers of the past believed the Golden Age of Chinese literature had long since passed, with prose peaking in the pre-Qin and poetry in the Tang and Song. Regarding the course of literary history as a process of gradual deterioration, the archaists espoused imitation, discipline, and adherence to rules established by the ancient masters, resulting in a ponderous prose style full of outdated syntax and vocabulary. In response to such conservatism, new generations of writers arose in the mid- and late-Ming championing self-expression, informality, and spontaneity. As Yuan Hongdao, leader of the Gongan school, famously put it, prose should "uniquely express one's personality and innate sensibility without being restrained by convention and form" (*dushu xingling, buju getao*). Yuan's key term *xingling* was rendered by James Liu as "natural spiritual powers," whereas Lin Yutang interpreted *xing* as one's character and *ling* as one's soul or spirit.

So radical a statement on self-expression, deemed by some "as close as one can come in traditional Chinese criticism to a conception of individualism as a principle of artistic creativity," did not come out of nowhere.[2] It represented a confluence of ideas that gained increasing popularity in an age of decadence, confusion, and decline. One such strand of intellectual development was the revival of Buddhism, which promulgated the belief that each individual is born with the "Buddha-nature" and only needs to become aware of it. Also, Wang Yangming (1472–1529), perhaps the most influential neo-Confucian philosopher of his time, emphasized the individual mind as opposed to external principles, maintaining that each person has within an essentially good "intuitive awareness" (*liangzhi*). Last, Li Zhi, a heretical, bohemian writer, carried Wang's idea of individualism to an extreme. He "called for reliance on one's own intuitions and desires, which associated with what he called the 'childlike mind.'"[3] To Li, a writer is one "who is aroused by his feeling, whose mind cannot stop acting, whose emotions having been stimulated, cannot restrain himself from revealing these emotions in words." Two hundred years later, this sentiment would find an echo in the Romantic dictum of William Wordsworth: "Poetry is the spontaneous overflow of powerful feelings."

Materialized in writing, these ideals of self-expression, spontaneity, and free thinking led to a prose style more lyrical than didactic, more vernacular than formal, and artful without artifice. With unlikely origins in a fifth-century collection of anecdotal vignettes adapted from Buddhist sutras, *xiaopin wen* in the Ming and Qing assumed manifold forms, including travelogues, epitaphs, prefaces, biographical sketches, epistles, discourses, and dialogues. Printing presses and a growing reading public also created an impetus for the genre, as many talented writers, facing increasing difficulties to achieve officialdom by traditional means, turned to selling occasional pieces as a way to make a living. In addition, the rise of the novel also cultivated a readership that looked for pleasure and entertainment rather than moral didacticism in literature. As a whole, *xiaopin wen* was defined, as Tina Lu puts it, by what it was not, situating the genre "in contradistinction to that associated official business . . . namely orthodox literature in the service of the state."[4]

Spanning more than three hundred years from the mid-sixteenth to the late-nineteenth centuries, the six occasional essays selected in this chapter represent the height of the genre's spectacular achievement. It may be true that, as David Pollard writes in a stunning statement, "China had no Montaigne, no background to produce a Montaigne, and no inclination to celebrate a Montaigne had he arrived as a freak of history. Neither his mindset nor the language he used had a place in China until the twentieth century."[5] But Montaigne never had to worry about the collapse of the European civilization, whose relative stability buttressed the kind of soul-searching and disinterested inquiry trademarked by the European discursive essay. China in the Ming and Qing period faced tremendous pressures from the outside, and the former Middle Kingdom was steadily losing its place in the world. As their civilization crumbled from internal decay and external assault, those Chinese contemporaries of Joseph Addison, Charles Lamb, Washington Irving, and Nathaniel Hawthorne, by virtue of their uninhibitedness and nonconformity, blazed a trail toward Chinese literary modernity.

The first *xiaopin* writer we will read is Gui Youguang (1506–1571), a transitional figure in mid-Ming, who led the canonization of the Eight Great Tang and Song Masters of ancient prose and paved the way for more radical writers to come. Born in Kunshan (in today's Jiangsu province) to a wealthy family, Gui was an excellent scholar of the classics, despite struggling in the exams and only eventually acquiring the *jinshi* degree as he approached sixty. A universally recognized grandmaster of ancient prose, Gui, on one hand, upheld the core principles of the Tang and Song masters, especially Han Yu's mandate for prose to be a carrier of *dao* (*wen yi zai dao*). On the other hand, he used the otherwise-hefty medium of *guwen* for ostensibly light, trivial subjects. The next essay "A Chronicle of the Xiangji Studio" offers a prime example. Literally "A Chronicle of the Studio of Nape and Spine," the essay was first written in 1524, when Gui was just eighteen. Over twenty years later, now a sadder and wiser man who had experienced many vicissitudes in life, Gui added two paragraphs at the end of the original piece.

Different editions of the essay have as its title either *Xiangjixuan Ji* or *Xiangjixuan Zhi*. Both *ji* and *zhi*, with cognate meanings of "record, or chronicle," fall under the rubric of *zaji* (miscellaneous records), as defined by Yao Nai. In his groundbreaking *Classified Anthology of Ancient-Style Prose* (*Guwenci leizuan*), Yao divided Chinese prose into thirteen categories, and *zaji* is the ninth category, a catchall repository for various subgenres that are hard to classify, including historical records, occasional records, personal chronicles, informal treatises, notes, analects, and dedicatory inscriptions.

C16.1 Gui Youguang, "A Chronicle of the Xiangji Studio"

歸有光 項脊軒志

The Xiangji Studio was formerly the South Loft. Ten square feet in size, it is barely big enough for one person. The structure is a hundred years old, dust falling from the roof, rainwater running down the walls. Every time I tried to move my desk, I looked around in vain for a place to put it. Facing north with no sunlight, the room would get dark in the afternoon. So, I had some repairs done to stop the leaks, and also had four windows cut in the front and a parapet built around the courtyard to catch the sun. With reflected sunlight, the room brightened up considerably. I also planted a mix of orchids, laurels, bamboos, and trees in the yard, thus enhancing the look of the old railings. Filling my shelves with borrowed books, I would lie back to read and chant, or sitting in solitude, listen to all the sounds of nature. In the stillness of the yard and terrace, small birds would occasionally come to feed, oblivious to the approach of human footsteps. On nights of full moon, radiant moonlight washed over part of the parapet, where laurels cast dappled shadows that moved with the wind—what a lovely scene! Living here, I experienced much joy, but also much sorrow.[1]

項脊軒，舊南閣子也。室僅方丈，可容一人居。百年老屋，塵泥滲漉，雨澤下注，每移案，顧視無可置者。又北向，不能得日，日過午已昏。余稍為修葺，使不上漏；前闢四窗，垣牆周庭，以當南日；日影反照，室始洞然。又雜植蘭桂竹木於庭，舊時欄楯，亦遂增勝。借書滿架，偃仰嘯歌，冥然兀坐。萬籟有聲，而庭堦寂寂，小鳥時來啄食，人至不去。三五之夜，月明半牆，桂影斑駁。風移影動，珊珊可愛。然予居於此，多可喜，亦多可悲。

The courtyard used to link the north and south quarters of the compound, but after my uncles divided up the property, they added doors and erected walls. Dogs on the east side barked at residents on the west side, guests had to pass through the kitchen to find dinner, and chickens came to roost at the reception hall.[2] At first fences were raised in the courtyard, then replaced by walls, and more changes were made. There was an old woman who once lived here. Maid to my grandmother, she had nursed two generations of my family. My late mother was very fond of her. The west side of the studio was linked to the inner chambers, and my mother would come here. The old woman often told me, "Here, this is where your mother once stood." Or again, "One time your sister was crying hard in my arms. Your mom tapped the door lightly with her fingertips, asking, 'Is the baby cold? Hungry?' I replied from this side of the door." Before she had finished, I burst into tears, and so did she.

先是，庭中通南北為一。迨諸父異爨，內外多置小門牆，往往而是。東犬西吠，客踰庖而宴，雞棲於廳。庭中始為籬，已為牆，凡再變矣。家有老嫗，嘗居於此。嫗，先大母婢也。乳二世，先妣撫之甚厚。室西連於中閨，先妣嘗一至，嫗每謂予曰："某所，而母立於茲。"嫗又曰："汝姊在吾懷，呱呱而泣。娘以指扣門扉曰：'兒寒乎？欲食乎？'吾從板外相為應答。"語未畢，余泣；嫗亦泣。

After knotting my hair at fifteen, I studied in this studio. One day my grandmother happened by. "My child," she said, "I haven't seen you at all for a while. Why do you stay all day here, quiet like a girl?" Upon leaving, she gently closed the door behind her and muttered, "This family hasn't had a successful scholar for some time. Maybe there's hope with this young man." Soon she returned with an ivory tablet in hand, saying, "This was what my grandfather, as Chief

---

[1] A masterly light stroke, switching the focus from joy to sorrow.

[2] A family's saga, its rise and fall, cohesion and disintegration, is all reflected by the behavior of barking dogs, roosting chickens, and visiting guests. Gui's mother died when he was still a child, a traumatizing event that would later inspire the composition of his timeless essay, "Brief Account of My Deceased Mother."

余自束髮讀書軒中。一
日，大母過余曰：「吾
兒，久不見若影，何
竟日默默在此，大類女
郎也？」比去，以手闔
門，自語曰：「吾家
讀書久不效，兒之成，
則可待乎？」頃之，持
一象笏至，曰：「此
吾祖太常公宣德間執
此以朝；他日，汝當用
之。」瞻顧遺跡，如在
昨日。令人長號不自禁。

軒東故嘗爲廚。人
往，從軒前過。余扃牖
而居，久之能以足音辨
人。軒凡四遭火，得不
焚，殆有神護者。

項脊生曰：蜀清守丹
穴，利甲天下。其後秦
始皇築女懷清臺。劉玄
德與曹操爭天下，諸葛
孔明起隴中，方二人之
昧昧于一隅也，世何足
以知之？余區區處敗屋
中，方揚眉瞬目，謂有
奇景。人知之者，其謂
與坿井之蛙何異！

余既爲此志後五年，
吾妻來歸。時至軒中從
余問古事，或憑几學
書。吾妻歸寧，述諸小
妹語曰：「聞姊家有閣
子，且何謂閣子也？」
其後六年，吾妻死，室
壞不修。其後二年，余
久臥病無聊，乃使人復
葺南閣子。其制稍異于
前，然自後余多在外，
不常居。庭有枇杷樹，
吾妻死之年所手植也。
今已亭亭如蓋矣。

[ZCXSJ 429–430]

Sacrificial Officer, used to carry when attending court in the Xuande reign. Hopefully someday you'll use it." Recalling these past things, vivid as yesterday, I couldn't hold back my tears.

To the east of the studio there was a kitchen, and to get there, folks would pass in front of the studio. I stayed inside with the windows shut, and after a while I could tell people apart by the sound of their footsteps. The studio caught fire four times, but was not destroyed, a sign that there might be divine protection.

Thus said the scholar of the Xiangji Studio [Gui's self-reference]: "In Sichuan there was a widow named Qing, who inherited a cinnabar mine and became the richest person in the world. Later, the Emperor of Qin built a memorial terrace to honor her. Zhuge Liang rose from the rice field and assisted Liu Bei to vie with Cao Cao for the rule of China. When these two were still living in obscure corners, how could the world recognize their merits? At present, I am merely an occupant of a ramshackle abode, and yet I feel proud, eyes glinting, as if in view of an unusual vista. Perhaps people would think of me as the proverbial frog living at the bottom of a well?"

Five years after I wrote the above article, I got married. My wife would often come to my studio, ask me about historical affairs, or practice calligraphy by the desk. When she visited her parents, her little sister, according to my wife, would ask, "They say there's a loft in your home? But what's a loft?" Six years later, my wife died, and my studio fell into disrepair. In another two years, I became bedridden for quite some time, and out of boredom I had the studio remodeled, making it look slightly different from before. But then I was mostly away from home and seldom stayed in the studio.

In the courtyard, there is a loquat tree, planted by my wife with her own hands the year she died. Today it has grown tall under a lush canopy.

The entire essay consists of a series of discrete fragments, all poignant, almost Proustian, remembrance of things past from the perspective of a scholar sitting inside a humble studio. Writing at a time when Chinese fiction was on the rise, Gui skillfully incorporates novelistic techniques of characterization through direct or indirect speeches of women in his family: the old maid, his grandmother, his wife, and his sister-in-law. Lin Shu, the famous translator of foreign novels and an admirer of Gui's prose, thus commented on this fictional aspect of the essay: "The old lady's words reported by Gui Youguang are extremely trivial, wholly immaterial, yet no one who has lost his mother in childhood can read them without shedding tears."[6] Although there is a passing reference to tears, emotions are distinctly understated, especially in the last paragraph in which the author deflects sentiment onto an object, describing a vibrant living tree rather than directly expressing sorrow over his dead wife who had planted the tree. Just as Chinese painters made great use of empty spaces, Gui left things unsaid.

In the wake of Gui Youguang's accomplishment, the writer who took xiaopin wen to new heights was Yuan Hongdao (1568–1610), an uncompromising reformer and a major poet and essayist of the Ming dynasty. Born in Gongan, Hubei, Yuan was the leader of the Gongan school, named after his native place and including his two brothers and their avid followers. Perhaps symbolic of the unusual significance of his rather short life, Yuan was born in the same year as Wei Zongxian and died the same year as Matteo Ricci—Wei was the notorious, power-grabbing eunuch responsible for much of the political repression and scandalous corruption plaguing late-Ming, and Ricci was one of the earliest Jesuit missionaries who introduced Western knowledge and technology to China. Living in a time of turmoil, Yuan fashioned a self-image of a bohemian recluse, modeled after the legendary Madman of Chu, who defied social norms and sang in protest. Acquiring the *jinshi* degree at the age of twenty-four, Yuan served for one year as the magistrate of Wu County (modern-day Suzhou) and then resigned out of boredom, declaring in a poem that "I would rather be a slave of the West Lake / than the master of the Wu Palace."[7] Traveling extensively in the south, he produced a corpus of landscape poems and essays that radically changed the traditional genre and had a major impact on later travel writers, such as Xu Xiake, the great geographer and explorer.

As mentioned earlier, Yuan was influenced by Buddhism; Wang Yangming's philosophy; and the radical viewpoints of his mentor and friend, Li Zhi, who promoted childlike innocence in literature. Seeking the expression of natural sensibility unrestrained by convention or form, Yuan advocated *wufa* (no style, no method) in writing, and emphasized *zhi* (substance) over *wen* (ornament), echoing Laozi's insight: "Truthful words are not beautiful; beautiful words are not truthful." He also promoted *qu* (zest, gusto, or flair), which he defined as "the color of mountains, taste in water, light in a flower, and charm in a woman," a quality deemed unattainable through study or cultivation.[8] Demonstrated in writing, these aesthetic ideas led to an impressive body of occasional essays addressing the mundane and trivial, such as cricket raising, spider fights, and other realms of life rarely depicted in classical prose. Giving credence to what Michel de Certeau would call "the practice of everyday life," these occasional essays about the ephemeral and quotidian signified Yuan's disillusionment with Ming politics and a yearning for self-expression.

During the New Culture movement in the early twentieth century, Chinese writers looking to abandon classical Chinese (*wenyan*) and replace it with the vernacular (*baihua*) found their inspiration in the works of Yuan and his fellows of the Gongan school. Proclaiming the three Yuan brothers the distant forerunners of the modern vernacular literary revolution, Lin Yutang especially extolled Yuan Hongdao's occasional essays as manifestos of a leisurely lifestyle. Echoing Yuan's interest in the quotidian, Lin declared a preference for writing about his toothbrush rather than national politics.

The essay "Record of a Trip to Manjing" was written in 1599, during Yuan's brief stint as an instructor at the Metropolitan Prefectural School in Beijing. The title phrase *youji* literally means "record of an outing," or simply, travelogue, an important subgenre of *ji* (record), a forum for countless informal essays throughout history, such as Yao Nai's "Record of Climbing Mount Tai" (*Deng taishan ji*) and Xue Fucheng's "Record of a Visit to a Parisian Oil Painting Exhibition" (*Guan bali youhua ji*). In some editions, Gui Youguang's "A Chronicle of the Xiangji Studio" and Zhang Dai's "Mid-July on West Lake" also contain the generic word *ji* in their titles. Traditionally, Chinese essays about journeys to mountains and streams focused on objective descriptions of the landscape. Yuan departed, as he often did, from such a formula and dwelled instead on his own feelings, thus breaking up the convention of landscape writings in the same way we have seen earlier in the works of Liu Zongyuan, Ouyang Xiu, Su Shi, and others.

袁宏道　滿井遊記

C16.2 Yuan Hongdao, "Record of a Trip to Manjing"

燕地寒，花朝節後，餘
寒猶厲。凍風時作，作
則飛沙走礫，局促一室
之內，欲出不得。每冒
風馳行，未百步，輒
返。廿二日，天稍和，
偕數友出東直，至滿
井。高柳夾堤，土膏微
潤，一望空闊，若脫籠
之鵠。於時冰皮始解，
波色乍明，鱗浪層層，
清徹見底，晶晶然如鏡
之新開，而冷光之乍出
於匣也。山巒爲晴雪所
洗，娟然如拭，鮮妍明
媚，如倩女之靧面，而
髻鬟之始掠也。柳條將
舒未舒，柔梢披風，麥
田淺鬣寸許。遊人雖未
盛，泉而茗者，罍而歌
者，紅裝而蹇者，亦時
時有。風力雖尚勁，然
徒步則汗出浹背。凡曝
沙之鳥，呷浪之鱗，悠然
自得，毛羽鱗鬣之間，
皆有喜氣。始知郊田之
外，未始無春，而城居者
未之知也。夫能不以遊墮
事，而瀟然於山石草木之
間者，惟此官也。而此地
適與余近，余之遊將自此
始，惡能無紀？己亥之二
月也。

[*YHDJZJ* 2: 681]

It is cold in the Beijing area. Even after the Flower Festival, the lasting chill was still ferocious. Icy gusts recurred, driving sand and pebbles into the air. Consequently, I was confined indoors and could not go out even though I wanted to. Every time I ventured out to brave the wind, I had to beat a retreat within a hundred steps.

On February 22, it warmed up a bit. Some friends and I went out of Dongzhi Gate and got to Manjing. Tall willows lined up along the dike, and fertile soil was soft and moist, presenting a broad vista that made me feel like a swan escaping from a cage. By this time the frozen surface of the lake had started to thaw, ripples glistening like fish scales. Like a new mirror beaming cold light out of a box, the lake was so limpid that one could see all the way to the bottom. Mountain ranges, washed by sunlight and melting snow, looked lovely and dazzling like a beautiful girl after bath, her face radiant, hair freshly knotted. Willow branches had not yet fully unfurled, their soft tips swaying in the wind. Wheat sprouts in the field stood like horsehair, about an inch in height. Though this was not the peak season, tourists could still be seen here and there, some of them drawing spring water to make tea, some singing over a jug of wine, some dressed gaudily while riding a donkey. Though it was a bit blustery, one would sweat after a brisk walk. Birds enjoying the sun on the sand and fish slurping on waves were all insouciant and smug. Joy seemed infectious among all the creatures, whether furry, feathery, scaly, or hairy. At this moment I realized that spring, unknown to the city-dwellers, had arrived in the suburbs.

Only a job like mine can let one go sightseeing without the guilt of negligence. Thus, I can enjoy myself among hills, rocks, grass, and trees. Also, this place happens to be close by, and with my tour starting from here, how can I not keep a record? Written in the second lunar month of 1599.

In this essay, Yuan assumes a sensualist attitude toward landscape and foregrounds the introspective aspects of sightseeing rather than geographical features of the place. "I am by nature a casual and carefree person," he once said, "I cannot put up with any kind of bondage . . . Whenever I stay indoors for one day, I feel as if I am sitting on a hot stove. Therefore, even on frosty, dark nights, when I have numerous things to do, my mind is always with my friends in the hills and lakes."[9] Also striking is the absence of any didactic message in the essay, when traditionally landscape writing was intended as moral calisthenics, a means of self-cultivation by Confucian literati for the purpose of better serving the State. In this sense, Yuan was a *sui generis* radical. A year after the composition of this essay, his elder brother died. Yuan became a recluse on a small islet in the middle of Willow Lake in his birthplace, Gongan.

Unlike Yuan Hongdao, who had sought and then forsaken an official career, our next writer, Zhang Dai (1597–1679), never held any official post, partly because he could afford not to and partly because, as the Chinese saying goes, he was "born in the wrong time." Scion of a prominent family in Shaoxing, Zhejiang, Zhang lived comfortably and sowed his wild oats for the first half of his life until the Manchu invasion in 1644. A loyalist to the fallen Ming, Zhang let loose his hair and fled to the hills, living frugally there to the end of his days. Such a cataclysmic change became the basis for his writings. His magnum opus, *Dream Recollections of Tao'an* (*Tao'an mengyi*), is a book of occasional essays full of nostalgia and lament over his "misspent youth"—a time of precarious living, drunkenness, and debauchery, in the twilight years of a dying dynasty. Described through the haze of memory and rendered in what Stephen Owen characterizes as "breathless, impressionistic prose," these *ubi sunt* scenes took on an elegiac coloring and somnolent tones.

"Mid-July on West Lake," like the other pieces from *Dream Recollections*, is an essay of hypnotic allure. July 15 on the lunar calendar is also called the Zhongyuan Festival, or the Day of the Dead. Residents of Hangzhou, Zhang's favorite city and adjacent to his birthplace, would customarily go out that night to watch the full moon, preferably from West Lake. Reminiscing about the scenic spot long commanding potent symbolic power in the Chinese cultural imagination, Zhang writes from his perch in the mountains: "I have been kept far from West Lake for twenty-eight years. Nevertheless, there has not been a day that West Lake has not been a part of my dreams, and the West Lake in my dreams has, in fact, never been gone for a single day."[10]

C16.3 Zhang Dai, "Mid-July on West Lake"

張岱 西湖七月半

There is nothing to watch on West Lake in mid-July save the people watching the mid-July moon. We may watch five kinds of mid-July moon watchers.[1] The first kind, on storied pleasure boats, flutes and drums playing, tall-caps seated at lavish banquets, accompanied by actors and servants, lanterns blazing, a riot of sound and light. These people pretend to watch the moon but in fact do not see the moon. The second kind, also on storied pleasure boats, society ladies and high-class maidens sit around the upper decks, together with handsome boys, laughing and crying, glancing left and right. They are under the

西湖七月半，一無可看，止可看看七月半之人。看七月半之人，以五類看之：其一，樓船簫鼓，峨冠盛筵，燈火優傒，聲光相亂，名為看月而實不見月者，看之；其一，亦船亦樓，名娃閨秀，攜及童孌，笑啼雜之，環坐露台，左右盼望，身在月下而實不在看月者，看之；其一，亦船亦聲歌，名

[1] This is a paragraph full of twists and turns. The opening sentence craftily sets up a drama, turning an essay that should have focused on the splendor of the full moon, a common motif in classical Chinese literature, into a piece about moon watchers. Dividing the moon watchers into five categories, the author creates a hierarchy not by wealth, class, or any worldly measure but by a person's ability to truly appreciate the art of moon watching, something only the fifth group of watchers seemed to understand.

妓閒僧，淺斟低唱，弱管輕絲，竹肉相發，亦在月下，亦看月而欲人看其看月者，看之；其一，不舟不車，不衫不幘，酒醉飯飽，呼羣三五，躋入人叢，昭慶、斷橋，囂呼嘈雜，裝假醉，唱無腔曲，月亦看，看月者亦看，不看月者亦看，而實無一看者，看之；其一，小船輕幌，淨几煖爐，茶鐺旋煮，素瓷靜遞，好友佳人，邀月同坐，或匿影樹下，或逃囂裏湖，看月而人不見其看月之態，亦不作意看月者，看之。

杭人遊湖，巳出酉歸，避月如仇。是夕好名，逐隊爭出，多犒門軍酒錢，轎夫擎燎，列俟岸上。一入舟，速舟子急放斷橋，趕入勝會。以故二鼓以前，人聲鼓吹，如沸如撼，如魘如囈，如聾如啞，大船小船一齊湊岸，一無所見，止見篙擊篙，舟觸舟，肩摩肩，面看面而已。少刻興盡，官府席散，皂隸喝道去；轎夫叫，船上人怖以關門，燈籠火把如列星，一一簇擁而去。岸上人亦逐隊趕門，漸稀漸薄，頃刻散盡矣。

moon but do not watch the moon. The third kind, also boating and carousing, famous singing girls and idle monks sip wine and croon ditties. On gentle flutes and soft strings, instrument and voice coalesce. They are also under the moon, also watching the moon, but wanting others to watch them watching the moon. The fourth kind, riding no boat or carriage, wearing no coat or cap, drunk and gorged, in a boisterous gang of four or five, barging into the crowds at Zhaoqing Temple and Broken Bridge, kicking up a hullabaloo, pretending to be drunk, singing out of key, these people watch the moon, watch the moon-watchers as well as those who don't watch the moon. In fact, they watch nothing. The fifth kind, in little boats with light screens, equipped only with clean tables and hot stoves, tea quickly boiled, white cups passed around quietly. Good friends and fair ladies invite the moon to sit with them, at times hiding in the shadow of the trees, at times escaping into the solitude of the inner lake. They watch the moon but others can't see their way of watching the moon, nor would they watch the moon purposefully.

When Hangzhou people visit the lake, they usually go out in late morning and return in early evening, avoiding the moon like the plague. But on this night, out of vanity, they come out in droves. Guards at city gates get extra tips, while palanquin bearers queue up along the shore, torch in hand, waiting. Once aboard, they order the boatmen to speed towards Broken Bridge to catch the festivities there. As a result, before nine o'clock there is a commotion of voices and music, boiling and earthshaking, like a scene of nightmare or muttering in sleep, blinding and deafening.[2] As big boats and small dinghies simultaneously make for the shore, one can't see anything except pole hitting pole, boat bumping boat, shoulder rubbing shoulder, and face watching face. After a while, the fun is over, the banquets of the officials break up and their servants yell to clear the way. The palanquin bearers call for the boaters, cautioning them against gate closure. One by one, or altogether, lanterns and torches depart like a constellation of stars. The onshore crowd also gathers and rushes for the gates, the throng gradually thinning out until everyone is gone in a twinkling of an eye.

Only then do we coax our boat near the shore.[3] The stone steps of Broken Bridge have cooled off. Sitting there, we call on guests to drink freely with us. Now the moon dazzles like a newly polished mirror, the hills have refreshed

---

[2] A scene of carnivalesque ballyhoo, without a word about moon watching. It sets the stage for the next paragraph when the moon and the ideal moon watchers, still hiding from the maddening crowd at this point, finally enter the scene.

[3] "Only then" marks the separation between the foolish crowd and "us." In contrast, there seems to be an unspoken harmony between "us" and nature: after the crowd clears, the moon appears like a newly polished mirror, hills refresh their makeup, and the lake washes its face anew. The anthropomorphic moon, like the lotus later, is a symbol of innocence and purity, uncontaminated by worldly dust, a poetic projection of the authorial self.

their make-up, and the lake has washed its face anew. Those who have been sipping and crooning now emerge, as do those hiding in the shadow of the trees. We send over greetings, inviting them to join us. Refined friends coming, famous singing girls arriving, cups and chopsticks set, woodwinds and vocals starting. We don't break up until the moon pales and the east blanches. Then we drift in the boat, slumbering among miles of lotus blossoms. Soaking in fragrance, our lucid dreams are so cozy.

吾輩始艤舟近岸。斷橋石磴始涼，席其上，呼客縱飲。此時月如鏡新磨，山復整妝，湖復面，向之淺斟低唱者出，匿影樹下者亦出，吾輩往通聲氣，拉與同坐。韻友來，名妓至，杯箸安，竹肉發。月色蒼涼，東方將白，客方散去。吾輩縱舟酣睡於十里荷花之中，香氣拍人，清夢甚愜。

[*TAMY* 62–63]

As David Pollard points out, Zhang Dai's spellbinding essays "would not have been conceivable in the literary sense without the Gongan school of prose."[11] Yuan Hongdao and his brothers had taught late-Ming writers to rely on intuition and personality and express themselves freely in the lingo of the street—or to borrow from Wordsworth, "in a language really used by man." The vocabulary of "Mid-July on West Lake" is more vernacular than formal. The parallel structures used to describe the five categories of moon watchers sound natural and poetic, not rigid as in parallel prose (*pianwen*). The entire piece painstakingly emphasizes the author's individuality, his resolute distance from the benighted crowd. Conceptually, the paradox of watching the moon while being watched by others would inspire numerous essays and poems in the future, most famously the lines by modernist poet, Bian Zhilin, in the twentieth century: "You stand on the bridge looking at the view—/the viewer on the balcony is viewing you."

Our next writer is perhaps one of the six best known to the English-speaking world, largely thanks to Arthur Waley's sympathetic biography, *Yuan Mei: Eighteenth Century Chinese Poet* (1956). Whether, as Waley suggests, Yuan Mei (1716–1798) truly resembled some of the Bloomsbury Circle figures, without question, his lifestyle and thinking flew in the face of repressive, orthodox Chinese culture of his time, making him one of the most fiercely independent and outspoken literati in Chinese history.

Born in Hangzhou to a father who moved around constantly from one small post to another, never reaching high office, Yuan Mei was a brilliant student and passed the *jinshi* exam at the rather young age of twenty-three. He was appointed to the Hanlin Academy, followed by several years of working as county magistrate in Jiangsu, where he became a local legend, à la Judge Dee, for his sharp wit and legal acumen. Shortly after being appointed governor of Nanjing in 1748, Yuan resigned from office, explaining his decision in a letter to a friend, "All I ask for is a village of some ten houses where I can live exactly as I choose, and rule the people merely by chanting to them the Way of the Former Kings; then I could end my days there in perfect contentment, though I held the rank only of a village constable."[12] Spurning a high post and the glamor of "coursing about the blazing streets of a great town," Yuan devoted the rest of his life to teaching and writing.

As a teacher, Yuan attracted controversy for accepting female pupils and was censured by his contemporaries for perverting the minds of the young by encouraging the commingling of sexes at his school. He also acquired a reputation for loose living at his estate, the Sui Garden, allegedly the origin of Daguanyuan, the sprawling mansion that is the setting for Cao Xueqin's *The Dream of the Red Chamber*. Yuan's critics accused him of "ransacking the neighborhood for whatever was soft and warm, not minding whether it was boy or girl."[13]

As a writer and scholar, he followed the Ming and Qing radicals by advocating *xingling* (personality and soul) and maintaining that literature should be an expression of individual temperament and feeling rather than a vehicle for moral edification. He argued against imitation of canonical masters and suggested that writers find their own idioms for their unique spirit and mind. Such an individualistic challenge to authority and tradition was a bold gesture, especially in light of Emperor Qian Long's infamous literary inquisition, a long and brutal campaign to which many of Yuan's friends and associates fell victim. Fortunately, his friendship with a number of influential Manchu figures enabled him to stay out of trouble and remain a leading literary figure in the second half of the eighteenth century.

The word *shuo* (discourse) in the title puts the essay in the *lunbian* (discourses and arguments) genre, the first category of classical prose, as defined by Yao Nai. Derived from the works of pre-Qin philosophers, *lunbian* includes *shuo*, *duiwen* (question and answer), *kao* (investigation), and *yu* (parable). The ancient sage Zhuangzi gave us the prototype of *shuo*, but Yuan Mei's essay finds its generic precedent in Liu Zongyuan's "A Discourse of a Snake-catcher" (☞ C13.2) and its successor in Liang Qichao's "Discourse on the Youthful China" (☞ *HTRCProse–CCC*, L30).

袁枚　黃生借書說

黃生允修借書，隨園主人授以書，而告之曰：書非借不能讀也。子不聞藏書者乎？七略、四庫，天子之書，然天子讀書者有幾？汗牛塞屋，富貴家之書，然富貴人讀書者有幾？其他祖父積子孫棄者，無論焉。非獨書爲然，天下物皆然。非夫人之物而強假焉，必慮人逼取，而惴惴焉摩玩之不已，曰：今日存，明日去，吾不得而見之矣。若業爲吾所有，必高束焉，庋藏焉，曰：姑俟異日觀云爾。

C16.4 Yuan Mei, "Discourse on Book Borrowing" (Huangsheng jieshu shuo)

A young Mr. Huang Yunxiu came to borrow books. I, the Master of the Sui Garden, lent him the books and said to him, "Books don't get read unless they're borrowed.[1] Have you heard about those book collectors? The Sons of Heaven own the Seven Divisions and Four Libraries, but do they read? The rich and noble own enough books to make the moving ox sweat or fill a house to the rafters, but how many of them read? Never mind the countless cases where books accumulated by grandfathers get thrown away by sons and grandsons. Not just books, but everything under the sky is treated in the same manner. When you do not own the stuff but have managed to borrow it, you must worry that the owner will want it back. So you cannot stop caressing it in trepidation and telling yourself, 'It's here today but will be gone tomorrow, and I won't be able to see it again.' But if I already own it, I will most likely wrap it up and leave it in a high place for safekeeping, saying things like 'I'll look at it later.'"

---

[1] The essay begins with a provocative statement, as striking as remarks made by another bibliophile, Walter Benjamin, of the twentieth century, discussed later. And then the author makes an adroit move, niftily switching from books to everything under the sky, deepening and expanding the spiritual lesson offered.

"Growing up, I loved books. But my family was so poor that books were hard to come by. There was a Mr. Zhang, who owned a huge library. When I went to borrow from him, he refused.[2] After I got home, I would dream about it—that's how eager I was. Thereafter, I would try to digest and remember every book I read. After becoming an official, I spent my salary on books, which piled up and filled my house. Oftentimes the bindings and pages would be eaten by worms and covered in dust and cobwebs. Then I sighed over how conscientious a book borrower is, and how precious the time of one's youth."

Now young Mr. Huang is as poor as I was, and he tries to borrow books as I used to do. The difference is that I share books whereas Mr. Zhang hoarded them. Yet was it really my misfortune to encounter Zhang, and is it really Huang's fortune to encounter me? Knowing fortune from misfortune, one would read with more concentration and return the books much sooner. I hereby offer these remarks, along with the books.

Contrary to the thesis put forward by Yuan Mei, German writer and bibliophile, Walter Benjamin, extols the virtue of hoarding and "non-reading of books" by collectors and borrowers. In his essay "Unpacking My Library," Benjamin relates an anecdote about Anatole France, who, like Mr. Zhang in Yuan's essay, owned a huge personal library. One day, a philistine came to visit. Admiring the vast collection, the visitor asks what Benjamin dismisses as "the standard question": "And you have read all these books, Monsieur France?" To which France replied, "Not one-tenth of them. I don't suppose you use your Sèvres china every day?"[14] To Benjamin, a personal collection encloses a book within a magic circle and releases it from its original function as an object of exchange or use. Owning a book but not reading it, in the eye of a Benjaminian connoisseur, constitutes the most intimate relationship that one can have to a book as an object. France's quip is a rebuke of his visitor's vulgar utilitarianism, a reminder that books, like china pieces on display in every bourgeois household, have values other than use or exchange. For this reason, Benjamin commends borrowers who hang on to the books, turn a deaf ear to reminders about return, and above all, fail to read the books. This appears to contradict the lesson that Yuan gives the young Mr. Huang with his remark: "Knowing fortune from misfortune, one would read with more concentration and return the books much sooner."

Despite their difference of opinion, both Benjamin and Yuan manage to express something quite profound in their respective essays by addressing seemingly trivial matters. "Unpacking My Library" gave Benjamin a venue to illustrate the concept of collection and thereby criticize the cultural logic of capitalism, a critique fully launched later in his magnum opus, *The Arcades Project*. Similarly, "Discourse

余幼好書，家貧難致。有張氏藏書甚富，往借不與，歸而形諸夢。其切如是。故有所覽，輒省記。通籍後，俸去書來，落落大滿，素蟫灰絲，時蒙卷軸。然後嘆借者之用心專，而少時之歲月爲可惜也。

今黃生貧類予，其借書亦類予。惟予之公書與張氏之吝書若不相類。然則予固不幸而遇張乎？生固幸而遇予乎？知幸與不幸，則其讀書也必專，而其歸書也必速。爲一說，使與書俱。

[*XCSFSWJ* 1620]

---

[2] Another interesting twist, describing poverty as an advantage and affluence as a burden for reading and learning, suggests a precious life lesson.

on Book Borrowing" provided Yuan an occasion to explicate a life lesson he had learned and wanted to pass on to posterity. A few hundred years apart and steeped in different literary traditions, both bibliophiles indulge us with gems of the occasional essay.

The last two *xiaopin* essayists featured in this chapter, Yao Nai and Xue Fucheng, belong to the same school, one as its poster child and the other a diehard follower. In some ways, their writings represent the final stage of classical Chinese prose. Born in Tongcheng, Anhui, Yao Nai (1732–1815) was closely associated with the school of prose named after his native place, the Tongcheng school, which includes his fellow townsmen Dai Mingshi, Fang Bao, and Liu Dakui. Tutored by Liu, Yao passed the *jinshi* exam in 1763 and was appointed to the Hanlin Academy. Like Yuan Hongdao, Yun Mei, and many other Chinese literati who kept alive the tradition of spurning the glamor and privilege of official position and seeking a reclusive lifestyle, Yao resigned from office in 1774 and devoted himself to teaching in private schools and promoting ancient-style prose (*guwen*). His compilation of *Classified Anthology of Ancient-Style Prose* was a groundbreaking achievement, and his energetic advocacy of *guwen* had a lasting influence on the development of Chinese prose. The Tongcheng members and their countless followers constituted a formidable force that dominated Qing literature for two and a half centuries.

Philosophically, the Tongcheng school subscribed to the neo-Confucian notion of *wendao heyi* (writing and the Way united in one); aesthetically, they exalted Tang and Song prose. As Fang Bao emphatically put it, "In scholarship we follow Cheng Yi and Zhu Xi [Neo-Confucian leaders], and in prose we are somewhere between Han Yu and Ouyang Xiu."[15] Yao specified eight elements that define a work of literature: *shen* (spirit), *li* (principle), *qi* (vital force), *wei* (taste), *ge* (structure), *lü* (measure), *sheng* (sound), and *se* (color). Following Liu Xie's observation that the vital force may be strong or weak, Yao distinguished two kinds of beauty in literature: the yang and the yin. His own essays, as exemplified by "Record of Climbing Mount Tai," are known for their simplicity and clarity, avoiding the superfluous in their ardent pursuit of the mild (*dan*). Also noteworthy in the following essay is the depth of Yao's scholarship (shown in the geographical names and historical references), and the supreme skill with which he made esoteric knowledge readily accessible to readers.

C16.5 Yao Nai, "Record of Climbing Mount Tai" (Deng Taishan ji)

姚鼐 登泰山記

泰山之陽，汶水西流；其陰，濟水東流；陽谷皆入汶；陰谷皆入濟；當其南北分者，古長城也。最高日觀峯，在長城南十五里。

To the south of Mount Tai, the Wen River flows westward; to the north, the Ji River runs eastward. All the valley water from the south side joins the Wen, while that from the north joins the Ji. At the watershed dividing the north and south stands the ancient Great Wall.[1] Five miles south of the wall lies the summit, the Sun Viewing Peak.

---

[1] Although the Great Wall stands for the crowning achievement and longevity of the Chinese civilization, climbing to the top of Mount Tai, a shrine to Confucianism, was for many Chinese literati a symbol of spiritual elevation. The weight of these references is lightened by the matter-of-fact way Yao composes this introductory paragraph.

In December 1774, braving a blizzard, I traveled from the capital city, passed Qihe and Changqing, through the valleys northeast of Mount Tai, cleared the Great Wall, and arrived in Taian.[2] On the twenty-eighth of the month, I joined the local governor, Mr. Zhu Xiaochun (also known as Ziying), and climbed the mountain from the south side. Over seven thousand stone steps had been laid on the mountain road, which extended for fourteen miles.

There are three valleys on the south side of Mount Tai. The stream from the middle valley wraps around the city of Taian, lending credence to the name "Surrounding Water," mentioned by Li Daoyuan in his book. We set off by following the middle valley, and nearly halfway, climbed over the middle ridge. Then we followed the west valley, all the way to the top. In the old days, people would take the east route, passing many of those Heavenly Gates. The water from the east valley used to be called the Heavenly Gate Stream, which we did not reach. From the middle ridge to the top, we found cliffs blocking our path like thresholds; hence the epithet, Heavenly Gate. There was a dense fog along the way, and the icy stone steps were very slippery, hard to scale. Upon reaching the summit, we saw blue hills covered in snow, the southern sky lit up as if by a bright candle. Further away, the setting sun shone on the city of Taian, the Wen River and the Culai Mountain looked as pretty as a picture, and fogs hovered around the waist of the mountain like a silk sash.[3]

At dawn on the last day of December, Ziying and I sat at the Sun Viewing Pavilion, awaiting the sunrise. Gusty wind blew snow up into our faces. East of the pavilion, below our feet, there was a sea of cloud, in the midst of which stood dozens of white dice, dimly visible—these were in fact mountains. At the edge of the sky there appeared a line of rare hue, instantly becoming rainbow-colored. The sun rose, pure red like cinnabar. Underneath, a field of red light shimmered and quavered, supporting the sun. Someone said that was the East Sea. Turning around and looking at the peaks to the west, we saw that some of them had been painted red by sunlight and others remained white. Differently hued as they were, all hunched their backs as if bowing.[4]

West of the pavilion there is the Dai Temple as well as the Bixia Yujun Temple, east of which lies the Temporary Royal Palace. That day, we examined stone carvings by the mountain path. They were dated as early as the Xianqing

余以乾隆三十九年十二月，自京師乘風雪，歷齊河、長清，穿泰山西北谷，越長城之限，至於泰安。是月丁未，與知府朱孝純子穎由南麓登四十五里，道皆砌石爲磴，其級七千有餘。

泰山正南面有三谷：中谷遶泰安城下，酈道元所謂環水也。余始循以入，道少半，越中嶺，復循西谷，遂至其巔。古時登山循東谷入，道有天門。東谷者，古謂之天門谿水，余所不至也。今所經中嶺及山巔崖限當道者，世皆謂之天門云。道中迷霧冰滑，磴幾不可登。及既上，蒼山負雪，明燭天南。望晚日照城郭，汶水、徂徠如畫，而半山居霧若帶然。

戊申晦，五鼓，與子穎坐日觀亭待日出，大風揚積雪擊面。亭東自足下皆雲漫，稍見雲中白若樗蒱數十立者，山也。極天雲一線異色，須臾成五采。日上，正赤如丹，下有紅光動搖承之。或曰："此東海也。"迴視日觀以西峯，或得日，或否，絳皓駁色，而皆若僂。

亭西有岱祠，又有碧霞元君祠。皇帝行宫在碧霞元君祠東。是日觀道中石刻，自唐顯慶以

---

[2] Yao's signature laconic style is well represented by his use of five single-character verbs: *cheng* (riding on), *li* (pass), *chuan* (penetrate), *yue* (clear), and *zhi* (arrive). Another example of Yao's masterful management of the heavy and the light: he glosses over the fact that this was a life-changing journey he was taking. He had just resigned from office in Beijing and was heading home to live the life of a civilian in the south.

[3] A scene of crepuscular serenity sets the stage for a contrast with the dramatic sunrise featured in the next paragraph.

[4] A sublime moment, popularly ingrained into the Chinese imagination by the popular saying, "When one reaches the top of Mount Tai, all the other mountains look tiny."

來。其遠古刻盡漫失，
僻不當道者皆不及往。

山多石少土，石蒼黑
色，多平方，少圓。少
雜樹，多松，生石罅，
皆平頂冰雪。無瀑水，
無鳥獸音跡。至日觀數
里內無樹，而雪與人膝
齊。桐城姚鼐記。

[*XBXSWJ* 220–221]

reign of the Tang dynasty. Inscriptions earlier than that had been erased or destroyed.[5] As for those lying off the roads, we had no time to look for them.

Mount Tai has more rocks than soil. The boulders are mostly dark green in color, flat and square in shape; few are round. There are few trees other than pines, which grow in rocky crevices, sporting flat canopies. On a day of snow and ice, there was no waterfall, no sound or sighting of any bird or beast. Within miles of the Sun Viewing Peak, there were no trees. Snow was knee-deep. The above was written by Yao Nai of Tongcheng.

Structurally, the essay is extremely well designed: The opening paragraph gives a geographical description, and the second paragraph provides the itinerary of the traveler who arrives at sunset—a peaceful moment, like the eve of a great battle. The sunrise is the climax of the piece, full of sound and fury, followed by a short paragraph full of human references, loaded with proper nouns but inked lightly like those illegible inscriptions. Against the onslaught of time, the essay ends with an emphasis on the emptiness of nature, like finishing up a feast with a sip of spring water, washing away all the flavors. Brevity is key, as brief sentences, no more than two or three words in length, dominate the paragraph. "Snow was knee-deep" is a haiku moment of harmony, the knee being a synecdoche for the human, who, like birds and beasts, disappears into the vast emptiness of nature. It is a perfect ending to an essay by a writer seeking an otherworldly life.

Unwittingly, Yao Nai's resignation from officialdom was a blessing for classical Chinese prose: in his new role as a highly sought-after private tutor in the lower valleys of the Yangtze River, he trained directly and indirectly some of the movers and shakers of late-Qing literature and culture. Xue Fucheng might not count as a titan, but he was certainly a titan's protégé. Representing the first generation of Chinese diplomats posted to Western countries and a dying breed of Chinese literati adhering to ancient-style prose, Xue Fucheng (1838–1894) was born in Wuxi, Jiangsu, to a prominent family. A key event in Xue's life was his becoming a disciple of Zeng Guofan, a powerful official and influential writer, who carried the banner of the Tongcheng school into the mid-nineteenth century. Serving as governor of Ningbo and Shaoxing, two coastal cities in Zhejiang, Xue participated in the Sino-French War (1884–1885) and witnessed the humiliating defeat of the Chinese military by the technologically superior French navy. A reform-minded servant to the Qing court, Xue authored several proposals advocating changes to the government, including the introduction of Western science and technology, strengthening diplomacy and knowledge of international laws, and building a modern navy. He was subsequently appointed the imperial envoy to England, France, Belgium, and Italy.

---

[5] In a few terse sentences, Yao refers to temple, palace, and inscription, all layered traces of history that seem to pale in comparison to the weight of the mountain. It is a delicate dance of yin and yang, warp and woof.

The essay "Record of a Visit to an Oil Painting Exhibition in Paris" was written during Xue's tenure as ambassador in Europe, the same period when he kept a detailed diary, later published as *Diplomatic Journals from Four Countries (Chushi siguo riji)*. Along with Yan Fu and Lin Shu, Xue represented the last generation of Tongcheng writers, who stood on the cusp of cataclysmic changes about to overtake China. In fact, they wrote the final chapter of the history of classical Chinese prose. Couched in the archaic form of *wenyan* but filled with neologisms, translationese, and other novelties, the prose of Xue and his peers embodied the struggles, wounds, aspirations, failures, successes, and anxieties of the Chinese literary mind in the wake of China's clash with the West.

C16.6 Xue Fucheng, "Record of a Visit to an Oil Painting Exhibition in Paris" (Guan Bali youhua ji)

薛福成　觀巴黎油畫記

On the *jiazi* day of the leap second month in 1890, the sixteenth year of the Guangxu reign, I visited the wax museum in Paris. The wax figures, all imitations of real people, showed striking resemblances in physique and demeanor, hair and skin color, height and size. Notable personages, ranging from princes and councilors to craftsmen and artists, would often have their effigies made by the museum. They may stand up or lie down, sit and stoop, laugh or cry, drink or gamble. At first glance, one would be astonished to see them as real. While I continued to marvel at the spectacular craftsmanship, my interpreter said, "The consummate skill of the Westerners is actually in oil painting. Why don't we proceed to the art gallery now and look at the painting of the Franco-Prussian War?"[1]

光緒十六年春閏二月甲子，余遊巴黎蠟人館。見所製蠟人，悉仿生人，形體態度，髮膚顏色，長短豐瘠，無不畢肖。自王公卿相以至工藝雜流，凡有名者，往往留像於館。或立或臥，或坐或俯，或笑或哭，或飲或博，驟視之，無不驚爲生人者。余亟嘆其技之奇妙。譯者稱："西人絕技，尤莫逾油畫，盍馳往油畫院，一觀普法交戰圖乎？"

The exhibition room was a large rotunda, with walls covered by huge canvases and light entering through the dome. Standing at the center of the room and looking around, I saw forts, hills, creeks, and woods laid out in crowded patterns, and two armies clashing in chaos: some galloping on horseback, some fallen to the ground, some running, some pursuing, some shooting, some setting off cannons, some waving banners, some pulling cannon carts, and so on. When a heavy shell lands, there is an instant blast, and smoke fills the air. The bombed areas are littered with broken walls and collapsed buildings, a ruin of charred houses and burned fences. The sight of soldiers who have lost arms or legs, their blood running like a rivulet across the field, the wounded lying on their backs, or the dead crouching facedown, is unbearably horrific. Looking up, I saw a bright moon hanging in a corner of the sky, set off partially by crepuscular clouds. Looking down, I found green grass as soft as velvet, a sprawling plain with no end in sight. It felt as if I were standing

其法爲一大圓室，以巨幅懸之四壁，由屋頂放光明入室。人在室中，極目四望，則見城堡、崗巒、溪澗、樹林，森然布列。兩軍人馬雜遝，馳者、伏者、奔者、追者、開槍者、燃炮者、搴大旗者、挽炮車者，絡繹相屬。每一巨彈墮地，則火光迸裂，煙焰迷漫。其被轟擊者，則斷壁危樓，或黔其廬，或赭其垣。而

---

[1] Given that the title promises a visit to an oil painting museum, this opening paragraph about a wax museum sounds like a digression, but in fact, it works as a prologue, setting the stage for more dramatic scenes later. Such freedom in choice of subject is also an indication that Xue was breaking away from formulas and rules laid down by his Tongcheng predecessors.

軍士之折臂斷足、血流
殷地、偃仰僵仆者，令
人目不忍睹。仰視天，
則明月斜掛，雲霞掩
映；俯視地，則綠草如
茵，川原無際。几自疑
身外即戰場，而忘其在
一室中者。迨以手捫
之，始知其爲壁也、畫
也、皆幻也。

　余聞法人好勝，何
以自繪敗狀，令人喪氣
若此？譯者曰："所以
昭炯戒，激起眾憤、圖
報復也。"則其意深長
矣。

夫普法之戰，迄今雖爲
陳跡，而其事信而有
征。然者此畫果真邪、
幻邪？幻者而同於真
邪？真者而同於幻邪？
斯二者蓋皆有之。

[*TCPWX* 441–442]

right next to the battlefield rather than in the middle of a room. Only when I reached out to feel with my hand did I realize that it was only a wall and a painting, all illusions.

I heard that the French liked to win.[2] Then why did they paint such a picture of defeat and make the viewer feel so demoralized? My interpreter replied, "This is intended as a lesson, to rile up the people so they become eager for revenge." Considered this way, the painting had indeed far-reaching significance.

Even though the Franco-Prussian War is already history, it is a real event with credible evidence. As for this painting, is it real or imaginary? Is it the imaginary that captures the real, or the real that fulfills the imaginary? Maybe it is a bit of both.

In a paper published in the *American Journal of Mathematics* in 1885, five years before Xue's visit to the Paris exhibition, Charles Sanders Peirce wrote: "So in contemplating a painting, there is a moment when we lose consciousness that it is not the thing, the distinction between the real and the copy disappears, and it is for a moment a pure dream—not any particular existence, and yet not general."[16] Xue probably had no way of knowing the semiotic theory propagated by the father of American pragmatism, who believed that an icon, such as a painting, is contiguous with the referent and thus enjoys an ontological closeness to the latter. Without the benefit of Peircean semiotics, Xue's reflections on the painting, were inspired instead by two well-known Tang essays, "Record of Paintings" (*Huaji*) by Han Yu and "An Essay in Memory of an Ancient Battlefield" (*Diao guzhanchang wen*) by Li Hua. In the former, Han, a universally acclaimed prose master, vividly and schematically limned the movements, gestures, and idiosyncrasies of horses and riders along with carriages, weapons, and other miscellaneous objects as portrayed in a portfolio of paintings. And Li, an early Tang talent, produced a lyrical masterpiece that reads like a cinematic recreation of ancient battles and their bloody devastation. Unlike his predecessors, however, when Xue immersed himself in the virtual space of a foreign painting, he did not simply get carried away by the wings of fancy or imagination. Instead, he was fully aware that he was studying and admiring the skill of a European painter who represented a new regime of episteme, at once enticing and menacing to the Chinese literati.

In their experience with the foreign, Xue's illustrious contemporaries, such as Yan Fu and Lin Shu, both Tongcheng disciples, had translated Western works by using ancient-style prose as a way to create a centaur of *zhongti xiyong* (Chinese body and Western use), a strange mixture of nostalgia and exoticism. Similarly, Xue tried to convey and contain his shock and awe at novel experiences abroad by using a literary language that dates back, almost uninterrupted, two thousand

---

[2] A somewhat-bittersweet remark on the French penchant for victory, given Xue's personal experience in a battle lost to the French earlier in his career.

years. In this sense, Xue's essay, written in the twilight years of the Qing dynasty, represents the last gasp of classical Chinese prose, before its painful death and miraculous reincarnation at the dawn of the next century.

Yunte Huang

NOTES

1. Shen Yongbao, ed., *Lin Yutang piping wenji* (*A Collection of Critical Essays by Lin Yutang*) (Guangzhou: Zhuhai chubanshe, 1998), 98.

2. Jonathan Chaves, *Pilgrim of the Clouds: Poems and Essays by Yuan Hung-tao and His Brothers* (New York: Weatherhill, 1978), 18.

3. Chaves, *Pilgrim of the Clouds*, 14.

4. Tina Lu, "The Literary Culture of the Late Ming (1573–1644)," in *The Cambridge History of Chinese Literature*, edited by Kang-I Sun Chang and Stephen Owen (Cambridge: Cambridge University Press, 2010), 2:92–93.

5. David Pollard, *The Chinese Essay* (New York: Columbia University Press, 2000), xi–xii.

6. Quoted in Pollard, *The Chinese Essay*, 150.

7. Chih-p'ing Chou, *Yuan Hung-tao and the Kung-an School* (Cambridge: Cambridge University Press, 1988), 105.

8. Chou, *Yuan Hung-tao and the Kung-an School*, 52.

9. Chou, *Yuan Hung-tao and the Kung-an School*, 105.

10. Jonathan D. Spence, *Return to Dragon Mountain: Memories of a Late Ming Man* New York: Viking, 2007), 250–251.

11. David Pollard, Editor's Introduction to "Zhang Dai, Six Essays," *Renditions*, no. 33 and 24 (1990): 155.

12. Arthur Waley, *Yuan Mei, Eighteenth Century Chinese Poet* (London: G. Allen and Unwin, 1956), 88–89.

13. Waley, *Yuan Mei: Eighteenth Century Chinese Poet*, 77.

14. Walter Benjamin, "Unpacking My Library: A Talk About Collecting," in *Illuminations*, translated by Harry Zohn (New York: Schocken, 1969), 62.

15. William H. Nienhauser, Jr., *The Indiana Companion to Traditional Chinese Literature* (Bloomington, IN: Indiana University Press, 1986), 502.

16. Charles Sanders Peirce, "On the Algebra of Logic," *American Journal of Mathematics* 7 (1885): 181.

SUGGESTED READING

ENGLISH

Chaves, Jonathan. *Pilgrims of the Clouds*. New York: Weatherhill, 1978.

Chou, Chih-p'ing. *Yuan Hung-tao and the Kung-an School*. Cambridge: Cambridge University Press, 1988.

Lu, Tina. "The Literary Culture of the Late Ming (1573–1644)." In *The Cambridge History of Chinese Literature*, edited by Kang-I Sun Chang and Stephen Owen, 2:63–151. Cambridge: Cambridge University Press, 2010.

Pollard, David. *The Chinese Essay*. New York: Columbia University Press, 2000.

Waley, Arthur. *Yuan Mei: Eighteenth Century Chinese Poet*. London: Allen and Unwin, 1956.

CHINESE

Chen Xingwu 陳興蕪 and Fu Demin 傅德岷. *Zhongguo gudai sanwen liubian shigao* 中國古代散文流變史稿 (*A History of the Transformations of Classical Chinese Prose*). Beijing: Zhonghua shuju, 2013.

Shen Yongbao 沈永寶, ed. *Lin Yutang piping wenji* 林語堂批評文集 (*A Collection of Critical Essays by Lin Yutang*). Guangzhou: Zhuhai chubanshe, 1998.

Wang Qizhen 王琦珍. *Tongchengpai sanwen jingpin shangxi* 桐城派散文精品賞析 (*Readings of Tongcheng School Prose*). Changchun: Jilin wenshi chubanshe, 1997.

Xiong Lihui 熊禮匯. *Ming Qing sanwen liupai lun* 明清散文流派論 (*A Study of Ming and Qing Schools of Prose*). Wuhan: Wuhan daxue chubanshe, 2003.

Yang Yang 楊揚. *Zhou Zuoren piping wenji* 周作人批評文集 (*A Collection of Critical Essays by Zhou Zuoren*). Guangzhou: Zhuhai chubanshe, 1998.

ABBREVIATIONS OF PRIMARY TEXTS

BZJJZ	Bao Zhao 鮑照 (ca. 414–466). *Bao Zhao ji jiaozhu* 鮑照集校注 (*The Annotated Collection of Bao Zhao*). Edited by Ding Fulin 丁福林 and Tang Lingling 唐玲玲. Beijing: Zhonghua shuju, 2012.
CCZZZ	*Chunqiu Zuozhuan zhu* 春秋左傳注 (*Annotated Zuo Commentary on the* Spring and Autumn Annals). Edited and annotated by Yang Bojun 楊伯峻. 4 vols. Beijing: Zhonghua shuju, 1990.
CWZ	*The Complete Works of Zhuangzi*. Translated by Burton Watson. New York: Columbia University Press, 2013.
CZJJ	Cao Zhi 曹植 (192–232). *Cao Zijian ji* 曹子建集 (*The Collection of Cao Zijian*). Sibu congkan edition.
DJMHLJZ	Meng Yuanlao 孟元老. *Dongjing meng hua lu jianzhu* 東京夢華錄箋注 (*A Record of Dreaming a Dream of Splendors Past in the Eastern Capital, with Annotations and Notes*). Edited by Yi Yongwen 伊永文. 2 vols. Beijing: Zhonghua shuju, 2007.
DSXZ	Du Fu 杜甫 (712–770). *Du shi xiang zhu* 杜詩詳注 (*Detailed Commentaries on the Poetry of Du Fu*). Compiled with commentaries by Qiu Zhao'ao 仇兆鰲 (1638–1717). Beijing: Zhonghua shuju, 1979.
FZYQJ	Fan Zhongyan 范仲淹 (989–1052). *Fan Zhongyan quanji* 范仲淹全集 (*The Complete Works of Fan Zhongyan*). Edited by Li Yongxian 李勇先and Wang Rongui王蓉貴 . 3 vols. Chengdu: Sichuan daxue chubanshe, 2007.
HCLSXNJS	Han Yu 韓愈 (768–824). *Han Changli shi xinian jishi* 韓昌黎詩繫年集釋 (*Han Yu's Poetry, Arranged Chronologically with Collected Commentaries*). Edited by Qian Zhonglian 錢仲聯. 2 vols. Shanghai: Shanghai guji chubanshe, 1984.
HFZXJZ	Han Fei 韓非 (ca. 280–233 BC). *Han Feizi xin jiaozhu* 韓非子新校注 (*Han Feizi, with New Collations and Commentaries*). Edited by Chen Qiyou 陳奇猷. Shanghai: Shanghai guji chubanshe, 2000.
HNZJS	Liu An 劉安 (ca. 179–122 BC). *Huainanzi jiaoshi* 淮南子校釋 (*Huainanzi, with Collations and Explanations*). Edited by Zhang Shuangdi 張雙棣. Beijing: Beijing daxue chubanshe, 1997.
HS	Ban Gu 班固 (32–92), ed. *Hanshu* 漢書 (*History of the Han*). Beijing: Zhonghua shuju, 1962.
HWLC	Zhang Pu 張溥 (1602–1641), ed. *Han Wei Liuchao bai san jia ji* 漢魏六朝百三集 (*One Hundred and Three Collections from the Han, Wei, and Six Dynasties*). Nanjing: Jiangsu guji chubanshe, 2002.
HYGWJZHJ	Han Yu 韓愈 (768–824). *Han Yu guwen jiaozhu huiji* 韓愈古文校注彙集 (*Annotated Edition with Collected Comments of the Prose of Han Yu*). Edited by Luo Liantian 羅聯添. 5 vols. Taipei: Dingwen shuju, 2003.

HYWJHJJZ	Han Yu 韓愈 (768–824). *Han Yu wenji huijiao jianzhu* 韓愈文集彙校箋注 (*Complete Works of Han Yu, with Collected Collations and Commentaries*). Edited by Liu Zhenlun 劉真倫 and Yue Zhen 岳珍. 7 vols. Beijing: Zhonghua shuju, 2010.
JYJ	Su Xun 蘇洵 (1009–1066). *Jia you ji* 嘉祐集 (*Complete Works from the Jiayou Reign [1056–1063]*). 3 vols. Shanghai: Zhonghua shuju, 1936? [Shanghai Zhonghua shuju ju Ming keben jiaokan 上海中華書局據明刻本校刊].
JZZZJS	*Jiaozheng Zhuangzi ji shi* 校正莊子集釋 (*A Collated Collection of Commentaries on the Zhuangzi*). Edited by Guo Qingfan 郭慶藩. 2 vols. Beijing: Zhonghua shuju, 1961.
LBQJJZHSJP	Li Bai 李白 (701–762). *Li Bai quanji jiaozhu huishi jiping* 李白全集校注彙釋集評 (*Annotated Edition with Collected Commentary of the Complete Works of Li Bai*). Edited by Zhan Ying 詹英. 8 vols. Beijing: Baihua wenyi chubanshe, 1996.
LCJ	Su Zhe 蘇轍 (1039–1112). *Luancheng ji* 欒城集. Edited by Zeng Zaozhuang 曾棗莊 and Ma Defu 馬德富. 3 vols. Shanghai: Shanghai guji chubanshe, 1987.
LDJZJS	Lou Yulie 樓宇烈. *Laozi Daode jing zhu jiaoshi* 老子道德經注校釋 (The Commentary to *Laozi Daode jing*, Collated and Explicated). Beijing: Zhonghua shuju, 2008.
LDMYSJ	Wang Xiuqin 王秀琴. *Lidai mingyuan shujian* 歷代名媛書簡 (Letters by Literary Ladies of China). Changsha: Shangwu yinshuguan, 1950.
LQZJJZ	Li Qingzhao 李清照 (1084–ca. 1155). *Li Qingzhao ji jianzhu (xiuding ben)* 李清照集箋注 (修訂本). Edited by Xu Peijun 徐培均. Shanghai: Shanghai guji chubanshe 2018.
LSCQXJS	Lü Buwei 呂不韋 (ca. 291–235 BC). *Lüshi chunqiu xin jiaoshi* 呂氏春秋新校釋 (Springs and Autumns of Mr. Lü, *with New Collations and Explanations*). Edited by Chen Qiyou 陳奇猷. Shanghai: Shanghai guji chubanshe, 2002.
LYJZ	*Lunyu jizhu* 論語集注 (*Collected Commentaries on the* Analects). In *Sishu zhangju jizhu* 四書章句集注 (*Collected Commentaries on the Four Books*). With commentaries by Zhu Xi 朱熹 (1130–1200). Beijing: Zhonghua shuju, 1983.
LZYJJZ	Liu Zongyuan 柳宗元 (773–819). *Liu Zongyuan ji jiaozhu* 柳宗元集校注 (*The Collected Works of Liu Zongyuan, Collated and Annotated*). Edited by Yin Zhanhua 尹占華 and Han Wenqi 韓文奇. 10 vols. Beijing: Zhonghua shuju, 2013.
MQSWJX	*Ming Qing sanwen jingxuan* 明清散文精選 (*Selected Essays of Ming and Qing Dynasty*). Edited by Guo Yuheng 郭預衡. Nanjing: Jiangsu guji chubanshe, 1992.
MQSWX	*Ming Qing sanwen xuan* 明清散文選 (*Selection of Ming Qing Essays*). Edited by Ye Chucang 葉楚傖, Liu Yanling 劉延陵, and Hu Lunqing 胡倫清. Taipei: Zhengzhong shuju, 1989.

MSZJ	*Mao shi Zheng jian* 毛詩鄭箋 (*Zheng Xuan's Comments on* The Mao Edition of The Book of Poetry). Sibu beiyao 四部備要 edition.
MZJG	Mozi 墨子 (ca. 470–ca. 391 BC). *Mozi jigu* 墨子集詁 (Mozi, *with Collected Glosses*). Edited by Wang Huanbiao 王煥鑣. Shanghai: Shanghai guji chubanshe, 2005.
MZJZ	Mencius (ca. 372–ca. 289 BC). *Mengzi jizhu* 孟子集注 (*Collected Annotations on the* Mencius). In Zhu Xi 朱熹 (1130–1200), *Sishu zhangju jizhu* 四書章句集注 (*The Four Books, with Passage-Line Commentaries and Collected Annotations*), 197–377. Beijing: Zhonghua shuju, 1983.
MZYZ	Yang Bojun 楊伯峻, ed. *Mengzi yizhu* 孟子譯註 (*The* Mencius, *with Translation and Annotations*). Beijing: Zhonghua shuju, 1960.
NATW	*A New Account of Tales of the World*. Translated by Richard B. Mather. Ann Arbor: University of Michigan Press, Center for Chinese Studies, 2002.
OYXQJ	Ouyang Xiu 歐陽修 (1007–1072). *Ouyang Xiu quanji* 歐陽修全集 (*The Complete Works of Ouyang Xiu*). Edited by Liu Shangrong 劉尚榮. 6 vols. Beijing: Zhonghua shuju, 2001.
QBZZ	Zhou Hui 周煇 (1127–1198). *Qingbo zazhi* 清波雜志 (*Uncategorized Records Written at Pure Waves*). In *Quan Song biji* 全宋筆記 (*Complete Song Dynasty Miscellanies*). Edited by Shanghai Normal University Ancient Texts Research Institute. Series 5, vol. 9. Zhengzhou: Daxiang chubanshe, 2003–.
QDSSW	Fang Bao 方苞 (1668–1749), ed. *Qinding Si Shu wen* 欽定四書文 (*Imperially Authorized Essays on the Four Books*). Taipei: Taiwan Shangwu yinshuguan, 1969.
SBCZCZS	Ma Chengyuan 馬承源, ed. *Shanghai bowuguan cang Zhanguo Chu zhushu* 上海博物館藏戰國楚竹書（二）(*The Warring States Bamboo Manuscripts of Chu Stored in the Shanghai Museum*, vol. 2). Shanghai: Shanghai guji chubanshe, 2002.
SGZ	Chen Shou 陳壽 (233–297), ed. *San guo zhi* 三國志 (*Record of the Three Kingdoms*). Beijing: Zhonghua shuju, 1982.
SJ	*Shiji* 史記 (*Grand Scribe's Records*). Edited by Gu Jiegang 顧頡剛 (1893–1980), He Cijun 贺次君, Song Yunbin 宋云彬, and Nie Chongqi 聶崇岐. Beijing: Zhonghua, 1959.
SKK	Takigawa Kametarō 瀧川龜太郎 (1865–1946). *Shiki kaichū kōshō* 史記會注考證 (*The Shiji, with Collected Commentaries and Investigations*). 2nd ed. Tokyo, 1957–1959.
SS	Shen Yue 沈約 (441-513), comp. *Song shu* 宋書 (*History of the Liu Song*). Beijing: Zhonghua shuju, 1974,
SSQJ	Su Shi 蘇軾 (1037–1101). *Su Shi quanji* 蘇軾全集 (*Complete Works of Su Shi*). Shanghai: Shanghai guji chubanshe, 2000.
SSWJ	Su Shi 蘇軾 (1037–1101). *Su Shi wenji* 蘇軾文集 (*Complete Prose of Su Shi*). Edited and collated by Kong Fanli 孔凡禮. 6 vols. Beijing: Zhonghua shuju, 1986.

SSWJJZ   Su Shi 蘇軾 (1037–1101). *Su Shi wenji jiaozhu* 蘇軾文集校注 (*The Prose Collection of Su Shi, Collated and Annotated*). Vols. 10–20 of *Su Shi quanji jiaozhu* 蘇軾全集校注 (*The Complete Works of Su Shi, Collated and Annotated*). Edited by Zhang Zhilie 張志烈, Ma Defu 马德富, and Zhou Yukai 周裕锴. 20 vols. Shijiazhuang: Hebei renmin chubanshe, 2010.

SSXYJJ   Liu Yiqing 劉義慶 (403–444). *Shishuo xinyu jiaojian* 世說新語校箋 (*A New Account of the* Tales of the World, *Collated and Annotated*). Edited by Xi Zhen'e 徐震堮. 2 vols. Beijing: Zhonghua shuju, 1984.

SYJZ   Liu Xiang 劉向 (77–6 BCE). *Shuoyuan jiaozheng* 說苑校證 (*The Garden of Persuasions, with Collations and Verifications*). Collated by Xiang Zonglu 向宗魯. Beijing: Zhonghua shuju, 1987.

SYJZSZJL   Yang Bing'an 楊丙安. *Shiyi jia zhu Sunzi jiaoli* 十一家注孫子校理 (*Eleven Masters' Commentaries on* Sunzi, *Collated and Rationalized*). Beijing: Zhonghua shuju, 1999.

TAMY   Zhang Dai 張岱 (1597–1689). *Tao'an mengyi* 陶庵夢憶 (*Dream Recollections of Tao'an*). Shanghai: Shanghai guji chubanshe, 1982.

TCPWX   *Tongchengpai wenxuan* 桐城派文選 (*Selected Prose of Tongcheng School*). Edited by Qi xubang 漆緒邦 and Wang Kaifu 王凱符. Hefei: Anhui renmin chubanshe, 1984.

WASQJ   Wang Anshi 王安石 (1021–1086). *Wang Anshi quanji* 王安石全集 (*Complete Works of Wang Anshi*). Edited by Wang Shuizhao 王水照. 10 vols. Shanghai: Fudan daxue chubanshe, 2016.

WJNBCWXSCKZL   *Wei Jin Nanbei chao wenxue shi cankao ziliao* 魏晉南北朝文學史參考資料 (*Reference Material on the Literature of Wei, Jin, and Southern and Northern Dynasties*). Edited by the Research Group on Chinese Literary History at Peking University. Beijing: Zhonghua shuju, 1962.

WWJJZ   Wang Wei 王維 (701–761). *Wang Wei ji jiaozhu* 王維集校注 (*Annotated and Collated Edition of the Works of Wang Wei*). Edited by Chen Tiemin 陳鐵民. 4 vols. Beijing: Zhonghua shuju, 1997.

WX   Xiao Tong 蕭統 (501–531), ed. *Wen Xuan* 文選 (*Selections of Refined Literature*). Compiled and commented on by Li Shan 李善 (630–690). Shanghai: Shanghai guji chubanshe, 1986.

WXDLSY   Zhu Yingping 朱迎平, ed. *Wenxin diaolong suoyin* 文心雕龍索引 (*Indexes to* Wenxin diaolong). Shanghai: Shanghai guji chubanshe, 1987.

XBXSWJ   Yao Nai 姚鼐 (1732–1815). *Xibaoxuan shiwen ji* 惜抱軒詩文集 (*Complete Poetry and Prose of Yao Nai*). Shanghai: Shnaghai guji chubanshe, 1992.

XCSFSWJ   Yuan Mei 袁枚 (1716–1797). *Xiaocangshanfang shiwen ji* 小倉山房詩文集 (*Complete Poetry and Prose of Yuan Mei*). Shanghai: Shanghai guji chubanshe, 1988.

XKJ   Xi Kang 嵇康 (223–263). *Xi Kang ji jiaozhu* 嵇康集校注 (*The Annotated Collection of Xi Kang*). Edited by Dai Mingyang 戴明揚. Beijing: Zhonghua shuju, 2014.

XWCJJJ   Xia Wanchun 夏完淳 (1631–1647). *Xia Wanchun ji jianjiao* 夏完淳集箋校 (*The Collected, Edited Works of Xia Wanchun*). Edited by Bai Jian 白堅. Shanghai: Shanghai guji chubanshe, 1991.

XXJ   Wang Shifu 王實甫 (1260–1316). *Xixiang ji* 西廂記 (*The Story of the Western Wing*). Hong Kong: Zhonghua shuju, 1965.

XZJJ   Wang Xianqian 王先謙 (1842–1917). *Xunzi jijie* 荀子集解 (*Collected Explanations on the* Xunzi). Edited by Shen Xiaohuan 沈嘯寰 and Wang Xingxian 王星賢. Beijing: Zhonghua shuju, 1988.

YG   Liu Xizai 劉熙載 (1813–1881). *Yigai* 藝概 (*Essentials of the Arts*). Shanghai: Shanghai guji chubanshe, 1978.

YHDJZJ   Yuan Hongdao 袁宏道 (1568–1610). *Yuan Hongdao ji jianjiao* 袁宏道集箋校 (*Complete Works of Yuan Hongdao with Collected Commentaries*). 3 vols. Shanghai: Shanghai guji chubanshe, 1981.

YTJ   You Tong 尤侗 (1618–1704). *You Tong ji* 尤侗集 (*Collection of You Tong*). Shanghai: Shanghai guji chubanshe, 2015.

ZBQQJ   Zheng Xie 鄭燮 (1693–1766). *Zheng Banqiao quanji* 鄭板橋全集 (*The Complete Works of Zheng Banqiao*). Edited by Bian Xiaoxuan 卞孝萱. Jinan: Qilu shushe, 1985.

ZCXSJ   Gui Youguang 歸有光 (1507–1571). *Zhenchuan xiansheng ji* 震川先生集 (*Complete Works of Gui Youguang*). Shanghai: Shanghai guji chubanshe, 1981.

ZGCJZ   Liu Xiang 劉向 (77–6 BCE). *Zhanguo ce jianzheng* 戰國策箋證 (*Stratagems of the Warring States, with Philological Glosses*). Edited by Fan Xiangyong 范祥雍 and Fan Bangjin 范邦瑾. Shanghai: Shanghai guji chubanshe, 2006.

ZGLJ   *Zhuge Liang ji* 諸葛亮集 (*Complete Works of Zhuge Liang*). Edited by Duan Xizhong 段熙仲 and Wen Xuchu 聞旭初. Hong Kong: Zhonghua shuju, 1972.

ZZ   *Zuozhuan* 左傳 (*Zuo Tradition*). Translated by Stephen Durrant, Wai-yee Li, and David Schaberg. Seattle: University of Washington Press, 2016.

ZZYL   Li Jingde 黎靖德 (thirteenth century). *Zhuzi yulei* 朱子語類 (*The Spoken Words of Master Zhu, by Category*). Edited by Wang Xingxian 王星賢. Beijing: Zhonghua shuju, 1984.

ACKNOWLEDGMENTS

We owe a debt of gratitude to the Center for Language Education and Cooperation for funding the How to Read Chinese Literature series and to Professor Yuan Xingpei for his indispensable help in securing this funding support.

We wish to thank Jennifer Crewe, associate provost and director of Columbia University Press, for her enthusiastic support of this book series and Christine Dunbar for her editorial guidance. Our thanks also go to Cara Ryan for her meticulous editing of all chapters, Christian Winting for assistance with clerical matters, and Matthew Ching Hang Cheng for his format editing, and Ben Kolstad for efficiently overseeing the production process, as well as three anonymous readers for their insightful comments and suggestions.

Finally, a personal note of thanks to my wife Changfen Zheng for her tolerance of my countless evenings, weekends, and extended leaves devoted to this and other projects instead of her and the family.

CONTRIBUTORS

Zong-qi Cai teaches at the Lingnan University of Hong Kong and the University of Illinois at Urbana-Champaign. Apart from publishing extensively on Chinese poetry and literary theory, he cofounded/founded and edits two Duke journals, *The Journal of Chinese Literature and Culture* and *Prism: Theory and Modern Chinese Literature*; the *Lingnan Journal of Chinese Studies* 嶺南學報; the Brill book series *Chinese Texts in the World*; and the Columbia book series *How to Read Chinese Literature*. At the 2021 MLA convention, he received the "Distinguished Editor Award," the highest honor given by the Council of Editors of Learned Journals.

Wai-yee Li is the 1897 professor of Chinese literature at Harvard University. She focuses on early China and late-imperial Chinese culture and literature in her research. Her publications include *The Zuo Tradition/Zuozhuan Reader: Selections from China's Earliest Narrative History* (2020), *Keywords in Chinese Culture* (2020), *Plum Shadows and Plank Bridge: Two Memoirs about Courtesans* (2020), *The Oxford Handbook of Chinese Literature, 1000 BCE–900 CE* (2017), *The Letter to Ren An and Sima Qian's Legacy* (2016), *Zuo Tradition/Zuozhuan: Commentary on the Spring and Autumn Annals* (2016), *Women and National Trauma in Late Imperial Chinese Literature* (2014), *The Columbia Anthology of Yuan Drama* (2014), *The Readability of the Past in Early Chinese Historiography* (2007), *Trauma and Transcendence in Early Qing Literature* (2006), and *Enchantment and Disenchantment: Love and Illusion in Chinese Literature* (1993).

Scott Bradley Cook received his doctorate in Chinese from the Department of Asian Languages and Cultures at the University of Michigan in 1995. He spent the next eighteen years teaching at Grinnell College, where he served as Cowles-Kruidenier Chair of Chinese Studies. Since 2014, he has served as Tan Chin Tuan Professor of Chinese Studies at Yale-NUS College in Singapore. He specializes in pre-Qin textual studies and early Chinese intellectual history. He is author of several books, including *The Bamboo Texts of Guodian: A Study and Complete Translation*, vols. 1–2 (Ithaca: Cornell East Asia Series, 2012), *The Pre-Imperial Confucian Texts of Guodian: Broad and Focused Perspectives* (*Guodian Chujian xian-Qin rushu hongweiguan* 郭店楚簡先秦儒書宏微觀) (Taipei: Xuesheng shuju, 2006), *A Multi-Perspective Survey of Lost Warring States Texts Among the Shanghai-Museum and Other Chu Manuscripts* (*Shangbo deng Chujian Zhanguo yishu zonghenglan* 上博等楚簡戰國逸書縱橫覽) (Shanghai: Zhongxi shuju, 2018), and *A Study of Recorded Conversations of Confucius Texts among the Shanghai Museum Manuscripts* (*Shangbo zhushu Kongzi yulu wenxian yanjiu* 上博竹書孔子語錄文獻研究) (Shanghai: Zhongxi shuju, 2021); editor of *Hiding the World in the World: Uneven Discourses on the Zhuangzi* (Albany: SUNY Press, 2003); and the author of more than eighty articles in English and Chinese.

Shuen-fu Lin is professor emeritus of Chinese literature at the University of Michigan. He is author of *The Transformation of the Chinese Lyrical Tradition: Chiang K'uei and Southern Sung Tz'u Poetry* (Princeton, 1978), *Through a Window of Dreams: Selected Essays* (in Chinese) *on Premodern Chinese Literature, Aesthetics, and Literary Theory* (Taiwan Tsing Hua, 2009), and *Interpretation of Texts and Cultural Significance* (articles in Chinese) (Nanjing, forthcoming); co-editor of *The Vitality of the Lyric Verse: Shih Poetry from the Late Han to the T'ang* (Princeton, 1986), *Constructing China: The Interaction of Culture and Economics* (Michigan, 1998), and *Senses of the City: Perceptions of Hangzhou and Southern Song Culture, 1127–1279* (Hong Kong & Columbia, 2017); co-translator of Tung Yueh's *The Tower of Myriad Mirrors: A Supplement to Journey to the West* (Berkeley, 1978; Revised Edition, Michigan, 2000); and contributor to Zong-qi Cai, ed., *How To Read Chinese Poetry: A Guided Anthology* (Columbia, 2007), Stephen Owen and Kang-i Sun, eds., *The Cambridge History of Chinese Literature*, vol. 1 (Cambridge, 2010), and Kim-chong Chong and Kai-Yuan Cheng, eds., *Dao Companion to the Philosophy of Zhuangzi* (Springer, forthcoming).

Paul R. Goldin is professor of East Asian languages and civilizations at the University of Pennsylvania. He is the author of *Rituals of the Way: The Philosophy of Xunzi* (1999); *The Culture of Sex in Ancient China* (2002); *After Confucius: Studies in Early Chinese Philosophy* (2005); *Confucianism* (2011); and *The Art of Chinese Philosophy: Eight Classical Texts and How to Read Them* (2020). In addition, he edited the revised edition of R. H. van Gulik's classic study, *Sexual Life in Ancient China* (2003), and has edited or co-edited seven other books on Chinese culture and political philosophy.

William H. Nienhauser, Jr. majored in Chinese literature at Indiana University and Bonn University receiving his doctorate in 1973 under Professor Liu Wuji 柳无忌. That year Nienhauser became assistant professor of East Asian Literature (University of Wisconsin); he has been Halls-Bascom Chair Professor of Chinese Literature since 1995. His publications include *Indiana Companion to Traditional Chinese Literature*, nine volumes of translations from the *Shiji* (*The Grand Scribe's Records*), and the Biographical Dictionary of Tang Dynasty Literati. He was a founding editor of *Chinese Literature: Essays, Articles, Reviews* (*CLEAR*). In 2003, he was awarded a Forschungspreis (Research Prize) for lifetime achievement from the Humboldt Foundation.

Liu Yucai received his doctorate from Peking University's Department of Chinese Language and Literature. He concurrently holds the positions of professor at the Department of Chinese Language and Literature and at the Center for Chinese Classical Texts 中國古文獻研究中心 of Peking University. He is chief editor of the *Newsletter for International China Studies* 國際漢學研究通訊, associate editor of the journal *Chinese Classics and Culture* 中國典籍與文化, associate editor of the *Journal of Chinese Literature and Culture* (*JCLC*), and one of the chief editors for *A Cultural History of Premodern China* 中國古代文化史. He is the lead researcher in the Chinese Academy of Social Science Foundation's major project on "Research for the Cataloging of Unpublished Manuscripts in the Archives of the National Library." His primary research interests are classical Chinese philology, the cultural history of China, and the history of cultural exchange in East Asia. His monographic publications include *Research on Qing dynasty Academies and the Evolution of Scholarly Discourse* 清代書院與學術變遷研究, *Cultural Transmission and Change* 傳承與新變, *Manuscripts from the Garden of Misty Wilds* 莽蒼園稿, and *Records on Collating the Commentaries and Subcommentaries to the Thirteen Classics* 十三經注疏校勘記.

Benjamin Ridgway is assistant professor of Chinese in the Department of Modern Languages and Literatures and the Asian Studies and Medieval Studies programs at Swarthmore College. His research interests lie in Classical Chinese Poetry; Life and Poetry of Su Shi; Travel Literature; Urban Space in pre-fourteenth-century literary texts; and Word and Image Relationships in Chinese Poetry and Painting. His articles have been published in *Chinese Literature: Essays, Articles, and Reviews*; *Frontiers of Literary Studies in China*; the *Journal of Chinese Literature and Culture*, the *Journal of Song-Yuan Studies*, and in the volume, *Senses of the City: Perceptions of Hangzhou & Southern Song China* (CUHK Press, 2017). He co-authored an extensive online bibliography on the great poet "Su Shi" for Oxford Bibliographies in Chinese Studies with late Kathleen Tomlonovic. He is completing a manuscript entitled, *Longing for Landscape: Displacement, Memory, and Literati Identity in the Song Lyrics of Su Shi (1037–1101) and the Crossing-South Generation*.

Xinda Lian is professor of Chinese language and literature at Denison University. Lian received his doctorate from the University of Michigan in 1995. His research interests include Song dynasty poetry, Song dynasty literati culture, and the stylistic analysis of the *Zhuangzi* text. He is the author of *The Wild and Arrogant: Expression of Self in Xin Qiji's Song Lyrics* (Peter Lang, 1999), as well as a variety of book chapters and articles on Song dynasty literature and the study of the *Zhuangzi*.

Alexei Kamran Ditter is associate professor of Chinese at Reed College. His research explores interactions between social and textual practices in late-medieval China, focusing in particular on questions of place, genre, and memory. Topics on which he has published include twentieth-century literary histories of the Tang dynasty (618–907), civil examinations and cover letters in late-eighth-century China, conceptions of urban space in Duan Chengshi's nineth-century *Records of Monasteries and Stupas*, and the commercialization of funerary writing in the mid- to late-Tang. He has also edited, along with Jessey J. C. Choo and Sarah M. Allen, a volume of annotated translations from the tenth-century anthology *Taiping guangji*. He is currently completing a monograph studying genre and memory in medieval Chinese literature and co-editing, with Jessey J. C. Choo, an anthology of late medieval entombed epitaph inscriptions.

Ronald Egan is Confucius Institute Professor of Sinology in the Department of East Asian Languages and Cultures at Stanford University. He received his doctorate in Chinese literature from Harvard University. His research focuses on Chinese literature, aesthetics, and cultural history of the Tang-Song period. His publications include books on the literary works and lives of Ouyang Xiu and Su Shi, the latter entitled *Word, Image, and Deed in the Life of Su Shi*. He has also published a general study of innovations in Song dynasty aesthetic thought, entitled *The Problem of Beauty: Aesthetic Thought and Pursuits in Northern Song Dynasty China*, now available in a Chinese edition from Shanghai Ancient Books Publishing Company. He is also the translator of selected essays from Qian Zhongshu's *Guanzui biani*, which appeared as *Limited Views: Essays on Ideas and Letters by Qian Zhongshu*. His most recent book is a study of the works and reception history of Li Qingzhao, entitled *The Burden of Female Talent: The Poet Li Qingzhao and Her History in China* (Harvard University Press, 2013), now also available in a Chinese edition from Shanghai Ancient Books Publishing Company (2017). He previously taught at the University of California at Santa Barbara, UCLA, Wellesley College, and Harvard University.

Anna M. Shields is the Gordon Wu 1958 Professor of Chinese Studies and chair of the Department of East Asian Studies at Princeton University. She received her master of arts from Harvard University and her doctorate from Indiana University and specializes in classical Chinese literature of the Tang, Five Dynasties, and Northern Song eras. Her particular interests include literary history and the emergence of new literary genres and styles in late medieval China; the sociology of literature; and the role of emotions in classical literature. Her first book, *Crafting a Collection: The Cultural Contexts and Poetic Practice of the* Huajian ji (*Collection from Among the Flowers*), published by the Harvard Asia Center (2006), examined the emergence of the song lyric in a path-breaking anthology. Her most recent book, *One Who Knows Me: Friendship and Literary Culture in Mid-Tang China* (2015), was also published by the Harvard Asia Center and is now available in Chinese translation from the Zhongxi Publishing Company (2020). It explores the literary performance of friendship in ninth-century China through a wide range of genres, including letters, prefaces, exchange poetry, and funerary texts. Other recent publications investigate emotions in medieval letters; the compilation of anthologies of Tang literature in the Northern Song; and the cultural influence of Tang dynasty anecdote collections. She served as president of the T'ang Studies Society from 2011–2018. She is a former editor of the East Asian section of the *Journal of the American Oriental Society*, and is an editorial board member of the Library of Chinese Humanities Chinese-English translation series, published by De Gruyter. Before her appointment at Princeton, she taught at the University of Maryland, Baltimore County, where she served both as director of the Honors College and as associate professor in the Department of Modern Languages, Linguistics, and Intercultural Communications, and at the University of Arizona. She is currently working on a new book that traces the shaping of the Tang dynasty literary legacy during the Five Dynasties and Northern Song.

Stephen H. West received his doctorate from the University of Michigan in 1972. He began his teaching career at the University of Arizona (1972–1985) before joining the Berkeley faculty in 1986. He teaches courses in the prose and poetry of late-medieval China (the Song and Yuan dynasties), urban literature of the twelfth and thirteenth century, and early Chinese drama. His research specialties are in early Chinese theater, urban culture of the late-medieval period, and cultural history of the same period.

Yugen Wang is professor of Chinese literature in the Department of East Asian Languages and Literatures at the University of Oregon. He received his doctorate in East Asian Languages and Civilizations from Harvard University and master's degree in comparative literature from Peking University. His primary research area is classical Chinese poetry and poetic thought, with a focus on the Tang and Song dynasties. He is the author of *Ten Thousand Scrolls: Reading and Writing in the Poetics of Huang Tingjian and the Late Northern Song* and, most recently, *Writing Poetry, Surviving War: The Works of Refugee Scholar-Official Chen Yuyi (1090–1139)*.

Manling Luo is associate professor of Chinese literature at Indiana University. She received her doctorate in Chinese and comparative literature from Washington University in St. Louis. Her primary research interests include the social life of narratives, literati culture, gender, and religious literature. Her first monograph, entitled *Literati Storytelling in Late Medieval China* (University of Washington Press, 2015), examines how both the literary and the social dimensions of stories intersect, making storytelling a powerful medium for educated men of the mid-eighth to the mid-tenth centuries to redefine themselves in response to sociopolitical transformations. She has also published a range of research articles in English and Chinese.

Rivi Handler-Spitz is associate professor in the Department of Asian Languages and Cultures at Macalester College. Her monograph, *Symptoms of an Unruly Age: Li Zhi and Cultures of Early Modernity* (University of Washington Press, 2017) compares writings by the late-Ming dynasty provocateur Li Zhi to works by his best-known European contemporaries including Shakespeare, Montaigne, and Cervantes. Along with co-editors Haun Saussy and Pauline C. Lee, she published a volume of translations from Li Zhi's writings, *A Book to Burn and A Book to Keep (Hidden)* (Columbia University Press, 2016). With the same collaborators, she co-edited a volume of critical essays titled *The Objectionable Li Zhi: Fiction, Criticism, and Dissent in Late Ming China* (University of Washington Press, 2021). She also writes and draws in the genre of graphic non-fiction.

Yunte Huang is Tong Tin Sun Chair Professor of English at Lingnan University of Hong Kong and a professor of English at the University of California, Santa Barbara. A Guggenheim Fellow, he is the editor of *The Big Red Book of Modern Chinese Literature*, and the author of *Transpacific Imaginations, Inseparable,* and *Charlie Chan,* which won the Edgar Award in 2011.

GLOSSARY-INDEX

This index does not contain thematic entries, as they are already provided in the thematic table of contents beginning on page xi.